A Companion to Romance

D1495185

Learning Resource Services: Coleg Powys

000445

Blackwell Companions to Literature and Culture

This series offers comprehensive, newly written surveys of key periods and movements and certain major authors, in English literary culture and history. Extensive volumes provide new perspectives and positions on contexts and on canonical and post-canonical texts, orientating the beginning student in new fields of study and providing the experienced undergraduate and new graduate with current and new directions, as pioneered and developed by leading scholars in the field.

Published

A COMPANION TO

ROMANCE

FROM CLASSICAL TO CONTEMPORARY

EDITED BY **CORINNE SAUNDERS**

Blackwell
Publishing

© 2004, 2007 by Blackwell Publishing Ltd
except for editorial material and organization © 2004, 2007 by Corinne Saunders and chapter 11,
"*The Faerie Queene* and Eighteenth-Century Spenserianism" © 2004, 2007 by David Fairer

BLACKWELL PUBLISHING
350 Main Street, Malden, MA 02148-5020, USA
9600 Garsington Road, Oxford OX4 2DQ, UK
550 Swanston Street, Carlton, Victoria 3053, Australia

The right of Corinne J. Saunders to be identified as the Author of the Editorial Material in this Work has
been asserted in accordance with the UK Copyright, Designs, and Patents Act 1988.

All rights reserved. No part of this publication may be reproduced, stored in a retrieval system, or
transmitted, in any form or by any means, electronic, mechanical, photocopying, recording or otherwise,
except as permitted by the UK Copyright, Designs, and Patents Act 1988, without the prior
permission of the publisher.

First published 2004 by Blackwell Publishing Ltd
First published in paperback 2007 by Blackwell Publishing Ltd

1   2007

Library of Congress Cataloging-in-Publication Data

A companion to romance: from classical to contemporary / edited by Corinne Saunders.
p. cm. – (Blackwell companions to literature and culture ; 27)
Includes bibliographical references and index.
ISBN 0-631-23271-0 (hardcover : alk. paper)
1. English literature–History and criticism. 2. Romances, English–History and criticism.
3. Romanticism–England. I. Saunders, Corinne, 1963– II. Series.

PR149.R65C66 2004
820.9–dc22
2004004336

ISBN-13: 978-0-631-23271-1 (hardcover : alk. paper)
ISBN-13: 978-1-4051-6727-7 (paperback : alk. paper)
ISBN-10: 1-4051-6727-0 (paperback : alk. paper)

A catalogue record for this title is available from the British Library.

Set in 11/13 Garamond 3
by SPi Publisher Services, Pondicherry, India
Printed and bound in the United Kingdom
by TJ International Ltd, Padstow, Cornwall

The publisher's policy is to use permanent paper from mills that operate a sustainable forestry policy, and
which has been manufactured from pulp processed using acid-free and elementary chlorine-free practices.
Furthermore, the publisher ensures that the text paper and cover board used have met acceptable
environmental accreditation standards.

For further information on
Blackwell Publishing, visit our website:
www.blackwellpublishing.com

Contents

COLEG POWYS
BRECON
BRECON

Illustrations

Acknowledgments

I have incurred a very great number of debts over the several years in which this volume has been in the making. I am grateful to the University of Durham for a term of research leave, and to the Arts and Humanities Research Board for a matching Research Leave Award, which allowed me to finish my work on the book. I am grateful too to my colleagues in the Department of English Studies at the University of Durham for their continued support, and to the fellows of Emmanuel College, Cambridge, in particular Barry Windeatt, for the Visiting Fellowship that gave me so pleasant a setting in which to complete the volume.

I should like to thank especially Andrew McNeillie and Emma Bennett for first being persuaded by the idea of a Romance Companion. The staff of Blackwell, in particular Karen Wilson, have from the start offered not only invaluable assistance and support, but also patience and good humor, as has my copy-editor, Sandra Raphael. I am most grateful to all those, too numerous to list here, with whom I discussed the volume, and who offered interest and advice at so many different stages. I owe a special debt to Helen Cooper, who has been a friend and mentor over many years, and to Derek Brewer, whose work on romance has been so formative, and who has offered me much generous encouragement. I am grateful to my parents and friends for their consistent support, and particularly to David Fuller, who has, as always, provided intellectual stimulus, unfailing interest, and much advice and encouragement. Most of all, however, I should like to thank the authors of these essays for their interest and belief in the volume, their generous and original contributions, from which I have learned so much, and their unstinting cheerfulness.

It is a particular sadness that Ray Barron, whose work and presence contributed so much to Authurian and Romance Studies, did not live to see the publication of this volume.

Notes on Contributors

Elizabeth Archibald is Reader in Medieval Studies at the University of Bristol. She is the author of *Apollonius of Tyre: Medieval and Renaissance Themes and Variations* (1991) and *Incest and the Medieval Imagination* (2001), and the co-editor of *A Companion to Malory* (1996), and has published widely on medieval romance.

W. R. J. Barron, having been a student at St. Andrews, Yale, and Strasbourg and taught at Aberdeen, Manchester, and Shiraz, was a Senior Research Fellow of the University of Exeter. He published widely on chivalric and Arthurian romance, and was the author of *English Medieval Romance* (1987). He died in April 2004.

Derek Brewer is Emeritus Professor of English in the University of Cambridge and Life Fellow (formerly Master) of Emmanuel College. He has published many books and articles, mostly on late medieval English literature.

Helen Cooper is Professor of Medieval and Renaissance Literature at the University of Cambridge, and was previously Professor of English Language and Literature at Oxford, and a Tutorial Fellow of University College. She is the author of *The English Romance in Time: Transforming Motifs from Geoffrey of Monmouth to the Death of Shakespeare* (2004).

Richard Cronin is Professor of English Literature at the University of Glasgow. His most recent books are *Romantic Victorians: English Literature 1824–1840* (2002) and the co-edited *Blackwell Companion to Victorian Poetry* (2002).

David Fairer is Professor of Eighteenth-century English Literature at the University of Leeds. His most recent book is *English Poetry of the Eighteenth Century, 1700–1789* (2003). He is also the author of *Pope's Imagination* (1984) and *The Poetry of Alexander Pope* (1989). With Christine Gerrard he has edited *Eighteenth-Century Poetry: An Annotated Anthology* (second edition, 2004).

Robert Fraser's books include *The Making of* The Golden Bough: *The Origins and Growth of An Argument* (1990; revised edition 2002); *Proust and the Victorians: The*

Lamp of Memory (1994); *Victorian Quest Romance: Stevenson, Haggard, Kipling and Conan Doyle* (1998); and *The Chameleon Poet: A Life of George Barker* (2001). He has taught at the universities of Leeds and London, and at Trinity College, Cambridge. He is currently Senior Research Fellow in Literature at the Open University.

David Fuller is Professor Emeritus and Public Orator at the University of Durham, and has written on a variety of Renaissance, Romantic, and Modernist subjects. His books include studies of Blake and Joyce, and editions of Marlowe and Blake.

Jerrold E. Hogle is Professor of English, University Distinguished Professor, and Vice-Provost for Instruction at the University of Arizona. A Guggenheim and Mellon Fellow for research, he has published extensively on Romantic poetry, literary theory, and Gothic romances of many kinds, most recently in *The Undergrounds of* The Phantom of the Opera (2002) and his editing of *The Cambridge Companion to Gothic Fiction* (2002).

Kathryn Hume is Distinguished Professor of English at Penn State University. She has written five books: *"The Owl And the Nightingale": The Poem and its Critics* (1975); *Fantasy and Mimesis: Responses to Reality in Western Literature* (1984); *Pynchon's Mythography: An Approach to Gravity's Rainbow* (1987); *Calvino's Fictions: Cogito and Cosmos* (1992); and *American Dream, American Nightmare: Fiction since 1960* (2000). Some of the authors influenced by the hero monomyth whom she has analyzed in articles include H. G. Wells, C. S. Lewis, David Lindsay, Kurt Vonnegut, Arthur C. Clarke, and Thomas Pynchon.

Susan Jones is Fellow in English at St Hilda's College, Oxford. She is the author of *Conrad and Women* (1999) and is co-editing *Chance* for the Cambridge Edition of Joseph Conrad. She is currently writing a book on literary narrative and dance.

Andrew King is Lecturer in Medieval and Renaissance English at University College Cork, Ireland, and the author of *The Faerie Queene and Middle English Romance: The Matter of Just Memory* (2000).

Edward Larrissy is Professor of English Literature at the University of Leeds. His books include *William Blake* (1985), *Reading Twentieth-Century Poetry: The Language of Gender and Objects* (1990), and *Yeats the Poet: The Measures of Difference* (1994), as well as the edited volume, *Romanticism and Postmodernism* (1999). He has just completed a monograph on *The Blind Man in Romantic Writing* and is now working on William Blake and Modern Literature.

Richard Mathews is author of *Fantasy: The Liberation of Imagination* (1997; 2002) and has written book-length critical studies of William Morris, J. R. R. Tolkien, Anthony Burgess, and Brian Aldiss. His poetry and criticism have also been widely published. He is Dana Professor of English at the University of Tampa, where he is director of the University of Tampa Press and editor of the literary journal *Tampa Review*.

Ulrika Maude is Lecurer in English at the University of Durham. She has research interests in modernism, post-war writing and American literature. She is currently finishing a book on Samuel Beckett.

Clare Morgan teaches English Literature at Oxford University, where she is Director of the Undergraduate Programme in Creative Writing. Recent publications include essays on George Orwell, Willa Cather, and Virginia Woolf and the Neo-Romantic imagination. She reviews regularly for the *Times Literary Supplement*.

Lori Humphrey Newcomb is Associate Professor of English at the University of Illinois at Urbana-Champaign. She is the author of *Reading Popular Romance in Early Modern England* (2002) and articles on popular print culture, women's labor in pastoral romance, and Shakespearean romance and its sources.

Francis O'Gorman is Senior Lecturer in Victorian Literature at the University of Leeds. His books include *John Ruskin* (1999), *Late Ruskin: New Contexts* (2001), and *The Victorian Novel* (Blackwell Guides to Criticism 2002), as well as *Ruskin and Gender* (edited with Dinah Birch, 2002) and *The Victorians and the Eighteenth Century: Reassessing the Tradition* (edited with Katherine Turner, 2004). His *Victorian Poetry: An Annotated Anthology* appeared in 2004 and he is currently writing about Victorian literature and immortal life.

Michael O'Neill is a Professor of English and the current Head of Department at the University of Durham. His most recent publications include *Percy Bysshe Shelley: The Major Works* (2003), which he co-edited with Zachary Leader, and *A Routledge Literary Sourcebook on the Poems of W. B. Yeats* (2004).

Leonée Ormond is Professor of Victorian Studies at King's College, University of London. She has published widely on Victorian and Edwardian literature and fine art, with books on George du Maurier, J. M. Barrie, and (with Richard Ormond) Frederic, Lord Leighton. She is the author of a Literary Life of Alfred, Lord Tennyson (1993).

Lynne Pearce is Professor of Literary Theory and Women's Writing at Lancaster University. She has written widely on romance including the edited collections *Romance Revisited* (with Jackie Stacey, 1995) and *Fatal Attractions* (with Gina Wisker, 1998), and her next monograph, *A Cultural History of Romance*, is due for publication in 2006.

Fiona Price has published on eighteenth-century aesthetics, Romantic women's writing, and Scottish common-sense philosophy. She is currently working on the monograph *Revolutions in Taste: Aesthetics, Politics and Women's Writing 1776–1832*, and is Lecturer in English at University College Chichester.

Clive Probyn is Professor of English at Monash University, Melbourne, Australia, and has taught in universities in England, West Africa, USA, and Australia. He is the author of several books on Jonathan Swift, the eighteenth-century English novel (1987), James Harris of Salisbury (1991), and others on English poetry and African fiction. He is the co-editor of the *Correspondence* of Henry and Sarah Fielding (1993), and of the letters and novels of the Australian writer Henry Handel Richardson

(1995–2004). He is a Fellow of the Australian Academy for the Humanities, and is currently completing a book on Swift and Anglo-Irish print culture.

Fiona Robertson is Research Professor of English at the University of Central England, and a former Reader in English at the University of Durham. Her publications on the prose of the Romantic period include *Legitimate Histories: Scott, Gothic, and the Authorities of Fiction* (1994). She has published extensively on the Romantic period, on Scottish literature, and on Anglo-American literary exchange, and is writing the volume on the Romantic period for the new Oxford English Literary History.

Andrew Sanders is Professor of English at the University of Durham. He is a former editor of the *Dickensian* and has edited a number of Victorian novels for various scholarly paperback series. His studies of Dickens include *Dickens and the Spirit of the Age* (1999) and *Charles Dickens* (Authors in Context, 2003). A third edition of his *Short Oxford History of English Literature* appeared in 2004.

Corinne Saunders is Reader in the Department of English Studies at the University of Durham. She specializes in medieval literature, in particular romance, and in history of ideas. Her books include *The Forest of Medieval Romance* (1993), *Rape and Ravishment in the Literature of Medieval England* (2001), and *Chaucer* (Blackwell Guides to Criticism, 2001). She is English editor of the journal *Medium Ævum*.

John Simons is Dean of the Faculty of Humanities, Management, Social and Applied Sciences at Edge Hill College of Higher Education. His most recent books include *Animal Rights and the Politics of Literary Representation* (2002), an edition of Robert Parry's prose romance *Moderatus* (2002), and a jointly edited collection of essays on Ronald Firbank. He is currently working on a book about Australian animals in Victorian England.

Raymond H. Thompson has recently retired as Professor of English at Acadia University in Wolfville, Nova Scotia. He is the author of *The Return from Avalon: A Study of the Arthurian Legend in Modern Fiction* (1985); an associate editor of *The New Arthurian Encyclopedia* (1991) and its supplements; co-editor of the *Merlin Casebook* and the forthcoming *Gawain Casebook*; and consulting editor of Pendragon Fiction, published by Green Knight.

Lisa Vargo is Associate Professor of English at the University of Saskatchewan in Saskatoon. She has published articles on eighteenth- and nineteenth-century women writers and is the editor of Mary Shelley's *Lodore* (1997) and volume editor of *Spanish and Portuguese Lives* in *Mary Shelley: Literary Lives and Other Writings* (2002). She is also co-editor of a *Romantic Circles* electronic edition of Anna Barbauld's *Poems* (1773).

Judith Weiss is a Fellow of Robinson College, Cambridge. Her publications are mostly in the fields of Anglo-Norman romance and historiography. She has done several translations of romances and is currently engaged in translating *Boeve de Haumtone* and *Gui de Warewic*.

Introduction

Corinne Saunders

...history is a pattern
Of timeless moments.

T. S. Eliot, "Little Gidding."

Romance, one might say, is situated in and speaks of timeless moments. The celebrated romance images that spring to mind often encapsulate such moments – the images of Tristan and Isolde drinking the fateful potion; of the Holy Grail appearing to the Knights of the Round Table; of Guinevere led out to the fire, clad only in her shift; of the hand clothed in white samite, "mystic, wonderful," taking back the sword Excalibur; of the black-robed queens who weep and shriek as they bear Arthur away in the barge. The imagistic nature of romance is clear from its recurrence as a subject in visual art, especially but by no means exclusively in the nineteenth century. These romance moments have a powerful appeal, not just because they are visually compelling, but because they convey fundamental human emotions: they are trans-historical. Classical writers used such moments long before the term romance emerged, and we inherit from them some of the most powerful instances of all – Dido and Aeneas, sheltering in the cave from the storm; Medea, weaving her fearful enchantments; Apollonius, guessing at the riddle of incest. These in part provided the medieval *romanciers* with their material, and certainly shaped their imagination. The story matters they wove, of Arthur, of Troy, of the Celtic other-world, have slipped in and out of fashion – more often in than out – ever since, but, even more importantly, the great motifs of medieval romance – the knight errant, the quest, the chivalric test – became foundation stones of literature, shaping and influencing subsequent writing across a whole range of genres.

The pervasive nature of romance, however, also means that it is inherently slippery, and the difficulty of compiling a *Companion to Romance* is that the *genre* of romance is

impossible adequately to define. This is not so surprising when we recall that the term
finds its origins in the French word *romanz*, meaning simply literature written in the
vernacular, the romance language of French. Such works could differ vastly, and were
linked most of all by their function as entertainment rather than serious moral
instruction. Yet what is striking is that in the course of the twelfth century, romance
became a literary genre – though a very fluid, varied one. Perhaps it is not fanciful to
view romance as a genre waiting to happen, a story already told, situated in those
moments of classical writing, inherent in the earliest of fictions and fundamental to
human nature. Medieval romances treated an extraordinarily diverse range of material:
classical (the subject of the earliest, twelfth-century romances), historical (the matter
of both England and France), legendary (in particular, Arthurian), and spanned both
popular and courtly, oral and literary culture. Despite their variety, however, the
romances of the Middle Ages are linked by the motifs that echo through the genre:
exile and return, love, quest and adventure, family, name and identity, the opposition
between pagan and Christian. Such motifs form the backbone of romance. Romances
require heroes and heroines, figures distinguished from the everyday by their ideal
quality, and offset by similarly extreme, negative figures; they typically oppose a
social, usually conservative, ideal of order with the threat of disorder of various kinds.
The focus is not the nation represented or protected by the hero so much as the
individual and the ideals he or she embodies. The pursuit of love, the special realm of
the individual, is the particular but by no means the only subject of the romance, and
love is often combined in medieval romance with the pursuit of chivalry. Romances
offer escape and frequently open onto an exotic or in some way aggrandized world,
whether that of faery or of Charlemagne's France. They can also allow for incisive
social reflection and comment, for the exploration of gender and relationships, for
engagement too with the deep structures of human existence, on a level that we might
call psychological, sometimes through a dream-like interweaving of fantasy and
reality. Romance is a genre of extraordinary fluidity: it spans mimetic and non-
mimetic, actuality and fantasy, history and legend, past and present, and is striking
in its open-endedness, if frustrating in its capacity to defy classification or resolution.

Most influential in developing a kind of grammar of romance has been Northrop
Frye, who argues in *The Anatomy of Criticism* that romance is both an historical mode
and a *mythos*, rather than a genre (1957: 186–206). The notion of a mode derives from
Aristotle's *Poetics*, which distinguishes types of heroes (lesser, greater, or the same as
ourselves): Frye argues that in the romance mode, the hero is superior in degree to
others (rather than of god-like or mythic status), as in medieval romance. By contrast,
classical literature tends to present mythic heroes, and later writing to focus on heroes
closer to reality, in mimetic or ironic modes. Frye also, however, elaborates a non-
historical notion of the romance *mythos* or generic narrative form. This grows out of a
sense that, both with regard to the hero and more generally, romance reflects a
"tendency...to displace myth in a human direction and yet, in contrast to 'realism,'
to conventionalize content in an idealized direction." Literature stemming from this
romance impulse suggests "implicit mythical patterns in a world more closely

associated with human experience," and hence plays on archetypes, large patterns, conventions, and repetition of motifs (1957: 137). According to Frye's definition, romance is not a genre, but rather a "generic plot"; it consists in a distinctive structure and form that may be found in novel, poetry, or drama (1957: 162). Frye elaborates the idea of this generic plot in his study, *The Secular Scripture*, the very title of which points to the powerful influence of romance structures on Western thought. Romance is "essentially a verbal imitation of ritual or symbolic human action" (1976: 55): it is characterized by a focus on the development of the hero, and the winning of the heroine, by an emphasis on the great cycles of life and death, by the opposition of the ideal to its converse, and by patterns of ascent or descent to "otherworlds," which are linked to the shaping of identity and the process of self-realization. As the *mythos* of summer, romance leads from a state of order through darkness, winter, and death, to rebirth, new order, and maturity. Adventure is central to romance, as is the quest form: the hero moves through conflict and death-struggle to self-realization. Frye notes the "wish-fulfillment" quality of romance: it both projects social ideals and reflects "new hopes and desires" of the individual; it is frequently nostalgic, seeking a Golden Age (1957: 186). Romance is thus both escapist and socially pertinent, looking backwards and forwards. Perhaps what Frye does not emphasize enough is the oddly mixed mode of much romance: at their most sophisticated, romance narratives are characterized by irony, parody, self-consciousness, and comedy – and sometimes by a sense of deep failure and loss.

Critics of romance have been divided between mimetic and non-mimetic approaches. Erich Auerbach in "The Knight Sets Forth" (in *Mimesis: The Representation of Reality in Western Literature*, 1953) identifies the archetypal pattern of medieval romance as the movement from court to forest, "setting forth" in search of adventure. For Auerbach, the function of romance is primarily social: it engages with and shapes the values of the new, chivalric class of twelfth-century France. Susan Crane (1986), similarly, has treated English medieval romance as growing out of and reflecting the conservative social concerns of the barony. Social contextualization offers critical analysis a valuable specificity, and such specificity may work as well for romance of any age as it does for medieval romance. At the same time, one of the striking aspects of romance is its universality, and it has proved fruitful to approach romance as Vladimir Propp (1958) did the folk tale, in terms of deep recurring structures. Cultural anthropology, myth-ology, and psychoanalysis provide further ways into the deep structures of romance, complementing Frye's work. Derek Brewer's *Symbolic Stories* (1980), for instance, considers romance from the point of view of the folk tale: Brewer traces the recurrent pattern of growing up, of separation from and return to the family. Romance can also be seen as about the liminal or transitional period between one state and another, in particular from boyhood to manhood, and as treating the *rites de passage*, the initiation or testing undergone within this period. The genre may be fruitfully interpreted from both Jungian and Freudian perspectives: Anne Wilson, for instance, in *How Stories Mean* (1976), reads the dream-like and ritual quality of romance narrative, in particular its magical elements, as providing keys to the unconscious mind.

What much criticism brings out is the universality and timelessness of romance: it is not a literary form or *mythos* specific to the Middle Ages, but is found prior to them, in Greek stories and late classical works, and survives long after in works of diverse genre, function, and status – Shakespeare's plays, Gothic novels, Romantic poetry, modern fantasy, Mills and Boon, postmodern fiction. As W. R. J. Barron argued in *English Medieval Romance* (1987), romance treats values that have remained constant, and is characterized across the ages by idealism and symbolism, evident especially in the use of familiar patterns and motifs. At the same time, there is frequently a mimetic aspect to romance, meaning that it is marked by a dualistic quality. The ideal is necessarily linked to models of social order, and thus romance often provides pertinent social commentary. The varying emphases of romance, its more or less mimetic aspects, and the precise shaping of its *mythos*, are closely linked to its social, intellectual, and literary contexts. Romance is often self-conscious, reflecting some degree of choice against realism, and demonstrating over the course of literary history the enduring power and relevance – social, intellectual, emotional – of a mode of writing underpinned by the imaginative use of the symbolic and the fantastic, by idealism, and by universal motifs such as quest and adventure.

This volume begins with a retrospective, as Elizabeth Archibald looks back at late classical fictions to find in them the seeds of the romance genre, as well as some of the story matters and motifs so formative for the Middle Ages. Her essay is telling in its demonstration that, although a cohesive group of classical romances did not exist, the "grammar" of romance very much did; perhaps, as Frye suggests, these late works were a step on in literary development from the highly sophisticated classical genres of the epic, drama, and pastoral. The next several essays treat the medieval period, when romance first became a recognizable genre, and when it connected with ideas of England and Englishness to gain a distinctive national identity, particularly apparent in the emergence of the new form of Anglo-Norman romance discussed by Judith Weiss. These narratives allowed for engagement with a variety of historical themes alongside the mythic, and with questions of values, behavior, and ideals. In Derek Brewer's exploration of the popular metrical romances of the Middle Ages, he illuminates how folk material, with its recurrent motifs, such as those of growing up and of the "fair unknown," may be both mimetic and non-mimetic, providing the "imaginative ground of culture" and fulfilling an educative function of a social and literary kind. Alongside this, W. R. J. Barron surveys the development of the most famous romance matter of all, that of Arthur, again showing the roots of romance in historical matter, and the impulse of the age to elaborate already present romance elements by creating works that explored new issues of nation, identity, and the ideal. As Barron and many subsequent contributors suggest, at their most sophisticated such works tend to question, undercut, or treat the failure of the ideal, and this is especially the case with Chaucer's writing, explored by Corinne Saunders. Chaucer both composes some of the most elevated of romance works in English, and calls into question the very foundations of the genre.

This questioning is taken forward in very different ways in the works of Malory, Sidney, and Spenser. In Malory's *Morte Darthur*, discussed by Helen Cooper, the use of prose allows for a new kind of English Arthurian romance. Malory's narrative of epic grandeur, arguably the most influential of all English romances, both looks back nostalgically to the never-never world of Logres, with its glimmering hopes and failed ideals, and is firmly rooted in contemporary mores and concerns, and the practical possibility of chivalric education. Cooper examines Malory's narrative in light of other transitional prose romances, to find in them elements of the realism and sentiment of their literary descendants, the novels of the eighteenth century. Lori Humphrey Newcomb looks further at prose romance in the Renaissance, and in particular at the relation between gender and genre, as women come to be specially associated with the writing and reading of romances. The mixed mode of Sidney's *Arcadia*, discussed by Andrew King, plays on the notion of a coterie of women readers and also addresses, often with a high degree of irony, more general questions of virtue, behavior, and rule, alongside experimental questions about writing itself. The variety of Renaissance romance is demonstrated by its very different manifestation in Spenser's epic poem, *The Faerie Queene*, also discussed by King, which employs the naïve veil of romance to treat the deeper issues of aspiration to perfection and the mutability of the fallen world. Shakespeare's equally questioning stance is shown by David Fuller, who argues for the worthwhile perspectives on the last plays that may be gained through an awareness of the structures of romance. Romance, he suggests, allows for the treatment of extremes of experience free from contingent circumstances, by using familiar motifs, idealized or stylized characters, and the qualities of magic and wonder so appropriate to stage performance. Like the writing of Chaucer and Spenser, however, Shakespeare's drama is sophisticated precisely in its uneasiness, its mixed mode, and its unanswered questions.

A transition to the eighteenth century and beyond is provided by John Simons' exploration of the specialized genre of chapbooks, in which some medieval romances maintained a half-life for centuries, and which as literacy increased provided the means for the motifs of romance to reach a much wider popular audience. Chapbooks functioned and were viewed in terms not so much of escape as of education, opening windows onto culture. David Fairer's essay also provides a transition, tracing the recovery of romance and the growth of Spenserianism in the eighteenth century. A new model of affective reading allowed for the rediscovery of "fairy ground" for the adult world, and for a new mode of writing that looked both to the real and beyond. One of the most popular forms of this new mode was to be the Gothic, and Jerrold Hogle explores the origins and cultural implications of this powerful sub-genre. Again, romance proves a mixed mode, employing old structures to new purposes, often at war within itself, and offering society a mirror in which its "ghostly" or "monstrous" aspect is reflected through a process of "abjection." Gothic writing, perhaps more than any other form, expresses the repressed, the unconscious, through the interplay of horror and wish-fulfillment. Lisa Vargo examines the special relation of women writers to the Gothic, going beyond the easy association of the form with profound conservatism to suggest how it could also prove liberating and experimental. Women writers wove together romance and realism in ways that probed

desire and voiced the conflict between public and private, often subverting expectations. Romance in the eighteenth and nineteenth centuries was not, however,
confined to the Gothic novel. Clive Probyn discusses the new eighteenth-century
mode of parodic romance, deeply influenced by *Don Quixote*, but also manifesting the
kind of irony already evident in the works of Chaucer and the *Gawain* poet. For
writers like Johnson, Lennox, and Smollett romance becomes "a licensed vehicle for
otherwise transgressive ideas." Parody was balanced by the new bourgeois and
national romance of Richardson, discussed by Fiona Price. Richardson's works
weave together the cynicism and idealism of earlier French romances, and the
conventions of the Gothic, to create a narrative where economics and spiritual
edification meet. His reliance on the reader's familiarity with the grammar of romance
illuminates the vast influence of the genre even while novelists were responding
against what they frequently saw as a clichéd and flawed form.

The nineteenth century would usher in another face of romance, that of Romanticism. So associated with a political and intellectual movement of the nineteenth
century has this term become that it has nearly lost its original association with
romance – but the root of the word rightly implies the fundamental influence of the
romance genre on the period. In the reactions of writers and artists against the
Enlightenment, and the growing emphasis on the individual, nature, the affective
and the sublime, medievalism and romance narrative more generally played formative
roles. Fiona Robertson surveys the especially influential place of Scott as both
medieval scholar and novelist, examining his use of romance motifs, patterning,
and symbolism, as well as story matters themselves, to shape a new kind of historical
narrative that looks both forward and back. Through close consideration of the poetry
of Coleridge and Keats, Michael O'Neill evokes the way that romance becomes "a
many-colored dome" in the poetry of the period: this visual image is crucial, for the
vivid strands and images of romance allow for a poetry of heightened imagistic effect,
as in Romantic art. Romance opens out new narrative matters, enchanted worlds of
pasts and futures at once familiar and unknown, worlds of dream and symbol, which
provide ways into the deepest fears and pleasures of the human psyche.

This extraordinary visual, enchanted effect is carried through into the Victorian
period, and is famously evident in the paintings of the Pre-Raphaelites with their
repeatedly medieval subjects, but also in much of the great literature of the period.
Like Scott, Tennyson was especially influential in the shaping of romance in his time,
and most of all the Arthurian material: Leonée Ormond traces Tennyson's reading of
medieval texts and his use of them to create works that address complex and
contemporary moral and psychological questions of ideals and reality, often in a
highly pictorial way. Richard Cronin's closely linked essay examines Victorian medievalism further, looking at a range of poets to tease out the complex balance between
seriousness and sport in their writing. The new and old are twisted together with a
self-consciousness that allows for the probing of human experience and of the
questions haunting the Victorian imagination, especially those of love, loyalty, and
adultery. The ambiguous relation of the Victorians to romance, their attraction to the

ideal but also their fear of failure, is traced in a different way by Francis O'Gorman, who examines the ways that romance influences autobiographical narratives, in particular that of Ruskin, for whom medieval aesthetics and the writing of Scott were important influences. The structuring pattern of the progress narrative, so closely related to the quest narrative, and the tension between real and ideal, are also evident more generally across Victorian prose. Andrew Sanders explores what the term "romance" meant in relation to the fiction of the period, and traces the use of this label by a series of writers, demonstrating how Dickens, for instance, chose to employ ideas of the marvelous and a certain ideality of incident. Dickens' Christmas books hint at a newly burgeoning sub-genre, that of fantasy, while romance elements are also evident in the historical novels of the period and in the sensationalism of another new genre, that of the mystery or detective novel. Fantasy is considered further by Robert Fraser, who shows how the apparently naïve and sentimental, fairy-tale type of romance may mask parody, satire, and self-referentiality: journeys that seem literal become internal, subjective, and symbolic in the works of writers such as Meredith, Carroll and Stevenson, so that fantasy and reality blur, and the darkness of the divided self is revealed. Ulrika Maude explore how these many new faces of romance manifest themselves in the other world of America, where the force of the primitive and the sense of distance infuse literature with new potential.

The motif of the journey, fundamental to romance from its earliest origins, finds a new manifestation in the transitional, "imperial romance" of the late nineteenth and early twentieth centuries, examined by Susan Jones. Here the imperialist venture of colonization provides the subject matter of a new mode of adventure story, which rewrites the motifs of quest, battle, and otherworld through different and ambiguous treatments of race, gender, and place, to raise uneasy political and psychological questions. Unease will be present throughout the writing of romance in the twentieth century, a crucial aspect of modern and postmodern perspectives. As Edward Larrissy shows, the modernist poetry of Yeats, Pound, and Eliot looks consciously back to the matter of romance, most famously the legend of the Waste Land and the Fisher King, but also the faery matter of Ireland and the material of the troubadours. These fragments of the past respond to the crisis of identity in the modern world by providing ways into other worlds, and hence opening the possibilities of social and sexual renewal – although they always remain fragments, shored against our ruin but never coalescing into the ideal beyond the moment.

The more unashamedly fantastic genres of the twentieth century are also more optimistic. It is striking that, as Raymond Thompson demonstrates, the Arthurian matter has retained its appeal right across the twentieth century and into the twenty-first, and he argues persuasively for the way that such retellings may react against but can never escape their romance identity. They rely on romance's building blocks – the marvelous, the archetypal, the struggle of dark and light, and nostalgia for an idealized past, though they play too with the dynamic between romance and realism, their effect rooted in the interweaving of difference and familiarity, this world and another, so characteristic of romance. Richard Mathews surveys the development of non-Arthurian fantasy in the twentieth century, looking back to the Victorian models of Morris and MacDonald to trace the ways in which writers play on the powerful ideas of quest and otherworld, often by using differences of perspective. Fantasy sets alternative realities against ideas of progress, time and change, and thus highlights questions of belief. The growth of fantasy is also closely connected to technological advances – the popular explosion of film, animation, and comics or "pulps," all forms that use the basic building blocks of the romance genre in what is, in one sense, a simplified way, though each new medium finds its own sophisticated forms. A similar use of the building blocks of romance is evident in the sub-genre of science fiction discussed by Kathryn Hume, in which the journey takes on a new aspect as the marvelous is replaced by scientific devices, and the otherworld becomes that of outer space. As Hume shows, however, the replacement is not as simple as it seems, for medieval notions of the spirit are succeeded by modern distinctions between mind and body, and a prominent theme of contemporary science fiction becomes the possibility of escaping or transforming the confines of the body, and even of remaking the mind.

Romance has not departed from the more mainstream genre of the novel in the twentieth century. As Clare Morgan shows, the twentieth century saw a neo-Romantic movement in both art and writing, which brought with it a new emphasis on ideas of Englishness as rooted in the past, in place, and in myth, on the power of archetypes, and on the possibility of the dream or fantastic world as opening out different kinds of knowledge. This neo-Romantic emphasis has been sustained from the 1950s to the present, so that both the postwar novel and the postmodern novel may become "narratives of enchantment," as Morgan demonstrates in her analysis of the writings of Iris Murdoch and A. S. Byatt. Her essay is in certain ways closely related to that of Lynne Pearce, whose first subject is that of popular romance of the Mills and Boon kind. As Pearce shows, however, no easy distinction can be made between popular and literary romance, for popular romance simply demonstrates more clearly how the deep structures of the mode allow us to access our traumas, fears, and hopes. It is an interesting phenomenon of postmodern, experimental writing that popular romance structures have found their way out of Mills and Boon into the much more self-conscious, ironized "literary" work of novelists such as Jeannette Winterson, as well as into film at all levels. Romance, as Pearce argues, provides an Ur-story that society cannot, does not wish to, escape.

This study, then, offers a way through the tangled web of romance. Its aims are several-fold: to clarify the definition(s) of romance; to consider the historical and literary development of this mode, from its classical origins to the present day (with a focus on English literary perceptions of romance); to survey both its continuity and its permutations; to examine the changing readership of romance (with particular emphasis on women readers); and to discuss a wide range of specific and influential literary examples. Essays may be read sequentially or in isolation; cross-references are offered at the end of each to suggest different paths through the book. It will be evident that the essays fit into chronological groups, but also groupings of other kinds: Arthurian romance, fantasy, poetry, prose fiction, travel writing. Perhaps they do not lead to the rose at the heart of the maze – but, at the very least, it is hoped that they will offer some delights along the way – and will open the possibility of many other worlds, many further quests into the romance world and its enduring promise of adventure and transformation, its constant potential for metamorphosis of the mundane into treasures untold.

References and Further Reading

Auerbach, Erich (1953). *Mimesis: The Representation of Reality in Western Literature*, trans. Willard R. Trask. Princeton, NJ: Princeton University Press. [First published in German, 1946.]

Barron, W. R. J. (1987). *English Medieval Romance*. Longman Literature in English Series. London: Longman.

Beer, Gillian (1970). *The Romance*. London: Methuen.

Brewer, Derek (1980). *Symbolic Stories: Traditional Narratives of the Family Drama in English Literature*. Cambridge: D. S. Brewer; Totowa, NJ: Rowman and Littlefield.

Butcher, S. H., ed. and trans. (1985). *Aristotle's Theory of Poetry and Fine Art*. London: Macmillan.

Campbell, Joseph (1968). *The Hero with a Thousand Faces*. 2nd edn. Princeton, NJ: Princeton University Press.

Crane, Susan (1986). *Insular Romance: Politics, Faith, and Culture in Anglo-Norman and Middle English Literature*. Berkeley: University of California Press.

Frye, Northrop (1957). *The Anatomy of Criticism: Four Essays*. Princeton, NJ: Princeton University Press.

Frye, Northrop (1976). *The Secular Scripture: A Study of the Structure of Romance*. Cambridge, MA: Harvard University Press.

Hume, Kathryn (1984). *Fantasy and Mimesis: Responses to Reality in Western Literature*. New York: Methuen.

Jameson, Fredric (1975). "Magical Narratives: Romance as Genre." *New Literary History* 7, 135–63.

Ker, W. P. (1926). *Epic and Romance: Essays on Medieval Literature*. London: Macmillan.

Krueger, Roberta (2000). *The Cambridge Companion to Medieval Romance*. Cambridge Companions to Literature. Cambridge: Cambridge University Press.

Parker, Patricia A. (1979). *Inescapable Romance: Studies in the Poetics of a Mode*. Princeton, NJ: Princeton University Press.

Pound, Ezra (1929). *The Spirit of Romance*. London: Peter Owen.

Stevens, John (1973). *Medieval Romance: Themes and Approaches*. London: Hutchinson University Library.

Wilson, Anne (1976). *Traditional Romance and Tale: How Stories Mean*. Cambridge: D. S. Brewer.

1
Ancient Romance

Elizabeth Archibald

In the case of ancient romance, the usual difficulties of defining and discussing the literary genre are compounded by the fact that there is no word for it in either Greek or Latin in the classical period (in Byzantine Greek, interestingly, the word for prose fiction was *drama*). There is no discussion of romance as a genre by literary critics or rhetoricians in antiquity; indeed there is very little comment of any kind about romance in ancient writers, either approving or disapproving. Until recently there was very little comment on it by modern classical scholars either; the few surviving Greek and Latin texts included under the umbrella term "romance" were thought to be minor works, of limited literary interest to both ancient and modern readers. In the last 20 years, however, there has been a remarkable surge of interest in ancient romance.

The main focus of this attention has been a group of five Greek prose narratives by Chariton, Xenophon, Achilles Tatius, Longus, and Heliodorus, which are all concerned with love, travel, and adventure, in various combinations. In these five stories, obstacles of various kinds divide the protagonists, but eventually love triumphs: enemies are overcome, ordeals are endured, identities are established, and the young lovers settle down to happy married life (in the complete texts, at least). A number of tantalizing fragments of what seem to be romances predate the five complete romances; though not all conform to the description above, they do all involve some combination of the same basic ingredients, love, travel, and adventure. These three ingredients could also be said to be the main components of the *Odyssey*, which is sometimes described as a romance. Although it is set in the context of epic (the Trojan War), it concerns the travels and tribulations of an individual hero trying to get home to his faithful wife, a hero who is tested not so much for martial prowess and courage as for resourcefulness and marital commitment. The same three themes, love, travel, and adventure, are central to *The Ass*, attributed to an anonymous Greek writer known as Pseudo-Lucian, and its better-known Latin analogue, Apuleius' *Golden Ass* (both written in the second century AD), precursors of the Bottom subplot in Shakespeare's

A Midsummer Night's Dream: the hero's interest in magic leads to his accidental transformation into a donkey. These two *Ass* texts have their fair share of vulgarity, but Apuleius ends his story on a higher plane, surprisingly, when his hero becomes a devotee of Isis after being restored to human shape. Lucian's own version of this comic tale is lost (if indeed he did write one), but we do have his fantastic travelogues in the ironically titled *True Story*, described by a recent translator as "an early Baron Munchausen tale" (Reardon 1989: 619); it includes journeys beyond the Pillars of Hercules, to the moon, and into the belly of a whale. Another recounter of fantastic travels is Antonius Diogenes, whose *Wonders Beyond Thule*, supposedly a source for Lucian, survives only in a summary by Photius. Equally fantastic in parts, for all its historical basis, is the *Alexander Romance* (third century AD in its present form); this very popular "biography" of Alexander includes an account of his historical conquests, but also finds room for more bizarre episodes such as the begetting of the hero by an exiled pharaoh disguised as a god, and some close encounters with strange life forms on the frontiers of the known world. It certainly features love, travel, and adventure, but it does not have a happy ending, since Alexander is poisoned and dies young. All these texts are in Greek, apart from Apuleius' *Golden Ass*. There are far fewer Latin texts that can be categorized as romances. A marginal candidate is the scurrilous *Satyricon* of Petronius (probably written under Nero in the first century AD), with its vulgar parvenus and its homoerotic encounters, travel, and shipwreck; it survives only in fragments (including the famous account of the lavish feast given by the freedman Trimalchio), but it could be described as a lowlife romance. A less problematic candidate is the anonymous *Apollonius of Tyre* (*Historia Apollonii regis Tyri*, written in the late fifth or early sixth century); like Alexander, Apollonius is a king who travels a great deal, though in the eastern Mediterranean rather than in fantastic landscapes; but he fights no battles, and his main focus is domestic rather than political. Like the protagonists of the five complete Hellenistic romances, he finds love only to lose it, and reaches the happy ending only after many vicissitudes and journeys.[1]

The motifs of separated families, discovery of identity, tests and ordeals, travels and adventures are common in classical stories of mythological and legendary heroes, yet such narratives are not described by critics as romances. The term is often applied to Shakespeare's late plays, but no one would use it for plays by Sophocles or Euripides. In fact, classicists tend not to use the term *romance* very much at all nowadays; they prefer *novel* or, if they wish to be more inclusive, *fiction*. The ancient romance/novel is a very fashionable area of scholarly activity at present, but it encompasses a range of texts which might seem surprising to non-specialists. In the Middle Ages the term *roman* could be used of a life of Christ, as well as of a chivalric adventure story. Classicists today often include in their discussion of romance/novel/ fiction some early Christian writings (second to third century) about the adventures of the early apostles and evangelists, stories which share a number of motifs and themes with the secular romances. One example is the *Acts of Paul and Thecla*, in which the young virgin Thecla falls in love (in a chaste, spiritual sense) with Paul and follows him through a series of adventures, repeatedly escaping attempts to martyr her, until the happy ending, which consists of her acceptance as a missionary. Another is the *Acts of Andrew*, in which Andrew not only converts many pagans but also rescues Matthias from the clutches of cannibals, and performs other heroic tasks, such as disarming robbers and killing a monstrous serpent, before going willingly to his death as a martyr. A third is the *Clementine Recognitions*, in which Clement is reunited with all the members of his long-separated family through the agency of St. Peter, who also converts Clement's pagan father. It seems very likely that early Christian writers used for their own purposes the secular narrative themes and structures popular at the time (perhaps in oral rather than written tradition): love at first sight, travel and shipwreck, separation and reunion. But Christian adventure narratives may also have contributed to secular romances. Bowersock (1994: chapter 5) has remarked on the popularity of the theme of apparent death (*Scheintod*) followed by apparent resurrection in the ancient romances, and speculates that these secular narratives were influenced by the death and resurrection of Jesus in the Gospel stories. He writes of the *Clementine Recognitions* that they "represent the appropriation, probably the inevitable appropriation, of a pagan and popular genre that itself owed so much to the miraculous narratives, both oral and written, of the early Christians" (Bowersock 1994: 141). He suggests a new name for this fusion of secular and religious narrative modes:

> The stories of Jesus inspired the polytheists to create a wholly new genre that we might call romantic scripture. And it became so popular that the Christians, in turn, borrowed it back again – in the *Clementine Recognitions* and in the massive production of saints' lives. (Bowersock 1994: 143)

In view of such arguments, *The Secular Scripture* seems a particularly apt title for Northrop Frye's wide-ranging discussion of romance from antiquity to the present day. He does not spend a lot of time on ancient romance, but does note that "with the rise of the romantic ethos, heroism came increasingly to be thought of in terms of suffering, endurance and patience … This is also the ethos of the Christian myth" (Frye 1976: 88). He argues that this emphasis on suffering accounts at least in part for the prominence of heroines in romance.

Other marginal texts included in modern discussions of ancient romance are pseudo-histories and biographies, such as Xenophon's *Cyropaedia*, a biography of the Persian king Cyrus the Great (fourth century BC); the *Life of Aesop* (the earliest fragments date from the second or third century AD); and Philostratus' *Life of Apollonius of Tyana* (third century AD). Also on the margins of romance are the supposedly eyewitness reports of the Trojan War by Dictys and Dares (actually produced in the late classical period); and Jewish novellas such as *Joseph and Aseneth* (possibly first century BC). It is impossible to include all such variations on romance in a short survey, so I shall discuss briefly the five complete Hellenistic romances, and then concentrate on the two narratives that were very well known in western Europe during the Middle Ages and the Renaissance, the *Alexander Romance* and *Apollonius of Tyre*.

The Hellenistic Romances

The five complete Greek romances are Chariton's *Chaereas and Callirhoe* (first century BC/AD); Xenophon's *Ephesian Tale* (second century AD); Longus' *Daphnis and Chloe* (later second century AD); Achilles Tatius' *Leucippe and Cleitophon* (second century AD); and Heliodorus' *Ethiopian Tale*, or *Ethiopica* (third to fourth century AD). A number of narratives also categorized by critics as romances are known only from fragments of manuscript or papyrus, or from summaries in ancient authors.[2] The most important of these fragments are the anonymous *Ninus*, which shows the king as a young man in love with his cousin (not named, but possibly Semiramis); Iamblichus' *Babylonian Tale*, apparently a story of separated lovers; Lollianus' *Phoenician Story*, two scenes of sex and violence which suggest that the original was a picaresque lowlife adventure perhaps comparable to the *Satyricon*; the *Iolaus*, also apparently a lowlife story told in both verse and prose, like the *Satyricon*; the *Sesonchosis*, about an Egyptian ruler; and *Metiochus and Parthenope*, a love story set in the court of the historical tyrant Polycrates of Samos. It is striking that some of these fragments seem to be about "historical" characters and events, as well as about love. This suggests that the five complete romances, which tend to focus on middle-class protagonists with no political connections, may not be especially representative of the genre – or perhaps that we need to change our definition.

The romances do not include mythological characters; they are realistic and everyday in their characters and setting (though not of course in the series of vicissitudes endured by the lovers, the startling coincidences and sensational crises). Some critics have been brave enough to offer broad definitions or rubrics for the analysis of the ancient romances. In his seminal study, Perry gave this definition:

> An extended narrative published apart by itself which related – primarily or wholly for the sake of entertainment or spiritual edification, and for its own sake as a story, rather than for the purpose of instruction in history, science, or philosophical theory – the adventures or experiences of one or more individuals in their private capacities and from the viewpoint of their private interests and emotions. (Perry 1967: 44–5)

Winkler (1994: 28) is much more succinct and focuses on the love story: "The entire form of the Greek romance can be considered an elaboration of the period between initial desire and final consummation" (see also Bakhtin 1981: 90). Frye (1976: 24) makes a similar claim for romance in general. Of course, this is to restrict the term *romance* to stories of star-crossed lovers, and the happy ending to sex and marriage. Not all the Greek romances fit this model. For example, in what seems to be the earliest complete romance, Chariton's *Chaereas and Callirhoe*, the lovers marry at the beginning of the story.

> Chaereas and Callirhoe, beautiful young people living in Syracuse, fall in love at first sight, and marry in spite of opposition from their families. Jealous enemies cause

Chaereas to doubt Callirhoe's fidelity. He kicks her, and she appears to die. When she recovers consciousness in her tomb, she is discovered by a tomb-robber and a pirate, who carry her off to Ionia and sell her as a slave. Her new master Dionysius falls in love with her and marries her; she is pregnant by Chaereas, but intends to persuade Dionysius that the child is his. Meanwhile Chaereas has found the open grave, and is searching everywhere for Callirhoe. Through the plotting of Dionysius' devoted steward, Chaereas is captured and sold into slavery, but still seeks his wife. Eventually the two husbands appear before the King of Persia to claim Callirhoe, but the King has to leave for war in Egypt, and takes Callirhoe with him. Chaereas and Dionysius both perform great feats in the hope of winning Callirhoe. Eventually Aphrodite decides to reunite the lovers, and brings about a recognition scene. The protagonists return to Syracuse and tell their story.

This is a fairly standard romance plot, though each of the five surviving Greek texts has some distinctive features. The *Ethiopica* begins in the middle of the heroine's adventures, and thus includes many accounts by various characters of earlier incidents; the happy ending involves revelations about her parentage and her return to claim the crown of Ethiopia. *Daphnis and Chloe* also involves revelations about the true identities of the lovers, but its most unusual feature is that the young protagonists do not travel more than a few miles for their adventures; it is set in the countryside, and the naïve protagonists remain extremely innocent, and extremely static, for most of the narrative. Daphnis has to be sexually initiated by an older woman, and after their wedding they continue to live a simple life in the country. The story does contain many of the usual romance motifs – pirates, foundlings, and a final recognition scene – but as Hägg comments (1983: 36), "the gradual awakening of love in two children of nature is the main theme, in contrast to the 'love at first sight' motif in the earlier novels."

One important trait of all these five romances is the prominence of female characters (see Wiersma 1990). Usually they share the limelight with their lovers, but in Heliodorus' *Ethiopica* Chariclea is clearly the central character. She is the daughter and heir of Ethiopian royalty, exposed at birth because of her white skin. She and her beloved Theagenes are repeatedly threatened, separated, and tested by a series of ordeals and adventures before the story ends happily, not just with her marriage but also with her discovery of her true parentage and identity and her return to her proper royal status in Ethiopia. Thus the romance has a political dimension, though this is not its main focus. In the other romances there is a more equal balance between the lovers in their adventures. In the works of Achilles Tatius, Chaereas, and Xenophon, the protagonists travel separately around the Mediterranean, enduring shipwrecks, pirates, brothels, slavery, amorous employers, unjust accusations, false deaths, and other ordeals before being reunited and reinstated in their original home.

Ordeals are important: in his discussion of these romances, Bakhtin uses the term *Prüfungsroman*, or "novel of ordeal" (Bakhtin 1981: 100). He discusses them in the context of his theory of the chronotope, "the intense connectedness of temporal and spatial relationships that are artistically expressed in literature" (Bakhtin 1981: 84), and points out that all the adventures in the ancient romances are extra-temporal in that they have no lasting effect on the protagonists: the ordeals leave no psychic trace (Bakhtin 1981: 90). He stresses the significance of chance and coincidence in the plots: the protagonists never take the initiative, but simply respond to, or endure, whatever happens to them, until the happy ending when they return to normal domestic life. He also stresses, as do other critics, the focus on the individual rather than the state or society: "Social and political events gain meaning in the novel only thanks to their connection with private life" (Bakhtin 1981: 109; see also Perry 1967: 44–5, quoted above). This focus on private life has much to do with the time when they were composed.

The dating of most of the romances is highly problematic; only a very few can be reliably attributed to a named author, and even then the identity of these authors is not always certain. It used to be thought that the romances were the product of the period of Greek cultural revival known as the Second Sophistic, in the second and early third centuries AD (see Hägg 1983: 104–8). But Chariton is now believed to have been writing much earlier, at the end of the Hellenistic period (330–30 BC) or perhaps in the first century AD, and some of the recently discovered papyrus fragments are also early; the *Ninus*, for instance, was written down between 100 BC and 100 AD. Various critics have considered the literary and social factors that contributed to the development of romance in the late Hellenistic period, a time when literary tastes and trends were going through some significant changes. In the political sphere as well as the literary one, the old order was changing. The city-state, which made so many demands on its citizens and dominated their imaginations, was giving way to great empires, in which individuals had very restricted roles and responsibilities. Perry comments (1967: 7):

> The age of Greek romance was similar to that of the modern novel in the centering of thought and feeling about the private concerns of the individual man apart from society, and the tendency to look outward in a spirit of wonder upon the endless varieties of nature and human experience, rather than inward to the nature of man in his more universal or more heroic aspects.

Reardon (1989: 7) makes a similar point: "The novel is a reflection of their personal experience, as the older forms of tragedy and Old Comedy had been a reflection of their civic experience." In Athens Old Comedy, with its concern for the safety and prosperity of the city-state, gave way to New Comedy, with its emphasis on individual lovers and their families. Hellenistic poetry focused heavily on love; the *Love Romances* or *Erotica pathemata* of Parthenius (first century BC) are prose summaries of verse and prose love stories featuring the vicissitudes of young lovers much like the protagonists of the romances, though they tend to have tragic endings (Hägg 1983: 122). New Comedy shares many motifs with the romances: problems of identity, the removal of obstacles separating lovers, recognition scenes and family reunions (see Trenkner 1958: many of these plays might be seen as the equivalent of the final episodes in the romances, when the lovers resolve all their problems, return home, and are recognized by or reunited with their families). Frye argues that there is a general tendency in literary history for romance to come to the fore when the major genres can no longer be reworked and improved: "the conventions wear out, and literature enters a transitional phase when some of the burden of the past is thrown off and popular literature, with romance at its center, comes again into the foreground" (Frye 1976: 29). One of his examples is the Greek romances; another is Gothic romance in late eighteenth-century Britain.

Romance has often been sneered at as an unsophisticated genre. It used to be said rather dismissively that the Greek romances were intended for a female readership, but that is no longer the accepted view. It has been pointed out that the five complete romances show great interest in literature and rhetoric, with many philosophical and literary allusions, and sophisticated techniques such as *ekphrasis* (elaborate description of a work of art).[3] When the romances were rediscovered in the Renaissance, they certainly found favor with sophisticated writers and readers (see Hägg 1983: chapter 8). Shakespeare assumed that some of his audience would recognize a reference to a moment of crisis for the heroine of the *Ethiopica* when he made Orsino contemplate killing his beloved Cesario/Viola: "Why should I not, had I the heart to do it, / Like to th'Egyptian thief at point of death, / Kill what I love?" (*Twelfth Night*, V.i.115–17). Racine loved the *Ethiopica* so much that after the sacristan at his Jansenist school had confiscated and burned two copies, he obtained a third and learned it off by heart before dutifully relinquishing it (Hägg 1983: 205–6).

Frye argues (1976: 23) that romance is "a form generally disapproved of in most ages by the guardians of taste and learning"; he mentions the legend that Heliodorus was a Christian bishop who was forced to choose between his bishopric and his writing, and chose the latter (107). It is suggestive that much of the action in the romances takes place in the eastern Mediterranean, where some of its authors lived. Winkler (1994: 35) sees romance as fundamentally un-Greek:

> The narrative pattern of romance (as I have defined it) is a resident alien in Greek culture, a literary form born in and (presumably) appropriate to the social forms of a Near Eastern culture, and which has been Hellenized in the wake of Alexander's conquests.

He draws attention to the fact that earlier Greek writers are not interested in sex and marriage, "*eros* leading to *gamos*," but rather in *eros* as a dangerous and destructive force (Winkler 1994: 35). In the romances, however, as in New Comedy, love conquers all. It is not destructive in any significant way; many minor characters die in the course of the narratives, but this is not tragic or disturbing, and there is no doubt about the desirability of the lovers' final reunion.[4]

The *Alexander Romance*

The definition of romance proposed by Winkler and others, an account of the events between the protagonists' first feelings of desire and their satisfaction in marriage (or reunion), may be appropriate for the five Hellenistic romances, but it does not work well for other classical narratives categorized today as romances, including the very popular *Alexander Romance*. There is nothing fictional about Alexander the Great, but within a few years of his death his history was being turned into a romance which proved so popular that versions of it survive not only in Greek and Latin and in all the European vernacular languages, but also in Arabic, Persian, Turkish, Malay, Ethiopian, and even Mongolian. This is the *Alexander Romance* of Pseudo-Callisthenes, so called because in the Middle Ages it was incorrectly attributed to Alexander's physician Callisthenes. In fact it is not the work of any single author, but a hybrid of history and legend which accumulated over many centuries; there are three main versions, which have produced hundreds of descendants (see Cary 1956; Stoneman 1991). Alexander died in 323 BC. The *Ur*-romance was probably begun soon after his death, in the third century BC, though the earliest surviving manuscript (written in Greek) dates from the third century AD; it was translated into Latin by Julius Valerius in the late third or early fourth century. The title *Alexander Romance* is a modern one, of course.

Nectanebus, Pharaoh of Egypt, flees his country before it falls to Persian invaders. He comes to Macedonia and falls in love with Queen Olympias. He tells her that the god Ammon wishes to sleep with her, and then visits her himself disguised as the god; Alexander is the result. Later Nectanebus foresees correctly that he will be murdered by Alexander; as he is dying, he reveals their true relationship. Aristotle becomes Alexander's tutor. The boy tames the man-eating horse Bucephalus. When his father Philip dies, Alexander campaigns in Italy and Greece. He goes to Egypt and founds Alexandria; he is hailed as the reincarnation of Nectanebus. He goes to Asia and begins his campaign against the Persian king Darius; eventually he burns Persepolis and on the death of Darius marries his daughter Roxane. He writes to his mother about his adventures and his attempt to reach the end of the world, during which he encounters many fantastic peoples and animals. Not all his adventures end in success: he is unable to get to the bottom of the sea in his bathysphere; he misses a chance to drink the Water of Life; he is warned to turn back from the Islands of the Blessed, and from his flight into the heavens; the oracle of the Trees of the Sun and the Moon foretells his imminent death. He also has some successes, however (often when he is in disguise): he rescues Candaules' wife from her abductors, and outwits the clever queen Candace; he is accepted by the Amazons as their overlord; he visits the City of the Sun and the magnificent palace of Cyrus. In India he meets the Brahmans, naked philosophers with whom he discourses, and he describes this visit in a letter to his tutor Aristotle. He then returns to Macedonia, where he is poisoned through the machinations of the regent Antipater, and dies.

Here the historical achievements of Alexander, extraordinary enough in themselves, are embellished with motifs taken from myth and legend. The first is the story of his clandestine conception, a familiar motif in legends of heroes; it is reminiscent of the story of Merlin's part in Arthur's conception, and also of the story of Christ's birth.

Clearly the insertion into the Alexander story of Nectanebus, the last Pharaoh of Egypt, represents the Egyptian desire to be connected to the story of the great conqueror, and to extend his Egyptian connections beyond the founding of Alexandria. But, as many critics have pointed out, the *Alexander Romance* in the form in which it has come down to us cannot be pure Egyptian propaganda, since Nectanebus is presented as a trickster rather than a noble hero. He dies an ignominious death in a ditch, pushed in by his own son; this is a far cry from the tragic fate of Laius and Oedipus.

The descriptions of the wonders encountered by Alexander in the East draw on the vogue for fantastic travelers' tales (for instance Lucian's *A True Story* and Antonius Diogenes' *Wonders Beyond Thule*). The account of the Brahmans would fit that category too, but it can also be linked to the vogue for histories of holy men or aretalogies popular in the imperial period. It is striking that in his fantastic travels Alexander does not achieve his goal of reaching the end of the world. Again and again he is advised to turn back, and is told that his goal is inappropriate. In the Middle Ages he was often used in exemplary literature as an example of overweening pride or *hubris*, and this tendency is already visible in the *Alexander Romance*. In the Land of Darkness, two birds with human faces deter him:

> "Why, Alexander, do you approach a land which is God's alone? Turn back, wretch, turn back; it is not for you to tread the Islands of the Blessed. Turn back, O man, tread the land that has been given to you and do not lay up trouble for yourself." (II. 40; Stoneman 1991: 121)

When he is carried up into the sky by huge carrion-eating birds, a flying man warns him: "O Alexander, you have not yet secured the whole earth, and are you now exploring the heavens? Return to earth as fast as is possible, or you will become food for these birds" (II. 41; Stoneman 1991: 123). The triumphs are balanced by the failures, and of course the whole story ends bleakly, with Alexander's betrayal and murder.

The abrupt shifts of both content and style that characterize the *Alexander Romance* are likely to strike the modern reader as peculiar and not altogether successful. One chapter is plain narrative, giving historically attested accounts of Alexander's journeys and military practices; but the next may be a rhetorically elaborate speech, or a letter reporting on his travels among fabulous peoples of the kind represented on medieval world maps. Realistic and practical details of warfare are juxtaposed with fantastic accounts of exotic peoples and customs. Clearly this mish-mash found favor, since the text in its various recensions was disseminated so widely. Of course, many classical histories contain episodes which strike modern readers as pure romance – for instance, that of Herodotus; but the proportion of history to romance in these works tends to be rather different. Paradoxically, some of the elements in the *Alexander* which seem most characteristic of romance are historically attested, for instance, Alexander's adoption of various disguises. Whether or not the exotic stories of Alexander's adventures had any basis in truth, we know that they were very popular: Strabo, writing in the first century AD, reports that "All who wrote about Alexander preferred the marvellous to the true" (2.1.9; Stoneman 1991: 9). Stoneman characterizes the *Alexander Romance* as "history becoming saga before our very eyes," a process familiar in more recent times too (1994: 120 and 118). But he sees it as more than just entertainment:

> The *Alexander Romance* is a text which uses the freedom of fiction to explore more fully, through philosophical and psychological means, the quality of a particular historical epoch. Like *War and Peace* or *Waverley* it adds to history in order to explain history.

This may be true, but it is also the case that Alexander, like many heroes, had become a magnetic figure who attracted many stories of very different kinds, and of whom almost anything could be believed. It is striking that the readership assumed by the romance as we know it was apparently equally happy to read about battle formations and philosophers, Amazons and underwater exploration.

Various versions of the *Alexander Romance* were known in the Middle Ages (as were some other classical accounts of his life), and he was a very popular literary figure (see Cary 1957). Some writers simply related his deeds and adventures, interspersing more or less fantastic material with reliable history; his letter describing the Brahmans was often circulated separately. But other writers, influenced by the Stoics and by Christian polemicists such as Orosius, were more hostile:

> Alexander was either fundamentally weak or fundamentally bad, and his continued prosperity, ascribed not to his own ability but to Fortune, encouraged his inherent weakness to yield to vicious influences, or his inherent wickedness to worsen as his power increased. (Cary 1957: 80)

It is instructive to compare the treatment of Alexander and Arthur. Arthur's mysterious and somewhat dubious birth story may well have been borrowed from that of Alexander. Both were raised to the throne when quite young, and both distinguished themselves early on by conquest. Both were included in the late medieval list of the Nine Worthies (three classical heroes, three biblical, and three medieval). Both stabilized and then enlarged their realms through war, and appeared unbeatable. Both died through treachery, before their time. But there the resemblance ends. In medieval romance Arthur is largely eclipsed by the knights of his Round Table, and especially by Lancelot. He rarely has adventures himself, or love affairs, and his final war against Rome ends in disaster. Alexander, however, is always the dominant character in his adventures; he is never eclipsed or even equaled by a lieutenant. He is constantly traveling, unlike Arthur.[5] He has no permanent court; and he has a complicated love life, though it is not central to his story. He marries Roxane, daughter of the defeated Persian king Darius, as a political move. Queen Candace becomes an object of his desire in some medieval versions of his story, but in the classical *Alexander Romance* she is merely a resourceful opponent (though she does have a portrait of him painted before she meets him, which no doubt encouraged medieval writers to develop her as a love interest). Apart from the opening story of Nectanebus' desire for Olympias, conquest and exploration are much more important in the *Alexander Romance* than romantic love. When Alexander meets his unhappy end, he writes a letter to his mother, and in one recension speaks his last words not to his wife but to his horse Bucephalus, which dies of sorrow after killing the treacherous slave who had administered poison to his master (Stoneman 1991: 157).

Apollonius of Tyre

Love is a very important element in the *Apollonius of Tyre* (*Historia Apollonii regis Tyri*), a narrative that may originally have been written in Greek, perhaps in the third century AD, but that survives only in a rather terse Latin form, written in the late fifth or early sixth century (see Archibald 1991, and 2001: 93–101). I have left it until last because, even more than the *Alexander Romance*, it both does and does not conform to expectations of ancient romance. At first glance the plot looks much like those of the five Greek romances, yet there are significant differences in the treatment of the familiar motifs of love, travel and adventure, separated families and recognition scenes.

> King Antiochus of Antioch seduces his only daughter, and sets a riddle for all her suitors, killing those who fail. Apollonius of Tyre solves the riddle, detecting the incest, but the king tells him he is wrong, and gives him a 30-day respite. Apollonius flees, pursued by Antiochus' assassin. He is shipwrecked in Cyrene, where he is befriended by the king, whose daughter he marries. Antiochus and his daughter are killed by a thunderbolt, and Apollonius is invited to rule over Antioch. On the way there, Apollonius' wife apparently dies in childbirth and is thrown overboard in a coffin. It arrives at Ephesus, where she is revived by a doctor and lives in the temple of Diana. Apollonius leaves his baby daughter Tarsia with foster parents at Tarsus, and goes off to Egypt in despair. Tarsia grows up to be beautiful and clever. Her jealous foster mother tries to murder her, but in the nick of time she is carried off by pirates and sold to a pimp in Mitylene. She manages to preserve her chastity in the brothel. Apollonius, in despair after being told that his daughter is dead, comes by chance to Mitylene; Tarsia is sent to entertain him. After he answers her riddles they discover their relationship. Tarsia marries the local prince, Athenagoras. In Ephesus Apollonius is reunited with his wife. The villains are punished. Apollonius inherits the throne of Cyrene, and has a son.

This narrative can be read as three separate romance plots combined. One features Apollonius, who loses a kingdom, finds a wife only to lose her as well as his daughter, then eventually regains them both, and ends up with several new kingdoms and a male heir. However, there is a major gap in his story when he goes off to Egypt in despair as a merchant for 15 years (during which Tarsia grows up). Then there are the stories of his wife and his daughter, who might be seen as two aspects of the standard Hellenistic romance heroine. His wife (unnamed in the earliest Latin versions) represents the motif of the protagonist separated from her beloved through the popular false death motif; but unusually, this is her only adventure. Once revived, she spends 15 years safe in a temple until it is time for the recognition scene.[6] It is their daughter Tarsia who stars in many of the other conventional romance episodes and undergoes most of the ordeals: she does not know her parents, is forced to leave her home because of a jealous foster mother, is carried off by pirates, and undergoes an ordeal in a brothel before the happy ending. It is Tarsia who revives the suicidal Apollonius, not his wife; but as soon as his daughter is identified, he marries her off without any concern for her own wishes. If there was a love story between Athenagoras and Tarsia in the *Ur*-text, involving passionate desire and obstacles to happiness, no trace of it remains. After the recognition scene with her father, Tarsia never speaks again. In the final scenes the focus is on Apollonius both as king – administering justice, rewarding his loyal helpers, and begetting a male heir – and as husband, inheriting his father-in-law's throne and begetting a son at last. It seems that there is only room for one extended love story in this romance: it is the love of Apollonius and his wife which is more fully explored, but even so this is very muted by the standards of the Greek romances. She falls in love at first sight, but he does not; he seems accepting rather than enthusiastic about his marriage, though after the wedding we are assured that the young couple loved each other devotedly and passionately. They are not faced with the typical challenges of the earlier Greek romances, however: they have no difficulty in remaining chaste, and face no temptations or ordeals before their final reunion. All the vicissitudes are piled onto their daughter Tarsia. And in order for her to grow up, the story has to span more than 15 years, unlike the Greek romances (the *Ethiopica* begins in the middle, when the heroine is already grown up, with flashbacks to the time of her birth).

Like the *Alexander Romance*, the *Apollonius* has some historical roots, though they are much less explicit and much less significant. I have argued elsewhere that one source for the plot may have been the struggles between Antiochus III and the Maccabees (Archibald 1991: 37–44). As in the five Greek romances, all the places that Apollonius visits were real cities (in the eastern Mediterranean); there are no fantastic episodes or travels beyond the bounds of the known world. Apollonius is a king, and by the end of the story he has acquired two new kingdoms (Antioch and Cyrene). It seems striking that the final aspect of the happy ending is the birth of a son, who can put an end to the problems caused by only daughters as heiresses. Yet there is little comment on the qualities of a good ruler, or on political issues; these are much stronger in some later versions of the story, most noticeably in Shakespeare's *Pericles, Prince of Tyre*. Most strikingly, Apollonius is no warrior, and fights no battles; instead, his main characteristic is his learning, which helps him to solve the initial riddle and causes the princess to fall in love with him. Both the female protagonists are very learned too. This is not a feature of other ancient romances, and makes one wonder all the more where this story was produced, and for whom.

Critics have also been very exercised over the opening incest episode, which is shockingly explicit: Antiochus rapes his virgin daughter and leaves her dripping blood on the floor. It has been argued that this scene was tacked onto the *Ur*-romance in order to create a catalyst for the flight and subsequent adventures of Apollonius, but this seems implausible. As many critics have noted, the shadow of incest hangs over the story from beginning to end. All the main male characters have daughters, and their relationships with these daughters are crucial to their moral status. Antiochus rapes his daughter, prevents her marrying, and lives in sin with her till they are struck dead by a thunderbolt from heaven. Archestrates admires and indulges his clever daughter, and allows her to marry a destitute stranger; the couple is reunited with him at the end just before his death, and he leaves his kingdom to them. Apollonius is separated early from his daughter, and when he meets her again their relationship is unknown to both of them. How will he treat her? He is strangely attracted to the clever girl sent to rouse him from his gloom, and she to him – but the recognition scene occurs before there can be any question of incest, and both are restored to their proper royal status. There is a clearly implied parallel between behavior as a father and behavior as a king; domestic tyranny indicates political tyranny.

Incest seems a dominant theme in the *Apollonius*, yet nothing is made of it at the end. One might have expected a final moral, such as is supplied in later versions of the story. Gower's narrator, the Confessor, explains to the young Amans "Lo thus, mi Sone, myht thou liere / What is to love in good manere, / And what to love in other wise" (*Confessio Amantis*, VIII.2009–11; "Thus, my son, you can learn what it is to love in a good way, and what to love otherwise"). Shakespeare is even clearer at the end of *Pericles* (Epilogue, 1–6):

> In Antiochus and his daughter you have heard
> Of monstrous lust the due and just reward.
> In Pericles, his queen and daughter, seen
> Although assail'd with fortune fierce and keen,
> Virtue preserv'd from fell destruction's blast,
> Led on by heaven, and crown'd with joy at last.

The phrasing here reminds us that Tarsia's ordeal in the brothel is reminiscent of the lives of virgin saints such as Agatha, Agnes, and Theodora, as much as of the vicissitudes of earlier romance heroines. The empire was officially Christian by the time the Latin text was composed: while there are no explicit references to Christianity in the text, apart from a vision of someone dressed like an angel, there may be some influence from hagiography and Christian romance in Tarsia's adventures, and in her characterization as a persecuted virgin.

It is not at all clear who might have constituted the intended audience of the Latin version as we have it. There are some literary allusions clearly aimed at the educated, but overall the style is not nearly as rhetorically polished and learned as that of the

Greek romances, which are all much longer and more leisurely in pace than *Apollonius*. Some strange gaps, inconsistencies, and failures of logic may be explained if it is an epitome of a longer and more complex lost Greek original. It is striking that the Greek romances do not survive in Latin translations, and were forgotten everywhere but in Byzantium until the Renaissance, when they were rediscovered, printed, and translated, and became very popular (see Beaton 1996; Hägg 1983, chapter 8). *Apollonius*, on the other hand, was read and referred to throughout the Middle Ages and into the Renaissance, when it was dramatized by Shakespeare as *Pericles, Prince of Tyre*. Versions of it exist in every European language, often much altered from the Latin original (see Archibald 1991): sometimes the story is made explicitly Christian, sometimes extra classical allusions are added to it; sometimes Apollonius is presented as Job, sometimes he becomes a chivalric hero, fighting both human and supernatural enemies, and showing a much stronger interest in love. It is curious that the most clumsy and undeveloped of the ancient romances should have had a much longer life than its more sophisticated and elaborate Greek predecessors. Was it really the only Latin version of a Greek romance of love and adventure? This seems unlikely, but until the sands of Egypt produce some papyrus fragments of lost Latin romances, we must treat it as a unique specimen.

Conclusion

Is there, or was there, really such a thing as ancient romance? It has become fashionable in modern literary criticism to say that "genres exist if readers think they exist," or that "genres are essentially literary *institutions*, or social contracts between a writer and a specific public."[7] The further back one goes in history, the harder it is to be at all clear about the generic expectations of contemporary readers. There is currently much debate about who read the ancient romances. Does the scarcity of texts, and of allusions to them, indicate that they were not very popular? The Greek papyrus fragments emerging from the sands of Egypt have already changed the critical picture considerably by proving the existence of romances unknown a hundred years ago and pushing back the time-frame for ancient romance, though some of the newcomers survive only in a few pages, and their plots are not easy to discover. They may have been read aloud, though there is no evidence of this practice. Or were they read to pieces, as has been argued for Malory a thousand years later? It may be true, as Reardon says (1989: 12), that "on the whole, the novel made little lasting impression on educated antiquity," but the novels we know are not the equivalent of Harlequin or Mills and Boon romances today. Certainly the intended audience was expected to catch the sophisticated literary and philosophical allusions, and admire the elaborate rhetoric: this suggests that the target audience was educated and as a consequence largely male. It seems clear, however, that, as Selden has argued (1994: 43), "there is no evidence that before the modern era the range of texts that we have come to call 'the ancient novel' was ever thought of together as constituting a coherent group." Indeed, modern critical expectations of ancient romance have changed considerably over the last two decades. Ancient romance remains a slippery and controversial topic.

See also: chapter 2, Insular Beginnings; chapter 3, The Popular English Metrical Romances; chapter 9, Shakespeare's Romances.

Notes

1. For translations of most of the Greek texts mentioned here, see Reardon 1989, which also includes some romance fragments and *Apollonius of Tyre*. Some variant versions of the *Alexander Romance* are added in Stoneman 1991. For details of editions and translations of both Greek and Latin texts, and critical comment, see recent studies of ancient fiction: Hägg 1983; Bowie and Harrison 1993; Tatum 1994; Morgan and Stoneman 1994; Schmeling 1996; Hock et al. 1998; Hofmann 1999.

2. For translations see Reardon 1989: 783–827. These discoveries have had a major impact on the study of ancient romance, in relation not only to date but also to content and popularity.

3. The romances themselves were sometimes incorporated into works of art: a mosaic in a villa near Antioch shows Ninus, Parthenope, and Metiochus, with their names beside them (see Hägg 1983: 18–23).

4. Cooper (1996: chapter 2) argues that the romances were intended to serve the common good by encouraging young lovers to do their civic duty by getting married and having children.

5. Such was his reputation as a traveler that in one medieval French romance, *Perceforest*, he visits England (Berthelot 1992).

6. The *Apollonius* seems to have been a source for Shakespeare's *Comedy of Errors*, where the long-lost mother emerges from a temple to bring about the family recognition scene in the final act.

7. The quotations are taken from Todorov and Jameson respectively, cited in Selden 1994: 45 and 47.

References and Further Reading

Archibald, Elizabeth (1991). *Apollonius of Tyre: Medieval and Renaissance Themes and Variations, Including the Text of the* Historia Apollonii regis Tyri *with an English Translation*. Cambridge: D. S. Brewer.

Bakhtin, M. M. (1981). "Forms of Time and of the Chronotope in the Novel: Notes towards a Historical Poetics." In *The Dialogic Imagination: Four Essays*, ed. Michael Holquist, trans. Caryl Emerson and Michael Holquist. Austin: University of Texas Press, pp. 84–258.

Beaton, Roderick (1996). *The Medieval Greek Romance*. 2nd edn., revised and expanded. London: Routledge.

Berthelot, Anne (1992). "La Grande Bretagne comme terre etrange/ère: le tourisme d'Alexandre dans le *Roman de Perceforest*." In Wolf-Dieter Lange, ed., *Diesseits- und Jenseistreisen im Mittelalter*. Bonn: Bouvier, pp. 11–23.

Bowersock, Glen (1994). *Fiction as History: Nero to Julian*. Berkeley and Los Angeles: University of California Press.

Bowie, E. L., and S. J. Harrison (1993). "The Romance of the Novel." *Journal of Roman Studies* 83, 159–78.

Braun, M. (1938). *History and Romance in Graeco-Oriental Literature*. Oxford: Clarendon Press.

Cary, George (1956). *The Medieval Alexander*, ed. D. J. A. Ross. Cambridge: Cambridge University Press.

Cooper, Kate (1996). *The Virgin and the Bride: Idealized Womanhood in Late Antiquity*. Cambridge, MA: Harvard University Press.

Frye, Northrop (1976). *The Secular Scripture: A Study of the Structure of Romance*. The Charles Eliot Norton Lectures, 1974–5. Cambridge, MA: Harvard University Press.

Hägg, Tomas (1983). *The Novel in Antiquity*. Berkeley and Los Angeles: University of California Press.

Hock, Ronald F., J. Bradley Chance, and Judith Perkins, eds. (1998). *Ancient Fiction and Early Christian Narrative*. Society of Biblical Literature Symposium Series 6. Atlanta, GA: Scholars Press.

Hofmann, Heinz, ed. (1999). *Latin Fiction: The Latin Novel in Context*. London and New York: Routledge.

Holzberg, Niklas (1995). *The Ancient Novel*, trans. Christine Jackson-Holzberg. London and New York: Routledge.

Kortekaas, G. A. A., ed. (1984). *Historia Apollonii regis Tyri*. Groningen: Bouma's Boekhuis.

Morgan, J. R., and Richard Stoneman, eds. (1994). *Greek Fiction: The Greek Novel in Context*. London and New York: Routledge.

Perry, Ben Edwin (1967). *The Ancient Romances: A Literary-Historical Account of Their Origins*. Sather Classical Lectures 37. Berkeley and Los Angeles: University of California Press.

Pervo, Richard I. (1987). *Profit with Delight: The Literary Genre of the Acts of the Apostles*. Philadelphia: Fortress Press.

Reardon, B. P., ed. (1989). *Collected Ancient Greek Novels*. Berkeley and Los Angeles: University of California Press.

Schmeling, Gareth, ed. (1996). *The Novel in the Ancient World*. *Mnemosyne*, Supplement 159. Leiden: Brill.

Selden, Dan (1994). "Genre of Genre." In James Tatum, ed., *The Search for the Ancient Novel*. Baltimore, MD: Johns Hopkins University Press, pp. 39–64.

Stoneman, Richard, trans. (1991). *The Alexander Romance*. London: Penguin.

Trenkner, Sophie (1958). *The Greek Novella*. Cambridge: Cambridge University Press.

Wiersma, S. (1990). "The Ancient Greek Novel and its Heroines: A Female Paradox." *Mnemosyne* XLIII, 109–23.

Winkler, Jack (1994). "The Invention of Romance." In James Tatum, ed., *The Search for the Novel*. Baltimore, MD: Johns Hopkins University Press, pp. 23–38.

2
Insular Beginnings:
Anglo-Norman Romance

Judith Weiss

When William the Conqueror and his knights invaded England in 1066, they ensured that their own language became the dominant one among the rulers of their new land, and that what was the current taste in northern France for epic literature became popular among the aristocracy here. The imported entertainment had a long life in insular society; nevertheless, in the first century and a half after the Norman arrival there was also an astonishing flowering of vernacular writing of many kinds, which owed little, sometimes nothing, to previous writing on the Continent. Recent scholarship has made us aware of the precocity of Anglo-Norman literature, and has convincingly linked this to England's multicultural and multilingual environment.[1] Among this writing in the French vernacular, romances occupy a prominent position. Long overlooked in favour of their Continental counterparts, they nevertheless appear earlier than many of them, and those early productions are of fine quality. Indeed, the beginnings of romance as a genre could fairly be said to be more associated with this country than with any other, as we shall see.

To distinguish insular from Continental romances too rigidly, however, would be a mistake: they are often written for patrons, and directed to audiences, who would have had lands and kin on both sides of the Channel, and who would have had similar interests and tastes; they are written by authors with similar education, influenced by the same classical school-texts. Above all, they are both written in the same language. If, by the thirteenth century, the orthography and grammar of Anglo-Norman are increasingly divergent from those of Northern French, up to about 1150 it is hard to distinguish them. Answering the question "what is Anglo-Norman?" is in any case complicated: for the purposes of discussing early romances I shall define it with some freedom. Crane's description, "broadly assigned to French texts produced in England" (Crane 1999: 38), provides a working definition, and allows some mention of those romances, such as *Amadas et Ydoine* and *Fergus*, which may have been written for insular patrons but are only fragmentarily, or no longer, extant in Anglo-Norman manuscripts.

Insular romance comes into being roughly halfway through the twelfth century. For those composing it, the memory of the long and peaceful rule of Henry I had been temporarily eclipsed by the horrors of the civil war of the 1140s, between the first cousins Stephen and Matilda. But this had been firmly brought to an end by the magnates on both sides; power had moved away from the king to them, and they were determined to see "the right heir of England" on the throne (Crouch 2000: 146, 242, from *Gesta Stephani*). Thus a second Henry had started a reign to compare with his grandfather's, and, like Henry I and his two queens, both he and his consort, Eleanor of Aquitaine, had wide cultural interests, not only in literature but in history, geography, and law. The production of historical work in England is especially remarkable: Latin historians of the first half of the century, such as William of Malmesbury, Henry of Huntingdon, and Geoffrey of Monmouth, prepared the ground for the blossoming of the *estoire*, the French verse history which appeared a century earlier in England than on the Continent and which was undoubtedly also indebted to Anglo-Saxon England's well-established vernacular tradition (see Damian Grint 1999). At least four of these histories are associated with the Angevin court: Wace's *Roman de Brut* and *Roman de Rou*, Benoît de Sainte-Maure's *Chronicle of the Dukes of Normandy*, and Jordan Fantosme's *Chronicle*.

It is important to see the birth of insular romance against this background of interest in history, for the two are often closely associated. The dedicatees and patrons of both kinds of work frequently seem to have taken a keen interest in the history (legendary and otherwise) of their adopted country. Historians and writers of romance are also alike in the contents and procedures of their texts. Chronicle writers like Geoffrey of Monmouth, Geffrei Gaimar, and Wace provide stories supposedly from the insular past which are taken up into romances and acquire a long life thereby: the most evident example is of course the material about Arthur, but Gaimar's story of the hero Haveloc was soon removed from its chronicle context into a *lai* or short romance, and thereafter to a full-blown English romance. Writers of romance similarly provided stories which were appropriated by chroniclers and passed off as factual. The styles of poets of fiction and nonfiction are the same: they use the poetic unit, the *laisse*, with its ten- or twelve-syllable line, familiar from the French epics, the *chansons de geste*, or the newer octosyllabic couplet, and in the latter especially, show the influence of classical rhetoric. The values they promulgate are similar: they praise *corteisie* (even if they may leave its definition to the context) and slate *vilainie*. They tend to draw attention to themselves, in prologues, epilogues, or the body of their work, as "truthful," authoritative, serious writers, keen to instruct as well as entertain their audiences. This self-validation is a device which will become increasingly ironic.

Gaimar's *Estoire des Engleis* (1138–40)[2] is a good example of history's close links with romance and the way it enables its production. The poet evidently regards himself as a serious scholar: he refers to his work as a *veire estoire* ("a true history," 756), meticulously lists its sources, and asserts that it is neither "fable ne sunge" ("fiction nor vision," Appendix, 16). Fictional elements, however, feature in his opening story, the Lincolnshire tale of Haveloc, probably chosen to please his patroness Constance, wife of Ralph FitzGilbert, who had estates there (Bell 1960: 9). This self-contained tale is carefully inserted into that little-known period immediately after the death of Arthur and connected to "the passage of dominion" from Britons to Saxons; it also has the function of explaining the later claim of the Danes to England because of the Danish Havelok's earlier rule (2071–84). It contains themes such as the dispossession and restoration of rightful princes, and the vulnerability of the female heir, which might seem calculated to appeal to an audience after the death of Henry I. It leaves history quite behind with its elements of magic – flames and horns which amazingly proclaim the true heir – and folk tale – the strong simpleton who nevertheless wins an heiress and two countries, and turns out to be a prince in disguise. Thus it is not surprising to see it reappearing, with a courtly gloss, as a *lai* at the turn of the twelfth and thirteenth centuries.[3]

Gaimar's work drew largely on the *Anglo-Saxon Chronicle* but he also knew the influential Latin "history," Geoffrey of Monmouth's *Historia Regum Britanniae* (late 1130s), whose influence was spread yet more widely by its Norman translator, Wace, in his verse *Brut*, supposedly presented to Queen Eleanor in 1155 (according to La3amon's *Brut*: lines 19–23). Wace rendered Geoffrey fairly faithfully, but he seems to have picked up local stories and details from travels in southern and western Britain, along with some English and Welsh words, with which to embellish his text. Though fascinated by these, and by the way changes in names mark transitions in language and culture, he takes pains to present himself as scholarly and skeptical in relation to his sources so that we may believe him truthful and authoritative. He refers, like Gaimar, to written accounts; in his later *Roman de Rou* he even invokes his own eyewitness experience. His justification for writing is to preserve the memory of the past, as an example and a warning to others. He helped to spread the fame of the Arthurian material he used – which from then on could travel into either genre, chronicle or romance – but also to bolster the taste for insular story which was increasingly characteristic of twelfth-century Anglo-Norman audiences. Wace, like Gaimar before him, chose the new octosyllabic couplets for his *Brut*, but his style is still clearly indebted to that of the *chansons de geste*. Though the line has shrunk, the formulaic phrases seeking to involve an audience – *Es vus* (here comes . . .), *or oiez* (now hear . . .), *dunc veissiez* (now you could see) – are still retained, as are the patterns of combat (see Rychner 1955). The early romances, like the histories,[4] have the option of using either style; the choice of the older one results in interestingly hybrid works.

The context for the birth of early romance in Angevin Britain, then, is an interest in insular history and topography and a choice of narrative styles. The three *romans d'antiquité* (the *Roman d'Eneas*, the *Roman de Thèbes*, and the *Roman de Troie*, 1150s–70s) provide another influence on Anglo-Norman romance, though they are always claimed as Continental works.[5] In fact they are a perfect example of the futility of countries attempting to stick nationalist labels on literature: their authors came from northern France but spent at least some time working for Henry II and his wife Eleanor (whether in England or Normandy) and there has been speculation but no proof that all three were involved in some kind of literary atelier at court

(Damian-Grint 1999: 59; Angeli 1971: viii–ix; Petit 1991: 10). It is certainly true, however, that they are not interested in insular material: "the new intellectual vitality of the twelfth century" (Short 1991: 231) has led them to take their stories from classical writers such as Virgil and Statius, and their representations of the tortures of love from Ovid, even if characters and combats are frequently still indebted to the *chanson de geste*.

In several ways these *romans antiques* remind us of the vernacular histories: their authors make us aware of their presence through comments on the action and on the importance of demonstrating one's learning by a story worthy of memory (as in the *Roman de Thèbes*), and through their desire to instruct their audiences. This last, however, has less to do with "truth" than with the writers' classical education and with the taste for the exotic stimulated by European contacts with the East. Here we see appearing a feature often said to be typical of romance. The three poems supply fanciful details of splendid and elaborate cities, tents, and tombs, and describe elegant, richly decorated interiors. The arts of refined living are slowly becoming as important as the martial struggles in the field, and by the end of the *Roman d'Enéas* include an interest in private feeling: Lavine and her Trojan hero both endlessly analyze their love.

The importance of women in these romances, as opposed to many of the *chansons de geste*, is undeniable, though it is striking how powerless they are: female rulers are unable to take care of their lands and are advised to remarry quickly; maidens may observe from watchtowers and comment upon their lovers fighting but cannot influence their fates, and though remarkably learned cannot prevent lovers abandoning them. There is a marked amount of misogynistic comment, more in *Enéas* and *Troie* than in *Thèbes*, and in all it is clear that though women may feel passionate desire, it is reprehensible for them to display it. In these respects the *romans antiques* do no more than reflect the society that produced them and resemble markedly many of the later Anglo-Norman romances. The *Roman de Thèbes*, earliest of the three, is also closest, despite differences of setting, to some of its Anglo-Norman successors in several of its themes: it chooses a pessimistic story about a fratricidal war in which the best die and the land is ruined, and it presents both Oedipus and Polynices in turn as wrongly disinherited sons who are rescued by a neighboring king. The first may be a response to civil war in England; the second broaches a subject used equally by *chansons de geste* and insular romance.

The *romans antiques* are quickly followed by – indeed, may be contemporary with – two talented and unrelated poets called Thomas, whose romances may unequivocally be called Anglo-Norman, though their settings and heroes are decidedly insular. The authors of *Horn* and *Tristan* could have written any time between the 1150s and 1170s; there have been persuasive attempts to link them to the royal court but (despite *Tristan*'s praise of London) no firm evidence (Short 1991: 231). They are, however, connected to each other by their use of very similar story material, some of which is also present in the earlier Latin account of Hereward, the *Gesta Herewardi*, equally difficult to date.[6] This provides the first example of what becomes characteristic of many if not most Anglo-Norman romances: their intertextuality.[7]

Thomas' *Tristan* (1155–75) seems to be the first extant version of a story already known some decades earlier Gaunt 1986: 108–13) and survives only in nine fragments. In its depiction of a love inextricably mixed with suffering, expressed in long, tortured, and intensely analytical monologues, it is reminiscent of the *romans antiques*; unlike them, the reflections of Tristan and Iseut on their contradictory emotions seem more important than the action, their *aventures* as much internal as external. Though Thomas has softened and given a courtly gloss to aspects of his story, in other respects the actions of his lovers are far from courtly: their passion is compulsive, not chosen, it involves sordid stratagems and lies, and their loyalty to each other entails breaking faith to others, whether spouses or king. The poet is prominent in his romance, making us aware of his choice of sources (perhaps passing off his own inventions as one of them) and presenting himself as more authoritative than his rivals, seeing his function as preserving the truthful memory of his story while simultaneously (and contradictorily) embellishing and instructing through it. Linguistic similarities link his work with the story of Tristan's madness, the *Folie Tristan d'Oxford* (1175–1200), which succinctly condenses the tale of the lovers into one short episode by the use of constant flashbacks.[8]

Thomas' *Tristan* may have been known to Marie de France when she wrote her *Lais* (ca. 1160–90); though the form of her stories limits lengthy analysis of emotion, they show familiarity with the story of Tristan (the *lai* of *Chevrefueille*), as well as with Arthurian legends (the *lai* of *Lanval*) and possibly (the *lai* of *Eliduc*) with the *Romance of Horn*. She too depicts love affairs often at odds with society and the value of *fei* (loyalty), and makes us aware of the poet's task of preserving a tale in the fashion best calculated to teach a truth or significant meaning, while drawing attention to her name; this self-advertisement is by now becoming the hallmark of romance written on the Continent as well as in Britain, as Chrétien de Troyes' works (1170s–90s) attest.

The second Thomas' *De Horn Bono Milite* (as its Oxford manuscript labels it), hardly known in comparison with the other work, nevertheless deserves equal fame. It is the first of the insular "hybrids," poems which successfully combine the form and much of the spirit of the *chanson de geste* with elements introduced by romances. The *Horn* poet, one *mestre* Thomas, who writes with a rich and varied vocabulary and some knowledge of English,[9] is adept at using and varying the epic form, so that his hero's three battles against "Saracens" have all the crusading zeal and impetus of the *Chanson de Roland*. But times of peace, and scenes away from the battlefield in richly decorated interiors, are presented with more panache, and less digressiveness, than in the *romans antiques*. Thomas' use of detail is perhaps driven by a compulsion to explain and connect, but it is strikingly successsful in some of the high points of the poem, such as the music-making at the Irish court or the rescue of the heroine at her wedding feast. Women have an important role to play: they are depicted somewhat in the manner of the *romans antiques*, with their forward desires revealed, if disapproved of, by a notably priggish hero; the epic form has relieved them of the burden of lengthy self-analyses, however, and their portrayal is softened by both sympathy and humor.

Thomas' material is a mixture of insular and more widely occurring themes: the exiled prince regaining his lands, and the man with two wives, are popular stories not confined to Anglo-Norman narratives. On the other hand, his material may have been shaped by twelfth-century insular history and by earlier Viking raids on Ireland and southern England, and he seems to have some knowledge of Ireland. He refers repeatedly to sources, apparently written ones, which may have been influenced by the *Gesta Herewardi*. These references may be not entirely trustworthy, for he refers to a preceding poem about Aalof, Horn's father, in a way that does not bear too much scrutiny. But in advertising his own name, works, and a projected poem about Horn's son, to be carried out by his own son, Willemot, Thomas repeats a feature of insular writing we have noticed so far: such poets (like the historians) are eager to persuade us of their reliability and learning. It is a pity we have no certain evidence of his patron and audience; we can at least assume that they knew some English, and something of Ireland (Weiss 1999: 7–9).[10]

Hue de Rotelande (fl. ca.1180–90), the talented poet of two romances (*Ipomedon* and *Protheselaus*), gives us, on the other hand, plenty of details of himself (his house and town), his friends or competitors (Walter Map, Hue de Hungrie), contemporary wars and figures, and his patron, Gilbert FitzBaderon, lord of Monmouth.[11] Apparently as keen as Thomas to authorize the sources of his two romances, which he insists are "translations" from Latin and a book in FitzBaderon's library, Hue's emphasis on the truth of his narratives is deliberately and comically undercut by a passage in *Ipomedon* asserting he never lies "except sometimes" (7177). His manipulation for parodic purposes goes far beyond just burlesquing authors' puffs: the intertextuality of insular romances emerges in his deliberate use of themes, motifs, and styles from the *romans d'antiquité* and probably from the *Romance of Horn* and various versions of the Tristan story.

Hue is not, however, a slavish plagiarizer. As much at home with the formulaic accounts of combat derived from the *chansons de geste* as with the newer *topoi* of romance, he excels at casting these in new lights. Familiar with Arthurian romance, probably through reading Chrétien, his use of it is indirect and subtle. Deliberately rejecting the insular history and topography of Horn or Tristan, he takes his settings from the Norman kingdoms of southern Italy and Sicily and his names from the *romans antiques*, but uses the latter obliquely or ironically: Ipomedon, the hero of a long section of *Thèbes* and a model of an active, responsible leader, is transmuted into a man who to most of his world seems to be quite the opposite; Meleager, valiant cousin of Eteocles in *Thèbes*, has become an Arthur figure, a *roi fainéant*; Ismaine, whose sensual relationship with Athon was celebrated in the same romance of *Thèbes*, has become much more wanton, and more despised, as she repeatedly tries to betray her mistress by seducing her true love; in *Protheselaus* she tries to seduce La Fiere's son, 20 years her junior. The theme of fraternal strife, a tragic one in *Thèbes*, reappears in both Hue's romances, but the stress falls mostly on reconciliation, not death. The *topoi* of disguise, concealment of names, prowess earning love, rings of recognition, rescues in the nick of time, and long tormented internal monologues become comical through repeated use. Above all, the frequent employment of delay and postponement of closure mocks the characteristic romance move toward a happy ending: Hue's heroes seem to abrogate their responsibilities to marry and settle down in favor of endless adventures. Their long-suffering mistresses, and all the other female figures, are presented in misogynistic, even obscene, terms, peppered with proverbs, suggesting a worldly cynicism presumably appealing to an audience plausibly characterized as small, intimate, even a coterie.[12]

In Thomas of Kent's Alexander romance, the *Geste d'Alisandre* or the *Roman de Toute Chevalerie*[13] (ca. 1175–85) insular settings are again eschewed, this time in favor of the distant and exotic settings of the Middle and Far East. The Alexander stories clearly appealed to the serious, moralistic, and philosophical bent of this poet, who has little in common with Hue de Rotelande except a love of proverbs. Unlike Hue and the poet of *Horn* he is not especially inventive: he has drawn on many other authors, as he repeatedly acknowledges, for the scenes in Alexander's life. In some ways this is what is most extraordinary about his account: that the backbone of the work is still the largely historical version we know initially from Arrian. Despite all the extraordinary and fantastic accretions over the centuries, it is this which accounts for both the shortcomings and the power of the *Roman de Toute Chevalerie*. Its episodic quality is characteristic of all biographies, nor has this poet been able to integrate scenes such as the encounters with Queen Candace smoothly and consistently into the narrative. His description of the marvels and monstrosities encountered by Alexander is lengthy and repetitive: monoceroses (unicorns) appear at least three times, and dragons are two a penny.

Yet the high points of the original biography – not directly available to Thomas but known through later histories of Alexander, like an epitome (abridgment) of Julius Valerius' *Res Gestae Alexandri Magni* and the *Epistola Alexandri ad Aristotelem* (Foster 1977: II, 62–3) – also move him to passages of great literary power, still affecting today. The dignified death of Darius, betrayed by his own men, and Alexander's own parting reflections on man's mortality, are both conveyed with rhetorical skill. Thomas also rises splendidly to the challenges of some incidents which early became part of the legendary tradition, such as the enclosure of the cannibalistic tribes of Gog and Magog, and the prophecy by the Trees of the Sun and Moon that Alexander will die at the hands of a traitor. The poet's choice of the *chanson de geste* form for his material is advantageous for such moments of brilliance in that it provides a more flexible unit and a longer line, more suitable for gravity and weight.

Once again, therefore, as with *Horn*, a narrative hybrid of romance and epic has been created, though the balance leans rather more toward epic. Marvelous adventures, fantastic creatures, exotic cities, and palaces are features of both late *chansons de geste* and romance; on the other hand, though Alexander is exceptionally well-educated and well-mannered, these are the only courtly facets to the poem which, in the depiction of its very few women, manages a combination familiar from epic (and indeed from *Horn*) of vivid appreciation of their attractions with irrelevant misogynistic comment on their lechery and deceit. "Amur fine" (7755) is in fact merely a coy way of alluding to sex; love as a source of moral worth has no part to play here, while the ethos of the poem as a whole is overwhelmingly militaristic, expressed in all the conventional epic formulae.

The Middle Ages inherited both antagonistic and admiring views of Alexander (Crane 1986: 108–9). Walter of Chatillon, a contemporary of Thomas of Kent, favors a more positive view in his *Alexandreis* (ca. 1182), and Thomas himself is more inclined to praise than blame. Alexander's obsession with exacting "tribute" wherever he goes, while refusing it to others, is critically observed, especially when he wishes to extend his conquests even to the Earthly Paradise. On the other hand, he is for the most part portrayed as a Christian *avant la lettre*, a monotheist whom God uses as His instrument to improve the world, and a forerunner of the Last World Emperor, holding back the barbarians before the arrival of Antichrist.[14] His admired *chevalerie* is inextricably bound up with the restless but honorable desire to explore the outer bounds of the earth.

The author tells us a great deal more about himself than just his tendency to philosophic reflection. Though he employs a vocabulary as wide and learned as that of his namesake who wrote *Horn*, he alludes a couple of times to his Englishness (4662, 4674–5) and *suffreite de romanz* (lack of French), though a positively Chaucerian invitation to his audience to amend whatever is superfluous in his poetry (6655–6) alerts us to a feigned modesty. He is by turns boastful and defensive of his work, asserting its authority, its truthfulness, and its Horatian function to supply both profit and delight. Moreover he tells us his name, refers to an (unnamed) patron (6645), and, through his frequent considerations of the fate of the *bosoignus*, the poor and needy, perhaps insinuates that he is one of them (see especially 4688–9). This is, in short, an author who insists that his distinctive voice be heard.

The narrative voice in *Boeve de Haumtone* (1190s) is less ironic and sophisticated, more comic, vigorous, and even crude. Much of this romance takes place, like the *Roman de Toute Chevalerie*, in the Middle East, but there is little of the supernatural or the marvelous in it. It has obviously been influenced by the crusading ethos of the *chansons de geste*: its hero fights for a pagan king, marries his converted daughter, a *bele Sarrasine* ("beautiful Saracen"), smashes idols, and is aided (and betrayed) by an Ethiopian giant straight out of the pages of Albert of Aix's History of the First Crusade.[15] The third of the narrative "hybrids," it began a story of astonishing popularity throughout Europe. This popularity may be surprising to us, since the romance as it stands is structurally unsatisfactory: its second part reads like an inconsistent continuation, planned in outline but careless in detail. The concerns of the first part resemble those of *Horn*: the exiled hero makes good abroad, securing land and a wife, who is threatened by unwelcome and forced marriages, before returning to claim his inheritance and defeat his enemies. The second part begins and ends with the unjust behavior of the English king, out to dispossess Boeve (supported by the barons) and his friends; in between, the hero's family is again scattered and reunited, lands are accumulated, and wars are fought, in a jerky and episodic narrative in which Boeve finishes as a French rather than an English champion and spends his final days far from his native land (Weiss 1986).

Boeve would appear to have drawn upon the *Romance of Horn*, recycling themes popular with an insular audience, but there is a great difference in construction and tone. While Thomas almost obsessively explained, motivated, and prepared actions, and set them against a detailed, substantial background, *Boeve's* author or authors do not bother with either. Geography is vague: Spain, North Africa, and Syria all appear as contiguous, while Hampton and Arundel both seem next door to London. Sarah Kay (1995: 224) has persuasively argued that the lawless ungoverned behavior in the romance points to a world where a society barely exists, and the same could be said of *Waldef* (see below). Certainly both social settings and constraints are never fleshed out. Thomas was expert at handling the *laisse* form. In contrast, the *Boeve* poet(s), after a promising beginning where short *laisses* are used to focus on the important features of the plot, allows the units to expand to unwieldy length.

Tone distinguishes these two romances most. The hero of *Boeve*, though described as *le curteis guerrer*, deserves only the last word: arrogant, stupid, rude, and rash, his nobility and dignity are too often abrogated in favor of vigorous, even brutal words and acts, whose details destroy idealism. Boeve's feigned snores when Josiane comes to his bed to woo him remind us of a similar crudely comic scene in *Ipomedon*. Yet the depiction of Josiane, whose experiences in the first half of *Boeve* are broadly similar to Rigmel's in *Horn*, is such as to contradict Simon Gaunt's assertion that writers of romance don't actually like or respect women:[16] she is sensual and violent but also talented in music and magic, enterprising and resourceful, more intelligent than her husband. She gives Boeve his horse Arundel ("swallow," 542), with which she is in several places in the narrative virtually identified. The horse's name may well refer to one of the Albini family's devices, probably taken from the town of Arundel's arms in the twelfth century, and since it was Adeliza of Louvain, Queen Dowager and wife of William II of Albini, who brought him the town at their marriage, the romance has perhaps hit upon a way of praising a patroness, whether mother or wife (Weiss 1986: 239). There were family connections between the Albinis, the Clares (possible patrons for *Horn*), and the FitzBaderons (patrons of Hue de Rotelande): the possibility of romance texts being passed between the families, serving as inspiration for the poets they employed, is a fascinating if unproven one.[17]

No patrons are either known, or have yet been plausibly suggested, for the lengthy and unfinished *Waldef* (early thirteenth century).[18] Neglected by critics, it is nevertheless a key text, as Field first pointed out, in the development of Anglo-Norman romance in that it draws heavily on previous insular narrative and in turn influences what comes next, notably the more popular *Gui de Warewic*.[19] Its author was indebted to Wace (and not merely its Arthurian section), the *Roman de Thèbes*, and the romances of Horn, Boeve, Tristan, and possibly Alexander, in addition to using classical stories such as Hero and Leander. Not only did it serve as a model for *Gui* but it was translated into Latin prose in the fifteenth century by Johannes Bramis, a monk at Thetford, a translation which provides us with an end to the romance though not necessarily quite the one envisaged by the poet.[20]

The author of *Waldef* cannot be identified, though tantalizingly he promises to identify both himself and his *duce amie* at the end. This lady, whom he praises (despite misogynistic outbursts about women) and serves, has apparently asked him to translate the *estoire englesche* (85) of Waldef, though the poem's editor has convincingly shown this is more likely to be an example of a contemporary device for authorization of a newly invented text than a genuine English source. The poet is clearly a native of East Anglia, as appears in his detailed knowledge of its topography, but he is geographically under-informed about both Continental settings and English ones beyond Norfolk and Suffolk; as Holden (1984: 20, 32) points out, the sea is so important to him that he moves all important towns to its shores, even Cologne. He enjoys intervening in his narrative, sometimes to stimulate the interest of the *seignurs* of his audience, by anticipating exciting events or raising the emotional register: he has a particular taste for dramatic irony, lamenting his characters' ignorance in a potentially fatal encounter. His fervent and frequent praise for "les Englois," superior to all other nationalities, especially the French and Germans, points to an audience the members of which were similarly proud of their adopted country, even if they did not speak its language, but, as in *Boeve*, his praise is not accompanied by any feeling for the kingdom as a whole (Holden 1984: 35–6; Field 2000: 35).

The poem is long without a corresponding density of detail. A narrative flaw is the insistence on retelling events rather than summarizing them. Threads are left hanging; there are inconsistencies and implausibilities; the pasteboard characters turn from baddies to goodies in an unprepared instant. Yet the romance also has some of the virtues of a long nineteenth-century novel: when enemies long at daggers drawn are at last reconciled, the scene is moving, and there is an undoubted climax in Guiac's triumphant coronation as emperor, swiftly followed by the news of his father Waldef's death and his own resolution to renounce power. The poet could draw on a larger emotional palette than *Boeve's* author and though he manages his narrative at a fast pace, he can also pause for moments of emotional intensity.

The poem's octosyllabic couplets provide the style most characteristic of romance, but epic also is milked for numerous elements which by 1200 have become clichés: Saracen invasions, noble pagans, the Christian hero fighting for a pagan king, the search for identity, exiled heirs, narrowly avoided incestuous unions and the killing of close relations in fights, rescues from forced marriages and rings of recognition are merely some of these. Field (2000: 35) has observed *Waldef's* "rejection of romance's expectations and values," most notably in the hero's death in the streets of Rochester. We do not expect the hero to die in romance. We also expect women to play a substantial role. Despite the poet's use of the Hero and Leander story, an emotional high point, women and love make rare appearances in a predominantly male world. They are given the obligatory monologue to express how far they are *susprise d'amor* ("seized by love") for a hero; they may even take the initiative in wooing him. But a ruler's consultation of his barons and the difficult life of a mercenary are issues that engage the poet as much or more, though his male characters also show the sensibility that gradually became fashionable for heroes during the twelfth century: they may dash out the brains of an innocent child one moment, then sigh, weep, and faint over followers or family the next.[21]

Like *Ipomedon*, this romance has incidents which recall Arthurian narrative. Field first pointed out that the episode of the mysterious palmer who appears at Guiac's court to warn him of the consequences of his arrogant determination to conquer Rome, Jerusalem, and the Earthly Paradise is the only known forerunner of the scene in the alliterative *Morte Arthure* where Sir Cradok, the palmer, gives a similar warning to the king (Field 2000: 29); this episode is closely followed by the scene with the messengers from England bringing news of Waldef's death and the usurpation of the family lands, reminiscent of scenes in Arthurian chronicle. Geoffrey of Monmouth, and especially Wace, have ambivalent attitudes to would-be conquerors (Weiss 2002: 90) which *Waldef* has absorbed; the many references to Belin, Brenne, Arthur, and especially Alexander, *celi qui tant fist sanc espandre* ("he who shed so much blood," 15538) warn us against endorsing Guiac's lust for power and prepare us for what might seem a rather abrupt about-turn when he relinquishes power and embraces the pilgrim's tattered clothes.

If the vocabulary of conquest increasingly dominates the narrative of Guiac's achievements, another linguistic repetition characterizes the latter stages of the poem. Words expressing betrayal and abandonment, above all *(de)guerpir* (forsake, desert), point to an important theme of the romance throughout: neighbors are attacked and betrayed by neighbors when they should support each other (15087–92); followers are abandoned by their leader, rulers of cities are betrayed by citizens; and most of all, the second generation deserts the first whether by death or departure. The emperor laments the death of his only daughter and heir, closely followed by his nephew's, making him powerless against the takeover of his empire by the English (20199–209). Waldef and his wife beg their sons to stay and seek adventure at home rather than abroad, and Waldef knows he will die alone without their help (15281–91) – anticipating his final words: "Ah, ah! my sweet sons, if you were now here, I would still be alive and well. Alas! now I shall be killed" (21343–56).

The England of the poem is a land of kinglets aggressively jostling for power, each with his power-base in a city. The importance of cities is signaled from the very start of the romance, when the Romans establish them to civilize and protect the land, and though centralized control and order break down when they depart, the kings of Norfolk and Suffolk follow the Roman example and construct more. Cities are powerful and wealthy centers, great prizes to be won, and their inhabitants play important roles throughout the poem, in both a negative and a positive way. Early on, the citizens of Colchester, besieged by Waldef, decide to abandon their young and rash ruler, Swein, and allow him to leave the city while they close the gates behind him, leaving him vulnerable to enemy attack. The citizens have made a sensible decision to back the winning side, but this is regarded as rank treachery; once Waldef has persuaded Swein to join forces with him and captures the city, 43 of the *burgois* are hanged. Merlin tells the story of Hertford whose *felun burgois* (villainous people) rebelled in the past against their ruler; the city was destroyed as a consequence and never recovered its former prosperity. A treacherous *vesquons* (sheriff) of London lures Waldef into a trap in Cheapside. The deep disapproval the poet expresses at such actions suggests a view of burgesses as disloyal, concerned only with their own skins and comfort. But there is an interesting counterview. When Fergus, king of London, proposes unjust action against one of his mercenary supporters, Okenard, the *vesquons* of the city, Edward, intervenes and rebukes him. Reminding him that a mercenary can't be punished in the way a liegeman can, Edward magisterially declares that the king's proposed action *n'est pas l'us de ceste cité* ("is not what this city usually does") and *ceste esguard n'avom pas veü* ("we have not seen this decision before"). The city is the audience and judge for the ruler's behavior. Fergus is forced to submit (10700–74).

The romance thus expresses an ambivalent view toward the growing power of cities and their citizens. It contains ideas familiar from older narratives, about the importance of the land, its defense, invasion, and devastation, but it also recognizes the concentration of power and wealth in towns and thus their importance to rulers. They sustain kings, judge and correct their actions, but they can also be easily persuaded to betray and kill them: Waldef dies in Rochester, not on the battlefield. Just as the Continental section of the romance charts the declining power of the empire, so the English portion makes us aware of the inexorable rise of the bourgeoisie.

The bourgeoisie play no part in *Gui de Warewic* (early thirteenth century)[22] but the decline of the empire is even more marked in this romance, which is closely dependent on *Waldef*. *Gui's* world is historically and geographically more precise than *Waldef's*: it encompasses the Byzantine empire as well as the Holy Roman one and knows the German part of the latter reasonably well. Its hero aids both emperors, but neither aims to conquer the world (like Guiac) nor to defend his patrimony (like the heroes of many previous insular romances); his most distinctive feature is in fact to abjure all lands and power in the second half of his career. The accommodation of religious piety with undiminished prowess is possibly one of the features which ensured the story's extraordinarily long life.

The poet seems familiar with the work of Wace, Chrétien de Troyes, and insular romance, though he makes his heroine far less forthcoming than any we have encountered so far. He refers, as we have come to expect, to an almost certainly nonexistent source and, apart from a prologue and epilogue of fairly conventional sentiments, makes little appearance in his narrative other than occasionally to augment interest by way of anticipations and promises. Clearly he knew the Oxford area, especially Wallingford, but he never addresses his audience in any way more specific than "seigneurs," and claims that the poem is an "ancestral" romance written for the d'Oilly family have attracted only muted support.[23]

While drawing on *Waldef*, the *Gui* poet obviously learnt from its deficiencies, and writes more succinctly. His fast-paced romance is apparently divided, not between the deeds of parents and children but between those of a hero driven by different impulses. Yet in fact the second generation does appear, in the adventures of Reinbrun after his father's death. There are signs that these are a later addition, stimulated perhaps by the success of Gui's exploits.[24] Fighting is the backbone of these, whether for Felice or for God, and two fights in particular are described at length: with the Saracen champion Amoraunt, and with the seneschal Berard. The close parallels between these fights perhaps serve to make the point that Christendom can provide treachery equal to any from Islam. In both cases they are also connected with Gui's identity. In his new role of religious warrior, he is modestly reluctant to disclose his name though insistent on his Englishness; nevertheless the revelation of his identity is always the climax of episodes like these.

In this overwhelmingly masculine world (Felice provides Gui with fashionable amatory laments, a spur to his initial adventures and thus his fame, and an heir, but otherwise has no existence or interest) the protagonists are constantly parted and constantly search for each other, often appearing as pilgrims *en route* to a deeply desired person, never to a shrine. It is homosocial, not heterosexual love, which most frequently gives rise to emotional scenes, and of these the temporary reunion of Gui and Terri at a stone cross outside the city is the most striking, with its suggestion that, for a moment, Gui with his battered and cracked feet has become a type of Christ, willing to lay down his life for his friends. There is more than a passing resemblance here to the contemporary Continental romance *Robert le Diable*, and in both works the corpse of the dead hero, emitting an odor of sanctity, becomes a highly desirable object transported from its original tomb to a specially constructed abbey.

Throughout the romance there is also an important stress on the injustices perpetrated under imperial rule, especially in the Holy Roman empire. The emperor is not personally wicked but allows his vassals – Seguin, Terri, Amis – to be appallingly maltreated. Only the peripatetic English hero can put matters right, while observing, as Crane has remarked, the proper judicial procedures (Crane 1986: 78–80; Weiss 2002: 101). *Gui*, like *Waldef*, testifies to the fact that in the early thirteenth century the French-speaking nobility of England regarded themselves as English and as equal, if not superior, to anyone in the imperial domains.[25]

Fouke le Fitz Waryn, a verse romance of the 1260s surviving only in a 1325–40 prose redaction, is undoubtedly indebted to earlier insular romance and historiography. But two aspects of it strike us: first of all, that it is written so long after the other romances. The gap between *Gui* and *Fouke* seems to have been filled, not by original compositions but by scribal copies, throughout the thirteenth century, of all the previous romances, which indicates their continuing popularity, if also a decay of the genre in Anglo-Norman. Secondly, this romance relates not pre- but post-Conquest history, about known, not legendary, figures. The localities of the authors of both the original poem and its prose *remaniement* (rearrangement) are clear, even if their names are unknown: the first knows Ludlow very well and is familiar with the major and minor towns on the borders with Wales; the second, the compiler of the single manuscript (British Library, Royal 12.C.xii), as also of British Library, Harley 2253, both trilingual miscellanies, is a priest, probably a canon of Hereford (Hathaway et al. 1975: xxxv–xliv).

It is clear that the poet's sympathies are with baronial opponents to the king (John), and we may assume that his audience (addressed only as "seygnours") shared his anti-royalist sentiments, but the narrative is no longer thought of as an "ancestral" romance, since although it celebrates the adventures of the FitzWaryn family, it also makes many mistakes about its history (Crane 1986: 17). If it originally stems from the 1260s, this was as turbulent a period of conflict between barons and king as was the era of Magna Carta, so the romance could have been enjoyed as particularly appropriate to contemporary events. It is a lively, fast-moving account in which fragments of the original verse still occur, or can be detected from rhyme-words, and contains an interesting mixture of realism and fantasy. The opening, apart from a FitzWaryn ancestor vanquishing a devil who inhabits the body of Gogmagog, reflects the historical apportioning of lands in the Welsh Marches to Norman and Angevin knights, and continues with the battles of Foukes One and Two against oppressors, culminating in the wicked John who disinherits Fouke Two. The latter's adventures, on the other hand, include visits to Saracen lands, fights with giants and dragons, and an encounter with a *bele Sarrasine*, as well as a fight between unknowing brothers, possibly an incident suggested by *Waldef* or *Gui*.

Fouke Two is the prototype for Robin Hood: the aristocratic outlaw and pirate whose only depredations are against the king's property – loyal to friends, proud and valiant, yet contrite and pious in old age. His *engin* is constantly celebrated in exploits of disguise and escape, and enlivened by passages of dialogue and pithy humor. His driving impulse is to regain his heritage: he is obsessed with John's *force e tort* and his own rights, in which he believes he represents *meint prodhome d'Engleterre* (many a worthy Englishman). The emphasis on law, however, sits oddly with his repeated capturing of the king, suggesting that in the end only strength of arms can secure justice.

Two much shorter mini-romances, one actually naming itself a *lai*, call for a brief discussion here. *Amis e Amilun* and the *Lai du Cor* both belong to the end of the twelfth century. *Amis* is an Anglo-Norman version of a popular Continental story, extant in many languages, about sacrificial male friendship. The poet has made an attempt to downplay the Continental coloring of the original (Weiss 1992: xxxiii). The two heroes, after death and burial in Lombardy, are, like Gui, venerated as saintly figures by pilgrims. The poet of the *Lai du Cor*, Robert Biket, light-heartedly and gracefully burlesques the Arthurian *topos* of the testing of the court, in this case by a horn which reveals the shortcomings of knights and ladies alike. Both these short works are familiar with Wace and with insular romance.

Two other works from the end of the twelfth or early thirteenth century merit inclusion in the corpus of Anglo-Norman romance, though both survive complete only in Picard manuscripts. Indeed, there are not even any fragments of an Anglo-Norman version of *Fergus*, if one ever existed, and its author, Guillaume le Clerc, probably hailed from and worked in Picardy; its tenuous claim to insularity can thus be derived only from its detailed knowledge of southern Scotland and unproven hypotheses about its patrons in Galloway.[26]*Fergus*, its hero based on a historical prototype, is inspired by the Arthurian romances of Chrétien de Troyes but is no mere derivative parody of them: its use of humor and irony make it entertaining in its own right. *Amadas et Ydoine* belongs more securely to the corpus: two Anglo-Norman fragments of this work survive as well as its Picard manuscript version. Its location, on the other hand, is not insular but firmly Burgundian and many references to it indicate early Continental as well as English popularity. It shows obvious familiarity with both Continental and insular romances – its opening situation is similar to that of *Gui de Warewic* – but the works with which it is most obviously connected are Chrétien de Troyes' *Cliges* and Thomas' *Tristan*, in that it provides a virtuous (and non-ironic) "solution" to the problem of a married woman with a lover (Reinhard 1926: iii–vii; Crane 1986: 181–6). It is like no other insular romance in that the lovers' affair remains center-stage from start to finish; fighting plays little part, apart from a crucial combat near the end. The resourceful Ydoine, just as important a figure as Amadas, despite the occasional misogynistic outbursts of the poet, is reminiscent of Rigmel or Josiane, and a welcome contrast with Gui's Felice.

The issue of what constitutes or defines romance has been skirted around in this chapter; by its end it should be possible to think at least about the characteristics of Anglo-Norman romance and whether or not it can be seen as distinct from the Continental French variety. Answers on both issues are inevitably and unsatisfyingly qualified. When Field (2000: 38) detected in *Waldef* anxiety and pessimism about "disorder, violence and injustice," not "the optimistic harmony of romance," she saw it as a forerunner of later texts in English with the same concerns. This "optimistic harmony" is also challenged in *Fouke*, *Boeve*, and, in a different fashion, by the sober philosophical reflections on power and transience in the Anglo-Norman *Alisandre*; it is, however, harder to see it as a feature of Anglo-Norman romances in general. Crane argued powerfully that these catered to insular baronial interests by portraying the importance of inheritance and landed rights, the necessity of orderly government and the rule of law. Again, this picture fits some narratives and not others – which appear quite unconcerned with issues of inheritance or legality – and is possibly over-influenced by the viewpoints of historians such as R. H. C. Davis.[27] Such concerns moreover do not appear solely in insular romance: they are evident in French *chansons de geste*, such as *Raoul de Cambrai*, *Aiol*, and *Mainet*, and romances such as *Ille et Galeron*, which use the "exile and return" theme, often cited as uniquely insular but, like the motif of the man with two wives, so popular in twelfth-century literature that they cannot be identified with any one country.[28]

There are, nevertheless, some distinct characteristics of Anglo-Norman romance. It is often closely connected to an interest in British history, topography, and story, which is evident in its precise references to localities. Although patrons are hardly ever directly mentioned, actual, probable, or possible ones came from families who were connected by links of kinship. These poems do seem to be written for a provincial rather than a royal court audience, though again our information is incomplete; a few of them support their hero against his king though it would be going too far to term them "anti-royalist." They are notably non-Arthurian and yet show a familiarity with Arthurian material, often in a way which casts an oblique or parodic light on it; this may again be connected with provincial rather than court concerns (Field 1999: 161, 164). Many of them depict female characters of marked initiative, activity, and sensuality, which challenge expected ideals of courtliness; these characteristics are inconsistently both admired and rebuked in a predominantly male world where women often have a rather small role to play (Weiss 1991). Finally, and not unexpectedly, the heroes of these romances from the thirteenth century onward refer repeatedly to their Englishness: a growing pride in nationality distinguishes these narratives.

In the end, distinctions matter less than the fact that, in island and mainland, the twelfth century saw the birth of a vigorous new genre, so fluid in its parameters that it remains impossible to define except as story used for both entertainment and instruction, usually ending happily after multiple adventures. Anglo-Norman romances, flourishing in the twelfth century, declining in the later thirteenth, represent within that short period a body of work often of high quality, flexible enough to challenge the genre's conventions, and an invaluable legacy to its Middle English successors.

See also: chapter 1, ANCIENT ROMANCS; chapter 3, THE POPULAR ENGLISH METRICAL ROMANCES; chapter 4, ARTHURIAN ROMANCE; chapter 5, CHAUCER'S ROMANCES; chapter 6, MALORY AND THE EARLY PROSE ROMANCES.

Notes

1. Domenica Legge (1963) was the trail-blazer, followed by Ian Short (1991).
2. Ian Short 1990: 156. Bell (1960) prefers 1135–40.
3. *Le Lai d'Haveloc*, ed. A. Bell (1925), trans. Judith Weiss (1992).
4. Jordan Fantosme's Chronicle uses *laisses*, as does the Harley *Brut*; some interpolations to Wace's *Brut* use monorhymed alexandrines. *Horn, Boeve de Haumtone, Le Roman de Toute Chevalerie* and the unedited *Otinel* are all in *laisses*.
5. The earliest, the *Roman de Thèbes*, ca. 1150–6, is called "notre premier roman" by its editor, Raynaud de Lage.
6. Judith Weiss 1999: 1–14; on the dating of the *Gesta Herewardi*, see Elisabeth Van Houts 1999: 201–23.
7. Rosalind Field 1999: 159. Matilda Tomaryn Bruckner maintains that this is characteristic of medieval writing in general: *Shaping Romance* (Philadelphia: University of Pennsylvania Press, 1993), p. 2.

8. Its only manuscript, Bodleian Library, Douce d. 6, also contains Thomas' poem.
9. "Mestre" indicates the poet was learned, probably a clerk. See *The Romance of Horn*, ed. M. K. Pope, vol. II (1964: 1–2, 75, 122–3).
10. See also R. Wadsworth [Field], "Historical Romance in England," unpublished D.Phil. thesis, University of York, 1972, pp. 141–9.
11. Hue de Rotelande, *Ipomedon*, ed. A. J. Holden (1979: 7–11); *Protheselaus*, ed. A. J. Holden, 2 vols. (1991); see Judith Weiss 1993: 17–18.
12. Field 1999: 159 suggests this was the audience of Anglo-Norman romance as a whole. For an excellent discussion of *Ipomedon*, see Susan Crane 1986: 158–73.
13. Both titles are given in the MSS. See Thomas of Kent, *The Anglo-Norman Alexander*, ed. Brian Foster (1977: II, pp. 2–3).
14. Alexander was the instrument of God in that he supposedly confined Gog and Magog and their 22 nations behind an iron gate: see Ian Michael 1982: 131–47.

15. On the *bele Sarrasine*, see Judith Weiss, 1991: 151–3; on Albert of Aix and Ethopian giants, see J. E. Martin [Weiss], "Studies in Some Early Middle English Romances," unpublished Ph.D. dissertation, University of Cambridge, 1967, p. 122.
16. See Simon Gaunt, "Gender and Sexuality in the *Roman d'Enéas*," *Romanic Review* 83 (1992), pp. 1–27 (p. 26).
17. Field 1999: 161; Short 1991: 243; Weiss 1993: 17–18. The FitzGilberts (Gaimar's patrons) were related to the Clares.
18. *Le Roman de Waldef*, ed. A. J. Holden (1984: 18). It survives in a single MS along with *Otinel* and *Gui de Warewic*. Holden has effectively demolished any argument that it is an "ancestral" romance, pp. 33–4.
19. Field 2000: 25–39. Holden first pointed out the extent to which *Waldef* influences Gui (pp. 29–32), which has been redated to before 1215, possibly even before 1205: see Emma Mason 1984: 25–40.
20. Holden 1984: 18. Despite some discrepancies between what the poet promises and what is written, toward the end of *Waldef* there are firm indications that the character of Guiac is intended to retire from the world and not reappear, as he does in Bramis.
21. The growing requirement for fictional figures of virtue to register strong emotion through swoons or tears is perhaps connected to the increasing use of the "dispersed family" *topos*, employed in *Waldef*, *Gui*, and Continental romances like *Octavian*. It provides more opportunities to mistake family members for enemies or potential new wives, and thus more emotional recognitions.
22. *Gui de Warewic*, ed. A. Ewert (1932–3). Ewert dated the romance to 1232–42 (I, vii), using what Holden calls "fragile" arguments (1984: 29). See note 19.
23. He may have known of Wigod of Wallingford, cup-bearer to Edward the Confessor (Ewert 1932–3: I, iv). Crane is sceptical of the poem being written for any particular family; Field, on the other hand, calls it a "foundation myth for the earls of Warwick" (Crane 1986: 16–17; Field 1999: 158).
24. One of Gui's last requests of his wife is that she bury his body in his hermitage near Warwick. When the body proves impossible to budge, she accedes to his wish and buries it in a marble tomb there. When she dies, she is buried with him; the poet says they are now in the company of the Virgin Mary, and prays we may come to as good an end, adding "Amen." This is usually the sign a romance has ended, and indeed the Royal MS stops here (as does the Caius MS of the English *Guy*). MSS CFM and especially E all show signs of interruption, and restart with a brief summary of Gui's end, followed by a contradiction of the previous events: Terri arrives, asks for Gui's body, and carries it off, unresisted, with him to Lorraine where it still remains (11645–56).
25. On "a developing sense of Englishness" in the twelfth century, see Gillingham 2000.
26. Guillaume le Clerc, *The Romance of Fergus*, ed. Wilson Frescoln (1983: 1–6, 28); Legge 1963: 161–2; Beate Schmolke-Hasselmann 1981: 342–53; D. D. R. Owen 1984: 47–81.
27. See Crouch 2000: 125–6, who disagrees with views that twelfth-century English barons were preoccupied with issues of inheritance and dispossession.
28. A. Fourrier (1960), observes a preoccupation with questions of marriage in the second half of the twelfth century, such as the *sponsa duorum*.

References and Further Reading

Angeli, Giovanna (1971). *L'Enéas e i primi romanzi volgari*. Milan: R. Ricciardi.

Bell, A., ed. (1925). *Le Lai d'Haveloc*. Manchester: Manchester University Press.

Bell, A., ed. (1960). *Geffrei Gaimar, Estoire des Engleis*. Oxford: Blackwell.

Crane, Susan (1986). *Insular Romance*. Berkeley: University of California Press.

Crane, Susan (1999). "Anglo-Norman Cultures in England, 1066–1460." In David Wallace, ed., *The Cambridge History of Medieval English Literature*. Cambridge: Cambridge University Press, pp. 35–60.

Crouch, David (2000). *The Reign of King Stephen, 1135–54*. Harlow: University of Minnesota Press.

Damian-Grint, Peter (1999). *The New Historians of the Twelfth-Century Renaissance*. Woodbridge: Boydell Press.

Dannenbaum, Susan [Crane] (1981–2). "Anglo-Norman Romances of English Heroes: 'Ancestral Romance'?" *Romance Philology* 35, 601–8.

Ewert, A., ed. (1932–3). *Gui de Warewic*. 2 vols. Paris: Champion.

Field, Rosalind (1999). "Romance in England, 1066–1400." In David Wallace, ed., *The Cambridge History of Medieval English Literature*. Cambridge: Cambridge University Press, pp. 152–76.

Field, Rosalind (2000). "*Waldef* and the Matter of/with England." In *Medieval Insular Romance: Translation and Innovation*, ed. Judith Weiss, Jennifer Fellows, and Morgan Dickson. Cambridge: D. S. Brewer, pp. 25–39.

Foster, Brian, ed. (1977). *Thomas of Kent, The Anglo-Norman Alexander*. 2 vols. London: Anglo-Norman Text Society.

Fourrier, A. (1960). *Le Courant réaliste dans le roman courtois en France au moyen-âge*, vol. 1 [all published]. Paris: A. G. Nizet.

Frescoln, Wilson, ed. (1983). *Guillaume Le Clerc, The Romance of Fergus*. Philadelphia: William H. Allen.

Gaunt, Simon (1986). "Did Marcabru know the Tristan legend?" *Medium Aevum* 55, 108–13.

Gillingham, John (2000). *The English in the Twelfth Century*. Woodbridge: Boydell Press.

Hathaway, E. J., P. T. Ricketts, C. A. Robson, and A. D. Wilshere, eds. (1975). *Fouke Le Fitz Waryn*. Oxford: Anglo-Norman Text Society.

Holden, A. J., ed. (1979). *Hue de Rotelande, Ipomedon*. Paris: Klincksieck.

Holden, A. J., ed. (1991). *Hue de Rotelande, Protheselaus*. 2 vols. London: Anglo-Norman Text Society.

Holden, A. J., ed. (1984). *Le Roman de Waldef*. Cologny-Geneva: Bodmer Foundation.

Kay, Sarah (1995). *The Chansons de Geste in the Age of Romance: Political Fictions*. Oxford: Clarendon Press.

Legge, Domenica (1963). *Anglo-Norman Literature and its Background*. Oxford: Clarendon Press.

Mason, Emma (1984). "Legends of the Beauchamps' Ancestors: the Use of Baronial Propaganda in Medieval England." *Journal of Medieval History* 10, 25–40.

Michael, Ian (1982). "Typological Problems in Medieval Alexander Literature: the Enclosure of Gog and Magog." In *The Medieval Alexander Legend and Romance Epic: Essays in honour of David J. A. Ross*, ed. Peter Noble, Lucie Polak, and Claire Isoz. Millwood, NY: Kraus, pp. 131–47.

Owen, D. D. R. (1984). "The Craft of Guillaume Le Clerc's *Fergus*." In Leigh A. Arrathoon, ed., *The Craft of Fiction: Essays in Medieval Poetics*. Rochester: Solaris Press, pp. 47–81.

Petit, Aimé, trans. (1991). *Le Roman de Thèbes*, Paris.

Pope, M. K., ed. (1964). *The Romance of Horn*. 2 vols. Oxford: Anglo-Norman Text Society.

Reinhard, John R., ed. (1926). *Amadas et Ydoine*. Paris: Champion.

Rychner, Jean (1955). *La Chanson de Geste. Essai sur l'art épique des jongleurs*. Geneva: Droz.

Schmolke-Hasselmann, Beate (1981). "Le Roman de *Fergus*: technique narrative et intention politique." In Kenneth Varty, ed., *An Arthurian Tapestry*. Glasgow: University of Glasgow Press, pp. 342–53.

Short, Ian (1980). "On Bilingualism in Anglo-Norman England." *Romance Philology* 33, 467–9.

Short, Ian (1990). "Gaimar et les débuts de l'historiographie en langue française." In Danielle Buschinger, ed., *Chroniques nationales et chroniques universelles*. Göppingen: Kümmerle, pp. 155–63.

Short, Ian (1991). "Patrons and Polyglots: French Literature in Twelfth-century England." *Anglo-Norman Studies* 14, 229–49.

Van Houts, Elisabeth (1999). "Hereward and Flanders." *Anglo-Saxon England* 28, 201–23.

Weiss, Judith (1986). "The Date of the Anglo-Norman *Boeve de Haumtone*." *Medium Aevum* 55, 238–41.

Weiss, Judith (1991). "The Wooing Woman in Anglo-Norman Romance." In *Romance in Medieval England*, ed. Maldwyn Mills, Jennifer Fellows, and Carol Meale. Cambridge: D. S. Brewer, pp. 149–61.

Weiss, Judith (1992). *The Birth of Romance.* London: Dent.

Weiss, Judith (1993). "The Power and the Weakness of Women in Anglo-Norman Romance." In Carol M. Meale, ed., *Women and Literature in Britain 1150–1500*. Cambridge: D. S. Brewer, pp. 7–23.

Weiss, Judith (1999). "Thomas and the Earl: Literary and Historical Contexts for the *Romance of Horn*." In Rosalind Field, ed., *Tradition and Transformation in Medieval Romance*. Cambridge: D. S. Brewer, pp. 1–14.

Weiss, Judith (2002). "Emperors and Antichrists: Reflections of Empire in Insular Narrative." In Phillipa Hardman, ed., *The Matter of Identity in Medieval Romance*. Woodbridge: Brewer, pp. 87–102.

3

The Popular English Metrical Romances

Derek Brewer

There are about 50 separate chivalric metrical romances in English composed from about 1250 to the early sixteenth century, mostly derived from French versions. They survive in slightly differing versions in 90 medieval manuscripts, most from the fifteenth century, and in mostly fragmentary printed versions of the sixteenth century. The stories are varied within a general pattern and draw from the vast ocean of European storytelling going back to oral origins, but whose themes and motifs survive even today. It is convenient to call this great mass of narrative "folktale" but it circulated among all classes and varied constantly in levels of artistry and structures of narrative. The term "folktale" has acquired patronizing and deprecatory overtones, but looked on simply as "traditional narrative" it is the basis of works from clumsy stories to the highest artistic achievements of such writers as Shakespeare, Chaucer, and Boccaccio, to go no further. The English chivalric romances shared this inheritance and a remarkably homogeneous style and ethos. The ethical assumptions are those of "the gentleman," based on valor, honor, piety, and the active life, opposing the ever-present enemy, the "Saracen," and various wicked kings, traitors, giants, and dragons. A central though not universal concern is the process of maturation of the hero. Another is the patience and endurance of ladies. Fantastic as the adventures often are, they reflect the real-life concerns of central issues of existence, and are set in a fantasy world of chivalry which was itself a genuine if distorted reflection of real-life social and psychological concerns.

It would seem that the probable audience and readership of these romances were the aspiring country gentry of the fourteenth century, which came later to include the richer bourgeoisie. The Auchinleck manuscript, discussed below, seems to be the product of a London-centered "bookshop" of the mid-fourteenth century and lends itself easily to the speculation that it or some book very like it was known to Chaucer, the son of a prosperous London vintner on the edges of the court. The mid-fifteenth-century Yorkshire gentleman Robert Thornton, who wrote out the manuscript now at Lincoln Cathedral, including many romances, probably represents the typical reader,[1] as did Chaucer himself when young, though he mocked the English metrical romances later for their artistic simplicity. The actual stories are as varied as the traditional Europe-wide folktale from which they derive (often from more sophisticated but similar French romances). An ancient classification was by subject matter, the fabulous histories of Greece, Rome, and Britain, but this leaves far too many out of account. The present essay attempts some grouping by date and theme but aims above all to evoke the nature of the stories by summaries and examples.

Among the earliest of the popular metrical romances in English is the story of *Guy of Warwick*, which illustrates many of the favored characteristics of the English romance.[2] The poem is closely based on an Anglo-Norman original composed about 1240. As usual there are variant versions in English, the earliest surviving being in the Auchinleck manuscript (ca. 1330), whose gaps can be filled with another manuscript, Caius College, Cambridge, 107. The essence of the story is pure chivalric folktale, and it is rich enough in folktale commonplaces to have pleased readers and hearers up till the nineteenth century, while displeasing critics. The poem begins with pious commonplaces and the poet's intention to tell of hitherto unknown adventures by men who loved "Faith with trewthe and stedfastness" (14). He tells of an earl who has a steward with a son, "a fayre yonge thynge" (24) called Guy, who loved "a mayden sheen," daughter of the earl, and how at last he married her and they had a son called Reynbroun. The poet wastes no time because he has some 12,000 lines before him. The setting is England, the maiden, called Felice, of surpassing beauty, well learned in the seven arts: the heroines of medieval romances are well educated, unlike most of their deprived sisters in real life. And this is the point. All is heightened, the good people are better, their enemies more evil, the festivals grander, knights stronger, ladies more beautiful, than in everyday life. The implied audience does not want to hear of peasants, nor of kitchen-sink realism. Life is harsh and dull enough. What is wanted is what is brighter, more exciting, more luxurious, a fantasy upper class. At a festival Guy performs well; 30 maidens fall in love with him, but he falls into a love-sickness for Felice. He finally brings himself to tell Felice, but she regards him as socially too inferior, as the son of her father's steward, and he swoons like Chaucer's Troilus. Eventually she agrees he must prove himself, so we enter into a series of adventures. Guy fights great battles against the Saracen, acquires a favorite lion (unfortunately killed at his master's feet), makes a sworn friend, fights a giant, slays a dragon, and so forth, all told in jog-trot couplet form that carries us effectively along, though without much variation. All these deeds are done for virtuous reasons of friendship or combating evil. Guy then returns home and is accepted by Felice. But immediately he has a religious revelation. All his fighting has been for worldly glory, but this is not good enough. He returns as a hero but remains only 50 days with his beloved Felice, who has accepted him with joy as a proven knight, and becomes pregnant. Then he departs again, this time in pilgrim guise. His new adventures are not so very different. He is a fighting pilgrim. In particular he helps a friend by killing the giant Amoraunt, then after helping his friend Tirri, he saves King Athelstan of England by defeating the invading Danes and their African giant ally

Colbrond, fighting "for England's sake." This part was at times treated as an episode on its own, as was the history of his equally heroic son Reinbrun. Typical episodes in the latter are the battles fought unwittingly against friends until all is made clear. Guy returns, still in disguise as a pilgrim, and at his deathbed sends the faithful Felice a ring she has given him – a favorite recognition device in romance. They are reunited, he dies, Felice buries him in a hermitage. She dies 40 days after him, and they live happily together in heaven. There are elements of a saint's life in the second part, but the general tone and activity are the same. The first section is almost equally imbued with a serious piety.

The story is aggregative. There is hardly any plot, only a series of typical episodes, into which various manuscripts sometimes divide it. It would not be quite right to call it "wish-fulfillment" except in the most general way that people wish to associate themselves with honor, success, and, in these stories, virtue. They expand the mind, entertain daydreams of vigorous action that deserves praise. There is no depth of characterization or complexity of personal relationship, and little description – just an archetypal story of growth, achievement, recognition, and a good death.

In this and other romances, within the manifest verbal content a latent significance is symbolically suggested, of the progress and maturation of the protagonist. The giants and dragons, the treacherous friends, the continuous struggle against the vaguely realized "Saracen" enemy are the imaginative counterparts of the struggle against the less dramatic forms of opposition or support that the growing adult encounters – parents, friends, rivals, the ordinary difficulties of life. Even the reluctance to consummate marriage, and the tendency of heroes to leave immediately after that, reflects the tensions, fears, and anxieties of sexual relationships, and especially of sexual commitment in a medieval society riddled with uncontrolled violence and deep injustices, which religion and law attempted to control with absolute injunctions impossible effectively to enforce. Living in such a society one needs to be able at least to imagine success. The very simplicity of the story helps this at one level, though the necessary complexity of great literature is thereby sacrificed. Thus the incidents in *Guy* arouse simple narrative interest which fulfills natural and worthy ideals, giving it a deserved popularity in progressively ever simpler form well into the eighteenth century. It provides the base line of chivalric romance and its ideals. When works such as this survive in separate manuscripts, it is common to find that some versions are reworkings by scribes who may also qualify as "editors" or even as contributory authors. Multiple origins, even multiple authors, with no concept of the personal ownership of a story, are characteristic of such premodern authors, even those as great as Chaucer and Shakespeare. In the case of *Guy*, the earliest version in the Auchinleck manuscript has an interesting change about midway from four-stress couplet to tail-rhyme verse, with stanzas of 12 lines, usually of three main stresses, rhyming a a b c c b d d b e e b. So many rhymes require much use of stock epithets and rhymes, which make the verse go with a swing and to some extent derive from the oral origins of the style, combined with bookishness. The tail-rhyme stanza has occasional variant details and sometimes incorporates a two-stress line. It came to be seen as the leading characteristic of the metrical romances, even though many are in couplets, and it is parodied in its most extravagant, unkind, and ludicrous form in Chaucer's *Sir Thopas*. Many romances handle the simpler four-stress short lines in couplet form with the same vigor and the same formulas. (The word "formulas," referring to style, is a more understanding way of describing clichés. Either way they are characteristic of traditional literature, associated with oral origins, but much used in undoubtedly literate styles.)

Guy has some other interesting aspects which are also reflected in later romances. They include the "Saracens" as the generic enemy, various giants, faithful or treacherous friends, lovesickness and faithful love leading to faithful marital love, a ring as a token of recognition. Courteous, noble, chivalric behavior is practiced by the hero. It is better to die in a manly way than to flee with shame and villainy – honor is an abiding issue, so important as to be taken for granted and easily overlooked by the modern reader, though it is fundamental to the hero's bravery and the heroine's chastity. The flattering call to the audience as "lordings," "Listen to me now" (l. 2449 only in the Auchinleck manuscript, absent in the Caius manuscript) is a call that echoes through romances, but implies at least the speaker reading from a book, as later in three lines of *Guy*, when the poem turns to tail-rhyme:

> God graunte hem heuen blis to mede
> That herken to mi romaunce rede
> Al of a *gentil kni3t.   noble
> (Auchinleck MS, stanza 1, 1–3)

The piety, the reading from a book, the emphasis on the noble knight – the honorable upper-class fighting man – are all typical. But women as well as men could be in the audience, and there could well have been at times a reader reading to or for himself or herself. The references to Guy being English, fighting "to saue ous the ri3t of Ingland" (Auchinleck MS, stanza 246, l. 11) as well as "for hym that dyed on rode," and a few lines later agreeing to fight, though now an old man "for God in Trinite / & for to make Ingland fre" (stanza 248, ll. 3–4), indicate a clear vein of nationalistic, patriotic feeling. Parallel to *Guy* in popularity was the equally long and less highminded *Beues of Hamtoun*.[3] Bevis is less chivalric, more closely a folk-hero, whose combativeness reaches a climax in a single-handed battle with the massed citizens of London, thousands of whom he slaughters. The six manuscripts vary in different ways, but there is no doubt that they each tell the same romance.

One of the most fundamental of the general themes of popular romance is that of "The Fair Unknown." The hero suffers when young from various disadvantages, such as being brought up out of society, like Perceval in all his European appearances or Libeaus Desconus of the early fourteenth-century English tail-rhyme romance of 186 stanzas that bears his name (mocked in *Sir Thopas*). Libeaus goes to King Arthur's court, is insulted, wins various battles with giants, etc., is temporarily entranced by a magic lady (shades of the return of Odysseus defeating Polyphemus and beguiled by

Circe – so ancient and natural are these motifs), acquits himself well in other adventures, concluding by disenchanting with a kiss a serpent with a woman's face whom he then marries. One does not have to have recourse to psychoanalytic theory to see that this is not only an entertainingly various adventure story but a symbolic account of maturation, of overcoming the hero's own early anxieties of adolescence, fears of rivals and opponents, of his own and women's sexuality, and his eventual success in becoming an adult. The poem was probably composed in the early fourteenth century, building on age-old motifs of folktale, and it survives in four fifteenth-century manuscripts, one of them British Library, Cotton Caligula A ii, which also contains two other romances. One is *Sir Launfal*. The theme is the virtuous if extravagant liberality of a knight who thereby becomes poor, but is rewarded by finding a rich fairy mistress – an endorsement of chivalric generosity. The other is *Octavian*, another collection of favourite motifs, including a noble hero brought up in obscurity by Clement, a Parisian butcher. The hero's inherent nobility becomes apparent through his incompetence at useful trade, his ignorance of commercial values, and his ability in fighting.

The general flavor and circumstances of the medieval English metrical romances are conveyed by the festival celebrating the success of the hero toward the end of the poem we call *Havelok*, composed toward the end of the thirteenth century, probably in Lincolnshire. The protagonist, Havelok, son of the king of Denmark, is abducted as a child, looked after by a poor fisherman called Grim (in the town later called Grimsby), lives to be strong but poor, and makes his way by strength and bravery from being a kitchen-porter to eventual marriage to a princess, to the slaughter of enemies, and finally to being crowned as king of England. In essence it is a typical folktale expressing the common and natural sense that we all have of starting with a child's sense of unrecognized "royalty" in himself, the need to struggle and suffer, and then self-realization in maturity of marriage and good status. Havelok's inherent royalty is signified in the story by a light that emanates from him when he is asleep. It is typical of the reliance of romance, like folktale, on underlying pattern rather than materialistic cause and effect that this light is only rarely seen and commented on. It is not accounted for in any way. The style is vigorous, not without artistry but plain and direct, with little elaboration. Toward the end, as Havelok's feats of strength prevail, he is accepted as king of England and a great feast is held for 40 days, the tone and detail of which encapsulate the imaginative appeal and perhaps the actual circumstances of many early romances. So many clothes were given, there was great quantity of good food, and wine as plentiful as the water of the sea. In this list is the very substance, setting, and style of the romances, and though heightened, the description is by no means totally remote from the actuality of royal and baronial feasts,[4] in which sometimes thousands of animals and birds, with proportionately huge quantities of other food and drink, were consumed, with great variety of entertainments. Lists and feasts are topics the romance-writers liked, but here we may concentrate for a moment on the line "romanz reding on the bok" (2326), and the following line, that men might hear "the gestes singe." In brief, we have here references both to reading from a book, whether to oneself or to a group, and to the singing of stories, but there is no mention of minstrels. The festive recreational nature of what is read or sung is clear. The songs and stories are secular and line up with the other amusements – jousting, wrestling, putting the stone, music, gambling, bull- and boar-baiting, as well as eating and drinking. No doubt individual tastes for the amusements might vary, but they share the same cultural pattern.

More detail which throws some light on the romances from a different perspective comes from a probably contemporary work composed not too far away from Lincoln-shire, perhaps a little to the north in County Durham. This is the work known as *Cursor Mundi* ("Runner over the World"), a history of Creation, of some 30,000 lines, composed from Biblical story and Christian legend, and therefore of clerical origin. It begins

Man *yhernes rimes forto here	yearns
And romans red on *manere sere	of various kinds
Of Alisaundre the conqueroure	
Of Iuly Cesar the emperour ...	

(1–4)

It continues by listing the wars of Greece and Troy, of Brut, first conqueror of England, of King Arthur and the marvels and adventures of his knights Gawain, Kay, and others, of Charles (that is, Charlemagne) and Roland, of Tristram and his love Ysote, of Ionec and Isumbras, Ydoine and Amadas. These are all the names mentioned, and it will be noticed how much priority is given to stories of war and battle. The love stories come last, though the author adds that in general there are many other stories, "of princes, prelates and kings." Moreover, the author comments that while good men are attracted to virtuous stories, bad men are attracted to "folly," and, in a word, lechers like dirty stories. Our clerical author is suspicious even of the romances he has named as well as others:

For now is halden non *in curs	in fashion
Bot qua that luue can *par amurs	who love passionately
That foly luue, that uanite –	
Tham likes now nan other gle	

(53–4)

[Those who love folly and vanity are now pleased with no other amusement.]

The clerical author recognizes the universal passion to hear stories, and especially love stories, but disapproves particularly of these.[5] He goes on for some hundred lines.

Cursor Mundi suggests that the medieval English understanding of romance em-phasizes "adventure story," "history of conquest," before the love interest. Other lists make the same point. *Richard Coer de Lyon* of about 1300, probably composed somewhere in the south Midlands, also begins with a list which, after a brief prayer to Jesus, who was never found coward, says it is good to hear in "iest," that is, serious story, of Richard's prowess and conquest (1–6). The usual list of heroes follows of "knights good and courteous" (15) but introduces another note:

> In Frensshe bookys this rym is wrougt
> Lewede men ne knowe it nou3t
> Lewede men cune Ffrensch non
> Among an hondryd vanethis on.
> Neuertheles, with glad chere
> *Ffele of hem that wolde here   Many
> Noble iestes, j. vndyrstonde
> Off dou3ty kny3tes off Yngelonde . . .
>
>   (21–7)[6]

The emphasis in the vernacular on the general ignorance of the French illustrates the social level aimed at, together with the usual rumble of English nationalism that surfaces here and there throughout writing in English up to the fifteenth century. Making of lists is an important device in traditional literature, as the Bible, Homer, and in English Chaucer, later poets, and the makers of nursery rhymes well know.[7] A good list has a shape and a point. The author of *Richard Coer de Lyon* lists many heroes but will not read about them because none did such doughty deeds as King Richard (ed. Brunner, 6723–42).

As it happens Richard did not make it to the other lists of romances but this, the story of this bloodthirsty English king and hero, who made his name in the romance by killing a lion and eating its heart, as well as slaughtering numberless Saracens and eating the boiled heads of a couple of them, was clearly popular, as the surviving eight whole or fragmentary manuscripts and three prints attest. (The losses of manuscripts of romances must have been enormous, owing to heavy usage, lack of clerical care [though a few were found having been kept in monasteries] and possibly fashionable contempt.) This last is illustrated in the most famous list of all, contemptuous on artistic and rationalistic rather than moral grounds. Chaucer's brilliant satire *Sir Thopas*, on the popular metrical romances, with all their absurdities and jog-trot rhythm, concludes with this comment:

> Now holde youre mouth, *par charite*
> Bothe knyght and lady free
> And herkneth to my *spelle: story
> Of bataille and of chivalry
> And of ladyes *love-drury   passionate love
> Anon I wol yow telle.
>
> Men speken of romances of prys
> Of Horn child and of Ypotys
> Of Beves and sir Gy
> Of sir Lybeux and Pleyndamour –

> But sir Thopas, he bereth the flour
> Of roial chivalry.
>
> (The Canterbury Tales VII, 891–902)

And he adds a comment that Sir Thopas drank water of the well "As dide the knyghte sire Percyvelle" (916), famous for his pious chastity and innocent ignorance. To this we may add the comment made by Chaucer on the most famous of King Arthur's "auntrous knights":

> Now every wys man, lat him herkne me
> This storie is also trewe, I undertake
> As is the book of Launcelot de Lake
> That wommen holde in ful greet reverence.
>
> (The Canterbury Tales VII, 3210–13)

In both these passages we should note Chaucer's easy assumption, not without a touch of mockery, that ladies were as eager to read or hear romances as were men. In *Troilus and Criseyde* Criseyde is found listening to a reading of the "geste / Of the seige of Thebes" with her ladies (*Troilus* II, 81–4). *Sir Thopas* as a literary parody usefully sums up many of those characteristics of the chivalric romance which, despite Chaucer's mockery, are of most interest to us. He characteristically neglects the militaristic ardor that not surprisingly engaged most interest in the medieval period of endemic war. Chaucer emphasizes the love element – Sir Thopas seeks an elf-queen of whom he has only dreamt. Such an element is only a very small part of the popular *Richard Coer de Lyon*. But Sir Thopas is indeed a knight, chivalric and chaste, which probably seemed ridiculous to the worldly Chaucer living in the amorous as well as militaristic courts of Edward III and Richard II. The hero seeks strange adventures, comes across a giant, and is described going through the well-established topos of arming,[8] though that is more frequent in French than in English romance. Chaucer has selected just those elements of love and adventure that have come to be accepted as characteristic of romance, especially as influenced by the French and Arthurian traditions. Romances of love and adventure may well have been more popular in England than the surviving number of manuscripts shows, partly as a result of the hostility of clerical writers, who were in a better position generally to preserve manuscripts of any kind, and preserved nearly a hundred of the dismal *Pricke of Conscience*.

The style of *Sir Thopas* is a notably comic parody of the vernacular tail-rhyme style of the fourteenth-century romances. Although, as is Chaucer's wont, lower-class style and subject matter are mocked (for example, in *The Miller's Tale*), and the point of *Sir Thopas* is to mock the lower-class style and naivety of the romances, he nevertheless expects his courtly audience to have read the romances he refers to in English. There are none of the chip-on-shoulder references to those who cannot read French, as found in *Richard Coer de Lyon* or more aggressively a little later in *Arthour and Merlin*, to Englishmen rightly speaking English and even "noble men" knowing no French.

Another characteristic of the audience of romances is implied by Chaucer's sarcastic remark about the story of Lancelot being "women's reading," or at any rate, believed by women, as it obviously is not by Chaucer. One final point to be made about *Sir Thopas* reflects the context of romances within the books in which they survive. *Sir Thopas* is placed within the group of *Canterbury Tales* known as Fragment VII, which contains an extraordinary variety of tales. This medley is, genius apart, quite characteristic of many of the manuscript placings of the English metrical romances, which correspond in some ways to the conglomeration of activities reported of the feast in *Havelok*. The English romances are in many respects simply one aspect of a spectrum of mingled tales, of a whole culture, which mingles comic and serious, religious and secular, side by side. A very few manuscripts contain predominantly romances, of which the most famous is the Auchinleck manuscript in the National Library of Edinburgh, Adv. 19.2.1, written in the London area, 1330–40. It has been cut about and a few items are now missing; even so, Guddat-Figge (1976) counts 44 separate items, of which 16 are romances, some relatively short, some, like *Guy of Warwick* and *Sir Beues of Hamptoun*, very long. There is some rough and ready grouping of types of items but a number of different sorts of text are interspersed, some devotional, some secular. Another famous manuscript which contains many romances is that largely or entirely written by a Yorkshire gentleman, Robert Thornton, about 1430–40. It contains ten romances, some known only from this manuscript, a few in prose or in alliterative verse. These are grouped together at the beginning, but even so with a few short pieces of very miscellaneous kinds interspersed. The last romance in the Lincoln Thornton, *Sir Percyuelle of Galles*, a unique text, is followed immediately by "Three charms for toothache" (Guddat-Figge 1976: 135–42). The latter part of the manuscript has religious pieces, though the last but one is a prescription "ffor the Scyatica," and the last of all a prose collection of medical prescriptions.

The accidents of arbitrary survival, the interchangeability of certain motifs, and the surprisingly homogeneous nature of the style whatever the subject matter and length, make systematic analysis very difficult. As a preliminary we may glance at a tentative chronology of the texts in English, following Pearsall (1988) for the most part. *Havelok* is usually dated about 1280 and serves well as a start. We may groupic with *Guy of Warwick*, *Beues of Hamtoun*, *Richard Coer de Lyon*, *Kyng Alisaunder*, and *Arthour and Merlin*. The latter five all appear in the Auchinleck manuscript. Of these *Kyng Alisaunder* receives most praise from critics for rich detail and rhetorical amplification. The story of Alexander, in real life as learnt from ancient sources, and in the romanticized form known in many medieval accounts, is the world's great success story, gilded in the Middle Ages with fabulous elements. It is notably well written, probably by a cleric, in couplets relatively free from formulaic tags, with subdivisions marked by lyrical passages on the seasons.[9] Besides this poem there are several fragmentary alliterative poems. Yet for all its popularity the Alexander story did not have the staying power of *Guy* or *Beues*.

Along with the early romances of war and adventure there also appear romances with a love interest more specific than the rather incidental references in *Guy*. The earliest of these, still not very "romantic," is the admirable *King Horn*, surviving in three manuscripts, of which the English original was written in the earlier part of the thirteenth century, probably based on an Anglo-Norman original of the latter part of the twelfth century. As with *Guy*, any apparently historical references may be disregarded as history of fact, though not of the English imagination.[10] The story is again one of the maturation of the hero. Horn is the son of a king, who is killed. The boy is set adrift with several other boys, one of whom, Athulf, is faithful, and one, Fikenild, is treacherous. They land in "Westerness," Horn proves his worth by killing many of the usual enemy, the Saracens, and the king's daughter Rymenild falls in love with him. She has a notably symbolic dream that he has broken her net. They love each other, Rymenild taking the initiative, but do not marry or sleep with each other. Soon Fikenild slanders Horn, who escapes to Ireland where again he fights well and is offered the king's daughter in marriage. He refuses but stays seven years until he hears that Rymenild is to be married. He returns disguised as a beggar, speaks punningly at the wedding feast of "horns" and fishing net, then drops a ring into Rymenild's cup, by which she recognizes him. He slays the bridegroom, King Mody, but again sets off without marrying to regain his own lost kingdom. There is more fighting, more treachery, another last-minute rescue of Rymenild, killing the traitor Fikenild. The whole is told in an irregular short couplet form, admirably terse and compact, with little description, nothing of motive or explanation. It is not a naturalistic story but a powerful psychodrama.

These are all variants of that ancient narrative theme, the exile and return of the hero, who is much the dominant figure. Rather different, though of a similar date to *King Horn*, is the romance *Floris and Blauncheflur*, figuring a prominent love interest, translated from French, and surviving in English in four incomplete versions, one of them in the Auchinleck manuscript, composed in three- or four-stress couplets. It has a touch of the exotic East; the style is brisk without the starkness of *King Horn* and introduces a new tenderness, which contributes strongly to our notion of essential romance by its concentration on the innocent passionate mutual love of hero and heroine, though all is nature, and there is no emphasis on strained courtly manners. Floris, son of the king of Spain, is born at the same time and brought up with Blauncheflur, daughter of a captured princess, who nurses both children. When Floris needs to go to school at the age of seven, Blauncheflur and he insist that she too be taught – the kind of detail of admittedly "idealized realism" of good nature which is typical of this romance, and not so very unusual in others, one of the incidental rewards of reading them. Eventually Floris' father, who tends like most fathers in medieval romance to be either excessively severe or dangerously fond of his daughter, wishes to ensure that the less well-born Blauncheflur does not marry Floris (though both are still children) and so wants her killed. The queen, like most mother figures being kind and loving (mothers-in-law by contrast are usually evil) saves her. Eventually Blauncheflur, after various adventures, finds herself imprisoned in a tower in rich and exotic Babylon, destined to be the emir's bride. Floris finds her and in a delightful image gets himself conveyed into Blauncheflur's bedroom in a basket of flowers, upon which, with pious exclamations of joy, they immediately strip off their clothes and go to bed together. They are concealed by Blauncheflur's faithful friend Clarice but eventually discovered. The emir wants to behead them. They have a magic ring which will preserve one life, but each insists the other wear it. The emir is won over by such selfless love and spares them. He goes further and marries the equally lovely Clarice. The incidental harshnesses of family life, the real dangers in medieval and not only medieval life of kidnap, rape, and murder are not denied. But the story is good-humored and decent. Devoted secular love between boy and girl conquers all difficulties, and in the original French we are assured they live happily ever after. In one of the French versions there is more fighting, but in the English version romance is the core: faithful love, brave endurance of suffering, and a happy ending.

So far some principal characteristics of the popular English metrical romances have been established. A number of later romances share them – the zest for fighting, youthful love and its pains leading to faithful marriage. Among the so-called Breton lays the best is rather different, a short medieval version in couplets of the story of Orpheus and his wife Eurydice, who is captured by the Otherworld. In the familiar classical version it is a story about the death of the beloved. In the English version, existing in three manuscripts, one of them the Auchinleck manuscript, King Orfeo's wife Heurodys is mysteriously carried away when asleep in her orchard in the afternoon. The distraught Orfeo, a famous harper, abandons his kingdom and lives wild in the woods. Eventually he is passed by a Fairy Hunt and recognizes his wife Heurodys with the Fairy King. He succeeds in winning her back and rewarding the faithful steward who has guarded the kingdom. The tale is delicately written and illustrates the fundamental optimism of romance, where the dead are found alive.

A poem also often thought of as derived from a Breton lay is *Sir Degarré*, interesting in itself and offering a bridge to a different kind of romance, more centered on family relationships between the protagonist and parents. Some half-dozen versions survive, one in the Auchinleck manuscript. The story, written in the early fourteenth century, has no direct source, but re-creates archetypal themes. It tells of a strong king with a lovely daughter, on whom he dotes to such an extent that he will allow no one to marry her unless he can defeat the king in a tournament. One year the daughter becomes lost in a forest and is raped by a knight who claims to be a "fairy," who has loved her many a year. He leaves her with a sword with a missing point. The baby when secretly born is left with a hermit and certain money and tokens, including a pair of gloves sent by the knight and a letter saying he is of noble birth. The child grows up, fostered by rich merchants (the mingling of high bourgeois with knights is not unusual), kills a dragon, and eventually arrives at the annual tournament for the king's daughter, and of course throws the king from the saddle, as the poet says, "tail over top." So he marries the daughter but first must try if the gloves fit the bride. They do, proving that she is his mother, and he thus narrowly escapes committing incest. More adventures follow, and Sir Degarré defeats another knight who owns the sword with the missing tip, which Sir Degarré is carrying. He has just met and defeated his father. Only in the timeless world of romance could such absurdities take place, yet it has a psychological and emotional truth. The hero defends a beautiful unrelated lady with rich lands and marries her. The tale is a classic presentation of one aspect of the family drama – the child's love of the mother, who is nevertheless legally and morally beyond marriage; he needs to defeat the threatening father images, and find through love the legitimate Other of the opposite sex. The original family is reunited in love and a new family begun, all centered on the protagonist. The other poems that are usually connected with the so-called Breton lay, *Lai le Freine, Emaré, Launfal, Sir Gowther, The Erl of Toulous*, deploy the usual folktale themes and have little to distinguish them from similar tales except their claim to be "Breton lays."

Although most of these English romances are centered on a male protagonist, not all are of maturing heroic young men. A significant number invoke the themes of endurance by older men, and by women. They are more evidently religious in structure, but even such a gung-ho hero as Bevis developed in a context of pious and no doubt sincere commonplaces. A very popular romance illustrating these points is *Sir Isumbras*, composed in tail-rhyme stanzas in the early fourteenth century, surviving in nine mostly incomplete manuscripts and five even more fragmentary prints from before 1550.[11] About 800 lines long, it is a version of the folktale type known as *The Man Tried by Fate*. Isumbras is a doughty knight with a wife and three sons, rich, "curteys and hende": "His gentylness [i.e. nobility] nor his curtesye / There kowthe no man but discryve [describe]" (ed. Mills: 21–3). But he is proud and a bird tells him he has forgotten what he is, a mortal man dependent on God, to whom he therefore owes all that is good in his life. One day, when he is enjoying himself inspecting his forest, he hears a bird reproaching him and offering him the choice of happiness either in youth or age. He chooses age. Soon all his property is gone. He and his family wander starving in the wild near the sea. A lion captures the eldest child, a leopard the second, but Isumbras, his wife, and the remaining child are left starving on the seashore. A pagan king with a fleet lands. He tries to convert Isumbras and buy his wife, but Isumbras refuses. The king takes the wife and beats Isumbras, and soon a griffin snatches away the remaining son. Bereft of all, Isumbras at last becomes a blacksmith and, after 14 years, wearing the armor he has made, comes to the aid of a king against the heathen. Then he becomes a pilgrim and after more extraordinary but interesting adventures too complex to relate here, meets his wife again. In battle she dons armor and helps him to a famous victory, while the three sons, now grown up and great warriors, arrive on strange steeds to come to their aid. The family is reunited and becomes rich and powerful.

The motifs are familiar. In many romances children are lost, for example, *Sir Eglamour* (one of those mocked by Chaucer), *Sir Torrent, Sir Octavian, Beues of Hampton, Valentine and Orson*. Children once lost but recovered in maturity through the recognition of rich tokens are also common. An unrecognized husband receiving alms from his wife occurs here, as in *Beues* and *Guy*. Another aspect of this story and many other romances is that of the proud man (or king) brought low into a degrading position. In a hierarchical society such a fantasy gives great satisfaction.

(Moreover, it could well happen in real life, as the fate of Edward II, Richard II, and many nobles who fell from favor could illustrate.) With repentance the fallen could be restored – another message giving religious, social, and psychological satisfaction, as in *Sir Gowther*, *Guy*, *Isumbras*, and *Amadas*. Critics complain of the piety and implicit didacticism of this and other romances but praise sections of vigorous action and "blunt realism." As to realism, "Barbary corsairs" were raiding and kidnapping on the south coast of England as late as the seventeenth century. The "Saracens" did not give up easily. But emphasis on "realism" may obscure the fundamental mythic quality of the structure of such folktales, which embody the hopes and fears of so many people, fortified by a simple piety. Loss of children is every parent's nightmare, and one that most medieval parents must have endured. So were local pillage and destruction, especially in the medieval period. Stories like *Sir Isumbras* were fortifying fantasies, parallel to real life, expressing both anxiety and hope, adding imagination, color, and variety to ordinary life.

Another popular romance, *Sir Eglamour of Artois*, composed in the mid-fourteenth century in tail-rhyme, survives in four medieval manuscripts (one of them Thornton), a later fragment, and the seventeenth-century Percy Folio. It is one of those listed by Chaucer. There is a love interest, a mixture of fabulous beasts, a near miss of marriage with the hero's mother, from whom he was separated at birth, and the cruel banishment of the heroine with her new-born baby. She is an example of the Calumniated Wife (as in Chaucer's *Man of Law's Tale* and *Emaré*). Other incidents are loss of children, combat between father and son, recovery of former wealth. Such recurring yet varying repetitions of familiar motifs are yet another way of fortifying experience. Repetition with variation consolidates the sense of the self, re-creating history, yet using the sense of the past as a mode of defense against anxiety in the present. A strong vein of archaizing has rightly been detected in the romances (Fewster 1987), and hence many formulaic stylistic characteristics, the introductory, probably fictional "minstrel's call," and much of the literary chivalric ethos. The romances do not begin formally with the fairytale opening, "Once upon a time ... " but in spirit they come near it. Such distancing helps to make the painfully real (the death of children, the hostility of parents, the difficulties of love) at once more imaginative and more bearable.

Within the themes of romance concerned with children come both the longing for a child and, less often, the conception of an evil child. Such a one occurs in *Sir Gowther*, a tail-rhyme romance composed about 1400 in 757 verses. It begins with in effect a rape of the virtuous wife by a man in the shape of her husband who suddenly reveals himself as a fiend. The child proves himself from a baby as cruel and unmanageable (and many a parent in any period may recognize the type if not the extreme). Eventually he forces his mother to confess who his true father is. Horrified, he goes to the Pope, who says he must live the life of a dog until a sign comes from heaven. Eventually, unknown and portraying himself as a fool, he is able to arm himself, defeat some attacking Saracens, save the emperor's captured daughter, and though wounded, cure the princess of her dumbness. Gowther is then absolved from his earlier sins by the Pope and rules over the land of Almayne, finally becoming revered as a saint.

The love of children appears in a different form when treated as a most powerful emotion set in unhappy conflict with another most powerful emotion, the love between friends. Such friendship is more common in a military society where a man may well owe his life to his friend, but it has more complex social roots. Most romances contain examples of true and treacherous friends (*Guy* and *Horn* are obvious cases) and friendship faithful or not is an obvious motif because it is a component of most people's lives. There are a few romances where a deeply committed friendship between men, not in the least sexual in nature, is part of or central to the story. Sworn brotherhood is an element in the fourteenth-century pseudo-historical *Athelston*, king of England, but is only part of complex domestic motifs (including the less familiar one of the enraged king kicking his wife and thus killing their unborn son). In hundreds of stories throughout Europe, trust in brotherhood is violated by a brother-in-law who attempts unsuccessfully to seduce the wife, a theme connected with that of the Calumniated Wife and her patient suffering, exile, and escape, vigorously presented in the late fourteenth-century *Le Bone Florence of Rome*, 2187 lines in tail-rhyme stanzas. Much less frequent are the stories which carry faithful friendship to an extreme, of which one popular throughout medieval Europe is that of *Amis and Amiloun*, surviving in English in four manuscripts, the earliest the Auchinleck one.

The basis is two friends, knights at a duke's court, indistinguishable from each other in appearance and honor. From their similarity arise various complications in the niceties of sexual honor, all of which depend on the knights placing the claim of friendship above the strict marital bond.[12] The final test comes when the friends are told from heaven that Amiloun's leprosy can be cured by the blood of Amis' two children. In agony Amis, with the consent of his equally distressed wife, kills his children and Amiloun is cured. At last, by a miracle the children are revived. Like many romances, the essence is a test of virtue. The story is distinguished by one high virtue (loyal friendship) taking precedence over other virtues – such as truth-telling in the case of both the steward (for which he is killed) and Amis, wifely faith on the part of Amis' wife, and parental duty, of both Amis and his wife to their children. As with several other romance narratives, including *Sir Gawain and the Green Knight* and Chaucer's *Franklin's Tale*, the improbable premises allow for the interesting presentation of the irreconcilable clash between the demands of two unquestionable virtues. Such stories could be set up as problems in the exercise of legal and moral arguments. As romances they have the advantage of engaging our imaginative sympathies with some of our deepest moral convictions and emotions, while the happy ending saves us from the distraction of real distress. It is necessary that the characters should be stereotypes, but the incidents in themselves have a parallel in the dilemmas of real life. Individual characterization and realistic motivation are secondary concerns. The structural moral problem is all.

Another aspect of the chivalric ethos is found in *Sir Amadas*,[13] which shows a profound ancient belief in generous giving without counting the cost, illustrated as widely as in the biblical Book of Tobit, in Proverbs 19: 17, in various Psalms, and in a different way in the North American Indian custom of potlatch.[14] This is exemplified in the spendthrift generosity of Sir Amadas, a key chivalric virtue, which leaves him almost penniless, needing to mortgage all his possessions (a nice practical point) and go away for seven years. As he wanders he comes across the rotting corpse of a merchant, whose burial is prevented by an unsatisfied creditor. Amadas spends his last few pounds settling the debt and paying for a grand funeral, thus satisfying the need for charity and the ancient requirement to bury the dead. Now destitute, he is met by a mysterious White Knight who directs him to a shipwreck where all are dead and their riches available. This nicely illustrates the focused non-naturalistic logic of folktale. Sir Amadas does not need to bury the drowned men and is free to use their wealth. This he does, meets a nearby king, wins a tournament, and marries the king's daughter, by whom he has a child. As we read in Proverbs 19: 17, "He that hath pity on the poor lendeth unto the Lord: and look, what he layeth out, it shall be paid him again." But there is a price to be paid. The White Knight, in first helping Amadace, made an agreement with him that all their gains should be shared. He returns and asks for his due, including even the half of Amadas' wife and child. In agony, but voluntarily, Amadas and his wife agree. At the last moment the White Knight, with a generosity at least equal to that of Amadas, but as a supernatural being, the "ghost" of the one-time merchant whose body Amadas has buried, releases him from his bond. The ancient themes of the sacred duty of burial, its refusal because of debt, the Grateful Dead, the duty to give without thought of return, the Testing of the Hero, and the ultimately optimistic but deservedly happy ending, have all been neatly woven together within a chivalric setting which even brings merchant and knight together. Only modern naturalistic assumptions can deny the poetic power of this story, as of those other Spendthrift Knights, Sir Cleges and Sir Launfal. In the end all possessions are gifts from God and he is the most generous giver of all. A generous circuit of mutual giving, entailing the exchange of both gift and obligation, in itself a part of honor, is set up.

Most chivalric romances have men as the protagonist, but a very important group center on women, especially those in which the heroine progresses from beautiful virgin to wife, often harshly treated, and mother. These romances usually begin with an unmarried heroine of great beauty, such as the one who gives her name to *Emaré*,[15] composed around 1400 in tail-rhyme 1035 lines long. Her own father falls in love with her and gets the Pope's permission to marry her. She rejects him and the enraged father banishes his daughter, sending her out to sea in a noble boat and a wonderfully embroidered garment, but with no money, food, or drink. Such unpractical details are "mythic" or "poetic." Emaré reaches another land and becomes a servant, but once seeing her, the king loves and marries her. In another familiar pattern (cf. Chaucer's *Man of Law's Tale*), however, her mother-in-law hates her and causes it to be believed that her new-born son is a devil. Once again Emaré is sent to sea in an open boat. Patient suffering acquires its own power to prevail, as in the case of Chaucer's Griselda and Constance. A complex religious, moral, and social message is sent by such episodes. Patient endurance, like love, "suffereth long and is kind" (I Corinthians 13: 4).[16] Although there is no direct evidence of women in the implied audience or readership of romances apart from those of Chaucer, tales of virtuous, persecuted, but ultimately justified wives must surely have appealed to women as well as men.

As a further complication, as the complexities of the various plots evolve it is often the children who by their presence, or by some positive action or merely their appearance, are the means by which the parents, separated against their will, are eventually brought together again. An extraordinarily complex version of such a pattern exists in only a brief fragment, the last 114 lines of the original poem of *Apollonius of Tyre*, composed in the late 1370s, though the manuscript is of the fifteenth century. The interest here is not so much in the fragment itself as the evidence it provides of the availability from the classical period of the whole story, which includes such well-known motifs as the Incestuous Father, the Faithful Servant, the Evil Stepmother, Tests for Suitors, the Dangerous Riddle, the Sea Journey, and the Fortunate Happy Reunion. The story has the distinction of being the only romance (apart from a reference to Alexander) known in Old English, but hundreds of versions exist in Latin and all European languages (Archibald 1991).

Among the lists given in medieval romances themselves there are a number of long historical accounts of Troy and Rome which, although they have a chivalrous tone, do not come within the scope of this essay. There are few properly Arthurian stories among the metrical romances. One is *Sir Perceval of Galles*. It is the usual story of the hero who starts from a disadvantage, being kept secluded in a forest precisely to avoid his becoming a knight. This rare note of maternal hostility to combative chivalry, found in all the Europe-wide versions of the Perceval story, deserves recognition, as it comes from the heart of chivalric tradition. The only other whole-hearted, or almost whole-hearted, condemnation of chivalry comes occasionally from the Church. That such condemnation was unsuccessful is witnessed not only in history but in the very course of the story of Perceval, another account of maturation seen in chivalric terms. The poet composed the poem in the early fourteenth century in tail-rhyme with a certain rollicking zest in 2286 lines, of which the unique copy is in the Thornton manuscript of about 1440. Once again, the number of surviving manuscripts is no index of the popularity of a given piece, since Chaucer knew it well enough to make a mocking reference to Perceval drinking water from the well, which no sensible knight would have done if he could help it. But the poem has touches of genuine humor, and though it is only part of the full Perceval story, with no mention of the Grail, and altogether inferior to the great European examples and Malory, it deserves recognition.

The same must be said of the solitary version of the Tristram story, preserved in the Auchinleck manuscript in 3344 lines of complicated tail-rhyme stanzas, probably composed late in the thirteenth century. It has lost the last page but otherwise is a competent if stark abbreviation of the original French romance, including parts that are now lost in French. Unusually for English romance it is a story of adultery. The story of Tristan and Isolde is too well known to need rehearsal here, though this is somewhat adapted to include the young Tristan's abduction and includes the slaying of a dragon earlier on and a giant toward the end. The essential elements of adultery, obsessive love, and the unconsummated marriage with Ysonde (as she is called here) of the White Hands remain, as do the inevitable but here assumed deaths of the principals. Although Tristan and Ysoude figure in various catalogues of famous heroes of romance, their story, since it ends in tragedy, does not conform to the usual optimistic pattern of romance, and for this reason may not have been particularly popular as a story. Tristan and Ysoude figure in one of Chaucer's lists along with Paris and Achilles, both famous as lovers in the Middle Ages, in *The Parliament of Fowls* (290). Chaucer's list, however, is specifically of those lovers who came to grief and died because of their love. They appear painted on the walls of the Temple of Venus, which is dedicated to obsessive, unfortunate, or immoral love.[17]

The stories of Tristan and Lancelot are relatively rare examples (contrary to a general impression) of heroically adulterous love. Adultery is more usually the subject of derisive jesting, as in *fabliaux* by Chaucer and in French. There are many instances of attempts on a maiden's or a wife's chastity by treacherous friends or servants, but there are very few examples of persistent adultery, though the late fifteenth-century romance *Generides*, revealing Chaucerian influence, is one exception. The stories of Tristan and Lancelot are further exceptions, until we come to the great prose work of Malory, *Le Morte Darthur*, close to the end of the fifteenth century. Among the metrical romances there is only one significant manuscript version of the story of Lancelot and Guinivere and the fall of Arthur and the Round Table, composed in 3969 four-stress lines in eight-line stanzas about 1400.

The Arthurian *Ywain and Gawain*, a compressed derivative of Chrétien de Troyes' great romance *Yvain,* in about 4000 lines in four-stress couplets, is one of the best-told English romances. Its effectiveness derives from Chrétien, and the story has some complexity. Some ancient topics are present – especially the hero's first victorious combat, departure, forgetfulness of his newly married wife, and return, rather better motivated than in simpler narratives. The essential inner story of maturation is more complex than in the usual English metrical romance, but it fails to achieve the resonance of Chrétien's original, or the strong symbolic undertow of cruder narratives of adventure and love.

Elements of romance appear in many different kinds of stories and are combined in different proportions. Romance is a mode rather than a genre and examples are found from Classical Antiquity to the present day. It may be more strictly limited to certain kinds of writing in the Middle Ages. Of these the popular metrical English romances are only a part. They are the folklore of chivalry. Time is that of a fantasy world. Seven years, twenty years, may pass without change in the stereotyped characters (Chaucer and the *Gawain* poet are unique in the precision with which they mark the passing of time). The metrical romances deal in a fantasy world of adventure and love by knights and ladies. Giants and dragons and the ever-present enemy, the Saracen, quest and desire are their base. They are secular but unfailingly pious. Their ethos is that of "the gentleman," unhesitatingly brave, willing to help the weak, careless of riches, suffering without complaint, and always with the confident expectation, normally fulfilled, of a happy ending. They have a fundamental optimism. Like so many fairytales, their underlying symbolic drive is often the process of maturation variously achieved by male or female protagonists against various opponents, unless it is of suffering bravely endured and ending in success. Only the greatest of them, discussed independently elsewhere in this book, achieve high art. The rest depend on a highly conventional style full of formulas, often in a jog-trot meter, whether couplet or tail-rhyme. Yet they constitute the imaginative ground of a substantial area of medieval and much post-medieval literary and social culture. They have close connections with saints' lives, though churchmen regarded them with a quite unwarranted suspicion. They reflected life's variety of love and suffering, grief and joy. In themselves as entertainment they contributed to that variety, and showed that life can have purpose and a general moral structure. It was well enough for that great upper-class poet Chaucer to mock them. His own achievement far surpassed them, but he himself grew up on them. Most of his gentry audience, and eventually the merchants and later many in a humbler walk of life, read versions of them, as Bunyan and Samuel Johnson did, and fed their imaginations on them, to their benefit. Whatever their limitations, these romances were all rooted in a culture of goodness, courage, and aspiration, and they have many points of interest inevitably unmentioned here.

This culture in the main continued in the fifteenth century and most of the manuscripts which contain them were written in the fifteenth century. But the metrical romances were increasingly replaced by lengthy romances in prose, suggesting a shift in reading habits. Their great exemplar is Malory's *Le Morte Darthur*. He used both the alliterative *Morte Arthure* and the stanzaic *Morte Arthur* as well as French prose sources, but it was prose that he preferred for writing the great climax of English Arthurian romance.

See also: chapter 1, ANCIENT ROMANCE; chapter 2, INSULAR BEGINNINGS; chapter 4, ARTHURIAN ROMANCE; chapter 5, CHAUCER'S ROMANCES; chapter 6, MALORY AND THE EARLY PROSE ROMANCES; chapter 9, SHAKESPEARE'S ROMANCES.

Notes

1. For discussion of the Auchinleck MS see H. M. Smyser in J. B. Severs 1967: 89–90. Caroline Barron finds little interest in English romance in the rich bourgeoisie of late fourteenth-century London, but few manuscripts written in the fourteenth century survive. They may have been regarded as trivial, or indeed have been read to pieces. See Barron 2002: 229–42.

2. *Guy of Warwick*, ed. J. Zupitza. Early English Text Society, Extra Series 42, 49 (London: Routledge and Kegan Paul, 1883–91).

3. *Beues of Hamtoun*, ed. E. Kölbing. Early English Text Society, Extra Series 46, 48, 65 (London: Routledge and Kegan Paul, 1885–94). But see also the valuable thesis by Jennifer Fellows (University of Cambridge Library) which prints versions in parallel, with fascinating variations.

4. Some examples, and further bibliography, may be found in Derek Brewer, "Feasts," in *A Companion to the* Gawain-*Poet*, ed. Derek Brewer and Jonathan Gibson (Cambridge: D. S. Brewer, 1997), pp. 131–42.

5. *Cursor Mundi*, 1–100, in *Early Middle English Verse and Prose*, ed. J. A. W. Bennett and G. V. Smithers (Oxford: Clarendon Press, 1966), pp. 184–9.

6. The principal edition is *Der mittelenglische Versroman über Richard Lowenherz,* ed. K. Brunner. Wiener Beiträge zur englischen Philologie 42 (Vienna and Leipzig, 1913), pp. 81–2.

7. W. H. Auden would make appreciation of lists a test of a true love of poetry ("Making and Judging," 1956), reprinted in W. H. Auden, *The Dyer's Hand and Other Essays* (London: Faber and Faber, 1963), p. 47.

8. See Derek Brewer, "The Arming of the Warrior in European Literature and Chaucer," in *Tradition and Innovation in Chaucer* (London: Macmillan, 1982), pp. 142–60.

9. *Kyng Alisaunder*, ed. G. V. Smithers. 2 vols. Early English Text Society 227 and 237 (London 1952–7).

10. The fullest analysis remains Anne Scott's illuminating essay "Plans, Predictions and Promises: Traditional Story Techniques and the Configuration of Word and Deed in *King Horn*," in *Studies in Medieval English Romances: Some New Approaches*, ed. Derek Brewer (Cambridge: D. S. Brewer, 1988), pp. 37–69.

11. See *Six Middle English Romances*, ed. M. Mills (1973), with valuable introduction. *Sir Isumbras* is on pp. 125–47.

12. There is a full and illuminating account of this story and its Latin and French sources and analogues in Jill Mann, "Excursus: Wife-Swapping in Medieval Literature," in *Feminizing Chaucer* (Cambridge: D. S. Brewer, 2002), pp. 152–73.

13. Ed. Mills 1973: 16–92. For an illuminating discussion see Ad Putter, "Gifts and Commodities in *Sir Amadace*." *Review of English Studies* NS 51 (2000), 370–94.

14. See M. Mauss, *The Gift*, trans. I. Cunnison (1925, reprint London: Cohen and West, 1954).

15. Ed. Mills 1973: 46–74.

16. Jill Mann, *Feminizing Chaucer* (Cambridge: D. S. Brewer, 2002), pp. xv–xviii, 114–25, 127–9. For Constance see also 100–12, etc.

17. *The Parlement of Foulys*, ed. Derek Brewer, second edition (Manchester: Manchester University Press, 1962), pp. 20, 30–2. This list of lovers is further evidence of Chaucer's lack of sympathy with the characteristic optimistic pattern of maturation in medieval chivalric love, exemplified in his mockery in *Sir Thopas*. He was equally unsympathetic to the story of Lancelot, derided as "women's stuff." He mocks the Tristan story by making an absurd allusion to himself as "Tristram the second" in the jesting poem *Rosemounde*, 20.

Further Reading

Aarne, A., and T. Thompson, eds. (1973). *The Types of the Folktale*. Helsinki: Academia Scientiarum Fennica.

Archibald, E. (1991). *Apollonius of Tyre: Medieval and Renaissance Themes and Variations*. Cambridge: D. S. Brewer.

Barron, Caroline (2002). "Chivalry, Pageantry and Merchant Culture." In Peter Coss and Maurice Keen, eds., *Heraldry, Pageantry and Social Display*. Woodbridge: Boydell Press, pp. 229–42.

Boardman, G. (1963). *Motif Index of the English Metrical Romances*. Helsinki: Folklore Fellows Communications 190.

Brewer, Derek (1980). *Symbolic Stories*. Cambridge: D. S. Brewer.

Brewer, Derek (1984). "The Relationship of Chaucer to the English and European Traditions." In *Chaucer the Poet as Storyteller*. London: Macmillan, pp. 8–36.

Brewer, Derek (1997). "Retellings." In Thomas Hahn and Alan Lupack, eds., *Retelling Tales* Cambridge: D. S. Brewer, pp. 9–34.

Cooper, Helen (1999). "Romance after 1400." In David Wallace, ed., *The Cambridge History of Medieval English Literature*. Cambridge: Cambridge University Press, pp. 690–719.

Fellows, J., R. Field, G. Rogers, and J. Weiss, eds. (1996). *Romance Reading on the Book: Essays in Medieval Narrative*. Cardiff: University of Wales Press.

Fewster, Carol (1987). *Traditionality and Genre in Middle English Romance*. Cambridge: D. S. Brewer.

Field, Rosalind (1999). "Romance in English, 1066–1400." In David Wallace, ed., *The Cambridge History of Medieval English Literature*. Cambridge: Cambridge University Press, pp. 152–76.

Field, Rosalind, ed. (1999). *Tradition and Transformation in Medieval Romance*. Cambridge: D. S. Brewer.

French, W. H., and C. B. Hale, eds. (1930). *The Middle English Metrical Romances*. New York: Prentice-Hall.

Gerould, G. H. (1908). *The Grateful Dead: The History of a Folk Song*. Publications of the Folk-lore Society 60. London: D. Nutt.

Guddat-Figge, G. (1976). *Catalogue of Manuscripts containing Middle English Romances*. Munich: Wilhelm Fink Verlag.

Hardman, Phillipa, ed. (2002). *The Matter of Identity in Medieval Romance*. Cambridge: D. S. Brewer.

Meale, Carol M., ed. (1994). *Readings in Medieval English Romance*. Cambridge: D. S. Brewer.

Mehl, D. (1986). *The Middle English Romances of the Thirteenth and Fourteenth Centuries*. London: Routledge.

Mills, Maldwyn, ed. (1973). *Six Middle English Romances*. London: Dent.

Mills, Maldwyn, J. Fellows, and Carol Meale, eds. (1991). *Romance in Medieval England*. Cambridge: D. S. Brewer.

Pearsall, D. (1988). "The Development of Middle English Romance." In Derek Brewer, ed., *Studies in English Romances: Some New Approaches*. Cambridge: D. S. Brewer, pp. 11–36.

Phillips, Helen (forthcoming, 2004). "Rites of Passage in French and English Romances." In W. M. Ormrod and Nicola McDonald, eds., *Rites of Passage*. Cambridge: D. S. Brewer.

Severs, J. Burke, ed. (1967). *A Manual of Writings in Middle English 1050–1500*. Fascicule I. *Romances*. New Haven: Connecticut Academy of Arts and Sciences.

Weiss, J., J. Fellows, and M. Dickson, eds. (2000). *Medieval Insular Romance*. Cambridge: D. S. Brewer.

4
Arthurian Romance

W. R. J. Barron

Of all the evocative names of romance, none is more charismatic than Arthur – king, conqueror, liege lord, lover, knight, fountain of nobility, Hope of the Britons, England's Messiah,[1] icon of evolving nationhood over many centuries. Yet even within the limited Arthurian corpus in English, his protean image is mirrored in a bewildering variety of forms: texts in prose and verse, in a few dozen lines and in many thousands, some in the simple linear structure of folktale and others as elaborately interlaced as their French exemplars, many patently derivative and a few highly original.[2] What can such variety contribute to our understanding of romance as genre or mode?

In the context of this volume it might seem helpful to seek guidance in the dominant cultural tradition of Europe in the later Middle Ages, from which both the name and the norms of romance emerged. But the evolution of the term from its original reference to the emergent vernaculars of the Latinate cultures, to the many varieties of secular texts written in it, to those forms particularly favored by aristocratic patrons, was prolonged and piecemeal. And even in France, where it was first applied to narratives of courtly life and values, it coexisted with other forms of secular narrative written in *romanz*.[3] The fact that France, at the height of its twelfth-century cultural hegemony, produced outstanding embodiments of secular social values in the work of Chrétien de Troyes was to give his *romans courtois* archetypal status. Unhelpfully and misleadingly so, since Chrétien's texts display evolving concepts of scope, structure, theme; they coexist with versions of earlier embodiments of aristocratic values in the *chansons de geste* and the *romans antiques*, and lead to vast prose cycles infinitely varied in form and content.

To all these varieties of romance, Britain was exposed by the cultural effects of the Norman Conquest even more powerfully than it would have been by Continental associations formed before 1066. The settlement of elements from the Conqueror's army – Normans, Bretons, Flemings, French – added to the cultural complexity of a society in which the Anglo-Saxon population was interspersed with regional groupings of Celts and Scandinavians. Each of the cultures represented in Britain was to produce texts conventionally identified as romances, and such texts survive in all the languages of the island, including Latin and Anglo-Norman (Crane 1986).

But despite the variety of models available, English Arthurian romance is rooted in a text in Latin prose predating any of those models, the *Historia Regum Britanniae* of Geoffrey of Monmouth (1138), the work of an ambitious provincial cleric based in Oxford – already an academic community though not yet a university – with his eyes on a future bishopric. Though he was apparently without court connections, the varied dedications to his *Historia* suggest an astute concern to catch the shifting currents of favor in an age of civil war, and its design and content show a shrewd judgment of his audience and its interests. The exalted rank of the dedicatees signals a work of serious importance. The proem announces a theme relevant to such men of authority, a blank in the regnal line: "I have not been able to discover anything at all on the kings who lived here before the Incarnation of Christ, or indeed about Arthur and all the others who followed on after the Incarnation" (§1).[4] The genre in which the theme is to be dealt with is simultaneously declared: a serious academic history in Latin prose, claiming the authority of an antique source, "a certain very ancient book written in the British language" (§2), brought by an eminent cleric *"ex Britannia"* (§208).[5] Characteristics of the genre are maintained throughout: occasional, but rare, concrete dating of events, supplemented by synchronic dating in relation to events in biblical and classical history; incorporation of elements from Gildas (ca. 516–70), Bede (673–735), and the *Historia Brittonum* (early ninth century) traditionally attributed to the Welsh historian Nennius; imitation of the procedures of Old Testament and Roman historians with occasional echoes of the heroic manner of Virgil. Every aspect of the presentation evokes the kind of history familiar to contemporary Latinists.[6]

But the content proved shocking, fascinating yet incredible, particularly to historians. Reassuringly rooted in the fallen Troy of their schoolbooks, it follows Aeneas to the west, attributes the founding and naming of Britain to his great-grandson Brutus, and includes in the long list of his successors legendary builders of British cities, future heroes of Shakespeare's plays, and Brenne and Belin, credited with the sack of Rome. This is fantasy; with the coming of Julius Caesar it is challenged by a reality which Geoffrey only reluctantly admits, the eventual success of the Roman conquest in the face of stubborn British resistance. When the Roman withdrawal leaves the island vulnerable to invading Saxons and the treachery of native usurpers, fantasy reasserts itself in the heroic resistance of the British under a dynasty which culminates in Utherpendragon and his son Arthur. The shadowy reality of Dark Age history is largely obliterated by Arthur's mysterious birth, his glorious career guided by the seer Merlin, repeated defeat of the Saxons, conquest of half Europe, defiance of Rome, and triumphant campaign against the imperial power. Then, as he is poised to capture the city, romance intervenes to circumvent a historical impossibility: news comes that Modred, left regent at home, has seized the throne and taken the queen adulterously, causing Arthur to return, kill his usurping nephew in battle, and, himself mortally wounded, depart mysteriously to Avalon. Reality reasserts itself as the Saxons, treacherously reintroduced by Modred, overwhelm the nation, driving the Britons into the west, until in AD 689 the last native king abandons the island to the victorious ancestors of the English.

The effect of this eclectic mixture was dramatic, first on historians, later on a wider readership. The chronicler Henry of Huntingdon, who came upon a copy at the abbey of Bec in Normandy in January 1139, within a few months of the *Historia*'s appearance, was astounded to read a detailed account of pre-Roman Britain, lack of information on which had inhibited his own work. But almost immediately doubt struck: reporting his discovery to a friend, Henry modified his account of the *Historia* to avoid disagreements with Bede, the *Historia Brittonum*, and his own *Historia Anglorum*, to which he appended this initial report rather than trying to reconcile his account with Geoffrey's.[7] His unease, like that of other historians, was rooted in the role attributed to Arthur. Even those who had long known Arthur as the hero of Celtic folklore and legend, localized largely in the southwest, were startled to meet him in the kind of historical context they nonetheless thought worthy of him. Yet, despite their professional doubts and occasional sarcasms at Geoffrey's expense, there are few medieval historians after 1150 who do not show extensive traces of his influence. The willing credulity of the less literate majority, for whom the landscape of the southwest was penetrated with Arthurian associations, is typified by the villagers of Bodmin, who in 1113 mobbed some visiting canons of Laon for doubting that Arthur was still living and would return to deliver the Britons. Their passion was rooted in a conviction widely shared among laymen; the ambivalence of the historians sprang from the frustration of their wish to echo that conviction by their professional discipline and critical instinct.

Frustration and self-conviction are the roots of romance, however defined. Early efforts to define the English corpus in terms of genre by comparing it – often unfavorably – with classic French examples have now been largely abandoned.[8] The iconic status attributed to Chrétien's *roman courtois* has been undermined by the fluidity of its characteristics, its interrelation with other genres – *chanson de geste*, hagiography, *lai*, *fabliau*, and beast fable – and its variation of theme and medium (Gaunt in Krueger 2000: 45–59). Attempts to contrive sub-definitions of the genre to which individual English texts can be related are rarely convincing.[9] Not surprisingly, critics increasingly prefer to define the medieval romance in terms of mode rather than genre. The critical basis for such a definition is supplied by Aristotle. In the *Poetics* he proposes to classify the fictions through which men attempt to express their relationship to the universe according to the hero's power of action: *mythic* fictions in which, as a divine being, he is superior to other men and their environment; *romantic* fictions in which he is superior to other men – often in rank but more significantly in personal qualities – and to his environment by virtue of his superlative, even supernatural, abilities; *mimetic* or realistic fictions in which he is superior neither to other men nor to the environment in that, however admirable his personal qualities, he is subject to the criticisms of others and to the order of nature in his actions. In classical and European literature these three fictional modes – mythic, romantic, mimetic – though associated with various genres, are not exclusively confined to any particular form. In application to periods and types of literature, the terms indicate the predominance of certain elements rather than the presence of a fixed canon of characteristics identified with a specific genre.[10]

The superior powers attributed to the heroes of romance represent means to an end: the achievement of an ideal of which lesser men would prove incapable. Across the ages romance has embodied a vast range of idealisms, personal, social, cultural, historical, religious, whose very formulation reveals the frustrations which the wish-fulfillment of the mode was designed to relieve.[11] Geoffrey of Monmouth's version of Britain's Dark Age history gave to a melting-pot of disparate nationalities, whose newest comers already declared themselves patriots ready to resist their Norman cousins as alien invaders (Davis 1976: 131), an impressively detailed chronicle of the triumph of a native dynasty, culminating in Arthur's Continental conquests, a fantasy empire foreshadowing the territorial ambitions of Geoffrey's patrons. Within the "historical" framework of Arthur's reign there are shadowy figures of romance: a king identified with a heroic ideal of national freedom, defending his people by personal prowess; a seer prognosticating greatness; a brotherhood of charismatic companions engaged in adventurous quests; a queen involved, willingly or not, with another man; an epic end in mystery and ambiguity.

In addition to the wish-fulfillment fantasy of national unity, the *Historia* had a special appeal for each racial component. For the native Celts it furnished an impressive racial history culminating in the apotheosis of a national hero still potent in folk memory and the assurance of Merlin's prophecy that the seed of Brutus would return to rule the land known by his name. To the English it offered sublimation of their recent humiliation through identification with ancient national tradition rather than Anglo-Saxon history, repeating the process by which the Celts they once defeated had turned that brutal fact into romantic fiction. For the Normans it provided legitimation of their conquest by putting it into historical perspective, showing Brutus as an invader bringing a superior culture, the Saxons as perfidious and brutal, unfit to rule.[12] Geoffrey's appreciation of the particular frustration of each component faction, victors and vanquished, in a Britain striving to become one nation and trace a dynastic link with a past in which they could all take national pride, was to give the *Historia* enduring appeal to their descendants in the centuries ahead. His skill as a storyteller, in the synthesis of disparate materials, in weaving together unconnected but evocative elements, echoing epic and *chanson de geste* to give historical resonance to native legend, was to attract the interest of other cultures, other ages. As far afield as Poland the *Historia*'s format was imitated, its material incorporated in national chronicles, making it one of the most seminal books of the Middle Ages, surviving today in over 220 copies. Vernacular versions quickly made it available to popular audiences; Wales alone produced at least five, of which some 60 texts still survive, and it remained current there long after the rational cynicism of the Renaissance had undermined its historical status in England. Shortly after its appearance, the poets of western Europe began to mine the vein of romance which was to give the story of Arthur currency round the world.[13]

The version of Wace, a cleric from Jersey educated in France, made in 1155 under the patronage of Henry II and presented to his queen Eleanor, was an instant success on both sides of the Channel. Its fluid octosyllabic couplets, the medium of the emergent courtly romance, heightened the chivalric overtones inherent in Geoffrey's material, giving the epic Arthur's relationship to his followers something of that idealization of contemporary reality familiar in narratives of Charlemagne and his *douzepers* (Twelve Peers). The effect is increased by extending the Arthurian section from one-sixth of the *Historia* to some 4,000 out of the 15,000 lines of the *Roman de Brut*, favoring his imperial conquests rather than victories over the Saxons, introducing new fictional elements, such as the founding of the Round Table, and expanding Geoffrey's somewhat cryptic account of the Hope of the Britons in Arthur's return. The fact that Wace did not make fuller use of the kind of material which had so convinced the patriotic citizens of Bodmin, most likely available in the brief prose *contes*, synopses of the lyric performances of Celtic bards currently wandering western Europe, may reflect a concern for the historical character of his work since he comments rather skeptically on the truth of such stories (9,793–8.) His descriptive elaborations are extremely brief; some, now interpreted as heralding a new age of courtliness, such as his description of Arthur's Whitsun feast at Camelot in which knights in distinctive livery contend for the admiration of ladies similarly dressed whose love inspires their chivalry, are closely based on Geoffrey. It is Wace's elaboration of detail, his choice of vocabulary, lively dialogue inserted among the formal speeches of the *Historia*, his gift for aphoristic summation, which give the *Roman de Brut* its courtly gloss, a first fleeting glimpse of England as a land of romance.[14]

A contrasting example of the romanticization of Geoffrey's *Historia*, similar in intent, radically different in execution, is provided by the earliest version in English. The work of Laȝamon, son of Leovenath, parish priest of Areley Kings, ten miles up the Severn from Worcester, it challenges by its very existence misconceptions about the status of the displaced culture. It came at a moment, most probably in the early thirteenth century, when, though the conquerors' dominance made Anglo-Norman the language of government, law courts, schools, good society, and courtly literature, the language of the native majority was beginning its slow climb out of dialectal parochialism to recolonize all those spheres. Early in that process, Laȝamon produced in the dialect of the southwest Midlands a work of over 16,000 lines, the second longest poem in the whole English canon. Its audience in that remote region is difficult to determine: his neighbors, literate and illiterate, in a small community, who could appreciate a lively narrative read aloud; the household of a local landowner – perhaps "the good knight" with whom Laȝamon is said to have lived, probably as domestic chaplain; feasibly some antiquarians among the ecclesiastical community at Worcester, renowned for its preservation of Anglo-Saxon traditions under the long-lived Bishop Wulfstan (d. 1095).

That it had an audience beyond Laȝamon's neighbors and his own age is shown by its survival in two British Library manuscripts, Cotton Caligula A.ix and Cotton Otho C.xiii, both independently derived from a common version which cannot have been the author's original. So at least four texts of this vast work, requiring quantities of expensive parchment, must once have existed. Their dating complicates our view of the cultural context of the *Brut*. The Caligula text, seemingly archaic in idiom, is largely devoid of French loan-words, rich in compound terms, some familiar from Old English, others apparently newly formed on traditional patterns; the Otho is simplified in syntax and vocabulary, French borrowings replacing many of the compound words. While it was assumed, on the dubious basis of internal allusions, now devalued, that the *Brut* was written between 1190 and 1199, it was natural to suppose its antiquated idiom was that of the end of the twelfth century and to see the "modernized" Otho as proof that it had ultimately become outdated. But paleographical evidence has conclusively undermined these assumptions, dating the Caligula to the second half of the thirteenth century and Otho some way into the fourteenth. Since such evidence cannot establish the period at which either version was composed, perhaps its greatest significance is to suggest how long the Caligula text remained viable, despite the contrast with other English writing of the second half of the thirteenth century and its archaic idiom.

Archaic or perhaps archaistic, the idiom of a past age was recreated by Laȝamon and faithfully reproduced by scribes who recognized its antique diction as an integral part of the poem, an emotive concomitant of its ancient historical subject matter. But a personal stylistic fantasy could not have ensured the longevity of the poem unless its audience through the ages shared at least something of the linguistic and stylistic tradition in which it was rooted. The issue is most sharply raised by the highly idiosyncratic verse medium: basically the long line of Old English verse whose two halves are linked across the medial caesura by the use of alliteration, but here with many irregularities, variations of stress and syllabic content, and, most notably, use of rhyme or near-rhyme to link almost 50 percent of the half-lines. The effect, often striking, sometimes bizarre, is of a poet with one ear attuned to past native tradition, the other to the contemporary octosyllabic couplet. Laȝamon may have been as much influenced by oral as by textual tradition, though the persistence of pre-Conquest poetic usage, literary or oral, into the second half of the thirteenth century is difficult to credit. Whatever its sources, Laȝamon's idiom does not suggest a literary pastiche: it is sustained, variable, self-consistent, a natural if highly idiosyncratic medium. And though the poet may have imitated and extended the idiom of his antiquarian reading, its components were apparently sufficiently current in an age of rapid linguistic change to be acceptable to a southwestern audience within the conservative ambit of the Worcester diocese.[15]

The emotive effect of the medium, part archaic, part hybrid, colors the *Brut* with its own distinctive romance tone. In content it remains essentially what Wace wrote, a verse chronicle, the historical pretensions of Geoffrey's original echoed in a conventional proem (1–35) giving the author's name, ancestry, habitation and profession, subject and sources. Of the prestigious works mentioned only Wace's *Roman* seems to have contributed materially to Laȝamon's *Brut*. Its length, however, is doubled, to some extent by verbal elaboration, by additional incidents and motifs, but above all by imaginative extrapolation, greater in some contexts than others, often adding hundreds of lines to the original narrative. Theories of the transmission of Arthurian material and of Celtic influences upon Laȝamon where he lived in the Welsh marches have led to much source-hunting, but the poet often seems to have embroidered upon established tradition rather than borrowed or invented outright. His version of the founding of the Round Table is characteristic: an episode prompted by Wace rather than borrowed from the Celtic tradition to which he alludes, but extended beyond his few lines to over 60 (11,357–421).[16] The focus of much of this extrapolation is the reign of Arthur, extended from one-fifth of Geoffrey's version to almost one-third of Laȝamon's.

Many of Laȝamon's additions and elaborations heighten the idealization of Arthur. Echoes introduced from Geoffrey's Prophecies of Merlin (§§111–17), omitted by Wace, establish his renown even before he has been born: " 'Longe beoð æuere, dæd ne bið he næuere; / þe wile þe þis world stænt, ilæsten scal is worðmunt' " ("As long as time lasts, he shall never die; while this world lasts, his fame shall endure," 9,406–7). The gift-giving "aluen" ("elves") introduced at his birth endow him with kingly qualities (9,608–15), including that liberality and munificence which make him supreme among monarchs (9,945–61). But his benevolence is matched with sternness and ferocity: "Arður wes wunsum þer he hafde his iwillen, / and he wes wod sturne wið his wiðer-iwinnen" ("Arthur was gracious whenever he achieved his purpose, and he was terribly stern with those who opposed him," 11,235–6). His function as lawgiver, sworn to at his succession, aged 15 (9,923–31), is periodically renewed at national hustings, his foreign conquests are confirmed by the establishment there of British law, and it forms the basis of his parting charge to his successor (14,273–6). But his justice is as often equated with punishment as with mercy. In Laȝamon's extension to the founding of the Round Table, those whose quarrel over precedence makes it necessary are dismembered by wild horses, their kinswomen brutally disfigured (11,357–414); disloyal Winchester, seduced and deserted by treacherous Modred, is utterly destroyed (14,195–202). Strong laws and stern justice; realism glossed with romantic idealization for an audience whose older members may have experienced the anarchy of Stephen's reign.

Other qualities of the ideal king, military genius and personal prowess, are similarly heightened in Laȝamon's amplification. To the general concept of the hero's arms as emblems of his valor, exploited by Geoffrey in a passage (§147) (barely altered by Wace) where names drawn from Celtic tradition are given to Arthur's shield, sword, and spear, Laȝamon adds further details of Celtic origin (that the sword Caliburn was made by magic skill in Avalon) and of Germanic coloring (that his helmet inherited from Uther was called Goswhit and his corslet was made by an elvish smith reminiscent of the magical weapon-smith Weland) (10,542–62). In a later addition to Wace (11,856–70) he attributes the spear Ron, inherited from Uther, to the Carmarthen smith Griffin. The splendor of Arthur's arming, the formality of his councils, the magnificence of his crown-wearing at Caerleon acknowledge the importance of ceremonial in medieval governance. Laȝamon shows his mastery of the refinements of courtly life, using a vocabulary which owes little to French culture, but he does no more than lip-service to Wace's rare passages of *amour courtois*, substituting for Gawain's praise of peace as conducive to amorous dalliance (10,767–72) a different idealism based on social good rather than personal happiness (12,455–8). Arthur's military prowess is demonstrated in his role as tactician marshaling forces from all over his empire against the might of Rome, in his personal valor in defending his people from the ravaging Giant of Mont St. Michel (12,960–13,040), and in his duel with the Roman tribune (11,951–69).

The evocation of Arthur as national champion reaches a poetic climax in a remarkable series of extended similes for which there is no counterpart in Wace, where the conventional comparison of warriors to raging lions occupies no more than a line or two. They come, significantly, at the height of his struggle against the Saxons, eight of them within 600 lines: Arthur leading the charge like a savage wolf rushing upon his prey from the snow-hung forest (10,040–3), falling upon the enemy as a fierce wind presses upon a lofty wood (10,047–8), or like a wild boar upon tame swine among the beech mast (10,609–10). His enemies flee before him like hunted prey: one leader like a wild crane pursued by hawks in the air and hounds on land (10,061–7), another like a frisking fox surprised by the hunt in the midst of his sport (10,398–417). Then three similes, continuous and interlinked, totalling 25 lines, mark the moment of triumph: Arthur as a preying wolf penning Colgrim like a goat held at bay in the hills above Bath (10,628–36); Childric fleeing before him as a hunter pursued by the horns of those who were once his prey (10,646–52); the final outcome envisaged in Arthur's image of slaughtered Saxons drifting in the Avon like dead fish (10,638–45), the whole river bridged with steel.

At moments of heightened significance Laȝamon's treatment of Arthur takes on mystical overtones. Portentous dreams warn him of danger to his kingdom: in one he cuts down the traitorous Modred and Guinevere as they strive to destroy the great wooden hall whose roof he bestrides (13,971–14,297). Structurally and thematically the episode echoes Geoffrey's; its imagery, evocative of the Anglo-Saxon hall as the seat of royal power, is characteristic of Laȝamon's inventive employment of native tradition. He similarly extends the mystic role of Merlin, conflating scattered passages of Geoffrey's Prophecies to declare even before Arthur's birth: "'Of him scullen gleomen godliche singen; / of his breosten scullen æten aðele scopes: / scullen of his blode beornes beon drunke" ("Of him shall minstrels splendidly sing; of his breast noble bards shall eat; heroes shall be drunk upon his blood," 9,410–12). The extrapolation from the concept of a hero's reputation serving as meat and drink to the bards who sing of him to the Eucharistic imagery of a Saviour on whose body and blood his people are spiritually nourished is characteristic of the verbal exaltation which overcomes Laȝamon in moments of heightened thematic interest. Christian and magical elements coexist in Arthur's public life as easily as the roles of feudal sovereign and fairy prince in his persona. It comes as no surprise that he invokes the fairy Argante for his bodily healing (14,277–82) and that it is Merlin who, like some Old Testament prophet, predicts his messianic return (14,293–7).

But, despite its impressive bulk, its imaginative development of the legend, its apparent longevity, Laȝamon's *Brut* was not to be central to English Arthurian tradition. Far more influential was another derivative of Geoffrey's *Historia*, more pedestrian, less creative, but enormously ramified and pervasive across the ages. It was rooted in the Anglo-Norman verse redaction made by Geoffrey Gaimar between 1147 and 1151 as the first part of a trilogy constituting a history of the nation from Trojan to contemporary times, the *Brut* being followed by an *Estorie des Engleis* based on the Anglo-Saxon Chronicle, the whole ending with a sketch of the reign of Henry I. It set the pattern of popular history for some three centuries, though in the four surviving manuscripts Gaimar's *Brut* has been replaced by the more prestigious version of Wace. Such composite chronicles appeared in all three literary languages, the Latin version attaining something of the status of an official history. Some 170 manuscripts preserve an English version, varying greatly in content, scale, and component sources and in the continuations which cover contemporary events well into the fifteenth century. Caxton recognized its national standing by publishing a version under the title *Chronicles of England* in 1480; a dozen more editions followed, from various presses, before 1530, and for the rest of the sixteenth century British history from Brutus to Arthur was the accepted prelude to contemporary records (Barron 1999: 32–8).

Though the pragmatic Prose *Brut* predominated in establishing Arthurian prehistory in the national consciousness, it was seconded by more literary versions, verse chronicles in all three languages, similarly tripartite in structure and rooted in Geoffrey's *Historia*. Disregarded until recently by historiographers for a supposed subservience of fact to art, the verbal skill which recommended them to the popular imagination is sometimes matched with scholarly precision. The chronicle attributed to Robert of Gloucester (late thirteenth or early fourteenth century) achieves coherence from a range of learned sources, sometimes conflicting, shaped by controlling themes and interests, embodying brief, rather uncharacteristic, passages from Laȝamon's *Brut* and thus suggesting attraction to an iconic work imperfectly known.[17] Its account of the *Historia* stresses Arthur's piety and exemplary leadership of a chivalric society. That attributed to Thomas of Castleford, ending with the accession of Edward III, includes the Prophecies of Merlin, whose gnomic prognostications were to fascinate popular audiences for centuries to come. The *Short Metrical Chronicle* (post 1307) provides an epitome of island history in some 900 lines in which the idealized model for contemporary kings is not Arthur but Hengist. Robert Mannyng's *Chronicle* (completed 1338) attempts to reconcile Arthurian history with romance narratives circulating contemporaneously by following Wace in assigning such adventures to the periods of peace which Geoffrey indicates in Arthur's reign (Johnson 1999b: 38–46).

The Arthurian material in these texts, prose and verse, remains manifestly in the romance mode, the golden age dream confirmed by its association with contemporary events. These dynastic chronicles are, however, progressively invaded by other genres: folklore, legend, lay, and romance. A passage in the *Short Metrical Chronicle*, telling how Lancelot holds Arthur's queen in specially designed caves under Nottingham castle, links the ancient legend of Guinevere's abduction with a possible echo of contemporary history, an incident of 1330 in which Roger Mortimer and Queen Isabella barricaded themselves in Nottingham castle; and ironically follows it with the bringing to court of a cloak which can detect adulterous wives, a folktale motif common to several Arthurian texts. The contemporary sections demonstrate the extent to which Arthur had penetrated English imaginations as the archetypal founding father: supposed relics of him are preserved in the royal treasury, ambitious nobles mimic his chivalric company in their 'round table' jousts, emulating Edward III's intended institution of the Order of the Round Table. In 1191 and 1278 reigning monarchs honorably reinterred Arthur at Glastonbury, affirming the dynastic succession while demonstrating to their rebellious Welsh subjects the futility of the Hope of the Britons.[18]

The elements of romance embedded in the chronicles suggest the kind of fugitive material available to Geoffrey, Wace, and Laȝamon for the embellishment of their histories. Such material was available also to Continental authors for whom stories of the mysterious Celtic world, known to them in forms and sources not yet fully defined, had greater inherent interest than British history. From motifs whose original meaning had been obscured by cultural change, magic machinery infinitely malleable, pervasive feminine influence, they evolved narratives to reflect their own interests: issues and values in courtly society, chivalric comradeship and conflict, idealized love as the inspiration of knightly prowess. The Arthurian setting gave historic perspective, a continuum of time and place, a renowned court where such things might once have been. The coincidence of a master storyteller exploiting new-found matter to express the concerns of a changing society produced in the work of Chrétien de Troyes a fresh encapsulation of the romance mode. In it Arthur drops into the background, the largely passive figurehead of a chivalric company whose members, embodiments of distinctive knightly virtues, pursue self-fulfillment through adventure, quest, and the inspiration of an idealized love. Complexity of theme is matched with subtlety of literary means: interrelation – often ironic – of thematic and narrative structure; literary self-consciousness evoked by the role of the often intrusive narrator, a stalking-horse for the poet as creator and controller; irony, humor, and a dialectic of words and images provoking the participation of the reader in the realization of meaning.

Though the originals were evidently read in English courts, Chrétien's romances apparently had little appeal for native redactors who have left only a single text of his *Yvain* (later fourteenth century), radically abbreviated not only by omission of descriptive detail and much of the verbal fencing conveying conflict between characters, but also the rhetorical art, analysis of feeling, verbal dialectic by which Chrétien queries his characters' advance in understanding in a circular narrative which poses and seemingly resolves a chivalric dilemma, so stimulating judgment of the values they profess. What survives is the narrative of adventures, tightened and quickened by omission of minor incidents, recounted in a clear swift-moving style unencumbered by verbiage, the fantasy realm of the original action replaced by the real geography of Britain, legal details specifically related to contemporary English law. Everything is designed for clarity, concreteness, and ready comprehension by less courtly readers of a story whose manners and values were some 200 years old. The moral ambivalences involved in the complementary and competing claims of chivalry and *fin' amor* are replaced by the single standard of *trowth* (loyalty, constancy) governing conduct in love and marriage as well as fellowship between knights. Its celebration of that aspiration places the English text firmly in the romance mode; its expressive means are characteristic of the English genre, basic human values replacing the social codes celebrated and queried in Chrétien's *romans courtois*.[19]

The French tradition was to develop its own version of Arthurian "history," providing a continuum for manifold varieties of social idealism and provoking corresponding variations of the romance genre to express them. The vast prose text known as the Vulgate Cycle, because it came to be regarded as the standard compendium, prefixed to the matter of Geoffrey's *Historia* a prehistory centered around the Grail, introduced in Chrétien's incomplete *Perceval* as a ritual object of undefined significance and developed into a potent Christian symbol, the cup of the Last Supper in which Joseph of Arimathea caught Christ's blood at the Crucifixion, brought by him to Glastonbury on a mission of conversion. This Christian prehistory incorporated in the first branch of the cycle, *L'Estoire del Saint Graal*, was followed by the *Estoire de Merlin*, which bridged the gap from the first to the fifth century by the devilish plot to mislead mankind through a prophet, half human half devil, that Merlin who later aided Uther in siring Arthur. The Arthurian world once established, the focus is on Lancelot, whose early adventures form a setting for Chrétien's romance *Le Chevalier de la Charette*. These lead on to the *Queste del Saint Graal* (probably written by a Cistercian monk) in which Lancelot's adulterous love for Guinevere exposes him, like many fellow knights, to humiliation in the spiritual experience of the Grail and, when renewed in *La Mort le Roi Artu*, to a breach with Arthur, civil war, and the downfall of the Round Table. Dynastic history has become little more than the background to endless variations on a romantic ideal of personal achievement given a gloss of spirituality by the exaltation of the Grail quest as a mission of mystic self-fulfillment and spiritual service in the course of which the inadequacy of worldly chivalry is repeatedly demonstrated.

From this romance massif in its many recensions English redactors chipped fragments which retained the allure while losing most genre characteristics. *Joseph of Arimathie* (ca. 1340) took from the opening of the *Estoire*, which recounted Joseph's early missionary adventures in the East, a saint's life with the scale (709 lines) and didactic tone of popular storytelling. Just as the late fourteenth-century hack responsible for *Arthur* compressed his whole reign, apparently using some version of Wace, into 642 octosyllabics, so two late linked ballads, *The Legend of King Arthur* and *King Arthur's Death* (255 lines in total), derived from the *Mort Artu*, cover the king's last battle and passing, prefaced with his personal account of his reign – they are manifestations of popular patriotism of the kind stimulated by the Prose *Brut*. The

Lancelot produced at one extreme a Scottish verse romance, *Lancelot of the Laik* (3,484 lines), ineptly disguised as a dream vision and incorporating a critique of Arthur's regnal failings probably aimed at James III, its didacticism blanketing a romantic reputation, and, at the other extreme, a ballad, *Sir Lancelot du Lake*, on one of the hero's many duels. The verse Chronicles have their counterpart here in the work of Henry Lovelich, a London skinner who translated the *Estoire* and the *Merlin* into octosyllabic couplets at enormous length which, like the contemporary prose translation of the *Merlin*, suggests the appeal of Arthurian prehistory to the commercial classes of the mid-fifteenth century, more interested in content than in genre. The Vulgate *Merlin* was also the primary source, much modified, of *Arthour and Merlin* (1250–1300), which reduced the narrative and psychological complications of the French, dismissing *fin' amor* as discreditable, in favor of action and an evident desire to convey useful information as an assertion of English national awareness (Burnley 1999: 83–90; Hodder 1999: 71–83).

National awareness was naturally most acute for native audiences at the dynastic climax, whether in the English or the French tradition. Two texts, both northern, both late fourteenth-century, provide informative contrasts of interpretation, genre, and medium in treating a classic example of romance mode: a troubled dream of the golden age of a nation brought to an end by inherent contradictions in the ideals on which it was built. The Alliterative *Morte Arthure* harks back to Laȝamon's *Brut* in its use of the long line even more rigidly alliterated and of some version of the chronicle tradition, probably Wace, intermixed with an eclectic range of other romance matters. The dynastic theme is here highly concentrated (4,346 lines), beginning with Rome's demand for homage, and the poem is structured in the epic manner, presenting detached, highly dramatic scenes in six major sections, five beginning with messengers whose nature or news characterizes the following episode. Arthur dominates as a Christian king defending his nation against pagan Rome, leading his lieges in fulfillment of their formal vows of vengeance, reminiscent of the competitive boasting of the *chansons de geste* but also of the Anglo-Saxon *beot*; and as a knight, leader of a chivalric order, defending his people against the bestial giant of Mont St. Michel, seeking out solitary adventures and killing the Emperor in single combat. Both roles are flawed by excessive aspiration. Gawain, Arthur's foil, displays in an episode borrowed from the romanticized epic *Fierabras* knightly prowess carried to grotesque extremes in single combat, and then, with the king's approval, applied to what has become a war of conquest. Laȝamon's strong ruler acts now as a tyrant warring against Pope and Church, warned by a prophetic dream of the Wheel of Fortune from which the overweening are hurled in the moment of triumph, his assault on Rome ironically counterpointed against the sub-theme of pilgrimage. A pilgrim brings him news of Modred's treachery, now seen as rooted in Arthur's imperial obsession since, by forcing the regency on his nephew, he had robbed him of his chance of military glory. As his forces invade their own country, Gawain is cut off in reckless pursuit of glory by his cousin Modred, and the dying Arthur recognizes the desolate end of worldly glory. By evoking the various genres associated with military idealism, the alliterative poet has infused chronicle material with the spirit of wish-fulfillment; but by using their conventions ironically and juxtaposing them with the moral and physical reality of war he has undermined their values to the point where he seems to be writing anti-romance (Johnson 1999a: 90–100).

The same impulse to find meaning in the failure of an ideal informs the Stanzaic *Morte Arthur*, otherwise radically different in every respect. Its medium, octosyllabic lines grouped in eight-line stanzas of two rhymes only, imposes narrative restrictions reminiscent of the ballad, and is expertly handled for thematic effect, blocks of stanzas balanced against each other, breaks between them allowing rapid changes of scene, speaker, or perspective, presenting an action followed by the reaction of various observers. As with the ballad, formulaic conventions, condensed speeches charged with suppressed passions, snatches of dialogue implying action not narrated, permit the presentation of moments of startling intensity in a narrative too familiar for recapitulation. The narrative, freely derived from the Vulgate *Mort Artu*, unravels its intertwined, long-running threads and recombines selected episodes to shift the thematic focus from Arthur, embodying the nation, to Lancelot, the archetypal representative of chivalry inspired by love. At the climax, the chronicle account of challenge from abroad and treason at home is combined with the inherent conflict between feudal duty and chivalric aspiration. The chivalric thread employs all the motifs of the romance genre: secret meetings between the lovers spied upon by jealous troublemakers, quest and tournament demonstrating the hero's prowess, a rival love breeding dissension, fidelity repeatedly proven in trial by combat, a bedroom siege, and rescue from the stake. But the chivalric and dynastic themes fatally interact: as a member of the Round Table, Lancelot's adultery with the queen is treason, Arthur's blind loyalty to all his knights tears the order apart, and Gawain's archaic impulse to avenge his kin turns his comradeship with Lancelot into bitter enmity. And under the feudal issues runs a moral current which, after Arthur's death, brings the lovers recognition of the disastrous consequences of their love, mutual renunciation, and retirement to the religious life (Weinberg 1999: 100–11).

In English examples of the classic chivalric romance celebrating an individual knight, the predominant hero is Gawain, perhaps because he could be most readily identified with the archetypal folk-hero seeking self-knowledge through adventure, renowned for his physical prowess, touched with mysticism in the waxing and waning of his strength with the power of the sun, largely indifferent to *amour courtois*, loving and leaving as the fancy takes him. The ambivalence of his chivalric status is reflected in English versions of an episode, *Le Livre du Chastel Orguelleus*, in the First Continuation of Chrétien's *Perceval*. In *Golagrus and Gawane* (Scots, ca. 1500), by putting his own reputation at risk, Gawain spares the honor and secures the independence of an opponent – a cipher in the original, whose worth is elaborately established by the redactor deploying all the tropes of romance – under the eyes of a rapacious, oppressive Arthur. This chapter in the hagiography of the English Gawain required the omission of an earlier episode in which he seduces and abandons the sister of an adversary, slaughtering her kin, material turned by the redactor of *The Jeaste of Syr*

Gawayne (southern, late fifteenth century) into little more than a bar-room anecdote, a burlesque of Arthurian chivalry (Barron 1999: 155–61; Mills 1999: 162–4).

An even more complicated reflection of the moral and social issues underlying contemporary chivalry characterizes *The Awntyrs off Arthure* (northwest, ca. 1400–30). Its twin episodes, in both of which Gawain acts as Arthur's surrogate, imply condemnation of Guinevere's adultery as the ghost of her mother rises to beg masses for the release of a guilty soul, and of Arthur's territorial rapacity when, having fought a challenger to a standstill before the court, Gawain restores his lands, which have been conferred by the king upon Gawain himself – echoing the ghost's warning that territorial acquisitiveness would lead to the downfall of the kingdom. The theme of disregard of self and generosity to others unites the chivalric and didactic levels of the text. The former relies on established conventions of the romance genre; the latter combines cultural motifs from exempla, folklore, stock personae, and settings with established associations. Parallels and inversions of characters and situations compound the complex interaction of the moral and chivalric levels of the poem, implying a sophisticated audience alert to its elaborate intertextuality (Allen 1999: 105–55).

Any tendency to underrate the sophistication of medieval English audiences could scarcely survive a reading of *Sir Gawain and the Green Knight* (northwest Midlands, later fourteenth century) in which Gawain's ambiguous reputation is exploited with extraordinary subtlety to demonstrate the inherent ambivalence of romance, the aspiration of fallible mankind to perfect achievement of an ideal. Every convention of the genre is deployed in development of the theme: the court assembled at Camelot in seasonal celebration of faith and fellowship, joining in games of love and war, jousting and kissing for forfeits, until Arthur's expectation of adventure brings a challenger to whom Gawain responds as representative of the Round Table. But every trope of romance is undermined by ironies of implication, ambiguous evocations of tradition, verbal ambiguity: sport gives way to earnest as mimic warfare is replaced by deadly challenge, Arthur's ceremonial usage evokes not narrative but action, the arrival of a monstrous figure, a fusion of the knight-challenger of romance and the Wild Man of folktale. His proposed game of forfeits threatens beheading, but is accepted by Gawain to save the reputation of his terror-stricken comrades, whose whispered criticism of the king undermines the reputed solidarity of Arthur's kingdom while the beheaded challenger departs, still mouthing with legal exactitude the terms of his deadly compact.

Thereafter the romance proceeds as it has begun, the audience constantly comforted by convention: the ceremonial arming of the departing hero, the perfection of his chivalry emblazoned in the perfect figure of his heraldic pentangle, symbol of *trawthe*, his wilderness quest opposed by a catalogue of conventional opponents, natural and supernatural, ending in a wayside castle which offers all the civilized amenities of Camelot. But the audience is also repeatedly discomfited by contradictions: the futility of armor against an undefended blow, the profusion of virtues, physical, moral, chivalric, subsumed in the pentangle, the parodic opponents of romance outclassed by the bitterness of the winter weather, the jovial host who challenges Gawain to another game of equal exchanges. The seductive hostess who engages him in a kissing game in the absence of her hunting lord evokes the tradition of wayside castles as places of trial and recalls Gawain's notorious susceptibility to women, while the varied deaths of the hunted beasts exchanged for the kisses on each of three evenings may seem emblematic of the fate awaiting a guest suspected of sexual treason with the wife of his host. Gawain's renowned courtesy allows him to fulfill the game of forfeits without apparent offense to either host or hostess, completing one romance structure and preparing for the expected crisis at the completion of the beheading challenge. But the moral crisis has already passed, in thought rather than action, as Gawain contemplates the value in that crisis of the protective girdle offered by the lady as a *drury* (love-token), not surrendered with her kisses at the nightly exchange with her husband but, as he arms for departure after priestly confession and absolution, superimposed upon the protective pentangle on his surcoat as a *luf-lace* seemingly emblematic of self-love. Submitting to the return blow, at the tryst he escapes with a scratch; challenge faced under twin talismans has proved a figment in the best manner of romance. Yet the blow is still to fall as the Challenger fuses with his wayside host, pardoning in confessional form the trifling fault, punished by the scratch, of retaining the girdle in breach of the castle compact. Gawain's violent reaction and bitter confessional outburst suggest awareness of absolution invalidated by retention of the coveted girdle, as he departs unreconciled, wearing the *luf-lace* across the pentangle on his chest like a bend sinister modifying his claim to *trawthe*. At his confessional recapitulation before the Round Table, not even his comrades' adoption of the girdle as a badge of honor can persuade him to accept comparative rather than absolute perfection.

His continued self-accusation of *untrawthe* may imply consciousness of flaws in his formal confession to which the reader could not be privy, a breach of *trawthe* with God. The gravity of such a possibility reflects the bitter realization of an idealist professing an absolute code that adventures do not come singly, that mere men cannot always distinguish between game and earnest, that failure may result from a momentary impulse to self-preservation as instinctive as a natural reflex. The issues have divided the critics and the poet provides no resolution, inviting instead reflection on all human aspirations by echoing his opening reference to the dynastic tradition of romance, that record of *blysse and blunder* since the fall of Troy against which chivalric idealism must appear profoundly comic. Then, beyond the hermetic structure of historical experience, he offers, under the guise of the tritest of terminal conventions in minstrel romance, an escape from the inevitable failure of human idealism: "Now þat bere þe croun of þorne, / He bryng vus to his blysse! AMEN" (2529–30).

The constant evocation of the romance genre in its classic form, the way in which its conventions are played with at every level from verbal ambiguity to structural complexity, above all the ironic and dialectic challenge to the reader's judgment on individual effects and overall meaning suggest familiarity with Chrétien's themes and methods on the part of both poet and audience. But the subtlety with which *Sir Gawain and the Green Knight* deploys and controverts conventions, the ambiguous outcome, the undermining of absolute ideals by human instinct, the implications of anti-romance are all too individual to be merely imitated. The community of treatment by two poets so widely separated by time and tradition seems rather the mutual appreciation by sophisticated minds of the inherent nature of romance.[20]

For the English, the natural protagonist of such an ambiguous adventure was Gawain, age-old exemplar of moderate, manly chivalry rooted in human qualities, all too often undermined by natural instincts and impulses. That is his role in a group of short verse texts composed in the Midlands or the north during the fifteenth century, six of which are preserved, partly mutilated, in the Percy Folio manuscript of ca. 1650. In them Arthur and his companions are subjected to the kind of tests by which popular heroes establish their identity. Where he serves as their champion, the action centers around Carlisle and Inglewood Forest, with which he was traditionally connected as Robin Hood was with Sherwood. In *The Avowynge of King Arthur*, Gawain surpasses his companions in fulfilling the vows they had made to requite the boasts of their demonic host, King Cornwall, so allowing Arthur to behead him. In *The Turke and Gowin*, the Turk challenges the Round Table to an exchange of buffets, Gawain courteously accepts and, riding north for the return blow, succeeds in a contest of strength against the giant retainers of the King of Man by the help of the Turk whom he then beheads at his request, so releasing the knight Sir Gromer from his enchanted form. Two versions of *The Carle off Carlile* represent variants of an original in which the giant Carl tests Arthur and his companions while they are his guests; only Gawain succeeds, obeying his commands to hurl a spear at his head, lie beside his wife, and finally to behead him, so transforming him into a knight who joins the Round Table.

There are analogues in French literature to many of the recurrent motifs here – tests imposed by a challenger, the fulfillment of vows or boasts, disenchantment by beheading; but they also have Celtic parallels, suggesting that the authors drew upon common folk-motifs which, their localization hints, may have derived from Galloway, the bridge to Gaelic Scotland known in the twelfth century as "the Kingdom of Gawain." Their material had already been demythologized, the tests imposed during a visit to some Otherworld being rationalized as the commands of an Imperious Host exacting obedience from his guests, giving them a rather half-hearted gloss as demonstrations of knightly qualities. The process is exemplified in the way in which the motif of the Loathly Lady Transformed, widespread in European folklore, has been associated with the Round Table in *The Weddynge of Sir Gawen and Dame Ragnell* and *The Marriage of Sir Gawaine*. Arthur is threatened with death by Sir Gromer Somer Joure unless he can tell what it is that women love most; Gawain, by promising to marry the hideous Dame Ragnell, learns from her that they desire sovereignty above all and, in the marriage bed, reluctantly kisses her and finds that he has freed a beautiful young woman from the enchantment of a wicked stepmother. The story may be rooted in an Irish legend of a hero whose fitness for the kingship is tested by his willingness to kiss a faery woman in the form of a hag. Chaucer, in his "Wife of Bath's Tale," used a version in which the roles of Arthur and Gawain were united in a young knight of the Round Table under sentence for the rape of a peasant girl and made it the vehicle, in the hag's pillow lecture to her unhappy bridegroom, for a noble restatement of the nature of chivalry as gentle deeds rather than gentle birth.

Chaucer's transformation illustrates the process by which folklore motifs, universal, age-old, and inherently ambiguous, could serve the idealism of chivalric romance. These late Arthurian texts, brief, sensational, in a variety of tail-rhyme stanzas evocative of ballad narration, suggest a popular audience more interested in incident than ideals. But the elements of parody involved need not imply a rejection of chivalric romance, any more than the dwindling of dynastic Arthur to a stereotyped Worthy. Critical attitudes to Arthur had been current since Chrétien, and in the earliest Celtic texts, in which a rash and foolish Arthur and his rumbustious followers serve as supernumeraries in the adventures of questing folk-heroes, there are traces of burlesque. So we are perhaps concerned with the coexistence of folktale and romance rather than differences of audience or degeneration in the status of the legend. These so-called folk romances are contemporary with the *Morte Darthur* in which, as perhaps in all forms of romance, heightened idealism coexists with awareness of human limitations.[21]

In every culture, every age, romances are fugitive dreams entertained in the sleep of reason. The English romances of Arthur suggest a troubled sleep broken by consciousness of human weakness, ideals undermined by social change, regnal authority resented as tyranny, chivalry distorted by conflicting loyalties. But day-dreaming is a form of thought, of envisaging a better world, past or future, disregarding human limitations. Where, as in *Sir Gawain and the Green Knight*, an ambivalent balance of aspiration and achievement is portrayed, challenging judgment, inducing understanding in a didactic age, there is a sense of literature fulfilling a valid social function, of romance as a catalyst of change, projecting from what is or has been to what might some day be. Malory's *Morte Darthur*, where the historical perspective is given by the dynastic tradition to the mass of chivalric adventures it frames, left to later ages a racial ideal glossed with patriotism which, for the Victorians, gave Arthurian romance something of the status of a national epic.

See also: chapter 1, Ancient Romance; chapter 2, Insular Beginnings; chapter 3, The Popular English Metrical Romances; chapter 5, Chaucer's Romances; chapter 6, Malory and the Early Prose Romances; chapter 26, Twentieth-century Arthurian Romance.

Notes

1. At Arthur's departure to Avalon, Laȝamon's *Brut* (ed. and trans. Barron and Weinberg 1995, l. 14,297) cites a prophecy of Merlin "þat an Arþur sculde ȝete cum Anglen to fulste" ("that an Arthur should again come to aid the people of England").

2. The variety of the corpus – some 50 texts ranging in date from ca. 1200 to ca. 1500 – is conveniently described and categorized in Barron 1999; the bibliography of that book lists editions of all the English texts referred to here and recent academic studies are reviewed in the notes.

3. The term was, for example, applied to the pseudo-chronicle of the *Roman de Brut*, the psychological allegory of the *Roman de la Rose*, the *Roman de Renart* beast fable, and even to a Life of Christ. On the range of references in English see Mehl 1968: 13–22.

4. References are to the chapter numbers of the edition of the Vulgate version of the *Historia* by Wright 1985 and quotations from the translation by Thorpe 1966.

5. It is not clear whether the reference is to a Welsh book brought from Wales or a Breton book from Brittany – though Geoffrey's usage throughout the *Historia* suggests that *Britannia* can only mean the latter. The present consensus of scholarly opinion dismisses the ancient book as the kind of fabulous source commonly claimed by medieval authors in search of authority for their own inventions. A partial source of Breton origin has, however, been suggested (Roberts 1991: 101) and the search for other components continues.

6. For recent, succinct characterizations of the *Historia* see Bromwich 1991: 97–116; 130-37 and Barron 1999: 11–18.

7. The significance of Henry of Huntingdon's reaction for contemporary historiography is brought out by Wright 1991: 71–113, which incorporates an edition and translation of Henry's initial report.

8. "It is doubtful whether the romance can be indeed regarded as a genre at all . . . The romance is in origin merely a narrative in the vernacular and the texts that we call romances merely a somewhat arbitrary selection from medieval narrative . . . It seems preferable to speak of a romance mode" (Gradon 1974: 269–70). "Even the works usually called romances today differ widely; thus insofar as observations about the generic nature of medieval romance can be made, they must be fluid and contingent, seeking to clarify the nature of single works rather than to classify them. Broadly speaking, medieval romances are secular fictions of nobility, 'storial thyng that toucheth gentillesse' [Chaucer, *Miller's Prologue*, 3179]" (Crane 1986: 10–11).

9. For two characteristic examples see Finlayson 1980: 44–62, 168–81 and Pearsall, 1980: 105–25.

10. "The words 'romantic' and 'realistic,' for instance, as ordinarily used, are relative or comparative terms: they illustrate tendencies in fiction, and cannot be used as simply adjectives with any sort of exactness" (Frye 1957: 49). Northrop Frye helpfully restates and extrapolates Aristotle's theory (see pp. 33–52) and in his later study, *The Secular Scripture* (1976), develops his own conception of romance more fully.

11. My conception of the mode and its embodiment in various literary forms and cultures is more fully outlined in Barron 1987: 1–10.

12. It is perhaps a tribute to Geoffrey's skill in shaping his narrative in a way that might appeal to various elements in his potential audience that modern analysts differ as to where his real sympathies lay. For an outline of the debate see Gillingham 1990: 99–118.

13. On the remarkably rapid and widespread dissemination of the *Historia*, see Crick 1991, and on the Welsh versions, Roberts 1991: 110–13.

14. For a modern edition and translation of the *Roman de Brut* see Weiss 1999 and for a recent summation of Wace scholarship, Le Saux 1999a: 18–22.

15. The implications of the idiom and dating of *Brut* texts for its cultural context and audience is conveniently summarized by Barron 2002: 157–84.

16. References to and quotations from the *Brut* are to the complete edition and translation by Barron and Weinberg 1995.

17. Of various insertions made in a second recension of Robert's *Chronicle* some time during the 1320s, three-quarters, some 560 lines, come from a Caligula text of the *Brut*. Though they have been somewhat modified linguistically, it is significant for the longevity of the *Brut* that the interpolator apparently understood its archaic diction without difficulty.

18. On the impact of the legend on later medieval history and ceremonial see Carley 1999: 47–57 and Vale 1999: 185–96.

19. For two complementary analyses of *Ywain and Gawain* see Barron 1987: 160–3 and Mills 1999: 117–24.

20. For a fuller analysis see Barron 1999: 164–83 and on the technical similarities to Chrétien's work, Barron 1988: 255–84.

21. The potential audience of these texts, their complex interrelations and bearing upon the folktale elements in such texts as *Sir Gawain and the Green Knight* are still at a preliminary stage of investigation. For a summary of current opinion see Gillian Rogers 1999: 197–224, and, on their counterparts in Celtic tradition, Ceridwen Lloyd-Morgan 1999: 1–9.

References and Further Reading

Allen, Rosamund (1999). "*The Awntyrs off Arthure*." In R. W. J. Barron, ed., *The Arthur of the English*. Cardiff: University of Wales Press, pp. 150–5.

Barron, W. R. J. (1987). *Medieval English Romance*. Longman Literature in English Series. Harlow and New York: Longman.

Barron, W. R. J. (1988). "Chrétien and the *Gawain*-Poet: Master and Pupil or Twin Temperaments?" In N. J. Lacy, D. Kelly, and K. Busby, eds., *The Legacy of Chrétien de Troyes*, II. Amsterdam: Rodopi, pp. 255–84.

Barron, W. R. J. (1999). "Geoffrey of Monmouth's *Historia*." In R. W. J. Barron, ed., *The Arthur of the English*. Cardiff: University of Wales Press, pp. 11–18.

Barron, W. R. J. (1999). "Prose Chronicles." In W. R. J. Barron, ed., *The Arthur of the English*. Cardiff: University of Wales Press, pp. 32–8.

Barron, W. R. J. (1999). "*Sir Gawain and the Green Knight*." In W. R. J. Barron, ed., *The Arthur of the English*. Cardiff: University of Wales Press, pp. 164–83.

Barron, W. R. J. (2002). "The Idiom and the Audience of Laȝamon's *Brut*." In R. Allen, L. Perry, and J. Roberts, eds., *Laȝamon: Contexts, Language, and Interpretation*. Kings College London Medieval Studies XIX. London: Kings College London Centre for Late Antique and Medieval Studies, pp. 157–84.

Barron, W. R. J., ed. (1999). *The Arthur of the English*. Arthurian Literature in the Middle Ages II. Cardiff: University of Wales Press. [A revised version was published in 2001.]

Barron, W. R. J., and S. C. Weinberg, ed. and trans. (1995). *Laȝamon's Brut*. Harlow: Longman.

Bromwich, Rachel, A. O. H. Jarman, and B. F. Roberts, eds. (1991). *The Arthur of the Welsh*. Arthurian Literature in the Middle Ages I. Cardiff: University of Wales Press.

Burnley, David (1999). "*Arthour* and Merlin." In W. R. J. Barron, ed., *The Arthur of the English*. Cardiff: University of Wales Press, pp. 83–90.

Carley, J. P. (1999). "Arthur in English History." In W. R. J. Barron, ed., *The Arthur of the English*. Cardiff: University of Wales Press, pp. 47–57.

Crane, Susan (1986). *Insular Romance: Politics, Faith, and Culture in Anglo-Norman and Middle English Literature*. Berkeley and London: University of California Press.

Crick, J. C. (1991). *The Historia Regum Britannie of Geoffrey of Monmouth, IV: Dissemination and Reception in the Later Middle Ages*. Woodbridge: Brewer.

Davis, R. H. C. (1976). *The Normans and Their Myth*. London: Thames and Hudson.

Finlayson, John (1980). "Definitions of Middle English Romance." *Chaucer Review* 15, 44–62, 168–81.

Frye, Northrop (1957). *Anatomy of Criticism: Four Essays*. Princeton, NJ: Princeton University Press.

Frye, Northrop (1976). *The Secular Scripture: A Study of the Structure of Romance*. Cambridge, MA, and London: Harvard University Press.

Gaunt, Simon (2000). "Romance and other Genres." In R. L. Krueger, ed., *The Cambridge Companion to Medieval Romance*. Cambridge: Cambridge University Press, pp. 45–59.

Gillingham, John (1991). "The Context and Purposes of Geoffrey of Monmouth's *History of the Kings of England*." *Anglo-Norman Studies* 13, 99–118.

Gradon, Pamela (1974). *Form and Style in Early English Literature*. London: Methuen.

Hodder, Karen (1999). "*Arthur, The Legend of King Arthur, King Arthur's Death, Joseph of Arimathie*, Henry Lovelich's *History of the Holy Grail* and *Merlin*." In W. R. J. Barron, ed., *The Arthur of the English*. Cardiff: University of Wales Press, pp. 71–83.

Johnson, Lesley (1999a). "The Alliterative *Morte Arthure*." In W. R. J. Barron, ed., *The Arthur of the English*. Cardiff: University of Wales Press, pp. 90–100.

Johnson, Lesley (1999b). "Metrical Chronicles." In W. R. J. Barron, ed., *The Arthur of the English*. Cardiff: University of Wales Press, pp. 38–46.

Le Saux, Françoise (1999a). "Wace's *Roman de Brut*." In W. R. J. Barron, ed., *The Arthur of the English*. Cardiff: University of Wales Press, pp. 18–22.

Le Saux, Françoise (1999b). "Laȝamon's *Brut*." In W. R. J. Barron, ed., *The Arthur of the English*. Cardiff: University of Wales Press, pp. 22–32.

Mehl, Dieter (1968). *The Middle English Romances of the Thirteenth and Fourteenth Centuries*. London: Routledge and Kegan Paul.

Mills, Maldwyn (1999). "*Ywain and Gawain*." In W. R. J. Barron, ed., *The Arthur of the English*. Cardiff: University of Wales Press, pp. 117–24.

Pearsall, Derek (1980). "Understanding Middle English Romance." *Review* 2, 105–25.

Roberts, B. F. (1991). "Geoffrey of Monmouth, *Historia* and *Brut y Brenhinedd*." In Rachel Bromwich, A. O. H. Jarman, and B. F. Roberts, eds., *The Arthur of the Welsh*. Cardiff: University of Wales Press, pp. 97–116.

Rogers, Gillian (1999). "Folk Romance." In W. R. J. Barron, ed., *The Arthur of the English*. Cardiff: University of Wales Press, pp. 197–224.

Thorpe, Lewis, trans. (1966). Geoffrey of Monmouth. *The History of the Kings of Britain*. Harmondsworth: Penguin.

Vale, Juliet (1999). "Arthur in English Society." In W. R. J. Barron, ed., *The Arthur of the English*. Cardiff: University of Wales Press, pp. 185–96.

Weinberg, Carole (1999). "The Stanzaic *Morte Arthur*." In W. R. J. Barron, ed., *The Arthur of the English*. Cardiff: University of Wales Press, pp. 100–11.

Weiss, Judith, ed. and trans. (1999). *Wace's Roman de Brut: A History of the British*. Exeter: University of Exeter Press.

Wright, Neil (1991). "The Place of Henry of Huntingdon's *Epistola ad Warinum* in the Text-history of Geoffrey of Monmouth's *Historia Regum Britannie*." In G. Jondorf and D. N. Dumville, eds., *France and the British Isles in the Middles Ages and Renaissance*. Woodbridge: Boydell, pp. 71–113.

Wright, Neil, ed. (1985). *The Historia Regum Britannie of Geoffrey of Monmouth*, I: *Bern Burgerbibliothek MS 568*. Woodbridge: Brewer.

5
Chaucer's Romances

Corinne Saunders

What did that most famous of medieval writers, Geoffrey Chaucer, make of the romance genre, so prominent in the Middle Ages, yet also so elusive?[1] In many ways, Chaucer's use of romance illuminates the complexity of the genre. Because the term originally referred simply to writing in a *romanz* language, it developed only loosely into a literary genre, and yet there does seem to have been an awareness in the later Middle Ages of romance as a distinctive mode. Notions of genre, however, remained much more fluid than our own – a work might be at once tragedy, history, and romance, as is Chaucer's *Troilus and Criseyde*, or saint's life and romance, as are the *Clerk's Tale* and the *Man of Law's Tale*, or comedy and romance, as is the *Merchant's Tale*.[2] It is possible to see Chaucer's mixed genre as looking forward to that of Shakespeare: both poets exploit the dramatic possibilities of shifts in genre and hence in tone, language, and subject matter. It is also clear that Chaucer distinguished between the kinds of romance that we might label metrical or popular romance, classical romance, Breton *lai*, Arthurian romance.

It is telling that Chaucer uses the word "romaunz" only rarely, and never to describe any of his own works. Indeed, such a label might well have displeased a writer keen to be viewed as cosmopolitan, courtly, and intellectual. The sole occurrence of the term in the *Canterbury Tales*, although they certainly include works that we would consider romances, is in the tale of *Sir Thopas*, which, as we shall see, satirizes the popular romance tradition: the eponymous hero is compared to other heroes of "romances of prys" as bearing the "flour / Of roial chivalry!" (897, 901–2).[3] The Nun's Priest makes a comparably mocking reference to Arthurian romance, assuring his audience that "This storie is also trewe, I undertake, / As is the book of Launcelot de Lake, / That women holde in ful greet reverence" (3211–13). This tale plays on the motif of women as mistaking readers: just as they falsely put their trust in romance, Pertelote trusts in Chauntecleer's translation of Latin and fails to trust in his actually prophetic dream. These women perhaps find a corrective in the Wife of Bath, who offers a dismissive comment on "the'olde dayes of the Kyng Arthour" when "Al was this land fulfild of fayerye": "This was the olde opinion, as I rede; / I speke of manye hundred yeres ago. / But now kan no man se none elves mo" (857–64); faeries have been replaced by lecherous friars. In these ironic references, it is hard not to hear the voice of Chaucer mocking Arthurian romance (see Windeatt 1992: 144).

Yet reading romances of one kind or another also comprises an essential and familiar part of aristocratic life, a pastime comparable to chess, or dancing, or hunting. We are told that the sleepless narrator in the *Book of the Duchess* calls for "a book, / A romaunce ... to rede and drive the night away": it offers better play than "ches or tables" (47–50). This "romaunce" with its "fables" (52) put into rhyme by clerks of old, including the tale of Ceyx and Alcyone, appears to be a collection of tales from Ovid's *Metamorphoses*. That a classical work is referred to as both fable and romance demonstrates the fluidity of genre terms: the classical content may also signal a higher status in the hierarchy of romance. The *Book of the Duchess* exploits too the familiarity of "romance reading on the bok," and its potential as a literary topos.[4] Similarly, in *Troilus and Criseyde*, both Criseyde and Pandarus are depicted as reading romances. It is interesting that Criseyde makes clear the classical content of her reading matter, "This romaunce is of Thebes that we rede" (II, 100); Pandarus nicely demonstrates his familiarity with other such romances, saying dismissively, "herof ben her maked bookes twelve" (II, 108). Barry Windeatt notes too Pandarus' ironic references to typical romance motifs (III, 891–3; 1992: 149). Perhaps Chaucer's most celebrated use of the term "romaunce" occurs in this work, when Pandarus has placed the lovers together: "And with that word he drow hym to the feere, / And took a light, and fond his countenaunce, / As for to looke upon an old romaunce" (III, 978–80). What better proof of Pandarus' internalization of romance conventions and expectations? The love affair is a romance both written and read by Pandarus as he manipulates Troilus and Criseyde into the conventions and intrigue of *fin'amors*. He is so knowing and confident a reader that, ultimately, he too will put too much trust in the workings of romance – assuming that reality may be shaped to follow romance's familiar, optimistic patterns.

Chaucer's potentially mocking stance on romance is elaborated most obviously in his parodic tale of *Sir Thopas*. When Harry Bailey asks Chaucer the pilgrim to tell a tale "of myrthe," he obliges with what he says is the only tale he knows, "a rym I lerned longe agoon" (706, 709) – a phrase that suggests immediately the mode of popular or metrical romance, with its traditional poetic formulae, and recalls that such works would have been Chaucer's own youthful reading (Brewer 1978: 32–3). It is tempting, as Derek Brewer has suggested in this volume, to imagine that Chaucer may have encountered the Auchinleck manuscript, which includes several of the romances named in *Sir Thopas*, and others containing analogous episodes (see Cooper 1991: 301). In his tale of just over 200 lines, Chaucer offers a superb pastiche of the form, using its conventions in the most clichéd manner possible. The tale begins in the manner of a minstrel addressing an audience, "Listeth, lordes, in good entent, / And I wol telle verrayment / Of mirthe and solas," its hero is a courtly knight, "fair and gent" (712–15), who follows a predictable course of action – riding out hunting, questing through a fair forest, falling in love with an elf-queen in a dream-vision, meeting a giant – all events likely enough to be found in a romance, but compressed to a space of only 200 lines and described in terms that employ one romance formula after another. The doggerel nature of the verse and the redundant language are immediately evident in the repeated interjections of the narrator, such as "I yow telle may," "al it was thurgh Goddes gras," "listeth, lordes, to my tale," "herkneth to my spelle" (749, 831, 833, 893), and the courtly images are often debased, as in the memorable description of Thopas:

> Sir Thopas wax a doghty swayn;
> Whit was his face as payndemayn,
> His lippes rede as rose;
> His rode is lyk scarlet in grayn,
> And I yow telle in good certayn
> He hadde a semely nose.
>
> (724–9)

Chaucer pokes fun at the conventional, sometimes unimaginative, language of popular romance in the empty clichés of Thopas' "semely nose" and "lippes rede as rose," and the foolishly uncourtly comparisons to saffron and bread. The story is set in Flanders rather than Logres, and its hero seems more bourgeois than courtly, his skills those of wrestling at a country fair, dressing in costly clothes, and leaving "many a mayde" mourning – though we are assured that he is "no lechour" (743, 745). The action too is deflated: Thopas only dreams of an elf-queen, and his battle with the three-headed giant never occurs, for he has no armor with him. Harry Bailey sums up the effect as he brings the narrative to an abrupt end, "Thy drasty rymyng is nat worth a toord" (930): the abortive tale is a brilliant joke at Chaucer's expense, but it also suggests Chaucer's negative view of popular vernacular romances – their repetition, their conventionality, their use of formulae and stock motifs, and most of all their bad verse.

Yet while Chaucer may not have approved of metrical romances, the larger notion of romance is crucial across his writing. In the *Canterbury Tales* he offers a series of generic variations. According to a broad definition of romance as secular, courtly narrative, of the *Canterbury Tales* not only *Sir Thopas*, but also the *Knight's Tale*, the *Squire's Tale*, the *Franklin's Tale*, and the *Wife of Bath's Tale* can be classified as romance, while the *Man of Law's Tale* might be termed a hagiographic romance and the *Merchant's Tale* merges romance and *fabliau*. The mode of these works is elevated and sophisticated in the use of convention by contrast to that of *Sir Thopas*, but at the same time Chaucer continues, though in a much more veiled and subtle form, to interrogate the straightforward, often transparent romance treatment of chivalric ideals. Within the fiction of the pilgrimage the romances work as more and less successful stories of love and adventure, offering insights into their tellers, but they also contribute to a meta-narrative that calls into question the foundations of the romance genre. In *Troilus and Criseyde*, Chaucer's most ambitious romance, the genre reaches an extraordinary poetic height which looks forward to Spenser and Shakespeare, yet its dramatic tension again lies in its unanswered questions, its troubled nuances, and its undercutting of the ideal.

The duality of romance in the *Canterbury Tales* is nowhere more evident than in the *Knight's Tale*. On the one hand, this could not treat a more appropriate story matter for the first teller, the "verray, parfit gentil knight," and the judgment of the pilgrims seems a fitting definition of the ideal romance, "a noble storie, / And worthy for to drawen to memorie"; it is especially admired by the "gentils everichon" (*General Prologue*, 72; *Miller's Prologue*, 3111–13). Its subject matter is elevated, situated in the classical world, and the epigraph affirms this in quoting Statius, not Boccaccio, who provides the story's real source; it also employs all the central *topoi* of medieval chivalric literature: fortune and *fin' amors*, knighthood and chivalry, kingship and justice, battle and tournament. Yet the tale raises disturbing questions regarding love, chivalry, and free will – questions that we cannot imagine the Knight asking. The narrative structures of *fin' amors* unfold in the context of a larger pattern of enforced marriage: the "fair, hardy queene," Hippolyta (882), has been defeated and captured by Theseus in his war against the Amazons (see Crane 1994: 80).[5] Emilye, her sister, appears in the Maytime garden as the archetypal romance heroine, but is also a trophy of war, who begins and ends the tale as an object to be fought over and won by men. The pattern is typical of chivalric romance, in which ladies are repeatedly won in battle by knights unknown to them, but in general these actions are validated by the ensuing experience of mutual "love," even if this is not always distinguishable from male wish fulfillment. In the *Knight's Tale*, by contrast, Emilye knows nothing of the knights' love for her, and when it is discovered, she has no preference for either suitor. She is a spectator in the enactment of mortal combat for her hand, her fate decided by Theseus.

Unknown and unknowing, Emilye is the "swete foo" for Palamon and Arcite (2780), eminently desirable, but also causing unhappiness, unease, illness, and strife. As in the *Parliament of Fowls*, in the *Knight's Tale* Chaucer places peculiar emphasis on the pains and tragic outcomes of love, pictured in both narratives on the walls of Venus' temple. The tale functions as a critique of the dynamic of romance, as the chivalric love ethic is taken to such an extreme that its destructiveness is revealed. Love, taken for granted as one of the highest, ennobling ideals, has changed sworn brotherhood into mortal enmity. This is particularly conspicuous in that the cousins Palamon and Arcite begin as blood brothers and friends but are reduced to the status of wild animals in their battle in the forest, as they abandon themselves to their passions:

> Thou myghtest wene that this Palamon
> In his fightyng were a wood leon,
> And as a crueel tigre was Arcite;
> As wilde bores gonne they to smyte,

That frothen whit as foom for ire wood.
Up to the ancle foghte they in hir blood.

(1655–60)

The tale hints more overtly at the silencing effect of the chivalric ethic on women through Emilye's prayer in the temple of Diana, "Chaste goddesse, wel wostow that I / Desire to ben a mayden al my lyf, / Ne nevere wol I be no love ne wyf" (2304–6); she asks that Palamon and Arcite should be turned away from "al hire hoote love and hir desir" (2319).[6] The stylized prayer places Emilye as a virtuous and chaste virgin, but also seems to provide a tiny window on the predicament of the woman objectified within the male romance structures of battle and love. Among the foreboding images painted on the temple walls is that of "wofull Calistopee" (2056), the nymph Callisto, metamorphosed into a bear as she flees the rape of Jupiter; for Emilye, however, there will be no metamorphosis. Death and force are interwoven in the image of Diana looking down to Pluto's "derke regioun," recalling both the story of the abduction of Proserpina and the very real possibility of death in childbirth for women – and we see too "a woman travaillynge" (2082–3), her cries an ominous sign of the future.

The darkness of the *Knight's Tale* is perhaps most apparent in the way that the authority and order of Theseus lead only to death. His interruption of the battle in the forest seems to replace chaos with civilization, battle with tournament, violence with pageantry: along with the construction of the great amphitheater in the forest, Theseus decrees that only blunted weapons shall be used (as royal decrees dictated for English tournaments from the thirteenth century). Yet in fact all remain subject to the arbitrary whims of the gods: Arcite wins the battle but is struck down by Saturn's decree as he rides triumphantly through the amphitheater, and the forest glade now becomes the setting for the funeral pyre. Arcite's death is a poignant reminder of the human suffering present beneath the strictures of order: the apparently harmonious concord of marriage at the end of the tale is founded on tragedy, grief and loss. Theseus' final speech describing the divine chain of love, which Chaucer draws from Boethius' *Consolation of Philosophy*, scarcely seems to fit the cruel and violent order of the tale in which only death can decide the chivalric question of who deserves the lady's hand. Most appropriate seem the words of Theseus' father Egeus, "This world nys but a thurghfare ful of wo / And we been pilgrims, passynge to and fro" (2847–8). The story draws attention to the difficulty of faith and the need "To maken vertu of necessitee" (3042), causing us to ask how we may believe in beneficent providence in a world of cruelly arbitrary destiny. Romance thus becomes a vehicle through which Chaucer can raise, if not answer, existential questions relating to free will, faith, and transience.

In different ways, and sometimes much more light-heartedly, this troubling quality recurs across the whole range of Chaucer's romance narratives. The *Knight's Tale* will in due course be followed by the peculiarly curtailed narrative told by his son, the Squire. The two stories form a definitive contrast: the Knight tells an elevated neoclassical romance whereas the Squire, fittingly for "a lovyere and a lusty bacheler" (*General Prologue*, 80), narrates a tale essentially of the marvelous, of magical gifts and talking birds, which relies on the physicality of adventure. The setting of the court of "Cambyuskan," Ghengis Khan, in "Tartarye," the Mongol empire (12, 9), immediately places this as a romance of the East, in which we can expect to hear of exotic marvels and strange adventures, and appropriately, the first part of the story tells of a strange knight's arrival on a great brass horse to present Cambyuskan with three magical gifts at his birthday feast. The tale self-consciously weaves together traditional romance motifs: the great feast, complete with "strange" foods – "swans and heronsewes" (67–8); the sudden appearance of the knight who rides into the hall, silencing the court in a manner reminiscent of "Gawayn, with his olde curteisye, / Though he were comen ayeyn out of Fairye" (95–6); the magical gifts themselves. The Squire's excessively self-conscious rhetoric and repeated use of incongruous or uncourtly asides, however, undercut the ethos of "merveille" (87): the court is full of "jangling" of "lewed peple" (257, 221); only Launcelot would be able to describe the festive dances "and he is deed" (287); these are "unkouthe" dances marked by jealousy and deception (284); the revellers have "Ful ... heddes of fuminositee" (358), rising late the next day; and the Squire suddenly announces that the horse, the subject of so much discussion, has vanished, "I noot in what manere / Out of hir sighte: ye gete namoore of me" (342–3). Much attention too is devoted to the possibility that this is not magic but science: the brass horse might be a "fayerye" but might also conceal Greeks, or be "an apparence ymaad by som magyk, / As jogelours pleyen at thise feestes grete" (201, 218–19); the Squire refers to writers such as Aristotle and Vitello on mirrors and perspective, and to the craft of Moses and Solomon. Chaucer complicates the unquestioning acceptance of marvel so typical of romance through an emphasis on astrology, natural science, and human debate and inquiry. In style and subject matter, the tale seems to offer an ironic comment on romance in something of the manner of the *Tale of Sir Thopas*.

Yet, startlingly, the second part of the *Squire's Tale* moves away from the grand world of the court to a narrative space much closer to that of Chaucer's *Parliament of Fowls*, when Canacee puts on the magical ring, which enables her to hear the speech of the birds. The unexpected pathos of the female falcon's lament is dramatically rendered: "Ybeten hadde she hirself so pitously / With bothe hir wynges til the rede blood / Ran endelong the tree ther-as she stod. / And evere in oon she cryde alwey and shrighte / And with hir beek hirselven so she prighte" (414–18). Again there are troubling narrative moments that stray into the burlesque – the voice is that of a bird not a human; Canacee holds out her skirts to catch the falcon but does not succeed, so that the bird falls swooning to the ground; the male tercelet finally chooses a "kyte" (624), a scavenger bird. Yet the overwhelming emphasis of the section is on lament, the pure expression of emotion and suffering. The motifs of Chaucer's *Legend of Good Women* recur – praise of female compassion; the idea that "pity renneth soone in gentil herte" (479); male dissembling and changeability ("Men loven of propre kynde newefangelnesse" 610); female steadfastness, *gentillesse*, and innocence (summed up in the falcon's simple promise "Lo, I am youres alle," 597); and the inexplicable male betrayal of *trouthe*. The falcon's speech is a beautifully rendered example of the genre of female complaint, set within the larger romance narrative – yet the very fact that this is a bird speaking reminds us of the distance between fantasy and reality. The salves and plasters applied by Canacee to heal the falcon are not available to the human victims of male betrayal, for whom the *remedye* tends to be death itself. As well, the lament functions as a critique of the customary subject matter of romance, reminding the audience that love and idealism may in reality be countered by betrayal, instability, change, deceit, and failure of *trouthe*.

It is not surprising that the *Squire's Tale* is unfinished: the final lines hint at an interlaced romance narrative so enormous that it would occupy the rest of the journey to Canterbury. Helen Cooper suggests that, had Chaucer completed it, he might have produced an epic romance with something of the "high chivalry, high sophistication and artistic mockery" of Ariosto (1991: 219). The tale suggests the difficulty of closure inherent in such a complex romance structure:

> The opening out of one tale into another in an accumulating series of narratives itself has the potential of infiniteness – which may be another reason for the unfinished state of the Squire's Tale. (Cooper 1991: 223)

Spenser too will adopt this interlaced mode – with the same difficulty of closure. The *Squire's Tale* raises as well the question of the forbidden, for the name Canacee evokes the classical incest story of Canacee and Machaire, and the conclusion of the narrative refers to Cambalo, the king's son, "That faught in lystes with the bretheren two / For Canacee er that he myghte hire wynne" (668–9). Thus the tale engages with unwritten romance, with its endless possibilities, with the stories that cannot be told, and with the voices that, as the falcon's would be without Canacee's magical ring, are silenced, oppressed, or repressed.

Whether or not he meant to finish the *Squire's Tale*, "the wordes of the Frankeleyn to the Squier," comparing the Franklin's son disparagingly to the Squire, suggest Chaucer's intention to follow it with the *Franklin's Tale*. The tales offer complementary perspectives on romance, treating a number of common themes: marvel and magic, betrayal and deception, pity and *gentillesse*, and the question of romance idealism (see Cooper 1991: 241). Unlike the Squire's sprawling, episodic narrative, however, the Franklin's story is as neatly contained as the garden in which Aurelius sees Dorigen, its subject matter the events that occur "at home" while Arveragus performs the kind of chivalric deeds relished by the Squire. The magic of the *Franklin's Tale* is humanly contrived and deceptive, and its emphasis is not action and adventure but high-flown philosophy and idealism. The tale is also generically contained, specifically identified in the Prologue as a Breton lay. Two romances in the Auchinleck manuscript, *Sir Orfeo* and *Lai le Freine*, begin with a celebrated definition of this genre:

> We redeth oft and findeth y-write –
> And this clerkes wele it wite –
> Layes that ben in harping
> Ben y-founde of ferli* thing.   marvelous
> Sum bethe of wer and sum of wo,
> and sum of joie and mirthe also,
> And sum of trecherie and of gile,
> Of old aventours that fel while*   once
> And sum of bourdes* and ribaudy –   jests
> And mani ther beth of fairy.
> Of all thinges that men seth
> Mest of love, forsothe, thai beth.[7]

The *Franklin's Tale* sets up the expectation that it too will be an ancient story of adventure and the marvelous, originating in Brittany or at least claiming to do so. Yet while its basic premise, a knight's attempt to win his beloved, is typical of the genre, its enactment is not: once again Chaucer is pushing the romance form to its limits. Dorigen is not the object of military combat, but rather the victim of deceit and illusion; the battle is one of words rather than swords, its enabling force *trouthe* not prowess. The Franklin offers at the start a description of the ideal marital relationship, based on *trouthe* in all its senses – faithfulness, loyalty, trust, truth, and, most important, mutuality – an ideal that explicitly opposes the romance model of love found in the *Knight's Tale*, where desire is focused in the male participants, and battle is the accepted mode of winning the lady's hand. The evocative, even radical lines, "Love wol nat been constreyned by maistrye. / Whan maistrie comth, the God of Love anon / Beteth his wynges, and farewel, he is gon!" (764–6), are crucial to the tale, for it is precisely constraint that the love-sick Aurelius attempts in his pursuit of another man's wife. His love, like that of Palamon and Arcite, is described in the traditional romance vocabulary of *fin' amors*, yet although this vocabulary fits the *locus amoenus*, the spring-time garden where Dorigen's companions dance, it clashes with the terms of faithful marriage: for Dorigen to consent to Aurelius' love would cause her to be an "untrewe wyf" (984) rather than a gracious lover. The sense of misdirected vocabulary is sustained as Dorigen is betrayed by the words she uses "in pley" to affirm her refusal of Aurelius' love. Ironically, she swears that she will not love Aurelius until the "grisly rokkes blake" disappear (859) – the very objects she would most like to see vanish, in that they seem to represent Arveragus' danger, yet also the objects she perceives as least mutable. The story centers on the possibility of false perception, a theme also evoked by the magical mirror in the *Squire's Tale*, as what has seemed eternal, a symbol of the possibility of death and destruction in the temporal world, becomes transient when the rocks disappear through the clerk of Orléans' magic. Whereas in the *Squire's Tale* the possibility that the magical gifts have some scientific explanation is raised but never verified, here we are aware from the start that what appears to be a marvel is actually an "illusioun," a piece of "magyk naturel" performed by a clerk who had studied magic arts (1264, 1155). Illusion and deception, false perspectives, call into question the solid foundation of the *trouthe* Dorigen has sworn, as suddenly she appears to belong to another man. The disappearance of the rocks authorizes what will effectively be her rape. As the falcon in the *Squire's Tale* discovers, to ignore the flux of the temporal world and to trust in appearances is dangerous. The rocks, which seem to represent the power and destructive potential of the natural world, in fact prove to be no more than a shadow in contrast to the god or gods by which perhaps Dorigen should have sworn.

Although Dorigen is shown to be imperfect, she is also the victim of illusion, and the tale derives its pathos from the predicament in which she is placed for no more fault than human uncertainty in divine governance. The usurpation of power by one individual over another, condemned at the start, is now demonstrated in all its cruelty; we are shown, indeed, that love cannot be constrained. The tale works within a world of absolutes, where words are fixed as true simply by being spoken: there is no question of Dorigen breaking her promise to Aurelius; there is not even a question of verifying the disappearance of the rocks. *Trouthe* is an absolute value, to be upheld at all costs, and the folly of foolish words must be paid for, even while the shame of submitting to Aurelius is portrayed as worse than death. Arveragus resolves this tension between death and dishonor through his assertion that *"trouthe* is the hyeste thyng that man may kepe"* (1479). The suicide contemplated by Dorigen is shown not to be the answer, as trust in absolute moral virtue brings its own solution: Arveragus' free action inspires first Aurelius' and then the magician's act of forgiveness; coercion is replaced with generosity. The tale sets up notions of mutual freedom and *trouthe* against the more traditional romance ideal in which the woman stands as an object to be fought over and won, and its focus is the action and reward of generous virtue.

The moral framework of the fiction is optimistic, and the story follows "the mythic cycle of romance" described by Northrop Frye (Cooper 1991: 235). Yet this tale with winter placed at its heart is also profoundly uncomfortable. Action and prowess are not only displaced by moral questions, but also are shown to be deeply threatening – it is only while Arveragus is absent, enacting the demands of knighthood, that danger arises. We wonder too what kind of moral perspective values words twisted wholly out of context above the marriage vow, and identifies the "right" moral action as the gift of one's own wife to another. And in a tale purportedly about freedom, Dorigen's fate is decided for her by first Arveragus and then Aurelius: her name certainly is not a possible answer to the Franklin's question, "Which was the moste fre, as thynketh yow?" (1622). The overt idealism of the story, as in the *Knight's Tale*, causes us to engage with the unreality of ideals, their untenability when taken to an extreme, and finally with the imprisoning nature of absolute morality. The structures and strictures of the moral code of the tale are presented as freeing the individual from the flux of the world – and yet we wonder precisely what kind of self emerges, and whether, within the real world, absolute morality would be so liberating. Chaucer instills in his audience a kind of double vision – the ending is so neat, so apparently positive in its upholding of *trouthe*, but also so disturbing in its unnaturalness – Arveragus' renunciation of his wife, Aurelius' denial of the fulfillment of his desire, Dorigen's obedience to a male chivalric ethic despite the Franklin's positive statement at the start, "Wommen, of kynde, desiren libertee, / And nat to been constreyned as a thrall" (768–9). We cannot but ask whether the extreme unquestioning idealism of romance may not form a cage every bit as constrictive as that imagined by the falcon in the *Squire's Tale* with its deceptive straw "faire and softe as silk," its "sugre, hony, breed and milk" (613–14).

Chaucer's *Wife of Bath's Tale* employs the romance genre to offer a still more provocative comment on the themes of desire, freedom, and *maistrye*. It seems at first surprising that the Wife of Bath, one of the strongest narrative voices and perhaps the most three-dimensional character in the *Canterbury Tales*, chooses to tell a romance, a tale of high ideals set in the distant Arthurian world. Yet this is also a romance with a difference, perhaps even a proto-feminist romance. The Wife's Arthurian knight is scarcely heroic, distinguished as he is by raping a maiden:

> And so bifel that this kyng Arthour
> Hadde in his hous a lusty bacheler,
> That on a day cam ridynge fro ryver,
> And happed that, allone as he was born,
> He saugh a mayde walkynge hym biforn,
> Of which mayde anon, maugree hir heed,
> By verray force, he rafte hire maydenhed.
>
> (882–8)

While the story has several analogues (including Gower's Tale of Florent in the *Confessio Amantis*), only Chaucer's version includes a rape, and his narrative is overtly constructed around the idea of rape as the most extreme form of male *maistrye*. Despite its Arthurian context, in actuality the tale explores not chivalric adventure but the virtue of *gentillesse* and the issue of what women truly desire, *sovereignté* – a theme that recurs in various guises across the *Canterbury Tales*.

The tale depicts rape as severely treated by the Arthurian court, in a realistic trial scene where the fitting punishment is stated to be death – but eventually the women are given the decisive choice of punishment. The closure of death is replaced by the action of quest as the knight is sent out to find the answer to the riddle, "What thyng is it that wommen moost desiren?" (905). The familiar pattern of the romance quest in which the knight meets with *aventure* as he rides, apparently aimlessly but guided by destiny, is subtly altered: this knight is no hero; his search takes him to towns and houses rather than wild forests; his encounters are with women; and the journey is a penitential and desperate one, a search for the right to live.

Yet we return to a sense of *aventure* with the knight's sight of the dance "under a forest side" of "ladyes foure and twenty, and yet mo" (990, 992). Their sudden disappearance and the traditional romance setting of the forest confirm the sense that this was indeed a faery vision, but the marvelous is undercut when their place is taken by an old hag, "a fouler wight ther may no man devyse" (999). The encounter, whether chance or destiny, provides the solution to the riddle, refuting the list of stereotypical female desires offered earlier as possible solutions – nobility, wealth, beauty, and also "lust abedde" (927). In the response that women desire "sovereynetee" or "maistrie" (1038, 1040), the old hag counters misogynistic notions of the female nature as sensual and material, provoking rape. Her answer refutes a "romance" code of love that ignores the female will.

The demand of the old hag that the knight marry her in return for saving his life wonderfully enacts the notion of the woman's *maistrye*, rectifying the rape through a novel kind of punishment. The rapist becomes the victim, the loathly old hag the aggressor:

> Greet was the wo the knyght hadde in his thoght,
> Whan he was with his wyf abedde ybroght;
> He walweth and he turneth to and fro.
> His olde wyf lay smylynge everemo.
>
> (1083–6)

The old wife becomes as well a voice of moral authority in her lengthy disquisition on *gentillesse*, her complex rhetoric demonstrating her reason, and thus refuting the clerical texts instanced by the Wife in her prologue, with their emphasis on female irrationality. Her rhetoric is successful: when offered the choice between a young faithless wife and an old true one, the knight resigns "maistrie" (1236) to his wife. The tale thus rewrites the act of rape and allows for the moral redemption of the knight. We accept the final transformation of the old and loathsome hag into a beautiful young woman as part of the marvelous potential of romance.[8] The tale returns, as it were, to the faery vision by the forest side.

Chaucer leaves us with troubling questions too – questions that emerge because of the intersection of romance and realism in the tale. Thus, as in the *Franklin's Tale*, it is difficult not to maintain a double perspective, whereby the conclusion, with the rapist's marriage to a young, beautiful lady and the complete silence of the victim, seem profoundly unfair. This is not, after all, a penitential romance: the knight's crime is not mentioned again. And in fact the tale ends with an assurance not of female sovereignty but of the wife's obedience to her husband: "And she obeyed hym in every thyng / That myghte doon hym plesance or liking" (1255–6). The tale is as ambiguous as its teller, the Wife of Bath, whose proto-feminism is founded in a collection of attributes drawn straight from anticlerical stereotypes of women – excessive sexuality, unfaithfulness, shrewishness to husbands. The tale seems as much about the Wife's hope for a new marriage, perhaps to a man as forceful as Jankyn, as about mutuality and *gentillesse*. She chooses *for* romance, for the happy ending with its traditional ideal of the marriage of the strong man and the beautiful lady. Youth triumphs over age as the old hag, with her rational dominance, is replaced by the obedient young lady – suggesting the Wife's own nostalgia for youth and romantic love.

Despite its problematic ending, the *Wife of Bath's Tale*, perhaps more than any other of Chaucer's writings, exposes the cracks in the romance ideal, establishing a counterpoint to the typical narrative mode as the chivalric knight is replaced with the rapist, the quest with the attempt to preserve life, the beautiful woman with the hag, and male force with female *maistrye*. The tale offers a rare instance of romance told from the woman's point of view, recalling the question asked by the Wife in her prologue, "Who peyntede the leon, tel me who?" (692). Woman not man narrates this romance and it does indeed paint a very different picture, responding to some of the silences and gaps of, for instance, the Knight's and Franklin's tales. Chaucer employs romance structures to create a dualistic tale and teller – at once championing women and rooted in patriarchal structures – a radical romance, though one of more questions than answers. Questions regarding the nature of chivalric ideals, their constraints, their potential failure, and their possible transformations are especially resonant when presented from the female viewpoint. As Custance in the *Man of Law's Tale* suggests, women may be seen as the "least free" within the patriarchal scheme of things: "Wommen are born to thraldom and penance, / And to been under mannes governance" (286–7).

It is no coincidence that in his greatest single work, *Troilus and Criseyde*, Chaucer also turns to the romance genre – but again, romance with a difference. As an epic romance of Troy, the fictional world of *Troilus and Criseyde* is very like that of the *Knight's Tale*, and it sustains and develops similar themes – the nature of *fin'amors*, the predicament of women, and the meaning of existence itself. Chaucer weaves together strands of romance and realism to ask uneasy questions regarding the possibility of the ideal, of free will, and of "truth" itself. In creating this self-conscious and highly wrought poem Chaucer radically rewrites the romance genre.

Through its first subject, "the double sorwe of Troilus" (I, 1), the work explores one of the great topics of romance – the sublimity of love, its capacity to elevate the individual to new realms of being, to open onto the ineffable, and to inspire creativity. Troilus' response to love is to compose songs (including the first translation of a Petrarch sonnet into English). Windeatt has argued persuasively that in *Troilus and Criseyde* love functions as *aventure* might in chivalric romance:

> Dragons and enchantments are there none, yet the all-possessing nature of the experience in love of Troilus makes that experience for him a kind of inward equivalent of *aventure*, just as the new strangeness of love, and that force of idealization which he brings to his experience, give it the momentum of a quest and the quality of a marvel, the marvellous inward adventure of love. (1992: 145)

The narrative is a "romance" not in the modern sense of the word, though the falling-in-love aspect is central, but in that it follows the transformative inner quest of its eponymous hero. Chaucer realizes powerfully the defamiliarizing experience of love in

Plate 1. Troilus and Criseyde, from a French prose translation of Boccaccio's *Il Filostrato*, written and illuminated ca. 1480. (Bodleian Library, Oxford, MS Douce 331, folio 26 recto.)

showing Troilus, so high a prince, completely overthrown by love, "with a look his herte wex a-fere, / That he that now was moost in pride above, / Wax sodeynly moost subgit unto love" (I, 229–31). Such experience, as Windeatt notes, is akin to religious epiphany:

> Chaucer's emphasis on the hero's *in*experience in love makes experience itself an adventure into an unknown, something marvellously out of this world, which is reflected in that language of heaven's bliss, of love as a religion, as worship, in which Chaucer's Troilus thinks of his experience. (1992: 148)

Troilus embodies the experience of *fin'amors*: suddenly struck by the God of Love's arrow, he is wounded through the eyes that lead to the heart, to manifest all the physical symptoms of the malady of love. His journey toward winning Criseyde is marked by stages of challenge, testing, and adventure – of more and much less humorous kinds – and the experience of gaining her parallels the romance experience of the marvelous or otherworldly. It is crucial to Troilus' characterization that he is a knight-hero, not just the one prostrated by love. As with the great Arthurian knights Launcelot and Tristan, the combination of extraordinary prowess and the ability to experience the extremes of love to the point of madness and malady proves not weakness, as it often seems to modern readers, but chivalric excellence.

It is typical of Chaucer's ironic vision, however, that we also see the other side of Troilus' extreme passion, his sometimes absurd inability to act: the story gains much of its comic momentum through Pandarus' promotion of the love affair, to the extent of physically placing Troilus in bed with Criseyde. But this passivity is tragic too, for it underlies Troilus' acceptance of Criseyde's departure as predestined. As we see Troilus suffering first the anguish of separation, then of betrayal, we cannot but question the good of this transformative experience of love. In the latter books, Troilus is literally unmade by love:

> He ne et ne drank, for his malencolye,
> And ek from every compaignye he fledde:
> This was the life that al the tyme he ledde.
> He so defet was, that no manere man
> Unneth hym myghte knowen ther he wente;
> So was he lene, and therto pale and wan,
> And feble, that he walketh by potente.
>
> (V, 1216–22)

Troilus' death partly comes about through his rash action in a battle in which he no longer cares for his life. His experience reflects that suggested in the inscription on the gates in Chaucer's *Parliament of Fowls*, that love may be both infernal and paradisal. We are left, as in the *Knight's Tale*, to ask whether great love must necessarily bring anguish with it.

The story is one of betrayal, and in many ways the enigma of Troilus' betrayer, Criseyde, lies at the heart of the work. In the twelfth century Benoît de Sainte-Maure had employed the episodes of the separation of the lovers and Criseyde's betrayal of Troilus to parallel the disastrous loves of Helen and Paris and of Achilles and Iphigenia; in Guido de Colonne's retelling, the story became an exemplar of feminine duplicity and weakness; and in Boccaccio's poem, a means of both celebrating sensual love and warning his lady of the consequences of infidelity. The place of Chaucer's poem as part of a long-standing literary tradition is made explicit when Criseyde laments: "Allas, for now is clene ago / My name of trouthe in love, for everemo . . . / Allas of me unto the worldes ende / Shall neyther ben ywriten nor ysonge / No good word, for thise bokes wol me shende. / O rolled shall I ben on many a tonge!" (V, 1054–64). The words suggest poignantly her regret but also draw attention to the self-consciously literary status of the text. Criseyde states that women will most abhor her name, but we are made conscious of the shaping and reshaping of that name by a whole series of male writers, reflecting the way that within the text she is passed from one man to another – from father, to uncle, to lover, to father; from Trojan to Greek. Chaucer's telling is remarkable for its extraordinary treatment of Criseyde: alone within this line of anti-feminist writers, including Henryson and Shakespeare after him, he constructs a narrative perspective that, if it does not wholly redeem Criseyde, does allow space for ambiguity, and for the possibility of pity and forgiveness, "she so sory was for hire untrouthe, / Iwis, I wolde excuse hire yet for routhe" (V, 1098–9). While Boccaccio's telling all too evidently leads toward Criseyde's betrayal of Troilus, Chaucer leaves her motivation uncertain, at once offering insight into her psyche and yet withholding details to ensure that compelling enigmatic quality.

Just as we are made aware of the predicaments of Emilye and Dorigen, so we see Criseyde as trapped within her own social situation as the daughter of Calchas, arch-traitor to Troy. Her widowhood becomes emblematic, for whereas in *Il Filostrato* this is an indication of sexual experience, in Chaucer's telling it suggests both independence and vulnerability – the lack of husband and protector in a chivalric world. It is this that allows Pandarus to manipulate her, and it is this that justifies the celebrated description of Criseyde as "slydynge of corage" (V, 825). Yet, as is apparent when we first see Criseyde in the temple, she is also assured, seeming to ask "What, may I nat stonden here?" (I, 292), and later, stating her value of her own independence, "I am myn owene woman" (II, 750). In her relation to Pandarus we also see her love of game-playing. This combination of assurance and hesitation does not allow us to construct Criseyde as a straightforward innocent victim of circumstance: rather, she appears as the victim of conflicting emotions, attracted to and yet afraid of the game that she is half-coerced into playing. She is, however, many steps closer to the damsel in distress than Boccaccio's bold, sensual figure.

Perhaps most striking in Chaucer's characterization of Criseyde is his use of images of force: in the consummation scene, Criseida's eagerness is replaced with a startlingly predatory image of the lark captured by the sparrowhawk (III, 1191–2). The violence of the image echoes that of Criseyde's dream of the eagle, which tears out her heart, and a similar subtext of force is suggested by the references to the Philomela story.[9] When Troilus first embraces Criseyde, Chaucer places most emphasis on her fear, "Criseyde, which that felte hire thus itake . . . / Right as an aspes leef she gan to quake" (III, 1198–1200). Even when this fear is replaced by joy, she is compared to the "newe abaysed nyghtyngale" (1233), again suggesting the story of Philomela. Like the *Wife of Bath's Tale*, *Troilus and Criseyde* raises questions about the relation of desire and force, and the nature of gender relations – not because Troilus is forceful, but because patriarchal society, and most of all Pandarus, are. Questions are raised too about the issue of secrecy, so often an aspect of *fin'amors*: are passionate love affairs fueled by their hidden intimacy, their games of concealment, as Pandarus seems to suppose, or do the differing social situations of Troilus and Criseyde simply preclude marriage? The poem certainly engages with the notions of honor and reputation, and of the potential shame of elopement. Despite the classical setting, Chaucer in part addresses the problem of how the fundamental romance conventions of *fin'amors* coexist with the mores of fourteenth-century England.[10]

The work not only interweaves realism and romance in its treatment of the lovers and their go-between, Pandarus, but also, like the *Knight's Tale*, goes beyond romance idealism to raise complicated philosophical questions regarding destiny and free will. Chaucer draws on Boethius' *Consolation of Philosophy*, which he was translating at about the same time, to align his three main characters with philosophical stances: Pandarus with opportunism, Troilus with fatalism, Criseyde with rationalism. All engage in different ways with the opposition between ideas of free will and predestination, and with the notion of fortune. That the plot unfolds within a pagan universe allows Chaucer to weave together a fabric of references to astrological influences, Fortune, Fate, and the classical gods, and thus to create a sinister aura of predestination, which is especially marked in the proems to each book. Thus, while the main actors within the game of love appear to make their own free choices, their free will is frequently called into question. On the one hand, the questions are those of Christian theology – Troilus in particular refers frequently to one all-powerful God and to the chain of love that binds the universe. Yet as in the *Knight's Tale*, the pagan world of *Troilus* lends great force to the impressions of looming tragedy and fall, of Fortune's turning wheel, and of the cruel nature of the gods. Especially disturbing is the conclusion of the poem, in which Troilus looks down from the eighth sphere of the heavens and laughs. The story's power comes precisely from its evocation of the passion and tragedy of the temporal world, and yet we are left with an assertion of "false worldes brotelnesse" (V, 1832). *Troilus and Criseyde* could not raise more profound existential questions regarding the nature and purpose of romantic love, and the human situation within a callous world, the untrustworthiness of which is finally symbolized by Criseyde's betrayal of Troilus.

Like the central characters, caught between their own free wills and the events predestined by the fates, the narrator is caught between his own affection for Criseyde and desire to portray her favorably, and his knowledge of the fixed end of the story, the "double sorwe of Troilus." Behind the narrator, with his fictional source of Lollius, stands the shadowy figure of Chaucer, who plays the complex literary game of presenting a fictional version of the author who translates and selects from his sources, even while he does this himself. We are made acutely aware of the difficulty of interpretation, of the subjective quality of the literary text, filtered as it is through the biases of the writer – and the narrator's bias for Criseyde is shown to be a powerful one. The poem presents layer upon layer of manipulation: by Pandarus, by Criseyde, by the gods, by the narrator, and by Chaucer himself. Yet Chaucer's free will is no more absolute than that of Pandarus; he is caught by the fixed points of the tragedy he tells, so that he too is subject to a kind of predestination. On all levels, then, the work engages with the opposition between free will and predestination – both within the human sphere of action, and symbolically, for the writer who undertakes to tell the stories already written in "olde bokes" (V, 1753), and must ask how far subjective interpretation can go. This romance, also a tragedy and an epic, tells of the difficulties of writing romance as well as "the double sorwe of Troilus": it is a romance about "the disenchantment of romance" (Windeatt 1992: 145).

Chaucer, as in all genres to which he turns his hand, shows himself to be a master of romance, and that mastery is demonstrated as much in his ability to transgress or trouble the conventions of romance as in his skill in their use. *Sir Thopas* may show his mocking view of romance at its least sophisticated, yet at the same time the romance genre allows for some of Chaucer's very greatest writing, and facilitates a kind of imaginative play that other genres do not. Chaucer's romances partly find their power in the tension between their mimetic and non-mimetic elements. Easy romance ideals are called into question, subverted, shown to be impossible, fractured, or failed – or simply set against the realities of the medieval world. Yet the ideals always remain, their potential glimmering – present in moments of transcendence, in recollections of delight, and in hope for those as yet unwritten possibilities. For in writing romance, Chaucer writes the story of the self – himself, ourselves – the journey of the individual not necessarily to encounter elf-queens, dragons, or giants, but to experience the heights of human passion, both love and despair, to plumb the depths of human nature, to discover both its best and worst, and to see into other, sublime, and transcendent worlds. The promise of the marvelous for Chaucer is perhaps most of all within – the *faery* company disappears, the consequences of history part the lovers, the cruel blow of fortune or destiny or the gods brings death – yet there remains always the possibility of transformation, of "something rich and strange" to be read of within books, to be recollected in the heart, and to be discovered within the self.

See also: chapter 1, Ancient Romance; chapter 2, Insular Beginnings; chapter 3, The Popular English Metrical Romances; chapter 4, Arthurian Romance; chapter 6, Malory and the Early Prose Romances; chapter 8, Sidney and Spenser; chapter 9, Shakespeare's Romances.

Notes

1. I should like to acknowledge at the start of this essay its debt to and dialogue throughout with the lucid and elegant discussions of Helen Cooper and Barry Windeatt, in their respective volumes of the Oxford Guides to Chaucer, *The Canterbury Tales* (1991) and *Troilus and Criseyde* (1992). Other particularly influential discussions of the texts under consideration may be found in Susan Crane 1994; Carolyn Dinshaw 1989; Elaine Tuttle Hansen 1992; Jill Mann 1991; Priscilla Martin 1990; and Angela Jane Weisl 1995.

2. On the fluidity of genre terms, see in particular Paul Strohm, "The Origin of Middle English 'Romaunce,'" *Genre* 10 (1977), 379–88, and "*Storie, Spelle, Geste, Romaunce, Tragedie*: Generic Distinctions in the Middle English Troy Narratives," *Speculum* 46 (1971), 348–59. Other useful discussions of the medieval romance genre include Erich Auerbach, "The Knight Sets Forth," in *Mimesis: The Representation of Reality in Western Literature*, trans. W. R. Trask (Princeton, NJ: Princeton University Press, 1953), pp. 123–42 (first published in

German in 1946); W. R. J. Barron, *English Medieval Romance*, Longman Literature in English Series (London: Longman, 1987); Derek Brewer, *Symbolic Stories: Traditional Narratives of the Family Drama in English Literature* (Cambridge: D. S. Brewer; Totowa, NJ: Rowman and Littlefield, 1980); Susan Crane, *Insular Romance: Politics, Faith and Culture in Anglo-Norman and Middle English Literature* (Berkeley: University of California Press, 1986); Carol Fewster, *Traditionality and Genre in Middle English Romance* (Cambridge: D. S. Brewer, 1987); John Finlayson, "Definitions of Middle English Romance," *Chaucer Review* 15 (1980–1), 44–62, 168–81; Roberta L. Krueger, ed. *The Cambridge Companion to Medieval Romance* (2000); Dieter Mehl, *The Middle English Romances of the Thirteenth and Fourteenth Century* (London: Routledge, 1968); Derek Pearsall, "The Development of Middle English Romance," *Mediaeval Studies* 27 (1965), 91–116; John Stevens, *Medieval Romance: Themes and Approaches* (London: Hutchinson University Library, 1973); Eugène Vinaver, *The Rise of Romance* (Oxford: Clarendon Press, 1971); Susan Wittig, *Stylistic and Narrative Structures in the Middle English Romance* (Austin: University of Texas Press, 1978).

3. All quotations from Chaucer's works are taken from *The Riverside Chaucer*, ed. Larry D. Benson, 3rd edn. (1987), and cited by line number.

4. In this volume, Derek Brewer discusses at greater length the question of reading romance, and adduces this phrase from *Havelok the Dane* (l. 2326) as one of the various references to reading found in the Middle English romances; see pp. 48–50.

5. For further discussion of the intersection of love and war, see in particular William F.

Woods '"My Sweete Foo": Emelye's Role in *The Knight's Tale*,' *Studies in Philology* 88 (1991), 276–306, John M. Ganim, "Chaucerian Ritual and Patriarchal Romance," *Chaucer Yearbook* 1 (1992), 65–86, and Susan Crane 1994: 76–84.

6. My discussion of the *Knight's Tale*, the *Franklin's Tale*, and the *Wife of Bath's Tale* in this essay draws on my earlier study, *Rape and Ravishment in the Literature of Medieval England* (2001): see especially pp. 286–310. My discussion of *Troilus and Criseyde* draws on that found in my critical guide, *Chaucer* (2001), pp. 129–36.

7. See Donald B. Sands, ed., *Middle English Verse Romances* (1966; 1986), *Lai le Freine*, ll. 1–12 (pp. 234–5).

8. For two positive readings of the learning process of the tale, emphasizing the concept of mutuality and the inclusion of feminine desire, see Carolyn Dinshaw 1989: 126–31, and Jill Mann 1991: 87–93; for a negative interpretation, see Elaine Tuttle Hansen 1992: 32–3.

9. See further Angela Jane Weisl's (1995) discussion of violent imagery in *Troilus and Criseyde*, and Jane Chance's more extreme interpretation in *The Mythographic Chaucer: The Fabulation of Sexual Politics* (Minneapolis and London: University of Minnesota Press, 1995), pp. 107–67.

10. See C. S. Lewis' famous discussion of the medievalization of Boccaccio's poem, "What Chaucer Really Did to *Il Filostrato*," *Essays and Studies* 17 (1932), 56–75; reprinted in Richard J. Schoeck and Jerome Taylor, eds., *Chaucer Criticism II: "Troilus and Criseyde" and the Minor Poems* (Notre Dame, IN: University of Notre Dame Press, 1961).

References and Further Reading

Primary

Chaucer, Geoffrey (1987). *The Riverside Chaucer*, ed. Larry D. Benson. 3rd edn. Oxford: Oxford University Press.

Sands, Donald B., ed. (1986). *Middle English Verse Romances*. Exeter Medieval English Texts and Studies. Exeter: University of Exeter Press.

Windeatt, B. A., ed. (1990). *"Troilus and Criseyde": A New Edition of "The Book of Troilus."* 2nd edn. London: Longman.

Secondary

Benson, C. David (1986). *Chaucer's Drama of Style: Poetic Variety and Contrast in the "Canterbury Tales."* Chapel Hill: University of North Carolina Press.

Benson, C. David (1990). Chaucer's *"Troilus and Criseyde."* London: Unwin Hyman.

Bloch, R. Howard (1991). *Medieval Misogyny and the Invention of Western Romantic Love.* Chicago and London: University of Chicago Press.

Brewer, Derek (1992). *Chaucer and his World.* Cambridge: D. S. Brewer.

Brewer, Derek (1998). *A New Introduction to Chaucer.* 2nd edn. London: Longman.

Brown, Peter (2000). *A Companion to Chaucer.* Blackwell Companions to Literature and Culture. Oxford: Blackwell.

Cooper, Helen (1983). *The Structure of the Canterbury Tales.* London: Duckworth.

Cooper, Helen (1991). *The Canterbury Tales.* Oxford Guides to Chaucer. Rev. paperback edn. Oxford: Oxford University Press.

Crane, Susan (1994). *Gender and Romance in Chaucer's* Canterbury Tales. Princeton, NJ: Princeton University Press.

Dinshaw, Carolyn (1989). *Chaucer's Sexual Poetics.* Madison: University of Wisconsin Press.

Donaldson, E. Talbot (1970). *Speaking of Chaucer.* London: Athlone Press.

Ferster, Judith (1985). *Chaucer on Interpretation.* Cambridge: Cambridge University Press.

Hansen, Elaine Tuttle (1992). *Chaucer and the Fictions of Gender.* Berkeley: University of California Press.

Klassen, Norman (1995). *Chaucer on Love, Knowledge and Sight.* Chaucer Studies 21. Cambridge: D. S. Brewer.

Kolve, V. A. (1984). *Chaucer and the Imagery of Narrative: The First Five "Canterbury Tales."* London: Edward Arnold.

Krueger, Roberta L., ed. (2000). *The Cambridge Companion to Medieval Romance.* Cambridge Companions to Literature. Cambridge: Cambridge University Press.

Laskaya, Anna (1995). *Chaucer's Approach to Gender in the "Canterbury Tales."* Chaucer Studies 23. Cambridge: D. S. Brewer.

Mann, Jill (1991). *Geoffrey Chaucer.* Feminist Readings. New York: Harvester Wheatsheaf.

Martin, Priscilla (1990). *Chaucer's Women: Nuns, Wives, and Amazons.* Iowa City: University of Iowa Press.

McAlpine, Monica (1978). *The Genre of "Troilus and Criseyde."* Ithaca, NY: Cornell University Press.

McGerr, Rosemarie P. (1998). *Chaucer's Open Books: Resistance to Closure in Medieval Discourse.* Gainesville: University of Florida Press.

Patterson, Lee (1991). *Chaucer and the Subject of History.* London: Routledge.

Pearsall, Derek (1992). *The Life of Geoffrey Chaucer: A Critical Biography.* Oxford: Blackwell.

Saunders, Corinne (1993). *The Forest of Medieval Romance: Avernus, Broceliande, Arden.* Cambridge: D. S. Brewer.

Saunders, Corinne (2001). *Rape and Ravishment in the Literature of Medieval England.* Cambridge: D. S. Brewer.

Saunders, Corinne, ed. (2001). *Chaucer.* Blackwell Guides to Criticism. Oxford: Blackwell.

Weisl, Angela Jane (1995). *Conquering the Reign of Femeny: Gender and Genre in Chaucer's Romance.* Chaucer Studies 22. Cambridge: D. S. Brewer.

Windeatt, Barry (1992). *Troilus and Criseyde.* Oxford Guides to Chaucer. Oxford: Clarendon Press.

6

Malory and the Early Prose Romances

Helen Cooper

Then was he ware where came from a wood there fast by a knight all armed upon a white horse, with a strange shield of strange arms.[1]

The mysterious knight on his charger (preferably white, as it is here), who emerges from the non-location of the forest to take on a chivalric or amatory adventure, is one of the most compelling images of romance. It fueled the earliest of the prose romances – the great Arthurian cycle, the vast *Tristan*, and the even more vast *Perceforest* – in thirteenth- and fourteenth-century France; it was taken over from there for the ever-multiplying sixteenth-century Spanish chivalric romances that told the stories not only of heroes such as Amadis de Gaule and Primaleon but of their sons and grandsons, stories that enjoyed huge popularity in almost every language of Europe, English included; it caught the imagination of Sir Thomas Malory, who is quoted here, and a century later of Edmund Spenser, who used it as the main structuring motif of the *Faerie Queene*, his allegorical epic for which, unusually for the date, he chose the medium of verse. Romantic and Victorian medievalism fed on such images, and recycled them in the poetry of Scott and Tennyson and the art of the Pre-Raphaelites. The new vogue for Malory's *Morte Darthur* in the late nineteenth and early twentieth centuries resulted in a crop of illustrated editions that often focused on just such moments. The same underlying scenario is still recognizable even in a Western television classic such as *The Lone Ranger*, though the stranger is no longer a knight, and a wood is too alien a landscape for the American West.

Malory apart, the early prose romances must be the least read substantial corpus within the whole canon of English literature; yet they were immensely popular from the late fifteenth to the early seventeenth century, and continued to exert an indirect influence long after the original texts had ceased to be reprinted. The form had been still more popular in Continental Europe, and the early conquistadors carried copies of Spanish chivalric quest romances with them to the New World and interpreted what they saw there accordingly (Goodman 1998; Leonard 1949). California was named after an island of Amazon women in *Esplandian*, one of the *Amadis de Gaule* sequels; Florida was discovered by Ponce de Léon in the course of a search for a fountain of eternal youth. Reprints of the prose *Lancelot*, the *Tristan*, and *Perceforest* dominated French bestseller lists throughout the great century of humanism. It was with good reason that it was early in the seventeenth century that Miguel de Cervantes created Don Quixote, the man who had read so many chivalric romances that he believed them to be true, and that his creation struck an immediate chord with readers across Europe. "I am a stranger and a knight adventurous," Malory has his Lancelot declare, "who laboureth throughout many realms for to win worship," and the line is used as the inspiration and the caption of the rousing frontispiece drawn by Edmund Sullivan to an Edwardian edition of *Don Quixote*, as if there were no difference between the two protagonists (628 (XVIII.13); Cervantes 1902). Cervantes' book was chosen in a recent poll of leading European writers as by far the most important work of prose fiction produced in the continent; yet however much it may parody the form it grows out of, it could not exist without those earlier prose romances. Don Quixote may not be able to afford a white charger, but the underfed and patient Rozinante is a walking reminder of what is missing – and it is telling that Sullivan's frontispiece recasts the beast as a steed in full gallop.

Just as Cervantes' work is an act of homage, in which Don Quixote's delusions become increasingly admirable in contrast to the commonplace inadequacies of the world around him, so the prose romances continued to seduce long after their fantastic elements had made them the mock of intellectuals. *Don Quixote* gave a continuing vicarious life to the very books it burned within the story, and acts of homage comparable to Cervantes' continued for long after the production of a serious chivalric romance would have killed any ambitious author's reputation. Henry Fielding's *The History of Tom Jones, a Foundling* (1749) relies on readers' continuing familiarity with both picaresque narrative structures and with the conventions of the "fair unknown," the young man of doubtful parentage who grows up to be recognized as a scion of noble stock and to win the lady. The genre could moreover still be reinvented in contemporary forms without any element of parody. A number of Dickens' novels tell stories of orphans recovered and virtue rewarded (whether to fulfill the full romance expectations of the form, or, as in *Great Expectations*, to foil them), though with their chivalric antecedents by now thoroughly overlaid: no white chargers here, nor any mysterious knight to act as a *deus ex machina* to set the plot to rights. The installment method of publication also meant the revival of the interlaced structure pioneered in the prose romances, where a series of simultaneous adventures happening to different characters can be pursued in parallel – a form that was to prove invaluable in radio and television soap operas. Complaints that the long and meandering structures of these narratives lack organic unity miss the point: their capaciousness, the ease with which they can accommodate new characters, their almost infinite capacity for deferral of closure, constitute much of their attraction for audiences medieval or modern, who can look forward to a new series of episodes day after day after day.

Naturalistic parodies or imitations or descendants of the prose romances none the less have very different aims from the early texts – their antecedents indeed are often invisible to their readers, sometimes even to their authors. The near-interchangeability of the terms "chivalry" and "romance" in the later eighteenth century was grounded rather in a deliberate scholarly antiquarianism, which justified itself by seeking out the manners and customs of the English past. Yet the chivalry the romances portrayed had always belonged in a bygone age, even while knighthood remained a compelling ideal. Not just medieval readers and writers, but also their immediate followers such as Sidney and Spenser, associated romance with chivalry as a nostalgic representation of what was still a living tradition; the seventeenth century increasingly scorned both together, along with the superstitious or barbarous Middle Ages that had spawned them. By the middle of the eighteenth century, however, there was a growing recognition that rationality was not enough, and that the scholarly recovery of early romance also had the capacity to feed that newly important faculty, the imagination. Thomas Warton undertook the first extensive research on medieval metrical romance as an adjunct to his study of Spenser; Thomas Percy brought many of the texts themselves into the public domain (Johnston 1964). Warton's work on the *Faerie Queene* also called serious attention to the *Morte Darthur*, and interest in the other prose romances followed on the back of that. In 1803, Robert Southey produced an abridged adaptation of the first part of *Amadis de Gaule*, the huge and unashamedly fantastic romance that in Antony Munday's translation had displaced the earlier generation of prose romances in popular affection around 1600; its success resulted in his version of Munday's *Primaleon* four years later.[2] The earlier English works had to wait for longer. It may have been the magical elements of the story of *Arthur of Little Britain* (despite its title, a non-Arthurian work) that lay behind the 1814 reprint of Lord Berners' early Tudor translation in what remains the standard edition. Malory's *Morte Darthur* was reprinted only after all these, perhaps because it was still quite widely available in its 1634 edition – an edition that had never been impressive, and that no doubt became tattier with increasing age. Southey owned a copy as a boy, and it had none of the rarity of the earlier prints. Malory was the most continuously read of any medieval English author after Chaucer, but unlike Chaucer, he had ceased to carry much in the way of cultural capital. His work seemed old-fashioned or middle-class rather than pristine or chivalric, an impression strengthened by the currency of Arthurian material in chapbooks and broadside ballads. The 1634 edition accordingly acquired financial value only as a consequence of the revival of serious interest in the *Morte*. It began to appear in sale catalogues in the 1790s, initially still for not much more than twice the price of Mrs Radcliffe's Gothick *Mysteries of Udolpho* (1794), but its value quintupled within 16 years.[3] Wider access to Malory was made possible in 1816 by two new editions in a popular format of the 1634 text, and more serious appreciation developed from the printing in the following year of the newly discovered Caxton print of the work. The dark imaginative spaces promised by chivalric romance had been initially filled by *The Faerie Queene*, and scenes from it, and especially of its women, became a favorite subject for artists in the later eighteenth century; but the *Morte Darthur* displaced it in both literary and artistic popularity in the nineteenth century, and it is Malory's Arthur who has remained the primary channel back to medieval romance ever since.

Arthurian material is so much a part of English tradition that is hard to imagine a period when the *Morte Darthur* was not an assumed element of cultural literacy. The new accessibility of Malory's work sparked something of a cult, as evidenced not only by the reworking of its stories (Tennyson's lament for a lost past; models of manliness and courage for boys; now, adoption into science-fiction form or by the agendas of feminism), but eventually also by films, musicals, and the whole paraphernalia of the heritage industry. In keeping with its centrality over so many centuries, whether popular or highbrow, much of this chapter is devoted to it. It was not, however, the only late medieval prose romance to exert a forward influence, nor does it exemplify all the new developments in romance that the advent of prose brought with it. Those are represented here by three other works, two from the decades following Malory, one contemporary with him, which represent different trends that later romanticism and prose fiction were to elaborate in different ways. One is *Valentine and Orson*, included both because it signals new areas of concern within the romance form, and because for centuries its story, in various simplified forms, remained as familiar a representative of romance in popular culture as *Cinderella* is now within the genre of fairytale: its omission from a volume of this kind would therefore misrepresent the history of romance. The second is *Huon of Bordeaux*, which makes perhaps the most extensive use of magic and the supernatural of any works of the genre, and which opens up a direct channel to fantasy worlds. And last is *Paris and Vienne*, which can lay a strong claim to being a precursor of the shift in prose fiction from romance to novel.

The Romance of Britain: *Le Morte Darthur*

Sir Thomas Malory's version of the Arthurian stories acquired its dominance in English literary history for three reasons. In the first instance, it was disseminated through print rather than manuscript, and so became available to a broad range of readership such as had not been available to Middle English writings even at the time it was composed. Second, it was the only work in English that gave a full account of the life of Arthur, the greatest British hero, and, incorporated within that, the adventures of his fellowship of knights. And third, it is quite exceptionally well written, not in any learned or rhetorical fashion, but in an understated style that requires its readers to fill in the hinterland of what is said, so giving them a deep imaginative and emotional investment in the text – a quality that conformed powerfully with the Romantic search for works that fed the imagination, and which is largely responsible for the ever-increasing number of modern rewritings.

The *Morte Darthur* was completed in 1469–70 and was printed by Caxton in 1485, within eight years of his setting up the first printing press in England. Prose romance was itself a new genre in English, and its late arrival on the literary scene made it the first to be disseminated primarily through the medium of print. The form had first appeared in France in the decades around 1220, in the great series of the prehistory and history of Arthur and the Grail known as the *Vulgate Cycle* or the *Lancelot-Grail*, and its non-cyclical variants and imitations. These had continued to be read ever since their composition, but they were enjoying a fresh wave of fashion in the fifteenth century in company with a range of newly composed prose romances. Caxton derived a particular interest in the genre through his connections with Burgundy, where the prose romance was experiencing a spectacular revival. He published his own translation of the Burgundian Raoul Lefevre's *Recuyell of the Histories of Troy* even before he moved his press across the Channel from Bruges to Westminster, and followed it up with a couple of others before turning his attention to Malory. It was the thirteenth-century texts that provided the sources for most of Malory's work: for Arthur's birth and exploits, the whole story of Lancelot and Guinevere, the *Tristram*, and the Grail quest. There had been earlier English adaptations of some of this material, but almost all before Malory had been in verse. The one exception was the prose *Merlin*, translated in the mid-fifteenth century, and there is no evidence that Malory knew that. He probably believed that he was breaking new ground in producing an English prose Arthuriad, and in effect that was true. The deliberate choice of his medium is shown by the fact that he incorporates adaptations of two late fourteenth-century Middle English verse romances, turning them into prose in the process: the Alliterative *Morte Arthure*, for the story of Arthur's war against the Romans, and the Stanzaic *Morte Arthur*, an increasingly dominant source for Arthur's downfall and death alongside the French *Mort Artu*. Prose was a fortunate choice in every way, though Malory could hardly have predicted how completely the fiction of the future was to reject verse. His earliest readers would have associated fiction with verse as readily as modern readers assume that it will take the form of prose.

The *Morte Darthur* exactly suited Caxton's business plan of transferring to England the Continental fashion for prose romance. He was especially intrigued by the three Christian heroes of the Nine Worthies tradition, Arthur, Charlemagne, and Godfrey of Bouillon, leader of the First Crusade: he published works on all three of them, and called attention to their role as Worthies in his prefaces. Arthur, as the one Briton among them, occupied a particularly important place in such a scheme. The famous introduction Caxton wrote for the work explains the value he saw in it – and therefore also the value he hoped readers would find: in the speculative world of print publication, as distinct from the commission-driven copying of manuscripts, advertisement takes on a new importance. Leading his sales pitch (and no doubt also driving his decision to publish the work) is the shameful lack of any English equivalent to the *Lancelot-Grail*, which his own edition can supply:

> Many noble and dyvers gentylmen of thys royaume of Englond camen and demaunded
> me many and oftymes wherfore that I have not do made and enprynte the noble hystorye
> of the Saynt Greal and of the moost renomed Crysten kyng, fyrst and chyef of the thre
> best Crysten, and worthy, Kyng Arthur, whyche ought moost to be remembred emonge

us Englysshemen tofore al other Crysten kynges … afferming that I ought rather t'enprynte his actes and noble feates than of Godefroye of Boloyne or ony of the other eyght, consyderyng that he was a man borne wythin this royame and kyng and emperour of the same, and that there ben in Frensshe dyvers and many noble volumes of his actes, and also of his knyghtes.   (xiii [preface])

He goes on to tackle the two main objections to Arthurian material, objections that were to be ever more insistently repeated over the next century. First is the question of Arthur's historicity. The *Lancelot-Grail* had taken the elements of flagrant fantasy in Arthurian romance to new heights, but Malory had made it part of his own agenda to cut those back, to convert the stories in content as well as style to something closer to chronicle (Field 1971). The earliest comprehensive account of Arthur's life, in Geoffrey of Monmouth's Latin *History of the Kings of Britain* (ca. 1138), had been presented as history, and the historical Arthur had remained the dominant English form of the legend. Caxton, in keeping with Malory's own approach, appeals to the evidence for such a figure behind the romance accretions, especially to material evidence: Arthur's seal, the great ruins at "Camelot" (probably Caerleon), the Round Table itself at Winchester – things that were still there in the physical world, and provided traces, signs in the present to confirm the stories from the past. The second objection was the one notoriously framed by Roger Ascham in the mid-sixteenth century, that the Arthurian stories told of nothing but open man-slaughter and bold bawdry. Malory was his particular target, since there were no other current English accounts of the adulterous love-stories of either Lancelot and Guin-evere or Tristan and Isolde; the near-invisibility of the French-invented Lancelot in earlier English Arthurian romance indeed suggests that the whole story had been regarded as a French slander on the greatest British king. Adultery had never figured as admirable or desirable in any English romance before Malory, and Caxton accord-ingly writes his way around the issue, beseeching his readers, both "noble lordes and ladyes with al other estates,"

that they take the good and honest actes in their remembraunce, and to folowe the same … For herein may be seen noble chyvalrye, curtosye, humanyté, frendlynesse, hardy-nesse, love, frendshyp, cowardyse, murdre, hate, vertue, and synne. Do after the good and leve the evyl, and it shal brynge you to good fame and renommee.   (xv [preface])

Caxton's Malory, unlike Ascham's, is a model for good living, and especially for good chivalric living. Not long before he printed the *Morte*, Caxton had published his translation of Ramon Lull's *Book of the Order of Chivalry*, a pan-European bestseller for the previous two centuries that expounds the theory of which Malory's Arthurian world appears to be the practice.

As the work progresses, however, that practice of chivalry increasingly falls short of the theory. Malory may offer his readers glimpses of a mysterious world of strange knights on white chargers in quest of adventures, but what most gives the work its sustained power is something altogether different. In keeping with the English emphasis on a historical Arthur, he draws much of his world as one of political possibility, especially so at the beginning, when the young king has to consolidate his hold on a disputed throne, and at the end, when factions split the old king's hold on his followers and subjects. Malory compares this directly to his own troubled age of the Wars of the Roses:

> Lo ye all Englysshemen, se ye nat what a myschyff here was? For he that was the moste kynge and nobelyst knyght of the worlde, and moste loved the felyshyp of noble knyghtes, and by hym they all were upholdyn, and yet myght nat thes Englyshemen holde them contente with hym. Lo thus was the olde custom and usayges of thys londe, and men say that we of thys londe have nat yet loste that custom.   (708 [XXI.1])

Despite its affiliations with romance, the *Morte* is finally about the impossibility of reaching or maintaining ideals in an imperfect and fallen world. The one ideal that is achieved, the Grail, can be reached only by a select group of knights who have opted out of the worldly business of sexuality and dynasty; they are led by Galahad, whose perfection defines itself by passing beyond the sphere of earthly adventures, and whose spiritual adventures reach their necessary and logical conclusion in death when he looks into the sacred vessel. For the knights who are left behind, the fellowship of the Round Table becomes increasingly fragmented and malicious. If Malory's evocations of Arthurian ideals and adventure captivate the imagination, his descriptions of crisis and disaster are more powerful still. The episodes that most compel attention for the sheer power of the writing are such occasions as the combat between the brothers Balin and Balan, neither recognizing the other until they are on the point of death; Gawain's grief and anger over Lancelot's accidental killing of his unarmed brother Gareth; the "day of destiny" on Salisbury Plain, when Arthur and Mordred, almost the last surviving representatives of their slaughtered armies, mortally wound each other; or Lancelot's parting from Guinevere after he finds her in the nunnery where she has taken refuge:

> "For I take recorde of God, in you I have had myn erthly joye, and yf I had founden you now so dysposed, I had caste me to have had you into myn owne royame. But sythen I fynde you thus desposed, I ensure you faythfully, I wyl ever take me to penaunce and praye whyle my lyf lasteth, yf that I may fynde ony heremyte, other graye or whyte, that wyl receyve me. Wherfore, madame, I praye you kysse me, and never no more."
> "Nay," sayd the quene, "that shal I never do, but absteyne you from suche werkes."
> (72 [XXI.9–10])

Yet the *Morte* is a wonderfully capacious work, encompassing with equal ease a shape-shifting Merlin and the pillagers on the field of battle, enchantresses and holy virgins, bloody combats and eucharistic miracles. Its iconic moments (the sword in the stone; Galahad and his white shield with its red cross; the corpse of Elaine of Astolat floating in a little boat down the river to Camelot; the arm that rises from the water to receive Excalibur back into the lake; Arthur's departure for Avalon in the barge full of weeping ladies) may have been reinvented by Tennyson and the Pre-Raphaelites and the film industry, but they all have their origins in Malory.

Readers of Caxton's version of the work – readers, that is, until the middle of the twentieth century, since even the 1634 text essentially reproduced that – accepted these changes of key, between romance fantasy and epic destiny, magic and piety, as part of the imaginative symphony of the work. The discovery of a manuscript of Malory's text in 1934 in Winchester College Library, and Eugène Vinaver's subsequent editing of it, led to the propounding of a rather different view. Vinaver published his magisterial edition under the title *The Works of Sir Thomas Malory*, since, he claimed, the manuscript layout showed that it consisted not of a single work with internal subdivisions into books and chapters such as Caxton had presented, but of eight separate works; the title of "Morte Darthur," he argued, properly referred to the last book alone, and should not be taken as a global title.[4] The claim set off an academic debate that has never been finally resolved. Scholars who studied the manuscript pointed out that it could be more properly divided into four parts, or just as plausibly into eleven, rather than Vinaver's eight. (The 1634 edition, without benefit of the manuscript, had presented it as a tripartite work.) As for the title, the opening and closing leaves of the manuscript are missing, and Caxton does not supply a title page; but although the colophon to the work in his edition first appears to distinguish between "the death of Arthur" and the whole "book of King Arthur," it then goes on to offer and justify a title he seems to have found odd: "Thus endeth thys noble and joyous book entytled *Le Morte Darthur*, notwythstondyng it treateth of the byrth, lyf and actes of the sayd kyng Arthur." In keeping with his treatment of the text, it should be noted, neither formulation allows for the volume's being a kind of Arthurian anthology on the Vinaver model. Vinaver's plural "works" does appear to solve the problem of narrative inconsistencies on both the large scale (the intrusive episode of the Roman War, the clash of ideologies between earthly and religious chivalry) and the small (such as some confusion as to when certain knights are killed); but it does not explain the whole pattern of connections that Malory built into his text and which he did not find in his sources. He goes to considerable trouble to incorporate numerous cross-references that offer chronological and other correlations between the stories of the various knights. So far as is known, it was he himself who enhanced the role of Gareth, giving him his own *Bildungsroman* within the work and turning him into one of the leading protagonists of the central and later books. It was certainly Malory who selected and rearranged material from the prose *Lancelot* so as to create the sequence of Lancelot's three defenses of Guinevere that encompass the fellowship's slide into catastrophe. On the first occasion, when she is charged with murder, she is indeed guiltless. The second charge is that she has slept with one of the wounded knights with whom she shared her chamber – an accusation of which she is innocent only on a technicality, since it was in fact Lancelot himself who had slept with her. On the last occasion, when Lancelot is found in her chamber in the middle of the night and fights his way out, she may or may not be guilty (and Malory refuses to commit himself, insisting only that "love that tyme was nat as love ys nowadays"),

but he has to defend her "whether ryght othir wronge." At the ending, the whole
weight of the earlier books – the love between Lancelot and Arthur and Lancelot and
Gareth, the increasing malice shown by Gawain and his other brothers in their
murders of good knights such as Lamorak, the assassination of Tristram – is brought
to bear on the self-destruction of the fellowship. Increasingly, Malory describes the
deaths of his best knights, not as they happen, but as they are reported and lamented
by surviving members of the fellowship, in ways that turn the later parts of the work
(and the singular is hard to avoid) into a threnody for its earlier hopes and achievements. The very last page of the work offers the culmination of the process, in Ector's
lament over the corpse of Sir Lancelot:

> "A, Launcelot!" he sayd, "thou were the hede of al Crysten knyghtes! And now I dar
> say," sayd sir Ector, "thou sir Launcelot, there thou lyest, that thou were never matched
> of erthely knyghtes hande. And thou were the curtest knyght that ever bare shelde! And
> thou were the truest frende to thy lovar that ever bestrad hors, and thou were the the
> trewest lover, of a synful man, that ever loved woman, and thou were the kyndest man
> that ever strake wyth swerde …"
> Then there was wepyng and dolour out of mesure.   (725 [XXI.13])

The speech expresses grief for more than one man's death, even if he was the best of
knights; it is grief for the loss of the whole beguiling vision of the Arthurian world.
The nostalgia in which the post-Romantics grounded their own images of knights
and ladies was already present in their medieval master-text.

There is one element recurrently associated since the early nineteenth century with
the Arthurian stories but which Malory rarely provides explicitly, and that is mys-
teriousness. His Grail has both miraculous and ethereal qualities about it, but it is
still very firmly an object rather than just an object of desire, and one moreover that
can be used to inculcate some good doctrinal lessons about the nature of transubstan-
tiation. Even his stranger knights are easily identified (usually, indeed, as Lancelot).
The weeping queens who set off with the dying Arthur for Avalon are later reported
to have delivered his corpse to Glastonbury, their scheme for curing him of his mortal
wounds presumably having failed. In all these episodes, however, as in more mundane
sections of the work, Malory's understatement leaves abundant imaginative space for
mystery to suggest itself, and later writers were eager to exploit the opportunities
offered. Bedivere has to return to the lake three times before he can bring himself to
restore Excalibur to its waters, and when he finally does so, in Malory "ther cam an
arme and an honde above the watir, and toke hit and cleyght [clutched] hit, and shoke
hit thryse and braundysshed, and than vanysshed with the swerde into the watir." But
it is Tennyson who describes the arm as "clothed in white samite, mystic, wonderful,"
both etherealizing and feminizing it in the process.[5] The association of the female
with the exotic and the dangerous is developed in the nineteenth century to a degree
that never occurs in Malory. His own women cover a range from the semi-supernatural
Lady of the Lake and the enchantress Hellewes to the innocently loving Elaine of

Astolat, but they do not include any *belle dame sans merci*. His Damsel of the Lake, Nenive or Nimue, shuts up Merlin inside a rock, but she does it because she is tired of being sexually harassed by him; it took the Victorian Tennyson to turn her into a vamp, the wicked Vivien who seduces the mage in order to steal his secrets, and Burne-Jones to illustrate her accordingly. The women of the *Morte*, even the ones with some element of the magical about them, are refreshingly down to earth. When Sir Pelleas thanks God for his rescue from loving a heartless woman by the same Damsel of the Lake, she tells him, "Thank me" (104 [IV.23]). Elaine of Corbin, on whom Lancelot begets Galahad in accordance with prophecy and by means of magic, never passes up any future opportunities to get him into bed with her even after the excuse of conceiving the perfect knight is long past, and even though she recognizes that Lancelot will never come to her wittingly. Morgan le Faye is Arthur's half-sister, with nothing inherently supernatural about her except that she learnt "nigromancy" in a nunnery; she, like Merlin, has the power to shape-shift, but her attempts to undermine Arthur's rule are invariably foiled by natural means. As in all the medieval Arthurian stories, and unlike many modern retellings, she is never allowed to become a rival focus to Arthur.

Reworkings of Arthurian material have been designed to convey different agendas ever since the twelfth century, when they first began to be produced in large numbers. Malory's move toward historicity helps to bring his protagonist out of French fantasy into the English past, and shows at the same time both the perfection that might have been, and the faction-fighting and downfall of the Round Table that does occur. In the Elizabethan period Arthur became contested ground, not only for Ascham's moral reasons but for political ones too. Spenser set out to produce an allegory that would show how the exercise of moral virtue, represented as chivalry on the Arthurian model, might yet move the world closer to perfection, but he never completed it, and perhaps could not have done so. The moment of closure that he foreshadows but never reaches will lie in the union of Arthur with Gloriana, figuring Elizabeth. But in 1586, a play entitled *The Misfortunes of Arthur* was presented before the Queen by a group of young men from Gray's Inn, which turned the Arthurian story into a revenge tragedy presided over by the ghost of Gorlois (the first husband of Arthur's mother), who had been killed the same night that Uther Pendragon slept with his wife (Hughes 1912). Gorlois's final speech celebrates the peace of Britain under Elizabeth in contrast with Mordred's rebellion: her reign is not one that will break down into the ultimate political evil of civil war. From being the great national hero, Arthur here becomes an exemplary warning against the failure of good rule.

Unhappy Endings: *Valentine and Orson*

The catastrophe that ends Arthur's life can make the whole category of 'romance' look questionable. The term might seem to fit the lesser stories of knights pursuing chivalric ideals inset within Malory's work, but the devastating and ugly last battle seems to belong to an altogether grimmer generic category. *Valentine and Orson* gives decisive demonstration that it was romance itself that was changing. The boundaries of the genre were fast expanding in the fifteenth century, to encompass many of the qualities more typically associated with tragedy or epic or with the disasters of history. Romance is generally thought of as a providential genre, where things work out for the best, often through the designs of God rather than the human characters. A strong movement in the late medieval prose romances presents the opposite scenario, where things go badly wrong despite the characters' best intentions, and often apparently in contradiction of any providential scheme (Cooper 1997).

Valentine and Orson started out as quintessential romance (ed. Dickson, 1937). Its earliest text is lost, but the evidence of surviving versions in other languages indicates that it was composed in French verse in the fourteenth century: late enough for it to be put together magpie-fashion out of all the most familiar story motifs and conventions from other romances. Like many French metrical romances, it was turned into prose in the fifteenth century, and from there translated into English – this time by Henry Watson, shortly after 1500, and printed by Caxton's successor Wynkyn de Worde. In this version (slightly changed in detail from the metrical original, but with no significant structural alterations), an empress is falsely accused of adultery and exiled by her husband; she gives birth in the forest to twin sons, one of whom, Valentine, is found and raised by King Pepin of France (the empress's brother, though it is long before the relationship is discovered), and the second, Orson, is carried off by a bear. Valentine eventually tames the wild Orson, their relationship is revealed (with the help of an angel and a talking brazen head), and they seek out their mother and reconcile her and themselves with their father. Encounters with giants and a love interest for each of the sons fill out the story. In the prose version, however, that whole loss and return series occupies only the first part of the text. It adds all kinds of further romance motifs (a "Green Knight," a dragon, a dwarf enchanter, a magical flying horse), and a generous range of further chivalric adventures, many of them involving battles against the Saracens – not a fantasy enemy, but the Turks whose advance across the Mediterranean and into Eastern Europe increasingly threatened the Christian West. In addition, however, Valentine abandons his first love; Orson betrays his wife for another woman, causing her to die of grief; King Pepin and his queen are poisoned by his bastard sons; and at the climax of the whole narrative, Valentine accidentally kills his father in battle. In modern terms, this incident might be called "friendly fire," but there is no such euphemism in the medieval vernaculars. Orson, who is the first to realize what has happened, cries out that it is "evill prowesse." Valentine describes it as "a dede before God detestable, and to the men abhomynable," and himself as "the moost cursed, unhappy, and evil fortuned" of men, who has lost any right to live or to be counted among the number of knights (308–9). As the older twin, he is entitled to inherit the empire, but he rapidly transfers it to Orson, and spends the rest of his life in penance for his action. His repentance is accepted by God, and he dies in a state of sanctity; but, as with the Grail quest, the narrative has to step outside the demands and vicissitudes of earthly secular and political life before such a point of rest can be achieved.

The later history of the story of *Valentine and Orson* is in effect a history of reactions to the generic transgressions enacted by the prose version (Cooper 1999). In abbreviated forms, it remained widely known in both England and France through to the late nineteenth century, though like the eighteenth-century Arthur it existed at a level below serious commentary. In a half-length version in the series of popular French texts called the *Bibliothèque bleue*, the most drastic excision is of the parricides – neither the bastard sons' poisoning of the king nor Valentine's killing of his father is explicitly recounted. From the early seventeenth century, an abridged but still substantial version was current in England, in which the omissions indicate a different kind of moral censorship: the parricides remain intact, but the sexual shenanigans are cut back. Other versions were still more selective. Like Don Quixote tilting at windmills, the episodes that were crucial for recognition came early in the narrative. Valentine and Orson, the armed knight and the wild man, appeared as pageant figures in the coronation celebrations for Edward VI, presumably on the strength of costume alone. A short rhymed version was produced ca. 1600, which reduced the story to its original metrical outline; and it may have been in a similarly truncated form that it was twice dramatized in the 1590s, though both texts are lost. By the eighteenth century, the story was circulating in a range of formats, lengths, and degrees of comprehensiveness, some including the disaster of the ending, some stopping short at the family reunion; the shortest version ran to just 12 leaves, printed, that is, on a single folded sheet. It was made into a pantomime in the Victorian era, complete with jokes about railways. With the disasters removed, the names of Valentine and Orson remained part of familiar nursery culture until around 1900, carrying with them a comforting reassurance about wildness tamed and virtue rewarded. Jan Huizinga famously characterized the fifteenth century as a time of moribund ideology; the history of this particular romance, like that of Arthur, suggests rather that it was an era that was prepared to challenge its own most admired ideals. It was later periods that turned the story back into something more reassuring, a fantasy about the putting right of whatever had gone wrong.

Exotic Romance: *Huon of Bordeaux*

Valentine is generous with its supply of magic and the out of the ordinary, but apart from the occasional giant and dwarf, who are simply the wrong size, it does not go in for the supernatural, for alternative orders of beings. Readers who wanted an otherworld of "faerie lands forlorn" had to look elsewhere. The two romances translated in the reign of Henry VIII by John Bourchier, Lord Berners, best known as the translator of Froissart, offered more possibilities in that direction. The hero of *Arthur of Little Britain* spends the romance in pursuit of his beloved with the help of a protective fairy queen, and *Huon of Bordeaux* serves the appetite for the marvelous still more generously. The earliest form of this story had been heavily martial in emphasis: at its core was an early thirteenth-century French verse epic about Charlemagne's attempts to have the hero done away with after he had accidentally killed the Emperor's treacherous son. This text acquired substantial accretions over the next century or so, and four of these continuations, together with the original poem, were put into French prose in the fifteenth century; it was this version that Berners translated (ed. Lee 1882–7). It received its last early modern printing in 1601, though, like *Valentine*, the work remained popular in France into the nineteenth century.

The story moves away from its concerns with Charlemagne's misrule as its setting moves away from France to more exotic locations. The emperor sends Huon on what is supposed to be an impossible mission to Babylon, on the assumption that he will be killed in the course of it. In the event, with the help of the fairy king Oberon, Huon not only accomplishes the mission but wins the love of the Emir's daughter. The distance of the work from any claim to serious historicity may be measured by the fact that Oberon is described as being the child of Julius Caesar and a fairy. He dwells in a forest that offers a short cut to Babylon, a crossing of 15 days as against 40 to go around it, but Huon is warned not to take the short route:

> The way is so full of the fayrey and straunge thynges, that suche as passe that way are lost, for in that wood abydyth a kynge of the fayrey namyd Oberon. He is of heyght bot of three fote, and crokyd shulderyd, yet he hathe an aungelyke vysage, so that there is no mortall man that seethe hym but that taketh grete pleasure to beholde his fase. And ye shall no soner be enteryd in to that wood, yf ye go that way, he wyll fynde the maner to speke with you; and yf ye speke to hym ye are lost for ever.   (63)

Huon of course disregards the warnings, and so in due course comes under Oberon's protection (mediated through a series of magic objects), but also under his sanctions for misbehavior. Oberon is dangerous, but he is not capricious (or only in the direction of mercy, when he occasionally lets Huon's misdemeanors pass unpunished); the conventional moralizing threat of God's displeasure for sin here becomes a much sharper and interventionist series of supernaturally directed punishments. Huon's later adventures include a period of isolation on a magnetic island that ships are unable to leave (he is eventually rescued by a griffin), his discovery of apples that renew one's youth, and a voyage in a magic ship ballasted with stones of supernatural powers. Eventually, in one of the continuations, he and his wife depart this earth for fairyland, and he overcomes a rival bid from Arthur to succeed Oberon as its king.

Part of the work's attraction to Tudor readers may have lain in its potential as a kind of travel writing: when unknown worlds were being opened up, a work about the strange things that could be found in unknown countries situated somewhere short of fairyland took on an edge of topical excitement, even of possibility. The work was popular enough for the rest of the sixteenth century for "Oberon" to establish itself as the standard name of the fairy king (*A Midsummer Night's Dream* being the most familiar, but by no means the only example), and for the work to be dramatized early in the 1590s, though the text does not survive.[6] Spenser was also familiar with the romance, and his fairy landscape of forests and enchanters and giants owes at least as much to *Huon* as to Malory. The boundary between the human and the fairy worlds is at its most permeable in *Huon*: not to the degree that humans can access the fairy whenever they wish, but that fairies can access the mortal world, and do so to its inhabitants' benefit and peril.

The Romance of Sentiment: *Paris and Vienne*

Paris and Vienne is very different. It cuts free from the meandering structures and sheer length of many of the other prose romances: although it was published by Caxton in the same year as the *Morte Darthur*, it runs just to some 30,000 words, only a tenth the length of Malory's text or an eighth of *Huon*. According to its French prologue (omitted from the text from which Caxton was working for his own translation), its redactor, Pierre de la Cypede, had always taken pleasure in reading romances such as those of Lancelot and Tristan, but found them impossible to believe; the attraction of *Paris*, by contrast, lay in the fact that the story is 'bien raisonnable et asses creable', within the bounds of reason and credibility.[7] Compared with the *Lancelot-Grail* or romances such as *Huon*, the claim is indeed true, even if the work is still very far from being an everyday story of medieval aristocrats. It is told with an abundance of circumstantial detail, starting with specific places and people and dates – it all begins in 1271, long enough ago to benefit from the glamor of distance, precise enough to suggest a basis in fact. The story concerns two young lovers who remain faithful to each other through numerous vicissitudes, of a kind much more plausible than most romances offered. The situations themselves are not altogether different from those encountered elsewhere, but the selection of motifs and their treatment all fall within the bounds of possibility, even if not of likelihood. Paris is of lower social standing than the beautiful Vienne, so although he is the winner in a tournament held for her hand, her father refuses his permission for their marriage. The lovers attempt to elope, but they are overtaken by her father's men when they are held up by a flooded river. Vienne is taken back to her parental home and made a prisoner there, where she has to fend off the wooing of the duke's son who has been chosen by her father to be her husband. Paris meanwhile sets off on a pilgrimage to Jerusalem, though he first learns "mouryske" (Moorish, i.e. Arabic), grows his beard, and familiarizes himself with the customs of the Moors. After curing the Sultan's favorite falcon of a sickness, he is given high office, and so finds himself in a position to arrange for the release from prison of Vienne's father, who has been betrayed to the Sultan while on pilgrimage. The disguised Paris asks for a gift of his own choosing as a reward, and eagerly accepts the offer of Vienne's hand. She refuses to consider any other husband than her first beloved, but he reveals himself to her by means of a ring she had given him; her father is reconciled to their marriage; and "Parys and Vyenne lyved togyder a grete whyle in ryght grete consolacyon and playsyr," have three children, and succeed to their parents' domains.

Caxton published *Paris and Vienne* just a few months after the *Morte Darthur*, but it comes across as a very different kind of work. It still contains plenty of chivalric action, but it reads much more like a precursor of the novel. The shift derives in part from the sympathetic, inward characterization, especially of Vienne, and the practical detail of how the plot is managed. The two are not unrelated: Vienne is of a very practical turn of mind. When she discovers that the unknown young man with whom she has fallen in love is in fact the lower-born Paris, it sounds for a moment as if she is going to demand of him that he go out and prove himself the best knight in the world (as is done by such well-known heroines as Guy of Warwick's lady, daughter to the earl of Warwick). She requires him to "assaye one thynge, which shal be moche dyffycile to doo and ryght peryllous" before she will marry him; but it turns out to be not the killing of a dragon, but rather "I wyl that incontinent ye say to your fader, that he goo to my lord my fader, and require hym that he gyve me in maryage to you" (31). Paris is appalled at the thought (much more, one feels, than he would be by a demand for dragon-killing), and his father is equally horrified when Paris plucks up the courage to present him with the demand. This very simple solution to the problem fails to work – hence the lovers' elopement. After Vienne has been put under close surveillance by her father, she has to resort to more ingenious methods to keep unwanted suitors at bay. She accordingly repels the duke's son not by any magic means but by tucking a quarter of rotten chicken under each armpit. The stink is enough to persuade him that she is, as she claims, seriously ill. When the seeming Moor comes to claim fulfillment of her father's promise of her to him, she plays the same trick; but although the men who accompany him cannot stand the stench, it "was to Parys a good odour, for he smellyd it not and sayd, I wote not what ye smelle, for I fele none evyl savour" (72). That may not quite be plausible, but it is a delightful way of putting into figurative form his single-minded longing for her, as if the rotting flesh were transformed into the odor of sanctity by the power of his love.

Paris and Vienne is one of the first of the prose romances to give extended space to naturalism of feeling, not least in the heroine herself. The possibility for readers, and especially women readers, to make a more personal connection with the material of such stories, as against the broad political analogies offered by the legendary romances, is enhanced by such treatment. It has the potential to be read as a kind of sentimental education, both in fine feeling and how to express it. The letters the lovers send to each other, and their conversations, could serve as models of how such things should be managed. Caxton's interest in the publication of courtesy literature is evidenced elsewhere, and he may well have thought of this romance as serving a comparable purpose. He saw no contradiction between the two. His prologue to a later publication, *Blanchardin and Eglantine*, in which he commends the work as especially valuable to "all vertuouse yong noble gentylmen and wymmen," could just as easily have prefaced *Paris*:

> In my jugement it is as requesyte otherwhyle to rede in auncyent hystoryes of noble fayttes and valyaunt actes of armes and warre, whiche have ben achyeved in olde tyme of many noble prynces, lordes and knyghtes, as wel for to see and knowe their valyauntnes for to stande in the specyal grace and love of their ladyes, and in lyke wyse for gentyl yonge ladyes and damoysellys for to lerne to be stedfaste and constaunt in their parte to theym that they ones have promysed and agreed to, such as have putte their lyves ofte in jeopardye for to playse theym to stande in grace, as it is to occupye theym and studye overmoch in bokes of contemplacion.

There were, however, plenty of moralists who found the diversion romances offered from "bokes of contemplacion" far less desirable, especially in view of their wide dissemination. The very act of publication takes such works out of the aristocratic worlds they describe and puts them into the hands of the middle classes, as textbooks for the upwardly mobile. The sheer length of the prose romances assumes a readership with competent vernacular literacy. Caxton is already making his own intervention in the debate about how that literacy should be employed, with its consequences for challenging both the practice of piety and social hierarchy.

Yet even from *Paris*, the road to the novel was not a clear way. The work was reprinted three times before 1505, and was still of sufficient interest for its license to be transferred in 1586; but by 1628 it had disappeared from sight sufficiently for Matthew Mainwaringe to present his own rewritten version of it as a new and original work. As *Vienna*, this went through two more editions, the last in 1650. Mainwaringe doubles the length, inserts a number of verses, and elaborates the style in a way that indicates that he had grown up both with euphuism and with Munday's *Amadis*. The characters lose their directness of speech and action and become little more than puppets. Vienna is allowed her rotten chickens, but they are treated with more sensationalism, and Paris is just being chivalrous when he says that he can't smell them. Something more than knights on white chargers had been lost from English prose when the original texts of the early romances disappeared from sight.

See also: chapter 1, ANCIENT ROMANCE; chapter 2, INSULAR BEGINNINGS; chapter 3, THE POPULAR ENGLISH METRICAL ROMANCES; chapter 4, ARTHURIAN ROMANCE; chapter 5, CHAUCER'S ROMANCES; chapter 8, SIDNEY AND SPENSER; chapter 10, CHAPBOOKS AND PENNY HISTORIES; chapter 14, PARADISE AND COTTON-MILL.

Notes

1. Sir Thomas Malory, *Morte Darthur*; see *Malory: Works*, ed. Eugène Vinaver, second edition (London: Oxford University Press, 1971), p. 618 (modernized spelling). In Caxton's edition, which is organized by book and chapter number numbers, the reference is XVIII.6. All quotations from the work are given double references in this form.

2. Although he did not admit it, Southey's *Amadis* as well as his *Primaleon* was based on Munday's translation: see Helen Moore, "Amadis and British Romanticism," in her *Amadis in English: A Study in the Reception of Romance* (forthcoming).

3. A list of sale prices is noted on the flyleaf of a copy in the Bodleian Library (Douce A 279), from 2 pounds 10 shillings in 1798 to 12 guineas in 1814. The 1634 edition is tripartite, like a three-volume novel; in the 1790s these cost around 10 shillings, though the four-volume *Udolpho* cost a pound (Peter Garside, James Raven, and Rainer Schöwerling, *The English Novel 1770–1829: A Bibliographical Survey* (Oxford: Oxford University Press, 2000), vol. 1, number 1794.46).

4. The edition first appeared in 1947 and is now superseded by the third edition, revised by P. J. C. Field, three volumes (Oxford: Clarendon

Press, 1990); see the introduction for the full discussion. The one-volume *Malory: Works* used elsewhere in this chapter is the student edition of this.

5. Malory, p. 716 (XXI.5); Tennyson, *Idylls of the King*, "The Passing of Arthur," line 312.

6. It was acted by Henslowe's company in 1593, but may have been written earlier. One scene of Huon material that may have been derived from the romance by way of the play, and in which Oberon puts in an appearance, is embedded in the *Tragical History of Guy of Warwick*, printed in 1661 (as yet there is no modern edition) but which, to judge from its heavily Marlovian verse, apparently also dates from the early 1590s.

7. From the introduction to the edition by MacEdward Leach, *Paris and Vienne*, Early English Text Society, OS 234 (1957), p. xv. All quotations are from this edition. Pierre claims to have translated the work from a Provençal original in 1432; it may possibly have had a Catalan antecedent.

References and Further Reading

Cervantes, Miguel de (1902). *The Adventures of Don Quixote de la Mancha*, trans. Peter Anthony Motteux. London: George Newnes.

Cooper, Helen (1997). "Counter-romance: Civil Strife and Father-killing in the Prose Romances." In Helen Cooper and Sally Mapstone, eds., *The Long Fifteenth Century: Essays for Douglas Gray*. Oxford: Clarendon Press, pp. 141–62.

Cooper, Helen (1999). "The Strange History of *Valentine and Orson*." In Rosalind Field, ed., *Tradition and Transformation in Medieval Romance*. Cambridge: D. S. Brewer, pp. 153–68.

Cunliffe, J.W. (ed.) (1912). *Early English Classical Tragedies*. Oxford: Clarendon Press.

Dickson, Arthur (1929). *Valentine and Orson: A Study in Late Medieval Romance*. New York: Columbia University Press.

Dickson, Arthur, ed. (1937). *Valentine and Orson*. Early English Text Society OS 204. London: Oxford University Press for the EETS.

Field, P. J. C. (1971). *Romance and Chronicle: A Study of Malory's Prose Style*. London: Barrie and Jenkins.

Garside, Peter, James Raven, and Rainer Schöwerling (2000). *The English Novel 1770–1829: A Bibliographical Survey*. Oxford: Oxford University Press.

Goodman, Jennifer R. (1998). *Chivalry and Exploration 1298–1630*. Woodbridge: Boydell Press.

Hughes, Thomas, and others (1912). *The Misfortunes of Arthur*. In J. W. Cunliffe, ed., *Early English Classical Tragedies*. Oxford: Clarendon Press, pp. 217–96.

Johnson, Arthur (1964). *Enchanted Ground: The Study of Medieval Romance in the Eighteenth Century*. London: Athlone Press.

Leach, MacEdward, ed. (1957). *Paris and Vienne*. Early English Text Society OS 234. London: Oxford University Press for the EETS.

Lee, S. L., ed. (1882–7). *The Boke of Duke Huon of Bordeux, done into English by John Bourchier, Lord Berners*. EETS ES 40, 41, 43, 50. London: N. Trubner for the EETS. [Two-volume reprint, 1973–98.]

Leonard, Irving A. (1949). *Books of the Brave*. Berkeley and Los Angeles: University of California Press. [Reprinted in 1992.]

Malory, Thomas (1971). *Malory: Works*, ed. Eugène Vinaver. 2nd edn. London: Oxford University Press. [First edition published in 1947.]

Malory, Thomas (1990). *The Works of Sir Thomas Malory*, ed. Eugène Vinaver. 3rd edn., revised by P. J. C. Field. Oxford: Clarendon Press.

Moore, Helen (forthcoming). *Amadis in English: A Study in the Reception of Romance*.

Saunders, Corinne J. (1993). *The Forest of Medieval Romance: Avernus, Broceliande, Arden*. Cambridge: D. S. Brewer.

7

Gendering Prose Romance in Renaissance England

Lori Humphrey Newcomb

That women's favorite reading is the faraway, repetitive, and improbable romance has itself been a much-traveled, much-repeated, and ill-supported critical myth. Nineteenth- and twentieth-century literary historians, linking the women readers in period references to the mass audiences of their own times, used to imagine a universal feminine taste that stretched from the Greek romance to formula fiction. This feminine taste was said to bloom with the Renaissance English prose romance. "Since women in general have never subscribed to realism," Louis B. Wright blithely asserted in 1935, "romance in strange opera lands and love stories with happy endings found favor with the Elizabethans even as with feminine readers today" (110). His evidence was the host of references in Renaissance texts to women reading prose romance – references derogatory in anecdotes, satires, and educational treatises, insinuating in the romances themselves. In the last generation, this evidence has been reexamined carefully by two overlapping groups: partisans of early fiction recovering its broad appeal, and feminist scholars validating women's reading experiences. These critics have argued that during the English Renaissance, while romance attracted a large audience of both genders, its association with women readers became a powerful literary convention. Educated men pretended to consign romance to women, displacing ambivalence about a genre long on appeal but short on cultural sanction.

When English Renaissance men did admit their own reading or writing of romance, they invoked Horace's praise of literature that mixes "profit and pleasure." Yet this commonplace too was polarized along gender lines: "profit" was seen as masculine and "pleasure" feminine; "profit" was linked to romance's treatment of war, "pleasure" to its treatment of love. Thus, the conventional "feminization" of the romance audience reveals further anxiety about the "femininity" of the reading pleasures it offered. Now that we have recovered the genre's diverse readership beyond the legend of its feminization, we also can recover its diverse uses beyond the dyad of "profit and pleasure." Renaissance romances were complex in their address to their audience, formal construction, and engagement with social issues; those subtleties were meaningful to both men and women. Romance "profits" were not exclusive to male readers, nor its "pleasures" to women readers. This essay replaces old truisms about Renaissance romance audiences with new questions about their profits and pleasures. It shifts from prose romance's derogation along gender lines to its positive contributions to the history of gendered reading, showing how the early Renaissance habit of consigning romance to women was replaced in the mid-seventeenth century by a growing appreciation of the genre, and grounded in new reading practices shared across genders.

For the prose romances that poured from London's presses through the sixteenth and seventeenth centuries, Horace's *utile et dulce* was the dominant generic rationale, conventionally repeated on title pages and in prefaces. Of course Horace's formulation, originally referring to poetry, was borrowed by most of the Renaissance genres, but none relied on it more heavily than prose romance. Beyond the newly recovered antecedents of the Greek romances, there was no classical theory justifying or governing prose narrative (Salzman 1999). Fiction's claim to dual benefit has often been mocked: narrative gives a sugar-coating to moral lessons, or spurious benefits to excuse guilty pleasures. Yet as we learn more about how and why romance was used by early modern writers and readers, the interdependence of profit and pleasure looks genuine and complex. If "profit and pleasure" elides worries that pleasure ran ahead of profit in romance's draw, it also names a dawning confidence, most explicit in Sir Philip Sidney's *Defense of Poetry*, that prose narrative could fulfill Horace's serious ambitions for poetry, indeed had unique capacities for "delightful teaching" (Sidney 1970: 21). While other genres were defined by form, romance was defined by its responsiveness to readers' needs and desires (N. Smith 1994: 234). However, such responsiveness slid easily toward the pole of feminized pleasure, making romance the genre most compromised by the discounting of women's reading – and most renewed when women's reading practices were embraced by men.

The association of Renaissance romance with women offers indirect access to the genre's gendered meanings, which prove to be highly contradictory. Literary references to a feminized romance audience are problematized by the predominance of male readers in the archival records, and the paucity of women authors writing in the genre. The profits that male romance authors and tellers of anecdotes reap by stressing the "feminine" qualities of romances militate against women readers taking pleasure from reading those romances. The fashionable habit of discriminating against romance as reading for uneducated women contradicts the growing interest of gentle readers of both sexes in new romance forms. By the end of the Renaissance, the derided taste for romance had wrought real changes in the practices of reading in leisure.

As men and women continued to find profit and pleasure in romance throughout the Renaissance, the genre's gender coding and perceived value altered considerably. For most of the period, romance could be justified only by insisting on its moralizing profits and defusing its indulgent pleasures – in short, by justifying the reading of romance to *men*. Reading for the profitable study of moral (though fictional) examples was common among educated men. Such profitable reading of romance was recommended to, shared with, or undertaken by women as well, more than has been acknowledged. On the other hand, reading romance for the pleasure of losing one's self in narrative was also familiar to men, although recurrently displaced onto women. The later seventeenth century saw an alternative approach that deconstructed the line between profit and pleasure. This approach celebrated not the reading practices of humanism, which were intensive, purposive, and rhetorical, but those practices once relegated to women and the uneducated, which were extensive, relaxed, and empathetic. This freer pleasure in reading increased in respectability with the late seventeenth century's more elevated romance forms, and would itself be redefined as aesthetic profit to justify the eighteenth-century novel.

How did Renaissance literature feminize the readership of romance? During Elizabeth's reign, prose romances increasingly featured or addressed women in titles, prefaces, narrative frames, asides to readers, and characterizations. The sheer number of such appeals seems to portray women as the majority of romance readers, as do dramatic and poetic texts satirizing women as addicted to the genre. However, this literary evidence cannot be taken at face value, for such appeals and satires partake of widespread Renaissance conventions for constructing and differentiating audiences. Elizabethan romance authors were especially brilliant at manipulating rhetorics of audience, at once soliciting patronage or purchase, experimenting with narrative form, establishing authority, and negotiating class and gender distinctions. Through the convention that Juliet Fleming (1993) calls "the ladies' text," male writers offered romances to female readers, adding disparagements that indirectly solicited the weightier approval of male readers. The convention apparently discharged ambivalence about the genre, widely felt by male readers and by male writers themselves. The ladies' text convention, however, both over-represents women readers' numbers and influence in the literary marketplace, and under-represents men's interest in romance. Decoding the convention may not yield a firmer estimate of the gender balance of romance readership, but it can recover more of the rich profits and pleasures that early readers derived from romance.

The first indicator that Renaissance romances made new appeals to women readers is a simple rise in titles that include women's names. This change in titling is particularly striking in the English tradition. In most of the English chivalric romances published before 1558, "the hero was the dominant character, and the male name was usually given to the story" (Hull 1982: 78). By the middle of Elizabeth's reign, several romances had been titled after a female protagonist alone, including Robert Greene's *Mamillia* (1583) and *Penelopes Web* (1587), and Thomas Lodge's *Rosalynde* (1590). Titles featuring women perhaps flattered Elizabeth (indirectly, for no prose romance directly named a *Faerie Queene*) or appealed to ordinary female readers; they may have invited male readers to possess a feminized text or asked them to sympathize with a female protagonist. All that can be claimed with certainty is a new interest in women's responses (if not their subjectivities). The focus continued in the mid-seventeenth century, when women were the central, titular characters in such long, politically pointed romances as *Parthenissa* (1651–69), *The Princess Cloria* (1653, 1661), *Theophania* (1655), *Panthalia* (1659), and *Aretina* (1660).

English Renaissance romances increasingly were framed by epistles to gentle-women readers, dedications to individual gentlewomen, or embedded remarks to "ladies." Indeed, the authorial appeal to female readers, collective or specific, became a signature feature of Elizabethan romance (though, again, no prose romance is dedi-cated to the monarch, confirming the genre's problematic standing). Early hints of this romance motif come from Italy: Boccaccio's narrator says that *Decameron* (written 1351–3) "should much rather be offered to the charming ladies than the men" (quoted in Fleming 1993: 159). This gallantry figures the book as a single man addressing a group of ladies, while in the book's frame, young men and women exchange tales of love on an equal footing. However, only male authors published Italian prose *novelle*. In mid-sixteenth-century collections by Matteo Bandello, Giam-battista Giraldi Cinthio, and Giovan Francesco Straparola (the latter's narrators are all women), a pose of address to ladies excuses male readers' interest in themes of love. Such asides to women readers are carried into English fiction via translated *novelle*, as in William Painter's *Palace of Pleasure* in three parts (1566, 1567, 1575), and Geoffrey Fenton's *Certaine Tragicall Discourses* (1567), and in George Pettie's more original "A Petite Pallace of Pettie his Pleasure" (1576). Pettie's narrator teasingly invites putative women readers to judge the stories' lovers. Above all, Pettie's collection gives the address to women a prefatory place of its own: a letter by one "R.B." is addressed "To the gentle Gentlewomen Readers," and begins, "Gentle Readers, who by my will I would have onely Gentlewomen" (2).

Several other English authors of fiction of the 1570s quickly imitated this example of a collective preface to women readers, nearly always with a preface to gentlemen as a counterbalance. Such gender play with the romance preface reached its zenith in John Lyly's *Euphues and His England* (1580), the sequel to his hugely popular *Euphues The Anatomy of Wit* (1578):

> I am content that your Dogges lye in your laps, so *Euphues* may be in your hands, that when you shall be wearie in reading of the one, you may be ready to sport with the other; or handle him as you doe your Junkets . . . for if you be filled with the first part, put the second in your pocket for your wayting Maydes: *Euphues* had rather lye shut in a Ladyes casket, then open in a Schollers studie. (9)

Lyly introduces fantasies about women's reading that later male romance-writers repeatedly echo: romance is a special taste of women, a generic sweet tooth; it is shared between ladies and their maids in cross-class intimacy; and the book itself is a Trojan fetish, giving male authors (and readers) illicit entry into women's fantasy lives. The reference to the "Schollers studie," however, signals rhetorical calculation, and suggests an educated male audience as the real audience for the sexual fantasy. The epistle continues, no longer concealing Lyly's contempt for the work of romance: "I would you would read bookes that have more shewe of pleasure, then ground of profit, then should Euphues be as often in your hands, being but a toy, as Lawne on your heads, being but trash" (10). Lyly labels pleasure as an ephemeral show, like fashion.

In doing so, Lynette McGrath comments, he also "acknowledges – and of course seeks to exploit for his own profit – women's ability to choose their reading pleasures" (2002: 106). Paradoxically, the unprofitability of romance, "being but trash," profits his reputation.

These ostensible appeals to women in titles and dedications merged in the feminine possessive title that Philip Sidney invented for *The Countess of Pembroke's Arcadia* (probably begun in 1579). Drawing his sister's aristocratic title into that of his romance, Sidney identifies his ambitious *jeu d'esprit* with a particular and exemplary noblewoman. Exceptionally, this ladies' text really was written for ladies: Sidney sent the romance "sheet by sheet" to Mary Sidney, or at times read it aloud to her and her "fair ladies," as narratorial asides suggest (Duncan Jones 1994: xiii). Beyond the family circle, however, Sidney also allowed a male coterie to read the romance in manuscript. Still, more than any previous address to women, Sidney's title "bestows a position as subject to a woman" and "grants to (the Countess's) reading a determinative role in the very production" of the work (Lamb 1990: 22). Indeed, the Countess did ultimately determine how the romance should be produced, more than Sidney could have anticipated: when his premature death and posthumous fame forced the publication of the romance, she gave his dedicatory letter for the first, incomplete edition of 1590, and assisted in the merging of two unfinished manuscripts into the composite edition of 1593. Later, however, the female subjectivity conjured by Sidney's romance would be more erotic than authorial.

If women readers of romance were a byword, why are traces of their readership and authorship so rare? The rhetorical linking of romance and women is corroborated by only the thinnest archival evidence of readership and female authorship. Before 1650, the readers of romance who left such traces as library inventories, commonplace books quoting romances, and signed and dated personal copies were, overwhelmingly, men. Helen Hackett has gathered the extant evidence of historic women reading romance titles. The most remarkable example is Lady Anne Clifford (1590–1676), who read the *Arcadia* many times, often with company. It was painted with other favorite titles in the retrospective portrait of her 16-year-old self (in the left frame of her triptych "Great Picture," painted in 1646); her diary for 1617 records a maid reading the work aloud; and Clifford's copy of the 1605 edition notes having read it "all ower" again during winter 1651 (Hackett 2002: 7). Clifford's sharing of the work with her maid does not fulfill Lyly's voyeuristic fantasies about romance, for the women similarly shared devotional and historical reading.

Few early modern women of any class recorded their reading choices as Clifford did. Keeping a reading list was a habit of scholars, and keeping a diary a novelty and luxury until mid-century, when nonconformist sects urged written self-examination. Naturally, that habit went along with devotional, not secular, reading choices: spiritual autobiographies speak frankly and specifically of the attractions of romance, even as their authors swear off the sinful books of youth. The tale of temptation, immersion, and renunciation is similar, whether the romance came in the form of cheap redactions of native chivalric tales or tomes of heroic romances, and whether the life-writer is male or female. The devout Lady Elizabeth Delaval rued having "vainley passed the blossom time of my life" on romance instead of reading "in such books as teach us heavenly wisdom." Her *Meditations*, written in her twenties, report reading four multi-volume French heroic romances when she was "but some few months past ten years old" (around 1659): a precocious literary blossoming (quoted in Charlton 1987: 467).

Statistical estimates stumble, counting not women readers of romance, but women readers of anything at all. Signatures on parish records, the basis for early modern "literacy" rates, in fact estimate ability in writing, not reading. Since children learned to read fluently before they started writing, those withdrawn early from school, including many women, may have been well-read, in romance and other genres, but lacked skills to write (Spufford 1982: 21–6). The depressingly low "literacy" rates for women are therefore a distortion in the historical record that makes women readers of romance more elusive, and the need to infer their existence more pressing.

Given that educational practice, it is not surprising that romance authorship, like readership, is dominated by men. Two Englishwomen are known to have published or written prose romances before 1650, and then only a handful more during the 1650s. Their circumstances are surprisingly distinct, and their courage evident. In 1578, an obscure but prescient woman named Margaret Tyler was the first person to publish an installment of a Peninsular romance in English translation, setting off a trend that male translators like Anthony Munday would exploit for decades. She apparently learned Spanish while in domestic service abroad. Her preface stoutly justifies the right of women to publish their own writing, much as men have "dedicated their labours, some stories, some of warre . . . some as concerning governent, some divine matters, unto diverse Ladies & gentlewomen." Making the most of the paradox of "the ladies' text," she reasons: "may we women read such of their works as they dedicate unto us . . . then it is all one for a woman to pen a story, as for a man to addresse his story to a woman" (quoted in Krontiris 1988: 23). Unlike later male writers, Tyler claims no female affinity for the chivalric cycles. Defending women's capacity to write about a genre of war, she defies later stereotypes that feminized romance as a genre of love.

During the Elizabethan heyday of the ladies' text, no other woman published an original or translated romance. A generation after Sidney used his noble sister's name to elevate his romance, his niece, Lady Mary Wroth, boldly borrowed his strategy for her own ambitious prose romance, *The Countesse of Mountgomeries Urania* (1621). The subjectivity that Sidney granted to his sister as a woman *reader* of romance ultimately licensed his niece as a woman *writer* of romance. For the first time, the romance was an original text of, by, and for the ladies. *Urania's* interwoven plots, narrated by both women and men, repeatedly explore female constancy and male inconstancy. Even more boldly, Wroth turned *roman à clef* references against her own circles, portraying one male aristocrat so scandalously that he circulated a verse epistle defaming her. Wroth wrote to him promising to have the work recalled, but 29 copies survive, including at least one with a female owner's signature on the flyleaf (Hackett 2000:

9). In 1651, a "young Gentle-woman" named Anna Weamys published a continuation of Sidney's incomplete *Arcadia*, again demonstrating its "narrative generosity" to women (Hackett 2000: 109–10).

Also writing after 1650, Margaret Cavendish and Aphra Behn risked moral and critical disapproval for their fearless romances. In her *Poems and Fancies* (1653), Cavendish explicitly alluded to the defamation of Wroth, commenting that men might well tell her to "*let writing* Books *alone*," as they had said "to the Lady that wrote the *Romancy*" (quoted in Hackett 2000: 183). Cavendish rewrote male ambivalence about romance: her autobiographical writings expressed contempt for women's reading of "romancies," while her own prose fictions, "The Contract" and "Assaulted and Pursued Chastity" (1656), repeat the condemnation yet rework the form (Hackett 2000: 184–5). Cavendish reconciled that ambivalence more fully in her astonishing *New Blazing World* (1666), which she described as part "*romancical*," part "philosophical," and part "*fantastical*" ("To the Reader"). Its heroine's planned elopement leads to a fantastic journey of discovery, female friendship, and authorship. While Cavendish's journey into published authorship was underwritten by her husband, the Duke of Newcastle, Aphra Behn actually supported herself by writing plays and prose fiction. Although such an enterprise was considered scandalous for a woman, Behn exploited her worldly reputation to write frankly about the hypocrisies of Restoration courtship, overturning the niceties of familiar romances in works like "The Unfortunate Happy Lady" (1696). For these five women writers, romance yielded at least intangible profits. Their evident pleasure in writing romance has been multiplied with their works' revival in modern classrooms.

What did male authors gain by stressing the "feminine" qualities of their romances? Elizabethan romance authors constructed women's reading as trivial, credulous, oversexed, or even dangerous, pretending to find the genre pleasurable only to women, and profitless to anyone. By exaggerating the profitlessness of romance, they posed as prodigals wasting their talents on women readers. This strategy may have been intended to profit the authors by advertising to *male* readers their fitness for weightier writing tasks (Helgerson 1976). Pushing further, Hackett, Fleming, and Lorna Hutson have argued that in appealing to women, romances compensate for male authors' shame at needing to publish their works (rather than finding patrons in an older tradition of authorship). For Fleming, Elizabethan romances are "ladies' texts" in an ironic, even violent, sense: they offset the degradation of publication in other men's eyes by rhetorically seducing female readers. Hutson argues that this homosocial strategy of seducing a woman to gain prestige in male eyes is enacted not just in prefatorial frames, but also at the level of plot in prose works: in Geoffrey Fenton's *Certaine Tragicall Discourses*, the heroine herself is "reduced to a profitable ground plot of invention" (1994: 98).

The self-contradictory gender positioning of Elizabethan romance is exemplified by Riche's *Farewell to Military Profession* (1581). The title page insists that this collection of novellas from the Italian is "Gathered together for the onely delight of the courteous Gentlewomen, bothe of Englande and Irelande, for whose onely pleasure thei were collected together." The claim of a solely female audience is undercut by the second epistle, to "Noble Soldiers," in which Riche dismisses the work as written only "to keep myself from idleness." The tales within the collection reward women for submission to men (Relihan 1994; Hackett 2000: 86). Despite Riche's evident contempt for his material, the work reached six editions by 1616. Similarly, Robert Greene's romances referred to female readers with a regularity beyond convention, but, as Hull notes (1982: 81), "none of his books has a direct dedication to women" as a group. Instead, many works included a "feminine" subtitle, a dedication to a prospective patroness, or a verse addressed to "ladies" – always counterpoised by a letter "to the gentlemen readers" or "to the gentle readers" (addressed as males). Even the frame-tales that took female virtues as their primary topics – the *Myrrour of Modestie* (1584) and *Penelopes Web ... a Christall Myrror of Faeminine Perfection* (1587) – maintained the usual addresses to gentlemen readers. The strategy creates a putative double audience, but with the rhetorical advantage given to male readers and the ideological burden placed on women, readers or not.

Although Greene's celebration of women's virtue earned him the epithet "Homer of women" (surely a left-handed compliment), modern critics question whether such a narrative could have pleased early modern women dedicatees or readers. For instance, *Penelopes Web* is dedicated to two noblewomen, the Countesses of Cumberland and Warwick, yet its epistle to "gentlemen readers" discounts such an appeal:

> I adventure to present what I write to your judgementes, hoping as my intent is to please all ... I was determined at the first to have made no appeale to your favorable opinions, for that the matter is womens prattle, about the untwisting of Penelopes Web. But ... *Mars* will sometime bee prying into *Venus* papers, and gentlemen desirous to hear the parlie of Ladies. (Grosart 5: 144–5)

After promising "to please all," Greene implies that women are easily pleased by "prattle," but that "gentlemen readers" exercise sterner "judgementes" – even over material in which they claim only vicarious interest. Yet that judgment quickly deteriorates to Lyly-like voyeurism: men wish to "pry into" women's written secrets or hear their "parlie." Like Boccaccio or Straparola, Greene frames his tales as women's narrations, but unlike those teasing Italian writers, his women are generally mouth-pieces for patriarchal teachings. *Penelopes Web* promises to give voice to women, then makes its women tell stories commending silence (Relihan 1994; Alwes 2000). In Greene's work, the role of women in textual creation and exchange unravels as fast as it is woven. An Elizabethan romance like *Penelopes Web* not only prevaricates about its appeal to women, but makes its appeal to men by insulting women, "requir[ing] its female readers to attend to the story of their own rejection" (Fleming 1993:161).

However, misogyny alone is too blunt an instrument to anatomize the ladies' text, produced by specific conditions of authorship, print culture, and gendered readership. As Fleming acknowledges, it is difficult to untangle the complex anxieties driving the convention:

Fear of the class impropriety of printing [publishing] a text may be disguised as a hesitation about doing it in front of women, and this fact alone could account for the prevalence of the ladies' text in early modern England. On the other hand, the interlock of the languages of print and gender could be read from its other end, so that "print anxiety" stands for a more generalized anxiety concerning the presence of women in the political and linguistic communities of early modern England. (1993: 163–4)

The association of this strategy with romance suggests that romance figured the new amplitude of print much as women readers figured the new breadth of the reading audience.

Significantly, the ladies' text strategy gendered men's acts of reading as well as women's. Men's disavowal of romance, by shifting anxieties about publication onto women, suppressed their knowledge of the genre's literary importance and social efficacy. Men's displacement of reading pleasures onto women's bodies made their own reading pleasure into a kind of "transvestite" experience (Fleming 1993: 158). These constructions would have to be undone to enable the mid-century recovery of romance as a profitable genre.

Why would women have enjoyed reading romances that seem to reproduce patriarchal values? Period stereotypes suggested that women read romances, especially chivalric translations, to indulge fantasies of sexual compliance. A 1615 prose satire describes a chambermaid who "reads Greenes workes over and over, but is so carried away with the *Myrrour of Knighthood*, she is many times resolv'd to run out of her selfe, and become a Ladie Errant" (Overbury 2003: 242). Men assumed that women read for sexualized pleasure, not considering that they could have read for profit, perhaps even for the profit of reflecting on gender constraints. Certainly archival records like Clifford's suggest that Lyly's preface and this chambermaid satire grossly exaggerate the titillation of women's romance reading. Nonetheless, as Hackett, Tina Krontiris, and Mary Ellen Lamb argue, romances *could* have allowed subversive reading experiences, for instance, by inviting women's capacity to love in the face of social obstacles. Drawing cautiously on Janice Radway's argument about contemporary women's reading of romance, these critics argue that in the Renaissance too, even apparently misogynist tales could be read to resistant ends (Krontiris 1988: 28). Furthermore, McGrath suggests (2002: 116), given men's hostility to women's reading of romance, women's choice of the genre for reading material constituted an act of resistance in itself. To appreciate women's pleasure in romance reading – itself, I have proposed, profitable in negotiating gender ideologies – we must read between the lines of men's fears.

According to McGrath (2002: 106), "In the cultural effort to control the experiences of readerly and writerly pleasure in women, the dominant ideology supported a wished-for overriding of pleasure by profit, and also at the same time needed constantly to countermand the inevitable alternative." Condemnations of romance-reading women dwelt on this danger of pleasure overriding profit. When they recognized that women did gain a measure of agency through exercising their will to read, if not through their reading matter, that agency was portrayed as mere pleasure, not profit. For instance, the gestures toward fashionable court ladies made by Rich, Pettie, and Lyly may acknowledge women's presence in court circles and desire for advancement. In 1617, Fynes Moryson recommended *Amadis de Gaule* as cosmopolitan reading since "the knights Errant and the Ladies of Courts doe therein exchange courtly speeches," – an acknowledgement that men and women both might exercise power by speaking the language of romance at court.

Some men gently portray women's acquisition of romance literacy in a mild rivalry with men; interestingly, this admission circulates especially in manuscript form. In his Jacobean manuscript poem *Fido*, William Browne has a chambermaid identify a letter of praise from a wooer to her mistress as "stol'n from *Palmerin* or *Amadis*" – again, chivalric romances (quoted in Newcomb 2002: 108–9). Browne jokingly reverses the homosocial ladies' text trope: he writes a scene of social rivalry between women, with a man as the victim. According to an anecdote in a manuscript of ca. 1655:

> A gentleman complimenting with a lady in pure Sir Philip Sidney, she was so well verst in his author, as tacitely she traced him to the bottome of a leafe, where (his memorie failing) he brake off abruptly. "Nay, I beseech you, Sir," says shee, "proceede and turn over the leafe, for methinke the best part is still behinde;" which unexpected discovery silenc't him for every after. (quoted in Garrett 1996: 22)

As the lady coolly promises that turning the leaf of the book will reveal its "best part ... still behinde," she extends her personal pleasures to elite readers of the anecdote – but only by denying them to the "silenc't" gentleman, who has lagged "behinde" her expertise.

Although we might sympathize with women readers' capacity to wield romance knowledge, acquiring such cultural literacy was repeatedly seen as a feminine sin, both personally and socially destructive. The accusation is harshest in the early humanists: Juan Luis Vives scolded that "verily they be but foolishe husbandes and madde, that suffer their wives to waxe more ungraciously subtyle by readinge of soche bokes," and Heinrich Bullinger warned that "Beves of Hampton [the English verse romance] ... and such lyke fables do but kyndle in lyers lyke lyes and wanton love" (quoted in Hackett 2000: 10). In 1609, the Earl of Northumberland warned his son against wives who would read "an Arcadia, or some love discourses, to make them able to entertain a stranger upon a hearth in a Privy Chamber" (Roberts 1988: 44). Even Cavendish echoed this fear: "The truth is, the chief study of our Sex is Romances, wherein reading, they fall in love with the feigned Heroes and Carpet-Knights, with whom their Thoughts secretly commit Adultery, and in their conversation and manner ... they imitate the Romancy-Ladies" (quoted in Charlton 1987: 467). If romance did not teach women to sin, it could invite them to imagine sinning. Yet this oft-repeated warning against romance reading itself may be reinterpreted: perhaps patriarchs feared that romances could model not falling from virtue, but resistance to abuse.

Why, if men insisted that romance was idle, was it relied on to furnish so many kinds of profit to both men and women? Throughout the English Renaissance, male writers and readers used the genre to treat war and love, to test questions of politics, class, nation, gender, and representation. For all their dismissal of romance to women, men led the way in articulating the unique value of its capaciousness and indirection – a value that women readers and writers also tapped. Men's deep commitment to the genre's profits required their belated acceptance of its pleasures.

Sidney's *Apology for Poetry* located fiction's profits in its "feigning of notable examples of virtue, vice, and what else" (1970: 21). Although elegant, Sidney's defense of fiction on those grounds is disingenuous, and his *Arcadia* made far greater demands than this on its readers. Naive theories of emulation persisted through the period, but Sidney was not the only reader to know that romance could do much more than make speaking pictures. He granted some value to chivalric romances, though humanists had decried them as works whose "whole pleasure ... standeth in two special points, in open manslaughter and bold bawdry" (Adams 1959: 33). As Roger Ascham's *Scholemaster* (1570) extends this tirade against sinful Elizabethan romances, his distrust centers not on their usual sexual pleasures, but on their misplaced political lessons. Ascham fears that these Italianate fictions will operate as papist spies: "and bicause our English men made *Italians* can not hurt but certaine persons, and in certaine places, therfore these *Italian* bookes are made English, to bryng mischief enough openly and boldly to all states, great and meane, yong and old, every where" (Smith 1904: 1:4; Maslen 1997). Italianate books entice readers to the humid thrills of papistry, and worse, they recruit them as spies themselves by teaching deceptive fiction-spinning skills. Ascham's fears intuit a power of fiction beyond the prevailing theory of emulation: fiction teaches not only through the examples it represents, but also through the ways of reading it models and invites. Indeed, many Elizabethan writers did recognize that romance could persuade, more or less covertly. Later, in the seventeenth century, authors and readers theorized what Ascham only guessed, and the processes of encryption and decryption, rather than the examples encoded, became the real profit and pleasure of romance.

Although Elizabethan romance authors were haunted by a sense of delinquency, by the sense that they wrote romance because more active service was not available to them, their romances were more topical, or at least politically efficacious, than they appeared. In the self-reflexive fictions of Lyly's *Euphues* and its sequel, Sidney's *Arcadia*, and George Gascoigne's *Adventures of Master F.J.* (1573/5), marginalized courtiers displayed, or at least, displaced, personal and political intrigue in the artistry of emplotment and persuasion. Like the prodigal-son narratives of Greene (published 1585–92), the cynical international adventures of Thomas Nashe's *Unfortunate Traveller* (1594) and Lodge's *A Margarite of America* (1596) explored the limitations of humanist codes (Helgerson 1976, Kinney 1986).

Seventeenth-century readers cultivated the art of decryption known as "application," in which selected readers read a text in selective ways (Zwicker 1998). Through application, romance readers undid fiction's displacement and reattached narrative to their personal and political lives. In the Caroline period, responding to what Annabel Patterson (1984) has called the "royal romance" of Charles and Henrietta Maria, the genre acquired a central role, addressing politics in the guise of love. As Martin Butler puts it, "romance and high politics are related activities; they share a vocabulary of 'courtship,' 'intrigue,' and 'service'" (quoted in Henderson and Siemon 1996: 110). Drawing on that duality to produce encrypted meanings, romance became the "secret" signature of the Caroline court and of Interregnum royalism (Potter 1989). Nigel Smith (1994: 236) argues that the phenomenon was even wider: "Romance was seen to be a political form by members of both sides in the political conflict," so that there were parliamentarian as well as royalist romances.

International strategies evolved for writing romances as *romans à clef*, and using application to read them. These strategies indirectly gave new weight to women readers. The idea of a long, primarily political prose romance was originated by John Barclay's *Argenis* (1621), written in Latin and translated into English several times. In the 1650s a longer, more heroic political romance began to appear in France. Barclay and the French heroic romance were imitated by well-read Interregnum writers of romance. Patterson proposes that *Clélie* (1654–61) debates, in embedded addresses, the "paired propositions that romance is not a serious form, and that women are not serious readers" (1994: 187). Apparently, readers of the period did not know that *Clélie*'s author was a woman, not Monsieur but Madame de Scudéry. If their female authorship was suppressed, the French heroic romances nonetheless provided a new role for women with their emphasis on the "unwritten events" behind court culture (Patterson 1994: 188–9).

No wonder, then, that most of these English political romances are named for women, from Barclay's *Argenis* to the anonymous *Theophania* (1655), *Panthalia* (attributed to Richard Braithwaite; 1659), Sir Percy Herbert's *The Princess Cloria* (1661), Sir George McKenzie's *Aretina* (tellingly subtitled *The Serious Romance*, 1660), and Roger Boyle, first Earl of Orrery's *Parthenissa* (1651–69). Each woman functions in an allegory that is political and also generic: "If Barclay's Argenis was the emblem of hereditary monarchy in France, and the Princess Cloria of England's national honor, Panthalia is the emblem of the historical romance itself" (Patterson 1994: 200). When the heroines of the Interregnum romance stand for allegorical principles while inviting the reading practice of application, they figure that practice as feminine. With them, romance achieved a new level of seriousness that need neither disavow nor exaggerate the female. Indeed, the English romances did interest both male and female readers, if not the large numbers of female readers apparently tackling Scudéry's French political romances. It is to the letter-writer Dorothy Osborne that we owe any awareness of two lost Interregnum romances, one by the royalist poet Edmund Waller, the other by the parliamentarian Lord Saye and Sele. Osborne comments that Waller's romance, if it "do's not mingle with a great deal of pleasing fiction cannot bee very diverting sure, the Subject is soe sad" (1987: 132). Osborne bridges profit and pleasure: a book on political events that she finds tragic will require leavening to be readable. She also evinces a growing sense, among both men and women readers, that romance applied to personal as well as national histories.

In the large and gifted family of the Earl of Cork, a daughter and two sons drew on romance reading to reflect on their lives, though in divergent ways. Cork gave his daughter Mary a copy of *Arcadia* when she was 12 (in 1636), and "devoured romances" in French (Mendelson 1987: 65). Grown up, Mary Rich, Countess of Warwick, repudiated her youthful romance reading in her spiritual memoirs. Her brother Robert, a 10-year-old convalescent (in 1637), "read the strange Adventures Amadis de Gaule [sic]; & other Fabulous & wandring Storys," which engaged his "restlesse Fancy." He grew up to become the distinguished scientist Robert Boyle. He recollected that youthful reading in the late 1640s, while his older brother Roger was drafting *Parthenissa*, reflecting through romance on his ambiguous place in the conflict (Hunter 1994: xvii, xxi). Each of these three brilliant young people both read romance avidly and wrote some form of autobiography. Their bridging of narrative forms confirms Nigel Smith's point that the inset tales of seventeenth-century romances taught a "fictionalised kind of selfhood" so that "where romances were read, they could become the dominant way in which an individual understood him or herself" (1994: 243).

How did the taste for romance make reading practices, men's and women's, more extensive, relaxed, and empathetic? Period comments mocking women's romance reading as insatiable, idle, and credulous recognize at some level that romances invited *all* readers to habits of reading that challenged period norms. These, as the last generation's work on the history of the book has reconstructed them, are intensive and extractive, purposeful, and detached (Zwicker 1998). Educated readers of the Renaissance were trained to digest books systematically though respectfully: to annotate, pull out apothegms, construct indices, compile commonplace books, compare, and translate. Lois Potter notes that the marginalia in a 1625 edition of Barclay's *Argenis* marks useful information, not just about politics, but also about animals; for this reader, Barclay's romance is not an "escapist fantasy," or even an exercise in political theory, but "a realistic genre from which much can be learned" (1989: 75). Although traditions from scholasticism to classical humanism to Protestantism shared this emphasis on intensive reading, Roger Chartier (1992) reminds us that more extensive reading experiences also existed; these were identified disproportionately with women (as, earlier, orality had been). The "rapid, inattentive, almost unconscious kind of reading habit" that Ian Watt links to the novel (1957: 49) can be linked to the reading of any fiction genre, particularly in an age of print (Ballaster 1992; Roberts 1998). The effects of extensive, relaxed, empathetic reading were first portrayed in the eponymous hero of *Don Quixote*, compelled to reenact romance plots because he could not read selectively or dispassionately. His characterization reflects the impact of printed chivalric romances on Spain: some 150 titles in the sixteenth century alone (Patchell 1947: 5).

In England, where the printed romance was more strongly tied to the emergence of female and popular literacy, male ambivalence about reading print for pleasure was

displaced onto women, especially lower-class women. Romance was constantly portrayed as downmarket. Its reputation for responsiveness to audiences pulled it
downward as its reputation for flexible political reference tried to pull it up.
Ultimately, romance was recovered for serious attention not by the assertion of its
profit and condemnation of its pleasures, but by the recommendation of its pleasures
to a more exclusive readership. A class line was drawn between popular and elite
romance forms, between credulous and knowing versions of female readers. In the
sixteenth century, the new audiences for printed romance were discounted so rapidly
that first chivalric imports and then native romances, even Sidney's *Arcadia*, were
relegated not just to women readers but to women *servant* readers. In the Jacobean
period and beyond, writers recover the literary and political capacities of romance by
splitting myths about its audience. That public commodity, cheap printed romance,
is left to the maidservant; the private grace of reading longer romances is elevated by
association with gentlewoman readers.

Print allowed for extensive readers: voracious, nonselective, passive, and hooked on
the formula. Romance seems to be the first genre seen as addictive because formulaic.
That addictive quality was admitted not to be exclusive to women; after all, Spain's
most famous romance addict was a (fictional) man. Before Don Quixote came Teresa
of Avila, whose spiritual autobiography confessed her youthful addiction, abetted by
her mother, to chivalric romances. To Teresa, growing up in the 1520s at the start of
the chivalric fad, "it seemed to me no evil to waste many hours of the day and of the
night in such a vain exercise, even though hidden from my father . . . if I didn't have a
new book, I could not be happy." In her provocative argument for continuity between
romance and novel, Margaret Doody takes Teresa's confession as a cultural watershed
in the history of pleasure reading, showing "no less than in Don Quixote an appetite
that could be at once stimulated and gratified by the new invention: the printing
press" (1996: 214).

Romance had always invited readers to lose themselves in narrative; printed
romance, offering an endless array of new titles, invited them to lose themselves
over and over again. A notoriously dilatory, infinitely expandable genre met the
technology for endless reproduction, and yet romance readers imply they could not
get enough. Richard Taverner, a devotional writer, admitted in 1545 that when he
found romances, he "gredily rede and rede agayne" (quoted in Charlton 1987: 452);
the 1615 chambermaid was said to read "Greenes works over and over"; and even
Margaret Clifford read *Arcadia* "all ower" late in life. But by the time that enforced
leisure and political reversals sent royalists and republicans to read and write
multiple-volume political romances, extensive reading had become acceptable behavior for well-educated Englishmen.

Similarly, the argument that romance reading was idle was reworked into a claim
that some romance reading was elegantly, gracefully relaxed. Jacobean male writers
claimed that women read the *Arcadia*, English translations of chivalric romances, and
shorter Elizabethan romances such as Greene's to indulge sexualized reading pleasures.
By the Caroline period, that claim had been divided by class, so that some works were

sexually damning and others erotically complimentary. The impact of this division of romance readership by class is most felt in the case of *Arcadia*. As Patterson puts it (1984: 171), Sidney's romance became "the center of a little Renaissance" in the Caroline court. That high reputation was not inevitable, for *Arcadia* risked disapproval with the chivalric romances. Wye Saltonstall, imitating the 1615 chambermaid in his 1631 *Picturae Loquentes*, satirizes a less than virtuous "maid" who "would not willingly dye in Ignorance": "she reades now loves historyes as *Amadis de Gaule* and the *Arcadia*, & in them courts the shaddow of love till she know the substance" (47).

Three years later, another gentle writer defended Sidney against Saltonstall, taking his insinuations as a class insult. The letter "To the Noble Reader" in Anthony Stafford's 1634 *Guide of Honour* rebuts Saltonstall's *ad hominem* attack on Sidney: the "detracting brood...have not spared even *Apollo*'s first-borne, incomparable and inimitable *Sir Phillip Sydney*, whose *Arcadia* they confine only to the reading of Chambermaids; a censure that can proceede from none but the sonnes of Kitchin-maids" (quoted in Garrett 1996). Stafford highlights Saltonstall's demotion of romance by rewriting his "maid" as chambermaid and then kitchenmaid. Stafford implies that Sidney's due is to be read by men, and men of gentle birth.

Stafford's was the most contentious voice in restoring the *Arcadia* as fit for upper-class men and women, helping to make the romance available for the Caroline court's emerging myth. It was a daunting challenge: English romances had been subject to decades of gender and class demotion, and Queen Henrietta Maria's romance exemplars were primarily French. What Stuart writers improvised was a thorough revision of the ladies' text trope: they dropped reference to lower-class women in order to pick up richer details of feminization. From comments like Lyly's they isolated the language of courtly love, the physical luxury amid which gentlewomen read, and the intimacy of gentlewomen (without their maids) and their books. This ensemble of features gave the imagined female readers of *Arcadia* a relaxed detachment, in sharp contrast to the coarse naivety still assigned in allusions to non-elite women as readers of popular and chivalric romances. Such an elevation of women's reading practice was introduced by Francis Quarles in his preface to *Argalus and Parthenia* (1629), his verse adaptation of the *Arcadia*'s famous love story: "Ladies (for in your silken laps I knowe this booke will choose to lye ...) my suit is, that you would be pleased to give the faire *Parthenia* your noble entertainment." The scene plainly alludes to Lyly, insisting more emphatically that these ladies are "noble," their laps "silken." In 1638, Richard Lovelace urged, "Fair ones, breathe: a while lay by / Blessed *Sidney's Arcady*": in the hands of "fair ones," the printed romance was not just purified but "Blessed" (Garrett 1996: 232). Even later, the royalist Charles Cotton's poem, "The Surprize," depicts a nymph warmed to "Desire" by "the happy *Object* of her Eye," "*Sidney*'s living *Arcady*." Finding herself blushing, she has "clos'd the Book" and taken up a "Lute" to "charm each wanton thought" into submission. The book inflames her desires, but also gives her the resources to curb them, even when the male narrator intrudes. Finally, the core charge against the romance – that its temptations will provoke misbehavior in female readers – has been answered – but only for the most socially refined. In their fair hands, this book can give both men and women sensual pleasure and social cachet.

So too, empathetic reading of romance came to be valued, first in women and then in men. The sort of emotional involvement and identification that misled Don Quixote would become the height of sensitive reading to Romantic sensibilities. In a 1998 article, Steven Zwicker pinpoints the cultural validation of empathetic reading in Goethe's *Sorrows of Young Werther* (1774), where two lovers weep together over a book. But then he notes an earlier empathetic reader, condemned rather than validated: Dante's famous portrayal of Francesca, doomed for identifying so much with the Arthurian romance she and Paolo read that they imitated its illicit love (*Inferno* V:137). Dante's episode is a seminal text in the condemnation of romance reading: it names romance as spurring excessive emotional identification, lays the blame disproportionately on the woman, and suppresses the extent to which the writer himself, like romance writers, echoes and emulates the pangs of past lovers. Goethe aestheticizes the act of reading and the immersion of his readers, and rescues empathy for artistic men and women.

Empathy is beginning to be accepted, I would argue, by the mid-seventeenth century in England, thanks to the changing uses of romance. It is not a new kind of reading pleasure, but a newly accepted one. Bullinger had theorized empathetic reading, though disapprovingly, when he wrote that romances would "kyndle in lyers lyke lyes and wanton love" (Hackett 2000: 10). In the very different world of the 1650s, Osborne takes empathy seriously. She asks her distant lover, Sir William Temple, about the characters in *Grand Cyrus*: "tell mee which you have most compassion for" (1987: 124). The word recalls *Don Quixote*, where the innkeeper's daughter says: "It is not the blows that my father likes that I like, but the laments that the knights utter when they are separated from their ladies; and indeed they sometimes make me weep with the compassion I feel for them" (quoted in Patchell 1947: 22). While the innkeeper's daughter is perhaps being mocked as a weak woman, Temple seems to accept and reciprocate Osborne's compassionate reading over the length of their correspondence. In a later letter Osborne responds to Temple: "the Judgment you have made of the fower Lovers I recommended to you do's soe perfectly agree with what I think of them, that I hope it will not Alter when you have read [the rest of] their Story's" (Osborne 1987: 128).

Nigel Smith claims that the inset tales of the mid-century romance newly offer, through their first-person narration, "a direct identification with the reader on the subject of love and morality" (1994: 242). Thus we observe the extraordinary level of identification – and theoretical subtlety – that Osborne reveals in reacting to a character from Scudéry's *Grand Cyrus* in 1653: "I know you will pitty Poore Amestris strangly when you have read her Storry. I'le swear I cryed for her when I read it at first though shee were but an imaginary person" (1987: 125). Crucially, Osborne assumes that Temple will share her feeling of pity. If she does not predict that he will cry, she does not apologize for her reaction as merely feminine. The power of romance to shape worldviews can be measured in Osborne's reaction to Boyle; having mocked one of his verbal tics, she applies it to her own situation (1987: 181). Smith's examples are drawn from the educated, those of Osborne's circle; but the same enthusiasm for reading personally is evident in Francis Kirkman, the erratically educated, headstrong future publisher. In a thinly veiled autobiography published in 1673, he boasted that reading endless chivalric romances made him dream of being a prince's son rather than a young bourgeois – and that the result of this dream was an addiction to romances. Luckily for his readers hooked on the formula, Kirkman kept a large stock of romances.

By the end of the seventeenth century, empathetic reading of romance was taken as seriously as application, and indeed merged with it. Osborne tells Temple that she is infuriated when a woman character in Boyle's *Parthenissa*, whom she read as a heroic resister of war, proves to rise to political resistance merely for love (Osborne 1987: 180). Writing to the man she loves across political lines, Osborne insists that women can read or act, in war or love, for principle as well as for pleasure. A practiced reader in her genre, Osborne still expects romance to lend what earlier writers called profit and pleasure, but the two notions are now seen as inextricable, flexible, powerful, and emotional. We can never fully recover early modern readers' pleasures, or distinguish the pleasures projected by men onto women readers from the uses that shaped shared reading practices. We can discern, however, that their joint impact, over the centuries, made prose romance a respectable genre, and the first defining form of printed pleasure reading. As a much later generation would find the personal to be political, the Renaissance found that in romance, the pleasurable could be profitable.

See also: chapter 1, ANCIENT ROMANCE; chapter 6, MALORY AND THE EARLY PROSE ROMANCES; chapter 8, SIDNEY AND SPENSER; chapter 9, SHAKESPEARE'S ROMANCES; chapter 13, WOMEN'S GOTHIC ROMANCE; chapter 15, "INCONSISTENT RHAPSODIES"; chapter 30, POPULAR ROMANCE AND ITS READERS.

References and Further Reading

Adams, Robert P. (1959). "'Bold Bawdry and Open Manslaughter': The English New Humanist Attack on Medieval Romance." *Huntington Library Quarterly* 23, 33–48.

Alwes, Derek B. (2000). "Robert Greene's Duelling Dedications." *English Literary Renaissance* 30, 373–95.

Ballaster, Ros (1992). *Seductive Forms: Women's Amatory Fiction from 1684 to 1740.* Oxford: Clarendon Press.

Benson, Pamela (1996). *Italian Tales from the Age of Shakespeare.* London: J. M. Dent, and Rutland, VT: Tuttle.

Charlton, Kenneth (1987). "'False Fonde Bookes, Ballades and Rimes': An Aspect of Informal Education." *History of Education Quarterly* 27, 449–71.

Chartier, Roger (1992). "Labourers and Voyagers: From the Text to the Reader." *Diacritics* 22:2, 49–61.

Doody, Margaret Anne (1996). *The True Story of the Novel*. New Brunswick, NJ: Rutgers University Press.

Fleming, Juliet (1993). "The Ladies' Man and the Age of Elizabeth." In James Grantham Turner, ed., *Sexuality and Gender in Early Modern Europe*. Cambridge: Cambridge University Press, pp. 158–81.

Garrett, Martin, ed. (1996). *Sidney: The Critical Heritage*. New York: Routledge.

Grosart, Alexander B., ed. (1881–6). *The Life and Complete Works in Prose and Verse of Robert Greene, MA*. 15 vols. London: Huth Library.

Hackett, Helen (2000). *Women and Romance Fiction in the English Renaissance*. Cambridge: Cambridge University Press.

Helgerson, Richard (1976). *The Elizabethan Prodigals*. Berkeley: University of California Press.

Henderson, Diana E., and James Siemon (1999). "Reading Vernacular Literature." In David Scott Kastan, ed., *A Companion to Shakespeare*. Oxford: Blackwell, pp. 206–22.

Hull, Suzanne W. (1982). *Chaste, Silent and Obedient: English Books for Women 1475–1640*. San Marino, CA: Huntington Library.

Hunter, Michael, ed. (1994). "An Account of Philaretus during his Minority." In *Robert Boyle by Himself and His Friends*. London: William Pickering, pp. 1–22.

Hutson, Lorna (1994). *The Usurer's Daughter: Male Friendship and Fictions of Women in Sixteenth-Century England*. London and New York: Routledge.

Kinney, Arthur (1986). *Humanist Poetics: Thought, Rhetoric, and Fiction in Sixteenth-century England*. Amherst: University of Massachusetts Press.

Krontiris, Tina (1988). "Breaking Barriers of Genre and Gender: Margaret Tyler's Translation of 'The Mirrour of Knighthood.'" *English Literary Renaissance* 18, 19–39.

Krontiris, Tina (1992). *Oppositional Voices: Women as Writers and Translators of Literature in the English Renaissance*. London and New York: Routledge.

Lamb, Mary Ellen (1990). *Gender and Authorship in the Sidney Circle*. Madison: University of Wisconsin Press.

Maslen, R. W. (1997). *Elizabethan Fictions: Espionage, Counter-Espionage, and the Duplicity of Fiction in Early Elizabethan Prose Narratives*. Oxford: Clarendon Press.

McGrath, Lynette (2002). *Subjectivity and Women's Poetry in Early Modern England*. Aldershot and Burlington, VT: Ashgate.

Mendelson, Sara Heller (1987). *Mental Lives of Stuart Women: Three Studies*. Amherst: University of Massachusetts Press.

Newcomb, Lori Humphrey (2002). *Reading Popular Romance in Early Modern England*. New York: Columbia University Press.

O'Connor, J. J. (1970). *Amadis de Gaule and Its Influence on Elizabethan Literature*. New Brunswick, NJ: Rutgers University Press.

Osborne, Dorothy (1987). *Letters to Sir William Temple*, ed. Kenneth Parker. Harmondsworth: Penguin.

Overbury, Sir Thomas (and others) (2003). *Character*, ed., with introduction and notes, by Donald Beecher. Ottawa: Dovehouse Editions.

Patchell, Mary (1947). *The Palmerin Romances in Elizabethan Prose Fiction*. New York: Columbia University Press.

Patterson, Annabel (1984). *Censorship and Interpretation*. Madison: University of Wisconsin Press.

Pearson, Jacquelyn (1996). "Women Reading, Reading Women." In Helen Wilcox, ed., *Women and Literature in Britain, 1500–1700*. Cambridge: Cambridge University Press, pp. 80–99.

Potter, Lois (1989). *Secret Rites and Secret Writing: Royalist Literature 1641–60*. Cambridge: Cambridge University Press.

Radway, Janice (1984). *Reading the Romance: Women, Patriarchy, and Popular Literature*. Chapel Hill: University of North Carolina Press.

Relihan, Constance C. (1994). *Fashioning Authority: The Development of Elizabethan Novelistic Discourse*. Kent, OH: Kent State University Press.

Roberts, Sasha (1998). "Shakespeare 'creepes into the womens closets about bedtime': Women Reading in a Room of Their Own." In Gordon Macmullan, ed., *Renaissance Configurations*. Houndmills: Macmillan, pp. 30–63.

Salzman, Paul (1985). *English Prose Fiction, 1558–1700: A Critical History*. Oxford: Clarendon Press.

Salzman, Paul (1999). "Theories of Prose Fiction in England: 1558–1700." In Glyn P. Norton, ed., *The Cambridge History of Literary Criticism*. Cambridge: Cambridge University Press, pp. 295–304.

Salzman, Paul, ed. (1987). *An Anthology of Elizabethan Prose Fiction*. Oxford and New York: Oxford University Press.

Salzman, Paul, ed. (1991). *An Anthology of Seventeenth-century Fiction*. Oxford and New York: Oxford University Press.

Sidney, Sir Philip (1970). *An Apology for Poetry*, ed. Forrest G. Robinson. Indianapolis: Bobbs Merrill.

Smith, G. Gregory (1904). *Elizabethan Critical Essays*. 2 vols. London: Oxford University Press.

Smith, Nigel (1994). *Literature and Revolution in England, 1640–1660*. New Haven and London: Yale University Press.

Spufford, Margaret (1982). *Small Books and Pleasant Histories: Popular Fiction and its Readership in Seventeenth-century England*. Athens: University of Georgia Press.

Watt, Ian (1957). *The Rise of the Novel*. Berkeley: University of California Press.

Wright, Louis B. (1935). *Middle-Class Culture in Elizabethan England*. Chapel Hill: University of North Carolina Press.

Zwicker, Steven N. (1998). "Reading the Margins: Politics and the Habits of Appropriation." In Kevin Sharpe and Steven N. Zwicker, eds., *Refiguring Revolutions: Aesthetics and Politics from the English Revolution to the Romantic Revolution*. Berkeley: University of California Press, pp. 101–15.

8

Sidney and Spenser

Andrew King

Contextualizing Elizabethan Romance

"Romance" as a term designating a literary genre or mode is not mentioned by Sidney in his *Defence of Poetry*. Similarly, Spenser never refers to *The Faerie Queene* as a romance or employs the term.[1] Yet both Sidney's *Arcadia* (ca.1580 and ca.1584; printed 1590, 1593) and Spenser's *Faerie Queene* (1590, 1596, 1609) demonstrate important and complex relations to the romance tradition. One of the difficulties inherent in defining romance is that a number of the texts that most clearly embody assumptions about the genre or mode are in fact reacting against it. *Don Quixote* (1605, 1615) is the great and obvious example, but *Arcadia* (especially in its "old" version) and *The Faerie Queene* also invoke and exploit romance conventions to ironic or otherwise complex rhetorical effect. They are both best thought of as texts in dialogue with romance; paradoxically, they presume a sense of what romance is even as they fail to assert it.

The rhetorical aims of each writer need to be examined separately; indeed, even their individual aims change through the different versions and stages of their works. We can begin our approach to these concerns, though, by distinguishing between a representational, surface level of romance narrative – signaled through stock elements such as aristocratic society, love interest, chivalry, the monstrous, and the supernatural – and a deeper notion of romance as a moral condition or kind of experience. The dominant idea here for both writers is romance as an aspiration toward an Edenic condition of perfect constancy, virtuous achievement, and the containment of mutability.[2] Romance in this deeper sense is attractive to both Sidney and Spenser, who are fascinated with the possibility of conceiving of their own age, especially in relation to the figure of Queen Elizabeth, in terms of perfected moral achievement. However, Sidney and Spenser engage thoughtfully with both Elizabethan politics and a fundamentally Calvinist assessment of human nature, and this ruminative aspect of their work often leads to an ironic handling of the narrative and representational conventions that should sustain the works as romances.

Sidney, Spenser, and their Elizabethan readers were the inheritors of a remarkably rich and varied romance tradition.[3] Native Middle English romance, beginning in the thirteenth century, remained popular and influential well into the sixteenth century, read both in printed editions and in manuscript (King 2000: 29–41). Intersecting with historical writings and saints' lives, native verse romances such as *Sir Bevis of Hampton* and *Guy of Warwick* (both ca.1300, but also existing in later versions) were key texts in a large tradition that gave special representation to God's providential care for the hero, and concomitantly England. The emphasis that a number of these texts give to England as the site of romance achievement makes them especially relevant to the political concerns of Sidney's and Spenser's work.

Continental and classical romance traditions also had an impact on Sidney and Spenser. Boiardo's *Orlando innamorato* (1483, 1494), Ariosto's *Orlando furioso* (1516, 1521, 1532), and Tasso's *Gerusalemme liberata* (1581) develop the narrative forms available to writers of romance. Ariosto's work in particular makes ironic play with romance conventions, emphasizing deferment and the generation of narrative rather than achievement and closure (Parker 1979). Also available and influential were romances of Spanish origin, such as *Amadis of Gaul*, and Hellenistic romances, such as Heliodorus' *Ethiopica* (translated into English by Thomas Underdowne, 1569, 1587).

Equally important is the figure of Queen Elizabeth as a generative force for romance narrative in the context of nationhood; neither the *Arcadia* (especially in its "old" version) nor *The Faerie Queene* could have assumed anything like their present shapes without her presence, since both works are largely written for and about her. But these texts are by no means naive celebrations of her. Indeed, much of the ironic and self-conscious relation that both works have to literary romance traditions relates to anxiety about the queen. In contrast, pageant literature, such as the Kenilworth pageants of 1575, provides simple examples of how a text is constructed into romance through the figure of the queen. At Kenilworth, for example, the "Lady of the Lake" escapes imprisonment because of Elizabeth's presence: "by Merlynes prophecie, it seemed she [the Lady of the Lake] could never be delivered but by the presence of a better maide than herselfe" (Nichols 1823: I.498). At this moment, it is not only the text that becomes romance, but also the English landscape in which Elizabeth stands. Iconography and narrative about the queen, whose personal motto *semper eadem* ("always the same") gave promise of perfect stability, could frequently take the form of an achievement of the romance condition in terms reminiscent of the Edenic myth; the Kenilworth pageants and other pageant texts present moments in which she and "we" cross through into a perfected romance version of our own experience. Sidney's Arcadian landscape and Spenser's faerie land are potentially romance versions of Elizabethan experience, but ultimately they fail to be so.

Elizabeth's ability both to generate and frustrate romance narrative in Sidney's and Spenser's perception is well illustrated in relation to the events of 1579, a seminal year for both writers and, in particular, the immediate political context for *The Old Arcadia*. Elizabeth's apparent intention to marry the French Catholic Duke, Alençon, was an imminent disaster for committed Protestants such as Sidney and Spenser, and the potential outcome was presented in a number of texts in terms of archetypal narratives of tragedy and fall – effectively, the loss of the romance world (see further McCabe 1995; Worden 1996). John Stubbes' *A Gaping Gulfe* (1579) defined the outcome of the intended match in terms of the fall from Eden, sharing with Sidney and Spenser a tendency to absorb the political into the imaginative and at the same time to confer upon narrative modes such as romance the strongest application to contemporary contexts. Stubbes writes concerning Alençon that the French nation "haue sent vs hither not Satan in body of a serpent, but the old serpent in shape of a man, whos sting is in his mouth, and who doth his endeuour to seduce our Eue, that shee and we may lose this Englishe Paradise" (1579: A.2[r]). Spenser's *The Shepheardes Calender*, published in the same year, similarly expresses anxiety about Elizabeth's planned marriage. Even more so than Stubbes, Spenser considers how Elizabeth's marriage to Alençon would be not only disastrous politically, but also calamitous for the writing of romance. Elizabeth's fall from Eden would make any romance literature that sought to engage with a sense of English nationhood irrelevant; in particular, it would invalidate epic, which presents nationhood in the context of the providential romance world. Accordingly, the great and anxious theme of *The Shepheardes Calender* is poetic vocation and the poet's projected Virgilian career. In "June" Colin, Spenser's poetic persona, describes himself in terms reminisicent of Aeneas: "I vnhappy man, whom cruell fate, / And angry Gods pursue from coste to coste" (14–15).[4] Like Aeneas, Colin is a figure of exile, but his quest is closer to Virgil's – to write an epic. Authorial self-reflexiveness is at the heart of Sidney's and Spenser's use of romance, because that use is in itself part of each work's theme and quest. Just as Aeneas' purpose is threatened by Dido, so too for Colin the death of Dido, which is the focus of "November," threatens to cancel the epic project, with the concomitant loss of the romance mode: "All Musick sleepes, where death doth leade the daunce, / And shepherds wonted solace is extinct" ("November," 104–5). But this "Dido" is better recognized by the other name she coincidentally bears in the *Aeneid*, Elissa, and the "death" of Elissa/Eliza is emblematic of the political tragedy that would accompany her marriage to Alençon.[5] In the *Aeneid*, her death, or at least abandonment, is necessary for Aeneas' progress and the development of the work toward closure in the romance mode. In Spenser's recontextualization of the narrative, by contrast, her death is foregrounded as tragedy and an impetus, however paradoxically, to the poet's own vocational quest.

The Old Arcadia

Sidney's first version of *Arcadia*, *The Old Arcadia*, also responds to the events of 1579, and it represents anxiety about the queen in terms of its ironic handling of romance narrative, mirroring *The Shepheardes Calender* in its sense that romance, given the context of political events, has become a deeply inappropriate literary form. For

English readers, Basilius' abandonment of his government at the start of the work is another version of the death of Dido, Eliza's sacrifice of the "Englishe Paradise." Tellingly, Philanax's injunction to Basilius to let "your subjects have you in their eyes, let them see the benefits of your justice daily more and more"[6] echoes Sidney's letter to the queen advising against the match.[7] Basilius' relinquishing of authority is one of a number of "unnatural" reversals of hierarchy in a work that exemplifies Sidney's maxim in the *Defence*, again invoking Edenic imagery, that because of "that first accursed fall of Adam . . . our erected wit maketh us know what perfection is, and yet our infected will keepeth us from reaching unto it" (Sidney 1973: 25). *Arcadia* exemplifies that dilemma at both the political and personal levels, and given that state of affairs, the generic signals of romance in the work are bound to prove ironic.

At the heart of *The Old Arcadia* is an analogy, also central to Plato's *Republic*, that reason must rule over the appetites in the individual, just as the prince must govern the commons in the state. Musidorus warns Pyrocles:

> Remember . . . that, if we will be men, the reasonable part of our soul is to have absolute commandment, against which if any sensual weakness arise, we are to yield all our sound forces to the overthrowing of so unnatural a rebellion. (*OA*, 17)

"Commandment" and "rebellion" are political words that enforce the macrocosmic analogy, and the two levels – individual and political – will come together explosively at key moments in the narrative.[8] Perhaps the figure in *Arcadia* who is closest to Elizabeth, and one of the most rebellious "sites" in the text, is Gynecia – appropriately the older woman lusting after a younger man (which Alençon was). More than any figure in the text, Gynecia threatens to push this world into violent tragedy in the pursuit of her desires. Her dream that she is "in a place of thorns which so molested her as she could neither abide standing still nor tread safely going forward" (*OA*, 102) is the dark underside to this "romance" – the antithesis to Elizabeth's freeing of the Lady of the Lake in the Kenilworth pageants. In its analysis of human nature and political structures, Sidney's work certainly goes beyond direct commentary on Elizabeth; however, her perceived personal and political failures generate a narrative that noticeably fails to fulfill its generic signals as romance, resulting in an ironic dislocation of those elements.

Allegory is another feature of Sidney's text that creates that ironic dislocation of romance motifs. Kenneth Borris has cogently analyzed some key scenes of *The Old Arcadia* in terms of their allegorical representation of the battle between "erected wit" and "infected will" – in particular, the attack of the lion and the bear (*OA*, 42), the outburst of a "mutinous multitude" interrupting Gynecia's wooing of Cleophila (*OA*, 108), and the attack of the "clownish villains" at the moment Musidorus is poised to rape Pamela (*OA*, 177; Borris 1999). In each case, the syntax carefully emphasizes the simultaneity of a sexually intense courtship or attack and an apparently arbitrary animalistic intrusion. At the narrative level, the two events appear unrelated, though at the allegorical level, they are one and the same; the animalistic is the externalized representation of the appetites within the wooing character, and the character's subsequent combat against those adversaries loses its heroic quality when we see exposed the violence within the "hero." Philoclea is chased by a lion, and Cleophila pursues the animal "seeing how greedily the lion went after the prey she herself so much desired" (*OA*, 42–3). Lion and Cleophila are united in their desire to consume Philoclea. A conventional romance "rescue" is complicated by the awareness that the greatest threat to the intended victim is the rescuer. Similarly, Musidorus' near rape of Pamela, the darkest scene in the work, is interrupted "to the just punishment of his broken promise, and most infortunate bar of his long-pursued and almost-achieved desires" by a sudden attack of "clownish villains" (*OA*, 177). The narrator's ambivalence – "just" and "infortunate" – both condemns Musidorus and supports his desires. The text strains in the direction of romance, where the reader's support for the hero should flow easily,[9] and yet most readers find the price of endorsing the sexually driven characters in Arcadia too high. Comparison with Cervantes' creation is appropriate here. Don Quixote thinks he is in a romance world, and of course he is not; if he were in the correct narrative context, his actions would be entirely decorous. *The Old Arcadia* provides just the opposite experience: on the surface level of narrative, the characters *are* in a typical romance world, but these characters are unable to rise to the level of that world, to cage the beast within. The disruptions of order within the individual characters spill out into the state, and political anarchy reflects the failure of personal government, even as it exploits it, widening the crack between this world and romance.

The Old Arcadia ends with the "resurrection" of Basilius and the pardoning of the princes and marriage. In this respect, the work "achieves" generic definition as romance, but after the preceding darkness, the ending is deeply unsatisfying. The unease that most readers feel is justified and part of the text's calculated rhetorical strategy. At this point, Sidney's ironic self-conscious manipulations of romance are comparable to the ending of Gay's *The Beggar's Opera*. Beggar, who is both character and "author" of the framed work, confesses to Player that for "strict poetical justice ... Macheath is to be hanged." Player objects: "this is a downright deep tragedy. The catastrophe is manifestly wrong, for an opera must end happily." Beggar complies with a reprieve for Macheath (just as Pyrocles and Musidorus are reprieved from their death sentences), though Beggar notes: "Had the play remained as I at first intended, it would have carried a most excellent moral" (Gay 1969: III.xvi.4–26). The irony of Beggar's remark applies well to *Old Arcadia*, for the uneasy nature of its "happy" ending enforces the reader's intellectual engagement. The rhetorical impetus of Sidney's work on the political level is clear: in the context of the Alençon crisis, England and Elizabeth cannot look for such a contrived and formulaic recovery. More generally, and perhaps more disturbingly, the depravities of human nature, revealed throughout *Old Arcadia*, suggest with the most condemnatory implications that romance as a literary mode is escapist and divorced from any relation to real life; the impossibility of a non-ironic yet credible depiction of human behavior in the romance mode emphasizes the triumph of the infected will.

The New Arcadia

The Old Arcadia was finished around 1580, and it circulated in manuscript and formed part of the literary culture supported by Sidney's sister, Mary, Countess of Pembroke. About 1584 Sidney began to rewrite *Arcadia*, making radical changes both to its narrative form and its thematic content. This revision was left incomplete at Sidney's death in 1586, and *Arcadia* subsequently reached a wider readership in two printed editions that both offer remarkable instances of the creation of literary meaning in the process of editing: the 1590 edition by Sidney's friend, Fulke Greville, which offers only the revised section, breaking off in Book III in mid-sentence; and the composite *Arcadia* of 1593, overseen by Mary Sidney, which concludes the work, however disjointedly, with the remainder of the "old" version.[10]

Despite its more complicated narrative structure, *The New Arcadia* presents a more straightforward, non-ironic version of romance. Sidney's model in the revised work is Hellenistic romance, chiefly Heliodorus' *Ethiopica*, and he follows Heliodorus in developing a narrative that unfolds its labyrinthine coils through retrospection, reported action, and interlaced stories. Little of the original version has been deleted, but the "old" text has been enmeshed with new adventures and new characters; the additional material is in fact longer than the original. Whereas in *Orlando furioso* the dilatory, interlaced narrative structure of deferred achievement suggests the ineffectuality of human ambition, *The New Arcadia* develops this kind of structure without irony. Instead, it exploits the opportunities for new narrative space to resuscitate the princes' moral and heroic worth. The first major episode in the revised work, for instance, presents both Musidorus and Pyrocles fighting in a war for altruistic rather than acquisitive reasons. Unknown to each other, they are on opposite sides, but irony gives way to good fortune as their mutual discovery is a means to resolve the conflict peacefully. Furthermore, in a major new character, Cecropia, Sidney creates a villain who changes the moral dynamics of the work. In *The Old Arcadia*, the evil was *within* the characters, and then projected outward, either in their explosive actions or through allegorical surrogate figures. Cecropia, however, is a more conventional figure of evil, and she simplifies the interpretative challenges of the earlier version, at the same time removing the ironic relationship of that work to romance. For example, Cecropia unleashes the lion that Zelmane/Pyrocles defeats,[11] so the allegorical nature of the attack in the "old" version, with its concomitant criticism of the prince, is lost. Cecropia wishes her son Amphialus to succeed Basilius as prince (*NA*, 181–2), and these narrative complications make her deeds independently motivated acts rather than an allegorical representation of dark impulses within Pyrocles. It is interesting, therefore, that in the 1593 composite *Arcadia* Musidorus' attempted rape of Pamela and Pyrocles' fornication with Philoclea are both omitted from the narrative of the "old" version used to complete the work. These changes may have been directed by Sidney himself or introduced by Mary Sidney; in either case, they are consistent with the direction of the revision toward a text that sits easily, rather than ironically, within the romance mode.

The most interesting aspect of the *New Arcadia* in relation to theorizing about romance is its presentation in Fulke Greville's edition of 1590. The remarkable aspect of this edition is not simply that Greville presents Sidney's text as incomplete, correctly judging that the changes in the revised text were too substantial to sanction an awkward joining with the conclusion of the first version. Rather, it is the calculated shock that the edition holds for the first-time reader. Without any prior warning or subsequent explanation, the 1590 *Arcadia* snaps off in mid-sentence on page 360r, during a fight between Zelmane and Anaxius: "Whereat ashamed, (as hauing neuer done so much before in his life)[·]"[12] In contrast, Hugh Sanford's preface to the 1593 edition comments on the "untimely death" of the author preventing "the timely birth of the child" (*NA*, 60). Greville's edition, however, offers no explanation or preparation – only a very teasing summation of the final chapter: "The Combattants first breathing, reencounter, and" (359r).

What the interrupted ending of the 1590 *Arcadia* does above all is reclaim the possibility of a future providential ending that could convince; in other words, it reclaims the text as romance, or at least the potential to be romance, in contrast to the parodic ending of the "old" version. Like the many narratives of Arthur's "death" which in fact suggest his healing in Avalon and eventual return, the suspended ending of Greville's *Arcadia* allows a loophole of recovery for its (in fact) dead author, Sidney. Greville is trying to save Sidney from being a "bare Was" of history, the victim of narrative and temporal closure. The Sidney constructed here by Greville, who has mysteriously put down his pen, is thus comparable to Arthur reading his own nation's history in *The Faerie Queene* – and necessarily stopping at the present:

> After him *Vther*, which *Pendragon* hight,
> Succeeding There abruptly it did end,
> Without full point, or other Cesure right,
> As if the rest some wicked hand did rend,
> Or th'Authour selfe could not at least attend
> To finish it.[13]
>
> (II.x.68)

This "vntimely breach" seems particularly apposite for Greville's *Arcadia*, which also ends "Without full point, or other Cesure right" because "th'Author selfe could not at least attend / To finish it." Moreover, Greville's *Life of Sidney* (ca. 1610) presents a fanciful resuscitation of Sidney, a romance hero whose early death still offers loopholes for a future recovery – like the 1590 *Arcadia*, an interrupted rather than a finished narrative. Greville writes:

> I do ingenuously confess that it delights me to keep company with him even after death, esteeming his actions, words and conversation the daintiest treasure my mind then lay up, or can at this day impart with our posterity. (Greville 1986: 71)

The notion of "keeping company" with Sidney goes deeper than a platitudinous sense of his memory living on. Greville's depiction of Sidney's manner of dying also sublimates finality and closure, emphasizing instead journey and change:

yet had the fall of this man such natural degrees that the wound whereof he died made rather an addition than diminution to his spirits; so that he showed the world – in a short progress to a long home – passing fair and well-drawn lines by the guide of which all pilgrims of this life may conduct themselves humbly into the haven of everlasting resting. (76)

Greville thus rewrites Sidney's death, as Sidney seems to have intended to rewrite the *Arcadia*, into a romance narrative that without irony achieves a lasting stability. The most famous passage in the *Life* – Sidney's offer of water to a dying soldier with the words "Thy necessity is yet greater than mine" (77) – similarly holds off narrative closure: Sidney is not yet confined by necessity, and his death, seemingly part of God's plan, remains an unfinished narrative rather than a foreclosed tragedy.[14]

The Faerie Queene: Elizabeth and Romance

Spenser's masterpiece is arguably the most complex experimentation with romance in English. The status of the text as a romance is not arbitrary, but essential. Overall, *The Faerie Queene* seeks a viable achievement of virtue – an attainment of constancy, in opposition to mutability, that can be related to "real" experience, that the reader "By certein signes here sett in sondrie place.../ may...fynd" (II.Proem.4). Romance, which aspires toward the Edenic mode of ultimate moral stability, is really the goal of the poem as much as it is its kind. The world of the poem on the representational, narrative level is recognizably that of romance, with its chivalric contests, enchantments, dragons, courts, love interest, and marvels. But it is also a deliberately naive veil over a deeper understanding of romance – one that is the object of the poem's quest and ultimately withheld. This "veiled romance" is the court and presence of Gloriana, the faerie land "which no body can know" (II.Proem.1). The attainment of this place and condition in the poem would be the defeat of mutability. Conversely, the failure to achieve this deeper level of romance means that the narrative world as we have it in the poem is indeed "painted forgery," rather than "matter of iust memory" (II.Proem.1) and that Mutability "beares the greatest sway" (VII.viii.1). When Merlin reveals that Britomart will marry Artegall and found a noble dynasty – a crucial aspect of the text's aspiration toward closure – the nurse Glauce asks: "what needes her to toyle, sith fates can make / Way for themselues, their purpose to pertake?" (III.iii.25). Glauce's question could be revised to assume the reader's perspective: why bother reading this work, since the generic signals at the most basic representational level tell us it is a romance, shaped toward moral victory and sustaining throughout a sense of providence? However, for reasons that may have more to do with the heuristic unfolding of the poem than with Spenser's death, that end never happens. Glauce's question, especially in our revised version, is simplistic because it fails to recognize how Spenser's work *struggles* to attain the values and meaning of romance – how *The Faerie Queene* is, at its deepest level, in the process of becoming romance, and equally in danger of failing to become that world. *King Lear* provides an interesting comparison. Shakespeare's tragedy is based on romance materials – the anonymous *King Leir*, with its happy ending, and Sidney's *New Arcadia*. It has classic romance narrative features of riddling questions, rival siblings, disguises, family separations and reunions, and "trial by arms" combat. Shakespeare therefore intensifies his tragedy by subverting the generic expectations signaled in the text, at the same time exploiting his audience's familiarity with the existing Lear narratives. A work that seems able to become romance right up to its last moments – "If that her breath will mist or stain the stone, / Why then she lives" (V.iii.236–7) – fails to do so. And the play's interaction with and loss of the romance world is its greatest meaning. The same struggle toward romance is at the heart of Spenser's poem.

Behind the anxiety and difficulty attached to romance and what it represents in *The Faerie Queene* is the figure of Elizabeth. She is seen "In mirrours more then one" (III.Proem.5), and the poem explores different representations of the queen in an effort to gain entry through her into a perfected romance version of experience. However, the most triumphant romance images of Elizabeth in the poem are frequently in danger of turning into ironic opposites. Belphoebe, for example, is one "mirror" in which Elizabeth is invited to view herself (III.Proem.5). But although Belphoebe embodies Elizabeth's "rare chastitee" (III.Proem.5) and thus might signify the queen's constancy, she is also disturbingly at odds with one of the principal means by which the text strives to become romance: the royal genealogy from Brutus to Elizabeth. That regenerative succession of monarchs is ideally an Edenic pattern of constancy, defeating mutability and sustaining romance. At the heart of Book III and central to the genealogical theme as it impinges on Britomart, Elizabeth's ancestor, is the Garden of Adonis – where, as in genealogy, all things are "by succession made perpetuall" (III.vi.47). The Garden of Adonis, however, is not the rearing place for Belphoebe, the virgin, but for her contrasting sister Amoret. In that sense, the Garden of Adonis (with its word-play on Eden) is a site of meaning from which Elizabeth, in Belphoebe, is excluded. As virgins, both Belphoebe and Elizabeth are unable to partake in the genealogy, and behind this is more than political anxiety regarding the royal succession in the 1590s. At issue here is an imaginative reception of Elizabeth that sees her unfitness to sustain a romance-epic narrative of ongoing perfection. She truly is Dido, a dead end for the quest. Interestingly, the description of Belphoebe at her first appearance is carefully picked up in Book V, when the Amazonian Radigund prepares to fight Britomart (compare II.iii.26–7 and V.v.2–3). Radigund is an aggressive, "proactive" Dido; she has imprisoned and emasculated Artegall on his quest, and in her opposition to Artegall's union with Britomart she threatens the direction of the work toward closure as romance. She is inimical to the genealogical line that will end in Elizabeth, and yet ironically she is, through her connections with Belphoebe, related to the queen. "End" is the operative word: Radigund expresses, more intensely than Belphoebe's exclusion from the Garden of Adonis, the anxiety surrounding the queen's lack of an heir. Merlin's prophecy of Britomart's and Artegall's descendants necessarily breaks off with Elizabeth:

> But yet the end is not. There *Merlin* stayd,
> As ouercomen of the spirites powre,
> Or other ghastly spectacle dismayd,
> That secretly he saw, yet note discoure.

(III.iii.50)

Like the "ending" of *Arcadia* in Fulke Greville's edition, this is an interrupted narrative that promotes both hope and anxiety. Tragic closure is at least temporarily withheld, but equally the presentation of English national experience within the romance mode cannot be assured.

The Faerie Queene: Moving away from Romance

Book I presents a unique set of concerns in its thoughtful interrogation of the romance tradition. On a simple narrative level, more than any other Book in the poem the legend of Holiness aligns itself with the generic signifiers of romance; Spenser has in fact drawn deeply on popular Middle English romance, especially *Sir Bevis of Hampton*, as well as related romances of displaced youths, "fair unknowns," and slandered ladies (King 2000: 126–59). The popularity of these texts, along with Spenser's self-conscious imitation of their antiquated language, would ensure that readers would recognize their imprint on Book I. At the same time, this native romance tradition was increasingly criticized throughout the sixteenth century on both literary and moral grounds. Although Middle English romance continued to circulate into the seventeenth century, with both Bevis and Guy of Warwick appearing in Drayton's *Poly-Olbion* (1613, 1622),[15] Thomas Nashe was not alone in viewing the old romances as "worne out absurdities" (1958: I.26). In a richer and more complicated way, Book I is saying the same thing. Rafe, the apprentice grocer in Beaumont's *The Knight of the Burning Pestle*, is a satiric portrait in line with Nashe's comment: a boy brought up on a literary diet of absurdity, whose language and actions represent escapist fantasies derived from popular romance. Of course he is in the wrong kind of world, and the same is true for the similarly Quixotic Redcrosse. But Redcrosse's world is not the mercantile London that renders Rafe's chivalric pretensions absurd, but the starkly Calvinist trial ground of holiness:

> What man is he, that boasts of fleshly might,
> And vaine assurance of mortality,
> Which all so soone, as it doth come to fight,
> Against spirituall foes, yeelds by and by,
> Or from the field most cowardly doth fly?
> Ne let the man ascribe it to his skill,
> That thorough grace hath gained victory.
> If any strength we haue, it is to ill,
> But all the good is Gods, both power and eke will.

(I.x.1)

"Fielde" maintains the language of chivalric romance, even as it describes the onslaught of "spirituall foes." Of course no romance hero can "most cowardly...fly" from the field, and the implications of this passage sound a death-knell for romance. Article 11 of the Thirty-Nine Articles of the Anglican Church, which are behind the Spenserian passage, has little time for romance heroes: "We are accounted righteous before God, only for the merit of our Lord and Saviour Jesus Christ by Faith, and not for our own works or deservings" (*The Book of Common Prayer*). The generic signals of romance in Book I are opposed at a deeper level, and resisting that impulse to the romance genre becomes the great test for both Redcrosse and the reader. Only when the hero has withdrawn an aspiration toward romance, as traditionally conceived in terms of knightly prowess and self-sufficiency, can the hero then begin to move toward a condition of moral stability that truly is romance in its deepest, Edenic sense. When Redcrosse "full of fire and greedy hardiment" (I.i.14) seeks out Error in her den, he is of course making a mistake – indeed, actually making the monster that confronts him. Bevis can fight a dragon and other monsters, and for him it is the right thing to do; he is even aided by God, but that never diminishes the sense of his heroic strength and personal achievement. But for Redcrosse, his assumption of self-sufficiency – his fundamental flaw of pride, perfectly expressed through his chivalric posturing – will create, not defeat, his enemies, since these enemies will be the allegorical projection of his own psyche. "With firie zeale he burnt in courage bold" (I.ix.37) as he approaches Despair, but again the despair is his, and he can only be saved from it by being reminded that he is not self-sufficient – not the sort of romance hero who can achieve victory with "courage bold." Una gives the correct insight: "In heauenly mercies hast thou not a part? / Why shouldst thou then despeire, that chosen art?" (I.ix.53). As in *Old Arcadia*, romance is ironically framed as an inappropriate representation of human behavior, given the fundamentally fallen nature of human-kind. Enmeshed in this emphasis on "that first accursed fall of Adam" is the idea that the true romance world, Eden, is inaccessible until, in Milton's words, "one greater Man / Restore us, and regain that blissful Seat."[16]

Given the highly subjective nature of Book I's landscape, reflecting the inclinations and mental and spiritual processes of the central character Redcrosse, we realize that the trappings of romance are part of the naive, "Rafe-like" attitude of that controlling perspective. The reader has to interrogate the romance narrative as a subjective and flawed perception – like Arthur's dream of Gloriana, a vision that may "delude," but that may also be "true" at a deeper level (I.ix.14). The romance mode on the representational level in Book I is not the record of an idealized world, but the record of a dangerous perspective that assumes an unwarranted self-reliance. What Redcrosse and the reader must perceive, therefore, is how the highly traditional romance narrative patterns on which Book I is based may, like Arthur's dream of Gloriana, have a "true" quality, once properly understood.[17] Ingeniously, Spenser exploits a narrative analogy between the well-rehearsed stories of the "fair unknown" and the displaced youth of noble birth but raised in deprivation and exile, struggling to regain his patrimony, and the Calvinist paradigm of salvation. Havelok, Bevis,

Perceval, Florent, Lybeaus, and several Malorian characters, including Arthur, are all instances of the character type. The crucial element in this story is that, although the hero may appear to be *earning* his noble identity as he overcomes his exile to regain his rightful place, the story has an ironic undertow in which the hero's birth, not his own merits or deeds, is the crucial factor that guarantees his eventual success. Chivalry or kingship are in the blood, and there are no self-made men in this kind of story; Malory's Gareth deliberately disguises himself as a "fair unknown" to gain respect for his deeds, but Lancelot insists that Bewmaynes (as he is named) proves that he is "com of full noble bloode," or else he will not knight him (Malory 1990: 326). The story has taken a number of forms, such as the narratives of Moses, Jesus, Luke Skywalker, and Harry Potter, and in all its manifestations the hero's eventual success is fundamentally a gift (through blood), no matter how much the hero struggles toward and seems to merit his final reward.

On a simple narrative level, Redcrosse is just such a hero. He is raised by a ploughman, but an innate attraction toward chivalry causes him to leave his step-father and "prickt with courage, and . . . forces pryde" (I.x.66) seek the court of Gloriana. An untested knight, he later departs from the court in borrowed armor (a common motif in this type of story, as in *Octavian*) and undertakes an adventure that leads to his discovery of who he truly is. Contemplation says: "For well I wote, thou springst from ancient race / Of *Saxon* kinges." A faerie placed him "in an heaped furrow," "Where thee a Ploughman all vnweeting fond . . . / And brought thee vp in ploughmans state to byde" (I.x.65–6). So Redcrosse learns he will be Saint George (I.x.61). But his identity as a "saint" rather than a knight or (despite his lineage) a king, is where the traditional story is redefined according to the analogy provided by Calvinism. The Calvinist meaning of "saint" is one of the Elect – those people chosen by God irrespective of their merits for salvation – and the whole narrative can be reevaluated from this perspective. The emphasis on the importance of birth in the romances of displaced youths and fair unknowns relates analogously to the central Calvinist doctrine that salvation is not earned, but given. Una tells Redcrosse that he is "chosen" (I.ix.53), and Contemplation reinforces the sense in which Redcrosse has not earned his saintly identity, but has been given it. What Calvin says about salvation could just as easily be said about knightly or kingly identity through birth: it "is freely offered to some while others are barred from access to it" (1960: III.xxi.I; p. 921). Just as one must be born a knight, so one must be born as one of God's Elect to be saved; both systems emphasize an identity given by or inherited from the "father," with God being the father in the second case. The fallen world is the form of exile analogous to the displacement suffered by heroes such as Bevis and Perceval, but the hero's striving, no matter how interesting and important it seems, is not what brings him to success. Appropriately, the defeat of the dragon in Book I is by an agentless "weapon bright / Taking aduantage of his open iaw" (I.xi.53). Redcrosse correctly gives praise to God, "Who made my hand the organ of his might" (II.i.33). Both the secular romance story and Spenser's revision are about the hero getting back to his father, but in creating in Redcrosse a version of this story that extends to God as father, Spenser has projected the achievement of the romance condition *beyond* this world. Redcrosse's realization that the Heavenly Jerusalem surpasses Gloriana's Cleopolis (I.x.58) creates the same *telos*, and the implications of it are that romance cannot be achieved in relation to even the most resonant human and cultural constructs, such as Elizabeth. However, this is a conclusion that *The Faerie Queene* will defer until *The Mutabilitie Cantos*, as the intervening Books now attempt to defeat mutability and recover Eden in the Elizabethan context.

The Proem to Book II, with its insistence that faerie land and Gloriana's court may be found, ignores the implications of Book I. If the discovery of "fruitfullest *Virginia*" (II.Proem.2) suggests the possibility of the hidden existence of faerie land – a romance condition achieved within the human context – then its eponymous queen may be the way into that land. The virginity of the queen will override her fruitfulness, and the paradox cannot therefore be made true in her. Genealogy becomes, from Book II onward, one of the dominant themes of the poem – not just part of its epic equipment, but a means by which it seeks to achieve the moral constancy of the romance world within its own context. However, the opposing genealogical chronicles read in Eumnestes' chamber (II.x) underline the problematic nature of this ambition – even though the chronicles are the product of memory, or Eumnestes, and not from the adjoining chamber of Phantastes. The violent and erratic history of the Britons, testimony to Mutability's sway, is opposed by the constant, secure faerie chronicle (see further O'Connell 1974); this is the opposition of history and romance, but the means of crossing over are not as clear as they were at Kenilworth. More critically, there is a danger, as the Proem has intimated, that the faerie chronicle has been mis-shelved and really belongs in Phantastes' chamber, where resides "all that fained is, as leasings, tales, and lies" (II.ix.51). The faerie queen of whom Arthur dreamed – "So fayre a creature yet saw neuer sunny day" (I.ix.13) – would fit well in Phantastes' chamber, where are things "such as in the world were neuer yit" (II.ix.50).

The way to Cleopolis is not clear, and the "certeine signes" in Book II are, despite the Proem, not encouraging. As in *Arcadia*, "that first accursed fall of Adam" casts a shadow over the credibility of human versions of romance. The apocalyptic defeat of the dragon at the end of Book I is diminished near the start of Book II with Guyon's inability to wash blood from Ruddymane's hands (II.ii.3). Because Ruddymane is a baby and has not sinned personally, the indelible stain is original sin (Article 16). The destruction of the Bower of Bliss at the end of Book II is in one sense a moral victory and a step toward Cleopolis. But even as that garden is destroyed, we are reminded of a greater garden that we have lost. Over a porch is an "embracing vine" with fruit that "seemd to entice / All passers by, to taste their lushious wine" (II.xii.54). Within this vine, some fruit "of burnisht gold . . . did themselues emongst the leaues enfold, / As lurking from the vew of couetous guest" (II.xii.55). The animated, coiling vine and fruit – "embracing" and "enfold[ing]" – and its equally personified secrecy – "lurking" – all suggest the Edenic serpent. The manner in which the serpent resides subliminally through association and is not revealed is a brilliant enactment within the lines of poetry of the serpent's own furtiveness. More than that, it demonstrates the intractable nature of sin and how it can easily lose urgency in our conscious deliberations. But it is there nevertheless, and as in Book I, we are directed to a theological framework that is at once the archetypal and informing narrative for all romance as well as the measure by which derived secular romance lacks credibility.

Books III and IV explore a different kind of romance narrative – the interlaced, polyvalent romance world of Ariosto. Allegory such as exists in the first two Books – characters named Despair and Mammon – is less present here, giving way to mythology and juxtaposed narratives that have a strong sense of thematic relations. Britomart is the central character, but a range of other characters expand her meaning, offering alternative perspectives on what she is, is not, and might be. The genealogical theme is central, and Elizabeth's relation to it, as discussed above, is problematic. Consequently, the poem's quest toward romance seems less viable, and other kinds of literary voices begin to challenge the seriousness of the poem.[18] In the Malbecco episode, for instance, Paridell's seduction of Hellenore is a framed *fabliau* that draws directly upon Chaucer. As Paridell's name suggests, he is a figure of parody – a fake Paris, and in fact the latter's illegitimate offspring (III.ix.36). Hellenore, or Helen-whore, similarly parodies Helen of Troy and her role in the city's destruction when she sets fire to Malbecco's treasury (III.x.12). Through these characters, Spenser draws the Trojan War into the debased world of *The Merchant's Tale*. Chaucer's May willingly cooperates in her seduction:

> Ther lakketh noght oonly but day and place
> Wher that she myghte unto his lust suffise,
> For it shal be right as he wole devyse.
>
> (IV.1998–2000)

Spenser picks up this line, allowing Hellenore an even more active role than May: "Nought wants but time and place, which shortly shee / Deuized hath, and to her louer told" (III.x.11). It is not just the characters, though, who lower the tone, but the narrative voice itself. The episode begins with the narrator's injunction to "listen Lordings, if ye list to weet" (III.ix.3) – a line that clearly echoes Chaucer's parody of native romance, *Sir Thopas*: "Listeth, lordes, in good entent ... " (VII.712).

The intrusion of this world of *fabliau* and parody is more than just the emergence of a new and ironic voice in the poem. Paridell is the only character in *The Faerie Queene* who unhorses Britomart (III.ix.16), and he is thus a challenge to the romance-epic poem that she is trying to sustain. Paridell is a proto-Mutability figure, and the threat he represents to the poem's deepest quest is especially clear when it falls to him to narrate the initial sequence of the British genealogy, from the fall of Troy to the arrival of Brutus, grandson of Aeneas, in Britain. Paridell's account is punctuated by "Thopas-like" flippancies – "that whilome I heard tell," "if I remember right," "so heard I say" (III.x.47–51) – and these militate against the seriousness of the discourse. Not surprisingly, his memory is in fact faulty, since he forgets to mention the crucial element for the poem's genealogical theme – that out of the sack of Troy came the founding of not only Rome, but Britain. Appropriately, Britomart inserts this part of the narrative:

> ...a third kingdome yet is to arise
> Out of the *Troians* scattered ofspring,
> That in all glory and great enterprise,
> Both first and second *Troy* shall dare to equalise.

> (III.ix.44)

Britomart is seeking to sustain the poem as romance not simply through her marriage with Artegall; she now also has to become an authorial, competitive voice within the poem, reinstating a vision that even the narrator, drawn into Paridell's style, seems to be losing interest in. Like *The Canterbury Tales*, *The Faerie Queene* is becoming a story contest, and the winning genre may not be romance. Without Britomart's interjection, Paridell's account of the Trojan War would have been another incomplete narrative – a *Thopas*-like text lacking proper romance closure and achievement.

Book V returns to the form of Book I, with a hero appointed to defeat a monstrous enemy, but it registers more profoundly than Book I an ironic gap between the representational narrative level of romance and the inappropriateness of human beings in that context. The recent historical allegory of Book V, as well as Spenser's Irish experiences, intensifies awareness of that disjunction, and the thoughtful quality of the Book emerges in its refusal to resolve difficulty. Consequently, Artegall is the most ironic and troubled of Gloriana's knights. The account of his adventures compares interestingly with a number of Arthurian texts, such as the Alliterative *Morte Arthure* and Malory's "Tale of Arthur and the Emperor Lucius," in both of which Arthur fights overseas, culminating in Malory's narrative in the conquest of Rome. Whereas this Arthur, like Guy of Warwick and other romance heroes, is supported by providence and by the context of his narrative world, Artegall is undermined by a context that refuses to follow the script. Don Quixote again comes to mind, as does Monty Python's Arthur, whose credibility and regality are considerably diminished by two peasants who are fluent in Marxist political theory![19] Indeed, Artegall encounters a "communist" giant who seeks to redistribute the world's wealth, and this is just one instance in which his authority is undermined by his own textual world. The knight's response to the giant, that all the planets "in their courses guide" and "euery one doe know their certaine bound" (V.ii.35–6) is unconvincing in the light of the Book's Proem: "the courses of the rowling spheares . . . all are wandred much" (V.Proem.5). In fact, the giant's awareness of "how badly all things present bee, / And each estate quite out of order goth" (V.ii.37) concurs with the Proem's narrator:

> Me seemes the world is runne quite out of square,
> From the first point of his appointed sourse,
> And being once amisse growes daily wourse and wourse.

> (V.Proem.1)

Talus' brutal dispatching of the giant (V.ii.49) is surely meant to feel like a crude and panic-stricken response.

Book V does not support Elizabethan imperialism, but rather demonstrates its lack of feasibility. More deeply, it realizes that the colonialist experience cannot be credibly constructed into the romance mode, though much early modern colonial and travel literature attempts to do precisely that (Greenblatt 1991). The contradictions within Artegall become intense, and with that crisis the work is retreating from romance and turning into the ironic mode. Whereas Redcrosse gradually discovers or remembers who he is, Artegall is in the process of forgetting. Crusading romance heroes should not become "contaminated" by their oppositional context, but that is precisely what happens to Artegall, and the crisis mirrors the complexity of Spenser's colonial experience in Ireland.[20] Guile is the quality that most strongly opposes justice in the Book, and it is manifested in numerous images related to insidiousness: trapdoors, such as Pollentes' bridge (V.ii.7, 12) and Dolon's bed (V.vi.7); nets and mechanical traps, such as Clarinda's metaphorical "subtill nets" and "engins of her wit" (V.v.52); and sleights of hand, such as Malengin's "slights" and "legierdemayne" (V.ix. 6,13). From the start, Artegall, whose sword is "gotten by . . . slight" by Astraea, is dangerously situated in this world. Consequently, he easily becomes a figure of hypocrisy, chastising Terpine for yielding to Radigund in words reminiscent again of the Proem – "runne so fondly astray / As for to lead your selfe vnto your owne decay" (V.iv.26) – and yet he will shortly submit to her himself. Furthermore, Artegall seems dangerously hypocritical when "faire semblant he did shew" to Clarinda in an effort to escape Radigund's prison; "Yet neuer meant he in his noble mind, / To his owne absent loue to be vntrew" (V.v.56). Is his "absent loue" Britomart or Radigund? "Noble" is deeply ironic. The Artegall seen by Britomart in Merlin's mirror was a romance ideal (III.ii.22–6); but this real Artegall, and by implication his descendant Elizabeth, is not allowing us to cross through that mirror into faerie land. No figure in Book V is more "astray" than Artegall; he seems like the survivor of a chivalric romance world who is now in a world/text that is no longer romance.

Book VI begins with a less than confident attribution of courtesy to courts (VI.Proem.1), and then the interest of the Book takes place far away from the court. The challenge here for *The Faerie Queene* to become romance is at its most critical. The pastoral world that dominates Book VI might be considered an alternative kind of romance experience. However, the forward momentum of the poem toward achieved virtue is dissipated in Calidore's pastoral sojourn, and even that world is then destroyed (VI.ix–xi). What is remarkable is that the poem turns so fully to pastoral; Richard McCabe notes (2002: 233) that "the unprecedented reversion to pastoral in book six signals no less than a radical reappraisal of the epic enterprise." Pastoral, for the vocational poet, is a stage *toward* epic, but now the Aeneas-like Colin of *The Shepheardes Calender* appears to have found his Dido and, like Calidore, abandoned his quest. As if in response to Paridell, *The Faerie Queene* is moving in the direction of other literary forms and away from romance.

No Book in the poem is so self-reflexive, so concerned with the writing of the poem as its own form of quest as Book VI. Not surprisingly, Colin Clout, Spenser's own poetic persona, appears in the Book (VI.x.16–31). The image of Colin's piping to the Graces represents a regularity and order that, like the regenerative cycles of the Garden of Adonis, suggest a defeat of mutability, but the image is tellingly transitory. At the heart of the concentric circles is not Eliza, as she was in "April" in *The Shepheardes Calender*, but Colin's love; Calidore, Gloriana's knight, does not so much achieve this vision of courtesy as mar it. The poem has clearly moved away from the figure of Elizabeth, and in doing so it has moved away from the search for the romance condition in the context of the public world. Calidore is ineffectual as a knight, ashamed at how he has abandoned his quest (VI.xii.12), and denied victory in the final escape of the Blatant Beast (VI.xii.38–41). The narrator reflects that the Beast will attack the poem (VI.xii.4), and the struggle of *The Faerie Queene* to become romance is now fully part of its own narrative. In Spenser's heuristic and self-reflexive process, the text becomes an element in its own imagined world, assaulted by the enemies of its own creation.

The Mutabilitie Cantos, published posthumously in 1609, is a remarkable "conclusion" to *The Faerie Queene*, even if it was never intended to be so. It completes the direction of the poem considered here, away from any sense that faerie land and romance can be found in its own world or that Elizabeth may be a means to keep, not lose, Stubbes' "Englishe Paradise." The images of Elizabeth in *The Mutabilitie Cantos* in fact stress the queen's own mutability; even as queen, she is "subject" to time and change. Drawing on well-established iconographical and textual traditions, Spenser shadows her in Cynthia, whom Mutability requires to "downe descend / And let her selfe into that Ivory throne" (VII.vi.11); and she appears in Diana, who curses and abandons Ireland since she has exposed there at her most vulnerable (VII.vi.54–5). Mutability's claim to rule the universe, including God, is disallowed by Nature, the judge, but the narrator-poet rejects that view, concluding that Mutability may be "vnworthy... Of the Heav'ns Rule," yet nevertheless "she beares the greatest sway" (VII.viii.1). In romance, the "unworthy" cannot rule, and at this point the poem accepts that the "Englishe Paradise," or indeed the Irish paradise, was lost long before Elizabeth. Romance, and *The Faerie Queene* itself, are in fact "painted forgery" (II.Proem.1), and the construction of human experience in the romance mode is Phantastes, or at best a deep-seated memory of the Edenic condition. Finally, the poem cannot be completed as a romance narrative, and its last canto, aptly titled "vnperfite," joins the other interrupted narratives – Merlin's prophecy, Greville's 1590 *Arcadia*, even *Sir Thopas* – waiting for its conclusion beyond this world;

> ... that same time when no more *Change* shall be,
> But stedfast rest of all things firmely stayd
> Vpon the pillours of Eternity.

                                                                        (VII.viii.2)

See also: chapter 1, Ancient Romance; chapter 5, Chaucer's Romances; chapter 6, Malory and the Early Prose Romances; chapter 7, Gendering Prose Romance in

RENAISSANCE ENGLAND; chapter 9, SHAKESPEARE'S ROMANCES; chapter 13, WOMEN'S GOTHIC ROMANCE; chapter 14, PARADISE AND COTTON-MILL; chapter 30, POPULAR ROMANCE AND ITS READERS.

Notes

1. My thanks to Thomas P. Roche, Jr., for checking Osgood's own corrected copy of *A Concordance to the Poems of Edmund Spenser*, ed. Charles Grosvenor Osgood (Washington: Carnegie Institute, 1915). Also, my thanks overall to Helen Cooper and Matthew Woodcock for expert proofreading and stimulating criticism.

2. On the informing nature of the Eden myth for romance, see further: Frye 1957: 186–206.

3. Useful summary essays are: Patricia Parker, "Romance" in Hamilton 1990; and Helen Moore, "Romance," in Hattaway 2000.

4. Edmund Spenser, *The Shorter Poems*, ed. Richard A. McCabe (Harmondsworth: Penguin, 1999). Cf. *Aeneid*, I.1–5. Colin's speech also draws on Meliboeus' opening speech in Virgil's first Eclogue.

5. From a more practical perspective, Stubbes' text also gives urgent consideration to what would happen to England should Elizabeth die in childbirth: [C.8.v].

6. Sir Philip Sidney, *The Old Arcadia*, ed. Katherine Duncan-Jones (Oxford: Oxford University Press, 1994), p. 7. All further citations will be to this edition. References immediately follow the quotation, with the abbreviation *OA* to indicate the version.

7. For Sidney's letter, see *Miscellaneous Prose of Sir Philip Sidney*, ed. Katherine Duncan-Jones and J. A. Van Dorsten (Oxford: Oxford University Press, 1973), pp. 56–7.

8. Sidney's *Astrophil and Stella*, 5, also represents the rebellion of the appetites over reason with reference to the political analogy.

9. Frye (1957: 187) notes that in romance "all the reader's values are bound up with the hero."

10. There are some crucial revisions in the 1593 text to the added portion of the "old" version, and these are discussed below. The fifth edition of 1621 contains a bridging passage by Sir William Alexander, attempting to make the transition from the revised text to the conclusion from the "old" version more coherent. Another major difference between the 1590 and 1593 editions is that the former divides the work into chapters with summary titles.

11. Sir Philip Sidney, *The Countess of Pembroke's Arcadia*, ed. Maurice Evans (Harmondsworth: Penguin, 1977), pp. 181–2, 446. All further citations will be to this edition, abbreviated as *NA* and with the reference directly following the citation. Note that in the *Old Arcadia*, Pyrocles adopts the name Cleophila when disguised as an Amazon; in the *New Arcadia*, however, the name is changed to Zelmane.

12. Sir Philip Sidney, *The Countess of Pembroke's Arcadia: A Facsimile Reproduction*, intro. Carl Dennis (Kent State University Press, 1970). There is no period or mark of punctuation after the closing parenthesis.

13. Edmund Spenser, *The Faerie Queene*, ed. A. C. Hamilton, Hiroshi Yamashita, and Toshiyuki Suzuki (Harlow: Longman, 2001), II.x.68. All further citations will be to this edition.

14. Greville also wants to keep Sidney "alive" since his career and works carry, in Greville's opinion, a potent political message for his own "effeminate age." Greville's antipathy toward James' rule is well documented, and the application of Sidneian values to Jacobean England may yet benefit an age whose "necessity is greater" than the previous age.

15. *The Works of Michael Drayton*, ed. J. William Hebel et al. (Oxford: Blackwell, 1961): Bevis, II.231–384 and pp. 46–7; Guy, XIII.327–52, and p. 286.

16. John Milton, *Paradise Lost*, I.4–5, in John Milton, *Complete Poems and Major Prose*, ed.

Merritt Y. Hughes (New York: Macmillan, 1957). Interestingly, Milton rejected earlier plans for an Arthurian romance-epic in favor of the fall.

17. On the interpretative anxiety pertaining to Arthur's account of the Faerie Queene, see further: Woodcock 2003: 94–8.

18. McCabe (2002) argues for the growth of a competing "Ovidian" satiric voice in the poem, especially in the 1596 installment and *The Mutabilitie Cantos* (249–51, 263–4).

19. *Monty Python and the Holy Grail* (Columbia Pictures, 1974).

20. Spenser's *View* provides a crucial context for the failure of romance in Book V and the irony that engulfs Artegall. Irenius notes that the Old English, or Anglo-Norman settlers in Ireland, "are degenerated and growne almost mere Irish, yea, and more malitious to the English then the Irish themselves"; Edmund Spenser, *A View of the State of Ireland*, ed. Andrew Hadfield and Willy Maley (Oxford: Blackwell, 1997), p. 54. See further: Nicholas Canny, "Introduction: Spenser and the reform of Ireland," in Coughlan 1989: 9–24 (20); McCabe 2002, passim.

References and Further Reading

Texts

The Book of Common Prayer (1999). Introduction by Diarmaid MacCulloch. London: David Campbell.

Calvin, Jean (1960). *Institutes of the Christian Religion*, ed. John T. McNeill, trans. Ford Lewis Battles. Library of the Christian Classics 20, 21. Philadelphia: Westminster Press.

Chaucer, Geoffrey (1987). *The Canterbury Tales*. In *The Riverside Chaucer*, ed. Larry D. Benson. 3rd edn. Boston: Houghton Mifflin.

Drayton, Michael (1961). *The Works of Michael Drayton*, ed. J. William Hebel et al. Oxford: Blackwell.

Greville, Fulke (1986). *The Prose Works of Fulke Greville, Lord Brooke*, ed. John Gouws. Oxford: Oxford University Press.

Gay, John (1969). *The Beggar's Opera*. In *British Dramatists from Dryden to Sheridan*, ed. George H. Nettleton et al. Carbondale: Southern Illinois University Press.

Malory, Sir Thomas (1990). *The Works of Sir Thomas Malory*, ed. Eugène Vinaver, rev. P. J. C. Field. 3rd edn. Oxford: Oxford University Press.

Milton, John (1957). *Complete Poems and Major Prose*, ed. Merritt Y. Hughes. New York: Macmillan.

Nashe, Thomas (1958). *The Works of Thomas Nashe*, ed. Ronald B. McKerrow, rev. F. P. Wilson. Oxford: Oxford University Press.

Nichols, John, ed. (1823). *The Progresses and Public Processions of Queen Elizabeth*. 3 vols. London.

Shakespeare, William (1992). *The Tragedy of King Lear*, ed. Jay L. Halio. Cambridge: Cambridge University Press.

Sidney, Sir Philip (1970). *The Countess of Pembroke's Arcadia: A Facsimile Reproduction*, introduction by Carl Dennis. Kent, OH: Kent State University Press.

Sidney, Sir Philip (1973). *A Defence of Poetry*, ed. J. A. Van Dorsten. Oxford: Oxford University Press.

Sidney, Sir Philip (1973). *Miscellaneous Prose of Sir Philip Sidney*, ed. Katherine Duncan-Jones and J. A. Van Dorsten. Oxford: Oxford University Press.

Sidney, Sir Philip (1977). *The Countess of Pembroke's Arcadia*, ed. Maurice Evans. Harmondsworth: Penguin.

Sidney, Sir Philip (1994). *The Old Arcadia*, ed. Katherine Duncan-Jones. Oxford: Oxford University Press.

Spenser, Edmund (1999). *The Shorter Poems*, ed. Richard A. McCabe. Harmondsworth, Penguin.

Spenser, Edmund (2001). *The Faerie Queene*, ed. A. C. Hamilton, Hiroshi Yamashita, and Toshiyuki Suzuki. Harlow: Longman.

Stubbes, John (1579). *The Discoverie of a Gaping Gulf Whereinto England is Like to be Swallowed by an Other French Mariage* ... London.

Criticism

Anderson, Judith H., Donald Cheney, and David A. Richardson, eds. (1996). *Spenser's Life and the Subject of Biography*. Amherst: University of Massachusetts Press.

Borris, Kenneth (1999). "Elizabethan Allegorical Epics: The *Arcadias* as Counterparts of *The Faerie Queene*." *Spenser Studies* 13, 191–221.

Burrow, Colin (1996). *Epic Romance: Homer to Milton*. Oxford: Oxford University Press.

Cooper, Helen (1999). "Romance after 1400." In David Wallace, ed., *The Cambridge History of Medieval English Literature: Writing in Britain 1066–1547*. Cambridge: Cambridge University Press, pp. 690–719.

Coughlan, Patricia, ed. (1989). *Spenser and Ireland: An Interdisciplinary Perspective*. Cork: Cork University Press.

Fichter, Andrew (1982). *Poets Historical: Dynastic Epic in the Renaissance*. New Haven and London: Yale University Press.

Frye, Northrop (1957). *Anatomy of Criticism: Four Essays*. Princeton, NJ: Princeton University Press.

Goldberg, Jonathan (1981). *Endlesse Worke: Spenser and the Structures of Discourse*. Baltimore, MD: Johns Hopkins University Press.

Greenblatt, Stephen J. (1991). *Marvellous Possessions: The Wonder of the New World*. Oxford: Oxford University Press.

Hamilton, A. C., ed. (1990). *The Spenser Encyclopedia*. Toronto: University of Toronto Press.

Hattaway, Michael, ed. (2000). *A Companion to English Renaissance Literature and Culture*. Oxford: Blackwell.

Helgerson, Richard (1992). *Forms of Nationhood: The Elizabethan Writing of England*. Chicago and London: Chicago University Press.

Hume, Anthea (1984). *Edmund Spenser: Protestant Poet*. Cambridge: Cambridge University Press.

Kay, Dennis, ed. (1987). *Sir Philip Sidney: An Anthology of Modern Critisism*. Oxford: Oxford University Press.

King, Andrew (2000). *The Faerie Queene and Middle English Romance: The Matter of Just Memory*. Oxford: Oxford University Press.

King, John (1990). *Spenser's Poetry and the Reformation Tradition*. Princeton, NJ: Princeton University Press.

McCabe, Richard (1996). "'Little booke: thy selfe present': The Politics of Presentation in *The Shepheardes Calender*." In *Presenting Poetry: Composition, Publication, Reception*, ed. Howard Erskine-Hill and Richard McCabe. Cambridge: Cambridge University Press, pp. 15–40.

McCabe, Richard (2002). *Spenser's Monstrous Regiment: Elizabethan Ireland and the Poetics of Difference*. Oxford: Oxford University Press.

McCoy, Richard C. (1989). *The Rites of Knighthood: The Literature and Politics of Elizabethan Chivalry*. Berkeley: University of California Press.

Norbrook, David (2002). *Poetry and Politics in the English Renaissance*. 2nd edn. New York: Oxford University Press.

O'Connell, Michael (1974). "History and the Poet's Golden World: the Epic Catalogues in *The Faerie Queene*." *English Literary Renaissance* 4, 241–67.

Parker, Patricia A. (1979). *Inescapable Romance: Studies in the Poetics of a Mode*. Princeton, NJ: Princeton University Press.

Woodcock, Matthew (2004). *Fairy in The Faerie Queene: Renaissance Elf-Fashioning and Elizabethan Myth-Making*. Aldershot: Ashgate Press.

Worden, Blair (1996). *The Sound of Virtue: Philip Sidney's Arcadia and Elizabethan Politics*. New Haven and London: Yale University Press.

Yates, Frances A. (1975). *Astraea: The Imperial Theme in the Sixteenth Century*. London: Ark.

9

Shakespeare's Romances

David Fuller

Shakespeare's romances contain some of his greatest and most experimental work. But Ben Jonson dismissed them summarily: *"Tales, Tempests*, and suchlike drolleries" (*Bartholomew Fair*, Induction); and Samuel Johnson objected magisterially:

> To remark the folly of the fiction, the absurdity of the conduct, the confusion of the names and manners of different times, and the impossibility of the events in any system of life were to waste criticism . . . upon faults too evident for detection, and too gross for aggravation. (Notes to his edition of Shakespeare, on *Cymbeline*)

The fundamental requirement of criticism of Shakespeare's romances is worthwhile perspectives. They are not easily come by.

The categorization of Shakespeare's last plays as romances begins with Coleridge (lecture on *The Tempest*, 1818), and was first elaborately formulated by Edward Dowden (*Shakespeare: A Critical Study of his Mind and Art*, 1875). Romance was not recognized as a dramatic category by Shakespeare, or by the compilers of the First Folio (who placed *The Winter's Tale* and *The Tempest* among the comedies, *Cymbeline* among the tragedies, and, for whatever reason – possibly because they could not acquire the right to print – did not include *Pericles*). The categorization has never been entirely accepted: the group is still often referred to simply as "last plays."[1] Though the plays evidently constitute a group, in that they deal with similar plot materials in some similar ways, there are also notable differences: they have, variously, elements in common with the tragedies and the earlier comedies; *Cymbeline* is in part a history; and these differences require some variation of critical perspective. One primary point of stressing genre with these works is to explain features which, if an audience responds in terms of assumptions, or a reader-critic judges by criteria appropriate to more realist modes, could seem – as they seemed to Jonson and Johnson – artistically inept. Adequate fundamental perspectives do not dissolve all critical problems, but they should obviate pseudo-problems about realism and that aesthetic consistency that neoclassical criticism calls (often with an expressive social resonance) "decorum." Shakespeare is (in this sense) no more "decorous" in the romances than in the mixed modes of his tragedies, comedies, and histories. "Tragical-comical-historical-pastoral": Polonius' apparently absurd proliferation of categories is no more than a plain description of *Cymbeline*.

The fundamental aim and method of romance is that some central experience should be presented as far as possible free of the contingent circumstances that realism – or any compromise with realism – is forced to hang on it. To see romance in these terms is to suggest that it is not so much a special mode as an extreme form of the tendency to embodiment by stylization to which all art – and, among literary forms, especially poetic drama – tends; and, insofar as Shakespeare's last plays are romances, in part they do simply intensify the mode of *Two Gentlemen of Verona* (a drama of erotic and chivalric quest), or *A Midsummer Night's Dream* (with its use of magic and the supernatural), or *All's Well that Ends Well* (with its use of folktale materials), just as, in more or less evident ways, they extend the matter and the manner of plays as diverse as *Measure for Measure* (with its Prospero-like Duke controlling the action) and *Othello* (to which *The Winter's Tale* adds a comedic sequel). Romance is difficult to define because, beyond the anti-realism that connects it more or less with all forms of fiction,[2] other delimiting features, however characteristic, may not be present in a given case.

Nevertheless, there are typical features: characters on a larger-than-life, heroic scale, often exemplifying extremes of virtue or vice; a quest (trial, test) – erotic, chivalric, both, or neither – which is almost always successful, and so (in keeping with the general heightening) leads to a state of ideal fulfillment in love, or of peace and justice in the social order, a Golden Age or New Jerusalem; a figure of disharmony or malice, or a concatenation of (literal or metaphorical) storm-and-shipwreck circumstances to be overcome; *en route*, pageantry, ceremonial, or organized festivity – elements that make life itself partake of the arrangement and formality of art; and a delight in the improbable, the mysterious, or the marvelous – magical, supernatural, or divine – which should not be obscured (apologetic implications of a preference for realism would betray the mode) but should rather be heightened so that fictionality may be relished.

Howard Felperin identifies three kinds of romance that would have been known to Shakespeare: classical prose romances (such as those of Longus and Heliodorus, and the *Apollonius of Tyre* that is the source of *Pericles*); chivalric romances of the Middle Ages (Chrétien de Troyes, Malory); and certain miracle and morality plays – sources that, he argues, converge in Shakespeare's romances (Felperin 1972: chapter 1). Shakespeare looks back to these classical and medieval sources sympathetically, albeit from a sophisticated distance. But sophistication does not mean that the attitude is detached. Quite the reverse: the stories present possibilities of participatory wonder at the marvelous which the tone of presentation often encourages. "It is required / You do awake your faith":[3] though addressed to the stage audience, this is also a hint to the audience in the theater. To take only the most extreme example of the wondrous, while the "miraculous" revival of Hermione is given a naturalistic explanation (which, though improbable, the play avoids inquiring into), that explanation can only be constructed after the event (from 5.2.103–6 and 5.3.126–9): Hermione's "resurrection" has the effect of magic or miracle, even though it is not ultimately presented as either. This is far from the only tone of these plays: that all range over a gamut from marvel and miracle to brothel-keeper, pedlar-thief, or drunken butler is vital to their mode. Nevertheless, quasi-religious wonder is an important tone in these plays, and, while some criticism has concentrated on this to the exclusion of more heterogeneous effects, there has been a tendency in would-be correctives to flinch from recognizing it at all.

Many of the typical features of romance we find in some degree in Shakespeare, albeit not only in the plays thought of as romances, and, in them, with qualifications that draw the stylizations and exaggerations of romance toward modes more obviously mimetic. Prospero may savor of Doctor Faustus and myth; he also smacks of Dr. Dee and science. And the materials Shakespeare incorporated in *The Tempest* from John Florio's translation of Montaigne's advanced anthropology (1603, "Of the Cannibals"), and a 1610 account of a Virginia Company shipwreck in Bermuda, not to mention the care he apparently took with details about how to handle a ship in a hurricane, were clearly meant to anchor the play's more romantic aspects in recognizable contemporary realities.[4] Then, contrary to romance norms, polarities of good and evil are not always kept clearly separate. In his readiness to engage with Iachimo's wager and the violence of his too ready jealousy, Posthumus, for example, can be understood not as the perfect romance hero he is apparently introduced as (1.1.17–55), but as a culpably active victim, who is therefore partly responsible for Imogen's sufferings. Similarly, both Britain and Rome partake of both good and bad: Cymbeline's rejection of a foreign conqueror in the name of native freedom cannot be imagined other than as commanding full assent from the first audience; but in the bad mouths of the Queen and Cloten similar sentiments, however humorous in their pungency, would appear unwisely confrontational (3.1). Nevertheless, the play presents a pattern of evil defeated and good triumphant. That Britain and Rome both partake of the good is part of that pattern. Their reconciliation is a subtle version of it: the wicked Queen, by whom the war was prompted, dies unmasked; though defeated militarily, Rome is reconciled to Britain when, from a position of strength derived from victory, Cymbeline accepts the old allegiance on a new basis.

"Chaste . . . blameless . . . true subject . . . jealous tyrant . . . innocent babe" – Apollo's oracle strikes the romance keynote of straightforward moral divisions: the good are wholly good, and the bad bad. Many central figures in these plays present romance moral polarities with similar simplicity. But not all. And the most strikingly problematic figure is the most central – Prospero. Criticism long took Prospero at his own valuation. But other points of view are possible, and in recent accounts of the play these have come routinely to predominate. Though Prospero's narrative to Miranda throws all the blame for the usurpation of Milan onto Antonio, even that bitter and self-justifying narrative allows other ways of seeing the events narrated to peep through: "I . . . to my state grew stranger, being transported / And rapt in secret

studies"; "I... neglecting worldly ends... in my false brother / Awaked an evil
nature"; this in a convoluted syntax wonderfully expressive of Prospero's being
gripped by a passion that blinds him to the alternative perspectives he is revealing
(1.2.66–116). Prospero's language of being transported and rapt, of neglecting what
he disdains as "worldly" but what another perspective might call properly attentive to
good government, and of awaking evils that, under a more observant regime, might
have slept, indicates what another way of balancing private interest against public
duty might see. Shakespeare takes some trouble not to allow the sophisticates in the
audience to acquiesce in that alternative simplicity: we see Antonio propose a ruthless
parallel reenactment of his crime (2.1). But if one feels unsure about Prospero's
valuation of himself, it follows that this will call into question his judgments more
generally. Caliban's view – that the usurped Prospero became in his turn, and again
with questionable justification, a usurper (1.2.331–44) – may then seem to have more
validity. Prospero's relation with Ariel, at times affectionate (4.1.48–9), at times
fiercely dominant (1.2.243–97), is similarly open to opposite readings. And finally
Prospero's magic too can be taken in different ways. Whether or not one recognizes
that in Prospero's climactic magical invocation Shakespeare is translating a speech
from Ovid by the wicked Medea (5.1.33–57), that "graves at my command / Have
waked their sleepers, oped, and let 'em forth" might suggest to the first audience that
this magic does not contrast so simply with the black magic of Sycorax, as Prospero

Plate 2. The Tempest, a design for a Shakespeare fresco by Henry Fuseli; pen and ink and brown wash,
1777–8. Left lunette (top): Trinculo and Stephano bent over Caliban (2.2); (bottom) Ferdinand and
Miranda (3.1). Spandrel (top): Prospero with Ariel whispering in his ear; inscription "Prospero" on a
plaque in the center; (bottom) Ariel confined in the cloven pine by the witch Sycorax (1.2). Right lunette
(top): the shipwrecked sailors leap overboard, protected by Ariel's spell (1.2); (bottom) Caliban shoul-
dering a tree-trunk (2.2). (British Museum, Roman Album, folio 45 verso, number 64.)

claims.[5] In Miranda, as in the parallel heroines, *The Tempest* has its extreme of good –
though even here with a difference: Miranda's virtue is less active and tested, more
naive, than that of Marina, Imogen, or Perdita. But though evil is powerfully present
in the play, its sources are open to interpretation.

Though the romances can be seen as a group, there are therefore important
differences between them. The special qualities of each work can be seen as related
in part to the various nature of their source materials. The sources of *Pericles* and *The
Winter's Tale* are themselves romances (*Apollonius of Tyre; Pandosto*), and Shakespeare
follows his originals relatively closely. The sources of *Cymbeline* are in part historical,
though they are so much reshaped as to draw little from Holinshed and to leave every
other putative source open to dispute. The sources of *The Tempest* are different again –
contemporary and philosophical (Montaigne) and, at least ostensibly, realist (travel
narratives) – though here the supposed realism is at least ripe for romance development. Readings that emphasize the play's relation to contemporary interests in
"science" (magic), in Prospero's relation to such figures as Giordano Bruno or John
Dee, may tend to qualify an understanding of the play as a romance – though, as with
travel narratives, this emphasis too can be Janus-faced: the Renaissance "scientist"
could still embody the Hermetic ideal of a return to the prelapsarian state of control
of nature and of the self – an early modern transmutation of romance idealism. Those
for whom one critical method fits all naturally attempt to understand all the romances
in terms of Jacobean politics and society – *Cymbeline* in relation to Jacobean problems
of nationhood, *The Winter's Tale* in relation to the court and family politics of James I.[6]
Readings that postulate a relation the first audience might understand to contemporary politics tend to draw attention from the qualities of the plays as romances; but no
way of reading has any necessary relation to the nature of their source materials, the
possible implications of which for interpretation are multiple. An awareness of the
different materials on which they draw helps mainly to bring out legitimate distinctions between the finished works.

The assumptions of romance are aristocratic. That royalty is treated as symbolic of
spiritual ideals is a standard romance topos that grew up in the context of fiction for
an aristocratic readership. That it should survive into the popular drama is an index of
how emphatically the romance mode at times insists on its fictionality. The assumption does not, of course, determine the moral status of particular royal or aristocratic
fictional characters, only the assumed tendency of royal or aristocratic being in a mode
of fiction the tendency of which is always toward the golden world of what should be.
The recognized stylizations of romance should mean that this is not confused with
political realities in the non-romance world; and even in the romance world it is
understood that true gentility is a matter of which birth should be, but is not
necessarily, an index. Primarily important is the recognition of nobility of mind
and spirit wherever that occurs, and this is not identified simply with nobility of
social status. Cerimon is a reliable guide: "I held it ever virtue and cunning [know-
ledge, skill] / Were endowments greater than nobleness and riches; / ... Immortality
attends the former [that is, the former pairing], / Making a man a god" (*Pericles*,

3.2.24–8). Posthumus, the son of an ennobled professional soldier, is infinitely superior to Cloten, a prince by adoption. He is utterly undervalued when his ethical worth is measured in terms of his social standing (2.3). Conversely, *arrivistes* show their *parvenu* vulgarity by their over-insistence on hierarchy, as when Cloten thinks it properly aristocratic to be rude to social inferiors (2.1). Guiderius twice, and with great emphasis, rejects taking Cloten at his social value (4.2; 5.4): though a prince, he was "a most uncivil one"; the wrongs he committed – rude behavior to a supposed social inferior of the kind about which he had earlier boasted – "were nothing prince-like." Nevertheless, aristocratic birth is also presented as having quasi-magical properties: it may reveal itself (semi-)independently of circumstance. That the royalty of Pericles should be discernible through his disguise as "the mean knight" may be taken as naturalistic. That Miranda should be "the top of admiration" is a plausible consequence of the special care taken with her education (1.2.172–5). Similarly, Guiderius and Arviragus, whose royal natures are evinced by their susceptibility to heroic action, although brought up away from court, have been educated by a courtier-soldier – though Belarius understands their desire for glory as an effect of their natures, not of his nurture (4.2.170–82; 4.4.53–4). Whether Marina's superiority to the child of Cleon and Dionyza is a result of nature or of chance is not investigated, but it is clearly the implication of her effect on clients in a brothel who profess themselves "out of the road of rutting for ever" that her nature is extraordinary. That Perdita, brought up by a shepherd, in all her actions "smacks of something greater than herself / Too noble for this place" (4.4.158–9) presents the romance equation of aristocracy and inherent virtue in its purest quasi-magical form.

Since this romance topos assumes a nature radically unconditioned by circumstances, the debates about nature and nurture in *The Winter's Tale* and *The Tempest* evidently bear on this, though only a determinedly thematic criticism would think of them as doing so other than remotely: primarily these debates arise from and express character in situation. What one makes of Prospero's abuse of Caliban as "a born devil, on whose nature / Nurture can never stick" (4.1.188–9) depends on one's wider estimate of their antagonism; and in any case, since Prospero may intend the ground of his abuse to be taken literally (2.2.319–20), Caliban presents too special a case to suggest any general truth.[7] In the grafting debate between Polixenes and Perdita (4.4.79–103) the main entertainment is the irony that Polixenes speaks with such patrician confidence, and in terms that draw attention to an analogy between breeding plants and breeding people ("marry... gentle... stock... noble race"), in favor of the method of improving nature that he will repudiate by joining the supposedly wild stock of (Princess) Perdita to his own noble race in Prince Florizel. If the debate is felt to resonate beyond the immediate confines of the scene in which it occurs it will be in the concluding *coup de théâtre*: nature outdoes art infinitely when the statue of Hermione is found to be Hermione herself.

Even outside the romances Shakespeare's characters often tend toward the symbolic. Underneath all the particular issues of character and situation that give rise to

Hamlet's special feelings, he seems so large a character because he is the epitome of basic responses to existence – *Unheimlichkeit, Weltschmerz* – that do not depend on those particulars. Whether or not particular motives can be found for Iago's will to destroy Othello, the opposition between the characters can be felt as embodying an inherent drive in cynicism to desecrate idealism. It is Othello, not Cassio, who has a beauty in his life that makes Iago feel ugly. Similarly, tragic characters are often felt as having a mythic dimension: Hamlet is both Oedipus (the son–husband) and Orestes; Lear is both Oedipus (the outcast–father) and Job. But these are not overt aspects of the presentation of the characters: rather, they are ways of understanding their breadth of appeal. In the romances, however, this presentation of representative figures and reference to mythic analogies is both more obvious and made with fewer concessions to the usual demands of individual characterization. Explicitly symbolic names are congruent with the romance mode, especially with the all-important daughters – Marina ("for she was born at sea I have named her so," 3.1.13), Perdita ("that which is lost," "counted lost for ever," 3.2.135, 3.3.32), Miranda ("O, you wonder," "admired Miranda . . . the top of admiration," 1.2.429, 3.1.37–8). If it is accepted that the traditional "Imogen" is an error for "Innogen" then its suggestion of innocence suits the character's assumed identity as Fidele (the appropriateness of which is, as with the other names, pointed in the text: "Thy name well fits thy faith, thy faith thy name" (4.2.383).[8] Perdita is welcome to Sicilia "as is the spring to th' earth" (5.1.151). Caliban is associated with earth (1.2.316), as Ariel is with air. The very title, *The Tempest*, in pointing to what is, as far as the plot goes, merely a mechanism setting in motion the basic scenario, suggests a symbolic reading, drawing attention to more metaphoric or metaphysical turmoils.

The relation of romance to symbol and to myth has been a central concern of one of the most influential critics of the mode, Northrop Frye, for whom romance is central to his account of literature and criticism more generally.[9] Distinguishing between supposed Iliad and Odyssey readers – those who read for reference to the world, and those who see literature as self-referential – Frye detaches Shakespearean romance from any view of art as (in Matthew Arnold's famous phrase) "a criticism of life," presenting it as an abstract mode in which all the particular materials and articulations are subordinated to the satisfaction that lies in experiencing a particular kind of structure. We may agree that, as with all Shakespeare's comedies, structural satisfactions that can be understood by reference to musical analogies – and may in part depend on unusually full use of actual music to point and heighten crucial moments – do contribute to the experience of these plays. But, though the romances are especially responsive to Frye's interest in the significance of structure, their repeated narrative patterns are made alive and vivid by Shakespeare's special manipulations in each case of dramatic shape – a principal difference between the four plays: though they are based on similar materials, they articulate and dispose it in dissimilar ways. Moreover, their relation to non-aesthetic experience is not finally less than that of tragic realism: it is only more oblique. Nor are the materials or the mode wholly different from those of Shakespearean tragedy. On the contrary, *The Winter's Tale* and *Cymbeline* both contain material that evidently links them to tragedy. Until near the end of Act 3 *The Winter's Tale* appears to be a tragedy, and even its dénouement of reconciliation and rebirth contains reminders of irrevocable loss. *Cymbeline* is dominated by tragic elements until the end of Act 4, and, despite its happy ending, was accordingly placed with the tragedies by the compilers of the First Folio. Interest in narrative structure requires a complementary sense of dramatic particulars, whereas Frye's overriding interest in archetypes leads to generalizations at odds with the specificity vital to most forms of aesthetic pleasure. Frye is right that audiences or readers do not get an adequate sense of the scale of these dramas unless they experience them as in part symbolic and archetypal – not, however, as though there is a mysterious key and all important meanings are ten leagues below the verbal and dramatic surfaces. Local effects of poetry, plot, and character remain central; but these usual satisfactions of drama operate within frameworks that point to other modes of meaning.

Frye's distinction between Iliad and Odyssey readers is not just a convenient simplification: it is a false dichotomy. The delight that the supposed Odyssey reader finds in an author's manipulation of form, convention, and genre ultimately recognizes meaning in such manipulations. Valéry is right: "syntax is a faculty of the soul."[10] That is, structure does not only express content; from the shape of a sentence to the shape of a whole narrative, structure is of itself expressive. The formal, conventional and generic shapes to which Frye's Odyssey reader responds are meaningful, just as, with music, while "meaning" is derived in part from melody, harmony, and instrumental color, structure (binary, ternary, or sonata form; rondo or variation form) is also in itself a mode of signification. Frye's distinction between different types of readers describes, at bottom, no more than gradations on a spectrum. In romance meaning is less involved with the more obvious aspects of subject matter than in realist fiction – and, insofar as it is so, meaning may be the more difficult fully to articulate. But though (as Frye says) we are conscious in Shakespearean comedy of a superficial unlikeness between the stage world and the non-stage world, we are also conscious, especially at crucial moments – usually moments critical to turns in the plot – of a deeper likeness, a recognition and stirring of emotions analogous to the life emotions on which the materials of the play draw. Shakespearean comedy generally, and romance more emphatically, posits that the disasters of life can be healed, or at least, where they cannot – as they cannot, finally, because of death – it posits that we know (or imagine we know) what it would feel like if they could. It is psychologically helpful, as well as deeply pleasurable, for the drama to remind us of this; and this deep pleasure is not disjunct from our knowledge of life experiences that involve some comparable overcoming of error or recovery of something lost.

Romance is inherently difficult to present as material for the stage. Characters tending toward the symbolic, stylized extremes of good and evil, improbable events, and grotesque horror, are not natural materials for drama. The killing of Cloten, and the exhibition of his head and headless body, exemplifies one typical problem. An audience responds to seeing the horrific differently from a reader, for whom it need not be described, and for whom it can be set in a distancing context of the stylized and fantastic. Here the horror of the severed head and decapitated trunk are presented without qualification. That Imogen then can, in a context that recalls the manner of tragedy, mistake Cloten's headless body in Posthumus' clothes for the body of Posthumus himself returns the drama abruptly to the expectations and plausibilities of romance. Similarly, combining characters whose presentation accords with romance conventions in the manner of Guiderius and Arviragus (princes whose nobility is not compromised by their being brought up in a mountain cave), or Cymbeline's Queen (the wicked stepmother of folktale), with characters such as Posthumus, Imogen, and Iachimo – beings who might exist in plays from *Romeo and Juliet* and *Troilus and Cressida* (Posthumus) to *As You Like It* (Imogen) to *Othello* (Iachimo) – places a comparable strain on the acceptance of romance conventions. Posthumus passes from the usual perfections of a romance hero to an antithesis of romance norms in a denunciatory tirade against women in the manner of Lear or Timon. Imogen too moves between romance perfections that suggest Griselda and an independence and fire that recall the heroines of the festive comedies. Iachimo inhabits a dramatic world of psychological plausibility that accords much less readily with Imogen as Griselda than with Posthumus as Timon. Romance plot conventions too, as well as incidents and character types, can impose strains. On dramatic romance and improbability of action Coleridge helpfully steers a course between what he sees as the pedantry of the Académie Française supposition that dramatic illusion must be consistently sustained (for example, by observing the unity of time and place), and the rationalist riposte of Samuel Johnson that illusion is always understood as illusory and does not, therefore, need to be consistent.[11] He argues that the acceptability of the improbable depends on its relation to other elements of the drama – that when it is a prerequisite of the plot, or when it obeys a kind of decorum in corresponding to other kinds of stylization, improbability may be entirely acceptable. Acceptability depends on context.

The romances embody their significances fully only in performance: they are, even more than is usual with Shakespeare, theatrical "happenings."[12] Requirements for music, dancing, spectacular effects, and non-naturalistic wordless action – the choreography of the "happening" – are, to an unusual degree, written into the texts in stage directions, accounts of dumb shows, and other forms of directions implied by the dialogue. That the dumb shows in *Pericles* are within the Gower choruses (2.0, 3.0) emphasizes their antique technique: they are dramatic archaisms, corresponding to Gower's characteristically archaic syntax and vocabulary. Neither dumb show advances the plot: as narrative their content is more clearly explained by Gower (2.0.15–26; 3.0.15–39). What the dumb shows contribute is a manifestation, the more powerful for being visual, of the crucial, framing Gower style – archaic formality. A similar formality marks the crucial turn of the action toward a comic ending in *Cymbeline*, the intervention of the Leonati. Uncertain in status – at first apparently a representation of Posthumus' dream, though finally a supernatural visitation (leaving behind a written prophetic riddle) – this too begins in dumb show, with directions for "solemn music," "music before," and "other music" that imply an elaborately formal entry, probably with musicians on stage, and with emblematic figures – Posthumus' mother as "an ancient matron" (apparently aged in the afterlife, since she died in childbirth); his brothers "with wounds as they died in the wars" (apparently without growing old in the afterlife, fixed as at the moment of death). The episode is set apart from its context by formally patterned verse, again archaic in style, as preparation for the climactic divine intervention, one of the most spectacular effects in all Shakespearean drama – "Jupiter descends in thunder and lightning, sitting upon an eagle." There are comparable moments of theatrical *éclat* in *The Tempest* – the harpies' banquet, with its visual spectacle, grand sound effects, music, dancing, and quasi-magical devices (3.3); and the final assembly, to "solemn music," of the court party, "frantic . . . charmed," into Prospero's magic circle (5.1). The main spectacular effect in *The Tempest* is not archaic (in the manner of *Pericles*) but notably modern, not a dumb show but a masque – with grandly attired goddesses, descending chariot, singing, and dancing, a playhouse version of the most up-to-date fashion in court entertainment in which the verbal text was often a less than equal partner to the other aspects (aural and visual) of *mise-en-scène*.

As these dumb shows, songs, and dances indicate, music too is an important aspect of these plays as theatrical "happenings."[13] In writing about the fundamental conception of his own verse dramas T. S. Eliot describes the "design" of music and words toward which he saw Shakespeare as moving in the romances:

> I have before my eyes a kind of mirage of the perfection of verse drama, which would be a design of human action and of words, such as to present at once the two aspects of dramatic and of musical order. It seems to me that Shakespeare achieved this at least in certain scenes . . . and that this was what he was striving towards in his late plays.[14]

Many of the central moments of these plays are marked by music. *Pericles* indicates something of the range. The first intimations of love between Pericles and Thaisa, Cerimon's revival of Thaisa, and the reunion of Pericles and Marina are all marked by music, with or without dance and song. The undeclared love of Pericles and Thaisa is covertly manifested in dance (2.3). One cannot wholly recover nonverbal aspects of the happening (choreography, music), but what Shakespeare apparently gives the opportunity for – in the group dance of knights in armor (with the "loud music" of its clangor), and the duet with Thaisa for which Pericles takes off his armor ("unclasp") – is a choreographic and aural contrast of war and love. As with the coming to life of the statue of Hermione (also accompanied by music), with Cerimon's recovery of Thaisa the audience cannot be sure, at the particular dramatic moment, whether what is presented is to be supposed natural or magical – whether we are asked to suppose extraordinary medical skill or miracle. The text implies both equally: an analogous Egyptian died and was revived: Thaisa "will live"; but also, she has been only "entranced" (in a swoon: 3.2.83–91). The music too may be understood as natural (restorative and animating) or as magical (a usual stage accompaniment of the supernatural). Either way, it marks a moment of peculiar intensity. Similarly Marina's song (5.1.74) is the prelude to an "artificial [skillful] feat . . . [of] sacred physic." Even in less exceptional circumstances her singing makes "the night-bird mute" (4.0.25), and "she sings like one immortal" (5.0.3). Here, whether music's effects are considered as natural or quasi-magical, it sets the emotional tone for the climactic restoration. That too is accompanied by music which the audience is directed to understand as an awareness of the divine usually imperceptible to human audition – the music of the spheres (5.1.223): it is a theatrical embodiment of the extreme of consciousness to which Pericles' joy has raised him, the epiphany or theophany to which the whole action is directed. What Lear hopes for hopelessly – "a chance which does redeem all sorrows / That ever I have felt" – Pericles experiences. Every aspect of the play moves toward that experience: music is a principal resource in its embodiment.

The other romances give music a similarly prominent role in marking central moments of the drama and intensifying dramatic atmosphere: in *Cymbeline*, with Cloten's aubade heralding dawn after the nighttime "hell" of Iachimo's machinations (2.3), the "solemn music" of Belarius' "ingenious instrument" by means of which Arviragus announces the "death" of Fidele (4.2.187), the great lyric dirge sung over Fidele's supposed dead body,[15] and the music accompanying the supernatural visitations (5.3); in *The Winter's Tale*, the songs and popular ballads of Autolycus and his customers, and the apparently spectacularly wild dance of satyrs, that help to set off the Bohemian countryside from the Sicilian court, and the utterly different music that accompanies the "resurrection" of Hermione; and, mostly remarkably, in *The Tempest*. There the "sounds and sweet airs that give delight," the ideal form of which should be imagined in terms of Caliban's dream of "a thousand twangling instruments," help to characterize magic and the supernatural – in the songs, instrumental music, and dances of Ariel and the spirits of the island, which Ferdinand, like Caliban, finds "sweet" and healing (1.2.394); the similarly therapeutic music, "cure" and "best comforter / To an unsettled fancy," that accompanies the performance of magic (5.1.58–60); and above all the wedding masque, accompanied throughout by music, and ending in song and dance (4.1.58–138). In making the performance of Prospero's magic beautiful, music is part of what suggests that the audience see it as beneficent.

Just as the most typically romance elements of these plays may require bold and frank stylization, and the opposite end of the dramatic spectrum a clashing relative realism, so it is also important in the romances that, as well as the exalted parts being sublime, the comedy should be funny. This is the Mozart comedy mode – from Papageno to Pamina, as from Touchstone to Rosalind. It makes the plays more inclusive in feeling that the tonal range extends from the humor of Boult, the Bawd, and the brothels to the sublime of Pericles' reunion with Marina, from the roguish jollity of Autolycus to the exalted tone of Hermione's "resurrection," from the tipsy banter of Stephano and Trinculo to the grandly solemn invocations of Prospero. Contrasts emphasize extremes, and the gamut of opportunities Shakespeare gives needs to be realized both in performance and in criticism. Laughter is a necessary part of the tonal experience of these plays – at the brothel workers who have values so inverted that they conceive of no perspective other than that from which "holy words" are "abominable"; at the brothel clients who are not just subdued by Marina but who, with romance's delight in extremes, are converted to holiness and chastity; at Auto-lycus when he draws out the credulity of Mopsa and Dorcas about sensational ballad narratives with his pedlar's patter ("Why should I carry lies abroad?"); at Trinculo, truculent with the adulation of King Stephano by his Mooncalf ("I am in case to jostle a constable... thou deboshed fish"). Only in *Cymbeline* is there little laughter: its comedy depends on Cloten, who is too unpleasant to prompt more than a smile.

Though laughter, at both sophisticated comedy and at clowning, is important, the central and characteristic effects of the romances involve wonder and exaltation. As with the trials of Job, in the romances the experience of suffering and the defeat of evil become bases of happiness even greater than that which was destroyed. This is so even in *The Winter's Tale*, where the end focuses not on the deaths of Mamillius and Antigonus but on the recovery of Perdita and the promise, more than simple renewal, epitomized by her marriage to Florizel. The pattern adduced by Jupiter in *Cymbeline* – "Whom best I love, I cross, to make my gift, / The more delayed, delighted" (5.5.195–6) – a pattern analogous to that not only of Job but also of the Christian "fortunate fall," in which evil and suffering are ultimately productive of even greater goodness or happiness, is explicit too in *Pericles* ("present kindness / Makes my past miseries sports"). It is also the pattern adduced by Gonzalo from the action of *The Tempest*: "Was Milan thrust from Milan that his issue / Should become kings of Naples?" As with Gonzalo's easily satirized sketch of Prospero's island as proto-paradise (2.1.149–75), his extrapolation from the action as a whole is simplistic: it supposes a more complete final harmony than the play shows. But, like Gonzalo's invocation of a myth of pastoral innocence and freedom, it does remind us of a pattern in the play against which harmony (and disharmony) can properly be registered.

Corresponding to this extrapolation of good from evil and happiness from grief, words of pardon and forgiveness resonate variously through the final scenes of the romances: Iachimo, Posthumus, Leontes, and (though his penitence is less central than that of the analogous figures) Alonzo all seek and find forgiveness. But again there are differences. In *Pericles* forgiveness is not relevant. The sufferings of Pericles came about in part as a result of error that involved no moral fault (the supposition that Thaisa had died), in part because of moral faults that, by the end of the play, can no longer be forgiven (Cleon and Dionyza's attempt to murder Marina has been avenged by their subjects). And the embodiment of joy in the various reunions could not be more complete. In *The Tempest*, on the other hand, first the reconciliations are only partial: Prospero's claim to forgive Antonio could scarcely be more undermined by its manner ("whom to call brother / Would even infect my mouth"); and Antonio shows no sign whatever of penitence. Then Prospero's rueful qualification of Miranda's innocent, joyous wonder – "O brave new world... 'Tis new to thee" – epitomizes a tone in which real and valid joy does not overcome what can be said to the contrary. The whole process that has brought about the repentance of Alonzo and the loving and politically appropriate marriage of Ferdinand and Miranda has been less radically purgative than parallel trials in the other plays. The deep melancholy of *The Tempest* – with its sadly vigorous hatreds (Prospero's of Antonio, Prospero's and Caliban's of each other), and its vivid individual expressions of *taedium vitae* (Caliban's weeping for the comfort of dreams [3.2.138–46]; Prospero's resonant account of the transience of all things [4.1.146–57]) – continues to be heard in Prospero's final contemplation of a return to life beyond the magic island on the terms on which life has to be lived outside fiction: events will not be arranged as the magician/artist wishes, and every third thought – not, the audience may reflect, just of this one old man, but of all those who have seen (whether in themselves or others) evils such as he has seen – will be of the sorrows epitomized by the grave.

As the criticism of Northrop Frye rightly emphasizes, structure is of crucial importance to the emotional impact and final significance of Shakespearean comedy. In the romances one central element of the emotional impact of the whole that is derived from structure is the focusing of the dramatic experience in a final peripeteia or theophany/epiphany.[16] (How one conceives the crucial turn has interpretative implications, especially about parabolic or more generally religious readings.) This crucial turn of the plot, which in the romances often involves for the central character(s) a heightened moment of clarification and an experience of the divine, brings about for the audience a feeling of release – a comic equivalent of the Aristotelian "catharsis" of tragedy. The importance of these numinous moments for the characters, and the way in which they act as an epiphany for the audience, focusing its experience of the dramatic structure, bears on the issue of the quasi-religious nature of the romances.

Though the romances are pagan in setting they do in some degree invoke Christian assumptions and a Christian frame of reference. *Pericles* is a play of Jupiter, Neptune, Diana, but it also refers at crucial points to a singular "God."[17] Shakespeare arranges the material precisely so that what it leads up to is an overpowering experience of the divine. Pericles hears the music of the spheres: he is for a moment drawn, by his experience of an extraordinary joy, into another level of being. That is why he has to sleep: not only for the sake of the plot (so that Diana can address him in a vision and so bring about the final stage of the action), but because he is exhausted by his experience of the farthest possible extension of his imaginative and emotional capacity. To embody this overwhelming experience is a central aim of the structure, the characters, the poetry, and the *mise-en-scène*. *The Winter's Tale* leads up to a similar moment of epiphany understood in more distinctly Christian terms. A "saint-like" penitence on the part of Leontes is the emotional basis for his reunion with Hermione. Though it also waits on fulfillment of the oracle's condition (that the lost be found), it would be quite different if based on that alone, without Leontes' years of active repentance. In the manner of the miracles of the Gospels, "It is required / You do awake your faith" as a prerequisite of Hermione's apparently miraculous "resurrection," which takes place in Paulina's chapel – not a specifically Christian place of worship, though given the play's (not unusual) anachronistic mixture of Apollo's oracle and references to "the gods" with invocations of "grace" and "him who did betray the best," it should not be specifically non-Christian either. When Perdita denies that her desire to express her reverence for the supposed statue by kneeling is "superstition" the first audience might well feel that, like a good ur-Protestant, she is dissociating her veneration from Roman Catholic worship of "idols." In *The Tempest* Gonzalo's extrapolation of good brought out of evil recalls the pattern of the "fortunate fall" (5.1.203–16) – the more so because Gonzalo's nobility is described in terms of that greatest of Christian virtues, "charity" (1.2.163). And finally "the rarer action is / In virtue than in vengeance" (5.1.27–8): whether Prospero does or does not forgive, his ethic is one of forgiveness in a potential revenge situation, and the terms in which he expresses this ethic imply a conception of it that is Christian.

The romances evoke Christian analogues and Christian conceptions. The significance of their doing so is open to interpretation.[18] The first audiences were accustomed to the idea, derived from Renaissance Platonism, that pagan myth, legend, and fable were to be understood as oblique conceptions of Christian truth – a view that can be stood on its head: the power of Christian myth can be understood as coming, not from its historical truth – irrelevant to the truth of poetry – but from its imaginative embodiment of purely human realities. On this view Shakespeare is not preaching Christianity covertly; he is drawing on the power of Christian myth in constructing romance stories, marvelous elements of which he treats in such a way as to imply Christian analogues. Quasi-religious readings need not carry belief implications.

Shakespearean romance is a mixed mode not all the elements of which sit easily together. These plays experiment with, and so do not wholly conform to romance expectations. They combine idealized or symbolic characters, stylized language, and plots that abound in elements of folktale and myth with realism of character, language, and dramatic mode. They exploit a range of tones from high mysticism to low comedy. They deal with ethical situations in ways that do not always respect romance polarizations of good and evil. They rework various elements of Shakespeare's earlier comedies, tragedies, and histories; and, despite obvious connections and correspondences, in many ways they are not, as a group, internally similar. In combining such disparate materials and styles they present problems for criticism and performance alike. Nevertheless, and despite the fact that some of their most typically romance materials can be difficult to stage, in these plays Shakespeare made drama a congenial and powerful vehicle for some of romance's most characteristic qualities and effects.

See also: chapter 1, ANCIENT ROMANCE; chapter 3, THE POPULAR ENGLISH METRICAL ROMANCES; chapter 5, CHAUCER'S ROMANCES; chapter 6, MALORY AND THE EARLY PROSE ROMANCES; chapter 7, GENDERING PROSE ROMANCE IN RENAISSANCE ENGLAND; chapter 8, SIDNEY AND SPENSER.

Notes

1. For objections see Stephen Orgel, "Shakespeare and the Kinds of Drama." *Critical Inquiry* 6 (1979), 107–23.

2. Cf. Robert Louis Stevenson, "A Humble Remonstrance" (1884). In *R. L. Stevenson on Fiction: An Anthology of Literary and Critical Essays*, ed. Glenda Norquay (Edinburgh: Edinburgh University Press, 1999), pp. 80–91.

3. *Winter's Tale* 5.3.94–5. References and quotations are from *William Shakespeare: The Complete Works*, ed. Stanley Wells and Gary Taylor (Oxford: Oxford University Press, 1988), except for *Pericles*, which this edition does not divide into acts. *Pericles* is quoted from and referenced in the edition of Doreen Del-Vecchio and Antony Hammond (1998).

4. For Montaigne, the Bermuda shipwreck, and Shakespeare's knowledge of seamanship see the appendices to Stephen Orgel's edition (1987).

5. For a well-informed account of modern (post-colonial) readings of Prospero, which intelligently historicizes New Historicist readings, see Howard Felperin 1990: chapter 9. For a positive view of Prospero's magic see John Mebane, *Renaissance Magic and the Return of the Golden Age* (Lincoln: University of Nebraska Press, 1989), and for a negative, D'Orsay W. Pearson, " 'Unless I be reliev'd by prayer': *The Tempest* in perspective," *Shakespeare Studies* 7 (1974), 253–82. For Prospero and Medea see Jonathan Bate, *Shakespeare and Ovid* (Oxford: Clarendon Press, 1993), pp. 249–54.

6. Such readings compare, for example, James I's absolutist view of royal prerogative with the imperviousness to advice of Leontes – an interpretation to which the King's Men must have relied on the King, when he saw the play, being likewise impervious; but the itch to find historical referents is willing to confront difficulties – comparing the death of Mamillius with the death of Prince Henry (a year after *The Winter's Tale* was written, but it would "add resonance" in later performances); or comparing the marriage negotiations of the Jacobean court with the problematic royal marriage in the play (unfortunately for this remote similarity any tempting plausibility lay as wholly in the future as Prince Henry's death: in 1611 Princess Elizabeth's suitor, later King of Bohemia, had not been named heir to that elective monarchy). For an intelligent critique of this kind of historical allegorization from a viewpoint not fundamentally unsympathetic see Simon Palfrey 1997: chapter 1.

7. For a more thematized discussion of the issues in relation to *The Tempest* see Frank Kermode's Arden edition (6th edition, 1964), introduction, sections 4 and 5 (Nature, Art).

8. The issue of whether the character's name should be Imogen or Innogen is fully discussed by Roger Warren in his edition of the play (1998).

9. Frye's principal accounts of Romance can be found in *Anatomy of Criticism* (1957), especially "The Mythos of Summer: Romance"; *A Natural Perspective* (1965), esp. chapter 1 (which begins from Frye's Iliad / Odyssey reader distinction); and *The Secular Scripture* (1976).

10. "Odds and Ends," *Collected Works of Paul Valéry*, ed. Jackson Mathews. 15 vols. (London, Routledge and Kegan Paul, 1957–75), vol. 14.

11. *Literary Remains*, in *Coleridge's Criticism of Shakespeare*, ed. R. A. Foakes (Detroit: Wayne State University Press, 1989), pp. 37–9.

12. A study that brings this out is Roger Warren's *Staging Shakespeare's Last Plays* (Oxford: Clarendon Press, 1990), principally an account of performances at the National Theatre, London, directed by Peter Hall in 1988.

13. Ideas about music and its symbolism axiomatic to Shakespeare's audience, and some music that may have been used in the first productions of the romances, are discussed by J. M. Nosworthy, *Shakespeare Survey* 11 (1958), 60–9. For a fuller account see John H. Long, *Shakespeare's Use of Music* (1961). On dancing see Alan Brissenden, *Shakespeare and the Dance* (London: Macmillan, 1981).

14. "Poetry and Drama" (1951), *On Poetry and Poets* (London: Faber, 1957), p. 87.

15. It is not certain whether this should be sung or said, but the text as it stands (which has the lyric spoken, not sung: 4.2.235–55) is usually assumed to have been written to deal with a practical problem about the singing ability of an actor of the role of Guiderius.

16. There were no interval breaks in contemporary performances that might interrupt the effect of overall dramatic structure (Gary Taylor and John Jowett, *Shakespeare Reshaped, 1606–1623*, 1993, chapter 1).

17. Simonides' blessing of the marriage of Pericles and Thaisa may be purely conventional

(2.5.85). Lysimachus' invocation of "the most just God" immediately before Pericles' reunion with Marina is more remarkable (5.1.54).

18. Religious readings of the romances range from those of Colin Still (1936) and G. Wilson Knight (1947), who claim to uncover timeless Christian meanings, to that of Velma Bourgeois Richmond (2000), who argues for a special compatibility between Shakespeare's imaginative vision in romance and that of Catholic Christianity. For a critique of religious readings see William Empson, "Hunt the Symbol," *Essays on Shakespeare* (1985), pp. 231–43.

References and Further Reading

William Shakespeare

Good modern editions of the plays include the following:

Cymbeline, ed. Roger Warren (1998). Oxford: Clarendon Press.

Pericles, Prince of Tyre, ed. Doreen DelVecchio and Antony Hammond (1998). Cambridge: Cambridge University Press.

Pericles, ed. Suzanne Gossett (2004). London: Arden Shakespeare.

The Tempest, ed. Stephen Orgel (1987). Oxford: Clarendon Press.

The Tempest, ed. Virginia Mason Vaughan and Alden T. Vaughan (1999). London: Arden Shakespeare.

The Tempest, ed. David Lindley (2002).. Cambridge: Cambridge University Press.

The Winter's Tale, ed. J. H. P. Pafford (1963). London: Methmer

The Winter's Tale, ed. Stephen Orgel (1996). Oxford: Clarendon Press.

Note: Among older editions, particularly notable are S. L. Bethell's of *The Winter's Tale* (Oxford: Clarendon Press, 1956; reprinted 1994), and Frank Kermode's of *The Tempest*, 6th edition (London: Methuen, 1964).

References and Criticism

Note: This list is confined to books and essays that specifically use, discuss, or challenge ideas about romance.

Adams, Robert M. (1989). *Shakespeare: the Four Romances*. New York: Norton.

Arthos, John (1953). "*Pericles, Prince of Tyre*: A Study in the Dramatic Use of Romantic Narrative." *Shakespeare Quarterly* 257–70.

Bergeron, David M. (1985). *Shakespeare's Romances and the Royal Family*. Lawrence: University Press of Kansas.

Danby, John F. (1952). *Poets on Fortune's Hill: Studies in Sidney, Shakespeare, Beaumont and Fletcher*. London: Faber, chapter 3.

Edwards, Philip (1958). "Shakespeare's Romances: 1900–1957." *Shakespeare Survey* 1–18.

Empson, William (1985). *Essays on Shakespeare*, ed. David Pirie. Cambridge: Cambridge University Press.

Felperin, Howard (1972). *Shakespearean Romance*. Princeton, NJ: Princeton University Press.

Felperin, Howard (1973). *Dramatic Romance: Plays, Theory and Criticism*. New York: Harcourt Brace Jovanovich.

Felperin, Howard (1990). *The Uses of the Canon: Elizabethan Literature and Contemporary Theory*. Oxford: Clarendon Press.

Frey, Charles (1980). *Shakespeare's Vast Romance: A Study of "The Winter's Tale."* Columbia: University of Missouri Press.

Frye, Northrop (1957). *Anatomy of Criticism*. Princeton, NJ: Princeton University Press.

Frye, Northrop (1965). *A Natural Perspective: The Development of Shakespearean Comedy and*

Romance. New York: Columbia University Press.

Frye, Northrop (1976). *The Secular Scripture: A Study of the Structure of Romance*. Cambridge, MA: Harvard University Press.

Gesner, Carol (1970). *Shakespeare and the Greek Romance: A Study of Origins*. Lexington: University Press of Kentucky.

Hoeniger, F. D. (1976). "Shakespeare's Romances since 1958: A Retrospect." *Shakespeare Survey* 29, 1–10.

Hunter, Robert Grams (1965). *Shakespeare and the Comedy of Forgiveness*. New York: Columbia University Press.

Jordan, Constance (1997). *Shakespeare's Monarchies: Ruler and Subject in the Romances*. Ithaca, NY: Cornell University Press.

Kay, Carol McGinnis, and Henry E. Jacobs, eds. (1978). *Shakespeare's Romances Reconsidered*. Lincoln: University of Nebraska Press.

Kermode, Frank (1963). *William Shakespeare: The Final Plays*. London: Longman.

Knight, G. Wilson (1947). *The Crown of Life: Essays in Interpretation of Shakespeare's Final Plays*. London: Methuen. [Reprinted with corrections, 1965.]

Lawlor, John (1962). "*Pandosto* and the Nature of Dramatic Romance." *Philological Quarterly* 41, 96–113.

Long, John H. (1961). *Shakespeare's Use of Music: The Final Comedies*. Gainesville: University of Florida Press.

Mowat, Barbara A. (1976). *The Dramaturgy of Shakespeare's Romances*. Athens: University of Georgia Press.

Palfrey, Simon (1997). *Late Shakespeare: A New World of Words*. Oxford: Clarendon Press.

Peterson, Douglas L. (1973). *Time, Tide, and Tempest: A Study of Shakespeare's Romances*. San Marino, CA: Huntington Library.

Pettet, E. C. (1949). *Shakespeare and the Romance Tradition*. London: Staples Press.

Richmond, Velma Bourgeois (2000). *Shakespeare, Catholicism, and Romance*. London: Continuum.

Ryan, Kiernan (1998). *Shakespeare: The Last Plays*. Longman Critical Readers. London: Longman.

Smith, Hallett (1972). *Shakespeare's Romances: A Study in Some Ways of the Imagination*. San Marino, CA: Huntington Library.

Still, Colin (1936). *The Timeless Theme: A Critical Theory Formulated and Applied*. London: Ivor Nicholson and Watson. [Includes a revised form of his *Shakespeare's Mystery Play: A Study of "The Tempest,"* 1921.]

Thorne, Alison, ed. (2003). *Shakespeare's Romances*. New Casebooks. Basingstoke: Macmillan.

Tobias, Richard C., and Paul G. Zolbrod, eds. (1974). *Shakespeare's Late Plays: Essays in Honor of Charles Crow*. Athens: Ohio University Press.

Uphaus, Robert W. (1981). *Beyond Tragedy: Structure and Experience in Shakespeare's Romances*. Lexington: University Press of Kentucky.

Wells, Stanley (1966). "Shakespeare and Romance." In *Later Shakespeare*. Stratford-upon-Avon Studies 8, ed. John Russell Brown and Bernard Harris. London: Edward Arnold, pp. 49–77.

White, R. S. (1985). *"Let Wonder Seem Familiar": Endings in Shakespeare's Romance Vision*. London: Athlone Press.

10
Chapbooks and Penny Histories

John Simons

The printing revolution, the subsequent revolution in literacy, and the development of sub-industries within and related to the book trade did not benefit only those who lived in households where income was sufficient to purchase books, to have access to collections of books, or later, to afford the not inconsiderable subscriptions to circulating libraries.[1] Many of those who lived on the margins of these groups – at most times the majority of the population – also learned to read and they quickly formed a market for books and reading material that could not possibly be satisfied, given their low income, from the production of those printers based, while the monopoly of the Stationers' Company was in force, in London, Oxford, and Cambridge, from which came the texts that make up our idea of the corpus of preindustrial literature and scholarship.[2] Nor, when the printing industry was liberalized, could the many provincial printers who soon set up shop satisfy this demand from their more prestigious output. Instead, the rural and industrial poor (though not exclusively these groups) depended for their reading matter on the chapbooks which circulated in vast numbers between the middle of the seventeenth century and the middle of the nineteenth. Of course, there were many other ways in which such people could have had access to reading material, but the chapbook formed the staple diet – at least until the end of the eighteenth century – and the industry and sub-industries of chapbook production operated almost exclusively to serve this large market.

This chapter is intended to show how romances were presented in chapbooks but, given the rather arcane nature of scholarship on the subject, it will be appropriate at this point to offer a brief account of chapbooks more generally.[3] The most common definition of chapbooks is probably "cheap books" but this does not really address the very specific qualities of these fragile little objects. For a start, although the most common price for a chapbook seems to have been one old penny, this was not an inconsiderable amount for an agricultural laborer living precariously in, say, the bad years of the 1790s. When gentlemen like James Boswell and Sir Walter Scott collected chapbooks as curiosities they would have found them cheap, but one of

William Cobbett's "chopsticks" would not have done.[4] Furthermore, there were other kinds of cheap books in circulation. Later in the nineteenth century there were the various series designed for the self-improvement of the working class, for example, and these – the first real books and periodicals aimed at this market – marked the end of the heyday of the chapbook.[5] In the later eighteenth century the religious revival (stimulated, in part, by fears of radicalism and revolution) and the resulting tracts, produced under the aegis of the Society for the Promotion of Christian Knowledge and with the guidance of figures such as Sarah Trimmer and Hannah More, also led to an influx into the marketplace of cheap texts that explicitly emulated the physical forms of chapbooks.[6]

Chapbooks have to be defined by price, but they also need to be defined by their format and by the ways in which they were produced and distributed. Chapbooks are small books that have been printed on both sides of a single leaf of paper. This is then folded into a small booklet, most commonly of 24 pages, although chapbooks of other sizes (especially smaller ones) are by no means uncommon. Chapbooks that have survived today are usually either still unfolded, or they have been cut and bound up for library use by a contemporary gentry collector or by a modern bookseller.

Distribution was also distinctive. There were huge printing operations for chapbooks in London and, later, Newcastle and Glasgow, with important centers also at Banbury, York, and Falkirk.[7] Many, if not most, of the smaller provincial printers also seem to have tried their hand at chapbooks, and examples with imprints ranging from Shrewsbury to Whitehaven and from Warrington to Worcester may be found. Chapbooks in Welsh circulated in Wales and there was a thriving market for chapbooks printed in Ireland. It was, of course, possible to buy chapbooks from local distributors but just as important – and more important in very remote areas – was the network of pedlars or chapmen who roamed the countryside on fixed routes, selling not only the everyday things that might add a little luxury to cottage life, such as equipment for needlework, combs, mirrors, and some fabrics, but also chapbooks. This distribution network meant that even isolated parts of the countryside, where the journey to a town with a printer or bookseller would have been arduous and not undertaken regularly, were part of the systematic circulation of printed information.[8] At the same time, it is likely that access to that part of the system represented by chapbooks was arbitrary inasmuch as an individual's choice would have been determined by what happened to be in the chapman's pack when he passed through. It is, however, probable that assiduous readers could ask chapmen to find particular texts and bring them on their next circuit, and it is not uncommon to find chapbooks that list on the last page the other titles available from the printer.[9]

Chapbooks covered a marvelously wide range of materials.[10] There were books of practical advice on such topics as letter-writing and courtship. There were books of jokes that continued the very old traditions of the Tudor jest books. There were rogue biographies and sensational accounts of lurid crimes. There were songbooks and collections of poetry. There were books of prophecy and prognostication, such as those of Mother Shipton. There were books of popular history, geography, and natural history. There were religious texts. There were abridgments of novels such as *Robinson Crusoe* and *Moll Flanders*.[11] There were freestanding tales, some of which were written especially for chapbook circulation. There were chapbooks aimed at children although, to some extent, most chapbooks doubled as children's books. In America, which depended largely, at least before 1776, on imports of chapbooks from Great Britain, there were also the distinctive forms of the Indian captivity narrative and the "Richard Rum" temperance story.[12] Lastly, there were versions of the romances that had descended from the chivalric poems of the thirteenth and fourteenth centuries and which had entered chapbook form via the initially prestigious prints of the early modern period. Added to these were chapbook editions of the second generation of chivalric romances produced in the later sixteenth and early seventeenth centuries by writers such as Richard Johnson and Emmanuel Forde. Both these types of romance became gradually less valued and increasingly viewed as representing an old-fashioned and unsophisticated taste. But they still had a place in the hearts of certain readers and it is these readers and, in particular, the chapbook romances they loved with which this chapter will be concerned.

It should be said very clearly that if some sections of the early modern readership saw the romances as unsophisticated, this judgment was based mainly on the view that anything to do with the Middle Ages carried with it the dust and superstitions that the scientific revolution and the Enlightenment were dedicated to sweeping away. But the criticism of taste and discrimination that is implied by a criticism of romance is not necessarily a criticism of any individual reader's ability to read or understand. In other words, this was a critique born out of the legitimate concerns of the educated elite and not necessarily an attack on humble readers. As the eighteenth century wore on, polite commentators also became anxious about the political effects of chapbook reading (and the growth of literacy more generally) and the risk that the lower classes might become discontented, and thus rebellious, if their imaginations and intellects were stimulated by the wrong kinds of reading matter.[13] Again, this is a critique of chapbooks that is rational and perfectly understandable within the norms of its time. Less forgivable is the perception implied in much literary scholarship on the eighteenth century whereby chapbooks are written off as unsophisticated and intended for the uneducated. Anyone who looks at chapbooks will notice that the language used in them is not particularly unsophisticated and might well share my conclusion that the humble consumer of chapbooks was not separated from more prestigious books by an inability to read them but by an inability to afford them.

Having briefly surveyed the forms and field of chapbook publication, let us now look at the place that romance occupied in this thriving market. As mentioned above, the chapbook romances were derived from two sources: the chivalric romances of the Middle Ages proper and the neochivalric prose texts of the Elizabethan and Jacobean periods. The medieval texts arrived in chapbook form in three ways. They were reduced from the early modern prints of the Middle English originals, they derived from versions of these texts that had already been modified into another form during the early modern period, or they appeared in chapbooks via much reduced ballad or folktale versions which may or may not have had explicit references to the original medieval text. It is worth adding at this point that there are few, if any, chapbooks that cannot be traced back to an earlier printed text of somewhat higher status, and the same may be said for most, if not all, ballads where these have been collected orally.[14] Where chapbooks do not have an obvious source, I think it would still be true to say that they have an obvious model.

Neochivalric prose followed an easier route and reduced forms of these often extensive and usually florid texts frequently began to circulate within a generation of their original appearance in print.[15] These reduced versions eventually evolved into the terse narratives of the chapbook versions, and there must have been a crossover period where chapbook versions of texts circulated in the same market as the full original versions. In fact, this phenomenon, in a slightly different form, was operative throughout most of the period during which chapbooks were the staple of popular reading: chapbook texts of *Moll Flanders* and *Robinson Crusoe* would have been read in cottages and nurseries while more prestigious editions of Defoe's novels were to be found in more polite libraries.[16] Similarly, while romances such as *Guy of Warwick* and *Bevis of Hampton* traveled the roads in the chapman's pack, scholars and antiquarians from Thomas Wright and Thomas Percy through to Joseph Ritson and George Ellis and, later, W. W. Skeat and Frederick Furnivall were taking a very serious interest in the problems and pleasures of the medieval originals.

In modern accounts of chapbooks, romances (both medieval and neochivalric) always feature heavily. Perusal of various trade lists and other documents from the eighteenth and early nineteenth centuries shows a slightly different picture, although romances still have a marked presence, particularly in the earlier period. The most common texts deriving from the medieval romances proper are *Guy of Warwick* and *Valentine and Orson*, with *Bevis of Hampton* being found slightly less often. Texts that are closely aligned to romances are common too, especially *The Seven Wise Masters* and the complex of narratives of the *King Edward and the Shepherd* type. Of the neochivalric texts Richard Johnson's *The Seven Champions of Christendom* is most common, with Forde's *Parismus* (sometimes in a form which included the sequel *Parismenos*), *Montelion*, and the independent text, *Don Belianis*, close behind in popularity. If we look at the most extensive trade list available, that of Cluer Dicey and Richard Marshall (issued in 1744), we find that of 145 items listed (counting two-part issues as single titles) 12 or just less than 8 percent derive from chivalric or neochivalric texts.[17] The chivalric texts are *Bevis of Hampton*, *Guy of Warwick*, and *Valentine and Orson*. The neochivalric texts are *Don Bellianis of Greece*, *Dorastus and Fawnia*, *Monetellion*, *Parismus of Bohemia*, and *The Seven Champions*. Texts allied to romance include *Courtier and the Tinker*, *King and Cobler*, *The Seven Wise Masters*, and the somewhat less authentic *Seven Wise Mistresses*.

This calculation does not take into account the relative stock levels or production levels of each text, so the actual number of romance chapbooks in circulation may have been considerably greater (or much less) than the 8 percent in stock when considered as a proportion of the total number of chapbooks available in the mid-eighteenth century. We can, however, assume that this proportion was more or less accurate across the country as we can see evidence of chapbook producers in many different centers dealing in the same range of texts.[18] Some 70 years after the compilation of the Dicey/Marshal stock list, the list produced by the Cheneys, who were stationers and printers in Banbury, shows only 15 items (again counting two-part productions as one title) with only one romance (*Valentine and Orson*; Neuburg 1964: 80–1). The stock levels suggest that this text was neither more nor less popular than others on the list, but there is plenty of evidence of the continued popularity of other romance texts in chapbook form well into the nineteenth century. Interestingly enough, the proportion of texts derived from chivalric romances which were part of the famous *bibliothèque bleue*, the extensive series of chapbooks published in the French town of Troyes, mainly but not exclusively in the eighteenth century, has also been estimated at 8 percent although here the range of texts is slightly different and included, for example, texts from the Charlemagne cycles which, as far as I am aware, were never produced in chapbook form in the British Isles.[19]

It is not usually possible to attribute Middle English romances to named authors, and exceptions such as the case that has been made for Thomas Chestre as author of *Sir Launfal* and *Lybaeus Desconus* are rare.[20] Where names are attached to particular texts we can also not be sure, as for example in the case of a number of manuscripts associated with an enigmatic "Rate," whether such attributions refer to an author or merely to the scribe.[21] However, we should not underestimate the role of scribal intervention in giving distinctive forms to individual variants of romance texts as they are copied from manuscript to manuscript: it is clear that scribes did, on occasion, consciously modify texts, sometimes very extensively. What is not clear is whether or not such modifications were the result of the scribe's urge to act as a kind of composite author-editor, the pragmatic need to produce a text of a certain shape and size in order to enable the construction of a manuscript book of a certain size and shape, or a deliberate attempt to reflect the interests and wishes of individual patrons.

The question of authorship of the chapbook romances is, for the most part, equally vague. There are a few known chapbook authors: Dougal Graham, "The Bellman of Glasgow," is one such and another is James Hogg, "The Ettrick Shepherd." Hogg, of course, went on to celebrity in more official literary circles, and it is instructive to compare the original chapbook versions of some of his tales with the revisions that are to be found in the printed volumes of his collected works.[22] What seems most likely is that chapbook texts were often produced by the printers themselves and by their apprentices. It is interesting to note, for example, that the novelist Samuel Richardson began life as apprentice to a printer who is known to have produced chapbooks. It may be of significance that the epistolary form of his work is mirrored in chapbooks designed to teach readers how to write letters (especially in the context of conducting courtship) and where the sequence of sample letters can often form a continuous narrative. It is certainly of significance that Mr Colbrond, one of the persecutors of Richardson's heroine Pamela, shares a name with one of *Guy of Warwick's* best-known opponents (Simons 1992: 130). It is likely that Richardson adopted this name not from any version of the full Middle English text of *Guy of Warwick* but rather from the common chapbook version. He could have had some confidence that this would have been familiar to most, if not all, of his readers and it is not unreasonable to speculate that, as a young man, he may have been involved in the production of a *Guy of Warwick* chapbook himself.

Guy of Warwick is, in fact, one of the few chapbooks for which we can trace an unbroken line from the Middle English versions. This romance was first printed by William Copland in 1569 and was, in various subsequent versions, popular throughout the remainder of the reign of Elizabeth I and into that of her successor.[23] In 1614, Samuel Rowlands, a writer largely of pamphlets in the manner of Robert Greene and miscellaneous other short works in prose and verse, produced a modernized and shortened version in stanza form and this became the basis for other versions over the next half-century or so.[24] Rowlands' version was, in turn, reduced and converted into prose by Samuel Smithson whose much-reduced narrative first appeared in 1688 (Simons 1998: 51–68). With minor variations, Smithson's version became the basis for the many *Guy of Warwick* chapbooks of the eighteenth and nineteenth centuries. This unbroken line of succession – which runs parallel with the history of *Guy* as an antiquarian/scholarly text and as a much longer narrative produced for the patriotic education of polite children – enables us to see very precisely just how a chapbook came into being and what kinds of changes were made as the text moved both from one form to another and from one period or audience to another. Some more detailed commentary on this will be found below.

Having considered some aspects of the production of chapbook romances, we may now look at the ways in which they were received. It will have been seen from the list of chapbook genres that a reader of chapbooks could have assembled an interestingly varied library which offered insights into a number of the main branches of official knowledge alongside less official studies such as palmistry, divination by moles, and prognostication.[25] It should also be remembered that the kinds of rural households where chapbooks may have been found would also, if reading matter were available at all, have had an almanac in which more practical concerns were considered (Capp 1979). These almanacs formed an important part of rural life and provided useful knowledge and a valuable tool. For example, I have a copy of the 1797 issue of *Old Moore's Almanac* in which the original owner has used the calendar pages to note the bulling, calving, and marketing times for various of his cows. If almanacs were used in this way, so might chapbooks have been. We can also be confident that another text to be found in most cottage libraries would have been the Bible. Bibles could be used for obvious devotional purposes, but they could also be used for less respectable needs, such as divination, by placing a key in the pages and reading the verse on which it fell when the book was opened. This was a humble version of the more polite *sortes Virgilianae* (Virgilian divination), most famously practiced by Charles I while he was a prisoner: there is a record of a *Guy of Warwick* chapbook being used in the same way (Vincent 1989: 176–7).

Of course, the possession of books did not necessarily mean an ability to read. For instance, a report of a pedlar working for the American Tract Society in 1844 mentions that a family in the Pines area of New Jersey proudly showed him a Greek lexicon that they thought was a Bible, and there is no reason to doubt that similar families may have existed in the United Kingdom.[26] On the other hand, an inability to read did not necessarily mean complete separation from print culture. The question of literacy rates in the English countryside during the eighteenth century is a vexed one, although we can be reasonably confident that rates in Scotland were higher.[27] When Edmund Burke said in 1792 that there were 80,000 readers in the country we should assume he meant that there were 80,000 consumers of polite culture and that his identification of what constituted a reader carried a very strong overtone of class or economic power.[28] It is likely that literacy rates in Jacobean London ran at something like 50 percent for adult males, with a slightly lower figure for women, and that there was a further lowering as the dwelling place became more remote from a town or city.[29] However, for every person who could read for himself or herself there was at least one to whom that person could read aloud. We know, for example, that devotional reading and prayers could form a part of the life of households where the master or mistress would read to the servants. There is also anecdotal evidence for the existence of reading or storytelling evenings, equivalent to the French *veillée* or the Italian *veglia*, in the English countryside, and it seems likely that even where these were not organized on a communal basis they would have taken place within individual cottages.[30]

Thus the romances circulated in both printed and quasi-oral form simultaneously. But what would a poorly educated or uneducated farm laborer have made of them? I am fairly sure that the one thing we can rule out is the commonest argument: that these texts served an escapist purpose. A number of factors militate against this possibility. The first is the problem of escapism itself. In what does this inhere? My view is that the idea of escapism rests on two related notions. The first is that people are dissatisfied with their lot. The second is that they use their imagination to compensate themselves for this dissatisfaction. Now, this is all very well in conditions of prosperity where mere imaginative extension suffices to project the individual out of the unsatisfactory situation. But in conditions of dire poverty this kind of emotional travel strikes me as being just as much a luxury as, say, hot meat on the table at every meal. I am not arguing here that villagers of the eighteenth century had no imagination, but rather that poverty is a condition that affects and determines intellectual as well as physical opportunities.

The second problem with escapism is the assumption that the literary world into which the escape takes place, or which stimulates the escape, is perceived and understood as being purely imaginary. Again, this seems to depend on a very clear understanding of the boundary between fact and fiction or reality and imagination. It also assumes a non-utilitarian reading of aesthetic texts. It seems to me that any such boundary was differently drawn in the eighteenth century from the way it is today, and also that the impulse to read was, almost invariably, driven by a desire to find utility in every action – for each action requires energy and, in conditions of poverty, energy is a commodity that needs careful husbandry.

Lastly, the notion of escapism depends on a sense of alternatives, some of which are realistic possibilities, while others are completely fantastic. Such a range of alternatives makes escapism possible as it grows out of the multiple stimulation that is the result of wide exposure, either physically or vicariously, to various experiences. For example, we may all dream of foreign travel, but this is because we have all either done some foreign traveling ourselves and want imaginatively to recreate its pleasures or because we know enough about the wider world through media representation to fantasize about it for ourselves. Again, the closed world and limited opportunity of the eighteenth-century laborer makes such imaginative consumerism difficult, if not impossible, to achieve.

So, what did the chapbook reader make of a romance chapbook? The first thing is that chapbooks did provide imaginative stimulation. However, I would argue that this stimulation grew, not out of an impulse to escapism, but rather as part of the structure of access to knowledge that chapbooks provided more generally. In other words, in reading, say, *Bevis of Hampton*, the reader was able to access a world which was not his or her own but which offered a credible and viable emotional alternative to it, just as reading history chapbooks (and the word "history" is richly ambiguous in this context) offered an image of a different world. Second, we must not necessarily assume that the chapbook reader did, in fact, make a hard and fast division between romances and other kinds of chapbooks: it may be that they all offered an equally "real" access to a world of knowledge and manners that gave a pleasing and instructive contrast to that of the village community. In this sense, there may have been little difference between reading the life of Guy of Warwick and reading, say, the life of Nelson in chapbook form. Third, romance chapbooks would have offered models of conduct for emulation: the values of heroism, decency, and politeness represented in romances could easily have been understood as transferable in modified form to the everyday life of the laborer and, again, the existence of chapbooks about conduct shows that there was an interest and demand for texts which offered this option much more explicitly. Finally, the growth of a national consciousness and the coalescence of models of Britishness alongside models of Englishness, Scottishness, and Irishness (Welshness is a more elusive construct in this sense because of the key role of the Welsh language in forming a national identity within the principality) made chapbooks such as *Guy of Warwick*, *Bevis of Hampton*, and *The Seven Champions of Christendom* obvious locations for the celebration of national superiority and virtue, especially in the context of a period when most of the foreign news concerned victories over the French.[31]

So the chapbook reader found in romance both diversion and edification. In other words, romance offered the uneducated reader not solely the imaginative and aesthetic literary diversions that were available to a more polite audience but, in equal measure, both useful knowledge and a sense of participation in a world of culture which would have been only dimly glimpsed through encounters with the local gentry. Chapbook romances are, when viewed through the lens of a speculative account of their reception by the core audience of the rural poor, somewhat different from the romances that, in fuller forms, constituted their sources. In the eighteenth and early nineteenth centuries this is of especial significance as the chapbook romances also need to be read against the rise of Gothic as an aesthetic fashion and medievalism as a newly important and systematized branch of scholarship.

In this respect we can use chapbook romances as a tool to stratify our understanding of the reception of romance more generally. In polite society the attraction to the medieval manifested in the vogue for Gothic (I am talking here of the fanciful "Strawberry Hill" Gothic of Horace Walpole and his imitators, not the much more rigorous and academically well-founded Gothic of Pugin in the next century) represents a significant split in the consciousness of well-to-do readers. On the one hand the representation of the Middle Ages, the Gothic, handed down from the early eighteenth century is of a time of uncultivated barbarism and viciousness. On the other hand, the Gothic romances of Walpole, Radcliffe, Reeve and others exploited this very distaste and made it a subject for fiction. Contrary to the current critical orthodoxy on Gothic fiction, which tends to see it as offering an otherwise repressed audience a titillating and almost pornographic alternative to mainstream literature and representing a revolutionary new direction in taste, careful reading of the sources will disclose that the Gothic actually reproduced very faithfully a body of opinion about the Middle Ages that had been current in one form or other for the best part of half a century.[32] At the same time, this perception was being contested by the careful scholarship of a new generation of antiquarians and scholars who found in the Middle Ages not barbarism but a sophisticated and complex culture, which offered a very real foundation for understanding the present. Thus, a contemplation of the medieval romances and their neo-Gothic imitators in polite contexts shows a picture of discontinuity not only in the transmission of romance from the Middle Ages into the Enlightenment but also within the polite audiences of the Enlightenment itself. When we turn to chapbook romances and chapbook readers we see a very different picture. Here we can see unbroken lines of transmission and a picture of continuity in both the production and the reception of texts.

This is not to say that the audience for romances in chapbook form was not in itself stratified. It may briefly be modeled as follows: agricultural laborers, urban workers, children of all classes, adult members of the gentry who had never grown out of their childhood tastes, adult members of the gentry who saw chapbooks as an antiquarian curiosity to be collected. Leaving aside children and the two groups of gentry, we can look at the humble readership in more detail. Where urban workers are concerned, the main complexity in assessing the extent and nature of chapbook readership is the fact that living in an urban environment offered both systematic access to reading materials and the possibility of involvement in radical politics (especially toward the end of the eighteenth century) which was likely to stimulate an entirely different kind of reading – although it might be noted that chapbook versions of the works of Tom Paine were available almost at the same time as the originals (Wood 1994: 94–5). Furthermore, towns quickly began to develop educational establishments for the working man (these evolved into the Mechanics' Institutes and, in the present day, a number of universities) which offered access to a wider range of material than anything comparable for the more remote parts of the countryside.[33] Looking to agricultural laborers, we can see three possible groups: those that regularly bought chapbooks, those that occasionally bought chapbooks, those that could not afford to buy chapbooks (or did not because they could not read) but did have the opportunity to hear them read. Of these groups, the first is by far the most important and must have been composed of the slightly more prosperous members of the village communities. It was these people who acted as "culture brokers" for their immediate neighbors and as a source of access to print other than the parson or the local gentry.[34] Considering this model we can begin to see how important it is not to assume a unified understanding of romance in chapbook form, and this explains why the scattered evidence that has come down to us represents a far from univocal response.

This account of chapbook romance has thus far been concerned almost exclusively with the British Isles and the heyday of the form between the late seventeenth and the mid-nineteenth centuries. Before moving to a detailed consideration of some examples, it is important further to contextualize the English chapbooks and chapbook romance in general by a very brief survey of the form in other countries and other times. I have already alluded to the chapbook industry in the American colonies and the early years of the United States. When we consider this market we see, in the colonial period, a large-scale importation of chapbook titles that have the same variation in subject matter, and an analogous proportion of titles, as those found in the old country. One important player in North America, both as author and producer, was Andrew Steuart, who first kept his links with Ulster alive by his importation of chapbooks produced by Belfast printers and subsequently produced his own American texts.[35] So *Guy of Warwick* circulated as widely across the Atlantic as it did in its home country, and we can find not only American versions of the conventional prose version, based on the original Smithson modification of Rowlands' poem, but also new verse chapbooks based on Rowlands and produced after the success of the American Rebellion.

In Continental Europe chapbook romances were also widespread, and examples may be found in various dialects of Italian, German, Dutch, Danish, and Czech (Bohemian) among other languages. In Spain the enormous and sprawling adventures of Amadis de Gaulle were reduced to chapbook size as early as 1515 (the earliest known edition of the long version dates from 1508) although here it might be argued that what we are dealing with is, in fact, a chapbook version of a ballad rather than a reduction of the complete text. The question must be, however, whether that ballad existed before the chapbook or whether the chapbook sought to deal with the intractable bulk of *Amadis* by adopting ballad form. In addition, there were Spanish chapbook versions of texts from the Charlemagne cycle. In Russia *Bevis of Hampton* seems to have been particularly popular, and there is an early chapbook, complete with a wonderfully naive woodcut of Prince Bova and his love, the Princess Dzinskaya. In more modern times the *folhetos* of Brazil maintain the tradition of chapbook romances today, while at the beginning of the twentieth century the chapbook author Yona produced romance chapbooks in Judeo-Spanish for the Sephardic community of Salonika.[36] I have already alluded to the French *bibliothèque bleue* (so-called because of the color of the paper wrappers that covered the little books) and no survey of chapbook romance could be considered complete without a little more detail on this extraordinarily comprehensive and systematically produced series of chapbooks. The popular literature produced in Troyes and its environs has been subject to considerably more study than have British chapbooks, or indeed, the chapbooks of any other country. Scholarship in this field has tended to see the *bibliothèque* as the carrier and sign of the *mentalité* of its readers, the "little people" so beloved of historians of pre-revolutionary France. At the most basic level this must, of course, be true. As for the English chapbooks, the *bibliothèque* could not have survived unless what it offered struck a chord that beguiled its readers and tempted them to invest their limited money in further purchases. However, as for English chapbooks, the crucial question has to be that of whether the *bibliothèque* constructed or reproduced that *mentalité*. At one level both possible answers will be true, especially if we abandon the pernicious habit of seeing groups of common people as an undifferentiated "class" and try instead to understand that they were individuals with different tastes.

We also need to concern ourselves with confronting the equally pernicious habits of assuming that the common reader in the pre-industrial period received what he or she was given quite uncritically. Even if the *bibliothèque bleue* or the chapbooks were a concerted attempt to inculcate a conservative worldview and a consequent political docility in the common reader – and there is no reason to think this; indeed, if anything the evidence suggests that polite thinkers feared rather the opposite – why should we assume that these readers would necessarily be compliant in such a project? I am afraid that in arguments of this kind we see the difficulties that some scholars have in coming to terms with the notion that the poor might be intelligent and that physical poverty and intellectual poverty might not necessarily be the same thing. Where the romances of the *bibliothèque bleue* are concerned I would rather fall back on the kind of arguments I have mounted above for the English chapbook romances and see a continuity that does not necessarily imply conservatism and a variation of response that arises naturally from the arbitrary stratifications of the chapbook audience.

The one major difference which seems to me important was that, while the English chapbooks presented the narratives of the old religion (romances are essentially a Roman Catholic art form and were clearly seen as such by the Protestant commentators of the English Reformation) within a Protestant context that was often rabidly anti-Catholic, the French texts circulated within a society that was broadly Catholic in outlook and within which the Roman Catholic Church operated a more or less explicit system of social control in the countryside.[37] This may be used as evidence for the romances of the *bibliothèque* as bearers of conservative messages, but perhaps that is possible only if one sees the social organization of the French village from a modern secular perspective and chooses to see the peasantry as an uncritical mass. I doubt if the religious implications of the medieval romances were important to their readers in the eighteenth century, and I believe that they would have been far more interested in the unfolding of the narratives and in what they could learn from the conduct of the heroes and heroines.

We may now turn to a detailed consideration of individual chapbooks. The best starting point is perhaps *Guy of Warwick* as this is the most commonly found text. The Middle English versions of *Guy of Warwick* are lengthy and comprehensive accounts of the interaction between the chivalric and pious dimensions of knighthood articulated though an exhaustive and occasionally repetitive catalogue of the hero's triumphs over various adversities. Guy is of relatively humble birth, and his desire for the hand of the Earl of Warwick's daughter Felice forms the first stimulus to adventure as he seeks to prove his worth in the field of martial adventure. His demonstration of chivalric prowess enables him to win his goal but he realizes how empty the world of chivalry is when it is separated from religious significance. The second part of the romance is therefore taken up with another set of adventures showing Guy as a crusader, and the poem ends with a recognition scene followed not long after by the deaths of both protagonists.

Samuel Rowlands' version of the story maintains most of the key elements but reduces the space given to description of fighting and slightly changes the emphasis of some incidents. The chapbook authors were faced with a very simple but daunting challenge – how to reduce such a sprawling (but coherent) narrative into the narrow compass of 24 pages. The chapbook carries out the task of reduction with perhaps surprising success and tact. There is no attempt to reproduce everything so that the multifarious descriptions of tournaments, battles, and single combats found in the original are pared down to a representative selection which, in itself, consists of shortened accounts. In fact, this tendency to reduce the space given to descriptions of battles is inherited from the popular romances of the early modern period where, already, we begin to see a stress on the interaction of characters and the examination of conduct within a social framework that is somewhat wider than that found in the medieval period, when texts concentrate almost exclusively on the realms of chivalry and the nuances of courtly behavior.

At the same time, the chapbook author recognizes two different aspects of the *Guy of Warwick* story and concentrates on these. The first concerns those things that make Guy's story distinctive. The second is a choice of key moments of high emotion that drive the longer narrative and give it shape. Thus we find the initial meeting with Felice (called Phillis in the chapbook), the winning and leaving of the Emperor's daughter, the acquisition of a pet lion, the Terry subplot, the dragon fight, the return and marriage, the penitential revelation and pilgrimage, the fight with Colbrond and the defeat of the Danes, the recognition scene, and the holy death. These are the main elements of any *Guy of Warwick* narrative, and they are all to be found in the chapbooks. In this primary regard the chapbook not only succeeds in retaining the basic shape and motivation of all *Guy* narratives but also does so in a manner that is relatively unhurried.

However, while some elements of the *Guy* story are dealt with briefly, others are expanded to occupy a much larger part of the chapbook version of the romance than they do, relatively speaking, in the medieval versions. This is particularly the case with regard to the initial narrative impetus surrounding Guy's courtship of Phillis and his initial rejection by her, Guy's penitential meditations after he has left Phillis to become a pilgrim and crusader, and his fight with Colbrond. The effect of the stress on these elements above the others is threefold. First, we are reminded of the social element that intervenes to complicate Guy's desire for Phillis. Second, we are given an insight into private attitudes and a religious mentality that enriches our sense of Guy as more than just a man of action. Last, at the end of the chapbook, Guy is fixed in our minds as a distinctively English hero.

These three aspects are important to our understanding of why this story should have had and retained such popularity with the readers of chapbooks from the end of the seventeenth century to the beginning of the nineteenth and slightly beyond. The first aspect might be seen to offer the humble reader an opportunity to consider how his or her own low status might be overcome by meritorious action. At the very least it enables the point to be made that virtue can coexist with lowly birth, and this is a key feature of a number of chapbook narratives, not just of the romances. The second aspect is more interesting and, at this point, most *Guy of Warwick* chapbooks interpose a scene that Rowlands added to the medieval original, Guy's meditation on a skull. Indeed, the American *Guy* chapbook in verse, produced by George Jerry Osborne at Newbury Port in 1794, concentrates more or less exclusively on this episode.[38] This interpolation is important as it marks the transition of the knightly hero from man of love and war to man of ideas (albeit in the crudest sense), and this enables Guy to be inserted into a more modern frame of reference in which martial prowess is balanced by a gentler, more reflective, mode of being. Certainly, when Rowlands added this passage Guy immediately became part of a late Renaissance tradition of contemplation that was quite different from the medieval *memento mori* that preceded it. By the eighteenth century this tradition had mutated into a more philosophical framework and the chapbook author's sense of this mutation means that the retention of the passage in question enables the narrative to continue to hold credibility. Finally, Guy's emergence as a national hero inserts the chapbook into a mesh of representation that was part of the project to create a national consciousness and a model of Englishness that stressed the superiority of the English over other European nations.

When we turn to chapbook versions of Richard Johnson's neochivalric *The Seven Champions of Christendom* we see a somewhat simpler process at work, but here too we can identify an attempt to do more than simply abridge a large work into the 24-page chapbook format (although in a Shrewsbury chapbook version I have seen this is achieved partly by switching to a smaller font of type halfway through the text). *The Seven Champions* first appeared in two parts (1596 and 1597) and can be read as a distinctively English attempt to create an interlaced chivalric story to rival the romance cycles of *Amadis*, *Palmerin*, and *The Mirror of Knighthood* series, which came into England from Spain and Portugal in the 1580s and retained their popularity until well into the Jacobean period and beyond.[39] Johnson's narrative is also part of the attempt to Protestantize the lives of the saints which surfaces sporadically throughout the late sixteenth century. The popularity of *The Seven Champions* may be gauged in part by the number of reprints but also by the fact that there were at least two continuations. The chapbook versions do not represent these later additions to the tradition.

The *Seven Champions* chapbooks operate by concentrating mainly on the adventures of St. George of England and paying less attention to the other saints (David, Patrick, Andrew, Anthony, James, and Dennis). This effect is inherited from Johnson's original version, but it is less marked there because of the greater spread of the narrative. In the chapbooks, however, St. George emerges unambiguously as the protagonist and the most heroic of these Christian adventurers. The chapbook therefore becomes a patriotic text and, like the *Guy* chapbook discussed above, forms part of a national discourse in which romance plays a clear and important role. In *The Seven Champions* chapbooks fighting is also reduced, but there is less opportunity to reflect on the finer points of behavior. The overall effect is therefore less subtle and complex than that encountered in *Guy of Warwick*, and the chapbook author has a far more difficult task in extracting the adventures of St. George while retaining some element of variety through the doings of the other saints.

Where *Guy of Warwick* remains entirely within the realm of the earthly, *The Seven Champions* depends very heavily upon enchantment, transformation, and other magic. The text therefore offers a provisional bridge between the world of literacy and print and the oral tales of the folk tradition. It also offered a very real bridge into the folk world, as the traditional mummers' plays appear to draw heavily on elements derived from a version of *The Seven Champions*.[40] Whether or not such a bridge does manifest itself in *The Seven Champions* is arguable. We can see chapbook readers such as John Bunyan and John Clare, both of whom were brokers between two different cultural layers, weaving together elements from the printed and the oral in their distinctive voices, but they were not ordinary readers; whether less imaginative consumers of the text found in it elements that connected the two cultural worlds must be left as speculation.

The chapbooks represent the end of a very long narrative tradition. They are the last works in which the heritage of Middle English romance was unselfconsciously deployed for the entertainment of adult readers and thus they are worthy of critical attention today. A survey of the field shows that while romances were important in the context of chapbook production and readership, they were not perhaps quite as important as more cursory surveys of general literary history would suggest. At the same time, it is important, given the nature of the chapbooks and the nature of their readership, not to separate romance chapbooks from the form more generally. It is better to see them as part of a generic continuum. When we do this we can see how their truncated versions of romance narrative acted as a further articulation of concerns and themes that were clearly of interest and, more important, of value to humble readers over a period of nearly two centuries. As this value changed so the chapbooks fell from favor and became the province of a last generation of child readers, bibliographers, and antiquarians.

See also: chapter 3, THE POPULAR ENGLISH METRICAL ROMANCES; chapter 4, ARTHURIAN ROMANCE; chapter 5, CHAUCER'S ROMANCES; chapter 6, MALORY AND THE EARLY PROSE ROMANCES; chapter 9, SHAKESPEARE'S ROMANCES; chapter 11, *THE FAERIE QUEENE* AND EIGHTEENTH-CENTURY SPENSERIANISM; chapter 15, "INCONSISTENT RHAPSODIES."

Notes

1. In 1798 the subscription to William Lane's London-based circulating library was one guinea and by 1841 this had doubled. Although there were facilities for borrowing at a lower rate, these kinds of prices were far in excess of anything that could have been afforded by the rural or urban poor (Neuburg 1977: 149–50). It was the case that many small shops, such as confectioners, also had stocks of books that were for sale or loan at a fee. But here too the price would have been high for the very poorest. In a fascinating study of a provincial circulating library and bookseller, which fills many gaps in our knowledge of the make-up of the eighteenth-century reading public, Ian Fergus notes that even where lending rates were as low as two pence and therefore competitive with the purchase price of popular books, few of the laboring class took up the opportunity to borrow (I. Fergus, "Eighteenth-Century Readers in Provincial England: The Customers of Samuel Clay's Circulating Library and Bookshop in Warwick 1770–1772," *Bibliographical Society of America Papers* 78 [1984], 155–213). Other detailed studies of eighteenth-century stationers and the role of chapbooks in their business include John Feather, "John Clay of Daventry: the Business of an Eighteenth-Century Stationer," *Studies in Bibliography* 37 (1984), 189–209, and I. Fergus and I. Portner, "Provincial Booksellers in Eighteenth-Century England: The Case of John Clay Reconsidered," *Studies in Bibliography* 40 (1987),147–63.

2. The Stationers' Company was first granted its monopoly in 1557. This had the effect of limiting printing to London, with some specialist work in Oxford and Cambridge. By 1692 the monopoly had been superseded by a licensing system and, by 1695, all attempts to regulate the press had been abandoned.

3. The best general description of all aspects of chapbooks remains H. B. Weiss, *A Book About Chapbooks* (1942). This very scarce book was originally privately produced in an edition of only 100 copies of reproduced typescript and is thus more rare than many of the chapbooks it describes. The 1969 facsimile, which also contains a range of useful illustrations, is more accessible. The only modern edition of chapbooks is John Simons, *Guy of Warwick and other Chapbook Romances* (1998): this has an introduction that sets out some of the issues involved in the description of chapbooks. Also valuable are J. Ashton, *Chapbooks of the Eighteenth Century* (1882, reprint1990?), R. Cunningham, *Amusing Prose Chapbooks* (1889), Victor Neuburg, *The Penny Histories* (1968), and P. Stockham, *Chapbooks* (privately published, n.d., reprinted from *Antiquarian Book Monthly Review*, September, 1976). All these books have introductions that remain useful and all contain facsimiles or transcripts of a range of chapbooks.

4. To put this in perspective, an agricultural laborer might have earned about 37.5 pennies per week in 1795. Thirteen years later Sir Walter Scott was offered a thousand guineas for a poem.

5. The expansion of the printing industry, stimulated by a combination of demand and technological advances between the 1820s and 1850s (the steam-driven press, stereotyping and electrotyping, and the development of wood-based, machine-made paper) enabled reading material to be produced for a mass audience to a price and volume that had not been possible before. In the early 1830s *The Penny Magazine* was being produced at the rate of 200,000 copies per week. B. E. Maidment, *Reading Popular Prints 1790–1870*, (Manchester: Manchester University Press, 1996), pp. 14–17, offers a concise summary of the ways in which these developments affected the mass production of images.

6. These tracts were almost certainly responsible, at least in part, for the demise of the chapbook. See Neuburg 1977: 249–64 for an excellent survey of this form. See also T. W. Lacqueur, *Religion and Sensibility* (New Haven: Yale University Press, 1976). I. Green, *Print and Protestantism in Early Modern England* (2000), looks in detail at all manner of popular religious (and other) texts.

7. There are a few specialist surveys of local chapbook printing operations or collections of materials relating to regional printing. See D. S. Bland, *Chapbooks and Garlands in the Robert White Collection* (Newcastle, 1969), R. Davis, *Kendrew of York* (York: Elmete Press, 1988), C. A. Federer, *Yorkshire Chapbooks* (London: Elliot Stock, 1899), D. Good, *Catalogue of the Spencer Collection of Early Children's Books and Chapbooks* (Preston: Harris Public Library, 1967), W. Harvey, *Scottish Chapbook Literature* (Dundee, 1903, reprint New York: Burt Franklin, 1971), P. G. Isaac, *William Davison of Alnwick* (Oxford: Oxford University Press, 1968), P. G. Isaac, *Halfpenny Chapbooks by William Davison* (Newcastle: Frank Graham, 1971), P. Isaac and B. McKay, eds., *Images and Texts* (1997), P. Isaac and B. McKay, eds., *The Reach of Print* (1998), E. B. Lyle, "A Checklist of Chapbooks Printed by William Scott of Alnwick," *Bibliotheck* 10 (1980), 35–48, B. McKay, "Books in Two Small Market Towns: The Book Trade in Appleby and Penrith," *Bibliotheck* 20 (1995), 128–43, P. O'Brien, *Eyres' Press Warrington* (Warrington: Owl Books), E. Pearson, *Banbury Chapbooks* (London: A. Reader, 1890, reprint Welwyn Garden City: Seven Dials Press, 1970), F. W. Ratcliffe, "Chapbooks with Scottish Imprints in the Robert White Collection," *Bibliotheck* 4 (1964), 88–174, P. Renold, "William Rusher: A Sketch of his Life," *Cake and Cockhorse* 11 (1991), 218–28, J. Simons, "Irish Chapbooks in the Huntington Library," *Huntington Library Quarterly* 57 (1995), 359–65, F. M. Thompson, *Newcastle Chapbooks* (Newcastle: Oriel Press, 1969), P. Ward, *Cambridge Street Literature* (Cambridge, 1978). The most comprehensive work on the topic, although chapbooks are mentioned only in passing, is John Feather, *The Provincial Book Trade in Eighteenth-Century England* (1985). Most of these works offer further insights into the spread and popularity of chapbook romances.

8. The chapman remains an obscure figure. For England the most comprehensive attempt yet to describe the nature of the trade is Margaret Spufford, *The Great Reclothing of Rural England* (1984). R. Leitch, " 'Here Chapman Billies Take Their Stand': A Pilot Study of Scottish Chapmen, Packmen and Pedlars," *Proceedings of the Scottish Society of Antiquarians* 120 (1990), 173–88, makes a beginning on the topic for Scotland. In fact, Scottish chapbook literature does offer some insight into the role of the chapman. James Hogg's celebrated tale *The Long Pack* started life as a chapbook and Dougal Graham's *John Cheap the Chapman* tells us something about the conditions in which chapmen lived and worked. Chapmen also distributed chapbooks in the United States. On this see J. C. L. Clark, *Notes on Chapman Whitcomb* (Lancaster, MA: reprint from *The Clinton Daily Item*, 1911), D. Jaffee, "Peddlers of Progress and the Transformation of the Rural North, 1760–1860," *Journal of American History* (1991), 515–35, L. Leary, *The Book Peddling Parson* (Chapel Hill: University of North Carolina Press, 1984), and H. B. Weiss, "Chapman Whitcombe," *The Book Collector's Packet* 3 (1939), 1–3.

9. For example, the chapbook of *The Seven Champions of Christendom* printed by Cotton and

Eddowes of Shrewsbury lists some 25 items (counting two-part issues as single titles) and ends with a tantalizing "etc. etc. etc."

10. The most comprehensive critical survey of chapbooks that includes detailed analysis of content is Margaret Spufford, *Small Books and Pleasant Histories* (1981). This deals exclusively with the later seventeenth century and draws its material solely from the collection gathered by Samuel Pepys and now in the Pepys Library at Magdalene College, Cambridge. However, the continuities of the chapbook trade mean that Dr Spufford's work is still of inestimable value for any study that includes work on the later period. See R. Thompson, *Samuel Pepys' Penny Merriments* (1976) for a selection of materials from the Pepys collection. Pepys himself categorized his chapbooks as either "Penny Merriments" or "Penny Godlinesses."

11. On these see P. Rogers, "Classics and Chapbooks" in I. Rivers, ed., *Books and Their Readers in Eighteenth-Century England* (Leicester: Leicester University Press, 1982), pp. 27–46. Two other works by Pat Rogers – "Defoe's Tour (1742) and the Chapbook Trade," *The Library*, 6th Series, 6 (1984), 275–9, and *Literature and Popular Culture in Eighteenth-Century England* (Brighton: Harvester, 1984) – are also of relevance.

12. The starting points for study of American chapbooks are Weiss's *Book about Chapbooks* and his "American Chapbooks 1722–1842," *Bulletin of the New York Public Library* 49 (1945), 491–8 and 587–96. More recently V. E. Neuburg (1989: 81–113) has commented in detail on the distinctive contributions of the American chapbook industry. A more general survey that offers some useful statistics on imports of British chapbooks may be found in J. D. Hart, *The Popular Book* (Berkeley: University of California Press, 1961). See also R. D. Brown, *Knowledge is Power* (Oxford: Oxford University Press, 1989), W. J. Gilmore, *Reading Becomes a Necessity of Life* (Knoxville: University of Tennessee Press, 1989), D. D. Hall and R. D. Brown, eds., *Printing and Society in Early America* (Worcester, MA, 1983), T. D. Mabbott, "Two Chapbooks Printed by

Andrew Steuart," *American Book Collector* 3 (1932), 352–8.

13. Locke was certainly worried about this from the perspective of his forward-looking educational programs, but by the 1790s radical publishers were explicitly using chapbook forms to disseminate subversive propaganda. See M. Wood 1994: 218–23. On the other hand, it has been argued that continuities in popular culture and overlaps between different groups of consumers mean that certain kinds of radical reading cannot easily be sustained. See J. M. Golby and A. W. Purdue, *The Civilisation of the Crowd*, revised edition (Stroud: Sutton, 1999).

14. For an example of this see J. Morris, "A Bothy Ballad and its Chapbook Source," in Isaac and McKay 1998: 85–102.

15. The best account of these texts is A. Johnston, *Enchanted Ground* (London: Athlone Press, 1964). See also the appendix to E. R. Wasserman, *Elizabethan Poetry in the Eighteenth Century* (Urbana: University of Illinois Press, 1947), where the eighteenth-century vogue for Elizabethan prose fiction is reviewed.

16. The celebrated bookseller James Lackington wrote, in 1792, of entering the houses of the rural poor and seeing *Tom Jones* and *Rasselas* "stuck up on their bacon racks." See Simons 1992: 122–43, p. 130, for some analysis of this important passage. By 1854 Charles Knight was claiming (probably falsely) that the cheaper circulating libraries had "banished *Robinson Crusoe* to the kitchen" (see Neuburg 1977: 195–200).

17. The list is reprinted, with some valuable analysis, in Neuburg 1964: 75–80.

18. Although there are plainly differences between regional cultures at the level of popular recreations and rituals, the same distinctions are by no means so clear where literature is concerned (except in the cases of the differences between English, Irish, Welsh, and Scottish chapbooks or chapbooks dealing with very specific local interests such as the "Pace Egg" or "Peace Egg" chapbooks found in some areas of the northwest and in Scotland). A pioneering examination of the regional topology of popular culture is

D. Underdown, "Regional Cultures? Local Variations in Popular Culture during the Early Modern Period" in T. Harris, ed., *Popular Culture in England c. 1500–1850* (London: Macmillan, 1995), pp. 28–47.

19. Chartier 1987: 242. Work on the *bibliothèque* first stimulated Spufford's interest in the Pepys collection, and Peter Burke's important *Popular Culture in Early Modern Europe* (1978) also depends on material from this source. The starting place for study on this series is C. Nisard, *Histoire des Livres populaires ou de la littérature de colportage*, 2 volumes (Paris: Amyot, 1854), closely followed by A. Assier, *La Bibliothèque bleue* (Paris: Champion, 1874, reprint Nîmes: J. F. Marcellin OLLE, 1991). R. Mandrou, *De la culture populaire au XVIIe et XVIIIe siècles*, 3rd edn. (Paris: Stock, 1985), is also of great value. A useful anthology with fairly extensive critical and historical detail is M.-D. Leclerc and A. Robert, *Les Livrets de la Bibliothèque Bleue*, 2 volumes (Troyes: CDDP, 1986). In 1999 Phénix Éditions of Paris began to publish a series of facsimiles of individual chapbooks, *Nouvelle Bibliothèque Bleue de Troyes*.

20. It has also been suggested that Chestre was the author of the southern version of *Octavian* (British Library, MS Cotton Caligula A.2) but the evidence for this is highly speculative.

21. On Rate see L. Blanchfield, "The Romances in MS Ashmole 61: An Idiosyncratic Scribe," in M. Mills, J. Fellows, and C. Meale, eds., *Romance in Medieval England* (Woodbridge: D. S. Brewer, 1991), pp. 65–87.

22. The works of Dougal Graham have been edited by G. MacGregor, *The Collected Writings of Dougal Graham*, 2 vols. (Glasgow: T. D. Morrison, 1883). Hogg is, of course, much better known, but much remains to be done on the relationship between his chapbooks and the later printed editions of his works.

23. R. Crane, "The Vogue of *Guy of Warwick* from the Close of the Middle Ages to the Romantic Revival," *PMLA* 30 (1915), 125–94,. gives a very full account of the history of this text. More recently V. B. Richmond, *The Legend of Guy of Warwick* (New York: Garland, 1996) offers an exhaustive survey of the *Guy* legend in all its manifestations. J. Zupitza, "Zur Literaturgeschichte des Guy," *Sitzungsberichte der philosophische-historische Classe der Kaiserlichen Akademie der Wissenschaft*, LXXIV (Vienna, 1873), 623–88 remains extremely valuable. Copland's version was edited by G. Schleich, *Guy of Warwick nach Coplands Druck*, Palaestra 139 (Leipzig, 1923).

24. See E. Gosse, ed., *The Complete Works of Samuel Rowlands*, 4 volumes (Glasgow: Hunterian Club, 1860). *Guy of Warwick* is to be found in volume 3.

25. Ashton, *Chapbooks* (1882), gives a flavor of some of these. J. Friedman, *Miracles and the Pulp Press during the English Revolution* (London: UCL Press, 1993), and T. Watt, *Cheap Print and Popular Piety* (Cambridge: Cambridge University Press, 1991), offer a good sense of the variety of popular print in the period slightly before the heyday of the chapbooks.

26. The reports of the "colporteurs" who traveled the poor rural areas of the United States to evangelize the population and distribute religious reading matter make fascinating reading. A full set of transcripts of these reports is lodged in the Huntington Library. B. Reay, "Popular Religion," in B. Reay, ed., *Popular Culture in the Seventeenth Century* (London: Routledge, 1988), pp. 91–128, certainly suggests that there were individuals who exhibited significant confusion and misunderstanding of religious matters and, one assumes, these people are likely to have been illiterate. See also D. Valenze, "Prophecy and Popular Literature in the Eighteenth Century," *Journal of Ecclesiastical History* 29 (1978), 75–92.

27. See R. A. Houston, *Scottish Literacy and the National Identity* (Cambridge: Cambridge University Press, 1985). M. Forsyth, "Lighting a Frugal Taper" (unpublished Ph.D. thesis, University of Lancaster, 2001), is a study of nineteenth-century working-class women poets that shows very clearly the particular strengths of literacy in Scotland.

28. Significantly, this observation was cited in Charles Knight's preface to the first issue of *The Penny Magazine* (1832). *The Penny Magazine* was probably the most important and influential venture in popular publishing as it not only achieved a vast market but also began to erode the barriers between different kinds of knowledge and, more important still, demonstrated a high expectation of the working-class reader's intellectual capacity. *The Penny Magazine* and its many imitators were an important element in the complex of forces that led to the extinction of the chapbook.

29. The fullest and best account of literacy in early modern England remains that of David Cressy, *Literacy and the Social Order* (Cambridge: Cambridge University Press, 1980).

30. See Spufford 1981: 4–7, and Vincent 1989: 60–1, for some memories of this practice.

31. See Spufford 1981: 1–18 and Simons 1992: 122–3 for some examples of responses to chapbooks. Similar evidence can also be found for Ireland (see J. Simons, "Irish Chapbooks in the Huntington Library"). For a survey of the issues surrounding the creation of the United Kingdom see L. Colley, *Britons* (London: Vintage, 1996).

32. The current critical vogue for the eighteenth- and nineteenth-century Gothic novel is difficult to understand as it appears, in most cases, entirely to reverse contemporary responses to the Middle Ages and its Gothic echo.

33. See Vincent 1989: 53–94, V. E. Neuburg, *Popular Education in Eighteenth-Century England* (London: Woburn Press, 1971), Jonathan Rose, *The Intellectual Life of the British Working Class* (2001). J. McAleer, *Popular Reading and Publishing in Britain 1914–1950* (Oxford: Clarendon Press, 1992), pp. 13–41, reviews the position of the working-class reader when chapbooks had all but ceased to exist.

34. This idea is given far more general application in P. Burke, *Popular Culture in Early Modern Europe* (1978).

35. Neuburg 1989: 87–91 cites and analyzes Steuart's stock list. Of its 70 items six are unambiguously romances (either medieval or neochivalric) so, once again, the proportion of romance material to other chapbooks resolves to around 8%.

36. On the Spanish chapbooks see F. J. Norton and E. M. Wilson, *Two Spanish Verse Chapbooks* (Cambridge: Cambridge University Press, 1979). On the Russian *Bevis* see D. E. Farrell, "The Origins of Early Russian Popular Prints and their Social Mileu in the Early Eighteenth Century," *Journal of Popular Culture* 17 (1983), pp. 9–47. On the *folhetos* see P. Burke, "Chivalry in the New World" in S. Anglo, ed., *Chivalry in the Renaissance* (Woodbridge: Boydell and Brewer, 1990), pp. 253–62, on Yona see G. Armistead and J. Silvermann, eds., *The Judeo-Spanish Chapbooks of Yacob Abraham Yona* (Berkeley: University of California Press, 1971).

37. For an interesting discussion of the clash of secular and religious traditions in the French countryside during the revolutionary period see A. Corbin, *Village Bells* (London: Papermac, 1999). See also D. R. Thelander, "Mother Goose and her Goslings: the France of Louis XIV as seen through the Fairy Tale," *Journal of Modern History* 54 (1982), 467–96. For eighteenth-century England, E. P. Thompson, *Customs in Common* (London: Merlin Press, 1991) contains a wealth of material exploring the interface of popular and "official" culture.

38. This is edited in John Simons, *Guy of Warwick and Other Chapbook Romances* (1998), pp. 69–77.

39. On these cycles see J. O'Connor, *Amadis de Gaulle and its Influence on Elizabethan Literature* (New Brunswick, NJ: Rutgers University Press, 1970), M. Patchell, *The Palmerin Romances in Elizabethan Prose Fiction* (New York: Columbia University Press, 1947), and H. Thomas, *Spanish and Portuguese Romances of Chivalry* (Cambridge: Cambridge University Press, 1920).

40. The relationship between Johnson's romance and the mummers' plays is explored in detail by A. Helm, *The English Mummers' Play* (Woodbridge: D. S. Brewer, 1981), pp. 57–64. See also R. J. E. Tiddy, *The Mummers' Play* (Oxford: Oxford University Press, 1923), E. K. Chambers, *The English Folk Play* (Oxford: Oxford University Press, 1933), and B. Hayward, *Galoshins, The Scottish Folk Play* (Edinburgh: Edinburgh University Press, 1992).

References and Further Reading

Ashton, J. (1882). *Chapbooks of the Eighteenth Century*. London: Chatto & Windus. [Reprint, London: Skoob Books, 1990]

Burke, Peter (1978). *Popular Culture in Early Modern Europe*. London: Temple Smith.

Capp, Bernard (1979). *Astrology and the Popular Press*. London: Geneva Publications.

Chartier, Roger (1987). *The Cultural Uses of Print in Early Modern France*. Princeton, NJ: Princeton University Press.

Cunningham, R. (1889). *Amusing Prose Chapbooks*. London: Hamilton, Adams.

Feather, John (1985). *The Provincial Book Trade in Eighteenth-Century England*. Cambridge: Cambridge University Press.

Green, I. (2000). *Print and Protestantism in Early Modern England*. Oxford: Oxford University Press.

Isaac, P., and B. McKay, eds. (1997). *Images and Texts*. Winchester: St. Paul's Bibliographies.

Isaac, P., and B. McKay, eds. (1998). *The Reach of Print*. Winchester: St. Paul's Bibliographies.

Neuburg, Victor E. (1964). *Chapbook Bibliography*. London: Vine Press.

Neuburg, Victor E. (1977). *Popular Literature*. Harmondsworth: Penguin.

Neuburg, Victor E. (1968). *The Penny Histories*. London: Oxford University Press.

Neuburg, Victor E. (1989). "American Chapbooks." In C. N. Davidson, ed., *Reading in America: Literature and Social History*. Baltimore, MD: Johns Hopkins University Press, pp. 81–113.

Rose, Jonathan (2001). *The Intellectual Life of the British Working Class*. New Haven: Yale University Press.

Simons, John (1992). "Romance in the Eighteenth-Century Chapbook." In J. Simons, ed., *From Medieval to Medievalism*. London: Macmillan, pp. 122–43.

Simons, John (1998). *Guy of Warwick and other Chapbook Romances*. Exeter: Exeter University Press.

Spufford, Margaret (1981). *Small Books and Pleasant Histories*. Cambridge: Cambridge University Press.

Spufford, Margaret (1988). *The Great Reclothing of Rural England*. London: Hambledon.

Thompson, R. (1976). *Samuel Pepys' Penny Merriments*. London: Constable.

Vincent, D. (1989). *Literacy and Popular Culture*. Cambridge: Cambridge University Press.

Weiss, H. B. (1942). *A Book About Chapbooks*. Trenton, NJ; reprint, Hatboro: Folklore Associates, 1969.

Wood, M. (1994). *Radical Satire and Print Culture 1790–1822*. Oxford: Clarendon Press.

11

The Faerie Queene and Eighteenth-century Spenserianism

David Fairer

It was through Spenser's *Faerie Queene* (1590–6), more than any other text, that the eighteenth century engaged with the nature and possibilities of romance. The response to both was often ambivalent, and one of the keys to understanding Spenserianism as a phenomenon is the notion of ambivalence itself. During this period, readers of *The Faerie Queene* were often conscious of a duality of head and heart, just as critics who discussed the poem were challenged by its power to compromise judgment; and Spenserian poets enjoyed exploiting doubleness in a variety of creative ways. If eighteenth-century readers and writers were in two minds about romance, they were also acutely conscious of the two-mindedness of romance itself, its ability to divert the mind onto a fictional plane where it could look around, beyond, or beneath the real – not losing sight of it altogether, but opening up another dimension of human experience. Still within reach of sense, the eighteenth-century imagination was licensed to play with phenomena by giving them color and feeling, finding new angles of vision, and hearing extra frequencies. This "allegorical" potential was something that Spenser helped to release in eighteenth-century poets. "Romance" need no longer be dismissed as childhood fantasy, but was reconceived as "fairy ground" where things usually beyond sight or hearing could enhance perception and test empirical truth. In this way the eighteenth century valued the imaginative Spenser and the moral Spenser, and saw them as continuous.

What might be called the "romantic" response to *The Faerie Queene* was firmly in place by 1737, when Elizabeth Cooper included an extract from the poem in *The Muses Library*, her influential anthology of earlier English literature. The introductory essay (written with the help of the antiquarian William Oldys) is effusive and confessional, and her attitude was echoed by many other readers of the period:

> [I]f I may judge of Others by my self, 'tis impossible to read his Works, without being in Love with the Author... No Writer ever found so near a Way to the Heart as He ... For my own Part, when I read Him, I fancy myself conversing with the *Graces*,

and am led away as irresistibly, as if inchanted by his own *Merlin* . . . with all his Imperfections, no Writings have such Power as his, to awake the Spirit of Poetry in others. (Cooper 1737: 253–5)

Elizabeth Cooper is aware of the double movement of romance: its simultaneous intimacy and strangeness. Spenser reaches directly inside her ("so near a Way to the Heart"), yet draws her imagination into strange worlds ("I . . . am led away . . . irresistibly"). The key to her heart is also the key that unlocks the magic casement.

If Cooper the reader is "inchanted," Cooper the critic is aware of having to "suspend as much as possible this Female Fondness" and recognize that Spenser "debauch'd his Taste with the Extravagancies of *Ariosto*," a fact that in her eyes prevented him from matching "the most venerated of the Antients." She finds it difficult to align her response as a reader with the act of critical judgment, and has to suspend the one to engage the other. Spenser's obvious appeal to the imagination created a problem of evaluation in a period when "fancy" and reason were thought to operate in separate spheres. His poetry once again highlights a duality, here of the critical and creative impulses, which characterizes many of the reactions to Spenser during the eighteenth century. Pope for one felt that Spenser represented something equivalent to a romantic attachment whose charms overrode one's better judgment. He told John Hughes: "[Spenser] is like a mistress whose faults we see, but love her with them all" (Sherburn 1956: I, 316). As Greg Kucich (1991) has shown, a "mode of equivocation" (40) lies at the heart of the Spenserianism of this period, with Spenser's achievement being seen as "a rare mixture of unparalleled poetic beauties qualified by enormous lapses in judgment" (44). If the author of *The Faerie Queene* encouraged poets to explore the allegorical potential of romance, he also helped critics to acknowledge what Cooper terms "the Spirit of Poetry," and to become more attuned to readerly responses and creative energies.

"Old Spenser"

By 1700 there was no doubting Spenser's status as one of the classics of English poetry. Together with Chaucer and Milton, he formed a canonical trinity repeatedly invoked by critics and persons of taste. In 1700 John Dryden remarked on the family resemblance between them in terms of a transmigration of souls: "*Spencer* more than once insinuates, that the Soul of *Chaucer* was transfus'd into his Body . . . *Milton* has acknowledg'd to me, that *Spencer* was his Original" (preface to *Fables Ancient and Modern*). But after establishing this poetic bloodline, Dryden refuses to connect himself with it. In particular, as a writer conscious of rapid linguistic change he is careful to distance himself from their ageing language. Spenser was mistaken in antiquarianizing his vocabulary, as was Milton in similarly "digging from the Mines of *Chaucer* and *Spencer*" (preface to *The Satires of Decimus Junius Juvenalis*, 1693). Haunting Dryden's mind was the fact that Chaucer was virtually unread in the original, and Spenser very little, and he suspected that by following them Milton was also heading for obscurity.

By the end of the seventeenth century the language and intricate stanza form of *The Faerie Queene* were viewed by many as obstacles. They were certainly not to be imitated. One anonymous "Person of Quality" decided to remove this problem and make Spenser both readable and respectable by rewriting Book One in heroic couplets. In the preface to *Spencer Redivivus* (1687) he (or she) declares that the poet's "antiquated Verse and tedious Stanza" are being "totally laid aside," so that his poem can appeal to the "knowing Discernment" of modern polite readers. The effect achieved is evident in the rewriting of the moment when the monster Error is decapitated by the Red Cross Knight. The Elizabethan poet uses the resources of alliteration and the final Alexandrine to strong effect:

> And stroke at her with more then manly force,
> That from her body full of filthie sin
> He raft her hatefull heade without remorse;
> A streame of cole black blood forth gushed from her corse.

(I. i. 24)

In the heroic couplet version this is less disturbed, but also less disturbing:

> And striking her with more than human strength,
> Her Head he sever'd from her Body's length:
> Whence her Infernal Life flow'd from her Veins,
> In Blood that fill'd the Ground with foulest stains.

(8)

In the couplet text the powerful active verbs that mark Spenser's encounter (*stroke, raft, gushed*) are sacrificed so as to clarify the syntax of the passage with subordinate clauses (*striking her . . . Whence . . . In Blood that . . .*). What we see gushing less controllably from Spenser's monster is not mere flowing blood, but the vivid black of sin. The 1687 description offers vague concepts (*Body's length, Infernal Life, foulest stains*) and we get no sense of the knight's feelings; but in Spenser's text the visual, emotional, and allegorical are knit tightly together. A child would see and understand.

Eighteenth-century Spenserianism was dogged by the association of romance with childhood reading. Arthur Johnston (1964: 32) has spoken of "the gradual descent of the romances to the literature of the nursery," and this decline appeared to reinforce history's official "progress of refinement" narrative, which saw human society as having emerged over recent time from primitiveness to elegance. The link between childhood and the barbarous tastes of the past was often made. In the preface to his *Fables* (1700) Dryden wrote that Chaucer "liv'd in the Infancy of our Poetry," and Dr. Johnson, who devoured romances in his youth, concluded that "at the time when very wild improbable tales were well received, the people were in a barbarous state, and so on the footing of children" (Boswell 1934–64: IV, 17). It seemed natural that a

well-read, ambitious young man like Joseph Addison could write in his "Account of
the Greatest English Poets" (1694 in 1914: I, 31–2):

> Old *Spenser* next, warm'd with poetick rage,
> In ancient tales amus'd a barb'rous age ...
> But now the mystick tale, that pleas'd of yore,
> Can charm an understanding age no more.

There is a mismatch here between the fervor of Spenser's "poetick rage" and the
lukewarm response that Addison offers (*amus'd*, *pleas'd*, *charm*). Not only is he severing
the link between present and past, but he has disengaged the poet from his reader's
imagination. In this polite panorama there is no excited individual, just an indifferent
"age." It is as though Addison himself had never read *The Faerie Queene*. The answer is
that when he wrote those lines he hadn't (Spence 1966: I, 74).

Recovering the "genuine" Spenser in the eighteenth century would involve a fresh
attitude to the past and a reassessment of poetry's character and function: fears of
linguistic obsolescence would have to be replaced by a delight in recovering an old
stock of words; a more capacious and historically sympathetic concept of the literary
canon would be required; new critical criteria would have to emerge that privileged
imagination and valued description; the ear would need to be attuned to intricate
sound-patterns and more spacious, less pointed phrasing; and romance would have to
shed its embarrassing associations; above all, more people would have to read *The
Faerie Queene*, so that Spenser would become part of the cultural fabric – discussed,
investigated, imitated, and absorbed. By 1760 all this had happened, and by helping
to set this agenda the poem not only encouraged developments favorable to its own
reception, but made Spenserianism a benign model of transmission and influence in
literary history (Kucich 1991: 45–7).

Celebration and Satire

What is thought of as "the Spenser Revival" is usually located, for valid reasons, in the
1740s and 1750s, but it was an earlier decade (1706–15) that saw the sudden
emergence of *The Faerie Queene* onto the literary scene. Given that *The Faerie Queene*
was a largely unread classic, there was a degree of daring involved when Matthew
Prior chose to address Queen Anne publicly in a version of the Spenserian stanza. *An
Ode, Humbly Inscrib'd to the Queen. On the Glorious Success of Her Majesty's Arms, 1706.
Written in Imitation of Spenser's Stile* (1706) proved a sensation on the London literary
scene, and Prior was amused at the flurry of excitement it caused in polite circles. He
wrote to Lord Cholmondeley later that year:

> As to Spencer, my Lord, I think we have gained our point, every body acknowledges
> him to have been a fine Poet, thô three Months since not one in 50 had read him: Upon
> my Soul, tis true, the Wits have sent for the Book, the Fairy Queen is on their Toilette

table, and some of our Ducal acquaintance will be deep in that Mythologico-Poetical way of thinking.   (Prior 1971: 896)

Prior is delighted to think of the wits and courtiers struggling with Spenser in their closets (it is a toilette table, not a coffee table) before venturing out in public to pronounce on the poem. The Whigs did their best to denigrate the ode for its "obsolete" verse; but everyone realized that Prior had opened up a new seam of political poetry, and that Anne would be flattered to see herself as a reincarnation of Queen Elizabeth:

> An equal Genius was in SPENSER found:
> To the high Theme He match'd his Noble Lays:
> He travell'd ENGLAND o'er on Fairy Ground,
> In Mystic Notes to Sing his Monarch's Praise:
> Reciting wond'rous Truths in pleasing Dreams,
> He deck'd ELIZA's Head with GLORIANA's Beams.
>
> (15–20)

A monarch knows the value of a romantic image, especially one that associates the crown with days of national greatness. Spenserian poetry tantalizingly offered to fulfill every spin-doctor's ideal by reconciling "wond'rous Truths" with "pleasing Dreams," or at least selling one in the guise of the other. Prior's very public move onto "Fairy Ground" gave a new dimension to romance by linking its mystique to the idea of monarchy itself. Behind Anne, Prior declares, is the divinely sanctioned Elizabeth. He implies that such a ruler deserves more than courtly wit and elegance, and that with royal support poetry can affirm its own divine sanction and recover its "Mystic Notes." Recalling Elizabeth's poet laureate, Prior simultaneously makes a claim for poetry's lost power and becomes a voice in national politics. What we might call this "Gloriana strain" of Spenserianism persisted throughout the century in royal celebration or elegy, and as late as 1787 we find the Poet Laureate, Thomas Warton, invoking Spenser's example as he decks George III (a little incongruously) in the garb of romance:

> From fabling Fancy's inmost store
> A rich romantic robe he bore;
> A veil with visionary trappings hung,
> And o'er his virgin-queen the fairy texture flung.
>
> (*1787 Birthday Ode*, 29–32)

Spenser helped Prior to make poetic flattery venerable and dignified. But the underside of the satiric and grotesque was not long in appearing. Once the wits and courtiers knew their *Faerie Queene*, fresh opportunities arose, this time for political satire. For all its celebration of Gloriana and her knights, the poem was also filled with embodiments of vice and deception. Satire's own "double-speak" could tap easily into Spenserian allegory and cloak seditious meanings in harmless fairy fictions. The very antiquity of Spenser allowed him to be a prophetic Merlin himself. In 1714 the Whig Samuel Croxall published *An Original Canto of Spencer: Design'd as Part of his Fairy Queen, but never Printed*, which he had recovered "from a dusty heap of this antiquated Poetry" (4). In an uncanny way the Spenserian text seemed to be voicing anti-Jacobite sentiments, and celebrating a distinctly Whiggish view of constitutional liberty. The "vile Enchantments" with which Archimago enthralled Britomart were given a Catholic character by two new characters, Burbon and Romania. Later that year a further canto materialized, which featured a Jacobite "House of Faction," an underground vault kitted out with all the machinery of the Inquisition ("Wheels and Gibbets, Enginry of Death, / And pois'ning Cups do furnish out her Den." 11). With their dim aura of strangeness, old Spenserian texts carrying a vague canonical authority could enter public debate as prophetic voices from Gothic antiquity and contribute to the quarrels of the present. An allegory of Stuart monarchy was easily countered by a Hanoverian triumph over tyranny and superstition.

In the years of Robert Walpole's supremacy, 1725–42, what Christine Gerrard (1994) has termed "political Spenserianism" continued to flourish, with Whigs and Tories competing to claim the old "Matter of Britain" for themselves. Queen Caroline stirred up a fresh wave of controversy by constructing Merlin's Cave in Richmond Gardens, with lifesize waxwork models representing Elizabeth I and an ambiguous Britannia/Britomart figure. This enterprise, Gerrard concludes (1994: 169), "suggests both the pressure on the Hanoverians to mythologize themselves . . . and the absence of either a Spenser or a Prior capable of doing it for them." The opposition responded gleefully by mocking the allegorical structure (in which Stephen Duck, the thresher-poet, was installed as keeper) and identifying Prime Minister Walpole as the evil enchanter Archimago, weaving his spells of corruption across the nation. Gilbert West's *A Canto of the Fairy Queen. Written by Spenser* (1739), one of the most accomplished Spenserian imitations of the century, offered a disturbing picture of state power and court decadence, all controlled by Walpole the wizard:

> And eke to each of that same gilded Train,
> That meekly round that Lordly Throne did stand,
> Was by that Wizard ty'd a Magick Chain,
> Whereby their Actions all he mote command,
> And rule with hidden Influence the Land.

(7)

West's Spenserian pageant showed how the materials of allegorical romance (magic chains, gaudy pageants, prophetic mirrors, etc.) could invigorate satire with cleverly directed fantasy. A succession of False Florimels, Bowers of Bliss, Houses of Pride, and wicked magicians allowed a satirist to intrigue the reader with an allegorical scheme that asked to be decoded. Then as now, the reader succumbed to the satirist's spell by becoming his surrogate, tracing meanings and searching out identifications. In this type of satire the reader is not an aloof spectator and critic, but becomes through imagination a participant in the follies of the scene. A romance narrative draws us into a world that is grotesque yet eerily familiar, and the satiric point is made more forcibly through the resistance we must exert to extract ourselves from it, head and heart entangled. The greatest example of this satiric enchantment (as we might call it) is Pope's *Dunciad* (1728; 1743). Behind its many allegorical pageants is the elusive fantasy queen, Dulness, who manipulates the imaginations of her followers by playing on their hopes and dreams. In this poem the allurements of romance provide not just the mechanism of the satire, but also its object. The nation's enchantress has everyone in thrall – to fashion, self-indulgence, and ambition, and in Pope's hands the dunces become infantilized worshipers of their all-providing "Mighty Mother." The heroic ingredients of classical epic are absorbed into a series of mock-chivalric romance scenarios and allegorical masques of folly.

> All these, and more, the cloud-compelling Queen
> Beholds thro' fogs, that magnify the scene.
> She, tinsel'd o'er in robes of varying hues,
> With self-applause her wild creation views;
> Sees momentary monsters rise and fall,
> And with her own fools-colours gilds them all.
>
> (I, 79–84)

The "fairy texture" that eighteenth-century poets associated with the allegorical style of *The Faerie Queene* is made to characterize Dulness, Pope's embodiment of delusion and intellectual anarchy who presides over "a new world to Nature's laws unknown" (III, 241). For the poet of the four-book *Dunciad* (1743) Spenser's imagined Britain, the "land of Faery," is irredeemable, and the false enchanter holds sway unchecked. There are no heroes, no fulfilled quests, no guiding providence, no embodiments of the moral virtues, only grotesque parodies of each. At the end of the poem eternal darkness falls, and nobody intervenes. Pope presents his allegorical tapestry as a cultural indictment of the age. In his epic there is no Una to embody the steadfastness of Truth, just a fantasy novelist; no Arthur to guide and protect the righteous, just dangerous teachers and crooked publishers; no Britomart to fulfill her vision of the nation's destiny, just a Poet Laureate with writer's block; above all, no Gloriana to inspire devotion, just "Dunce the Second."

"The Fairie way of Writing"

Prior in 1706 can be seen to have inaugurated a twin tradition of Spenserian celebration and satire – or in the case of *The Dunciad*'s brilliant irony, satiric celebration. A few years later it was Addison who helped establish a sympathetic critical context for appreciating the poetry of *The Faerie Queene*. He had now read the poem (perhaps he was one of Prior's "wits" who "sent for the Book"), and his influential paper on "the Fairie way of Writing," published as issue 419 of *The Spectator*, July 1, 1712, does two important things: it implies that criticism has a duty to accommodate Spenser, rather than vice versa, and it celebrates English poetry's achievement over that of classical writers.[1] It does so by identifying a type of non-mimetic poetry that works outside the boundaries of "Nature," the touchstone of literary judgment since Aristotle. Addison praises Spenser's "admirable Talent" for a kind of poetry in which the poet "entertains his Reader's Imagination with the Characters and Actions of such Persons as have many of them no Existence, but what he bestows on them. Such are Fairies, Witches, Magicians, Demons, and departed Spirits." In this directly imaginative appeal, Addison argues, the three English poets, Shakespeare, Milton, and Spenser, have outdone the classical writers ("Among all the Poets of this Kind our *English* are much the best"). Spenser becomes a defining example of "how many ways Poetry addresses it self to the Imagination, as it has not only the whole Circle of Nature for its Province, but makes new Worlds of its own, shews us Persons who are not to be found in Being, and represents even the Faculties of the Soul." In a few phrases Addison identifies a poetry that leads its reader delightedly "as it were, into a new Creation."

Not only did this paper suggest a fresh critical approach to *The Faerie Queene*; it rehabilitated the nursery. To master "the Faerie way," Addison says, is "difficult" because it requires from the poet "an Imagination naturally fruitful and superstitious" (he uses the word in a positive sense). "Besides this," Addison continues,

> he ought to be very well versed in Legends and Fables, antiquated Romances, and the Traditions of Nurses and old Women, that he may fall in with our natural Prejudices, and humour those Notions which we have imbibed in our Infancy.

It is startling to find Addison, the most influential critic of his day, implying that the romances "imbibed" by a child's imagination can offer a model of primal experience that a modern poet might tap into. In this kind of poetry "Nature" is recast as "natural Prejudices." Addison associates the three great canonical poets with fairy legends and romantic fables, while opening up possibilities for a playful romantic vein in eighteenth-century poetry, in which a world of spirits might "humour" our childlike "Notions."

One poet who seems to have been intrigued by this idea was Pope, who had been welcomed into Addison's literary circle at the beginning of 1712, and had published his two-canto mock-heroic *The Rape of the Lock* just six weeks earlier (Spence 1966: I, 60). It is evident that Pope saw how the "Fairie way of Writing" offered him possibilities for developing his miniaturized epic in that direction. In his greatly expanded five-canto version of 1714 the heroine Belinda is now placed at the center of an imagined world of spirits who act out allegorically the little drama of pride, love, shame, and anger in which she is entangled. The airy sylphs and earthy gnomes are projections of the coquetry and prudishness that compete to claim her, and through them the world of "Idea" becomes manifest: .

> Just in that instant, anxious *Ariel* sought
> The close Recesses of the Virgin's Thought;
> As on the Nosegay in her Breast reclin'd,
> He watch'd th'Ideas rising in her Mind.

(III, 139–42)

The "Idea" that is rising inside Belinda is her love for the Baron, which will soon sweep her away from the lighthearted sylph-world of coquettish innocence, and bring her into the embrace of the gnomes, the spirits of splenetic melancholy. In a Spenserian reworking of the epic descent into Hell, the "gloomy spirit" Umbriel explores the thoughts Belinda normally keeps hidden. As he enters the interior womb-like space of her "Cave of Spleen," Belinda's darker fantasies are touched, and her hysteric potential aroused. Pope's description of the cave and its occupants is a *tour de force* of dark comedy which reaches back through Spenser to the Cave of Envy in Ovid's *Metamorphoses* (II, 768–82; one of Spenser's own sources, and mentioned in Addison's paper), but adds an element of robust humor:

> Unnumber'd Throngs on ev'ry side are seen
> Of Bodies chang'd to various Forms by *Spleen*.
> Here living *Teapots* stand, one Arm held out,
> One bent; the Handle this, and that the Spout.

(IV, 47–50)

This is a world where a hyperactive imagination gives bodily form to adolescent sexual confusions and frustrations: "Men prove with Child, as pow'rful Fancy works, / And Maids turn'd Bottels, call aloud for Corks" (IV, 53–4). Whether or not it was Addison's paper on "the Fairie way of Writing" that prompted Pope to add this allegorical dimension to his poem, he is certainly writing in its spirit and ends up creating a poem in which his imagination "makes new Worlds of its own, shews us Persons who are not to be found in Being, and represents even the Faculties of the Soul."

The reader of *The Rape of the Lock* experiences a clash between heart and head similar to that voiced by eighteenth-century readers of *The Faerie Queene*, and critics of Pope's poem have tended to be divided by how far they emphasize its competing elements of celebration and satire. An enthusiast for Spenser, as we have seen, could acknowledge in *The Faerie Queene* a direct emotional and imaginative response that short-circuited strict judgment ("No writer ever found so near a Way to the Heart as He . . . For my own Part, when I read Him, I fancy myself conversing with the *Graces*, and am led away as irresistibly, as if inchanted"). Spenser, as Addison recognized, opened the way to the possibility of enchantment, and prepared readers for a kind of poetry that set an emotional response in tension with judgment. In *The Rape of the Lock* Pope has the confidence to play with this idea, acknowledging the way in which his beautiful and fanciful heroine suspends our criticism ("If to her share some Female Errors fall, / Look on her Face, and you'll forget 'em all," II, 18–19). Many critics were prepared to do exactly that with *The Faerie Queene* and with Pope's poem, which along with *Eloisa to Abelard* was extremely popular among devotees of sensibility who found the poet's later work unsympathetic.[2] With those two poems, written when he wandered "in Fancy's Maze,"[3] Pope contributed to the ascendancy of sensibility in the mid-century.

Eighteenth-century Spenserianism, as this essay has argued, was more than just imitating Spenser: it encouraged a creative and critical flirtation with romance, which involved a degree of self-allegorizing, a giving rein to indulgence or fondness, while being conscious of a judgmental responsibility delightfully suspended (but not erased). Addison, Pope, and Elizabeth Cooper all register this, and we find Pope himself being the cause of two-mindedness in one of his severest critics. Aaron Hill, an early avatar of sensibility and an admirer of Spenser, was a tenacious opponent of Pope's, but *The Rape of the Lock* clearly delighted and influenced him. As Hill wrote to Samuel Richardson, in Pope's verse there was "something so expressed to bewitch us, that I cannot, for my soul, help admiring him."[4] One of Hill's poems celebrating female enchantment, "Bellaria, at her Spinnet," offers itself as an example of a romance-allegorical mode that could draw from both Spenser and Pope. Bellaria at her keyboard combines Pope's vision of the sylph-encircled Belinda with the scene in *The Faerie Queene* (III. xii. 8) where "Fancy" (Imagination) leads an allegorical procession of love while fanning the air with his plumes. Hill's symbolic picture of Bellaria's effect on her audience draws out the Spenserian soul through its Popean embodiment:

> Spirits, in fairy forms, inclose the *fair* …
> *Pity*, with tears of joy, stands weeping near;
> Kneeling *devotion* hangs her list'ning ear,
> *Candor*, and *truth*, firm-fix'd on either hand,
> Propping her chair, two sure supporters stand!
> Round her, while wrong'd *belief* imbibed new *strength*,
> And hugs th' instructive notes, and aids their length,
> *Love*, and his train of *Cupids* craftier cares
> Scatter, with plumy fans, the dreaded airs.
>
> (Hill 1753: I, 143–4, ll. 44–58)

Bellaria's playing wins the hearts of all around her, and the atmosphere is made palpable by the spirit-forms who express the emotions of the scene. *Imbibed* (line 55) is again an important word in suggesting how her music is absorbed into the soul. At the same time *candor* and *truth* stand guard, firm and unmoved. In this passage Hill develops the potential of allegory to represent the complexity of textual "meaning" in non-mimetic art. As a performance, Bellaria's music creates a force field of imaginative and emotional response, while its art remains "true" to something more steadfast. Style does not betray principle, and truth stands guard for imagination. It is an allegory in little of some of the issues that confronted eighteenth-century critics and editors of *The Faerie Queene*.

The Critical Debate

It is necessary once again to return to the decade 1706–15 to locate the first substantial impact of *The Faerie Queene* on literary criticism. The ground-breaking work was John Hughes' six-volume *Works of Mr Edmund Spenser* (1715), which along with a 25-page glossary of "Old and Obscure Words" includes a substantial critical introduction premised on a recognition that Spenser poses a fundamental challenge to "those who have laid down Rules for the Art of Poetry" (I, xxviii). Hughes' response is to use *The Faerie Queene* to define a specific category of "Allegorical Poetry" with its own features and principles. He characterizes it in Addisonian terms as "the *Fairy Land* of Poetry, peopled by Imagination" (xxxiv), but with an extra dimension. It is "a kind of continued Simile" in which the text's meaning develops simultaneously along two levels, which he terms the "literal" and the "mystical":

> [T]he Fable or Story consists for the most part of fictitious Persons or Beings, Creatures of the Poet's Brain, and Actions surprizing, and without the Bounds of Probability or Nature. In Works of this kind, it is impossible for the Reader to rest in the literal Sense, but he is of necessity driven to seek for another Meaning under these wild Types and Shadows. (I, xxxvi)

This kind of poetry, Hughes believes, has "a License peculiar to it self," and a reader who approaches *The Faerie Queene* in these allegorical terms may "excuse some of its Irregularities." He admits, however, that the poem's "most obvious Defects" are attributable to its being "so romantick a Story," and thus lacking the unity to be expected from an epic. It is at this point, with head and heart entangled, that Hughes steps boldly out of the impasse and uses Spenser's poem to challenge the universality of the "rules":

> [T]he whole Frame of it wou'd appear monstrous, if it were to be examin'd by the Rules of Epick Poetry, as they have been drawn from the Practice of *Homer* and *Virgil*. But as it is plain the Author never design'd it by those Rules, I think it ought rather to be consider'd as a Poem of a particular kind, describing in a Series of Allegorical Adventures or Episodes the most noted Virtues and Vices: to compass it therefore with the Models of Antiquity, wou'd be like drawing a Parallel between the *Roman* and the *Gothick* Architecture. (I, lx)

The limitations of the classically derived "rules" had been acknowledged before,[5] but Hughes went further by positing a separate *Gothick* pantheon, a whole alternative style and tradition – and at a time when "Gothic" tended to be a term of abuse equivalent to "barbarous." Such relativism, with its suggestion that the accepted standards of judgment (based on matters of structure and probability) were not universal principles but mere historical constructions, questioned the nature of the critical act itself. The need to come to terms with Spenser's poem challenged criticism to acknowledge an historical dimension.

Hughes's idea that *The Faerie Queene* was a monument to "Gothic" principles (if there were such things) and could defy classical authority was a challenge taken up by the poem's next important editor, John Upton, who made it his task to defend the poem, especially its structure, from the imputation of "romance" and from Hughes' suggestion that it fell short of classical standards. In his preliminary *Letter concerning a New Edition of Spenser's Faerie Queene* (1751) Upton outlined a "defence" of the poem on Aristotelian principles. His impressive two-volume edition (1759) takes this further by setting out to show, in the words of Jewel Wurtsbaugh (1936: 81), "not how the *Faerie Queene* neglected, but how it conformed to classic laws." Upton offers a sustained parallel between *The Faerie Queene* and Homer's *Iliad* with the aim of vindicating the unity and probability of the poem's action. In his notes he pours scorn on "silly romances," making it clear that he thinks Spenser much above that sort of thing. Upton's *Faerie Queene* is an unfinished classically structured epic, in which Arthur was intended to fulfill a role equivalent to that of Achilles in the *Iliad*. Finally entering the fray and "eclipsing all the other heroes," Arthur would have appeared before Gloriana in his full magnificence (I, xxiv). Upton preferred to conjecture about how Spenser would have completed his epic rather than acknowledging romance elements in the poem.

Upton, however, was out of step with the critical trends of the age, which were beginning to open up the issue of "romance" to historical investigation. This move was represented by a book that Upton's edition pointedly ignored, Thomas Warton's *Observations on the Faerie Queene* (1754). Warton's scholarly and critical study was in part directed at Upton, who had shown himself contemptuous of the elements of romance and chivalry that for Warton were at the heart of Spenser's poem.[6] In his book (extended to two volumes in 1762) Warton offers the first historical study of Spenser's romance sources, and presents *The Faerie Queene* as the "consummation" of a British line of imaginative allegorical writing deriving from Chaucer and Arthurian romance. For the first time Spenser was placed within literary history not as an isolated "classic," but as part of a national allegorical tradition in which the poet's imagination played a vital part. By contextualizing Spenser in terms of the tastes of the Elizabethan period Warton was able to characterize *The Faerie Queene* as primarily a work of "romance":

> [T]oo many readers view the knights and damsels, the turnaments and enchantments of Spenser with modern eyes, never considering that the encounters of Chivalry subsisted in our author's age . . . that romances were then most eagerly and universally read; and that thus, Spenser from the fashion of his age, was naturally dispos'd to undertake a recital of chivalrous atchievements, and to become, in short, a ROMANTIC POET. (1754: 217)

It is a challenging declaration. Warton homes in on the act of *reading*, linking the reading fashions of the Elizabethans with his ideal modern sympathetic readers who will place themselves imaginatively in Spenser's setting. This dual move, of historicizing enchantment while locating it in the imagination of the modern reader, recalls the "double movement" (the strangeness and intimacy of romance) noted at the beginning of this essay. It is perhaps not surprising that in Warton is encapsulated the struggle of head and heart that characterizes much eighteenth-century Spenserianism:

> [T]he FAERIE QUEENE . . . engages the affection of the heart, rather than the applause of the head; and if there be any poem whose graces please, because they are situated beyond the reach of art, and where the faculties of creative imagination delight us, because they are unassisted and unrestrained by those of deliberate judgment, it is this of which we are now speaking. To sum up all in a few words; tho' in the FAERIE QUEENE we are not satisfied as critics, yet we are transported as readers. (1754: 12–13)

Such emotional blackmail of the critic by the reader encourages a kind of romantic literary appreciation, bypassing classic criticism, and leaving the latter isolated in a world of judgment out of touch with the act of reading. This kind of reader-response theory developed during the eighteenth century partly in response to the critical problems posed by *The Faerie Queene*.

Imitation and Seduction

It is clear that Spenser offered a model for a more intimate and complex relationship between poet and reader. *The Faerie Queene*, as we have seen, raised issues of "enchantment" (a combination of imaginative engagement and emotional response), and through its "allegorical" potential, its layering of literal and mystical meaning, it allowed poets to work between the tangible and intangible. In poems like *The Rape of the Lock* and "Bellaria at her Spinett" emotions of fear or desire could be realized, along with elements of ambivalence and suggestiveness. In various ways Spenser and Spenserian poetry were amenable to the kind of affective reading associated with romances and their modern descendents, novels.

During the 1740s poets began to be excited by the creative potential of the language and stanza form of *The Faerie Queene*. Pope's death in 1744 marked a kind of watershed, and younger poets who came to prominence during the second half of the decade (Gray, Shenstone, Mason, Akenside, Collins, the Warton brothers) were all keen to place themselves in the tradition of Spenser and Milton, rather than to continue the work of Pope. Thomas Gray, for example, would always read some Spenser before sitting down to compose,[7] and William Collins in "Ode on the Poetical Character" (1746) chooses as his emblem of poetic power the girdle of Venus from *The Faerie Queene*, woven ("as Fairy Legends say") when the divine mind and the youthful imagination coupled together. Young poets of the 1740s found it difficult to place Pope within the native literary tradition, and they preferred to look back to Spenser and Milton for inspiration. This is the ironic message of William

Mason's *Musaeus: A Monody to the Memory of Mr. Pope* (1747), in which Spenser (along with Chaucer and Milton) appears before the dying poet to pay tribute to him. The result, however, is to distance Pope from his three visitors. Each speaks in his own distinctive language (Spenser in the stanza of *The Faerie Queene*) and at the end Pope resists their generous gestures of accommodation. Having been reminded of the early poetry he wrote under their influence, Pope angrily dismisses it: "Ah! why recall the toys of thoughtless youth? / When flow'ry fiction held the place of truth; / When fancy rul'd," 17). But in the late 1740s tastes were changing, and it was fiction and fancy that were wanted. In *The Pleasures of Melancholy* (1747) the 19-year-old Thomas Warton specifically rejects even the "happiest art" of *The Rape of the Lock* and celebrates his preference for Spenserian romance:

> Yet does my mind with sweeter transport glow,
> As at the root of mossy trunk reclin'd,
> In magic SPENSER's wildly-warbled song
> I see deserted Una wander wide
> Thro' wasteful solitudes, and lurid heaths.
>
> (155–9)

For a generation of young poets in the 1740s, *The Faerie Queene* represented the main current of English poetry that many saw as having been diverted during the period from 1660 to 1740. In the words of Joseph Warton (Thomas' brother) they were attempting "to bring back Poetry into its right channel," back toward "Invention and Imagination."[8]

The verse form of *The Faerie Queene* ceased to be a mere historical curiosity. The nine-line Spenserian stanza (or variants of it) became popular, and poets discovered along with it new possibilities of subject, vocabulary, and rhythm. It offered poets room to look around them and indulge in more extended description; a scene's atmosphere could be explored and details picked out, without the syntactic tightness that made the couplet such a powerful tool for wit and satire. One of the most popular imitations of the century, William Shenstone's *The School-Mistress*, had begun in 1737 as a 12-stanza parody, using quaint antiquated language to describe the poet's memories of his village school. But by 1748 it had swelled to 35 stanzas, in which the parodic became less evident as Shenstone began to use the stanza to enter the imaginative world of childhood, when wonder, fear, and delight were all around – often in combination:

> A russet stole was o'er her shoulders thrown;
> A russet kirtle fenc'd the nipping air;
> 'Twas simple russet, but it was her own;
> 'Twas her own country bred the flock so fair;
> 'Twas her own labour did the fleece prepare;
> And, sooth to say, her pupils, rang'd around,
> Thro' pious awe, did term it passing rare;

> For they in gaping wonderment abound,
> And think, no doubt, she been the greatest wight on ground.
>
> (64–72)

In the course of the stanza Shenstone catches the way a child's imagination can transform the ordinary into the magical. His language, like the schoolmistress' "russet" garments, is simple, homespun, and honest – nothing glitters or is there for show – but out of it emerges the possibility of enchantment. It is this sense of the potential *wonderment* of everyday experience, the possibility of recapturing something rare and strange, which characterizes much Spenserian imitation. "Imitation" in fact ceases to be the appropriate word for something that comes closer to "absorption." Shenstone, like his schoolmistress, wears his native material naturally.

Critics and poets alike sensed the seductive fullness of Spenser, and many of them entered his imaginative world with an awareness of its risks. This ambivalent attitude to enchantment was memorably exploited in James Thomson's *The Castle of Indolence* (1748), which began as a few stanzas "in the way of raillery" on himself and his friends, but grew into a two-canto exploration of poetry's delights and dangers. It was a poem he couldn't leave alone, and which kept drawing him back over the years, so that it becomes virtually an allegorical diary of the text's hold over him. Thomson's castle embodies the allurements of romance, with Indolence as the wizard who casts a spell on all who enter ("Till clustering round th' Enchanter false they hung, / Ymolten with his Syren Melody," I, 69–70). In Thomson's hands the Spenserian stanza is expressively used to represent the enchanter's power to detain the poet's imagination and prevent him from moving on:

> The Wise distrust the too fair-spoken Man.
> Yet through the Gate they cast a wishful Eye:
> Not to move on, perdie, is all they can;
> For do their very Best they cannot fly,
> But often each Way look, and often sorely sigh.
>
> (I, 185–9)

The Spenserian stanza itself seemed to enchant its users, and tempt them to linger.

In the poem's second canto the mood suddenly changes as Thomson introduces the power who will free him (and us) from these entanglements. The "Knight of Arts and Industry," however, is not an anti-Spenserian figure, but a representative of the moral allegory of *The Faerie Queene*. Thomson recognizes that Spenser may be the poet of imagination, but he is also a poet who (like Milton after him) appreciates imagination's dangers. This knight is the Sir Guyon who will destroy the dangerous Bower of Bliss: "Then strait a Wand / He wav'd, an anti-magic Power that hath, / Truth from illusive Falshood to command" (II, 596–8). It is often forgotten that the eighteenth century also recognized the pull of this "anti-magic" element in *The Faerie Queene*. Thomson draws out of Spenser's poem both its delightful magic and its spiritual and moral dimension, and he employs Spenser the moralist to challenge Spenser the enchanter.

The awareness that Spenser's poetic character included both imagination and wisdom made him ideal as an instrument of education. He could capture the young with his romantic fairyland, but then lead them on to maturer thoughts and social responsibility. A Spenserian style often included severer tones and an element of sober reflection. In his poem *Education* (1751) Gilbert West used Spenserian imitation to call for educational reform. Here the crafty enchanter is "Custom," whose "lore inur'd by usage long" (457) entraps the nation's youth "by disciplines and rules" (363). Only when Custom has been overthrown by the Gentle Knight can the nation's energies renew themselves. In Robert Bedingfield's *The Education of Achilles* (1747) the future Greek hero receives his lessons from various allegorical figures such as Modesty, Exercise, and Temperance, all of whom (in a duality characteristic of Spenserian writing) "temper stern behests with pleasaunce gay" (101).

This is one of the themes of another poem in the Spenserian stanza, James Beattie's *The Minstrel: Or, The Progress of Genius* (1771–4), which in a double structure similar to *The Castle of Indolence* traces the education of Edwin, a simple child of nature. In the first canto the youth is a potential romantic poet who imbibes not only the beauties of nature, but also (to recall Addison's list) "Legends and Fables, antiquated Romances, and the Traditions of Nurses and old Women":

> Her legend when the beldam 'gan impart,
> Or chant the old heroic ditty o'er,
> Wonder and joy ran thrilling to his heart;
> Much he the tale admir'd, but more the tuneful art.
>
> (I, xliii)

In the second canto Edwin meets a philosophical hermit who leads him away from "the gay dreams of fond romantic youth" (II, xxx), and teaches him that "Fancy enervates, while it soothes, the heart" (II, xli). It is clear that this impressionable youth has to grow up and become a responsible adult. The mid-century ambivalence over imagination and judgment has given place to an educational trajectory that offers an escape route from enchantment. In the 1770s it is noticeable how Spenserian allegory has become a vehicle for displaying the morally enervating and self-indulgent tendencies of "romance." When William Julius Mickle wants to show how wealth and pleasure are weakening the moral fibre of the nation, he finds the language of *The Faerie Queene* ideal for his purposes. His poem *Sir Martyn* (1778) traces the decline of a man of fortune and influence who gives way to "levity, love of pleasure, and dissipation" and, as he explains in his preface, for this subject the Spenserian descriptive style, with its tendency to luxuriance and wantonness, fitted his purposes best:

> Some reasons, perhaps, may be expected for having adopted the manner of Spenser. To propose a general use of it were indeed highly absurd; yet it may be presumed there are some subjects on which it may be used with advantage . . . the Author will only say, that the fulness and wantonness of description, the quaint simplicity, and above all, the

ludicrous, of which the antique phraseology and manner of Spenser are so happily and peculiarly susceptible, inclined him to esteem it not solely as the best, but the only mode of composition adapted to his subject.

The assumptions behind this passage are revealing: *The Faerie Queene* is characterized in terms of the "quaint," the "antique," and the "ludicrous," and is dismissed as a model for poetry generally. It does seem that by this date Spenserian poetry, and its associated language of romance and pleasure, was facing a degree of reaction. Mickle's patronizing remarks serve to remind us that the critical debate over the value of *The Faerie Queene* never went away. For the poet's admirers in the next generation of Leigh Hunt, Keats, and Shelley, the inspirational potential of *The Faerie Queene* needed to be reasserted.

See also: chapter 5, Chaucer's Romances; chapter 7, Gendering Prose Romance in Renaissance England; chapter 8, Sidney and Spenser; chapter 9, Shakespeare's Romances; chapter 10, Chapbooks and Penny Histories; chapter 12, "Gothic" Romance; chapter 16, Romance and the Romantic Novel; chapter 18, Victorian Romance: Tennyson.

Notes

1. In *The Spectator*, ed. Donald F. Bond, 5 vols. (Oxford: Clarendon Press, 1965), III, pp. 570–3. All subsequent references to Addison are from this issue.
2. Joseph Warton wrote approvingly that in *The Rape of the Lock* Pope "has displayed more imagination than in all his other works taken together" (*Essay on the Writings and Genius of Pope* [1756], p. 257).
3. "[N]ot in Fancy's Maze he wander'd long, / But stoop'd to Truth, and moralized his song" (Pope, *Epistle to Dr Arbuthnot*, 340–1).
4. Hill to Richardson (*The Correspondence of Samuel Richardson*, ed. A. L. Barbauld [1804], I, p. 110). Hill duly appears in *The Dunciad*.

5. Hughes makes this same point by quoting Sir William Temple's remark that rules "may possibly hinder some from being very bad Poets, but are not capable of making any very good one" (*Works of Spenser*, I, p. xlvi).
6. In his *Critical Observations on Shakespeare* (2nd edn., 1748) Upton argued that chivalric romances pandered to a "childish fancy." The ensuing quarrel between Warton and Upton is reconstructed in Fairer 2000.
7. Norton Nicholls' "Reminiscences" of Gray (1805), in *Correspondence of Thomas Gray*, ed. Paget Toynbee and Leonard Whibley, 3 vols. (Oxford: Clarendon Press, 1935), III, p. 1290.
8. Joseph Warton, *Odes on Various Subjects* (1746), Advertisement.

References and Further Reading

Texts

Addison, Joseph (1914). *The Miscellaneous Works of Joseph Addison*, ed. A. C. Guthkelch. London.

Anonymous (1687). *Spencer Redivivus: Containing the First Book of the Fairy Queen . . . Deliver'd in Heroic Numbers by a Person of Quality*. London: Thomas Chapman.

Beattie, James (1775). *The Minstrel . . . In two books.* London: E. & C. Dilly.

Boswell, James (1934–64). *Life of Johnson*, ed. G. Birkbeck Hill and L. F. Powell. 6 vols. Oxford: Clarendon Press.

Cooper, Elizabeth, ed. (1737). *The Muses Library: or, a Series of English Poetry, from the Saxons to the Reign of King Charles II.* London: J. Wilcox etc.

Hill, Aaron (1753). *The Works of the Late Aaron Hill, Esq: in Four Volumes.* London: Printed for the Benefit of the Family.

Mickle, William Julius (1799). *The Poetical Works . . . With the Life of the Author.* London: C. Cooke.

Pope, Alexander (1743). *The Dunciad, in Four Books.* London: M. Cooper.

Pope, Alexander (1956). *The Correspondence of Alexander Pope*, ed. George Sherburn. 5 vols. Oxford: Clarendon Press.

Prior, Matthew (1971). *The Literary Works of Matthew Prior*, ed. H. Bunker Wright and Monroe K. Spears. 2nd edn. Oxford: Clarendon Press.

Spence, Joseph (1966). *Observations, Anecdotes, and Characters of Books and Men*, ed. James M. Osborn. Oxford: Clarendon Press.

Spenser, Edmund (1715). *The Works of Mr. Edmund Spenser. In Six Volumes*, ed. John Hughes. London: Jacob Tonson.

Thomson, James (1748). *The Castle of Indolence. An Allegorical Poem. Written in Imitation of Spenser.* London: Andrew Millar.

Warton, Thomas (1754). *Observations on the Faerie Queene of Spenser.* London: R. and J. Dodsley; Oxford: J. Fletcher.

Warton, Thomas (1802). *The Poetical Works of the Late Thomas Warton, B. D.*, ed. Richard Mant. 2 vols. Oxford: Oxford University Press.

West, Gilbert (1739). *A Canto of the Fairy Queen. Written by Spenser. Never before Published.* London: G. Hawkins.

West, Gilbert (1751). *Education, a Poem: in Two Cantos. Written in Imitation of the Style and Manner of Spenser's Fairy Queen. Canto I.* London. R. Dodsley.

Criticism

Cummings, R. M., ed. (1971). *Edmund Spenser: The Critical Heritage.* London: Routledge and Kegan Paul.

Dowling, William C. (1992). "Ideology and the Flight from History in Eighteenth-century Poetry." In Leo Damrosch, ed., *The Profession of Eighteenth-Century Literature: Reflections on an Institution.* Madison and London: University of Wisconsin Press, pp. 135–53.

Erskine-Hill, Howard (1990). "Pope." In A. C. Hamilton, ed., *The Spenser Encyclopedia.* Toronto and Buffalo: University of Toronto Press.

Fairer, David (2000). "Historical Criticism and the English Canon: A Spenserian Dispute in the 1750s." *Eighteenth-Century Life* 24, 43–64.

Fairer, David (2001). "Creating a National Poetry: The Tradition of Spenser and Milton." In John Sitter, ed., *The Cambridge Companion to Eighteenth-Century Poetry.* Cambridge: Cambridge University Press, pp. 177–201.

Frushell, Richard C. (1986). "Spenser and the Eighteenth-century Schools." *Spenser Studies* 7, 175–98.

Frushell, Richard C. (1990). "Imitations and Adaptations, 1660–1800." In A. C. Hamilton, ed., *The Spenser Encyclopedia.* Toronto and Buffalo: University of Toronto Press, pp. 166–84.

Gerrard, Christine (1994). *The Patriot Opposition to Walpole: Politics, Poetry, and National Myth, 1725–1742.* Oxford: Clarendon Press.

Guillory, John (1983). *Poetic Authority: Spenser, Milton, and Literary History.* New York: Columbia University Press.

Johnston, Arthur (1964). *Enchanted Ground: The Study of Medieval Romance in the Eighteenth Century.* London: Athlone Press.

Kramnick, Jonathan Brody (1996). "The Cultural Logic of Late Feudalism: Placing Spenser in the Eighteenth Century." *ELH* 63, 871–92.

Kramnick, Jonathan Brody (1998). *Making the English Canon: Print Capitalism and the Cultural Past, 1700–1770.* Cambridge: Cambridge University Press.

Kucich, Greg (1991). *Keats, Shelley, and Romantic Spenserianism.* University Park: Pennsylvania State University Press.

Levine, Joseph M. (1987). "Eighteenth-century Historicism and the First Gothic Revival." In J. M. Levine, ed., *Humanism and History.* Ithaca, NY: Cornell University Press, pp. 190–213.

Patey, Douglas Lane (1988). "The Eighteenth Century Invents the Canon." *Modern Language Studies* 18, 17–37.

Ross, Trevor (1996). "The Emergence of 'Literature': Making and Reading the English Canon in the Eighteenth Century." *ELH* 63, 397–422.

Ross, Trevor (1998). *The Making of the English Literary Canon: From the Middle Ages to the Late Eighteenth Century.* Montreal: McGill-Queen's University Press.

Tucker, Herbert F., Jr. (1977). "Spenser's Eighteenth-century Readers and the Question of Unity in *The Faerie Queene*." *University of Toronto Quarterly* 46, 322–41.

Wasserman, Earl R. (1947). *Elizabethan Poetry in the Eighteenth Century.* Urbana: University of Illinois Press.

Wellek, René (1941). *The Rise of English Literary History.* Chapel Hill: University of North Carolina Press.

Wurtsbaugh, Jewel (1936). *Two Centuries of Spenserian Scholarship (1609–1805).* Baltimore, MD: Johns Hopkins University Press.

12

"Gothic" Romance: Its Origins and Cultural Functions

Jerrold E. Hogle

So-called "Gothic" romance came into being long after the Middle Ages, the tribes and the architecture of which are most associated, rightly or wrongly, with the racial term "Gothic." The first work of prose narrative to call itself "a Gothic Story" (and then only in its second edition) was Horace Walpole's *The Castle of Otranto*, first published in England in 1764 as supposedly a recent translation by the Anglican "William Marshall" of an Italian and Catholic text of 1529 printed "in the black letter" (a Gothic, as opposed to a roman typeface) that itself supposedly retold a story set and composed "between 1095, the aera of the first crusade, and 1243, the date of the last" (Walpole 1996: 5). When Walpole revealed the several ruses behind all this in the 1765 reprinting, he not only added the "Gothic" label – a word by then loaded with several contradictory meanings, as we shall see – but helped define it in a new preface that proposed his work as the avatar of a new kind of "romance" (as he put it himself) that partly embraced and partly rejected the medieval-chivalric, Renaissance, and seventeenth-century French traditions of *romans* that Walpole knew from his extensive reading and antiquarian collecting. Given that the mainly aristocratic romance of quests, long separated lovers, recovered nobility, and occasionally divine intervention had by now given way for the increasingly literate middle class to fictions of domestic life and individual development more suited to the growing ideology of "self-made men" (see Watt 2001), Walpole proposed to "blend the two kinds of romance: the ancient and the modern" (1996: 9), while still calling *both* "romance," given that the French *roman* then referred to virtually any kind of long fiction in prose. In doing so he began the codification of a very mixed genre, one that now extends from novels and plays to myriad films and even video games, a genre that was and remains rooted in a Janus-faced series of conflicts that look backwards and forwards in history simultaneously, making "Gothic romance" or "the Gothic" a mode inherently at war with itself *inside* itself while also at odds with other literary conventions (those of the older "romance" among them). The result has been a form of romance, and sometimes *anti*-romance, that has become a haunting staple in

Western culture, one of the longest-lasting of the symbolic modes by which that culture looks at itself in flagrantly imaginary, and in this case "ghostly" and "monstrous," disguises. In the process, this curious variation on romance has helped us, for two-and-a-half centuries of modern (in the sense of post-Enlightenment) existence, both confront and distance many of the most profound contradictions in our cultural lives, at least for the Western middle class (the Gothic's main readership). Symbolizing and masking deep conflicts, after all, is an especially fitting cultural role for a mode of fiction-making fundamentally at odds with itself in its origins, its forcibly mixed ingredients, and its history full of controversy and unsettling change.

Walpole's claims in his 1765 preface about his new "blend" are clear indications of the struggles over fiction, belief, and status that swirled around it, and finally helped bring it about, in the latter half of the eighteenth century. When he writes that in "ancient romance" on its own "all was imagination and improbability" (1996: 9), he is echoing, among others, one of the most prominent of the more "realistic" *new* romancers of the day, Tobias Smollett, who in his preface to *Roderick Random* (1748) sees older romance as the product of a time "when the minds of men were debauched by the imposition of priest-craft to the most absurd pitch of credulity" and so "filled their performances with the most monstrous hyperboles" (Smollett 1979: xliv). Romance so defined, based on quite partial knowledge, of course, was obviously abhorrent to the English Protestant middle class as much because of its Catholic basis as because of its fated or supernatural predestinations that assumed an aristocratic sense of ordained entitlement. When Walpole refers to "modern romance," though, as fiction where "nature is always intended to be, and sometimes has been, copied with success" (1996: 9), an achievement by now linked to the writings of Defoe, Richardson, Smollett, and Fielding in the wake of Cervantes, this claim is immediately undercut by the worry that "the great resources of fancy have been dammed up, by a strict adherence to common life" (Walpole 1996: 9). That is so much the case for Walpole that he finds himself "desirous of leaving the powers of fancy at liberty to expatiate through the boundless realms of invention, and thence of creating more interesting situations" than the "nature" which has "cramped imagination."

Such a statement quite directly echoes the justifications used in the revival of chivalric romance earlier in the 1750s and 1760s in England, which coincided with the revival of seemingly "Gothic" architecture in which Walpole participated by restyling his house at Strawberry Hill, using bits and pieces from old castles and churches. This deliberate retrogression was announced most forcefully in writing by Thomas Warton's *Observations on the Faerie Queene of Spenser* (1754; enlarged in 1762) and Bishop Richard Hurd's *Letters on Chivalry and Romance* (1762), as well as by the popularity of James Macpherson's faked old Celtic *Ossian* poems, gathered together in books of 1762 and 1763 (see Clery in Hogle 2002: 25 and 29). The motivation behind such a counter to the Smollett position, if we believe Hurd, was this: "we have lost . . . a world of fine fabling" and with it "the liberty of transgressing nature," one of "the real properties and powers of human nature," a freedom desirable to the "self-made" middle class, to be sure, yet available to readers now mostly in "Gothic" works, such as *The Faerie Queene,* that reflect the most progressive sides of England's old "FEUDAL CONSTITUTION" in a belated and less tyrannical form (Hurd in Clery and Miles 2000: 77 and 69). For Walpole to revert at least halfway to "ancient romance," then, is for him to reclaim a fading imaginative (as well as *broadly* Christian) birthright, to some extent a national mythology, highly desirable for the modern mind as long as he also fulfills the newer Enlightenment dictum "to conduct the mortal agents of his drama according to the rules of probability," more common in a narrative by Smollett than in one by Spenser (Walpole 1996: 9–10).

The label "Gothic," in fact, though it caught on only sporadically in fiction for decades after Walpole used it (Clery in Hogle 2002: 21–2), came to him already attached to versions of this same tug of war. It could mean so many things by then because its first use to describe medieval architecture and culture retrospectively was a *mis*nomer, used by Italian art critics of the fifteenth century to classify pointed-arch and castellated structures as "barbarous" by their Greco-Roman standards, as though the "Goths" who conquered Rome were somehow connected to much later Catholic churches and castles they never knew (Frankl 1960: 259–60). This initial stealing of the term from its original contexts thus helped it come, by Walpole's time, to mean "uncivilized" to the point of "rude" or "low class," "crumbling and decayed," "tyrannically Catholic" (like Smollett's sense of "romance"), "archaically medieval and outdated," "tastelessly ornate," "filled with old superstitions," and even "racially different," since it came to be applied to several non-English races ranging from war-mongering medieval Italians to black African Moors, one-time conquerors of realms beyond their own now long supplanted by a supposedly more enlightened British imperialism and Protestant Christianity (see Tucker 1967: 149–55). Even so, for Walpole, as the son of a former Whig Prime Minister opposed to the Tory government under King George III after 1760, "Gothic" was just as associated with the medieval English freedom thought to have been initiated by the Magna Carta in 1215, a replica of which Walpole kept posted over his bed (Kallich 1971: 42–50). The old English "Constitution" was construed as one, according to James Beattie in 1783, in which "All the Gothick institutions were, in their purest form, favorable to liberty" and thus this freedom even encompassed a "grand style of architecture" full of "chambers supposed to be haunted with spirits; and undermined by subterraneous labyrinths as places of retreat in extreme danger" (Clery and Miles 2000: 89–90).

As pejorative as it often still was, "Gothic" for Walpole also meant "superstitious" leaning towards "spiritual," "originally free" compared to more recent and decadent times, "happily elaborate and vast" as opposed to classically staid and confined, "imaginative" beyond restricted modern knowledge, and "more natural" given a rural, estate-based economy, compared to the more modern world – which Walpole also valued – of urban mercantilism and greater international exchange (see Kliger 1952). The initial "Gothic" romance really *had* to be as caught between backward- and forward-looking tendencies as it was, especially since what was coming to be valued in a more middle-class-controlled and preindustrial era was regarded as both opposed to archaic "Gothic" hierarchies and seeking to revive the primordial freedoms, including the "sublime" freedom of the mind, which was being projected back into a ruder "Gothic" Eden.· It was as if, like Walpole's *Castle* and its author, modern individuals were gaining their free-enterprise range to "expatiate" boundlessly only by deriving a pedigree for doing so from the very times and accoutrements they were pushing into the past, even as the remains of that past still surrounded them thoroughly, if mostly in ruins and pictures.

Walpole's second preface hopes that his "Gothic Story" can resolve this conflict in a new "blend," of course, by making "the mortal agents in his drama . . . think, speak, and act as it might be supposed mere men and women [as in modern fiction] would do in extraordinary positions" such as "the dispensation of miracles" and "witness[ing] the most stupendous phenomena," elements much more common in older romance than in Richardson or Smollett (Walpole 1996: 9–10). But the result in *The Castle of Otranto* itself turns out to be a series of juxtapositions that only reenact and expand the conflicts. As in romances all the way back to the Greek texts, Walpole's plot turns partly on a displaced aristocrat, the impoverished Theodore, severed from his true noble origins without his knowledge and forced to overcome several obstacles to regain his original status, especially the threats posed by Manfred, the reigning Prince of the castle and principality of Otranto, finally revealed as Theodore's stolen birthright. Hidden supernatural intentions of an obviously divine kind, meanwhile, do push all events toward this restoration, as in the thirteenth-century Vulgate French *Lancelot* and *Quest of the Holy Grail*, particularly as, in giant armored fragments, the ghost of Otranto's original owner, Alfonso, gradually forces the revelation of his age-old murder by Manfred's grandfather and hence of Manfred's continued usurpation of the true line of inheritance. The fragments finally come back together in one specter "dilated to a huge magnitude" at the end, who announces "Theodore, the true heir of Alfonso!" before "rising solemnly towards heaven" to be received by "the form of Saint Nicholas" in a "blaze of glory" reminiscent of a painted Catholic cathedral ceiling, to such an extent that all the characters are left "acknowledging the divine will" (Walpole 1996: 112–13). But these features are placed oxymoronically beside a domestic drama, clearly rooted in Shakespeare and the Aristotelian "unities" of the classical theater (as admitted in both prefaces; Walpole 1996: 6 and 10–11), which remains entirely confined to the castle, the adjacent abbey, and the underground vaults that pass between them, despite characters who narrate past exploits from the crusades within these claustrophobic spaces.

Gone is any expansive quest across many locations, and what replaces it is a very private, even middle-class-sounding dispute of claimants over the inheritance of money and property, all of which is laced with the eighteenth-century psychology of personal (and usually upper middle-class) "sentiment" whereby the "passions that ensued must be conceived" mentally and in words, since "they cannot be painted" in any old allegorical style like that in the quasi-Catholic fresco to which Alfonso ascends (Walpole 1996: 57). The ensuing internal quandaries about identity's very foundation – as when Manfred, simultaneously longing and fearing to know his roots, "forgot his anger in his astonishment; yet his pride forbad his owning himself affected" – end up seeming more convincingly "real" than the machinery of the "medieval romance" frames around them. Even "William Marshall" in the first preface reveals that he and, he hopes, his reader do not believe in the most Catholic icons he uses, calling them "ancient errors and superstitions" (Walpole 1996: 5), leaving the final ascent to Saint Nicholas as conceptually and physically empty as the ghost of Alfonso is largely fragmented. It was the modern hollowness of once Catholic symbols, it turns out, that helped make them appealing to Horace Walpole here and elsewhere. In such relics, he writes in one of his many letters, the "dead have lost their power of deceiving" and so the teller of the "Gothic Story" has "no reason to quarrel with their emptiness" (Walpole 1937–83: 10, 192).

Astonishing as it may seem, *The Castle of Otranto*, though not widely imitated until the 1790s, thereby established a great many of what have become the conventional features of "the Gothic" and "Gothic romance" even into the twenty-first century: the antiquated and haunted setting; some dark secret or secrets from the past hidden in the depths; the rising of these secrets in the form of some ghost or monstrosity; the pulling of characters back into that past in a tug of war with their aspirations to transcend it; the problem of establishing "correct" inheritance so that present figures can seem to gain the support of something past while they leave it behind; the determination of love objects more by these tensions than by mere preference; the mental terror of the looming unknown that may be founded in the supernatural (the ghost of Alfonso) or the natural (murder and its earthly consequences, for example) or the mental hesitation between one and the other (Manfred's condition for most of *Otranto*); and the consequent psychological state in the major characters of guiltily fearing and trying to escape a possible instability of identity both inside and outside the self. Yet these elements are all as conflicted within themselves as Walpole's central characters are, especially since what is most "real" in such fictions has been called into question by the emptied-out figures that seem to provide groundings from the past but also deny any solid grounds at the same time, since they have been uprooted. On the whole, though there are pieces of older romance everywhere in them, "Gothic" fictions with the above ingredients *neither* continue *nor* complete most of medieval romance's fundamental drives. They are rather *haunted* by chivalric-romance elements in a fragmented way to the point where the longing to repossess the security in their ultimate closure is usually as disappointed as it is almost always desired. *The Castle of Otranto,* strictly speaking, does not end with a supernatural apotheosis of simple restored lineage. In the dénouement, Theodore must assume his princely role without the love of Matilda, Manfred's now murdered daughter, whom Theodore (and she) saw as his self-completing other, the Una of this once-disguised Redcrosse Knight. Instead he must face a substitute marriage with *Otranto*'s other young heroine, Isabella (pursued earlier by Manfred), who, while highly interchangeable with Matilda throughout the tale, to the point where Manfred stabs his daughter *thinking* her to be Isabella, can only be the image of what Theodore has lost forever in the past. "He [is ultimately] persuaded," in *Otranto*'s odd and sad final sentence, that "he could know no happiness but in the society of one with whom he could forever indulge the melancholy that had taken possession of its soul" (Walpole 1996: 115). No earlier romance worthy of the name has ever ended this way, even though a few of them are tragic. *The Castle of Otranto*, for many the "father" of "Gothic" romance, clearly skews the tradition while continuing many elements from it piecemeal by pulling out the rug from under the usual union at the completion of most romantic quests to leave readers only with a desire for a past object – perhaps old romance itself – irretrievably lost behind an image that does not finally contain it.

This "blend" of inconsistencies that do not really blend at all, I would argue, immediately helped establish the Gothic romance as a vivid indicator of the deep cultural tensions, not of the Middle Ages or the Renaissance, but of increasingly "modern" times. The tug of war between Walpole's ingredients reenacts a conflict of values in himself and in his readers at a moment in history when "the feudal origins of an aristocratic order," the remnants of which were still powerfully visible and even sought by the rising middle class, confronted the more and more insistent "perspective of bourgeois capitalism with [its] different category of 'family' and a different concept of the relation between self and property" (Clery 1995: 76). *The Castle of Otranto* thus hyperbolically plays out the mid-eighteenth-century "contradiction between the traditional claims of landed property and the new claims of the private family; a conflict between two versions of economic 'personality'" (Clery 1995: 77). Hence the old accoutrements, including the Catholicism, of the fading aristocracy are both empty and fragmented in this tale, yet the characters can pursue alternatives to them only by reusing the old elements, such as male inheritance, restored lineage, claims for "divine will," and political marriages, which still have strong symbolic powers to articulate *and* confine human possibility. Walpole's people are haunted, in other words, not just by hollowed-out fragments of formerly aristocratic romance and religion but by the irreconcilable opposites that those ghosts or monstrosities are now made to contain: their being empty and still powerful, simultaneously broken apart and longed for, both models for desire and blocks to its attainment, all because they are the most available avenues to economic and familial foundations that most of the aspiring characters would like to gain, but cannot, through more middle-class means. Diane Long Hoeveler is quite right to conclude that the Gothic in its always contradictory forms "charts the death of the old world of Catholicism, communalism, feudalism, and the rise in its place of the Protestant subject, individual, modern, secular," but with such a strong sense that these opposites continue to play upon each other that the same mixed mode shows us all to be still "haunted by [a] bifurcation that [has] plagued definitions of the self" since shortly before and long after Walpole's inaugural "Gothic Story" (Hoeveler 2001: 9 and 4).

Rising along with the emergent mercantile and preindustrial capitalism celebrated in Adam Smith's *Wealth of Nations* (1776) less than 12 years after *Otranto*, we must realize, the Gothic romance was a striking new mixture of genres that registered the contradictory hopes, fears, and hesitations which accompanied that transition. In the first place, as Walpole demonstrates, the Gothic "extends the Protestant tradition of self-scrutiny into a critique of [developing] bourgeois values" by wondering about a future centered on "the modern materialistic individual" (Manfred) in which such "detached individuals" might devolve into "predatory and demonic relations" if unchecked by regulators from the past (such as the ghost of Alfonso) that carry with them, like "Gothic," "both an oppressive feudal past and a [supposed] golden age of liberty" that might or might not be more attractive than a "modern alienated and estranged world" (Kilgour 1995: 11–15). In the second place, simply leaving the past behind in its ruins may not be psychologically possible even for members of the middle class who fancy they welcome such a brave new world. As Leslie Fiedler has written (1966: 129),

> the guilt which underlies the gothic and motivates its plots [Manfred's guilt, for example, and perhaps that of Walpole and many of his readers] is the guilt of the revolutionary haunted by the ([apparently] paternal) past which he has been striving to destroy; and the fear that possesses the gothic and motivates its tone is the fear that in destroying the old ego-ideals of Church and State, the West has opened the way for the inruption of darkness: for insanity and the disintegration of the self.

After all, the newer choices being offered by bourgeois capitalism for symbolizing and anchoring identity may be only "the abstraction of capital investment and profit" (Clery 1995: 74), an inconclusive and finally ungrounded pursuit of acquisitions that (like Manfred's) must always be seeking fragments of the past as indications of wealth and thus as objects of desire, possibly like Walpole at Strawberry Hill. Gothic romance as *both* pro- and anti-romance consequently deals, from its very beginnings, with the "darker impulses" in the developing modern sensibility (Fiedler 1966: 129) as they *both* strive toward and against capitalist alienation using pieces of past orders *and* harbor fears of the radical inconsistency and multiplicity, the Janus-faced "bifurcation" underlying conscious modern quests for some wholeness in the self. We can hardly be surprised that the Gothic from Walpole on has therefore influenced much of the topography in the psychoanalytic vision of the human mind, the haunting of consciousness by the older and fragmentary unconscious, promulgated most by Sigmund Freud in the late nineteenth and early twentieth centuries, the very psychoanalysis that has more recently provided one of the most useful interpretive lenses for reading the Gothic romance (see Morris 1985, for example).

The key to the Gothic's conflicted nature and function since Walpole, it turns out, is not the use of old romance elements simply to haunt the present with the past. It is the use of those features, now anamorphosed and "dilated" into such monstrous specters as the huge and fragmented Alfonso, as a repository for what is feared as deeply *inconsistent and unresolved* about a modern state of mind after 1750 that wonders if there is an "identity" at the heart of itself or if there is only a welter of nonidentical multiplicities, of various "dark others" basic to us, including desires both to kill and to possess the past symbolized by old romance, all of which are "buried within [the bourgeois-based construction of a] partial and inherently false self" (Hoeveler 2001: 4). The fear aroused by the Gothic, we might say, is not on one side of the tug of war within it. It is the fear that the contest fundamental to *us* between possible states of being is always there in one way or another, pulling us perpetually toward and away from empty past modes (or ghosts) of symbolic self-fashioning. The French theorist and psychoanalyst Julia Kristeva has therefore provided a very apt descriptor for what the Gothic does for its authors and readers when she explains the process of "abjection" in her 1980 book *Powers of Horror.* Developing the history of that word, which in its roots means both "throwing off" and "being thrown under," Kristeva sees the abjection of preconscious conflicts in "horror" fiction as "sending over there" into an archaic or monstrous "other" those aspects of Western middle-class existence that are too multiple and inconsistent for "selves" to claim clear identities; such aspects include for her the birth-state of being half inside and half outside the mother, as well as being half-dead and half-alive *and* both self and "other" at that moment, "an immemorial violence" still in the visceral memory "from which a body [works to become] separated" simply "in order to be" (Kristeva 1982: 10). At a social and cultural level, similar "violences" include being caught between irreconcilable class positions and ideologies to the point, if one wishes to produce a coherent selfhood over against this morass, of casting it into an abhorrent repository of that fundamental "otherness" and then throwing the resulting ghost-like monstrousness "under" an authority that seems to contain it, while also fearing it. This process, as we have seen, is precisely what Walpole performs for himself and others in *The Castle of Otranto,* making that "Gothic Story" itself, along with its specters and main characters, a site of the "othered *abject*." Such a "throwing off and down" both half-reenacts/half-resists the conflicted foundations of the emergence of the middle-class *and* shunts this whole Janus-faced "birth" off into a seemingly fantastic past that keeps its complex reality half-hidden, though still looming over us, behind a veneer of fake antiquity and thus extreme fictionality.

It is in this way that Gothic romance, born from social movements and symbolic ingredients pulling in opposite directions like the term "Gothic" itself, becomes the locus of the cultural function that David Punter has rightly attributed to it: a realm of words from different sources in which the Western middle class, as Walpole did, "displays the hidden violence of present social structures, conjures them up again as past, and falls promptly under their spell" (Punter 1996: 2, 218), simultaneously longing for (as its "mother") and distancing itself from (as the denier of its claims to self-made coherence) the abjected mix of contraries that is the underlying basis for the modern middle-class effort at viable self-construction. The hollowed vestiges of old romance in the Gothic thus continue to serve cultural purposes by both helping to produce the quite deliberate and falsely antique "unreality" into which this conflicted process can be "thrown" and providing the stylistic heightening and exaggeration of perceived existence that allows what has been abjected to show itself to us, albeit in disguise, as a return of the repressed that unsettles the ideological "norms" behind the "realistic" explanations with which we protect our conscious psyches from facing the complete history of our modern "selves." As a result, about a century after *Otranto,* an American variation on the Gothic, *The House of the Seven Gables* (1851) by Nathaniel

Hawthorne, can identify itself in a Walpolean preface of its own as emphatically a "romance." In the words of its author, it "mingle[s] the Marvellous . . . as a slight, delicate, and evanescent flavor" with features from "the ordinary course of man's existence" so as to "connect a bygone time to the very present that is fleeting from us" and thereby reveal, just as *Otranto* did, that "the wrongdoing of one generation lives on into successive ones" as the repressed realm of multilayered conflict that really underlies the physical and mental conditions of a modern "locality" (Hawthorne 1962: 15–16).

The text of this work, like several of Hawthorne's other fictions, fulfills this promise at very particular moments. One occurs when the narrator "transfigure[s]" the garden around the budding lovers Phoebe and Holgrave with "a charm of romance" in which a "hundred mysterious years were whispering among the leaves," thereby drawing the two together almost fatefully to heal past wounds in both families (Hawthorne 1962: 197). Later the same speaker, after offering a modern apology, surrounds the suddenly dead Judge Pyncheon with a "visionary scene" full of ghostly "ancestral people" who reembody the dark history of New Englanders taking from the Indians, then taking from each other using accusations of witchcraft, on the way to replacing rural property rights with urban mercantile acquisition and its suppressions of the past behind "respectable" surfaces (1962: 252–4). "Romance" thereby resurrects the complexities and "immemorial violence" in the roots of American history, as well as hopes for ameliorating them, from their burial beneath supposedly "realistic" illusions. Because of such "flavoring," ghostly remnants of many kinds now half-reveal, while also still veiling, what the nineteenth-century American middle class has abjected from itself and put away into the past, even though it is all really part of its present, in order to construct its most powerful public stances by way of repressions it has long tried to deny. Though finally more "psychological" than traditionally supernatural, like much of the extremely Gothic writing by Hawthorne's American contemporary Edgar Allan Poe (see Eric Savoy in Hogle 2002: 180–5), this blurring of generic boundaries, clearly endemic to Gothic romance, also breaks down ideological barriers enough to allow for "the return of the irrational 'other' to dismantle the fundamental propositions of [the American] national experiment" (Savoy in Hogle 2002: 172). In one way or another, no matter how distant from Walpole it gets, Gothic romance, as long it retains most of its major features, uses its mixture of discourses to reveal abjected cultural, and within these psychological, anomalies that are both fundamental and crucial enough to be as haunting *for* us as they are "thrown off" into "Gothic absurdities" *by* us.

To arrive at the form this process takes in Hawthorne and even more recent versions, however, Gothic romance after Walpole has enacted such abjections and revelations only in fits and starts, during which some different types or strands of Gothic have developed out of its original tortured "blend" of "the ancient and the modern." These developments too, as they have proceeded through the striking changes in and public debates about them, have gradually expanded and deepened the kinds of abjection that Gothic romance can enact by both responding creatively to new historical uncertainties and intensifying the interplay of different kinds of fiction that the Gothic has always been. Befitting its theatrical sources, Walpole's initial mixture found some of its immediate imitators on the English stage, first in this writer's own *The Mysterious Mother* (penned in 1768, though never staged before his death in 1797) and then in Robert Jephson's *The Count of Narbonne* (1781), almost slavishly imitative of *The Castle of Otranto*. These seemed fairly isolated works until they helped prompt an effusion of florid plays, rife with heavily Gothicized spectacle and quasi-Shakespearean posturing, which accelerated in the 1790s and lasted until the 1830s (see Cox 1992), all live theatrical preludes to the effulgence of "monster" films with towering Gothic settings that began a century later. In prose narrative, meanwhile, the two decades after *Otranto* offered occasional experiments with aspects of it that tried to define its features more precisely. In 1773, John and Anna Laetitia Aiken published "On the Pleasure Derived from Objects of Terror" alongside their Walpolean "Sir Bertrand," a short fictional fragment with a missing beginning and end about a knight encountering an outsized specter in a "large antique mansion" (Clery and Miles 2000: 130). Their essay tries to justify "the old Gothic romance" in general as defined by both Hurd and Walpole (Clery and Miles 2000: 128) by bringing forward the value in them of the "sublime" heightening of emotion based on "terror," promulgated as the most powerful of human emotions by Edmund Burke in *A Philosophical Enquiry into the Origin of our Ideas of the Sublime and Beautiful* (1757). Provided that the spectator of fiction or art feels enough distance from the threats of death in vast or haunting images, as Burke insisted, for the Aikens these open a "new world" that allows the mind to feel "the expansion of its powers" (Clery and Miles 2000: 129), as though the latter were no longer possible without such archaic aid in a world of mundane commercialism. Gothic romance thus provides a locus in which the early modern psyche can abject its contradictory condition of that time by "throwing off" *both* fears of death, regression, and guilt linked to the lasting pull of the more Catholic and aristocratic past *and* "the resistance of the [middle-class] mind to the torpor induced by humdrum reality" (Clery1995: 81).

This joining of romance to the "terror sublime," however, allows the Gothic to move in different directions – and to abject different combinations of conflicts – for its growing middle-class readership, as the eighteenth century hurtles toward its final decades of revolution and gives way to the even faster changes of the nineteenth. The "Sir Bertrand" fragment suggests that the Gothic could obliquely help readers face the horror of the violence connected to change, as when the title character cuts off the threatening specter's "dead cold hand," leaving a "bloody stump," and "gigantic statues of black marble . . . in Moorish habit" raise their swords, hinting at threats from foreign and racial blackness, just before the "whole building" falls "asunder with a horrible crash" (Clery and Miles 2000: 131–2). Clara Reeve's imitation of Walpole in her prose romance *The Old English Baron* (1777–8), by contrast, minimizes the supernatural and the violent in favor of relatively static debates about property rights and modes of inheritance, as though the ghosts that briefly appear, possibly as the hero's mere dream images, are mainly goads toward facing these middle-class issues and prompting cultural solutions, however illusory, to vague class conflicts subsumed within a clearly bourgeois morality focused on "the redistribution of land" (Clery 1995: 85). By the 1790s, when the Gothic exploded in England, Continental Europe, and newly independent America, it was therefore poised to divide into what became its two most distinct types. One variation came to be known as "terror" Gothic, somewhat in the tradition of Reeve, where threats to life and limb are generally more implied, potential, or imaginary than real, and the social or mental roots of such threats consequently become quite prominent (see Clery and Miles 2000: 163–72). The other alternative was later termed the "horror" Gothic, and it developed the most lurid and graphic possibilities in "Sir Bertrand" whereby "romance" confronts gross destruction and violent transgression explicitly, if quite fictionally, in a way that pierces social veneers to register very deep cultural and psychological impulses in antiquated and grotesque disguises. The middle-class Western audience that so embraced Gothic romance by 1800 was clearly torn within itself in many ways, nearly all reflected in Gothic fictions. One of these levels harbored an oscillation in the culture, which the oscillation of Gothic between "terror" and "horror" revealed and disguised, between a tenuous wish for rational and legal protections from threats to modern middle-class security and a profound fear that such constructions were illusory in the face of destructive forces threatening Western humanity externally and internally, in the public sphere and in the depths of the psyche.

The "terror" mode came most fully into its own in the 1790s in the long prose narratives, interspersed with some poems, by Ann Radcliffe, which she and most others called simply "romances" (even directly in book titles, such as *The Romance of the Forest* in 1791). Radcliffe's work, which will be discussed further by Lisa Vargo in the next essay, furthers the transition, briefly visible in the mental quandaries of Walpole's characters, in which the archaically (as opposed to the deistic Protestant) supernatural is turned into a psychological effect. Gothic romance in Radcliffe, we find, announces the middle class's attempt at mastering history and physicality with the power of the individual mind, so long as it breaks with old superstitions and any retrograde "sensibility" – though this form of "terror Gothic" also exposes the distance from reality that inevitably results, even when everything *un*real is supposedly "explained." Another attraction is Radcliffe's indirect, but definite, support, starting in *A Sicilian Romance,* for the greater freedom of women and their subjectivity from excessive dominance and commodification by the patriarchy (Miles 1995: 95–9), one expressed tenet of the French Revolution as well as of some dissenting Protestants. By the end of *The Mysteries of Udolpho,* the heroine Emily St. Aubert, thanks mostly to her own self-discipline, has "escaped from so many dangers... become independent from the will of those, who had oppressed her, and found herself mistress of a large fortune" as well as still loved by a chastened Valancourt (Radcliffe 1980: 619). She attains the ultimate "romance" fate for a rising middle-class woman at the turn of the eighteenth into the nineteenth century, in other words. In doing so, she carries out the wish-fulfillment that many women readers have sought in perusing

Radcliffe and the legions of her successors in "female Gothic" right through to Daphne du Maurier and Victoria Holt in the twentieth century.

At the same time, however, such stirrings of hope are matched with equal force by a fear of feminine excess of sensibility in Radcliffe's romances, especially the later ones. Radcliffe's female Gothic thus becomes a symbolic site where the resulting conflicts over the rights and construction of "woman" in Western culture are played out at the "romantic" distance of the sixteenth to seventeenth centuries in a setting both avowedly progressive and insistently "spectralized." Again, Gothic romance, in its mixture of tendencies and even genres (including poetry for Radcliffe and a number of her successors), has served to abject an unresolved tug of war. This time it has cast its culture's indecision about the status of women into an extreme fictionality where it seems romantically "put away," on the one hand, and yet also haunts its readers fearfully, on the other, as a problem only momentarily sequestered in the past and yet to be completely faced and resolved. In so advancing *and* restraining bourgeois romance, we can now say, Radcliffe initiated a pattern and a problem that has been approached again and again by women writers throughout two centuries, as Lisa Vargo will show.

The "horror Gothic" in the 1790s, meanwhile, took a very different turn in its own reactions to this age of revolution and the relative restraint of Reeve and Radcliffe. With its own distinct, though still anti-Catholic, take on the potentials opened up by Walpole, the *Schauerroman* (or "shudder-romance") became so prominent in Germany after the French Revolution began that it soon attracted international interest, enough to lead to English versions of such exemplars as C. F. Kahlert's *The Necromancer* (translated in 1794), Friedrich Schiller's *The Ghost-Seer* (translated in 1795), and Karl Grosse's *Horrid Mysteries* (translated in 1796). Since even in Germany, as well as in an increasingly repressive England, "revolutionary violence was now the great unmentionable that could be expressed only through displaced representations" (Miles in Hogle 2002: 56), these works concentrated on covert rebellions or clever deceptions by secret societies or magicians working against the Protestant norm in which the actual supernatural was frequently invoked, violence could erupt quite suddenly and extensively, seemingly "holy" disguises of lascivious intentions were commonplace, and (especially for Grosse) the prospect of liberation through more rampant sexuality vividly rose from beneath religious repression (see Miles in Hogle 2002: 50–7). Those tendencies, along with the concurrent importation of ghostly German poetry (such as G. A. Burger's *Lenore* in 1796) and *Sturm und Drang* plays (especially Schiller's *The Robbers* from the 1780s), reached their peak most forcefully in Matthew G. Lewis' *The Monk* (late 1796), the most luridly extreme Gothic romance ever produced in England, or anywhere else, up to that time.

Here a mixture of genres careers wildly between Walpolean hauntings (including paintings come to life), intrusive ballads, love tragedies in verse, allegorical dream-visions, explicit critiques of the Catholic Inquisition in Europe (following Schiller), and highly theatrical tableaux and spectacles (since Lewis was also a prominent Gothic playwright). The work follows Ambrosio, a Spanish priest of the late Renaissance, as he falls in love with a portrait of the Virgin Mary; feels a strong attraction to the boy novice Rosario; gives way to sexual abandon with the succubus Matilda (the actual body behind both the Virgin's portrait and Rosario); lusts, with Matilda's magical aid, for the virgin Antonia, who turns out to be his sister after he has kidnapped, raped, and killed her; smothers Antonia's (and, as he finally learns, his own) mother incestuously on her bed; strikes a bargain with the Devil himself, who first appears to Ambrosio as "a Youth seemingly scare eighteen, the perfection of whose form and face was unrivalled" (Lewis 1973: 276–7); indirectly helps incite an urban riot against the Catholicism that has provided the images which tempt him, to the point where Madrid's conniving Prioress is literally torn to pieces by a mob; and "escapes" being executed by a hypocritical Inquisition, though they know very few of his crimes, only because he is finally wafted away by Satan in the Devil's most horrible form, to be dropped on rocky crags and die in a brutal reversal of Genesis in seven agonizing days (Lewis 1973: 441–2). This stunning shift in the development of Gothic romance, ranging widely from the rationalized to the unquestionably supernatural, as well as the *sub*natural, was quickly condemned as religiously, politically, and sexually licentious, as well as too popular – an indication of the very Revolution from which it seemed Gothically displaced – and so helped solidify a controversy that has lasted to this day about how much Gothic romance should be allowed to combine "low" culture and "high" culture in one symbolic form (see Clery and Miles 2000: 185–91).

This reaction shows, however, that *The Monk*, as well as the later "horror Gothics" in its wake, really abjects more than just combined fears about and attractions toward contemporary rebellion (though it does that too, just as Radcliffe did differently). To begin with, it clearly acts out a "return of the repressed" well prior to Freud, in which archaic vaults surrounded by a veneer of traditional sanctity actually harbor, albeit in supernatural guises, what may *underlie* the Revolution: the most insatiable human desires, from the heterosexual to the homosexual to the incestuous, envious, and murderous, all intermixed and blurring into each other, the various avenues of what Freud would later call the drives of the id (see Paulson 1981). The "horror Gothic" helps Western people realize that these are deeply *within* us while also seeming to remove them *from* us in body, time, and place. More shockingly, too, this kind of romance suggests, in its hyperbolic distension of impulses in action, how these are aroused and furthered by the very public symbols that seem to deny and suppress them (such as, for the Protestant Lewis, the gilded Catholic church, its ubiquitous figure of the Virgin, and the belief in the sensuous image that seems to lie behind both). On the one hand, this irony points to how much the attempt to transcend old constructs by *using* them remains trapped inside them, and indeed punishable by them, the more it tries to break beyond their confines. On the other hand, though – and even more frightening to a middle-class audience both encouraged by and fearful of revolutionary change – the fact that old symbols can become hollowed out and disbelieved, as in Walpole's use of Catholic icons, can mean that the acquisitive and future-oriented middle-class self (who *does* identify with Ambrosio, despite, or even because of, his extremes) is still left with having to find direction for his or her impulses in images and icons, like Walpole's Theodore, now without any definite foundation in lasting belief-systems that promise a firm substance or Spirit behind them.

The modern individual is left, *The Monk* and "horror Gothic" imply, in the daily, and quite theatrical, circumstance of having to construct identity and pursue objects of desire through external fragments, like the ghost of Alfonso's, sundered from solid past foundations and not yet well attached to newer ones either. The ghosts and monsters called up in this frantic process that can end only with death, such as Lewis' shape-shifting and homosexual Devil, are *both* existing forms, however anomalous, that the bourgeois person seizes on from the past to advance vague personal ambitions *and* externalized symbols of the mixed monstrosity that the self is becoming by using such "others" as mirrors by which it composes itself. It is this unfounded and multiple foundation of identity, its being always other than itself in fashioning itself in the modern world, that may be most incarnated *and* abjected in *The Monk* and the forms of "horror" romance that have become its progeny since. The extreme crossing of boundaries, generic and cultural, in this kind of fiction is ultimately emblematic of the modern self being alienated into many social molds and longing for a place in which to "throw off" this anomalous condition. Because "horror" romance provides this place, we can fancy we see the "monstrosity" of the modern self as the attractive but fearsome "other" in a Gothic fantasy, however close that fantasy is to who we really are in the West since the eighteenth century.

This profound cultural function for Gothic romance, to be sure, did not reach its full potential in either Radcliffe or Lewis, partly because they divided up the social conundrums that needed to be abjected for and by their readers. It could be argued that this potential is still being pursued, since these quasi-descendents of Walpole have prompted many more strands of Gothic branching off from their variations (see the histories offered in Punter 1996 and Hogle 2002). Some of these were subsumed in aspects of Victorian fiction and theater or even (as we have noted) in Freudian psychoanalysis, while others have reappeared in modern Gothic films, a barrage of short stories, and a wide variety of "romance" forms ranging from du Maurier's *Rebecca* (1938, released as a film in 1940) to the current "historical romance" to *The X-Files* on television from 1993 to 2002 (see Smith, Mason, and Hughes 2002: 74–210). But I would argue that the most thorough conflation of the Gothic's possibilities for both genre-crossing and the abjection of multiple cultural conflicts in the years that followed the major works of Radcliffe and Lewis is still Mary Shelley's *Frankenstein* (1818, revised in 1831), which is discussed more fully in the next essay. This work not only figures in many film and stage versions, but also opens up the vast possibilities of Gothic romance for cultural abjection later realized further in such classics of this form as Robert Louis Stevenson's *Dr. Jekyll and Mr. Hyde* (1886), Bram Stoker's *Dracula* (1897), and Gaston Leroux's original *Phantom of the Opera* (first published in French in 1910).

The wide-ranging mixture of initially incompatible sources in *Frankenstein*, manifest as much in the stitched-together creature – Shelley's "gigantic shadowy form" – as in the text and allusions in the book itself, shows how creatively *and* shockingly multiple the Gothic romance can be, extending while still valuing the tradition of Walpole, Radcliffe, and Lewis (a visitor to Byron and the Shelleys in 1816 already known in reviews as the author of a "monstrous literary abortion"; Botting 1995: 5). By now the *Otranto*-esque "blend" of the archaically fantastic and the contemporaneously real, more complicated but still in force, collates in one "monstrous" set of images a mass of developing fears and problems in the wider life of Western culture – one reason for *Frankenstein*'s long endurance as the most reread and adapted Gothic romance over the last two centuries. The original *Frankenstein* re-abjects in a still Gothic way the problem of modern identity-construction suggested in *The Monk*, this time offering a quite earthly "monster" as the complex distorting mirror of that self-fashioning in its creator and readers. Yet Shelley's novel does so, too, by gathering around the quest for identity the amazingly numerous cultural indecisions connected to it and at the root of its many consequences in the early nineteenth century during the expanding industrial revolution. We still live with *Frankenstein* because we still live with those in the postindustrial Western world, and that is possible because the hybrid that is Gothic romance reached one apogee of its abjective cultural function in Mary Shelley's masterpiece, so influential on the more recent romances of horror, science fiction, and bourgeois self-reflection.

The history of Gothic romance, of course, lasts well beyond the early developments presented here and has not yet come to an end even today. But the forms it has taken since, while prone to change as much as the Gothic was between *The Castle of Otranto* and *Frankenstein*, still gain their ongoing power – if they are well constructed – because the ever unstable mix of uneasily compatible ingredients in such works is especially adept at symbolizing and disguising the lingering cultural uncertainties and terrors (irrational mixtures themselves) that keep troubling us in modern Western life since the Enlightenment. Even Stephen King, the most prolific and popular Gothic romancer of recent years in the West, has recognized the deep modern *and* "postmodern" needs for this type of abjection, whether in books, films, or computer graphics, in his nonfiction study *Danse Macabre* (see King 1982). Only because the Gothic has both retained and rejected aspects of older forms of romance while mixing what it has kept with different modes of discourse, we now see, has it been able to become the mass-produced oracle of the myriad, changing, and most feared quandaries of our culture in fictions as varied as Charlotte Brontë's *Jane Eyre* (1847), Oscar Wilde's *The Picture of Dorian Gray* (1891), Henry James' *The Turn of the Screw* (1898), W. H. Hodgson's *The Night Land* (1912), H. G. De Lisser's *The White Witch of Rosehall* (West Indian, 1929), Isak Dinesen's *Seven Gothic Tales* (Danish/English, 1934), Shirley Jackson's *The Haunting of Hill House* (1959), William Peter Blatty's *The Exorcist* (1971), King's *Carrie* (1974) and *The Shining* (1977), Anne Rice's *Vampire Chronicles* (starting in 1976), Angela Carter's *The Bloody Chamber* (1979), Toni Morrison's *Beloved* (1987), Joyce Carol Oates' *Haunted: Tales of the Grotesque* (1994), and Peter Straub's *Magic Terror: Seven Tales* (2000), along with many films ranging from the silent *Phantom of the Opera* of 1925 and the *Dracula* or *Frankenstein* of 1931 to *The Others* of 2001, the last of which is a vivid revival of all the most classic "Gothic" elements in one production. As readers, viewers, students, or analysts, we therefore have a choice – as indeed readers have always had with the Gothic romance – as to whether we see its manifestations as symbolic of unresolved cultural anomalies still needing our attention or whether we can use its overtly fictional surfaces, including its ghosts and monsters, as ways to keep concealing, avoiding, and "othering" the multiple problems we have abjected into them. We can let these oracles speak their depths to us, if we read them that way in the contexts of their times, or we can simply ask to be scared or thrilled at a safe aesthetic distance from what really frightens us most in the Gothic. The options are ours, but at least we have them to choose from because of the foundations, history, and development of the Gothic romance.

See also: chapter 8, SIDNEY AND SPENSER; chapter 11, THE FAERIE QUEENE AND EIGHTEENTH-CENTURY SPENSERIANISM; chapter 13, WOMEN'S GOTHIC ROMANCE; chapter 14, PARADISE AND COTTON-MILL; chapter 15, "INCONSISTENT RHAPSODIES"; chapter 21, VICTORIAN ROMANCE: ROMANCE AND MYSTERY; chapter 24, AMERICA AND ROMANCE; chapter 27, ROMANCE IN FANTASY; chapter 28, QUEST ROMANCE IN SCIENCE FICTION.

References and Further Reading

Anonymous (1969). *The Quest of the Holy Grail*, trans. P. M. Matarasso. Baltimore, MD: Penguin.

Botting, Fred, ed. (1995). *Frankenstein: Contemporary Critical Essays*. New Casebooks. London: Macmillan.

Castle, Terry (1987). "The Spectralization of the other in *The Mysteries of Udolpho*." In Felicity Nussbaum and Laura Brown, eds., *The New Eighteenth Century: Theory, Politics, English Literature*. London: Methuen, pp. 231–53.

Clery, E. J. (1995). *The Rise of Supernatural Fiction, 1762–1800*. Cambridge: Cambridge University Press.

Clery, E. J., and Robert Miles, eds. (2000). *Gothic Documents: A Sourcebook, 1700–1820*. Manchester: Manchester University Press.

Cox, Jeffrey N., ed. (1992). *Seven Gothic Dramas, 1789–1825*. Columbus: Ohio State University Press.

Fiedler, Leslie (1966). *Love and Death in the American Novel*. Rev. edn. New York: Dell.

Frankl, Paul (1960). *The Gothic: Literary Sources and Interpretations through Eight Centuries*. Princeton, NJ: Princeton University Press.

Hawthorne, Nathaniel (1962). *The House of the Seven Gables*, introduction by Richard Harter Fogle. London: Collier-Macmillan.

Hoeveler, Diane Long (2001). "Inventing the Gothic Individual: Revolution, Secularization, and Suffering." Lecture delivered at *Romantic Subjects: The Ninth Annual Conference of the North American Society for the Study of Romanticism* (August 18). Seattle: University of Washington.

Hogle, Jerrold E., ed. (2002). *The Cambridge Companion to Gothic Fiction*. Cambridge: Cambridge University Press.

Kallich, Martin (1971). *Horace Walpole*. New York: Twayne.

Kilgour, Maggie (1995). *The Rise of the Gothic Novel*. London: Routledge.

King, Stephen (1982). *Stephen King's Danse Macabre*. New York: Everest House.

Kliger, Samuel (1952). *The Goths in England: A Study in Seventeenth- and Eighteenth-Century Thought*. Cambridge, MA: Harvard University Press.

Kristeva, Julia (1982). *Powers of Horror: An Essay on Abjection*, trans. Leon Roudiez. New York: Columbia University Press.

Lewis, Matthew (1973). *The Monk*, ed. Howard Anderson. Oxford: Oxford University Press.

Miles, Robert (1995). *Ann Radcliffe: The Great Enchantress.* Manchester: Manchester University Press.

Morris, David B. (1985). "Gothic Sublimity." *New Literary History* 16, 299–319.

Paulson, Ronald (1981). "Gothic Fiction and the French Revolution." *ELH* 48, 532–54.

Punter, David (1996). *The Literature of Terror: A History of Gothic Fictions from 1765 to the Present Day.* 2nd edn. 2 vols. London: Longman.

Radcliffe, Ann (1980). *The Mysteries of Udolpho*, ed. Bonamy Dobree and Frederick Garber. Oxford: Oxford University Press.

Shelley, Mary Wollstonecraft (1982). *Frankenstein or the Modern Prometheus: The 1818 Text*, ed. James Rieger. Phoenix edn. Chicago: University of Chicago Press.

Smith, Andrew, Diane Mason, and William Hughes, eds. (2002). *Fictions of Unease: The Gothic from Otranto to The X-Files.* Bath: Sulis Press.

Smollett, Tobias (1979). *The Adventures of Roderick Random*, ed. Paul-Gabriel Bouce. Oxford: Oxford University Press.

Tucker, Susie I. (1967). *Protean Shape: A Study in Eighteenth-Century Vocabulary.* London: Athlone Press.

Walpole, Horace (1937–1983). *The Yale Edition of Horace Walpole's Correspondence*, ed. W. S. Lewis et al. 24 vols. New Haven: Yale University Press.

Walpole, Horace (1996). *The Castle of Otranto: A Gothic Story*, ed. W. S. Lewis and E. J. Clery. Oxford: Oxford University Press.

Watt, Ian (2001). *The Rise of the Novel: Studies in Defoe, Richardson, and Fielding.* Rev. edn. Berkeley: University of California Press.

13

Women's Gothic Romance: Writers, Readers, and the Pleasures of the Form

Lisa Vargo

The ascendancy of women's Gothic romance in eighteenth- and early nineteenth-century English writing marks a shift in what romance means and who reads it. From the time of its first appearance, Gothic romance has been viewed as a source of entertainment for middle-class female readers. Kay J. Mussell suggests that a part of this enjoyment comes from the predictable nature of its plot which "always has a dual character; through identification with the heroine, the reader finds in escape fiction a world in which excitement, mystery, danger, and action occur side by side with the domestic activities and social roles that women have traditionally performed" (Mussell 1983: 58). That pleasure may seem the sugar coating of what is often seen as a bitter pill – women's Gothic romance performs the difficult maneuver of inscribing social roles for women while also affording an escape from those roles. In other words, Gothic romance is seen to perform a confinement for women equivalent to that which occurs within its pages. The narrative traced in this essay, while being mindful of this perspective, will explore a slightly different point of view. To consider the excitement that must have been felt by those women writers, critics, and readers to whom in its very newness Gothic romance was neither predictable nor formulaic suggests a liberating sense of pleasure, the significance of which extends far beyond the pleasures of the romance plot of marriage and happily ever after. The pleasures of authority, of theorizing, of literary conversation, and of exploring new terrain will form the focus of this essay.

Contexts: Recent Critical Discussions

While Gothic romance developed out of one set of specific conditions, its critical scrutiny is the product of another set of cultural forces. Critics such as Edith Birkhead,

Eino Railo, Montague Summers, and J. M. S. Tompkins set down the basis for its scholarship in the 1920s and 1930s, followed by Devendra Varma in the 1960s, but sustained interest in the form belongs to the last 25 years, a period that coincides with the development of feminist criticism.[1] In fact Ellen Moers coined the term "female Gothic" as recently as 1977 (Miles 1983: 7). Michael Gamer perceives a "prevailing – and warranted – nervousness over defining Gothic in anything but the most open-ended terms" (2000: 9) and Maggie Kilgour calls the genre "as difficult to define as any gothic ghost" because it mixes with so many other sources that it becomes a sort of Frankenstein's monster (Kilgour 1995: 3–4). Critical approaches emphasize indeterminacy, fragmentation, and a carnivalesque nature, as well as such forces as Protestant middle-class values, the French Revolution, notions of British national identity, and the body. Fred Botting prefers the union of the terms "Gothic" and "romance" rather than "Gothic" and "novel" because "it highlights the link between medieval romances, the romantic narratives of love, chivalry and adventure that were imported from France from the late seventeenth century onwards, and tales that in the later eighteenth century were classified as 'Gothic'" (1996: 24). It is in David Punter's terms "a mode of writing in which middle-class audiences and writers attempt to come to grips with their changing relations to a myth of aristocracy, and simultaneously try to invent myths to justify their own dominance" (1981: 116). Its hybrid nature means Gothic romance is associated with other popular modes of the day, including sensibility and the sentimental, and the melodramatic, which spilled over from the theater into prose fiction. Strands of male and female Gothic romance are teased out, the masculine "horror" Gothic being associated with the figure of the rebel and the writings of Matthew "Monk" Lewis, while the feminine "terror" Gothic is tied to the marriage plot of romance and defined by the novels of Ann Radcliffe (Kilgour 1995: 37).

When female Gothic romance is taken as a subject on its own, the form is commonly read through notions of fears of sexuality, of woman as a commodity in a consumer culture, of a struggle against a developing idea of a domestic sphere for bourgeois women that simultaneously values institutions like marriage and the family, of balancing seeming conformity and victimization with subversion during a period undergoing political, economic, religious, and social transformation. Two recent feminist readings of the genre stress the movement between resisting domestic ideology and promulgating it. Kate Ellis's *The Contested Castle* (1989) asks why Gothic fiction became popular just as women were gaining prominence as readers. Ellis looks to the rise of the doctrine of separate spheres, which imprisons women in the home. The Gothic novel both constructs and subverts, "creating, in a segment of culture directed toward women, a resistance to an ideology that imprisons them even as it posits a sphere of safety for them" (Ellis 1989: x). For Diane Hoeveler in *Gothic Feminism* (1998: 9–10), "the typical female gothic novel presents a blameless heroine triumphing through a variety of passive-aggressive strategies over a male-created system of oppression and corruption, the 'patriarchy'" and "was born when women realized that they had a formidable external enemy – the raving, lustful, greedy patriarch – in addition to their own worst internal enemy, their own consciousness of their own sexual difference perceived as a weakness rather than a strength." Accordingly the Gothic consists of an "enigmatic code" in the words of Roland Barthes, experienced by the characters and mirrored in reading: "For the female gothic heroine, that 'enigmatic code' generally clusters around questions of properly gendered behavior, power / property, and the relation of both to sexuality" through which she "creates her own self-serving ideology of the companionate family" (Hoeveler 1998: 21).[2]

And it was enormously popular. E. J. Clery points out there were over 50 women writers between the 1790s and the 1820s working in a form "that sees women writers at their most pushy and argumentative" (2000: 2–3). A clear sign of its prevalence exists in the set of assumptions invoked by the opening sentences of Jane Austen's *Northanger Abbey* (1818): "No one who had ever seen Catherine Morland in her infancy, would have supposed her born to be an heroine. Her situation in life, the character of her father and mother, her own person and disposition, were all equally against her" (Austen 1933: 13). Catherine is neither an orphan, nor plotted against by wicked guardians, nor possessed of a devoted lover who is far away and unable to protect her. In spite of these disadvantages, her adventures demonstrate that true treachery is not to be found in haunted abbeys but in the "dreary intercourse of daily life" with its plots and pitfalls in the business of love and marriage. That Austen can assume her readers will get the jokes in her satire on Gothic conventions suggests how well-established a genre it was in the first decades of the nineteenth century. And it is Austen who reminds us that men were readers of Ann Radcliffe as much as women were. Michael Gamer examines how the example of Henry Tilney is meant to overturn the stereotype voiced by critics of the day that its readers were women who should "avoid Romances, Chocolates, Novels and the like Inflamers" (2000: 52). Although one needs to be wary of the notion that romance is exclusively the domain of women, the Gothic romance offered women the pleasures of a space for expression because its ascendancy is contemporary with the rise of the female writer.

The sorts of assumptions that Austen draws upon point to the fact that, as David Richter and others suggest, the origins of the Gothic novel "present an admirable clarity" (Richter 1996: 1). The progenitor of the form is commonly viewed as Horace Walpole, who states in the preface to his second edition of *The Castle of Otranto*, first published in 1764, that he wishes "to blend the two kinds of Romance, the ancient and the modern" (Walpole 1969: 7). From here the genealogy is given to women: Clara Reeve in *The Champion of Virtue* (1777) later known as *The Old English Baron*, Sophia Lee in *The Recess* (1783–5), and Ann Radcliffe in *A Sicilian Romance* (1790) and her subsequent novels, *The Romance of the Forest* (1791), *The Mysteries of Udolpho* (1794), and *The Italian* (1797). But the Gothic was given a push in another direction with Matthew Lewis' *The Monk* (1796), which strengthens the identification of men's and women's forms of Gothic that might be said to begin with Walpole and Reeve. Within writing at the end of the eighteenth century and the beginning of the nineteenth a kind of working canon of women's Gothic romance exists in Reeve, Lee, Radcliffe, Joanna Baillie, Charlotte Smith, Mary Robinson, Mary Wollstonecraft,

Charlotte Dacre, and Mary Shelley. "By the time we reach Mary Shelley," David Punter explains (2000: viii), "the question of whether the 'original Gothic' has already fallen apart, become transmuted into different forms, left only traces to be picked up and re-utilised by later writers – for perhaps quite different purposes and often perhaps quite anxiously – is already a vexed one." In tracing this genealogy I wish to recognize the conversation among women writers who confidently explore different notions of pleasure that Gothic romance allows: the thrill of horror, escapist fantasy, power in one's authority, or even pleasure in perversity.

The Contemporary Scene: Critical Progresses of Romance

One of the forms of pleasure romance provided for women in the eighteenth century was the opportunity to practice literary criticism. Harriet Guest points out that Richard Hurd's *Letters on Chivalry and Romance* (1762), which predate Walpole's novel, provide the theoretical basis for the form to which women soon contributed innovative critical perspectives. Guest (1992: 121) traces a male/female split in opinion about the Gothic, which for men is described "as an unchaste or prostituted pleasure: for them, it is ravished and wanton." Elizabeth Montagu, in the "Essay on the Praeternatural Beings" from her *Essay on the Writings and Genius of Shakespeare* and in the third of her "Dialogues of the Dead" (both 1769), and Clara Reeve in *The Progress of Romance* (1785) locate a different sort of pleasure, which is "neither corrupt nor unambiguously trivial" (Guest 1992: 121). While Reeve's fictional and critical responses to Walpole are usually seen as the origins of female Gothic romance, Guest demonstrates an earlier model in Elizabeth Montagu, who makes clear her debt to Hurd. Montagu captures the importance of Gothic as well as the importance of reading for women. In an analysis of the ghost in *Hamlet*, Montagu notes the pleasure to be found in Shakespeare's use of "national superstitions" (1785: 165). Her third dialogue of the dead, where Charon introduces a Modern Bookseller to Plutarch, includes an account of the book trade in which the bookseller suggests that women "have greater obligations to our writers than the men" because while men can learn from "the commerce of the world," women "who in their early youth are confined and restrained, if it were not for the friendly assistance of books, would remain long in an insipid purity of mind, with a discouraging reserve of behaviour" (Montagu 1785: 307–8).

To this group might be added Anna Aikin, later Barbauld, who contributed the Burkean title "An Enquiry into Those Kinds of Distress Which Excite Agreeable Sensation" to *Miscellaneous Pieces in Prose* (1773), which was jointly authored with her brother John.[3] Barbauld was acquainted with Montagu, who wrote to praise her recently published essays and poems (Le Breton 1874: 37–40), and Montagu's arguments are echoed in the essay. Barbauld (2001: 196) explores "a phenomenon of the human mind difficult to account for, that the representation of distress frequently gives pleasure." She distinguishes between kinds of pain that are pleasing and those that "are really painful and disgusting" and insists that any scenes of misery must also be connected with moral excellence (Barbauld 2001: 197–8). In this respect the essay is critical of modern forms of romance which lead away from virtue and from realistic depictions of life, and offers the suggestion that it might be better "if our romances were more like those of the old stamp" that raise human nature and inspire notions like honor (Barbauld 2001: 207). In the same volume was also included her essay "On Romances: An Imitation," an imitation of Samuel Johnson's essay in *The Rambler* 4 on the dangers of romance. Barbauld notes the attractions of the form, in which the writer of romance "relates events to which all are liable, and applies to passions all have felt" (Barbauld 1825: II, 173). If she is critical of romance for steering readers away from "the investigation of truth" to "exhilarate his mind with new ideas, more agreeable, and more easily attained," she also notes the role of sympathy that can be found through romance, and states that romances "teach us to think, by inuring us to feel: they ventilate the mind by sudden gusts of passion; and prevent the stagnation of thought, by a fresh infusion of dissimilar ideas" (Barbauld 1825: II, 173, 175). Her mixing of pleasure and morality, and of old and new literary forms, anticipates Clara Reeve's more systematic weighing of romance and novel in her writings. But critical discussion continues throughout the period, as witnessed in the prefaces that Anna Barbauld wrote for her edition of *British Novelists* (1810; see Moore 1986) and in Ann Radcliffe's posthumously published "On the Supernatural in Poetry," which was both a preface to her novel *Gaston de Blondeville* and appeared on its own in the *New Monthly Magazine* in 1826.

Clara Reeve

Clara Reeve (1729–1807) is remarkable not only for writing the first female Gothic romance but also for making a sustained theoretical statement about the genre. Reeve, the daughter of a clergyman, was born in Ipswich in 1729. Her first publication was a volume of poems (1769) and her translation of John Barclay's Latin romance *Argenis* (1621) was published in 1772 under the title of *The Phoenix*. Six novels followed between 1777 and 1799, as well as a prose treatise on romance, and one on education. Another novel, *Castle Connor, an Irish Story* was lost in 1787. She wrote *The Old English Baron*, originally titled *The Champion of Virtue* (1777) as a response to Horace Walpole's *Castle of Otranto*. *The Old English Baron* is called by Reeve (1967: 3) "the literary offspring of the *Castle of Otranto*, written upon the same plan, with a design to unite the most attractive and interesting circumstances of the ancient Romance and modern novel." Part of the attractive nature of ancient romance is its ability to convey pleasure. As opposed to history, which "represents human nature as it is in real life; – alas, too often a melancholy retrospect! – Romance displays only the amiable side of the picture; it shews the pleasing features, and throws a veil over the blemishes" (Reeve 1967: 3). Like Barbauld, Reeve understands the principle of Horatian pleasure and instruction, the need to "excite the attention" of the reader and "to direct it to some useful, or at least innocent, end." Reeve seeks to avoid the defects she finds in Walpole, namely the violence of its "machinery" (1967: 4). She situates supernatural elements within dreams, stories, buried evidence, and displays of sensibility. The novel, set during the reign of Henry VI, begins with the return of Sir Philip Harclay, who discovers his best friend Lord Lovel dead and the brother-in-law of the present Lord Lovel, Lord Baron Fitz-Owen, resident in the castle. The plot focuses on the story of a humble but gifted peasant, Edmund, who is steward to the sons of the Baron. Edmund distinguishes himself in battle and in so doing inspires jealousy. He is forced to sleep in some haunted apartments of the castle and has dreams in which he is visited by Lord Lovel and his wife, who inform him that they have been murdered. With the help of Oswald and a faithful servant, Joseph, Edmund is discovered to be the rightful son of Lovel. He seeks out Sir Philip, who adopts him as his son. They return to Lovel's castle, Sir Walter Lovel confesses his crimes on his deathbed after he is wounded in battle with Sir Philip, Edmund is united with the daughter of Fitz-Owen, and his legitimate right to the castle and his title are restored. Reeve's tale is accompanied by a strong moral message about "the over-ruling hand of Providence, and the certainty of RETRIBUTION" (1967: 153).

E. J. Clery explains that in its own time opinion about *The Old English Baron* was fractured. Walpole predictably attacked it for reducing all "to reason and probability," and Anna Barbauld, who included it in a single volume with *Otranto* in her *British Novelists*, suggests that "we foresee the conclusion before we have reached twenty pages" (1810: 22, ii). Yet the work was an enormous success, engaging "readers on multiple levels, through the marvelous, the probable and the sentimental" (Clery 2000: 31). Fred Botting (1996: 55) believes that, as well as aesthetic considerations, class comes into Reeve's "educated middle-class" perspective, "reflected in the novel's highlighting of gentility and merit, dissociated from social position." The story stresses, according to Botting (1996: 56), "virtue, morality and social and domestic harmony," which is "divinely sanctioned and protected." Reeve is adapting the past to show a tradition of morality that is inherent in British history as well as championing the cause of the humble and virtuous as opposed to the corruption of the aristocracy.

If Reeve took Walpole to another level, equally important was her desire to theorize about romance. *The Progress of Romance* (1785) is a dialogue in which three characters, Euphasia (Reeve's alter ego), a male antagonist (Hortensius), and a female arbiter (Sophronia) discuss romance and the novel over twelve weekly meetings. Like Barbauld, Reeve involved herself in a defense of romance, responding to Samuel Johnson and James Beattie, who registered their concerns about the potential dangers of romance. Euphasia creates a defense of romance as a form suitable for women readers and writers in her clever alignment of the form with epic and with the powers of romance to educate its readers. The sorts of rhetorical strategies employed in the dialogue, as Laura Runge suggests (1997: 157–8), allow for the female voice to claim a space, which will not disrupt male authority. Reeve sorts out those female writers who present moral forms of entertainment and teaching (Sarah Fielding, Charlotte Lennox, Frances Sheridan, and Frances Brooke) from those like Aphra Behn and Mary

Delarivière Manley, whose works are "very improper" (1785: 117). Eliza Heywood presents a case of a writer who in the end atones for her errors and devotes her later works to "the service of virtue" (Reeve 1785: 121). If Reeve seems excessively moral to twenty-first-century readers, Runge (1997: 161) reminds us that *The Progress of Romance* received critical condemnation by Anna Seward for Reeve's preference of Richardson's novel *Pamela* over *Clarissa*, which demonstrates the sorts of aesthetic restrictions under which Reeve labored (Runge 1997: 163). The presence of Sophronia as arbitrator between the male and female disputants illuminates Michael Gamer's point (2000: 53) that "the romance's feminizing effects were linked less to its content than to the reading experience that they reportedly produced," particularly with respect to unsupervised forms of pleasure. Gamer takes the reading of the *Progress of Romance* that Runge presents a little further in arguing that Reeve wants to make romance more masculine as a strategy to render it more acceptable, "by prescribing to it the masculinity of antiquarian history and the same strictures of socially acceptable femininity – temperance, sense, and social duty – that constrain women writers in the period" (2000: 58). Gamer believes "her 'improved' version of Gothic seeks to blend two genders (male and female) and two types of discourse (history and fiction) under the assumptions that each will correct, enhance, and complement the other" (2000: 59). Reeve echoes Barbauld's perspective in her belief that pleasure can be united to moral instruction, and her defense of female authority is borne out by the subsequent works her writings inspired.

Sophia Lee

Devendra P. Varma (1972: xiv) declares that if *Otranto* and *The Old English Baron* "sounded the knocker of the castle door, it is Sophia Lee's *The Recess; or, a Tale of Other Times* (1783–85) that turned the key letting the castle gates creak open to admit the reader into the murky and sensational world of the dark and mysterious gothic courtyard." Sophia Lee (1750–1824) was the eldest of five daughters and one son. Her father, John Lee, was a member of David Garrick's company and eventually settled in the fashionable resort of Bath, where he ran a theater. Lee's first work, a comedy, *The Chapter of Accidents*, produced at the Haymarket Theatre in 1780, provided the profits with which she set up a school with her sister Harriet between 1781 and 1803. Lee published *Warbeck, a Pathetic Tale* (1786), a ballad called *The Hermit's Tale* (1787), and a blank-verse tragedy, *Almeyda; Queen of Granada*, was produced in 1796 with Kemble and Mrs. Siddons in leading roles. She contributed to her sister's collection of short fiction, *Canterbury Tales* (1797–1805), and an epistolary novel, *The Life of a Lover*, was published in 1804. A third play, *The Assignation*, appeared at Drury Lane in 1807 but was not a success.

Varma (1972: xiv–xv) suggests that Walpole's *Castle of Otranto* forms the inspiration for *The Recess* as well as its Gothic machinery and use of suspense, while Clara Reeve and French writer Baculard d'Arnaud also influenced her work (Varma 1972: xxv).

Lee's romance captured the favor of readers and received generally positive reviews in spite of reservations about its unrelenting gloom and inaccuracies of history. It went through a number of editions between 1785 and 1840 and was translated into French and Portuguese. Varma (1972: xxv) argues that it began the historical novel as a genre as well as influencing Radcliffe, who was acquainted with the Lee sisters (Miles 1995: 23; Clery 2000: 37), Jane and Anna Maria Porter, Sir Walter Scott, and other lesser-known novelists (Varma 1972, xxvii–xxx). *The Recess* mixes history and romance in its narrative of the tragic careers of Matilda and Ellinor, twin daughters of Mary, Queen of Scots, who is imprisoned by her rival Queen Elizabeth. The work plays with notions of romance and history by taking the form of Matilda's deathbed memoir addressed to a friend, and contains corroborating documents of a diary and letters, a device later used to advantage by Mary Shelley in *Frankenstein*. The "recess" is an underground dwelling inside a ruined monastery where the sisters live in hiding from the Queen. They do not escape the world for long, and their beauty and virtue cannot save them from the evils of the world. Matilda falls in love with Leister, and after he is murdered in her arms, she is kidnapped and exiled to Jamaica with her daughter by Leister. Upon her return to England, she finds her sister is insane. Ellinor has been forced into marriage by Elizabeth but falls in love with the Earl of Essex and is driven into madness through persecution and imprisonment by Elizabeth. After Ellinor's death Matilda lives in Richmond with her daughter Mary, who becomes the object of the affections of Henry, Prince of Wales, son of James I. Following the death of Henry, Mary meets Somerset, whose jealous wife poisons her. Matilda resolves to die in peace in France.

Lee presents a counter-reading to the kinds of pleasure Barbauld and Reeve locate in Gothic romance. While, like Reeve, Lee makes use of a historical setting, the differences between the two works can be traced through the influence of Samuel Richardson. If Reeve attracted criticism for her liking of *Pamela* (the story of a servant who maintains her virtue and marries her master) over *Clarissa* (a tragedy in which a virtuous woman is drugged and raped and suffers insanity and a long decline to death) this preference is reflected in the happy ending of *The Old English Baron*, in which as Kate Ellis suggests (1989: 68) she has "transformed Walpole's Gothic experiment into a vehicle for domestic optimism." Lee unsettles Reeve's perspective with what Ellis calls "pessimistic Gothic, which offers a much more radical critique of the idealization of home than even a heroine who defies her father can provide." Ellis views the work as a "radical warning to those parents and moralists who would allow passion no place in the bourgeois ideal marriage, who make female sexuality a secret that cannot move out of its hiding place in the world, and who demand obedience from their children in order to further their own worldly interests" (Ellis 1989: 73). Lee's critique is continued by Charlotte Smith and Mary Wollstonecraft (Ellis 1989: 97). Megan Lynn Isaac (1996) examines how Lee decries secrecy as an evil. One of those secrets seems to be what romance itself hides. Lee looks to recover a lost history of women, which therefore can only be written as romance. Yet she also calls attention to how romance and history trap women. She would remind readers of the terrors of the patriarchal that lie beneath the pleasures of the marriage plot.

Ann Radcliffe

Though it is unlikely Ann Radcliffe (1764–1823) attended the Lee sisters' school as critics have speculated, her admiration of *The Recess* was noted in the *Annual Register*'s obituary notice for Lee (Miles 1995: 23). Little is known about Radcliffe, who led a retired and thoroughly private life. She was born in London in 1764, the daughter of a haberdasher, but spent much of her youth in Bath, where she came into contact with Bluestockings including Elizabeth Montagu and Anna Barbauld. In 1787 she married William Radcliffe, owner of a liberal newspaper, the *English Chronicle*, and their marriage was happy but childless. She died after a period of ill health in 1823. Radcliffe published five novels: *The Castles of Athline and Dunbayne* (1789), *A Sicilian Romance* (1790), *The Romance of the Forest* (1791), *The Mysteries of Udolpho* (1794), and *The Italian* (1797). She produced a travel book co-authored with her husband and a final novel, *Gaston de Blondeville*, was published in 1826, three years after her death. In her novels, in which a heroine leaves her family home, is subjected to a series of thrilling adventures, and marries the man she loves, Radcliffe seems to reject Lee's pessimism and instead conveys, Frederick Garber insists, a pleasure that 'comes from a suspension of disbelief that leads to an enjoyment of the world of her fiction in and for itself' (Radcliffe 1981: x). When Keats playfully insists in a letter to his friend Reynolds, "I am going into scenery whence I intend to tip you a Damosel Radcliffe – I'll cavern you, and grotto you, and waterfall you, and wood you, and immense-rock you, and tremendous sound you, and solitude you" (Keats 1958: 1, 245), he alludes to her ability to create a mood and effect through her descriptions of landscape and her evocation of terror. Yet it would be misleading to restrict Radcliffe's artistry to mere enjoyment. If Radcliffe goes beyond Walpole, Reeve, and Lee to explore the pleasures of terror, she is putting into practice the theories of Barbauld and of Edmund Burke's *Philosophical Enquiry into the Origins of Our Ideas of the Sublime and Beautiful* (1757). This is something she makes clear in her posthumously published essay which she called "Introduction to the romance or Phantasie which is about to follow – a dialogue between two travelers in Warwickshire" in which she explains that "Terror and horror are so far opposite, that the first expands the soul, and awakens the faculties to a high degree of life; the other contracts, freezes, and nearly annihilates them" (Clery and Miles 2000: 168). In evoking the names of Shakespeare, Milton, and Burke to argue for the value of terror, Radcliffe writes what are essentially novels of education through recourse to the imagination and the passions used to teach reason and restraint.

E. J. Clery (2000: 51) calls Radcliffe's heroines "the co-authors of their own stories." In this respect Radcliffe's novels are both a defense of romance and a statement of the powers of the female mind. The rumor that her early death was the result of a mental derangement brought on by a morbid imagination (Miles 1995: 25–6) resembles the story of Keats being killed by bad reviews in betraying anxieties about the nature of her authority. As Robert Miles points out (1995: 8), she was the most popular novelist of the 1790s, read not only in Great Britain but throughout

Europe in translations. Walter Scott named her "among the favoured few, who have been distinguished as the founders of a class or school" (Miles 1995: 9–10). If Reeve is the innovator and Lee admits the reader into the courtyard, Radcliffe must be seen as taking that reader right into the castle in her place as the so-called "Shakespeare of Romance Writers" (Clery 2000: 51). And like Shakespeare she was less a founder than a consolidator. What is notable about Radcliffe's writing is that in articulating the "crucial narrative matrix" of female Gothic of a daughter searching for a lost mother (Miles 1995: 18), Radcliffe places the heroine at the front and center in her narratives. Her romances conclude with marriage, and in this respect critics have suggested that Radcliffe resembles Lee in that "these marriages are less celebrations than they are quiet acceptances of their new keepers" (Hoeveler 1998: 36). This is to overlook the words "joy," "happy," and "happiness" that dominate the final paragraphs of her novels. Radcliffe rewrites romance into a form where women have agency. It is not the knight who is rewarded with the lady, as is the case in Reeve, but the lady with the man she has chosen, and both live thereafter in a state of "domestic blessedness" (Radcliffe 1980: 672). She transforms old romance into a form that demonstrates, as Robert Miles suggests (1995: 42), how "the Gothic myth empowered women in a quite different way, for the myth insisted upon female equality. In Gothic society, women were the 'friends and faithful counselors' of men, their partners and equals."

Radcliffe's practice as a writer troubles the notion that her novels celebrate women's power to write individual history. One question is that of why Radcliffe shunned notoriety and stopped publishing romances at the age of 33: whether it was a horror of violating middle-class propriety, or some other cause of reticence, or a feeling that her books were no longer a source of interest is not known. Another puzzle is the nature of her politics. While her husband was a noted political liberal of the day, most critics view her as a conservative. Robert Miles (1995: 175–6) takes an opposing perspective, suggesting that she stopped writing because of pressures of censorship and conservative reaction. A third aspect concerns what might be seen as Radcliffe's response to Lee – not only are her heroines given a sense of a place in history, but also they gain a happy marriage. If this can be seen as a triumph for its originative pleasures, the fact that it then becomes the standard form of the romance is another matter. Maggie Kilgour (1995: 141) laments it as "sadly appropriate" that "the revolutionary form she perfected became a new type of generic tyranny, which hasn't changed much in the last 200 years." But it was new to Radcliffe and her readers, and because the Gothic genre takes a number of directions, the pleasure of the familiar form is not the entire story.

Monk Lewis, Radcliffe's *The Italian*, and Charlotte Dacre

At the very time that Radcliffe was bringing the female Gothic to a place where, according to a contemporary, she had "almost solitary sway over the regions of romance" (Miles 1995: 7), the form was subject to challenge, most notably by Matthew Lewis' notorious novel *The Monk*, discussed by Jerrold E. Hogle in the preceding essay. Robert Miles (1993: 167) suggests that Lewis "scandalously reworks" the Burkean contradiction of delight in terror "by hinting that the solution to the mystery is sexual in nature" through the story of Ambrosio. who is seduced by Matilda, rapes and kills his sister, and murders his mother before he is claimed by Satan. Radcliffe responded with her own tale, *The Italian*, which David Punter (1981: 109) calls "a kind of deparodization of *The Monk*." The work presents a happy ending for its lovers, Ellena and Vivaldi, but careful attention to the villains, the Marchesa and most notably Schedoni, suggests Radcliffe takes Lewis seriously and would reclaim the turf of the romance as her own. If this literary conversation is read as illustrating male and female kinds of romance, Charlotte Dacre contests these categories. In her guise as the Della Cruscan poet Rosa Matilda, Dacre had experience of dialogue with other women writers, but it is *The Monk*, the so-called male form of Gothic, to which she chooses to respond in *Zofloya*. In so doing Dacre pushes women's Gothic into a different realm. This dialogue is perhaps underscored in the choice of "Matilda" as her pen name, a possible allusion to the character in Lewis' novel (Clery 2000: 103).

Little is known about Dacre's life. She was the daughter of John King (or Jacob Rey) and it is speculated that she was born in 1772, though she suggests in her 1805 volume of poems that she is 23, ten years younger than this date would suggest. E. J. Clery (2000: 102) argues that she has a "separate 'authorial' age, for youthfulness is part of her writing persona." In 1798 Charlotte published a book of poems, *Trifles of Helicon*, with her sister Sophia King, author of a volume of poetry and four novels. In 1802 Charlotte took on the pseudonym of "Rosa Matilda" and published poetry in the *Morning Post* for which she gained notoriety, including the notice of Byron in *English Bards and Scotch Reviewers* (1809): "Far be't from me unkindly to upbraid / The lovely ROSA'S prose in masquerade, / Whose strains, the faithful echoes of her mind, / Leave wondering comprehension far behind" (quoted in Clery 2000: 106). Soon after she began an affair with Nicholas Byrne, the married editor of the *Post*, with whom she had three children. They married in 1815. A collection of poems called *Hours of Solitude* appeared in 1805 along with her first novel *Confessions of the Nun of St. Omer*, which is dedicated to Lewis (Clery 2000: 107). *Zofloya, or The Moor: A Romance of the Fifteenth Century*, appeared the next year and *The Libertine* in 1807. *The Passions* appeared in 1811 and a poem about George IV and some lyrics were published in 1822. She died in 1825.

It is clear that Dacre was aware of notions of literary dialogue, especially with respect to an interrogation of romance. While in *The Italian* Radcliffe revises *The Monk* through a "reassertion of sensibility" (Miles 1995: 173), in *Zofloya* Dacre replaces Ambrosio with Victoria, thus destabilizing notions of female behavior. From the time of its publication reviewers noted the similarities with Lewis' work and were critical of the novel's lack of morals and errors in grammar and usage (Clery 2000: 108). What is so daring about *Zofloya* is Dacre's attempt to make the heroine an anti-romance figure who embraces evil as she makes a pact with the devil and pursues a career of rape, kidnapping, murder, and, after joining a group of *banditti* led by her brother, descends to hell when the Moor reveals his identity as Satan. Critics have puzzled over Dacre's account of the source of Victoria's evil actions, though several possibilities are raised by Dacre herself, the two most prominent being that Victoria is spoiled and that her mother presents a bad example by entering into an affair which leads to the death of her husband and the breaking up of the family unit.[4] Robert Miles (1993: 183) suggests that "the primacy of desire in the self's economy, together with its sexual equality" dominate the work. Dacre seems to believe that the various roles romance creates for women all lead them to different forms of betrayal: Victoria's mother Laurina is too weak to resist desire while the virginal Lilla is stabbed and pushed off a cliff by Victoria. *Zofloya* demonstrates the problematic nature of viewing male and female Gothic as strictly gendered formulations or as a form encouraging women writers to indulge in pat conclusions.

Gothic Passions: Charlotte Smith, Mary Wollstonecraft, Mary Robinson, and Joanna Baillie

Other writers depart from what Kilgour calls Radcliffe's "generic tyranny" in a less drastic manner than Dacre to explore the nature of passion. Charlotte Smith's first novel *Emmeline; or, The Orphan of the Castle* (1788), called by Diane Hoeveler "the forgotten ur-text for the female gothic novel tradition," was satirized by Jane Austen through the story of Catherine Morland in *Northanger Abbey* and attracted the criticism of Mary Wollstonecraft for its depiction of adultery, but it sold 15,000 copies within the first six months of its publication (Hoeveler 1998: 37). *Emmeline* tells the story of two women – the beautiful and virtuous Emmeline, who marries for love after submitting to a number of trials, and her friend Adalina, who is forced into a loveless marriage, has an extramarital affair and a child, and eventually gains happiness through marriage with her lover. Emmeline is raised by a servant in the isolated location of Mowbray Castle and under the care of neglectful guardians. She rejects as a suitor her cousin Delamere, who has her kidnapped and tries to force her to marry him, and she also resists the suits of the caretaker of the estate, an elderly businessman, and a French aristocrat named Bellozane. Delamere is killed in a duel with Bellozane, who has had an affair with Delamere's sister. Emmeline discovers she is not illegitimate but the heir to Mowbray Castle and marries the worthy Lieutenant Godolphin. As Eleanor Ty points out (1993: 126), it is when Emmeline is outside the castle, which turns out to be her rightful home, that the world is threatening. The castle is not inherited, as in Reeve's novel, by a son, but by a daughter left to her own devices and besieged by dangers of passion and sexuality that are more explicit than those portrayed by Radcliffe (Ellis 1989: 86). When she marries a soldier, Emmeline and her husband "gently displace the undeserving representatives of the old aristocracy" which both rustic and aristocrat celebrate. As Ellis comments (1989: 92), "A more explicit acting out of the aesthetic and political program of the later Gothic revival would be hard to imagine."

If Mary Wollstonecraft overcame her qualms about the positive depiction of adultery, she seems less confident that women's passions can lead them to a happy ending. Her unfinished *Maria, or The Wrongs of Woman* (1798) moves across classes as it tells the story of the horrors of male power when a wife comes to dislike a husband, who separates her from her daughter and imprisons her in an asylum. In her prison she befriends her keeper Jemima, a former prostitute, and falls in love with Darnford, whose books and annotations she reads. Wollstonecraft died before she finished her novel, but it is clear she did not imagine a happy ending for Maria, who was intended to commit suicide. And yet, like Smith, Wollstonecraft defends female sexuality, which she writes about in pointedly revolutionary terms: "Marriage had bastilled me for life" (Wollstonecraft 1980: 154–5).

The use of Gothic romance to explore passion does not restrict itself to fiction. When poet and novelist Mary Robinson (1758–1800) wrote her memoirs, begun in 1798 and left incomplete at the time of her death, she looked to Radcliffe's heroines for a means to account for the events of her life as an actress and notorious mistress of the Prince of Wales. She traces her birth in Bristol in a house built on the site of a former monastery which became a ruin and was never "reraised to its former Gothic splendours" (Robinson 1994: 17). Time spent in Bristol's Gothic cathedral exposed her, she says, to "the progressive evils of a too acute sensibility" (Robinson 1994: 21). Anne Mellor calls the memoirs a version of sexual desire in which Robinson is a victim of a Gothic romance: she undergoes an early marriage to a man who is unfaithful, escapes rape by libertines, to find true love with the Prince of Wales (2000: 287, 294). Yet her illicit passion leads her neither to Adalina's happiness nor to Maria's suicide. Robinson's daughter completed the memoir, emphasizing Robinson's devotion as a mother and dedication as a writer (Mellor 2000: 292–4). In the fragment of the first part of the memoir, passion frees Robinson from her loveless marriage to pursue her own destiny as a desiring individual whose agency includes passion and sexuality. She neither dies nor finds love and marriage but a different plot of freedom and authority.[5]

If Robinson's allusion to the heroines of Radcliffe in her account of sexual notoriety strains credulity, a closer parallel exists between Radcliffe and Joanna Baillie. The anonymous publication of *A Series of Plays: In Which It is Attempted to Delineate the Stronger Passions of the Mind* in 1798 led to rumors that Ann Radcliffe was author of the plays (Miles 1995: 26). When *De Monfort* was produced at Drury Lane with Sarah Siddons and her brother John Philip Kemble in 1800, Baillie came forward and claimed her writings, though the play proved not to be a success and closed after eight performances. The daughter of a Scottish clergyman and professor of divinity, Baillie was born in 1762, and after her father died, she and her sister joined her brother in London: she eventually settled in Hampstead, where she lived until her death in 1851. She published poems and expanded and revised her plays to three volumes. A "great monster book" of her complete works was published in the year of her death.

As Elizabeth Fay and other critics have noted, in writing a series of comedies and tragedies illustrating the passions, for which she also composed a theoretical introduction, Baillie demonstrates she is "deeply concerned with the problem of subjectivity and of vision turned inward" (Fay 1998: 203). E. J. Clery (2000: 91) suggests that in so doing "Baillie brilliantly refashions tragedy along Gothic lines for an age of possessive individualism and state surveillance." *De Monfort* is meant to illustrate hatred through its account of a man raised by his devoted sister, Jane De Monfort, and of his irrational hatred for his childhood rival Rezenvelt. De Monfort goes to a small German town, Amberg, to escape his enemy, but Rezenvelt unfortunately comes to the town. Despite the efforts of Jane and his friend Count Freberg, De Monfort, who has become suspicious that his sister is in love with Rezenvelt, kills him in a wood full of what seem supernatural portents to the disturbed mind of De Monfort. After the murder, De Monfort is confronted with the corpse of Rezenvelt in the chapel of a convent and dies on the spot from remorse. As Michael Gamer notes (2000: 138), "Baillie resembles Reeve and Radcliffe in almost never haunting her characters with anything other than their own minds" but she goes beyond earlier writers "in making the mind the sole source of gothic effects." How far Baillie's critique of the conflict between the subjective and the social goes is a matter of debate. According to Jeffrey Cox (1992: 12), *De Monfort* demonstrates how a writer might represent ideological struggles during a period of censorship. Female figures like Jane De Monfort represents how class tensions might be resolved through virtuous actions. But E. J. Clery (2000: 98) calls the purpose of instruction in the play a "fig-leaf" for the audience's wonder at the tragic hero; "the fundamental pleasure is amoral" and vicarious. Without solving this critical crux, it is possible to consider the pleasure Joanna Baillie found in exploring passions in a manner where private desire and public value were enjoined in her writing.

Mary Shelley: Progress and Romance

Reference was made at the beginning of this essay to David Punter's vexed question of whether by the time of Mary Shelley "the 'original Gothic' has already fallen apart, become transmuted into different forms ... for perhaps quite different purposes and often perhaps quite anxiously" (2000: viii). The response that will be given here is that with Mary Shelley (1797–1851) the pleasures of the Gothic reach their fullest political significance. Mary Shelley purposefully employs romance in a manner that permeates her writings and represents a legacy of her reading of female writers, including her mother, Mary Wollstonecraft, as well as the political ideals of her father, William Godwin. Partly because he doubts we can ever know the truth of events and partly because he believes history can inspire reform, Godwin takes Reeve's coupling of history and romance farther, when in an essay unpublished in his lifetime he calls romance "one of the species of history." Because romance generalizes and selects instances "most calculated to impress the heart and improve the faculties of his reader," he suggests, "we should be apt to pronounce that romance was a nobler species of composition than history" (Godwin 2000: 464). It is this sort of ingenious reversal that Mary Shelley employs to impress and improve her own readers. Her version of Gothic romance is both profound and liberating; she adapts the genre to a form that is not duplicated again in writing by women.

Mary Shelley's first novel *Frankenstein* (1818), the story of the student who creates a being who is rejected because of the horror his appearance inspires, is her work most directly associated with Gothic romance. Nora Crook (2000: 58) wittily observes that it "contains most of the props of Gothic terror fiction, albeit disguised," including the castle as the workshop of the cloistered monk/student, a buried incest theme in the union of Victor and Elizabeth, beings like the transformed specter who is compared to vampire and mummy, pursuit, the sublime landscapes of the Alps and the Arctic, and the unspeakable secret of the creation of life. Mary Shelley's suggestion (1994: 195) that "her hideous progeny" is a story written out of a desire "to speak to the mysterious fears of our nature and awaken thrilling horror" invokes the notion of pleasure through the Gothic in an absolute sense that her other works do not approach. But as Crook suggests (2000: 63), elements of Gothic romance "permeate her later works" in a form which "revitalises the link between historical romance and the older Gothic conventions" of Walpole. Her two historical novels, *Valperga* (1823) and *Perkin Warbeck* (1830), her domestic novels, *Lodore* (1835) and *Falkner* (1837), her short fiction, her apocalyptic novel about plague, *The Last Man* (1826), *Mathilda*, her unpublished novella about incest (composed 1819), her writings of the lives of European writers and scientists for the *Cabinet Cyclopaedia* (1835–9), and her travel writings merit reconsideration. They employ Gothic romance to suggest alternatives for tyranny in a spirit not unlike Elizabeth Montagu's location of moral value in the supernatural in Shakespeare or Anna Barbauld's belief that romance can inspire sympathy and new ideas. *The Fortunes of Perkin Warbeck: A Romance* concludes with a statement by Richard of York's widow, Katherine Gordon: "The more entirely we mingle our emotions with those of others, making our well or ill being depend on theirs, the more completely do we cast away selfishness, and approach the perfection of our nature" (Shelley 1996: 398). Perhaps the most subversive and suggestive element of romance is how it conveys pleasure in the exploration of thought through which reader and writer might work together to change the world.

See also: chapter 7, Gendering Prose Romance in Renaissance England; chapter 12, "Gothic" Romance; chapter 14, Paradise and Cotton-mill; chapter 15, "Inconsistent Rhapsodies"; chapter 21, Victorian Romance: Romance and Mystery; chapter 27, Romance in Fantasy; chapter 28, Quest Romance in Science Fiction; chapter 30, Popular Romance and its Readers.

Notes

1. See Edith Birkhead, *The Tale of Terror: A Study of Gothic Romance* (New York: E. P. Dutton, 1921); Eino Railo, *The Haunted Castle: A Study of the Elements of English Romanticism* (New York: E. P. Dutton, 1927); Montague Summers, *The Gothic Quest: A History of the Gothic Novel* (London: Fortune Press, 1938); J. M. S. Tompkins, *The Popular Novel in England, 1770–1800* (London: Constable, 1932); Devendra Varma, *The Gothic Flame, Being a History of the Gothic Novel in England, Its Origins, Efflorescence, Disintegration, and Residuary Influences* (New York: Russell and Russell, 1966). Some more recent significant studies include Robert Miles, *Gothic Writing 1750–1820: A Genealogy* (1993); Steven Bruhm, *Gothic Bodies: The Politics of Pain in Romantic Fiction* (1994); E. J. Clery, *The Rise of Supernatural Fiction, 1762–1800* (1995); Anne Williams, *Art of Darkness: A Poetics of Gothic* (1995); Maggie Kilgour, *The Rise of the Gothic Novel* (1995); Fred Botting, *Gothic* (1996); David H. Richter, *The Progress of Romance* (1996); David Punter, ed. *A Companion to the Gothic* (2000); and Michael Gamer, *Romanticism and the Gothic* (2000).

2. Other significant studies include Ellen Moers, *Literary Women* (London: W. H. Allen, 1977); Juliann E. Fleenor, ed. *The Female Gothic* (Montreal: Eden Press, 1983); Elizabeth Fay, *A Feminist Introduction to Romanticism* (1998); and E. J. Clery, *Women's Gothic: From Clara Reeve to Mary Shelley* (2000).

3. Some critics look to the essay "On the Pleasure Derived from Objects of Terror with Sir Bertrand, a Fragment" which was thought by Walpole to be written by Barbauld (see Fay 1998: 133–4), but a number of critics and editors of Barbauld, including William McCarthy, Elizabeth Kraft, Dan White, and Laura Mandell, believe the essay and fragment to be by her brother John. I am grateful to Dan White and Laura Mandell for sharing this information with me.

4. For discussions of Victoria's actions, see Adriana Craciun, introduction to her edition of *Zofloya* (Dacre, 1997a), Kim Ian Michasiw, introduction to his edition of the work (Dacre, 1997b), Craciun 1995, and Wilson 1998.

5. In "Mary Robinson's Memoirs and Gothic Autobiography," delivered at *Romanticism and History: The Tenth Annual Conference of the North American Society for the Study of Romanticism* (August 24, 2002), London, Ontario: University of Western Ontario, Anne Close examines Robinson as a Gothic heroine, arguing that Robinson rewrites the Gothic to suggest that sexual knowledge helps women to survive. I am thankful for the opportunity of hearing this paper and discussing its contents with the author.

References and Further Reading

Austen, Jane (1933). *Northanger Abbey and Persuasion*, ed. R. W. Chapman. Oxford: Oxford University Press. [*Northanger Abbey* first published in 1818.]

Baillie, Joanna (2001). *Plays on the Passions*, ed. Peter Duthie. Peterborough: Broadview Press. [First published in 1798.]

Barbauld, Anna Laetitia (1810). "Clara Reeve." In *The British Novelists*, vol. XXII. London: F. C. and J. Rivington.

Barbauld, Anna Laetitia (1825). *The Works of Anna Laetitia Barbauld. With a Memoir by Lucy Aikin.* London: Longman, Hurst, Rees, Orme, Brown, and Green.

Barbauld, Anna Laetitia (2001). *Anna Laetitia Barbauld: Selected Poetry and Prose*, ed. William McCarthy and Elizabeth Kraft. Peterborough: Broadview Press.

Botting, Fred (1996). *Gothic*. London and New York: Routledge.

Bruhm, Steven (1994). *Gothic Bodies: The Politics of Pain in Romantic Fiction*. Philadelphia: University of Pennsylvania Press.

Clery, E. J. (1995). *The Rise of Supernatural Fiction, 1762–1820*. Manchester: Manchester University Press.

Clery, E. J. (2000). *Women's Gothic: From Clara Reeve to Mary Shelley*. Tavistock: Northcote House.

Clery, E. J., and Robert Miles, eds. (2000). *Gothic Documents: A Sourcebook, 1700–1820*. Manchester: Manchester University Press.

Close, Anne (2000). "Mary Robinson's Memoirs and Gothic Autobiography." Lecture delivered at *Romanticism and History: The Tenth Annual Conference of the North American Society for the Study of Romanticism* (August 24). London, Ontario: University of Western Ontario.

Cox, Jeffrey, ed. (1992). *Seven Gothic Dramas, 1789–1825*. Athens: Ohio University Press.

Craciun, Adriana (1995). "'I hasten to be disembodied': Charlotte Dacre, the Demon Lover and Representation of the Body." *European Romantic Review* 6, 75–97.

Crook, Nora (2000). "Mary Shelley, Author of Frankenstein." In *A Companion to the Gothic*, ed. David Punter. Oxford: Blackwell, pp. 58–69.

Dacre, Charlotte (1997a). *Zofloya, or The Moor*, ed. Adriana Craciun. Peterborough: Broadview Press. [First published in 1806.]

Dacre, Charlotte (1997b). *Zofloya*, ed. Kim Ian Michasiw. Oxford: Oxford University Press. [First published in 1806.]

Duncan, Ian (1992). *Modern Romance and Transformations of the Novel*. Cambridge: Cambridge University Press.

Ellis, Kate (1989). *The Contested Castle: Gothic Novels and the Subversion of Domestic Ideology*. Urbana: University of Illinois Press.

Fay, Elizabeth (1998). *A Feminist Introduction to Romanticism*. Oxford: Blackwell.

Gamer, Michael (2000). *Romanticism and the Gothic*. Cambridge: Cambridge University Press.

Godwin, William (2000). "Of History and Romance." In *Caleb Williams*, ed. Gary Handwerk and A. A. Markley. Peterborough: Broadview Press, pp. 453–67.

Guest, Harriet (1992). "The Wanton Muse: Politics and Gender in Gothic Theory after 1760." In *Beyond Romanticism: New Approaches to Texts and Contexts 1780–1832*, ed. Stephen Copley and John Whale. London and New York: Routledge, pp. 118–39.

Hoeveler, Diane Long (1998). *Gothic Feminism: The Professionalization of Gender from Charlotte Smith to the Brontës*. University Park: Pennsylvania State University Press.

Hogle, Jerrold, ed. (2002). *The Cambridge Companion to Gothic Fiction*. New York: Cambridge University Press.

Isaac, Megan Lynn (1996). "Sophia Lee and the Gothic of Female Community." *Studies in the Novel* 28, 200–19.

Keats, John (1955). *The Letters of John Keats*, ed. Hyder Edward Rollins. 2 vols. Cambridge, MA: Harvard University Press.

Kelly, Gary, ed. (2002). *Varieties of Female Gothic*. 6 vols. London: Pickering and Chatto.

Kilgour, Maggie (1995). *The Rise of the Gothic Novel*. London and New York: Routledge.

Le Breton, Anna Letitia (1874). *Memoir of Mrs. Barbauld. Including Letters and Notices of her Family and Friends*. London: George Bell.

Lee, Sophia (1972). *The Recess, or, A Tale of Other Times*. Foreword by J. M. S. Tompkins; introduction by Devendra P. Varma. 3 vols. New York: Arno Press. [First published in 1783–5.]

Lewis, Matthew (1980). *The Monk*, ed. Howard Anderson. Oxford: Oxford University Press. [First published in 1796.]

Mellor, Anne K. (2000). "Making an Exhibition of Her Self: Mary 'Perdita' Robinson and Nineteenth-century Scripts of Female Sexuality." *Nineteenth-century Contexts* 22, 271–304.

Miles, Robert (1993). *Gothic Writing, 1750–1820: A Genealogy*. London and New York: Routledge.

Miles, Robert (1995). *Ann Radcliffe: The Great Enchantress*. Manchester: Manchester University Press.

Montagu, Elizabeth (1785). *An Essay on the Writings of Genius and Shakespear. To which are Added Three Dialogues of the Dead*. 5th edn. London: Charles Dilly. [First published in 1769.]

Moore, Catherine E. (1986). "'Ladies ... Taking the pen in Hand.' Mrs. Barbauld's Criticism of

Eighteenth-century Women Novelists." In *Fetter'd or Free? British Women Novelists, 1670–1815*, ed. Mary Anne Schofield and Cecilia Macheski. Athens: Ohio University Press, pp. 383–97.

Mulvey-Roberts, Marie, ed. (1998). *The Handbook to Gothic Literature*. Basingstoke: Macmillan.

Mussell, Kay J. (1983). "'But Why Do They Read Those Things?': The Female Audience and the Gothic Novel." In *The Female Gothic*, ed. Juliann E. Fleenor. Montreal: Eden Press, pp. 57–68.

Norton, Rictor, ed. (2000). *Gothic Readings: The First Wave, 1764–1840*. New York: Leicester University Press.

Poovey, Mary (1984). *The Proper Lady and the Woman Writer: Ideology as Style in the Works of Mary Wollstonecraft, Mary Shelley, and Jane Austen*. Chicago: University of Chicago Press.

Punter, David (1981). "The Social Relations of Gothic Fiction." In *Romanticism and Ideology*, ed. David Aers, Jonathan Cool, and David Punter. London: Routledge and Kegan Paul, pp. 103–17.

Punter, David (1996). *The Literature of Terror: A History of Gothic Fictions from 1765 to the Present Day*. New York: Longman.

Punter, David, ed. (2000). *A Companion to the Gothic*. Oxford: Blackwell.

Radcliffe, Ann (1980). *The Mysteries of Udolpho*, ed. Bonamy Dobrée. Oxford: Oxford University Press. [First published in 1794.]

Radcliffe, Ann (1981). *The Italian*, ed. Frederick Garber. Oxford: Oxford University Press. [First published in 1797.]

Reeve, Clara (1785). *The Progress of Romance and the History of Charoba, Queen of Aegypt*. New York: Facsimile Text Society. [First published in 1785.]

Reeve, Clara (1967). *The Old English Baron*, ed. James Trainer. Oxford: Oxford University Press. [First published in 1778.]

Richter, David H. (1996). *The Progress of Romance: Literary Historiography and the Gothic Novel*. Columbus: Ohio State University Press.

Robinson, Mary (1994). *Perdita: The Memoirs of Mary Robinson*, ed. M. J. Levy. London: Peter Owen. [First published in 1801.]

Runge, Laura (1997). *Gender and Language in British Literary Criticism 1660–1790*. Cambridge: Cambridge University Press.

Shelley, Mary (1994). *Frankenstein*, ed. Marilyn Butler. Oxford: Oxford University Press. [First published in 1818.]

Shelley, Mary (1996). *The Fortunes of Perkin Warbeck: A Romance*. In *The Novels and Selected Works of Mary Shelley*, ed. Doucet Devin Fischer. Vol. 5. London: Pickering and Chatto.

Ty, Eleanor (1993). *Unsex'd Revolutionaries: Five Women Novelists of the 1790s*. Toronto: University of Toronto Press.

Varma, Devendra (1972) *see* Lee, Sophia (1972).

Walpole, Horace (1969). *The Castle of Otranto*, ed. W. S. Lewis. Oxford: Oxford University Press. [First published in 1764.]

Williams, Anne (1995). *Art of Darkness: A Poetics of Gothic*. Chicago and London: University of Chicago Press.

Wilson, Lisa M. (1998). "Female Pseudonymity in the Romantic 'Age of Personality': The Career of Charlotte King / Rosa Matilda / Charlotte Dacre." *European Romantic Review* 9, 393–420.

Wollstonecraft, Mary (1980). *Maria, and The Wrongs of Woman*, ed. Gary Kelly. Oxford: Oxford University Press. [First published in 1788 and 1798.]

14

Paradise and Cotton-mill: Rereading Eighteenth-century Romance

Clive Probyn

Almost all the fictions of the last age will vanish, if you deprive them of a hermit and a wood, a battle and a shipwreck.

Samuel Johnson, *Rambler* 4 (1750).

That there is a Castle, any Man who has seen it may safely affirm. But you cannot with equal Reason, maintain that there is no Castle, because you have not seen it.

Charlotte Lennox, *The Female Quixote* (1752), IX, XI.

In a famous passage in *Reflections on the Revolution in France* Edmund Burke declared that the age of chivalry had come to a shameful end on (Tuesday) October 6, 1789. On this day of infamy republicans and *sans-culottes* had laid their grubby hands on the person of Marie-Antoinette, Queen of France. Burke's image of an "innocent" aristocratic oligarchy demeaned by physical contact with its great unwashed subjects is one of the great rhetorical moments in his writing. Its power reverberates in the writing of others because it grounds the mysteries of nationhood, majesty, monarchy, and the eternal-feminine in the frailty of a single human body. Only a male reader untouched by what Burke called "that generous loyalty to rank and sex" would find this event other than repellent. On November 6, 1794, Major Watkin Tench, the first historian of the Botany Bay Settlement, was taken prisoner in revolutionary France. His account of that experience enlists the Burkean moment: he writes of the "brutal and unmanly spirit that dictated the charges upon which [the Queen] was tried" and that the "violent death inflicted upon this unhappy princess" was a "stain, which will be indelible, while sentiments of tenderness and generosity towards women, and principles of equity towards the accused, are cherished in the human breast." When speaking of the imprisonment of Lady Anne Fitzroy in 1795, furthermore, Tench was struck by an historical irony: it was in the very home of "courtesy and gallantry" that "a young, helpless, and beautiful woman" had been immured "within the walls of a common prison."[1]

Here are some of the lineaments of what might be called, somewhat speculatively, an Enlightenment view of romance. Its first characteristic is its self-consciousness: romance always contains the ingredients of what it denies, and it is conscious of its own excluded origins; what it suppresses is always present. It may not make good history, yet its opposite is not realism but an unreflective materialism and the unpoetic. Except when the authors of the romance are male (as in the examples above), its (female) exponents are usually shown by their (male) critics to be suffering from a generally *unconscious* "disorder" of the senses, and therefore lacking a "knowledge of life and manners."[2] Romance is both a product and a function of gender politics, and in some undeclared ways. Although it is conventionally centered on sexual politics (the position of woman in a patriarchal society, as in the example from Burke above), its character is constructed from some broader and not always positive issues: loss of origin, an indifference to history, a disbelief in providential order, a desire for self-fashioning, a resistance to the present, a dislike of the embodied, valorization of the other, a sublimation or fear of sexuality, and a pleasure taken in deferral. It is not accidental that the heroic romance has been called the *roman de longue haleine*.[3] At the micro-level of the novel, and in the perhaps unexpected context of eighteenth-century literary parody, romance may also be read as a safety valve, a licensed vehicle for otherwise transgressive ideas, an experiment with ideas whose time has yet to come.

Neither chivalry nor romance-writing took any notice of Burke's declaration. Nevertheless, something momentous had taken place on November 6, and not only in the real political world. For one thing, the English novel had already integrated romance into its repertoire and gone on to invent new interests and strategies, and the beginning of its own critical literature. In the revolutionary year of 1789, Clara Reeve's *The Progress of Romance* (the first critical monograph of its kind, and the only one to be written in dialogue form), was four years old. Charlotte Smith's career as a romance novelist had hardly begun when she published her three-volume translation from the French entitled *The Romance of Real Life* in 1787, followed by *Emmeline: or The Orphan of the Castle* (four volumes) in 1788. In the revolutionary year itself, English readers of romance could immerse themselves in Charlotte Smith's five-volume *Ethelinda: or The Recluse of the Lake*, and Mrs. Ann Radcliffe's Gothic-Scottish-medieval *The Castles of Athlin and Dunbayne*. Radcliffe's *Sicilian Romance* came in 1790, *The Mysteries of Udolpho* in 1794, and by 1800 *The Romance of the Forest* (1791) had gone through at least ten editions. If we figure the earlier history of romance as a meandering and intermittent country lane, then its eighteenth-century section presents a multi-lane highway. In the words of one observer, "the gradual change from one reigning style of fiction to another does indeed occur, and whether one calls this 'the rise of the novel' or 'the decline of the romance', the fact is the same: older fictive conventions were modified, qualified, or rejected, in favour of other conventions more suitable to a middle-class audience that offered, particularly in its female population, a market to be exploited."[4] As in politics, so in literary history: the *ancien régime* gives way not to anarchy but to another *régime*.

As a genre in the eighteenth century, romance enjoys perhaps the poorest of public reputations. Today, and to a postmodern reader, heir to a post-Lockean, post-Enlightenment, post-industrial, and post-patriarchal social realism, romance may seem morally and aesthetically ludicrous, a whisper from a "Paradise of Fools,"[5] the primal urge for a lost world of artifice, a pandering to innate hankerings after aristocratic origin, a dangerously naive belief in the triumph of hope over experience, a desire for the invincible power of love and youth over materialism and its class oppressions, the vehicle of a latent but barely respectable belief in a golden world generated in a brazen one. It is, one might say, a willfully perverse way of rewriting in art a life that in empirical terms has always already let us down.

Its virtues, if it has any, include its resistant popularity, but this is hardly to be disentangled from a broader defamation of the status of women readers and writers. And yet, if we think of the people who read romances as "women," then romance may also be seen as a genre with a transformational power, a way of seeing how the world might be in the present if only it *could* be rewritten. In this view, romance springs from a perceived disjunction between the world and the word: again, it is not the daughter of social realism (or in Ian Watt's terms "circumstantial realism") but the daughter of the Imagination (or Despair), the stepchild of Hope (or Boredom), a second chance at life, the vehicle of Desire.

The heroine of Charlotte Lennox's novel *The Female Quixote* (1752) chooses to live not in the real world but in an already-written romantic narrative: she thus becomes *the* heroic subject, the center of all attention, and thereby takes charge of her own life, both in the present and in a predictable (i.e. write-able) *future* (VII, xiv). We should be clear at the outset that Arabella temporarily defers but cannot escape the patriarchal tyranny of the present. She defers it by erecting a fantastic fictional paradigm, already drawn from a misreading of history, superimposed upon the dreary and uninteresting world of the real. Arabella's astonishing insistence is that all men and women should conform to her interpretation of the heroic/chivalric French romance tradition of the previous century. Like Flaubert's Emma Bovary (though without her adultery), Arabella becomes her own author-God and marginalizes the hard truths of experience of what Fielding – another careful reader of romance – was to call "the vast Doomsday-Book of Nature" or "History," or "Records."[6] Her success is so radical that it can only be explained as a kind of pathological state – madness – and so it is that the good male doctor (of theology), like a modern ego-psychologist, is sent to "cure" Arabella and close the novel by laying down the law of the father once again.[7] This appropriately *unnamed* vicar of the patriarchy addresses himself to all those ungoverned by a proper belief in divine providence. He excoriates the reading and writing of romances for encouraging "young minds to expect strange adventures and sudden vicissitudes . . . often to trust to chance," whereas "the order of the world is so established, that all human affairs proceed in a regular method, and very little opportunity is left for sallies and hazards, for assault or rescue" (419). Neither the reader, nor Charlotte Lennox, nor Arabella, nor, come to that, Jane Austen and her indefatigably romance-oriented Catherine Morland, can credit such a cruel orthodoxy. Romance may deny providence and elevate the random and unpredictable to a fictional principle, but for each of them the "atrocities" (Henry Tilney's word) of the everyday are every bit as alarming as anything dreamt up in romantic fiction. Henry Tilney's reassurance at the end of chapter 23 of *Northanger Abbey* (1818), "Remember the country and the age in which we live. Remember that we are English, that we are Christians," is no sooner uttered than flatly contradicted by an act of his own father which seems irrational and freakish. The measure of Lennox's achievement is not only the fact that Samuel Johnson was her champion,[8] but the distance she had traveled from Congreve's warning to the reader back in 1692: "Romances" will leave the reader "flat upon the Ground wherever he gives of[f], and vex . . . him to think how he has suffer'd himself to be transported, concerned and afflicted at the several Passages which he hath Read, viz. These Knights success to their Damosels Misfortunes, and such like, when he is forced to be very well convinc'd that it is all a lye" (ii–iii). Arabella is vexing in exactly this way, but the novel itself is not a lie. The thoughtful reader (then and now) is encouraged to see Arabella's irritating romance mania as an admirable and understandable bid for self-determination, though worked out in false terms, in a fable which offers her illusory freedom and real imprisonment. The conclusion we are asked to condone, the domestication or taming of an intelligent, middle-class Englishwoman, is both an edifying and a deeply troubling experience.

The romantic novel, then, is an interlude, a temporary game enacted between the jaws of patriarchy. Every page insinuates a vision of a world in which a woman may take power over her own subjectivity. For almost the whole book (itself a brief interlude in her life), Arabella has a starring role in a castle of her own construction before being obliged to move into Mr. Glanville's house as wife and domestic companion. For all its ridiculous comedy, Lennox's novel imagines not so much a female utopia but a world in which female intelligence is licensed to operate as the agent of its own self-definition (conventionally read as self-destruction, of course). The fact that Arabella is a perverse misreader, like Catherine Morland and Emma Bovary after her, is not, however, the central point. We can hardly argue that the social text waiting to enclose each of them after their return to "normality" is any more rational, any more liberating, or any less tyrannical. Just as Jane Austen closes her novels with the marriage state, so Arabella's brief flight is ended when she recognizes the propriety (in every sense of the word) of becoming the partner of Mr. Glanville. Congreve sensed that romance does indeed tap into deep psychic needs, and Virginia Woolf noted in another context that it effects powerful social myths, what she saw as a process in patriarchy itself: "Women have served all these centuries as looking-glasses possessing the magic and delicious power of reflecting the figure of man at twice its natural size" (*A Room of One's Own*, 35). Romance already knows that reading is a dangerous liaison; it can disavow its own sinfulness from within at the same moment as offering an irresistible seduction to those skeptics without. This is where its "danger" lies. When the 14-year-old Delia in *The New Atalantis* (1709) is sent to the country, she meets "an old out-of-fashion Aunt, full of the *Heroick Stiffness* of her own *Times*; [who] would read Books of *Chivalry* and *Romances* with her Spectacles. This sort of Conversation infected me, and made me fancy every Stranger, that I saw, in what Habit soever, some disguis'd Prince or Lover." Memories of what never was are converted into a script for a fervid non-present, and the mind is truly not present to itself. Madness is the result, a temporary syndrome shared by Sheridan's Lydia Languish – "the girl's mad! Her brain's turned by reading" (*The Rivals*, 1775, Act IV, ii) – and by Marianne Dashwood in *Sense and Sensibility* (1797–1811) – whose "opinions are all romantic" (I, xi).

We can be certain that Arabella's world after marriage to her cousin is not the stuff of which novels are made. As a *subject* (legally in the real world and actually in the fictional world), her life is over at this point.[9] On the other hand, her life is saved (as Emma Bovary's is lost) by dialogue, compromise, and capitulation to the social legislators. The irresistible attractions of romance in no way diminish the gender issues in Lennox's fine novel: the real and the fantastic fight a deadly comic duel for control of an intelligent and perceptive young mind. It is this contest which keeps us turning the pages.

It may be for more than a comic effect that Oliver Goldsmith has the vicar of Wakefield disavow his wife's aberrant choice of two "romantic names" for his daughters Olivia and Sophia, selected because "during her pregnancy she had been reading romances."[10] Romance may be a magnet for the intellectually feeble: but it is much more productive to see it also as a response to foreknowledge of mortality, pain, and loss. When the narrator in Laurence Sterne's *A Sentimental Journey* (1768) takes the name of the dead court jester in *Hamlet*, he does so to remind us that life is a comedy informed by death. When Yorick visits Paris in *A Sentimental Journey*, the "glittering clatter" of this city of pleasure suggests nothing less to his English mind than the whole world of French chivalric romance, a thought which provokes both melancholy and joy. Yorick is an apologetic shadow of Don Quixote – as is La Fleur of Sancho Panza – and it is the former who says: "Tis going, I own, like the Knight of the Woeful Countenance, in quest of melancholy adventures – but I know not how it is, but I am never so perfectly conscious of the existence of a soul within me, as when I am entangled in them."[11] Having finished this Quixotic masterpiece on the subject of the split psyche, and in the middle of "writing a Romance" (possibly the *Journal to Eliza*), the tubercular and maritally unhappy Laurence Sterne enquired of Mrs. Montagu how it could have been possible for Cervantes to "write so fine and humorous a Satyre, in the melancholy regions of a damp prison."[12] Sterne supplied a response to his own question in *A Sentimental Journey*: "Sweet pliability of man's spirit, that can at once surrender itself to illusions, which cheat expectation and sorrow of their weary moments! – long – long since had ye number'd out my days,

had I not trod so great a part of them upon this enchanted ground" (87). Sterne's
romantic fiction, his "enchanted ground," is a lifesaver: those who walk upon it may
decelerate time, and defer death for a time, thus transcending the painful facts of
physical deterioration and marital unhappiness. His romance is bad history and bad
autobiography, for it is predicated on and made possible by the art of forgetting pain.
Similarly, in *Tristram Shandy* Uncle Toby replays the scene of his war-wounding at the
siege of Namur by fabricating its simulacrum in the garden of Shandy Hall, where the
disaster is never to be reenacted and in which he is *never again* to be wounded.

As well as such erotic (and martial) episodes of romantic transcendence, there are
spiritual and psychological variants. John Bunyan composed his spiritual allegory
Pilgrim's Progress in the town gaol on Bedford Bridge; John Cleland worked at *The
Memoirs of a Woman of Pleasure* (1748–9) in the Fleet debtors' prison; Tobias Smollett,
racked with ill health and facing death, penned the wondrously recuperative *Expedition of Humphry Clinker* (1771) in "Il Giardino," his Italian mountain villa in
Antignano, set in a "romantic and Salutary situation." Here, at the miserable end of
his life Smollett turns his back on the crusty and intransigent horrors of his previous
picaresque narratives only to assert the power of transformative fiction.[13] Odd though
it has seemed to 200 years of critics and historians, it is perfectly plausible that
Smollett, the exponent of a sometimes horrendous and visceral realism, should have
wanted to translate *Don Quixote* (1755).[14] In each case, an anti-mimetic narrative
mode is both regressive and progressive, rejecting the world of the real by transfigur-
ing it into a cure for "too much reality."

Such a double response lies at the very source of the appeal of romance in this
period. For all Samuel Johnson's "extreme distance from those notions which the
world has agreed, I know not very well why, to call romantic" (Piozzi 1974: 142),
Boswell called *Rasselas* "his admirable philosophical Romance."[15] *Rasselas* echoes
many of the traditional romance types (the adventure tale, the traveller's tale, the
utopian/dystopian/arcadian allegory, the quest), as well as some of its common
features of setting and plot (the high-born characters, the exotic setting, the kidnapped heroine, and so on). The overt discussion of its own genre is itself a familiar
topic in the romance tradition. Imlac's dialogue with the astronomer in chapter 44
recalls, for example, the interview between Quixote and the Canon in *Don Quixote*,
(Part I, chapters 47–50), and parallels the interview between Arabella and "the good
divine" in *The Female Quixote* (Book IX, xi). But Boswell's shrewd comment points
beyond the question of the status of fiction to Johnson's core preoccupation with the
state of the human soul, the "philosophical" or psychological basis of the need for
whatever romantic fiction offers. Johnson defines the undesirable effects of the
imagination and the pejorative effects of romance as "airy notions," the "power of
fancy over reason," "madness" when "ungovernable," "the power of fiction," "impossible enjoyments," "luscious falsehood," and "dreams of rapture or of anguish."[16]
Rasselas concludes that even when presented with the empirical evidence, the human
imagination shrinks from accepting it as an answer to deep needs. Religion and
romance compete for the same therapeutic status, it seems. The last chapter of

Rasselas, like the skeptical postmodern reader of *The Female Quixote*, acknowledges the ineradicable human yearning for alternative and better worlds in flat contradiction to the laws of history and probability. To adapt the last lines of Johnson's *Vanity of Human Wishes* (1749), the "Mind . . . makes the Happiness she does not find." This is the comi-tragic error for the Augustinian in Johnson, not only the species of delusion called romance or fiction but restless desire itself, specifically the aching need to realize in this world the visions of the imagined, what he elsewhere thought of as the triumph of hope over experience. The transforming imagination may be deplored for its errancy (both knightly and epistemological) but it can never be denied, for this is precisely the power that makes Shakespeare the "poet of Nature" and Milton the poet of the "sublime." It is the transformative engine, the means of human greatness, as well as its greatest single tormentor. And this is why Johnson, it seems to me, addresses the problem of romantic "transport" in writing: he sees it as a narrative contest: it has existed as a dilemma within narrative ever since Plato's *Phaedrus* drew a distinction between speech/presence and writing/absence.

Romance and realism are competitors, not alternatives. Romance fools nobody except those who fail to recognize its interpretive rules, and such readers include the very people who populate it. If it damages nobody but the already naive, its hostile critics nevertheless regard it as a danger because they recognize its irresistibly powerful origins. Romantic fiction is written by solitary minds heated "with incredibilities . . . without fear of criticism, without the toil of study, without knowledge of nature, or acquaintance with life" (*Rambler* 4, 31 March 1750). Stern exponents of the idea of literature as a vehicle for self-improvement must repudiate its antithesis in romance because it is the negative term in the binary that validates and makes possible the idea of rational control and "common sense." It is always a matter of relativities. Fielding's famous invention of an ancient lineage for the new-born "novel" or comic epic poem in prose tracing its descent back to Homer, in the 1742 preface of *Joseph Andrews*, defines itself *against* romance but not in order to *deny* romance. His criticism is directed against those voluminous and relatively recent French heroic romances of the seventeenth century from which nothing "useful" can be learned, what H. K. Miller rather unhelpfully calls "the effeminate salon romances" of Madeleine de Scudéry (*Clélie, Artamène, ou le Grand Cyrus*) and which, in Fielding's words, "hath made us so cautiously avoid the Term Romance, *a Name with which we might otherwise have been well enough contented.*"[17]

Most contemporary critics preferred a cleaner break between the novel and the romance, and the new novelists (Defoe, Richardson, and Fielding) themselves preferred the descriptive label "History." Even so, Fielding was commended for doing more than he intended. One commentator (probably not the generally attributed Francis Coventry) complimented him for his "new Species of Writing" because it had opened a "new Vein of Humour" which would cure the "disease" of "Romances, or Novels, Tales, &c." that had become "epidemical."[18] The writer not only elided French heroic romance and romance as such: he also missed the vigorous continuity of romance conventions *within* the histories of Joseph and Tom, their combination of a linear/historical mode of narrative (the eponymous life-histories) and a circular, endlessly/recurrent narrative mode (departure/exile, initiation, and return) enacted through already-written providential circumstances which only *appear* to be coincidence, mysterious births, strange meetings, and the quest.[19] Coleridge's famous praise (*Table Talk*, 5 July 1834) for the consummate plotting of Fielding's *Tom Jones* (1749) cannot be fully understood until one has experienced the rambling miscellaneity of heroic romance, or the factitious pretense of shape and purpose in the English baggy-monster "romances" such as Eliza Heywood's *The Fortunate Foundlings: being the Genuine History... containing Many Wonderful ACCIDENTS that befel them in their Travels... The Whole calculated for the Entertainment and Improvement of the Youth of both Sexes* (1744). At the same time we should recognize that a large element in that consummate plotting has to do with traditional romance practice, the "mythopoeic ritual patterns that generalized and dramatized fundamental and recurrent human experience," as Miller puts it (1976: 23).

Romance persists vigorously in the "new novel" and transcends distinctions we have more recently learned not to make too hastily between "high" and "low" literary culture, both in the readership and in the reading subject matter. Chapter 44 of *Rasselas* is entitled "The dangerous prevalence of imagination": the reader is warned. Imlac here proposes a universal psychological account for the disease of fiction:

> no human mind is in its right state. There is no man whose imagination does not sometimes predominate over his reason ... No man will be found in whose mind airy notions do not sometimes tyrannise, and force him to hope or fear beyond the limits of sober probability. All power of fancy over reason is a degree of insanity ... To indulge the power of fiction, and send imagination out upon the wing, is often the sport of those who delight too much in silent speculation ... the mind, in weariness or leisure, recurs constantly to the favourite conception, and feasts on the luscious falsehood whenever she is offended with the bitterness of truth. (Johnson 1976 [1759]: 133)

Johnson focuses here on two key themes: the dangers of solitariness (the fertile ground of delusion), and (implicitly) the issue of gender. The mind and the imagination are "naturally" here conceived as a female sensibility. Reading romance (signed by either a man or a woman) is an encounter with an already gendered prose, an early version of *écriture féminine*. Its historical burden would suggest that a woman's book (the book read by or for a woman) should carry a government (mental) health warning.[20] We might put the case in other terms: the book of the mother is bad or dangerous not only because it fails to measure up to the father's good book but also because patriarchy demands that the mother must concede everything in order that the male be guaranteed freedom and sovereignty. As Nietzsche put it, "Woman gives herself away, man acquires more." This principle should come as no surprise to the reader who recalls Freud's potent claim that culture itself depends on this "momentous" step: "This turning from the mother to the father [the triumph of patriarchy over matriarchy] points ... to a victory of intellectuality over sensuality – that is, an advance in civilization, since maternity is proved by the evidence of the senses while paternity is an hypothesis, based on an inference and a promise."[21] The assumption is that although the former may be valuable insofar as it transmits initiating, even nurturing social values, such values or experiences constitute only the unmediated, immature stage of an individual reader or culture, a stage prior to entry into the "proper" public sphere. By the age of 7, Rousseau tells us, he had exhausted his mother's library of romance novels, and had thereby recognized a split in perception itself, the "error" of allowing *"feeling* before *understanding."* Sterne makes much the same point in *A Sentimental Journey* – "When the heart flies out before the understanding, it saves the judgment a world of pains" (16). The law of Rousseau's maternal grandfather's "good books" – histories, Plutarch's *Lives*, Ovid's *Metamorphoses*, Fontenelle's *Dialogues with the Dead* – supplants the mother's presence and influence and with "maturity" comes the "natural" preference for "Agesilaus, Brutus, and Aristides to Orondates, Artamenes, and Juba."[22] Similarly, the first reading experience of Lennox's quixotic heroine is in her absent (because deceased) mother's books, now physically incorporated within her father's library, before the end of her sixteenth year (the year which inaugurated St. Augustine's career of immorality by the act of stealing pears). She is, we are told by the orthodox wisdom, hereby initiated into the folly of believing that "Love was the ruling Principle of the World; that every other Passion was subordinate to this; and that it caused all the Happiness and Miseries of Life" (7). The "rational" choice (the law of the father) is signaled in Lennox's book by overt textual references to the literary works of Samuel Richardson and Johnson.[23]

Johnson's anxiety about the power of fiction was grounded in his own personal experience. As we have seen, he knew what he was talking about because he had traveled the same route. Bishop Thomas Percy told Boswell that the young Samuel Johnson had read *Felixmarte of Hircania*[24] by the age of 16 and had been "immoderately fond of reading romances of chivalry, and [that] he retained his fondness for them throughout his life." The Bishop also transmitted Johnson's appreciation of their dangerous fascination, adding that the great critic and lexicographer did "attribute to these extravagant fictions that unsettled turn of mind which prevented his ever fixing in any profession."[25] If this were true, then we would need no more vivid testament to the dangerous and long-term effect of early exposure to injudicious and unsupervised romance-reading. In this light, *Rasselas* is Johnson's "philosophical" response to such fatal attraction, a solemn, lengthy, and measured critical engagement with a universal and a highly personal dilemma that finally admits that its power is insuperable.

Reading romances in the English eighteenth century is thus presented to us as educationally dangerous, psychologically risky, and socially disabling. Men *might* read them before their minds had been properly formed by induction into the patriarchy, women *did* read romances because (at best) there was nothing else for them to read (their libraries were already constructed for them), or because (at worst) they were incapable of truly creative "genius" and "real" love (Rousseau's argument).[26] The convention of the deluded, ill-educated, female reader persists in Jane Austen and in

Dorothea's remark about "the shallows of ladies'-school literature" in George Eliot's *Middlemarch* (1871: chapter 3). It is most sharply defined in Flaubert, that implacable enemy of romance who admitted that Emma Bovary's absorption in a sentimentalized chivalric myth – again in her sixteenth year – was no less powerful than his own. Emma's tragedy is caused, in Flaubert's words, by a failure to exorcize the "romantic demons that hover about literature" – of which the phenomenology was "damsels in distress swooning in lonely lodges, postillions slaughtered along the road, horses ridden to death on every page, gloomy forests, troubles of the heart, vows, sobs, tears, kisses" (chapter 6).[27] *Madame Bovary* was written in the intervals between readings of *Don Quixote*.

Cervantes' hidalgo is the first and definitive misreader of romance. His book enables the paradoxical to become a literary topos: ridiculous tragedy embroiled with new materialism and old idealism. In all discussions of romance in this period, the "sleeper" is *Don Quixote*. Its pervasive cultural influence dovetails with the English eighteenth century's dominant modes of irony, parody, and satire (Paulson 1998). Its influence was diffuse and topical rather than systematic and wholesale, and to a large extent it remained above and beyond assimilation. It was recognized as a monumental narrative, *sui generis*, challenging imitators and intimidating those who would copy it. Translation is the sincerest form of imitation: *Don Quixote* was a foreign classic, but like Homer it simply had to be made English.[28] Henry Fielding regarded the book quite simply as "the history of the world in general" (*Joseph Andrews*, Book III, i). In his three-act ballad opera *Don Quixote in England* (1734) he used the Spanish narrative as a platform for broad social satire on political corruption and professional venality (Courtiers, Lawyers, Poets, Women), and as a means to recycle the old joke that a foreign madman would be perfectly at home in England, since everybody there was mad already. More interesting is his remark about the anxiety of Cervantic influence. In the preface he states that the

> Impossibility of going beyond, and the extreme Difficulty of keeping pace with him, were sufficient to infuse Despair into a very adventurous Author... Human nature is every where the same. And the Modes and Habits of particular Nations do not change it enough, sufficiently to distinguish a Quixote in England from a Quixote in Spain. (A5–A5v)

Incidents in Fielding's ballad opera anticipate aspects of plot and themes of *Joseph Andrews* (Mr. Wilson's narrative) and, almost 20 years later, *Tom Jones* (the Man of the Hill). It includes this stanza (Act 2, p. 40), for example, on the universal topography of morality:

> The more we see of Human-Kind,
> The more Deceits and Tricks we find,
> In ev'ry Land, as well as Spain:
> For wou'd he ever hope to thrive,
> Upon the Mountains he must live;
> For nought but Rogues in Vales remain.

Swift read *Don Quixote* at Moor Park, where he inherited Sir William Temple's admiration for the "matchless writer of Don Quixot" ("Of Poetry," 1690), borrowed Quixotic ideas for *A Tale of A Tub* (1704), and in his defense of John Gay's *The Beggar's Opera* nominated *Don Quixote* as the benchmark for "true Humour" (*Intelligencer* III). Pope invoked Swift as his dedicatee in the *New Dunciad* (1742): he was the master of "Cervantes' serious air" (line 19). So much was it a commonplace to think of Cervantes and Swift in the same moment that both friends and enemies needed to go further: Lord Bathurst and Lady Mary Wortley Montagu believed that Swift had "stolen" his humor from Cervantes, and the former said that in Spain "one 'would find that Don *Suifto* is in the highest estimation, being thought to be lineally descended from *Miguel de Cervantes*, by a daughter of *Quevedo's*" (Swift 1963–5: IV, 390). The great Spanish comedy remained in the English imagination even, perhaps especially, among those who had never read it. It was generally spared the savaging of the French heroic romances of the seventeenth century.

Lennox's *The Female Quixote* is the closest female English descendent of Cervantes, just as Smollett's *Launcelot Greaves* (1760–1) is his closest English male relative: each novel, though very different from the other, is characterized by random events, stock turns of plot, strange coincidences, a rambling structure, and a constant and covert intertextual reference to the Cervantic model. As we have seen, Lennox's book finally disavows the "madness" of Quixotic romance in recommending the "new" novels of Richardson and the reflective moral journalism of Johnson: these are better models on which to form the mind and on which to model conduct. And yet, in writers most resistant to romantic "nonsense" one catches a glimpse of fundamental stresses in contemporary critical debates on the respective truth-value of literature and history. It is in the eighteenth century that questions of the historicity of romance are taken seriously. In lecture XXXVII on "Romances and Novels," Hugh Blair provides a standard history of romance ("fictitious histories") in both eastern and western cultural history ("Indians . . . Persians . . . Arabians" as well as "Greeks and Romans"), and tracks such narratives from medieval chivalric tales and the "Provençal Troubadores," through Ariosto, and the bewitching Amadis de Gaul until "the ingenious Cervantes, in the beginning of the last century, contributed greatly to explode it."[29] The English had established zones free of dragons and enchanted castles with Durfey's *Astraea*, the *Grand Cyrus*, *Clelia*, *Cleopatra*, and Sydney's *Arcadia*, which effectively moved the genre from "magnificent heroic romance, [until it] dwindled down to the familiar novel" (III, 75–6), with exceptional examples being Le Sage's *Gil Blas*, Marivaux's *Marianne*, and Rousseau's *La Nouvelle Heloïse*. Defoe's *Robinson Crusoe* and Fielding's *Tom Jones* are among the praiseworthy novels of serious moral value ("characteristical novels formed upon nature and upon life, without extravagance and without licentiousness": III, 78).

Unsupervised by their male counterparts, women read romances because of a deficiency of male presence. It may seem to be the case that romance is the woman's choice by default: but I hope I have indicated other ways of reading romance as the vehicle of desire and (in Johnson) a wrestling with the most threatening of psychological demons. Moreover, romance enacts a real-life battle, in Harold Bloom's sense, between weak and strong readers. The modern knight-errant (Swift, Samuel Johnson, Mr. Glanville, Mr. Knightley, Flaubert) contests with romance for the soul of his reader. The strong reader speaks for the dominant patriarchy; the weak maiden is always to be rescued from Giant Fiction, but reality is not the victor.

Reading multi-volume folios of French romance is exceedingly time-consuming. That, after all, is part of their original *raison d'être* and attraction. They are a compensation for part-membership of the patriarchy and its (imperfect) public world. The 26-year old Lady Dorothy Osborne knew this very well. When she recommended La Calprenède's 23-volume collection of short stories, *Cléopâtre* (1642), to her husband-to-be Sir William Temple on February 26, 1653, she wrote, with a delicious play of voices:

> have you read Cleopatra? I have sixe Tomes on't heer that I can lend you, if you have not, there are some Story's in't you will like I beleeve. but what an Asse am I to think you can bee idle enough at London to reade Romances. noe I'le keep them till you come hither, heer they may be welcome to you for want of better Company. (Osborne 1928: 21)

One reads romances in lieu of anything better to do, as a substitute for a public life, as a substitute for lack of human company, in order to taste life in the metropolis. Dorothy Osborne knew very well that the purpose of reading was also to "divert myself withal." An alert reading of romance therefore will always require this doubling, a knowing suspension of disbelief, a consciousness that the real world is generally indifferent to the world of fiction, but also that writing and reading fiction provide a substitute life in a world of action otherwise proscribed for a woman. Although she throws herself into the Thames at one point, Arabella's world is Quixotic comedy, recuperative and forgiving. She will escape tragedy (unlike Emma Bovary) because there is a good man (Glanville) who can speak to her from *outside* the world of heroic romance. It is the bad man (Sir George Bellmour) who learns to speak "the language of romance" in order to mask a perversion of moral purpose. It is another woman, the Countess, already tamed by her experience (VIII, 7), who knows that society's rules are culturally and historically specific: she is a better reader of history than Arabella, and she provides the knockout blow: "The same actions which made a man a hero in those times would constitute him a murderer in these; and the same steps which led him to a throne then, would infallibly conduct him to a scaffold now." Arabella eventually hears this message, Emma Bovary does not, and there is a terrible and sardonic irony to follow Charles Bovary's death and Emma Bovary's suicide: their orphaned daughter is sent to earn her living in a cotton-mill. There is no more poignant reminder that romance can only exist through mechanisms of exclusion.

For another and earlier audience, and within its own generic terms of political *roman à clef*, romance provided other transgressive possibilities, notably a narrative mode for "dangerous" political allegory or for a vision of otherwise forbidden sexual preferences. In Mary Delarivier Manley's *Secret Memoirs . . . from the New ATALANTIS* (1709), the thematic structure is the revolutionary challenge of "the Power of Love, that Leveller of Mankind; that Blender of Distinction and Hearts."[30] The subjects include bigamous marriage (Don Marcus to Delia), incest (Urania and Polydore), illegitimacy, transvestism, and lesbianism. The cabal of ladies is defined thus: "the New Cabal; what an irregularity of Taste is theirs? They do not in reality love *Men*; but doat on the Representation of *Men* in *Women*" (206). In the hands of a greater talent, as Samuel Richardson was to show in *Pamela* (1740–2) and *Clarissa* (1747–8), the dominant power relations between the predatory male patriarchy on one side and female victimhood on the other could be suborned: all this in the genre of what Delarivier Manley calls, pointedly, "Airy Romances" and "Dangerous Novels" (53). Yet the description of sexual intercourse in *The New Atalantis* reminds us of the metonymic grotesqueries, the weirdly baroque circumlocutions (not to mention the hyperventilating typography) characteristic of a narrative mode in which everything is permitted except verisimilitude – no social *praxis* except through an extravagant, oblique, and unlimited *poesis*:

> [Diana] suffer'd all the *glowing* pressures of his roving Hand, that Hand, which with a Luxury of Joy, wander'd through all the rich *Meanders* of her Bosom; she suffer'd him to *drink* her dazzling naked Beauties at his Eyes! to *gaze*! To *burn*! To press her with *unbounded Rapture*! taking by intervals a thousand *eager, short-breath'd* Kisses. Whilst *Diana*, lull'd by the enchanting Poison Love had diffus'd throughout her form, lay *still*, and *charm'd* as he! – she *thought* no more! – she *could not* think! – let *Love* and *Nature* plead the weighty Cause! – let *them* excuse the beauteous Frailty! – *Diana* was become a *Votary* to *Venus*! – obedient to the Dictates of the Goddess! –[31]

No modern reader can read this without a smile. We may no longer tolerate such indirection in erotic narrative, nor such prevarication about the topic of female desire, yet the overblown language and the broken syntax indicate how, in eighteenth-century terms, such silences and censorship may be nevertheless coded, represented, and thereby circumvented, if only by an apparent collapse of denotative language into a series of gasps.[32] Again, successful romance narrative requires in its reader a play of awareness, an oscillation between the desirable, the possible and probable, a recognition that such play may also be the merest foolishness, no more than an artifice of the book, an episode within a complex, brutal, and repressive present. When Arabella looks with her intelligent eye at what the "real" world has to offer in the modern metropolis, she finds the royal court, the Tower of London, St. Paul's cathedral, and Vauxhall Gardens all equally disappointing. Even though London constitutes the inevitable and "proper" site of her social being, the real contest all along has been for ownership of Arabella's mind and body, her subjectivity and her social duty as a woman to acknowledge and accept the role prescribed for her (her future objectification by the patriarchy). In the end, and almost disastrously, Arabella's practice of chivalric codes excludes *all* men except the machiavellian fortune-hunter Sir George. Her private desires are excluded from her repertoire of action by the sheer banality of her social role: romance is her only outlet. In her own words, the alternatives are dire indeed: "the usual Topicks of Conversation among young Ladies, such as their Winnings and Losings at *Brag*, the Prices of Silks, the newest Fashions, the best Hair-Cutter, the Scandal at the last Assembly" (360). As Congreve rightly put in his preface to *Incognita* (1692), "Romance gives more Wonder, Novels more delight" (iii): romances were not read for their realism but for their poetry.

Lennox's novel remains more than a highly readable exercise in intertextual comedy because it performs what Samuel Johnson says *Don Quixote* also provides, the transmission through fable of a mimetic statement on the nature of interpretation and the business of living: "When we pity him [Quixote], we reflect on our own disappointments; and when we laugh, our hearts inform us that he is not more ridiculous than ourselves, except that he tells us what we have only thought" (*Rambler* 2, 24 March 1750). Thus does romance offer us a double mimesis of the "golden" world of the reader's desire and an allusion to our leaden origins and destinations. In Arabella's habitually literary mode of understanding, the past determines the present, and history is, or should be, repetition without difference. But if a fictional model of conduct is enacted in real life, then fiction and romance cease to exist because they have become the real thing. Romance therefore becomes a series of looping typologies: there is no progression because everything desirable has been always already written. Here is her great discovery and her great disappointment. Arabella and (for a time) the reader of romance forget the nature of metaphor and allegory, and forget to distinguish truth from the figurative medium of its representation (see Book XI, chapter II). She misreads both Mr. Glanville and history. In order to assimilate with the patriarchy, Arabella must denounce her practice of romance as a false paradise: the consequence is that although she certainly will escape the cotton-mill, she may never again practice her dream of self-determination. As the new Mrs. Glanville, she is invisible to us. Perhaps she will provide *Rasselas* and *Clarissa* for her own daughter to read. We cannot answer such questions with any certainty, but the eighteenth century is the time during which foundational questions are posed about the genre, value, and meaning of romance. In the work of its leading exponents and readers, there is a recognition of the ironic playfulness of romance, signaled by a "knowing" critique of its own artifice and of its self-consciousness. Charlotte Smith's comment, in *Letters of a Solitary Wanderer* (1800), shows how easily this serious and ironic play of awareness can vanish under the harsh scrutiny of a moralistic gaze: "a young woman who is so weak as to become in imagination the Heroine of a Novel, would have been a foolish, frivolous and affected character, though she had never heard of a circulating library" (I, vi).

See also: chapter 6, MALORY AND THE EARLY PROSE ROMANCES; chapter 12, "GOTHIC" ROMANCE; chapter 13, WOMEN'S GOTHIC ROMANCE; chapter 15, "INCONSISTENT RHAPSODIES"; chapter 21, VICTORIAN ROMANCE: ROMANCE AND MYSTERY; chapter 27, ROMANCE IN FANTASY; chapter 28, QUEST ROMANCE IN SCIENCE FICTION.

Notes

1. Watkin Tench, *Letters Written in France to a Friend in London between the Month of November 1794 and the Month of May 1795* (1796); quoted from the edition by Gavin Edwards, *Letters from Revolutionary France* (Cardiff: University of Wales Press, 2001), pp. 51, 96, 155–6. For Burke's remark, see *Reflections on the Revolution in France* (1790), ed. Conor Cruise O'Brien (Harmondsworth: Penguin, 1968), p. 170.

2. Charlotte Lennox, *The Female Quixote or The Adventures of Arabella* (1752), ed. Margaret Dalziel (London: Oxford University Press, 1970), p. 380. Subsequent references are to this edition and are given by page number (see also Duncan Isles, "Johnson, Richardson, and *The Female Quixote*," pp. 418–27).

3. See Paul Salzman's discussion in *English Prose Fiction 1588–1700* (1985), p. 177. This also contains a typology of romance.

4. Henry Knight Miller, "Augustan Prose Fiction and the Romance Tradition," in *Studies in the Eighteenth Century III: Papers Presented at the Third David Nichol Smith Memorial Seminar*, Canberra: Australian National University Press, 1976), p. 243.

5. Swift's or Sheridan's phrase; see A. C. Elias, "Swift's *Don Quixote*, Dunkin's *Virgil Travesty*, and Other New Intelligence: John Lyon's 'Materials for a Life of Dr. Swift,' 1765," *Swift Studies* 13 (1998), 103.

6. *Tom Jones*, I, 489. Cf. this comment: "*Sancho Pancho* was the original by which M. *Fielding* drew his *Partridge*, who indeed is not so entertaining as the 'Squire of *Don Quixote*, but however cannot fail of pleasing an *English* taste," in "A Literary Article from Paris," *Gentleman's Magazine* XX (March 1750), 117–18.

7. Cf. Freud's comment on the triumph of patriarchy over matriarchy in "Notes upon a Case of Obsessional Neurosis" ("The Rat Man"): "A great advance was made in civilization when men decided to put their inferences upon a level with the testimony of their senses and to make the first step from matriarchy to patriarchy." *Case Histories II: The Penguin Freud Library*, trans. James Strachey and others, vol. 9 (Harmondsworth, 1991), pp. 112–13.

8. For Johnson's response to Lennox's *Memoirs of the Countess of Berci* (1756), translated and adapted from two French romances of 1616 and 1735 respectively, see *The Letters of Samuel Johnson*, ed. Bruce Redford, 5 vols. (Oxford: Clarendon Press, 1992–4), I, 136–7. Johnson championed Lennox's work, although he may have done so in this case without necessarily having read it or its original sources. For Henry Fielding's enthusiastic review of *The Female Quixote*, see *Covent-Garden Journal* number 24 (March 1752).

9. "By marriage, the husband and wife are one person in law... the very being or legal existence of the woman is suspended during the marriage, or at least is incorporated into that of the husband: under whose wing, protection, and cover, she performs every thing." William Blackstone, *Commentaries on the Law of England* (1765–9) (New York: Garland, 1978), I, 442. Cited in Ngaire Naffine, "Possession: Erotic Love in the Law of Rape," *Modern Law Review* 57 (1994), 10–37. I am grateful to Nina Puren for this reference.

10. The reference is not to Chaucer, Boccaccio, or Petrarch, but to *A Collection of Old Ballads* (1727); see *The Vicar of Wakefield*, ed. Arthur Friedman (Oxford: Oxford University Press, 1981), p. 193 (note for p. 31). The Vicar's own preference for the name "Grissel" is hardly free of romantic associations, of course.

11. *A Sentimental Journey through France and Italy*, ed. Ian Jack (London: Oxford University Press, 1968), p. 113. Further references are to this edition and are given as page numbers.

12. *Mrs Montagu "Queen of the Blues": Her Letters and Friendships from 1762 to 1800*, ed. Reginald Blunt, 2 vols. (London: Constable, 1923), I, 192.

13. Smollett's widow remarked in 1773: "It Galls me to the soul when I think how much that poor dear Man Suffered while he wrote that novel." See *The Expedition of Humphry Clinker*, ed. Lewis M. Knapp (Oxford: Oxford University Press, 1984), p. viii.

14. The story of the 200-year-old resistance to the idea that Smollett could be credited with this translation is told by Martin Battestin in "The Authorship of Smollett's Don Quixote," *Studies in Bibliography* 50 (1997), 296–327. In his *Continuation of the Complete History of England* (1761) Smollett remarked that "The genius of Cervantes was translated into the novels of Fielding, who painted the characters, and ridiculed the follies of life with equal strength, humour and propriety." An acknowledgment like this, of course, enabled Smollett to take his own rather different path: *Launcelot Greaves* (1760–1) was the result.

15. *Boswell's Life of Johnson* (1791), ed. George Birkbeck Hill, rev. L. F. Powell, 6 vols. (Oxford: Clarendon Press, 1934, reprinted 1971), I, 89. Subsequent references given by volume and page number.

16. Johnson's *Dictionary* (1755) defines the term romance as "1. A military fable of the middle ages; a tale of wild adventures in war and love...2. A lie; a fiction. In common speech."

17. *Joseph Andrews*, ed. Martin C. Battestin (Oxford: Clarendon Press, 1961), p. 7; *Tom Jones*, ed. Martin C. Battestin, 2 vols. (Oxford: Clarendon Press, 1974), II, 489; my italics. Swift said he would ban "French Romances...for young Ladyes" ("Hints: Education of Ladyes" in *Prose Works*, ed. Herbert Davis and others, 16 vols. (Oxford: Clarendon Press, 1939–74), XII, 308.

18. Francis Coventry[?], *An Essay on the New Species of Writing founded by Mr. Fielding* (1751), ed. A. D. McKillop, Augustan Reprint Society 95 (Los Angeles: W. A. Clark Memorial Library, University of California, 1962). See further Martin C. Battestin with Ruthe R. Battestin, *Henry Fielding: A Life* (London and New York: Routledge, 1989), p. 531, and *Monthly Review* 4 (March 1751), 375.

19. Miller 1976: 9, 23 argues that *"Tom Jones* is in all major essentials a 'romance'" and "it shares with romance what Joseph Campbell calls 'The Monomyth' of Exile, Initiation, and Return."

20. Ian Watt's reservation (1957: 151) – that "most women read only romances and novels, as was endlessly asserted, is not likely. Many were certainly devoted to English literature" – also understates the polyglossic nature of the novel itself. For reading as a "promiscuous activity," see Probyn 1987: 4.

21. Cited by Peggy Kamuf, "Writing like a Woman," in McConnell-Ginet, Borker, and Furman 1980: 289.

22. *The Confessions of Jean-Jacques Rousseau* (1765), trans. J. M. Cohen (1953: 20). See also *Persuasion*, chapter 4: Anne Elliott, having been "forced into prudence in her youth...learned romance as she grew older – the natural sequel of an unnatural beginning." Jocelyn Harris alerted me to this example of the binary.

23. Johnson may or may not have written or rewritten chapter II of Book IX of Lennox's *The Female Quixote*, but Richardson said he would have been happier without the compliment of being mentioned here as a readerly model: see Lennox's *The Life of Harriot Stuart Written by Herself* (1750), ed. Susan Kubica Howard (Madison and London: Associated Universities Presses, 1995), p. 287; Duncan Isles (note 2 above); and Henson 1992: 111–41.

24. One of the romances (variously entitled *Florismarte of Hyrcania* or *Felixmarte of Hyrcania* by Melchor de Ortega, 1556) tossed onto the bonfire in *Don Quixote* (Part I, chapters vi and xxxii).

25. *Life*, I, 49. He was reading another, the sixteenth-century chivalric romance spared from the bonfire of such books in *Don Quixote*, *Il Palmerino d'Inghilterra*, "but did not like it much" on the night he stayed in Loughborough, in his sixty-seventh year. He "read it for the language, by way of preparation for his Italian expedition" (*Life*, III, 2). Notwithstanding their "fertility of invention, the beauty of style and expres-

sion" and their intrinsic historical interest, these "wild improbable tales" were essentially the product of an immature or "barbarous state" (*Life*, IV, 17). For his view that Lennox's talent was genius near allied to madness, see *Letters*, ed. Redford, III, 354.

26. See note 20 above and Rousseau's *La Lettre à d'Alembert sur les spectacles*, cited in Kamuf, "Writing Like a Woman," p. 290: "They are all cold and pretty like their authors. They may show great wit but never any soul. They are a hundred times more reasonable than they are passionate. Women know neither how to describe nor experience love itself." In her own eyes, Lennox's Harriot Stuart was a practiced same-sex gallant at 11 years of age, able to look *back* at her romance-reading in Scudéry's *Clélia* and *Artamène*, in La Calprenède, and Nathaniel Lee's play *The Rival Queens* (1677). See *The Life of Harriot Stuart written by Herself*, ed. Susan Kubica Howard (1995), p. 66.

27. *Madame Bovary*, trans. Alan Russell (Harmondsworth: Penguin, 1950), pp. 50 and 8. See further Margaret Low, "Madame Bovary, c'est moi!" in *Towards the Real Flaubert*, ed. A. W. Raitt (Oxford: Clarendon Press, 1984), pp. 15–28, and *Madame Bovary: Moeurs de province*, ed. Pierre-Marc de Biasi (Paris: Imprimerie Nationale Éditions, 1994), pp. 23–5.

28. Captain John Stevens revised Shelton's 1612/20 translation (1700), which was then overshadowed by Peter Motteux's four-volume translation in the same year (1700–3; the Modern Library edition until recent times); E. Ward's Hudibrastic version

appeared in 1711–12; Peter Motteux's translation in John Ozell's revision in 1719; Sarah Hyde's Dublin edition of 1733; Charles Jervas' version of 1742 (issued more than 100 times in England and the United States); Tobias Smollett's version of 1755 (19 editions and reprints to 1799); G. Kelley's version of 1769; and C. H. Wilmott's version of 1774. Swift's friend John Carteret produced a carefully edited and illustrated Spanish edition, with a *Life* of the author, in 1738; and Giuseppe Baretti was working slowly on another translation in 1773.

29. Hugh Blair, *Lectures on Rhetoric* (1820), III, 75; further references in text above. Smollett traces the "fable in prose" from romance to Cervantes to Le Sage in his *Preface to Roderick Random* (1748). See also Richard Hurd's *Letters on Chivalry and Romance* (London: A. Miller, 1762).

30. All quotations are from the facsimile of the first edition, *The Novels of Mary Delarivière Manley*, ed. Patricia Köster, 2 vols. (Gainesville: Florida University Press, 1991).

31. Pages 228–9. Regrettably, the typographical signals in the original text are removed in the modernized version: see *New Atlantis*, ed. Rosalind Ballaster (Harmondsworth: Penguin, 1992), p. 246.

32. Janine Barchas discusses Sarah Fielding's use of the dash as "a form of expression... which, in part, symbolize[s] a socially dictated silence peculiar to the women of the novel" ("Sarah Fielding's Dashing Style and Eighteenth-century Print Culture," *ELH* 63 [1996], 645).

References and Further Reading

Belsey, Catherine (1994), *Desire: Love Stories in Western Culture*. Oxford: Blackwell.

Blackstone, William (1978). *Commentaries on the Law of England*. New York: Garland. [First published in 1765–9.]

Blair, Hugh (1783). *Lectures on Rhetoric and Belles Lettres*. 3 vols. London: A. Strahan and T. Cadell.

Fielding, Henry (1742). *The History of the Adventures of Joseph Andrews ... Written in Imitation of the Manner of Cervantes, Author of Don Quixote*. London.

Henson, Eithne (1992). *"The Fictions of Romantick Chivalry": Samuel Johnson and Romance*. London: Associated University Presses.

Johnson, Samuel (1976). *The History of Rasselas, Prince of Abyssinia*, ed. D. J. Enright. Harmondsworth: Penguin. [First published in 1759.]

Lennox, Charlotte (1970). *The Female Quixote or The Adventures of Arabella*, ed. Margaret Dalziel. London: Oxford University Press. [First published in 1752.]

McConnell-Ginet, Sally, Ruth Borker, and Nancy Furman, eds. (1980). *Women and Language in Literature and Society*. New York: Praeger.

Manley, Delarivière (1991). *Secret Memoirs and Manners of Several Persons of Quality, of Both Sexes. From the New Atalantis, an Island in the Mediterranean*, ed. Rosalind Ballaster. Harmondsworth: Penguin. [First published in 1709.]

Miller, Henry Knight (1976). *Henry Fielding's Tom Jones and the Romance Tradition*. Victoria, BC: University of Victoria.

Osborne, Dorothy (1928). *The Letters of Dorothy Osborne to William Temple*, ed. G. C. Moore Smith. Oxford: Clarendon Press.

Paulson, Ronald (1998). *Don Quixote in England: The Aesthetics of Laughter*. Baltimore, MD, and London: Johns Hopkins University Press.

Perry, Ruth (1980). *Women, Letters, and the Novel*. New York: AMS Press.

Piozzi, Hester Lynch (1974). *Anecdotes of the Late Samuel Johnson, LL.D.*, ed. Arthur Sherbo. London: Oxford University Press. [First published in 1786.]

Probyn, Clive (1987). *English Fiction of the Eighteenth Century 1700–1789*. London and New York: Longman.

Radway, Janice (1987). *Reading the Romance: Women, Patriarchy and Popular Literature*. London: Verso.

Reeve, Clara (1785). *The Progress of Romance*. 2 vols. London.

Richetti, John J. (1969). *Popular Fiction before Richardson: Narrative Patterns 1700–39*. Oxford: Clarendon Press.

Rousseau, Jean-Jacques (1953). *Confessions*, ed. J. M. Cohen. Harmondsworth: Penguin. [First published in 1781.]

Saled, P., and S. Žižek, eds. (1996). *Gaze and Voice as Love Objects*. Durham, NC, and London: Duke University Press.

Salzman, Paul (1985). *English Prose Fiction 1558–1700: A Critical History*. Oxford: Oxford University Press.

Swift, Jonathan (1963–5). *The Correspondence of Jonathan Swift*, ed. Harold Williams. 5 vols. Oxford: Clarendon Press.

Watt, Ian (1957). *The Rise of the Novel: Studies in Defoe, Richardson, and Fielding*. London: Chatto and Windus.

Williams, Ioan M. (1970). *Novel and Romance 1700–1800: A Documentary Record*. London: Routledge and Kegan Paul.

15

"Inconsistent Rhapsodies": Samuel Richardson and the Politics of Romance[1]

Fiona Price

In Clara Reeve's *Progress of Romance* (1785) the character Euphrasia defends Samuel Richardson against the charge that he makes young women "wiredraw their language," arguing that they "improve" by reading, unlike the "ladies of the last age." "Truly," answers her friend Sophronia, "for their studies were the French and Spanish Romances, and the writings of Mrs *Behn*, Mrs *Manly*, and Mrs *Heywood*" (1785: I, 138). Reeve's praise of Richardson at the expense of earlier romances follows a contemporary trend. Still read in the century's opening decades, the "vast French romances, neatly gilt" gradually experienced a decline in status. Attacks on the epistemology of romance became commonplace, notably in the prefaces of defensive mid to late eighteenth-century novelists. Literary historians both presented the prose romance as an outdated form and underplayed its importance; in her essay "On the Origin and Progress of Novel Writing" Anna Letitia Barbauld describes *The Grand Cyrus* and *Clelia* as "novels," implying their desultory nature: "Some adventures and a love story was all they aimed at" (1810: I, 37).[2] This denigration of romance continues in the sometimes triumphalist twentieth-century accounts of the rise of the novel.[3] In spite of a growing interest in romance's relation to discourses of nationalism and romanticism, critics represented the eighteenth-century romance as a poor cousin to the novel, particularly in relation to "realism."[4] Current scholarship on the relation between the romance and the novel in the mid-eighteenth century is marked by this heritage. Yet the key to both the subsequent low status of romance and its great influence on the novel is to be found in its complicated genealogy during this period.

Although frequently cited as hostile to romance, Samuel Richardson's work demonstrates this complexity. In his guide to epistolary style, *Letters Written to and for Particular Friends*, Richardson criticizes "romantic Rhapsody in Courtship," mocks the "idle Rants of Romance," and argues that the modern lover proceeds very differently from the genre's "greatest Hero[es]."[5]However, alongside the "idle Romances," he also attacks "pernicious Novels."[6] In 1741 he wrote to his friend Aaron Hill: "I am introducing a new species of writing which might possibly turn young people into a course of reading different from the pomp and parade of romance writing, and dismissing the improbable and the marvellous, with which novels generally abound, might tend to promote the cause of religion and virtue" (p. 41). As well as singling out the romance for criticism, Richardson's strategy for establishing his didactic credentials involved the tactical dismissal of all other fiction characterized as scurrilous.[7]

In fact, there was a disjunction between his commentary and his practice, a gap indicative of careful maneuvering for literary space. The successional difficulties of the late seventeenth and early eighteenth centuries had generated a need to produce a new narrative to describe – and stabilize – authority within the state and the family. A shift from the Stuart emphasis on divine right and kingship made the aristocratic idealism of the French romance inappropriate, while the political environment engendered more scandalous, still less acceptable narratives. Aware of both British and French romance models, Richardson criticizes these older forms yet exploits their motifs. Moderating their aristocratic elements, he promotes a new heroic code, in which not only the bourgeois sensibilities of the middle class are evident, but also a broader national agenda. Investing the figure of the heroine with new political significance, the resulting narratives of affective influence were immensely important to the later development of the romance. Writers after Richardson ironized the genre, but they also drew upon its idealism to interrogate the use of authority. Particularly after the publication of Jean-Jacques Rousseau's *La Nouvelle Héloïse* (1761), modes of private behavior depicted in the romance became important counters in constructing British national identity. The ideological quarrels of the first half of the century had ensured the low status of the prose romance; however, they also made its language central to political debate.

The association of the romance and patriotism was in part determined by late seventeenth-century scholarly practice. While English scholars remained naive about the history of the romance, French commentators undertook firsthand research, generating a patriotically interested criticism. Medieval French romances led the Comte de Caylus to propose that the English, reading of Charlemagne, had created the legends of Arthur in competition.[8] Similarly, Pierre Daniel Huet in *A Treatise of Romances and Their Original* (1672) stressed the superiority of French romance.[9] Significantly, his description of romance as "Fictions of Love – Adventures writ in Prose with Art, for the delight and Instruction of his Readers," and his suggestion that war and politics are less appropriate subjects, indicate that his interest was primarily in the contemporary romances of France. British readers, ignorant of medieval romance, made the same assumption. In Charlotte Lennox's *The Female Quixote* (1752), for example, the heroine Arabella is satirized for reading a "great Store of Romances, and, what was still more unfortunate, not in the original *French*, but very bad Translations."[10] As Lennox's remarks suggest, despite the fact that these works were still read by some early to mid-century readers, their status was on the decline. On the one hand, an incipient patriotism insisted that their idealism was unnecessary in the English environment. On the other, they were characterized as too erotic.

At the heart of the problem was their presentation of an evolved form of "courtly love." Despite an emphasis on the denial and deferral of passion, this was seen as arousing, particularly for female readers. Addison's description of the ladies' library in *The Spectator* mentions as virtually the only books that show any sign of being read "*The Grand Cyrus*," with a strangely phallic "pin stuck in one of the leaves," and "*Clelia*, which opened of itself in the place that describes two lovers in a bower" (Barbauld 1810: 137). Equally troubling was the romance's insistence on ideal love as the hidden cause for political transactions, a blurring of motivational boundaries that ultimately ensured the politicization of the romance heroine. The translations suggested, according to Lennox, that "Love was the ruling Principle of the World; that every other Passion was subordinate to this; and that it caused all the Happiness and Miseries of Life" (p. 90). Ironically, subsequent satirists and scandal writers, in drawing attention to this convention, arguably added to the heroine's politicization. However, the love described in the French heroic romance itself was less directly political, but rather a heroic code. The tendency of "the *Grand Cyrus*'s, [and] the *Cleopatra*'s" was to depict the passion of hero or heroine not as earthly lust but as a desire for perfection.[11] Henry Knight Miller points out that this was very different from the way love was depicted in the medieval romance: "Mme de Rambouillet would have been scandalised at the forthrightness of such medieval heroines as Rimenhild or Josian or Belisaunt" (Miller 1976: 246–7). These works used the conventions of *bienséance* (decorum) and *vraisemblance* (truth to nature), not to aim at realism, but to provide an idealized image of passion. Nonetheless, these exemplars of heroic love were accompanied by an emphasis on the psychology and origin of passion that ultimately interested British writers. The popular romance, Gauthier de Costas de La Calprenède's *Cleopatra* (1647), translated by Robert Loveday in 1736, for example, began with Prince Tyridates who, despite unexplained melancholy, rescues Queen Candace from "the Jaws of Neptune"; he subsequently narrates his life story (1736: 1). Describing lovers separated by shipwrecks, seductions, and battles, the romance is episodic enough to allow the development of emotion to be thoroughly explored. Particularly important is the convention of the *surprise de l'amour*, where the hero suddenly becomes aware of the state of his feelings. This was a feature of some of the most popular romances, occurring in the work of both La Calprenède and Madeleine de Scudéry, author of *Artamène, ou le grand Cyrus* (1649–53), perhaps the most influential of its type in Britain.

The hero's lack of self-awareness led Enlightenment critics to present romance's (female) readers and characters as fantasists easily stirred to hysteria. However, ironically, in the French heroic romance, while the male characters struggled with love, the heroines were restrained, often presenting a model of bravery based on sexual renunciation. Instead it was the shorter French *histoire* or *nouvelle*, with which romances were often confused, which provided descriptions of illicit love. Probably the best-known of these, Mme. La Fayette's *La Princesse de Clèves* (1678), involved extensive self-deception on the part of the sexually awakening heroine. Often alluding to contemporary intrigue, in Britain these works gave rise to more popular abbreviated adaptations that had strong political relevance. Gone was the emphasis on the *vraisemblance* that improved upon reality; sexual and ethical restraint was replaced by desire and self-interest. These "secret histories" by Aphra Behn, Delarivière Manley, and later, Eliza Haywood, challenged as unreal the standards of chastity and political behavior put forward by the French heroic romance. Although often connected by critics with extravagance, effeminacy, or sexual indulgence, ironically their works hastened the decline of the heroic form.

In particular, while disgust with court life and praise of the country figured heavily in Tory narratives, the decade before the publication of *Pamela* showed explicit hostility to Robert Walpole. *Celenia, or the History of Hyempsal, King of Numidia* (1735–6) is in part a political allegory, arguing in favor of the Tory Jacobite cause. In this model, the Jacobite claim to the throne is backed up by the narrative of divine justification that, the romance posits, Walpole and the Whigs lack. In addition, such court fictions attacked the alternative narratives supporting the Hanoverian regime. In the process, they undermined, as Miranda Burgess puts it (2000: 13), "not only Robert Filmer's insistence that worldly kings are lineal descendants and heirs of the biblical Adam . . . whose God-given subjects were his wife and children, but also John Locke's Genesis-story of a created masculine authority operating in the putatively natural, pre-political realm of the household." The "secret histories" insisted on the disruptive force of passion; moreover, what might disrupt the family might disrupt the state, destabilizing both narratives of divinely sanctioned authority and disinterested political sensibility (see Ballaster 1992). Oriental tales also contained this threat. Haywood's *Adventures of Eovaai, Princess of Ijaveo* (1736) used its exotic setting to attack Sir Robert Walpole, but, more dangerously still, shows its heroine sexually aroused. The narrative suggests that all the careful education the heroine receives is worthless, forgotten in an instant of pride or lust; self-interested passion proves the ultimate motivation.[12] Notably, the villain, a scheming politician, is lowborn and knows no limit to his thirst for power; his essential baseness is, however, hidden by trickery. The narrative offers a contrast between divinely protected kingship and the self-interested politics of Hanoverian Britain, depicting the latter as threatening the social order.

However, an alternative to these narratives of political fervor was available: the didactic romance. This described a more restrained relationship between public and private life. Romances such as Fénelon's *Télémaque* (1699–1700), which went through five editions between 1700 and 1739, had a continuing popularity which showed the form's potential as a response to the secret histories. Unlike Haywood's *Adventures*, such narratives insist on the educational benefits of fiction. For example, Andrew Ramsay's *The Travels of Cyrus* (1727), which reached its seventh English edition by 1745, begins by recounting a mother's tuition of her son in a way that enforces the value of history and literature. The emphasis is on the importance of a life of virtuous action, condemning the intrigue and luxury of court life. However, far from advocating retreat from the court in all circumstances, it suggests that good conduct ameliorates the moral danger of political life. As such, Ramsay's work reflected contemporary preoccupations; eighteenth-century Britain was concerned with rewriting its narratives to elevate economic endeavor, trade, and production, but it was fearful of excessive consumerism. In particular, Ramsay's work offers a counter to the stories of self-interested passion often connected with luxury in the court fictions. His narrative's inset stories combine a critique of public life with a warning concerning private motivations, including love. In the first book, for example, Zarina, a female warrior, and her would-be lover are brought together by their bravery and military prowess, but she persuades him to remember his duty to his wife: Spartan values are encouraged by self-discipline – political responsibilities are fulfilled.

For Richardson both the idealism of the French romance and the cynical secret histories that challenged them needed restraint. Attacking the latter's portrayal of sexuality, in the preface to the *Collection of Entertaining Histories and Novels* (1739) Richardson praised Mrs. Aubin for raising the standard of romance in contrast to other women who brought fiction into "Disreputation" by trying "to make it their Study to corrupt the Minds of others" (Keymer and Sabor 2001: I, xiv). However, he also disapproved of the erotically charged optimism of the French romance; the way it provoked desire by deferral; and its projection of a supposedly improved reality: its "inconsistent Rhapsodies" seemed unrepresentative of courtship in England. Even while he rewrote the romance, Richardson's suspicion extended to other French fiction. In response to a suggestion by William Warburton that he "pursued in [his] former Piece the excellent Plan fallen upon lately by the French Writers," Richardson, with a defensiveness approaching Francophobia, claimed that "all that know me, know, that I am not acquainted in the least either with the French Language or Writers."[13] Nonetheless, parallels (sometimes extremely speculative) were traced between Richardson's writing and that of Marivaux (see McKillop 1960: 36; Munro 1975). In Marivaux's *La Vie Marianne* (six of the eleven parts of which had been translated into English by 1737) the young and low-ranking Marianne is courted by the older, treacherous Monsieur de Climal. Both Marivaux's work and Richardson's first novel *Pamela; or, Virtue Rewarded* (1740) contain echoes of French heroic romance. Richardson and Marivaux each emphasize the importance of reflection. Both are interested in tracing the psychological trials produced by love. Both used the romance convention of the sudden revelation of a previously ambiguous love. "What a pity his heart is not as good as his appearance! – Why can't I hate him?" Pamela asks ([1740] 1985: 172). However, in contrast both to the heroic romance and to Haywood's *Adventures*, the most notable similarity between the stories is the low rank of both heroines. The aristocratic romance had been rewritten.

In adapting key features of French romance, Richardson challenged those who, like Haywood, replaced its idealism with portrayals of female sexual desire and political self-interest. His efforts reflect a deep unease. Horace Walpole, writing the first British Gothic romance, *The Castle of Otranto*, in 1764, could satirize with a light touch both fictions of Jacobite divine authority, popular attacks on his father, Robert, and accounts of ruthless sexuality. For Richardson, writing 20 years earlier, these secret histories created a more serious need for an alternative "new species" of writing. Taking both the didacticism and the psychological interest of other forms of romance, he created a narrative of sensibility, stripped of the uncontrolled fervor of passion in the works of Behn, Manley, and Haywood, and disciplined by the self-restraint of Christianity. For this new vehicle, in which private virtue and private passion were balanced, Richardson created an explicitly British model of romance that rejected "foreign" narratives of authority. In Richardson's story of Mr. B.'s attempts to seduce his virtuous serving-maid, Pamela, Mr. B.'s "horrid romancing" is connected with Switzerland and France (1, 156; 2, 110). In addition, his threats of "torture" and complaints of Pamela's "treasonable behaviour" are signs of his belief in "arbitrary" authority reminiscent of the Jacobite emphasis on divine right (1, 207). Foreign romances, misuse of authority, particularly the law, and the promotion of excessive consumerism, are all linked by Mr. B's actions. Nonetheless, his behavior is so resolutely bourgeois that he remains a largely comic figure. The heroism of the older romance is unsuited to him, as a comparison with Sir Philip Sidney's *Arcadia* illustrates. Like Sidney's work, *Pamela* contains various common features of romance, including cross-dressing. However, Mr. B's attempt to disguise himself as the serving-woman, Nan, in order to gain access to Pamela's bedchamber, is considerably less courtly than Pyrocles' Amazonian disguise in the *Arcadia* (1, 177–9). Mr B. lacks the stature to represent even the dark side of the aristocratic model.

Richardson reinforces the point by containing Mr. B.'s French romance within references to Sidney.[14] Richardson knew the *Arcadia*: in 1724–5 his firm printed the fourteenth edition of Sidney's *Works* (Beer 1989: 23). Like John Barclay's *Argenis* (1621), Sidney's pastoral romance combined an exploration of government with a humanist insistence on the excellences of character and gifts of speech necessary for public life. In *Pamela* Richardson adapts Sidney's model of romance as a guide to authority but, most important, in doing so he steers carefully between the idealism of the old form and the cynicism of the secret history. The narrative tries to establish that it is possible for power to be unaristocratic, unconnected with absolutism, without degenerating into self-interest. A significant part of this modification is Richardson's interest in the relation between public authority and private behavior in the middle and lower ranks. His title character shares her name with Sidney's more dignified heroine. "Pamela" had also been recognized by Biddy Tipkin in Richard Steele's *The Tender Husband* (1705) as a name which epitomized the high-ranking women of romance. Richardson's selection of it for his serving girl reflects his change in focus. By contrast to seventeenth-century French romance, the passions of the lower orders are taken seriously. However, in avoiding the idealism of the older form, Richardson brings bathos to the usual pastoral imagery (Doody 1974: 23–9). Pamela is, for example, prevented from escaping Mr. B.'s clutches by the presence of, not a bull, but "two poor Cows." This is an anticlimax even more extreme, considering the attack of a ferocious bear and a lion on the two princesses in the *Arcadia*. Although later the imagery becomes more pastoral, Pamela's origin, sometimes disguised, is never rewritten. In *Pamela II*, when Sir Jacob Swynford describes "Pamela" as "A *queer* sort of name! ... Linsey-woolsey – half one, half t'other – like thy girl," his comments operate as shorthand reminders of Pamela's birth (2, 163).

To avoid the threat to the social order and the charges of scheming that Haywood levelled at Walpole, Pamela, Mr. B, and other members of his society constantly revisit their anxiety over Pamela's origin. Reminded of her class, they are then brought to terms with it by her virtue and eloquence. Pamela's writing, evidence of both her desire and restraint, causes the hostile members of the upper ranks to relax their authority. In Sidney's *Arcadia* it is the aristocrats Musidorus and Pamela who are most aware of the politics of the letter, Musidorus struggling for expression, and Pamela wondering "Shall I ... second his boldness so far as to read his presumptuous letters?" (pp. 138–9). In Richardson's work, on the other hand, it is a woman of low class whose words are ultimately the most influential. As a result of her comparatively powerless social position, her love letters, traditional conveyors of emotional truth, appeal to the law of her country: "the torture is not used in England." However, these appeals are ultimately less important than the emotional power her virtue (and particularly the written evidence of it) yields. Written evidence succeeds in transforming Mr. B from a tyrant to a sympathetic judge – after their marriage "she stood before [Mr. B], as criminals ought to do before their judge, but said, 'I see, Sir ... less severity in your eyes than you affect to put on in your countenance'" (1, 203; 2, 73). Richardson emphasizes the importance of legal and economic safeguards, yet curbs his narrative's revolutionary content by indicating that the greatest guarantee of domestic order is the affective eloquence of Christian virtue. Both Sidney and Richardson use language as a signal of merit; however, whereas the French romances and Sidney's *Arcadia* implicitly assume that distinguished birth is the basis of this linguistically marked nobility, according to Richardson, "VIRTUE *is the only nobility*." Standing in for the female body, Pamela's letters ensure virtuous behavior but also (since this is a fiction legitimizing a commercial social order) fair trade. Pamela is correctly "rewarded."

As such, *Pamela* is cognizant with other attempts to construct new narratives of political authority in the face of eighteenth-century political satires and secret histories. John Barrell and Michael Meehan have both noted a need to rewrite the classical discourse of civic humanism, which proved unsatisfactory as a way of interpreting eighteenth-century politics because it suggested that fitness to participate in public life was linked with active heroism, and with a disinterestedness unavailable in mercantile Britain (Barrell 1986: 2; Meehan 1986). The aristocratic romance similarly needed an overhaul in the face of a growing emphasis on its political and sexual unavailability. Richardson's attempt simultaneously to provide this and tackle the prevalent cynicism, was, however, weakened from the outset. At the same time as denying the prevalence of self-interest, Richardson maintained the didactic technique of allowing his heroine to be "rewarded." This confusion of greed and the conventions of romance had been noted earlier in "An Antediluvian

Romance" (*The Spectator* nos. 584–5, Monday, August 23 1714, Wednesday, August 25, 1714).[15] Addison replaces the gentle providential system of rewards and punishments that generally operate in such narratives with a thoroughgoing emphasis on economic motivation. The parody remains ambiguous; it is unclear what relationship Addison is advocating between fictional depictions of morality and economic punishment and reward. However, his romance indicates the growing awareness of the problematic relation between the ideal and the financial. Given this preceding debate, Richardson's attempt was open to radical misreading from the start.

Pamela's identification of Christianized sensibility with commerce created a grand fictional controversy that had a profound effect on Richardson's later work.[16] *Pamela* was praised for promoting virtue; it was also attacked. Most famously, Henry Fielding's *An Apology for the Life of Mrs. Shamela Andrews* (1741) portrayed Richardson's heroine as a sexually active woman with no genuine virtue. Eliza Haywood's retributive rewriting in *Anti-Pamela* (1741) insisted on the financial self-interest and manipulating sexuality of her heroine, Syrena. Suspicious of *Pamela*'s economic and moral framework, detractors allied it with the very fiction from which Richardson had wished to distinguish it. A.W.'s *Enormous Abomination of the Hoop-Petticoat* (1745) complained at the lack of time spent considering "the Bible and other books of Religion" compared to the "Reading of *Plays, Pamelas, Novels, Romances,* nay *Tatlers* and SPECTATORS themselves." Similarly, in James Miller's comedy *The Picture* (1745), the father remarks: "These confounded Romances have been the Ruin of thee; I warrant thou canst say more of *Pamela*, or *Joseph Andrews*, than thy Catechism" (McKillop 1960: 81–2). Instead of being allied to religion and restraint, an authoritative rebuttal of the self-interested passion of Tory narrative, *Pamela* was placed in relation to a consumer culture of luxury and licentiousness. These were the very associations that had harmed both the French heroic romance and the fiction of Behn, Manley, and Haywood.

The *Pamela* controversy left Richardson acutely aware of the ambiguity which parody generates. Indeed, the use of romance conventions to support opposing agendas became part of the confusion (and disgrace) surrounding romance and its readers throughout the eighteenth century. Earlier the French heroic romance had used the maxim to define and limit its heroic code of love. Mary Davys and Eliza Haywood adapted this feature to entirely different ends in their amatory works. By reexamining the ideological use of fiction, and the maxim in particular, Richardson attempted to shelter his second epistolary novel, *Clarissa* (1747–8), from such misreading. As the heroine's persecution by her family, her experience of being "tricked off" by Lovelace, and her rape and eventual death are recounted, romance comes in for a share of criticism (1964: 83). However, Richardson indicates, a variety of other fictional forms are vulnerable to use as a method of self-justification, particularly when unsupported by Christianized sensibility. Like *Pamela*, *Clarissa* reinforces such sensibility with the language of profit, loss, and legality. Nonetheless, Richardson wished firmly to distinguish Clarissa's spiritual economics from more prosaic narratives of middle class self-interest, social aspiration, or aristocratic corruption.

If Marivaux had taken the convention of the *surprise de l'amour* from seventeenth-century romance and explored the effects of such self-deception in the area of pride, Richardson took the examination of self-deceit even further. By throwing into question all sources of advice on conduct, he highlighted the arbitrary element in any act of self-justification. In *Clarissa* Richardson's use of the maxim was extensive but arguably ironized. Most obviously and consistently sententious are the speeches of Lord M., who remarks that Clarissa is "the most accomplished of *women*, as everyone says; and what *every one says, must be true*" (II, 323; XCI). His utterances at once provide a foil to the more intelligent correspondents and hint at the facile nature of the maxims they cite as guides. Lovelace himself makes use of similar techniques, although his sources occasionally have higher status: some culled from a range of classical and contemporary dramatic sources; others, such as the rake's motto *"Once subdued, always subdued"* based partly on experience; still more given authority through supreme egotism (II, 326; XCII). Even Miss Howe adopts the use of the maxim, internalizing the language of romance to propose "I knew by experience that love is a fire that is not to be played with without burning one's fingers" (III, 8; I).[17]

This questioning of the maxim is part of a larger interrogation of the way literary models are used to provide excuses. Although Richardson himself wished *Clarissa* to be associated with Aristotelian tragedy rather than with romance, he also questions higher-status genres, notably classical learning. If at times, Richardson suggests, the romance offers a mode of conduct colored by too much idealism, the classics, typically associated with male readers, give too little. Amusing himself while his friend is dying, Mowbray finds in Belton's library "chiefly classical and dramatical," "a passage in Lee's *Oedipus*":

> When the *Sun Sets*, shadows that show'd at *noon*
> But small, appear most long and terrible:
> So when we think fate hovers o'er our heads,
> Our apprehensions shoot beyond all bounds.
>
> (IV, 150; LVIII)

When Mowbray attempts to use this to increase his friend's courage, his classically supported, unchristian stoicism is rejected and he turns to alcohol with another, now markedly bathetic, classical allusion: "Betty, bring me a bumper of claret; thy poor master and this damned Belford are enough to throw a Hercules into the vapors." The most disturbing product of classical learning, however, is Mr. Brand (forerunner of the clergyman Mr. Collins in Jane Austen's *Pride and Prejudice* [1813]), whose university education has made him pedantic, misogynistic, and wildly inaccurate. Inclined to the misuse of Latin tags and maxims, his learning leads him to rely on gossip and prejudice, as when he assumes Clarissa is Mr. Belford's mistress. Providing a model for Mr. Collins' rejection of romance in favor of the ineffectual Fordyce's *Sermons to Young Women* (1766), Brand began a trend. After Richardson, commentators on romance frequently expressed reservations about classical education, suggesting that, untempered by genuine Christianity, it promotes licentiousness to as great a degree as the romance.

Richardson indicates that the binary opposition of classical learning and romance degrades both men and women. In particular, it leads the classically educated male to underestimate the female romance-reader and, adopting the gallant conventions of romance, to debase himself in the attempt to disgrace her. Shortly before Mr. Brand's misuse of the classics, Morden criticizes romance, remarking to Lovelace:

> Men had generally too many advantages from the weakness, credulity and inexperience of the fair sex: that their early learning, which chiefly consisted in inflaming novels, and idle and improbable romances, contributed to enervate and weaken their minds. (IV, 220; LXXXI)

Morden's comments on female education (often cited as Richardson's own view on romance) are in fact clearly compromised both by his failure to recognize Clarissa's virtue and his status as a man of the world. His background makes it all too easy for him to adopt the standard assumption that women and the romance material they read are open to corruption; he himself has participated in amorous intrigues and been debased by them. Arguably, such contempt increases the danger of romance-reading for women since, as Anna Howe suggests, romance is likely to promote an incompatible desire for power. Observing the supposed female preference for the hero over "sober fellows" such as Hickman, she comments: "As may be observed in [women's] reading; which turns upon difficulties encountered, battles fought, and enemies overcome, four or five hundred by the prowess of one single hero, the *more* improbable the better in short, that their man should be a hero to every one living but themselves; and to them know no bound to his humility" (I, 243; XLVI). This connection between romance and unthinking slavery later became a trope commonplace among radicals in the debate after the French Revolution, but for Richardson the influence of classical literature was equally questionable.

Having mitigated the romance association with licentiousness, Richardson both utilized the form's idealism and indicated its mimetic value. Like later commentators who found the rhetoric of romance a potential vehicle to describe oppression, Richardson used its motifs to depict social injury. Like Jane Austen in *Northanger Abbey* (1818), even while Richardson criticizes the deceptive hyperbole of romance, he shows the resonance of its motifs of persecution and flight. Richardson points out the real potential for tyranny by parents and the possibility of capture and imprisonment.[18] In addition, he insists on the romance element of the ideal, most strongly represented through the narrative of Christian virtue. When Clarissa briefly escapes from Lovelace, he rages:

> Purchased by a painful servitude of many months; fighting through the wild beasts of her family for her, and combating with a wind-mill virtue, which hath cost me millions of perjuries only to attempt; and which now, with its damned air-fans has tossed me a mile and an half beyond hope! (III, 518; CXXIX)

Lovelace compares his struggle against Clarissa's virtue to Don Quixote's fight against the windmills which the knight, interpreting by the rules of romance, has mistaken for giants. In attempting to place Clarissa's virtue within a parody of romance, however, Lovelace paradoxically reaffirms it – Clarissa's virtue is not an illusory "windmill" but, by implication, has the ideal quality sought by Don Quixote.

After establishing the ideal elements of the romance, Richardson protects them from the kind of misinterpretation *Pamela* had suffered by contrasting them with more self-interested frameworks of value. In contrast to *Pamela*, *Clarissa* constructs a spiritual narrative of profit and loss, reward and punishment, while insisting on the weakness of other, more prosaic economies which value wealth, status, or luxury. The middle ranks are condemned for their confusion of financial with moral good in their desperation to gain money – the mercenary Harlowes read Mr. Solmes's willingness to settle his estates on Clarissa as virtuous, whereas Clarissa interprets it as an *immoral* lack of duty and consideration. Similarly, Richardson emphasizes the dangers of aspiration to the middle ranks. In the final pages of the novel, the education of Polly Horton, the prostitute, is outlined. Directed by her mother, her reading of "romances and novels, songs and plays, and those without distinction, moral or immoral" leads her to identify with "every heroine" and adopt an affected rhetoric of social aspiration. The result is moral disaster when she is seduced by Lovelace. Finally, representing aristocratic decadence and much sought-after luxury, Lovelace states that "My predominant passion is *Girl*, not *Gold*" (III, 63). Possessing enough money no longer to care or account for it (generosity is an important trait in his character), he has ceased to audit his actions spiritually. In contrast, Clarissa avoids both the excessive middle-class measuring of money and Lovelace's failure to account adequately for cash or time spent. Instead, she follows a spiritual economy, constantly measuring the cost not in fiscal but in moral terms. Richardson is careful that Clarissa's virtue is not tarnished by financial considerations. In returning her estate to her before she dies, he makes it clear that she dies because of principle rather than out of financial need, avoiding the possibility of "Mandevillian misread[ing]" that had occurred with *Pamela* (Richardson 1964: 43). In *Clarissa* the only system of economy worth observing is spiritual; all others are faulty, and call for spurious non-Christian frameworks of self-justification. Yet, as in Richardson's earlier novel, Clarissa's sensibility is the ultimate guarantee. The heroine's spiritual economy is justified, not only by the Bible, but by recourse to her heart. Unlike other systems of self-justification, it is uniquely private. The reader's virtue is confirmed, as Mr. B.'s is, by his or her emotional reaction. As Henry Fielding uncharacteristically put it, "Let the Overflowings of a Heart which you have filled brimfull speak for me...I...melt with Compassion, and find what is called an Effeminate Relief for my Terror."[19] A humane social order is reinforced by the disinterested sensibility of the private citizen.

Charles Grandison (1753–4) continues this romance based on the profit and loss of the spirit, by adjusting the concept of hero to one suitable for eighteenth-century Britain. On certain levels *Grandison*'s deployment of romance is similar to that in Richardson's earlier work. Superficially, the rhetoric associated with romance is unfavorable, connected with mistaken sensibility – Harriet Byron, arguing against women marrying too young, suggests that a woman's "fluttering, her romantic age...is over by twenty-four...and she is then fit to take her resolutions, and to settle" (1, 109). Similarly, Mrs Shirley, considering Clementina's behavior, reveals that, in her youth, she "had romantic notions" of love and happiness as a result of reading romances such as "*Cassandra* and *The Princess of Cleves.*" As she confesses, "I was over-run with the absurdities of that unnatural kind of writing" (6, 223). Alongside such warnings, however, as elsewhere, Richardson utilizes the techniques of romance.

Most important, he establishes links between the idyllic pastorals of romance and ethical, prudent living. When Harriet Byron goes to the masquerade her dress is established as a parody of Arcadianism:

> They call it the dress of an Arcadian Princess: But it falls not in with any of my notions of the Pastoral dress of Arcadia.
> A White Paris net sort of cap, glittering with spangles, and incircled by a chaplet of artificial flowers, with a little white feather perking from the left ear, is to be my head-dress.
> My masque is Venetian.
> My hair is to be complimented with an appearance, because of its natural ringlets, as they call my curls, and to shade my neck.
> Tucker and ruffles blondlace. (1, 115)

The dress suggests an international but inappropriate consumerism. Its insensitive jumble of styles signals that Harriet is in moral danger, a warning fulfilled when, after the masque, she is abducted by Sir Hargrave Pollexfen. The episode indicates that international consumerism leads to luxury and that, as in *Clarissa*, the hallmark of such degradation is a corrupt view of romance. Harriet, passively dressed by others, ultimately escapes danger, but Pollexfen is one of a number of aristocrats in whom an incorrect notion of the genre is accompanied by an unfortunate economic and spiritual obtuseness. Like those who chose Harriet's dress, Pollexfen misuses the terms of romance, calling Grandison a "*Quixote*" for his honorable behavior (2, 254). The language of romance is also used pejoratively by Sir Charles' fashionably corrupt father, Sir Thomas. When the eminently suitable Lord L. asks for his daughter's hand in marriage, her father's worry is that: "Both his daughters would now be set a romancing" (2, 324). Yet he himself is a "*slave* to [the love of pleasure], and to what he called *freedom*" (2, 320).

In contrast, Richardson places Sir Charles who, as Harriet Byron's description immediately suggests, has the aristocratic appearance required in romance: "In his aspect there is something great and noble, that shews him to be of rank. Were kings to be chosen for beauty and majesty of person, Sir Charles would have few competitors" (1, 181). His name recalls William Villiers, Viscount Grandison, one of the leading Royalists in the Civil War, whom, as Margaret Ann Doody points out (1974: 249), Clarendon praises as "a young Man of so virtuous a habit of mind, that no temptation or provocation could corrupt him . . . and of that rare Piety and Devotion, that the Court, or Camp, could not shew a more faultless person." This reference suggests a British tradition of loyalty and virtue. Sir Charles's "value" is as a moral hero, as Charlotte recognizes:

> Once Miss Grandison, speaking of her brother, said, My brother is valued by those who know him best, not so much for being an handsome man; not so much for his birth and fortune; nor for this or that single worthiness; as for being, in the great and yet comprehensive sense of the word, a *good man*. (1, 182)

Crucially, a large part of his virtue consists of a sense of moderation. In both his behavior generally and in his personal expenditure he is prudent (1, 209; 1, 183). Unlike his cousin who gambles, Sir Charles invests. This attitude is typified in their reactions to the masquerade. While Sir Charles disapproves of its effects spreading down the social scale, his brother comments:

> Well, Sir Charles, and why should not the poor devils in *low life* divert themselves as well as their betters? For my part, I rejoice when I see advertised an eighteen-peny masquerade, for all the pretty 'prentice souls, who will that evening be Arcadian Shepherdesses, Goddesses and Queens. (2, 428)

Despite their superficially attractive libertarianism, Mr. Grandison's remarks illustrate that he has no concern for the economic or moral well-being of the lower ranks – indeed, as a rake, he represents a threat to them. Sir Charles, on the other hand, described by his sister as "knight-errant," refers to people as "property" that must be cared for, and comments that he at first gives new acquaintance a "short lease only in [his] good opinion," thus preserving his "charity, and . . . complacency" (2, 428). Financial and spiritual prudence are intimately connected, producing a private happiness that is conducive to public health. However, Sir Charles remarks: "And yet, by what I have seen, abroad, and now lately since my arrival, at home . . . I cannot but think, that Englishmen are not what they were. A wretched effeminacy seems to prevail among them" (3, 10). Sir Charles' remarks imply that this "effeminacy" is a foreign contagion; unlike later romance characters, including Falkland in William Godwin's *Caleb Williams* (1794), he resists the influence of supposedly older ideals of romantic honor, often associated with southern Europe and represented by dueling. For Grandison, the revenge ethic and its accompanying passion and violence are essentially un-British.

Richardson's insistence on the connection between prudence, restraint, and British virtue was to have a lasting influence on romance, partly due to the reaction against the French writer, Jean-Jacques Rousseau. While Richardson's reputation was, as McKillop put it (1960: 226), "international," in Britain a growing unease concerning Rousseau's epistolary novel *La Nouvelle Héloïse* (1803) generated renewed critical interest in the earlier writer. Although Rousseau himself never acknowledged any direct debt to Richardson, the critics were keen to make the comparison, particularly as the moral tendency of Rousseau's sentiment came under suspicion.[20] Most troubling was the first part of Rousseau's novel, in which the youthful Julie (Heloïse) has a sexual relationship with her tutor, St. Preux. St. Preux travels to Paris, where his experiences suggest the corruption of luxurious city life beside the comparatively innocent pastoral environment he has left. In the meantime, however, Julie conforms to her father's wishes and becomes a faithful wife to Wolmar. St. Preux, eventually returning from self-imposed exile, becomes the platonic friend of the newly dutiful Julie. For critics including Clara Reeve, the novel would have been better had Rousseau concentrated on the sections emphasizing self-restraint. In fact, as it stands, unlike Richardson's socially effective (if at times racy) sentiment, Rousseau's tantalizing account connects a sexualized sensibility, however briefly, with individualism. Rousseau's defenders claimed that this story might operate as a corrective to the French women who were inclined to licentiousness once married. However, in England it became associated with Rousseau's potentially revolutionary politics – the sexual danger to young women reading the novel would not only cause their corruption but also damage the state. Rousseau's narrative presents a threat to the Richardsonian fiction that British society rests on and is legitimized by affective ties assured through (economic and sexual) prudence.

Richardsonian sensibility itself seemed in need of defense or adjustment. Frances Brooke, for example, distances herself from Richardson but shows his influence in *Emily Montague* (1769) and *The Excursion* (1777); in both she adds a healthy dose of comedy and anti-sentimentality, protecting her reader from both the excessive idealism associated with romance and Rousseau's sexualized vision. Similarly, Elizabeth Griffiths in *The Delicate Distress* (1769) employs the epistolary technique along with a Richardsonian sensibility, but provides decidedly practical advice on how a woman should manage a husband she suspects of infidelity. A more fruitful path was suggested by Clara Reeve in *The Progress of Romance*. Attempting to distance romance from the French influence so often connected with rampant consumerism, licentiousness, and effeminacy, she evokes nostalgia for a hardier Gothic past. As Richardson does in *Grandison*, she makes this alternative implicitly British. Even in the 1790s, when the rhetoric of romance became politicized by association, not only with Rousseau, but with Edmund Burke's chivalric defence of Marie Antoinette (1968: 179), the notion of a British romance remained relatively untainted. In *Belinda* (1801), for example, Maria Edgeworth connected romance with slavery, irrationality, and radical (French) politics through the figure of Harriet Freke. The book's model family, however, are called the Percivals, suggesting a post-Enlightenment romance suitable for a rational Britain; similarly, in *Helen* (1834) Continental travel is connected with illicit romance, while one of the most morally upright (if inflexible) characters is entitled General Clarendon. The same Richardsonian influence sheds light on that critically debated reference to "English verdure, English culture, English comfort" in Jane Austen's *Emma* (1816: 3, 98). Although the novel's

French romance heritage is suggested by Austen's use of the *surprise de l'amour*, her hero's name, George Knightley, proclaims even more explicitly than "Sir Charles Grandison" that Austen is calling upon English heritage to reconstruct the romance (p. 199).

It is a critical commonplace that romance, particularly in prose, was awkwardly positioned in the eighteenth century. In part, this was due to its connection with an exaggerated idealism and concentration on love. In part, the Tory narratives of political passion hastened the downgrading of the extravagant emotion of the French heroic romance; aside from associations with Jacobitism, romance was often connected with self-interest, the arbitrary use of power, luxury, and licentiousness. Richardson attempted to adjust romance, retaining its idealism while urging the importance of legal and economic constrictions. Its private passions, tainted with anti-Walpole satire and accusations of self-interest, were rewritten, placed in a context of restraint; heroism was redefined in terms of spiritual and moral prudence. However, as well as generating disturbing sadomasochistic overtones, Richardson's emphasis on restraint, when applied to financial matters, was difficult to integrate into romance. Not only did it make his work a target for satirists, it also meant that most of his followers who tried to retain it (Clara Reeve, for example, in *Destination* [1799]) did not fully succeed. Consequently, one main strand of Richardson's legacy became sensibility, the passion and idealism of romance more successfully portrayed than the prudence. As such, the romance remained relatively low-status, its symbolism pervasive but contentious. Its influence was particularly marked in those genres neglected by most twentieth-century critics – the Gothic, the novel of sensibility, and the writings of the debate after the French Revolution. It was left to Austen to balance Richardson's model of spiritual restraint with the economic prudence implicit within his romance. As such, she provides the quintessential English romance that Richardson had attempted to create. Sir Walter Scott offers an alternative, his work revisiting Richardson's difficulties. For Scott romance remains associated with Jacobitism, arbitrary authority, and the French influence, but belongs to a sublime past; legal and economic restraints form the unromantic present. Unlike Richardson's, Scott's account suggests that romance and the modern social contract belong to different historical phases. In fiction they can coexist but they cannot be successfully united.

See also: chapter 7, Gendering Prose Romance in Renaissance England; chapter 8, Sidney and Spenser; chapter 12, "Gothic" Romance; chapter 13, Women's Gothic Romance; chapter 14, Paradise and Cotton-mill; chapter 21, Victorian Romance: Romance and Mystery; chapter 27, Romance in Fantasy; chapter 28, Quest Romance in Science Fiction; chapter 30, Popular Romance and its Readers.

Notes

1. Samuel Richardson, *Letters Written to and for Particular Friends* (1741), XCVI (142).

2. See also Barbauld's "On Romances," University of Pennsylvania, 20th June 2000, http://www.english.upenn.edu/~mgamer/Romantic/barbauldessays.html#.

3. Crucial to the debate is Ian Watt, *The Rise of the Novel* (1957), p. 298; subsequently Watt. See also critics replying to and adjusting Watt, for example, Michael McKeon (1987: 20).

4. Determination to praise realism leads to the downplaying of the romance's influence upon Richardson. See, for example, A. D. McKillop (1960: 152), and Ronald Paulson (1967: 24).

5. *Letters Written to and for Particular Friends* LXXXIX (123–4), LXXXIII (114), LXXIX (112).

6. *Letters Written to and for Particular Friends* CXLVII (206).

7. As both critical debate and Richardson's imprecision in referring to "romance-writing" and the novel suggest, the usage of the terms was not always consistent. See Williams 1970: 8.

8. See Arthur Johnston (1964) for a fuller account of romance criticism in France.

9. [Pierre Daniel] Huet, *A Treatise of Romances and Their Original: Translated out of French* (1672). Huet describes it as "truly a subject of wonder," that, despite the loss of the "Bayes for Epick Poesie and History, we have carried these to so high a pitch, that the best of their Romances do not equal the very meanest of ours" (103). English editions of Huet 1672, 1715, 1720; original date of publication 1670.

10. Charlotte Lennox, *The Female Quixote*, ed. Margaret Dalziel, introd. Margaret Ann Doody (Oxford: Oxford University Press, 1998), p. 9; the novel was read, approved, and printed by Richardson.

11. Henry Seymour Conway to Horace Walpole, 18 April 1745, in *The Yale Edition of Horace Walpole's Correspondence*, 37, p. 189.

12. The *Adventures of Eovaai, Princess of Ijaveo* was reissued in 1739 as *The Unfortunate Prince: or the Life and Surprising Adventures of the Princess of Ijaveo: Interspersed with several curious and entertaining Novels* (London: Hodges), I, 38.

13. Samuel Richardson, *Selected Letters*, ed. John Carroll (1964) p. 85. See also his letter to Aaron Hill (late January 1741) and Johannes Stinstra (June 2nd 1753) in which Richardson explains the origins for *Pamela* in a way which discounts any influence from French fiction (pp. 39–41, 228–35, particularly p. 232).

14. Sir Philip Sidney, *The Countess of Pembroke's Arcadia (The Old Arcadia)*, ed. Katherine Duncan-Jones (1999).

15. Joseph Addison, *Works* (1854–6).

16. The expression is used in the title of *The Pamela Controversy*, ed. Keymer and Sabor (2001); see that for a full account and reprints of the response to *Pamela*.

17. Broadly deconstructionist readings which emphasis the battle for control of meaning within the text include Terry Castle, *Clarissa's Ciphers* (1982), and William B. Warner, *Reading Clarissa: The Struggles of Interpretation* (1979).

18. Other minor motifs also suggest the underpinning romance: James Harlowe's plot to kidnap his sister by employing the sea captain; Lovelace's fantasy of capturing Anna Howard and her party when they journey to the Isle of Wight; Lovelace's self-fictionalization and his fantasies of cross-dressing.

19. Henry Fielding to Samuel Richardson, 15 October 1748, in Fielding 1993.

20. See McKillop 1960: 232–3 for details of the relevant reviews.

References and Further Reading

Addison, Joseph (1854–6). *The Works of Joseph Addison: With Notes by Richard Hurd D.D.* 6 vols. London: Bohn.

[Austen, Jane] (1816). *Emma: A Novel in three volumes.* By the author of *Pride and Prejudice.* 3 vols. London: John Murray.

Ballaster, R. (1992). *Seductive Forms: Women's Amatory Fiction from 1684–1740.* Oxford: Clarendon Press.

Barbauld, Anna Letitia [Aikin] (1810). *The British Novelists; With an Essay; and Prefaces, Biographical and Critical.* 50 vols. London: Rivington [and others].

Barbauld, Anna Letitia (2000). "On Romances." University of Pennsylvania. 20th June 2000. http://www.english.upenn.edu/~mgamer/Romantic/barbauldessays.html#.

Barrell, John (1986). *The Political Theory of Painting from Reynolds to Hazlitt: "The Body of the Public."* New Haven: Yale University Press.

Beasley, Jerry C. (1976). "Romance and the 'new' novels of Richardson, Fielding and Smollett." *Studies in English Literature* 16, 437–50.

Beer, Gillian (1989). "Pamela: Rethinking Arcadia." In Margaret Anne Doody and Peter Sabor, eds., *Samuel Richardson: Tercentenary Essays.* Cambridge: Cambridge University Press, pp. 23–9.

Burgess, Miranda J. (2000). *British Fiction and the Production of the Social Order, 1740–1830.* Cambridge: Cambridge University Press.

Burke, Edmund (1968). *Reflections on the Revolution in France*, ed. Conor Cruise O'Brien. Penguin: Harmondsworth. {First published in 1790.}

Castle, Terry (1982). *Clarissa's Ciphers.* Ithaca, NY: Cornell University Press.

Dalziel, Margaret (1970). "Richardson and Romance." *Journal of the Australasian Universities Language and Literature Association* 33, 5–24.

Doody, Margaret Anne (1974). *A Natural Passion: A Study of the Novels of Samuel Richardson.* Oxford: Clarendon Press.

Fielding, Henry (1993). *The Correspondence of Henry and Sarah Fielding*, ed. Martin C. Battestin and Clive T. Probyn. Oxford: Clarendon Press.

Huet, [Pierre Daniel]. (1672). *A Treatise of Romances and Their Original: Translated out of French.*

London: Heyrick. [Original work published in 1670.]

Johnston, Arthur. (1964). *Enchanted Ground: The Study of Medieval Romance in the Eighteenth Century.* London: Athlone Press.

Keymer, Thomas, and Peter Sabor, eds. (2001). *The Pamela Controversy: Criticisms and Adaptations of Samuel Richardson's* Pamela, *1740-1750.* 6 vols. London: Pickering and Chatto.

La Calprenède, Gauthier de Costas (1736). *Hymen's Praeludia: Or, Love's Master-piece. Being that so-much-admir'd romance, intitled, Cleopatra*, trans. Robert Loveday. London: Watson. [Original work published in 1647.]

McKeon, Michael (1987). *The Origins of the English Novel, 1600–1740.* Baltimore, MD: Johns Hopkins University Press.

McKillop, A. D. (1960). *Samuel Richardson: Printer & Novelist.* Hamden, CT: Shoe String Press.

Meehan, Michael (1986). *Liberty and Poetics in Eighteenth Century England.* London: Croom.

Miller, Henry Knight (1976). "Augustan Prose Fiction and the Romance Tradition." In R. F. Brissenden and J. C. Eade, eds., *Studies in the Eighteenth Century III. Papers presented at the Third David Nichol Smith Memorial Seminar, Canberra.* Toronto: University of Toronto Press, pp. 241–55.

Munro, James S. (1975). "Richardson, Marivaux, and the French Romance Tradition." *Modern Language Review* 70, 752–9.

Paulson, Ronald (1967). *Satire and the Novel in Eighteenth-Century England.* New Haven: Yale University Press.

Ramsay, Andrew (1727). *The Travels of Cyrus; To which is Annex'd a Discourse upon the Theology and Mythology of the Ancients.* London: Woodward and Pearce.

Reeve, Clara (1785). *The Progress of Romance, through Times, Countries and Manners; With Remarks on the Good and Bad Effects of It, on them Respectively; In a Course of Evening Conversations.* 2 vols. Colchester: Keymer; [London]: Robinson.

Richardson, Samuel (1741). *Letters Written to and for Particular Friends, on the Most Important Occasions. Directing not only the Requisite Style and*

Forms to be Observed in Writing Familiar Letters; But how to Think and Act Justly and Prudently in the Common Concerns of Human Life. London: Rivington; Osborn; Bath: Leake.

Richardson, Samuel (1967). *Clarissa or, the History of a Young Lady,* ed. John Butt. 4 vols. London: Dent; New York: Dutton. [First published in 1747–8.]

Richardson, Samuel (1985). *Pamela; or Virtue Rewarded,* ed. Peter Sabor. Harmondsworth: Penguin. [First published in 1740.]

Richardson, Samuel (1964). *Selected Letters of Samuel Richardson,* ed. John Carroll. Oxford: Clarendon Press.

Rousseau, Jean-Jacques (1989). *Eloisa, or a Series of Original Letters,* trans. William Kendrick, 1803. 2 vols. Revolution and Romanticism, 1789–1834: A Series of Fascimile Reprints. Oxford:

Woodstock. [Original work published in 1761.]

Sidney, Sir Philip (1999). *The Countess of Pembroke's Arcadia (The Old Arcadia),* ed. Katherine Duncan-Jones. Oxford: Oxford University Press.

Walpole, Horace (1937–83), *The Yale Edition of Horace Walpole's Correspondence,* ed. W. S. Lewis et al. 48 vols. New Haven: Yale University Press.

Warner, William B. (1979). *Reading Clarissa: The Struggles of Interpretation.* New Haven: Yale University Press.

Watt, Ian (1957). *The Rise of the Novel: Studies in Defoe, Richardson and Fielding.* London: Hogarth.

Williams, Ian, ed. (1970) *Novel and Romance, 1700–1800: A Documentary Record.* London: Routledge.

16
Romance and the Romantic Novel: Sir Walter Scott

Fiona Robertson

The main subject of this essay, with Spenser and Morris one of Northrop Frye's "three major centers" of the romance tradition in English (1976: 6), was uniquely important in the history of romance. A first-rate scholar, critic, and textual editor, steeped from boyhood in medieval and Renaissance tales and committed throughout his life to promulgating and interpreting them for a much wider audience, Walter Scott also had the creative and technical brilliance to reassert the place of romance at the heart of a literary culture, nationally and internationally. To read Scott is to be made aware of the strong shaping force of stories in a wider culture, and in literary history. It is fitting, then, that the period in which he was so prominent has been modeled along fictional lines of special interest to readers and historians of romance. The retrospective delineation of the "Romantic Period" is clear proof of the strong narrative drive of romance: bounded, in Frye's terms, by a rebirth-death (the French Revolution: 1789) and by a death-rebirth (Scott's death and the passing of the first Reform Act: 1832), a 40-year period has been marked out as a special world caught between eighteenth-century and Victorian rationalism and materialism. Conceptions, and misconceptions, of the period stem partly from our sublimated sense of it as a form of the enchanted, removed, or heightened worlds and interludes found in many romances. Medieval and Renaissance "romance" may be the ghost form of "Romanticism," but it is also permanently inflected by the writings of Scott and his contemporaries.

The argument of this essay takes shape from two episodes – one factual, one fictitious – which I hope to use to suggest the blurred boundaries of the romance world in texts and in literary histories. In 1831, near the end of Scott's life, Sir Frederic Madden of the British Museum wrote to him with news of an important discovery, that of the Museum's manuscript Cotton Nero A x, which Madden had begun to transcribe, and which contains the only extant copy of *Sir Gawain and the Green Knight* (along with *Pearl*, *Patience*, and *Cleanness*). Madden offered to edit *Gawain* for the Bannatyne Club. Madden's communication left Scott keen to secure this "great curiosity," which he described in letters to friends as "an old Scottish romance" and "supposed to [be] written by Clerk of Tranent lamented in the poem of the Makers by Dunbar" (Scott 1932–7: 11, 494–5). When he visited London in October 1831 before sailing for Malta, his researches in the British Museum were dominated by work toward a new edition of his novel *Woodstock*, and his *Journal* makes no mention of his taking this opportunity to read *Gawain*. The Bannatyne Club eventually published Madden's edition of the romance in 1839, seven years after Scott's death. The episode is a reminder of the complex transmission history of individual romances and of some ironies faced by interpreters and historians of romance. For the Middle English text that seems most in keeping with the elements of Scott's work explored in this essay is *Sir Gawain and the Green Knight*, the one romance he could not have known while he was writing his novels. And what can only be called a strong imaginative and critical affinity is not at all the pattern into which Scott tried to fit *Gawain* (that of a specifically Scottish "lost text"). I shall be examining two particular links between the technical conventions and experiments of texts like *Gawain* and those of "the Wizard of the North" later in this essay: Scott's use of hunting scenes and of the narrative form of *entrelacement* or narrative interlace.

The fictitious episode, liminal in a different way, comes from Scott's third novel, *The Antiquary* (1816). The central figure in this novel, Jonathan Oldbuck, has as his study in Monkbarns a cluttered, jumbled "sanctum sanctorum" ("holy of holies"), the walls of which are hung with a "grim old tapestry" depicting the wedding of Gawain and the Loathly Lady. This detail (a jest at the expense of the avowedly misogynist bachelor) is characteristic of the mass of brief references to romance tales in the Waverley Novels, and also prepares for a more sinister scene in which Oldbuck's young friend, Lovel, spends the night in the haunted Green Chamber of Monkbarns. The Green Chamber (like the Green Knight, suggestive of the natural world), is presided over by another grim old Flemish tapestry depicting hunting scenes and embroidered with extracts from *The Floure and the Leafe* (in Scott's time thought to be by Chaucer) and from the dream sequence of Chaucer's *Book of the Duchess*. Caught up in nightmares, Lovel thinks himself a bird, then a fish: hunted creatures, they suggest that underneath the ostensible cause of his restlessness (his rescue of Sir Arthur and Isabella Wardour) lies a paranoid insecurity. Eventually the tapestry rustles the hunt into life, "with all the fury of the chace," and from it steps one figure whose bugle-horn turns into an ancient book ([1816] 1995: 79). Lovel wakes with the motto "Kunst macht gunst" ("art wins favor") impressed on his memory. In *The Secular Scripture*, Northrop Frye (1976: 109) refers to this episode during his discussion of "the pictures, tapestries, and statues which so often turn up near the beginning of a romance to indicate the threshold of the romance world." Noting that the episode was an important influence on William Morris, Frye reads it in terms of "metamorphosis dreams" and as a stage in the hero's discovery of his mother. But he firmly distinguishes it from what he calls a "more complex level" of "novels with a symbolic visual emblem" (*The Scarlet Letter*, *The Golden Bowl*). *The Secular Scripture* has its origins, as Frye tells us, in an "abandoned" essay on Walter Scott (the term recalls the abandoned steamboat, the "Walter Scott," in Mark Twain's *Huckleberry Finn*), and the heroes, heroines – light (practical, domestic) and dark (virginal, quixotic), plot structures, and resolutions of Scott's fiction are a constant point of reference, despite Frye's disparagement of what he sees as the purely narrative comforts of Scott's "stagecoach style" (1976: 5). Frye has had an entirely beneficial impact on studies of Scott, but his reading of the Green Chamber episode disavows emblematic complexity, an aspect of Scott's work which remains neglected, but which was crucial to its influence on romancers as various as Tennyson, the Brontës, the Rossettis, Morris, and Stevenson.

Discussing the continuity of human passions in different stages of society in the first chapter of his first novel, *Waverley* (1814), Scott elaborates (1986: 5):

> Upon these passions it is no doubt true that the state of manners and laws casts a necessary colouring; but the bearings, to use the language of heraldry, remain the same, though the tincture ["gules" in the past, "sable" in the present] may be not only different, but opposed in strong contradistinction.

Critics tend to take his meaning and ignore his figure of speech. But Scott's interest in color, in formal patterns approximating to the rules of heraldry, and in visual metaphor, are part of his response to medieval and Renaissance romance. Scott is only superficially, and sometimes stylistically, a haphazard writer; only in part, too, a mere "story-teller" in E. M. Forster's dismissive formulation (1927: 33). He is a much-underestimated constructor of set-piece scenes and of moments of heightened visual and symbolic suggestion which set up insistent, even imprisoning, patterns within avowedly loose, meandering narrative prose. Everything in Scott evokes dynamism and change, even if the social and intellectual movements he describes remain, as Frye perceptively detects, "caught" in the cycles of history (1976: 164). In fact Scott is also a very still, formal, and consciously "composed" writer.

The study of romance links Scott's earliest and latest literary interests. Before he was 10 years old, he had collected over 100 chapbooks, many of them retelling tales from romance; later in life he was to collect over 2,000. In the "General Preface" to the collected Waverley Novels (the so-called Magnum Opus edition, 1829–33) he recalls childhood days in Edinburgh in which he and a friend "told, in turn, interminable tales of knight-errantry and battles and enchantments, which were continued from one day to another as opportunity offered" (1, iii). "Spenser I could have read for ever," he emphasizes (1, 50); and Ariosto and Tasso, whose works he read in translation as a child, inspired him to learn Italian and to read voraciously in a wide range of Italian literature. The passion continued throughout his life. His manuscript *Commonplace Book*, kept from 1792 to about 1803 (now in the National Library of Scotland) includes notes on Arthur, Italian poetry, romance, and assorted antiquities. More practically, it was through his efforts that the Advocates' Library in Edinburgh acquired in 1806 a manuscript containing *Sir Gowther*, *Sir Isumbras*, *Sir Amadace*, and *The Huntyng of the Hare*: the manuscript (MS 19. 3. 1) has a list of contents in his hand. And although we cannot tell whether he read *Sir Gawain and the Green Knight* before his voyage to Malta in 1831, he certainly worked on romance manuscripts during his stay there, in spite of his conspicuously failing health. At the end of January 1832 (he died in September that year) he recorded in his journal (1972: 698) that he was transcribing a manuscript of *Bevis of Hampton* in the Royal Library of Naples, for a planned reprint by the Roxburghe Club. The results of this lifetime's work are everywhere in his novels. In *The Heart of Mid-Lothian* he compares his digressive style to that of Ariosto; Frank Osbaldistone, hero of *Rob Roy*, translates *Orlando Furioso*; witch figures throughout the novels are invariably negotiated through Spenser; Tasso, Spenser, Froissart, and Cervantes are points of reference from *Waverley* in 1814 to *Count Robert of Paris* in 1832; a key chapter (32) in *Kenilworth: A Romance* begins with a quotation from Boiardo's *Orlando Innamorato*; characters and narrators alike refer to Tristrem, Arthur, Bevis, Colbrand, Gan, Merlin, Morgan la Fay, Ryence. In some novels, discussed later in this essay, romance is the key to structure and meaning and a way of exploring the changing relationship between the romancer and the readership for which he writes.

Before turning in detail to a range of Scott's novels and to a discussion of how they interact creatively with the patterns and conventions of romance, this essay considers, first, the wider fortunes of romance in the prose works of the Romantic Period, and, second, the importance of Scott's work as an editor and critic of romance.

The status of romance in the Romantic Period is complex aesthetically and politically. "Kidnapped" in Frye's sense ("romance formulas used to reflect certain ascendant religious or social ideals," that is, in the service of an ideology) (1976: 30) romance was also kidnapped formally. Politically, Edmund Burke had thrown down the gauntlet in *Reflections on the Revolution in France* (1790): "the age of chivalry is gone" (1968: 170). In *Caleb Williams* (1794), William Godwin specifically targeted an excessive attachment to the codes of chivalry and romance in the figure of Falkland, whose mind is "fraught with all the rhapsodies of visionary honour" (9). Anticipating several of Scott's heroes, Falkland's enthusiasm begins in youth with a deep love for the heroic poems of Italy; he pens an "Ode to the Genius of Chivalry." Unlike any of Scott's heroes, he murders and lets others hang for his crime because he is "too deeply pervaded with the idle and groundless romances of chivalry" and "the lustration which the laws of knight-errantry prescribe" (97) to overlook a public humiliation. ("Unlike" Scott's heroes, that is, because the novel's narrator stands firm about the "poison of chivalry" [326]; the heroes of the Waverley Novels are increasingly darkly caught up in the guilt of the illegalities they perform "passively," and they are rescued rather than redeemed.) Other novelists of the 1790s approach romance more equivocally, as Charlotte Smith does in *The Old Manor House* (also 1794) with its "true heir" Orlando Somerive. The most decisive refashioning of Burke's denunciation of modern society, however, comes in the work of Thomas Love Peacock. In *Melincourt* (1817), a love of Italian poetry and of Tasso in particular unites the romantic enthusiasts Anthelia Melincourt and Sylvan Forester, both of whom are mocked by pragmatic friends for having unrealistic ideas about love. "The age of chivalry is gone," the Honourable Mrs Pinmoney chides Anthelia, who replies "It is, but its spirit survives" (1948: 1, 113). That spirit lies in "disinterested benevolence": it is social, active, useful. In a chapter pointedly entitled "The Spirit of Chivalry" Anthelia maintains that "the spirit of the age of chivalry, manifested in the forms of modern life, would constitute the only character on which she could fix her affections" (1, 146). The novel is full of allusions to romance: to Valentine and Orson, to the Squire of Dames, to *Orlando Furioso*. It contains an updated type of the Savage Man in Sir Oran Haut-Ton and a risqué joke about the girdle of Florimel. Although Forester declares that "Italian poetry is all fairyland: I know not any description of literature so congenial to the tenderness and delicacy of the female mind" (1, 187), this novel places its faith in such a land and in the female mind. Comparable reworkings can be found in Peacock's other romances, *The Misfortunes of Elphin* (1829) and *Maid Marian*, published in 1822 but finished, apart from the last three chapters, in 1818, before the publication of *Ivanhoe*. Based on Joseph Ritson's *Robin Hood, a collection of all the ancient poems, songs, and ballads now extant relative to that celebrated outlaw* (1795), *Maid Marian* insists that romance speaks not for dead tradition and aristocratic restriction but for liberty of thought and action.

If, as these examples suggest, romance was part of a political debate in the years following the French Revolution, the issues involved in its aesthetic or formal transformations are even more complex. The novel in this period often seems a schizophrenic form, generically unstable but also both innovative and exploratory: Frye's view of it as a "realistic displacement of romance" or "parody-romance" featuring protagonists "confused by romantic assumptions about reality" (1976: 38, 39) disguises something far more vigorous and more actively expansionist. Aesthetic-ally, "romance" was a changing and contested category. Works declaring themselves in subtitles to be romances include many we now call "Gothic" (all Radcliffe's novels except *The Castles of Athlin and Dunbayne*, Eleanor Sleath's *The Orphan of the Rhine*, Charlotte Dacre's *Zofloya*, Maturin's *Fatal Revenge* – which Scott described in the *Quarterly Review* in 1810 as "his strange chaotic novel romance" – but not Maturin's *Melmoth the Wanderer*, "A Tale") (Scott 1834–6: 18, 171). They also include many which explore the meeting points of history and fiction, such as Jane Porter's *The Scottish Chiefs* and Mary Shelley's *Perkin Warbeck*. "Romance" in these subtitles clearly indicates the dominance of fiction or invention over something regarded as "real."

Reviewing Mary Robinson's novel *Hubert de Sevrac: A Romance, of the Eighteenth Century* (1796) for the *Critical Review* in 1798, Coleridge derided "the prevalence of the present taste for romances" but pronounced "that this taste is declining, and that real life and manners will soon assert their claims."[1] The tendency to contrast "real life" and "romance" (the descendents of Richard Hurd's "good sense" and "fine fabling") reverberates throughout the period, not least in poetry and in the aesthetic subsequently claimed for one of Coleridge's other excursions into print in 1798, *Lyrical Ballads*. In *Modern Romance* (1992), Ian Duncan points out that the contrast was a tired convention in these years, but this makes its resilience as a rhetorical ploy all the more interesting. (Hazlitt seized on it in *The Spirit of the Age*, 1825, to suggest that Scott proves that there is no romance like the romance of real life: the formula echoes Charlotte Smith's 1787 collection of tales from Gayot de Pitaval's *Causes célèbres*, *The Romance of Real Life*, a project in turn echoed in the frame narrative of *The Heart of Mid-Lothian*). Twelve chapters before the end of *Waverley* the young hero, lying low on the shores of Ulswater after the skirmish at Clifton which has broken his involvement with the Jacobite army, "felt himself entitled to say firmly, though perhaps with a sigh, that the romance of his life was ended, and that its real history had now commenced" ([1814] 1986: 3). The allusion is to John Logan's "Ode on the Death of a Young Lady":

> The dear Illusions will not last;
> The aera of Enchantment's past;
> The wild Romance of Life is done;
> The real History is begun.[2]

Nine years on in Scott's career, it takes the hero of *Quentin Durward* (1823) only five chapters to feel that the song of his lady-love "was a chapter of romance, and his uncle's conversation had opened to him a page of the real history of life" (2001: 68). The difference marks the later novel's more ruthless unveiling of the cruelties and hypocrisies concealed by the codes of chivalry; but it also marks a more ironic relationship between history and romance. The two read, in many of Scott's works, like parallel narratives, in which the dark freight of history is carried by a surface plot of romantic escapades, rescues, and miraculous resolution. Quentin Durward's loyalty to the patterns of courtly love ensures his survival even in the anti-chivalric world of Louis XI, and in the face of taunts directed at his "happy journey through Fairy-land – all full of heroic adventure, and high hope, and wild minstrel-like delusion, like the gardens of Morgaine la Fay" (2001: 268). *Quentin Durward* has heavily foregrounded elements of romance – the hero is entranced by the newly printed *romaunt* of "The Squire of Low Degree," among the mazes of the royal castle of Plessis is Roland's Hall, hung with tapestry and ancient (ugly) paintings of the Paladins of Charlemagne, and there are warnings about the folly of reading romances. At the end of *Quentin Durward* the author draws attention in an ironic coda to his failure to provide details of nuptials and offspring, declares that he "will steal away from the wedding as Ariosto from that of Angelica," and closes with an adaptation of a stanza from Canto 30 of *Orlando Furioso*. It is obvious that the romance of Quentin's life has not closed at the end of chapter 5.

The ending of *Quentin Durward*, with its highly self-conscious incorporation of an image of the "romantic" reader guiding the author's pen, is a reminder of the growing importance of actual readers and of the often stereotyped image of the reader in the Romantic Period. In *Caleb Williams*, Falkland's love of reading considerably compli- cates the gender roles of the novel, feminizing him even as he tyrannizes over Caleb. Just as the reading of romance offered in the eighteenth century feminizes Spenser (a characterization still very clear in works such as Keats's sonnets "Written on the Day that Mr Leigh Hunt left Prison" and "On Sitting Down to Read *King Lear* Once Again"), so the heroes of the novel in the Romantic Period become, especially in the works of Scott, enchanted and emasculated, while the image of the reader is feminized with ostensible mockery but discernible anxiety. In the tradition of Charlotte Lennox's *Female Quixote* (1752) come works such as Sarah Green's *Romance Readers and Romance Writers* (1810) and Eaton Stannard Barrett's *The Heroine; or, The Fair Romance Reader* (1813). In Scott's work, meanwhile, the engagement of writers with readers is manifested in several of the frame narratives of the first editions of his works (frames set up to maintain his anonymity but allowing him to puzzle over the nature of modern romance through a variety of antiquarian alter egos). In the frame narrative of *The Monastery* (1820), for example, Captain Clutterbuck frets about the novel as a form of "light reading" enjoyed by a "half-bred milliner's miss" (2000a: 7), while the "Author of Waverley," replying to Clutterbuck, describes Sir Isaac Watt as "as shameless and obstinate a peruser of novels as if he had been a very milliner's apprentice of eighteen" (26). Scott's consciousness of the dangers of reading, especially romance-reading, can be found in all his works, although his male characters are rescued from the consequences of their romantic visions more consistently than his female characters ever are.

The progress of romance scholarship in the first two decades of the nineteenth century quietly underpins the new imaginings of the age. Scott was at the center of a group of scholars, collectors, editors, and writers scattered through the British Isles but in regular contact with each other either through personal correspondence or through the periodical reviews. These collectors and scholars of romance – including Robert Southey, Francis Douce, Joseph Ritson, George Ellis, Henry Weber, Richard Heber, Sharon Turner, William Owen, and William Taylor of Norwich – still actively debated the theories of the origins of romance proposed in the eighteenth century, but they were more immediately committed to the collection and publication of romance texts, creating for them a new readership and a new lease of life in a wide rather than a specialized literary culture. Editorial practices were changing too. In the wake of Percy's *Reliques*, the prevailing fashion was for edited collections and "specimens" of authentic and native materials, such as Edward Jones' *Musical and Poetical Relics of the Welsh Bards* (1784, 1794), or for translations, such as Gregory Lewis Way's appealingly modernized *Fabliaux or Tales* (1796, 1800). But increasingly readers were to have access to the actual texts of the past (as in William Owen's editions of the poems of Dafydd ap Gwilym (1789) and Llywarch Hên (1792) and texts of early Welsh literature in the *Myvyrian Archailogy* (1801–7)). These decades also saw the beginnings of two monuments of romance publishing, the series of editions and reprints of old texts produced by the Roxburghe Club from 1812 and by the Bannatyne Club from 1822. In addition, and following on from the work of Hurd, Reeve, and Warton, scholarly histories of fiction such as that of John Dunlop (1814) integrated the stories of romance and of the novel, scrupulously registering differences in form and emphasis but giving the modern prose forms of the genre tradition and identity. (It is fitting that Dunlop's summative history appeared in the same year as *Waverley*, the form's new point of origin.)

Characteristic of these works is George Ellis's three-volume *Specimens of Early English Metrical Romances* (1805), which brought samples and extracts of old romance to a new reading public. As well as working with books and manuscripts in the British Museum, Lincoln's Inn Library, and Caius College, Cambridge, Ellis drew on the manuscript collections of Francis Douce (1757–1834) (now in the Bodleian Library, Oxford) and texts transcribed by Scott from the rich holdings of the Advocates' Library in Edinburgh (the foundation of the collections of the National Library of Scotland). Ellis's introduction to the *Specimens* is an impressive survey, written with an excited sense of discovery and debate. It is also a reminder of the nationalistic aspects of the romance revival, especially during the long years of war against Napoleonic France: Ellis puts bards native to the British Isles firmly at the center of the romance tradition, and it was he who first suggested to Scott that the earliest metrical romances written in English were the work of Scottish minstrels, an idea crucial to Scott's edition of *Sir Tristrem*. Ellis's book was followed by works such as that of Scott's friend and protégé Henry Weber, *Metrical Romances*, also in three volumes, published in 1810.

Scott was a key collaborator in his friends' projects, but in 1804 he produced a work which clearly outshone them. In the judgment of the historian of romance scholarship Arthur Johnston, Scott's 1804 edition of *Sir Tristrem* "even with its wild conjectures, still stands as the first great edition of a medieval romance" (1964: 187). Scott transcribed *Sir Tristrem* from the Auchinleck Manuscript. The fifth oldest extant collection of romances in English, given to the Faculty of Advocates in 1744 by Alexander Boswell (father of James), it spent months at a time in Scott's study between 1789 and 1803. Scott himself supplied a conclusion to the romance, in Middle English verse. The first run of 150 copies sold briskly: it was extended by 750 more in 1806 and by 1,000 in 1811. The 12 rarest copies are those Scott presented to fellow medievalists, in which – an indication of the tastes of the times – he was permitted to include a line excised from the standard run, with the word "queynt" in it. The edition was well received, stimulating debate even when scholars disputed Scott's theories about the authorship and origin of the romance, as William Taylor of Norwich did. Scott argued that *Sir Tristrem*, a redaction of the work of Thomas of Brittany, was not French but Scottish in origin, and that the author was the legendary Thomas of Ercildoune, the "Rhymer" of his own Borders territory. He suggested that Thomas of Ercildoune (to whom he also attributed *King Horn*) had been part of a group of thirteenth-century lowland Scots romance-writers writing in English (rather than in French, as English romancers of the time did). Scott's work on *Sir Tristrem* involved him in a great deal of detailed research to support his scholarly annotation, introduction, and glossary – his information on medieval hunting, for example, which he later put to use in many of his own novels, came from George Ellis's copy of the fifteenth-century hunting treatise known as *The Book of St. Albans* and attributed to Dame Juliana Berners. Scott's absorption of this hunting terminology surfaces often in his work, as in Cedric's scornful reference to "the new-fangled jargon of *curee, arbor, nombles*, and all the babble of the fabulous Sir Tristrem" in *Ivanhoe* ([1820] 1998a: 49), and it can take on sinister connotations, as when Edgar Ravenswood, "hero" of *The Bride of Lammermoor*, is likened to Tristrem, and his beloved, Lucy Ashton, to a "lily-white doe" and a "wounded deer." The hunt may be "normally an image of the masculine erotic," as Frye suggests (1976: 104), but Scott uses it far more widely, psychologically (as we have seen in the Green Chamber episode) and structurally. In *Quentin Durward*, a boar-hunt near the outset of Quentin's adventures precisely foreshadows the hunt for the "Wild Boar of the Ardennes," William de la Marck, during the French-Burgundian attack on Liège in the final pages of the novel. Nobody could miss the linking imagery of the boar, but Scott's patterning is more ambitiously precise, in both "hunts" showing that the true danger comes from a lesser beast which crosses the track of the main prey. Throughout *Quentin Durward*, charac-ters double, track, and stalk, and the image of the boar rushing on a fixed poniard, killed by its own weight, ties in with a macabre obsession (more noticeable in this novel than in any of Scott's others) with death by hanging (death again by the weight of one's own body).

As a critic, Scott's first significant published contribution to the debate on romance came in his 1803 review of new translations of *Amadis de Gaul* by Robert Southey (in prose) and by William Stewart Rose (in verse), in which he disputes details of interpretation and emphasis (such as Southey's claim that the Portuguese knight Vasco de Lobeira was the original author of *Amadis*), openly addresses the sexual improprieties of romance tales (those who imagine otherwise have read nothing earlier than Scudéry, he observes), and emphasizes the value of imaginative freedom when dealing with older materials: "too close adherence to his original is the greatest defect" of Rose's poetical *Amadis*. He reviewed Godwin's *Life of Chaucer* in 1804, the collections of Ellis and Ritson in 1806, wrote a conclusion to Joseph Strutt's romance *Queen-Hoo-Hall* in 1808, planned a history of romance, wrote in 1814 (while working on *Waverley*) an essay on chivalry for the *Encyclopaedia Britannica* (published in 1818), and wrote an essay on romance itself for the same publication.

The "Essay on Romance," published in the Supplement to the fourth, fifth, and sixth editions of the *Encyclopaedia Britannica* in May 1824, is the product of a section of Scott's career that almost seems to parody the opposition between romance and real life. In May 1823 he published one of his most romance-saturated texts, *Quentin Durward*. In December 1823 he followed it with his most experimental novel of modern manners, *St. Ronan's Well*. "Instead of some haunted fountain, connected with the fate, the adventures, and the traditions of a knightly race," grumbled the *British Critic*, "lo and behold we are introduced to a watering place of the nineteenth century."[3] The "Essay on Romance" is the product of a lifetime's thought, but also the product of a year of intense creative struggle between opposed forms of fiction.[4] At the start of the "Essay," Scott defines romance as "a fictitious narrative in prose or verse; the interest of which turns upon marvellous and uncommon incidents," presenting it in opposition to the novel ("a fictitious narrative, differing from the romance, because the events are accommodated to the ordinary train of human events, and the modern state of society"). Scott's conception of the form is fluid and inclusive: he traces its history not to an identifiable "origin" (it is "like a compound metal, derived from various mines") but to local and national circumstance. Throughout, his underlying interests are in the production and reception of the form: how romance had begun with records of events and traditions (so that "romance and real history have the same common origin"); how it had changed in response to the inclinations of its hearers and later readers; and how the authors of prose romance had striven, after the advent of the press, to satisfy a "newly-awakened and more refined taste." He considers the social status in different cultures of minstrels, scalds, and bards, the varying degree of their originality, the emergence of new ideas of authorship in, for instance, Malory's *Morte Darthur*, and the move toward a more sophisticated depiction of character and manners, and, in "the divine Ariosto" in particular, the ingenious interweaving of complex narrative. He berates the decline of seventeenth-century heroic romance ("the most dull and tedious species of composition that ever obtained temporary popularity") in the "interminable folios" of D'Urfé, Gomberville, La Calprenède, and Scudéry. Throughout the essay, Scott brings to bear on the analysis of romance a sophisticated awareness of changing methods of literary production and their impact on the literature itself.

Romance elements pervade Scott's works and have been permanently reshaped by them. The journey or quest, usually involving a search for identity, provides the basic structure of all his novels, even those which (like *The Heart of Mid-Lothian*) more obviously foreground forms of "real life." They are all, to follow Frye's terms, tales of spring, youth, and the struggle away from childish dependence and ignorance – "I do not like being borne in hand as if I were a child," Quentin Durward declares – even as they compulsively revisit the subjugations of childhood. The formulas Frye uses, especially in *The Secular Scripture*, suggest that in spite of his distrust of Scott's artistry he reads romance in the terms offered, and scrutinized, by the Waverley Novels. What Frye calls "the horror of being totally known" (1976: 123) is blatantly the condition of a modern, social, "fallen" romance, and the horror from which all the Waverley Novels recoil, to varying degrees. As Scott's novelistic career progressed, forms of shorthand increasingly characterize the endings of the novels, which are the surest warnings against the conservative social politics ostensibly offered in the fictions themselves. But even his first novel ends with a self-conscious "Postscript, which should have been a Preface." To read this pattern politically: Scott's works obsessively trace states of dissolution, decay, chaos, in order eventually to reinstate civic stability. But the nature of historical fiction means that any "Postscript" is always also a "Preface," and in the endings of Scott's novels fictionality asserts itself with a force sometimes amounting to irony. Only once in Scott's career did a formal recognition of this condition take shape (the first sequel in the history of the novel – the *Monastery/Abbot* sequence discussed below), but his obsessive interlinking of his fictions, through shared "editors," mutually reflexive frame narratives, novels taken from "manuscripts" in the collections of families within the Waverley group – shows that he was always setting his works in a context that is not just "playful" about fictive convention, but fundamentally skeptical about the nature of endings. The superficially conservative politics of Scott's fictions must be read in the context of intricate formal disavowals.

The whole venture of the Waverley Novels begins with the unnamed author setting out, in chapter 1 of *Waverley*, "like a maiden knight with his white shield" ([1814] 1986: 3; see also *Don Quixote*, Part 1, chapter 2). *Waverley* cannily blends romance and anti-romance, seeming to make the first a youthful, faulty manner of perception but actually reinforcing the reassuring structures of the form. Chapter 9, in which Waverley approaches Tully-Veolan for the first time, shows him imagining it as the castle of Orgoglio approached by Prince Arthur (*The Faerie Queene*, 1.viii.29); the perspective has shifted to parody by the time the narrator describes the scene as "not quite equal to the gardens of Alcina" (37), and as translating Armida's entrancing handmaidens (in Tasso's *Gerusalemme Liberata*) into the shapes of two washerwomen. While encouraging Waverley's attachment to the "enchantress" Flora, her brother Fergus continually mocks Waverley's inclination to understand life through "his romances." This feminized, "wavering," imaginative hero, "whose life was a dream" (170), is both cured of his romantic misconceptions and left fixed in the aesthetic space not only of the painting at the end of the story but also of his own happy married life at Waverley-Honour. In moving beyond romance he also moves out of history. Something comparable happens at the end of *Rob Roy* (1817), already a significantly darker response to the patterns of *Waverley*. In *Rob Roy*, the hero and heroine, both avid readers of Ariosto, play the parts of characters from romance: Diana Vernon's sprightly but embittered references to herself as a "distressed damsel of romance" mark the extent to which these two imprisoned characters fictionalize themselves. The fact that Diana has died before her husband begins to tell their story is another example of the way in which characters emerge from romance only to be voided from history. "I have no more of romantic adventure to tell" records Frank at the close of his story, while the "editor" notes "[Here the original manuscript ends somewhat abruptly. I have reason to think that what followed related to private affairs]" (1998b: 452).

It is Scott's second novel, *Guy Mannering; or The Astrologer* (1815), which, early in *The Secular Scripture*, anchors Frye's argument for the continuity of romance plots. Unlike *Waverley*, it is not rich in allusion to romance, working instead by an inverted notion of quest in which all the key figures return to their common point of origin. Quest elements are intertwined – most obviously, Harry Bertram's journey to Ellangowan takes up aspects of Guy Mannering's journey on the night of his birth – but many romance elements are buried or ironically refashioned. There is a "light" and a "dark" heroine, for example, but no choice between them, for each is already in love with her future husband by the time the second-generation story begins. *Guy Mannering* is a good example of the sometimes odd blend of "displaced" elements of romance – what Fredric Jameson, disputing Frye's hermeneutic of romance, suggests we regard instead as its "sediment" or "substitute codes" in later fiction – with motifs used structurally and symbolically. Some elements of magic and otherness are translated in *Guy Mannering* into modern social forms, but other elements which seem entirely incidental, hooks for a "realistic" depiction of regional manners, turn out to offer clues to an underlying symbolism. To take an example drawn from hunting, and with Scott's research for *Sir Tristrem* in mind: *Guy Mannering* is full of caves and den-like hovels such as those at Derncleugh (meaning "dark chasm"), typically approached in darkness. These caves and huts are where the smugglers hide the child Harry Bertram, and where the adult Bertram hides in shadow with the aid of Meg Merrilies. The climactic scene of confrontation and revelation involves Bertram, Dinmont, and "young Hazlewood" crawling down the secret passage to Hattaraick's cave. As historical accident has decreed, *Guy Mannering* is famous for its terriers. "Dandie Dinmont" terriers are named after the Borders farmer who, as if in a parody of the complex genealogy which takes up chapter 2 of the novel, boasts of "auld Pepper and auld Mustard, and young Pepper and young Mustard, and little Pepper and little Mustard" (1999: 119). Bertram's stay at Dinmont's farmhouse of Charlies-Hope is usually read as a pastoral interlude in the novel, but it is also a showcase for different types of hunting and different "degrees" of prey. Dinmont's terriers are active in the fox-hunt which takes place in a deep glen filled with mist, after which there is "a sort of salmon-hunting" by night, a scene Harry Bertram likens to Pandaemonium (1999: 136); then, mentioned merely, an otter hunt, and finally a badger baiting in which young Pepper loses a paw and young Mustard is "nearly throttled." Bertram pleads for the honorable release of the badger, and leaves his own terrier, Wasp, with the Dinmonts, on the undertaking that he will not be imperilled in such hunts. The effect is of a progression upward to the "noble" prey and the honorable compromise reached at the end of the novel between two former antagonists, Bertram and Guy Mannering, the lesser beasts of Glossin and Hattaraick having grappled to the death in their dark prison. Like his master, Wasp never has to be "entered" into his lower calling.

Another way of approaching the patterns suggested by romance, and a way of opening up more generally the motifs of romance apparent in *Waverley* and *Guy Mannering*, is to consider the technique of *entrelacement* or narrative interlace which, in differing forms and degrees of complexity, links romance writing from the works of Chrétien de Troyes, Ariosto, Malory, and the *Gawain* poet to Tolkien's *Lord of the Rings*. The first book of *The Faerie Queene* alone places in parallel the adventures of Una and the Red Cross Knight, interlinking episodes, recognitions, phrases and images and gradually making the two quests aspects of one more complex quest. This structure demonstrably affected Scott deeply, although, characteristically, he chose to present it as an "inartificial" style of composition. "Like the digressive poet Ariosto, I find myself under the necessity of connecting the branches of my story, by taking up the adventures of another of the characters," the narrator announces at the beginning of chapter 16 of *The Heart of Mid-Lothian* ([1818] 2004: 143). In fact, the character introduced in this chapter is Madge Wildfire, whose role in the novel, on a symbolic level at least, is to represent the more agonizing aspects of Effie Deans's experiences. In the central section of *Redgauntlet* (1824), two parallel and interlocking quests structure the narrative, as Darsie Latimer, held captive and dressed in female clothes, seeks the truth of his inheritance while Alan Fairford seeks his kidnapped friend. (The two are a displaced version of twins in romance, Frye suggests.) At the start of this novel, Alan continually chides Darsie for his romantic and romanticizing tendencies, yet Alan's experiences turn out to be far more tightly caught up in the webs of romance. Scott specifically describes Alan's journey as a quest; in it, he is confronted by characters in disguise, travels through secret passageways, and undergoes a swoon or death-state in Nanty Ewart's brig. Symbolically, the land in which he finds himself resurrected is a parallel land of romance; and his first resting-place within it is the enchanted house of Fairladies, where he encounters and is tested by the disguised Stuart prince, Charles Edward. Aspects of Darsie's struggle against his uncle's powers of enchantment are explored through Alan's more stalwart but also more hazardous experiences: when Darsie wins his inheritance by refusing to participate in rebellion – by doing, in effect, nothing at all – the active part of his struggle has actually been suggested to us through Alan's story. (The same story is told in a different key in the interpolated "Wandering Willie's Tale.") *Entrelacement* works here to express one experience in terms of another, and also to refine one of the connections between works like *Redgauntlet* and older romance: that the qualities tested throughout a quest are those that characterize not only the quester but also the strengths and flaws of the society out of which he (or, more rarely, she) journeys.

At the central point of the three volumes of *Ivanhoe* (beginning in chapter 7 of the 16 chapters in volume 2) comes a particularly intricate interlace, the siege of Torquilstone. Most of the key characters are being held captive in the castle of Front-de-Boeuf where, as Frye puts it, "terrible things almost go on" (1976: 135). It is pointedly formalized: each section is interrupted by the blast of the trumpet heralding the messenger of the attacking force, sounded "with as much violence as if it had been blown before an enchanted castle by the destined knight" ([1820] 1998a: 178). This is indeed the castle of modern romance, and the summons is from Richard, the destined, the disinherited. Each character – Athelstane, Rowena, Isaac, Rebecca – is tested along perceptible fault-lines, but with the result of making all their separate resistance eloquent of a larger resistance to Norman, Christian, masculine rule. At the climax of the sequence – the scene eloquently and purposively imitated, though now, for many readers, imperceptibly, in the events leading to the death of Bertha Rochester in *Jane Eyre* – the abused Saxon captive Ulrica sets fire to the castle and dies in defiant song, the final representative of the fate so narrowly escaped by Rebecca and Rowena.

The Torquilstone episode suggests a larger pattern of feint and substitution at work in this most influential of Scott's romances. For readers familiar with Malory, in particular, the novel is full of echoes and ironies: the nameless champion of the tournament of Ashby de la Zouche echoes the tournament of King Bagdemagus in Malory's "Lancelot," while Ivanhoe's last-minute rescue of Rebecca recalls the preparations for Guenevere's death at the stake. The novel features two disinherited knights, Wilfred of Ivanhoe and Richard I of England, and, closely echoing their situtations, two disinherited women, Rebecca the Jew and Rowena the true descendent of the Saxon royal line. The relationship between them is complex, and is traced through a series of tightly interconnected scenes of masking and unmasking. Ivanhoe spends most of the novel injured, carried around by others, while Richard takes on the more active role; but Ivanhoe's is the legitimate quest, Richard's a dangerous indulgence. These interlaced quests become bizarre at the novel's close, when, instead of witnessing Ivanhoe's reunion with Rowena, the reader is presented with a much more charged unveiling, as Rebecca unveils Ivanhoe's bride of two nights. As boy readers like Thackeray understood immediately, this has not really been a novel about men. A paragraph later, and with the grammatical distinction between Ivanhoe and Richard blurred ever so slightly, the novel ends as follows:

> With the life of that generous, but rash and romantic monarch [Richard], perished all the projects which his ambition and his generosity had formed; and to him may be applied, with a slight alteration, the lines composed by Johnson for Charles of Sweden –
>
> > His fate was destined to a "foreign" strand,
> > A petty fortress and a "humble" hand;
> > He left the name at which the world grew pale,
> > To point a moral, or adorn a TALE.
>
> (1998: 401)

The self-conscious quotation marks make "barren" and "dubious" (the actual readings in Samuel Johnson's "Vanity of Human Wishes") hang over this ornate but unexpectedly disengaged closure. Since it was common practice to end a novel with the word or words of its title, "the name" readers expect at this moment is "Ivanhoe," not "Richard"; and Richard's fate has in any case been strangely mangled by association with that of Charles of Sweden via Samuel Johnson. The muted ending of *Ivanhoe* is very strange, but, on successive readings, also very expressive.

Although romance elements feature in all Scott's novels, those written in the years 1819 to 1825 are particularly insistent in their echoes and their conscious swervings. *Ivanhoe: A Romance* was followed by the first novel in English to have a sequel. *The Monastery: A Romance* (1820) and its sequel *The Abbot* (also 1820; with no categorizing subtitle) allow Scott to contrast stories and approaches, and to complicate on a larger scale the contrast between "romance" and "real life." Ironically, *The Monastery* (the "romance"), is stubbornly down-to-earth, although it is set in a highly symbolic landscape – contrasting the Monastery of St. Mary at Kennaquhair and the Tower of Glendearg, the Red Valley – and centers on the two Glendinning brothers, dark-haired, masculine, Protestant-to-be Halbert and fair, feminized Edward, later Abbot of St. Mary's. As this contrast starts to suggest, romance assumes a new role as the characteristic form not only of the feminine but also of the Catholic. The land to be reclaimed in these novels is the supposedly male fiefdom of Avenel, a castle on an island whose emblem is a female figure shrouded. Put in their simplest form, the elements of the *Monastery–Abbot* sequence are very powerful: a series of disinherited Marys, two ladies of the lake – Mary, "the Spirit of Avenel," and Mary Stuart, imprisoned on an island in Lochleven – the monastery itself and the tradition it represents, a spectral White Lady guarding a mysterious Black Book, and, in *The Abbot*, a young unknown called Roland.

One of the most persistently underestimated achievements of Scott's career, the *Monastery–Abbot* sequence sets out ideological and historical complexity through a forcefully emblematic narrative. The sequence allows Scott for the first time to follow through the darker implications of his tale, and it is significant that the narrative model which allows him to develop this brilliant new type of fiction successfully is not "history," but romance. At the end of *The Monastery*, the song of the vanishing White Lady keeps readers in the realm of a distinctly Arthurian form of romance:

> "The knot of fate at length is tied,
> The Churl is Lord, the Maid is Bride!
> Vainly did my magic sleight
> Send the lover from her sight;
> Wither bush, and perish well,
> Fall'n is lofty Avenel!"

([1820] 2000a: 353)

The Abbot begins nearly ten years later, with Halbert and Mary childless and Mary frequently alone. An orphan child rescued from the lake by the stag-hound, Wolf, becomes her consolation, the seed of discord, and in due course the true lost heir of Avenel, "Child Roland" ([1820] 2000b: 33) Graeme. Roland is secretly at the disposal of his fanatical Catholic grandmother, who enlists him in the service of another Mary/Lady of the Lake, Mary Stuart, imprisoned at Lochleven. (Once again romance parallels offer additional insights: in the "Essay on Romance" Scott had described the generic character of Charlemagne's Roland as "brave, unsuspicious, devotedly loyal, and somewhat simple in his disposition" [75], which is what Roland's grandmother assumes he will be.) The crisis of Mary's reign at Lochleven, which riveted Scott's imagination for many years, is explored through codes of substitution, servitude, emasculation, and a highly ambiguous religious and political loyalty.

Given the significance of Scott's work on *Sir Tristrem*, it seems appropriate to close with the novel that most reprises that central story of romance. Like several of the other novels discussed in this essay, it still suffers from a residual tendency in Scott criticism to discriminate between the "serious" and the "decorative" uses of history. The first and less famous of the two *Tales of the Crusaders* (1825), *The Betrothed*, presents a love triangle between Eveline Berenger – after her father's death, commander of the castle of the Garde Doloureuse in the Debatable Land of the Welsh Marches, and "something of a damsel-errant" – the Constable of Chester, Hugo de Lacy, to whom she contracts herself in duty, and his nephew Damian. The romance parallels are insistent. Eveline rides a palfrey called Yseulte, Damian is described as "a second Sir Tristrem in sylvan sports," and, prompted by the song of a knowing minstrel, in his dreams the Constable has "some confused idea of being identified with the unlucky Mark of Cornwall" (1829–33: 37, 244). *The Betrothed* seems liberated by these parallels to explore psychology and situation in highly patterned ways. As two men vie for Eveline's hand, the narrative is structured around two sieges of her castle.

Eveline and Damian undergo paralleled testing (she in the haunted chamber of Baldringham, he in prison, questioned by the Constable in disguise). And just before she is captured by Welsh bandits, Eveline is taking part in a heron-hunt which becomes a precise evocation of her own "hunting." (The hawk brings down the heron with difficulty; Eveline dismounts in order to disable its legs and facilitate the hawk's attack; her own arms are immediately bound and the bandit-chief pronounces himself "a hawk".) She is then taken, blindfolded, down an earthen passage into a burial chamber. Eveline's ordeal translates the mimic-death states of romance, in which a knight enters another world as if in a swoon, only to find the secrets of his own situation (Mammon's cave in *The Faerie Queene*, the fairy world in *Sir Orfeo*). Throughout *The Betrothed*, Scott tests the ethics of chivalry, its mixture of personal honor, obstinacy, quixotry and superstitious adherence to vows and prophecies; but his questing knight is a woman. Eventually, Eveline's marriage to Damian emends rather than emulates the Tristrem story, the novel resisting archetype and convention just as its characters must learn to do. To achieve this complex fiction Scott adopts the conventions of romance, testing the ethic while echoing and elaborating the conventions just as the *Gawain* poet, Malory and Spenser had done before him.

At this stage in the history of romance, therefore, had come not a passively pivotal or "middle" figure ("Spenser, Scott, Morris") but an active shaper of romance stories and of the story of romance. Scott's combination of scholarship, creativity, and worldwide popularity suggests Tolkien, most nearly, among later romancers. All the advanced paratexts – appendices, glossaries, prehistories – of *The Lord of the Rings* evoke the Waverley Novels. Scott's greater complexity lies in the fact that one is never entirely "in" the world of Waverley romancing. His paratexts fragment rather than consolidate. In a period pondering its status as the "end" of the age of chivalry, and which readers of our own time see just as partially as the "beginning" of a recognizably modern (even postmodern) form of romance, Scott made and continues to make readers reconsider such boundaries.

See also: chapter 3, THE POPULAR ENGLISH METRICAL ROMANCES; chapter 4, ARTHURIAN ROMANCE; chapter 6, MALORY AND THE EARLY PROSE ROMANCES; chapter 8, SIDNEY AND SPENSER; chapter 11, *THE FAERIE QUEENE* AND EIGHTEENTH-CENTURY SPENSERIANISM; chapter 12, "GOTHIC" ROMANCE; chapter 13, WOMEN'S GOTHIC ROMANCE; chapter 17, POETRY OF THE ROMANTIC PERIOD; chapter 18, VICTORIAN ROMANCE: TENNYSON; chapter 19, VICTORIAN ROMANCE: MEDIEVALISM; chapter 20, ROMANCE AND VICTORIAN AUTOBIOGRAPHY.

Notes

1. *Critical Review* 23, 472.
2. John Logan, *Poems*, 2nd edn., 1782 (London: T. Cadell), lines 49–52.
3. *British Critic*, NS 21 (1824), 16–26.
4. Quotations from the "Essay on Romance" in this discussion come from Scott's *Essays on Chivalry, Romance and the Drama* (1880?), pp. 88, 67, 89, 107.

References and Further Reading

Burke, Edmund (1968). *Reflections on the Revolution in France and on the Proceedings in Certain Societies in London Relative to that Event*, ed. Conor Cruise O'Brien. Harmondsworth: Penguin. [First published in 1790.]

Cottom, Daniel (1985). *The Civilized Imagination: A Study of Ann Radcliffe, Jane Austen, and Sir Walter Scott*. Cambridge: Cambridge University Press.

Duncan, Ian (1992). *Modern Romance and Transformations of the Novel: The Gothic, Scott, Dickens*. Cambridge: Cambridge University Press.

Dunlop, John (1814). *The History of Prose Fiction: Being a Critical Account of the Most Celebrated Prose Works of Fiction, from the Earliest Greek Romances to the Novels of the Present Age*. 3 vols. Edinburgh: Ballantyne; London: Longman, Hurst, Rees, Orme, and Brown, and John Murray.

Elam, Diane (1992). *Romancing the Postmodern*. London and New York: Routledge.

Ellis, George, ed. (1805). *Specimens of Early English Metrical Romances, Chiefly Written during the Early Part of the Fourteenth Century*. 3 vols. London: Longman, Hurst, Rees, Orme, and Brown.

Forster, E. M. (1927). *Aspects of the Novel*. London: Edward Arnold.

Frye, Northrop (1976). *The Secular Scripture: A Study of the Structure of Romance*. The Charles Eliot Norton Lectures, 1974–1975. Cambridge, MA, and London: Harvard University Press.

Godwin, William (1982). *Things as They Are; or The Adventures of Caleb Williams*, ed. David McCracken. Oxford: Oxford University Press. [First published in 1794.]

Jameson, Fredric (1981). *The Political Unconscious: Narrative as a Socially Symbolic Act*. London: Methuen.

Johnston, Arthur (1964). *Enchanted Ground: The Study of Medieval Romance in the Eighteenth Century*. London: Athlone Press.

Mitchell, Jerome (1987). *Scott, Chaucer, and Medieval Romance: A Study in Sir Walter Scott's Indebtedness to the Literature of the Middle Ages*. Lexington: University of Kentucky Press.

Peacock, Thomas Love (1948). *The Novels of Thomas Love Peacock*, ed. David Garnett. 2 vols. London: Rupert Hart-Davis.

Scott, Sir Walter (1829–33). *The Waverley Novels*. 48 vols. Edinburgh: Cadell; London: Simpkin and Marshall, Whittaker.

Scott, Sir Walter (1834–6). *The Miscellaneous Prose Works of Sir Walter Scott, Bart.*, ed. J. G. Lockhart. 28 vols. Edinburgh: Cadell.

Scott, Sir Walter (1880?). *Essays on Chivalry, Romance, and the Drama*. London: Frederick Warne.

Scott, Sir Walter (1932–7). *The Letters of Sir Walter Scott*, ed. H. J. C. Grierson et al. 12 vols. London: Constable.

Scott, Sir Walter (1972). *The Journal of Sir Walter Scott*, ed. W. E. K. Anderson. Oxford: Clarendon Press.

Scott, Sir Walter (1986). *Waverley; or, 'Tis Sixty Years Since*, ed. Claire Lamont. Oxford: Oxford University Press. [First published in 1814.]

Scott, Sir Walter (1995). *The Antiquary*, ed. David Hewitt. The Edinburgh Edition of the Waverley Novels 3. Edinburgh: Edinburgh University Press. [First published in 1816.]

Scott, Sir Walter (1998a). *Ivanhoe*, ed. Graham Tulloch. The Edinburgh Edition of the Waverley Novels 8. Edinburgh: Edinburgh University Press. [First published in 1820.]

Scott, Sir Walter (1998b). *Rob Roy*, ed. Ian Duncan. Oxford: Oxford University Press. [First published in 1817.]

Scott, Sir Walter (1999). *Guy Mannering; or The Astrologer*, ed. P. D. Garside. The Edinburgh Edition of the Waverley Novels 2. Edinburgh: Edinburgh University Press. [First published in 1815.]

Scott, Sir Walter (2000a). *The Monastery*, ed. Penny Fielding. The Edinburgh Edition of the Waverley Novels 9. Edinburgh: Edinburgh University Press. [First published in 1820.]

Scott, Sir Walter (2000b). *The Abbot*, ed. Christopher Johnson. The Edinburgh Edition of the Waverley Novels 10. Edinburgh: Edinburgh University Press. [First published in 1820.]

Scott, Sir Walter (2001). *Quentin Durward*, ed. J. H. Alexander and G. A. M. Wood. The Edinburgh Edition of the Waverley Novels 15.

Edinburgh: Edinburgh University Press. [First published in 1823.]

Scott, Sir Walter (2004). *The Heart of Mid-Lothian*, ed. David Hewitt and Alison Lumsden. The Edinburgh Edition of the Waverley Novels 6. Edinburgh: Edinburgh University Press. [First published in 1818.]

Scott, Sir Walter, ed. (1804). *Sir Tristrem: A Metrical Romance of the Thirteenth Century, by Thomas of Ercildoune, called The Rhymer*. Edinburgh: Constable; London: Longman and Rees.

Wilt, Judith (1985). *Secret Leaves: The Novels of Walter Scott*. Chicago: Chicago University Press.

17
Poetry of the Romantic Period: Coleridge and Keats

Michael O'Neill

Although this essay will concentrate on two poets, Coleridge and Keats, and will discuss only a few poems by each poet, it is worth noting at the outset that "romance" is a many-colored dome in poetry of the Romantic period, splitting the white light of modal and generic purity into diverse stainings. It may, as in Shelley's *Alastor* (1816), signify a mode of quest adapted to "one of the most interesting situations of the human mind."[1] It can imply (Keats's *The Eve of St Agnes* [1820] is a complex instance) an experience of enchantment involving the conjuring into existence of a bygone era, often thought of as in some way medieval, sometimes with and sometimes without any basis in supposed historical fact. It certainly names a creative space in which connections are made, as Coleridge has it, between, on the one hand, "persons and characters supernatural, or at least romantic" and, on the other, "human interest" and a "willing suspension of disbelief."[2] And it often signals the reader's capacity to entertain and enter into hitherto unexperienced states of thought and feeling, as "the romancer's tale becomes the reader's dream," to borrow Walter Scott's formulation from the introductory stanzas to *Harold the Dauntless* (1817; Robertson 1904).

At the same time, romance, as in Byron's *Childe Harold's Pilgrimage: A Romaunt* (1812–18), may consort with its own self-ironizing shadow, the mock- or anti-romance. Byron deflates the idealizations of some forms of romance when he remarks in the preface to *Childe Harold*: "I fear that Sir Tristram and Sir Lancelot were no better than they should be, although very poetical personages and true knights 'sans peur', though not 'sans reproche'" (1986: 21). Moreover, for all its air of withdrawal into what Keats calls "faery lands forlorn,"[3] romance may contain within itself the desire to make sense of the past or even the present: hence the Romantic phenomenon of the romance with notes, where the storyteller or autobiographer joins hands with the chronicler or (as in the case of Byron in *Childe Harold*) the roving reporter or cultural commentator. So dominant is the mode of historical romance introduced for the Romantics by Scott that he is able to joke about the absence of notes at the conclusion of *Harold the Dauntless*: "Then pardon thou thy minstrel, who hath wrote / A Tale six cantos long, yet scorn'd to add a note."

Romance and English Romantic poetry are more than chance etymological neighbors; they are decisively twinned, living one another's life. Romance, like a Metaphysical conceit, yokes together the dissimilar, fusing or holding in tension the ancient and the novel, the marvelous and the ordinary. For a period consumed with dreams of political Utopia, romance can be the mirror in which social hopes regard themselves in all their finery – and potential illusoriness. So, Wordsworth recalls with rueful irony the fervor of his initial response to the French Revolution, a time or "times, / In which the meagre, stale, forbidding ways / Of custom, law, and statute took at once / The attraction of a Country in Romance" (1984: X, 693–6). Hamlet's disenchantment in his first soliloquy is echoed, only to be set aside as the youthful poet enters a world in which "Reason" appeared "A prime Enchanter to assist the work / Which then was going forwards in her name" (1984: X, 699–700). Again, many poets of the period use romance to explore issues of gender. Felicia Hemans in *Records of Woman* (1828) and elsewhere, for example, feminizes romance, as Gary Kelly has argued (2002: 30), by presenting experience "in terms of individual subjective and emotional experience and the 'domestic affections'." All these different possibilities actualize themselves in many of the poems treated in the remainder of this chapter.

Coleridge

If in certain moods imagination for Coleridge is a God-like force, "the living power and prime agent of all human perception," romance in his work opens up visions that induce terror as much as religious awe (*Biographia Literaria*, 1985: 313). A re-creation for Coleridge's culture of the traditional ballad, *The Rime of the Ancient Mariner* can legitimately claim to be a romance. The very epigraph (from Thomas Burnet's Latin) to the much-revised version in *Sibylline Leaves* (1817) repeats to us the genre's quintessential message (in a recondite manner that mirrors the nature of the matter): there are more things in heaven and earth than are dreamt of in our philosophy, and we do not understand them. Here is the first part of the epigraph, in translation:

> I can easily believe that there are more invisible creatures in the universe than visible ones. But who will tell us what family each belongs to, what their ranks and relationships are, and what their respective distinguishing characters may be? What do they do? Where do they live? Human wit has always circled around a knowledge of these things without ever attaining it. (46)

From its epigraphic outset, then, the poem's radar tracks the presence of "invisible creatures," even as Coleridge, via Burnet, concedes that the ensuing poetic journey will involve us in a seeking after unattainable "knowledge." The ingredients for romance are all there; Coleridge's master cooking makes of them something rare and strange.

Like all romances, the poem tells a story, but its narrative is full of, indeed thrives on, hiatuses, abruptness, the inexplicable. We are led up hill and down dale, or rather, across a wide, wide sea. When a safe port and the calmness of terra firma arrive at the close, they seem at simplistic odds with what has gone before. The mariner draws from his trials the seemingly trite lesson that "He prayeth best, who loveth best / All things both great and small; / For the dear God who loveth us, / He made and loveth all' (614–17). It would be wrong, however, to see these lines either as naive or as calculatedly ironic. Because of the repetition of "loveth," the rhythm has an effect of emphasis. We hear the tone of someone seeking to reassure himself as well as to instruct his listener. Indeed, we may feel that the mariner experiences as much need as trust in the act of asserting that the universe is controlled by a loving God. Romance always divines the hidden springs of destiny, and frequently, as here, a proffered solution reminds us, paradoxically, of the difficulties on which any solution is likely to be snagged.

Chief among those difficulties are the meaning of the mariner's ordeal and the nature of the God he supposes to be a loving maker. The mariner is at once the protagonist and the romancer; throughout, we are reminded of his role as storyteller. At the start we witness the mariner's hypnotic quelling of the wedding-guest's resistance: "He holds him with his glittering eye . . . The Mariner hath his will" (13, 16). This role is a source of both authority and torment; it gives the mariner's words a compelled and compelling quality, and makes him into a surrogate for Coleridge the contemporary poet, as well as a figure who steps before us with achronological vividness in the poem's first line. That line, "It is an ancient Mariner," breaks out of the dark backward and abysm of time where romance locates its originating power and enters an ongoing, haunting present. As a surrogate for the contemporary poet, the mariner presents a figure subject to forces he cannot understand. If he has "strange power of speech" (587), the impulse to tell his tale is involuntary, beyond his control, as his account of his first telling makes clear:

> Forthwith this frame of mine was wrenched
> With a woful agony,
> Which forced me to begin my tale;
> And then it left me free.
>
> (578–81)

Freedom for this romancer occurs only after the "woful agony" of the telling, an "agony" that seems, if anything, more "woful" than that experienced by the mariner during his time at sea when "never a saint took pity on / My soul in agony" (234–5).

One reason for the "agony" of the tale is that what it "teaches" (see line 590) – against the will of the poem's final moral – is a lesson about the self's ultimate and abiding loneliness in the cosmos. At the poem's center is not the shooting of the albatross or the blessing of water-snakes, vital as both events are. Rather, it is the brooding lament that breaks from the mariner in "Part the Fourth": "Alone, alone, all,

all alone, / Alone on a wide wide sea" (232–3). The four repetitions of "alone" magnetize the two uses of "all" toward themselves; in this romance, aloneness, rather than ripeness, is all – or if not all, then certainly close to the heart of the poem. Later, reaching out to his chosen listener, the mariner repeats the central terror of his experience: "O Wedding-Guest! this soul hath been / Alone on a wide wide sea: / So lonely 'twas, that God himself / Scarce seemed there to be" (597–600). Straight after the reference to "the little vesper bell, / Which biddeth me to prayer" (595–6) and just before the poem's last appeal to "the dear God who loveth us," these lines speak out of the transgressive terror which the God-fearing Coleridge cannot banish from his poem: that the universe, however populated by "invisible beings," may, in the end, be an atheist's void.

If God is not absent, he can be made, under the shaping influence of the images on which romance feasts, to seem a figure not of love but of hate. As has often been noted, an early simile equivocates queasily: "Nor dim nor red, like God's own head, / The glorious Sun uprist" (97–8). Below the overt meaning (like God's head, the glorious sun is neither dim nor red) runs a shadow meaning (the glorious sun is neither dim nor red the way that God's head is dim and red). Romance may be Manichean, a conflict between good and evil, but it is alert, in Coleridge's hands, to possible blurrings and confusions. Later, building on this equivocation, the movement of the specter-bark containing Death and Life-in-Death catalyzes a change of cosmic scenery:

> And straight the Sun was flecked with bars,
> (Heaven's Mother send us grace!)
> As if through a dungeon-grate he peered
> With broad and burning face.
>
> (177–80)

The "Sun" here puns on the "Son" whose Mother is invoked in the next line; but this Son peers "through a dungeon-grate," a ferocious gaoler gazing at those imprisoned in this life, a pitiless onlooker such as those who stare at the beheaded John the Baptist in Caravaggio's masterpiece in Valletta, which Coleridge might have seen at the end of a voyage to Malta aboard the *Speedwell* in 1804 – a voyage in which he appeared to have become his own mariner. And yet, even at its most grim, the poem retains its contact with enchantment. The stanzas paint discrete pictures, as though gathering themselves up again and again for a new, hallucinatory jolt of intuition. The meaning of the mariner's journey runs like an electric current through a series of images. These images are raids on the strange and the marvelous, brought uncannily into neighborhood with the ordinary: "Fear at my heart, as at a cup," says the mariner on watching the specter-bark's departure, "My life-blood seemed to sip!" (204–5). Sipping "life-blood" is vampiric yet homely, the homeliness having about it a distinct unhomeliness. In the midst of self-consuming "fear," the horror of a nature turned unnatural, the mariner expresses his feelings through the deeply natural image of sipping a drink. The image has the more impact for the reference earlier in "Part the Third" to one of the mariner's few actions in the poem. Unable to speak because his throat is parched, the mariner hails the boat (which turns out to be the specter-bark) in this way: "I bit my arm, I sucked the blood, / And cried, A sail! A sail!" (160–1). Life-blood has already been shed, before the later image internalizes and makes figurative such a loss. But whereas the first shedding permitted speech, the second sipping implies a dread beyond language.

Images are agents in Coleridge's romance, at once vehicles of narrative and figures for internal states. Reflecting Coleridge's (and Wordsworth's) reading of travel-stories, the poem records a voyage into the new, a polar region where "it grew wondrous cold: / And ice, mast-high, came floating by, / As green as emerald" (52–4). "Wondrous" is an intensifier expressive of wonder, a wonder that never vanishes from the poem and gives it a mingled air of endurance and expectancy. The ice will grow claustrophobic in a stanza or two, but for an unforgettable moment, it has a life and motion of its own, and the color of a gem. Throughout, Coleridge brings together realms of experience normally thought of as separate, suggesting, that in his hands, romance is a medium for the exploration of boundaries. The Protestant Romantic chooses a dimly Catholic period and narrator for his profoundest moral investigation; the glosses added in 1817 seem also to adopt the character of a mind far removed from Coleridge's own time and place. Romance as much as opium, one may speculate, frees Coleridge to reconceive, to dissolve fixities and to recreate. Ultimately, the poem modifies romance – especially in its exploitation of the genre's resistance to "logic or causality"[4] – to free itself from restrictive understandings of experience, as Coleridge hints in his reported rejoinder to Anna Letitia Barbauld's complaint that the poem "had no moral": "I told her," Coleridge replies according to *Table Talk*, "in my judgement the chief fault of the poem had too much." He felt that

> It ought to have had no more moral than the Arabian Nights' tale of the merchant's sitting down to eat dates by the side of a well, and throwing the shells aside, and lo! a genie starts up, and says he *must* kill the aforesaid merchant, *because* one of the date shells had, it seems, put out the eye of the genie's son. (593–4)

Coleridge evidently delights, here, in the mockery of cause and effect implied by that teasingly emphasized "*because*."

Northrop Frye ventures the opinion that the romance is a form characteristically falling into three stages: the "perilous journey," the "crucial struggle," and the "exaltation of the hero" (1957:187). *The Rime of the Ancient Mariner* dramatizes the perils of journeying; it even hints at a struggle that is resolved by the blessing of the water-snakes. But nothing is more Romantic about the poem than the way that it holds back from any straightforward exaltation of the hero; the mariner, infamously grumbled at by Wordsworth for having "no distinct character,"[5] is hardly exalted. And yet Coleridge may suggest a new kind of heroism, one in which suffering and guilt provide the creative artist with a distinctive identity, even if that identity is more the mark of Cain than an unambiguous honor. In *Kubla Khan* a similar kind of heroism emerges from a lyric that compresses into itself many of the elements of romance. Grouped by Frye among "the poems of self-recognition, where the poet himself is involved in the awakening from experience into a visionary reality" (1957: 302), the poem teems with narrative suggestions that are never realized fully. The tale it tells of its own composition is the tale of the romance of inspiration. The author, an adventurer into strange places ("a lonely farm-house between Porlock and Linton on the Exmoor confines of Somerset and Devonshire"), occupies a boundary space; he takes "an anodyne," which bewitches his senses, as surely as though it were a potion administered by Circe, before he undergoes the experience of beholding the grail of the perfect inspired state ("in which all the images rose up before him as *things*"), only to have it snatched from him by a representative of the forces of evil (here, evil takes on the form of dull ordinariness, embodied in "a person on business from Porlock"). The preface even discounts the worth of the poem; this "Vision in a Dream" is offered "rather as a psychological curiosity than on the ground of any supposed *poetic* merits." In this brief narrative, this romance of an introduction, Coleridge dispraises the eventual product of his imagination, but he exalts the original processes of creative reverie. Quoting from his own poem *The Picture*, he sums up the disenchanted emergence from enchanted trance typical of romance in the words, "all that phantom-world so fair / Vanishes," and yet he holds open the possibility of a final recovery of perfection in the ensuing lines, "And soon the fragments dim of lovely forms / Come trembling back, unite, and now once more / The pool becomes a mirror."[6]

The poem itself sustains a doubleness of effect. It is both narrative and lyric, fragmentary and complete, an assertion of poetic power and an elegy for a lost vision. The sounds that arise from it pull in conflicted directions: counterpointing the "Ancestral voices prophesying war" (30) is "the mingled measure / From the fountain and the caves" (33–4). The poem distills and crystallizes many of the ambivalences of romance. Sexuality, especially female sexuality, is enticing and threatening, associated with creativity, and located in the eroticized geography of "that deep romantic chasm" (12) of the second verse paragraph, a chasm that refuses any submission to the girdling round decreed by Kubla Khan in the poem's opening. This lyric romance takes us into the realm of the sacred and the profane, the holy and the dread-inducing. Its metrical virtuosity attempts to girdle round what is at the same time acknowledged to be "measureless to man" (27).

The river is an image central to other romances of the poetic vocation in the Romantic period (Wordsworth's *The Prelude* or Shelley's *Alastor* are examples). That which flows through *Kubla Khan* carries as its symbolic cargo awareness of the unknown. Possibly recalling the close of the second paragraph of Coleridge's poem, Shelley has his Poet comment as follows on a "stream" in *Alastor*: "O stream! / Whose source is inaccessibly profound, / Whither do thy mysterious waters tend? / Thou imagest my life" (502–3). What the stream images is the romance of lost, unknowing but questing consciousness. Coleridge may anticipate this emphasis in his reference to the "caverns measureless to man," 27), but he places his stress on momentary intuitions of supra-rational coherence and order. In the third section, he shapes a virtual world, a secondary creation, in which the dome's "shadow" (31) harmonizes with "the mingled measure" to create a marvel, or "miracle of rare device, / A sunny pleasure-dome with caves of ice!" (35–6). Here, one might feel, Coleridge has found his way into an imaginative clearing in which what is revealed is of the essence of romance: a quality of enchantment, a "miracle" that is at once "devised" and capable of effortlessly uniting the seemingly discordant.

The poem could have ended here, a clinching couplet announcing a miraculous resolution. What makes this lyric romance typically Romantic is the restless fashion in which it recommences the process of adventure, this time through a recollection of an original purity of "symphony and song" (43). The creator of this music, the "damsel with a dulcimer," belongs to another "vision" (38). The narrative complexities begin again: the damsel's music seems both kin to and beyond the "mingled measure"; her relationship with the "woman wailing for her demon-lover" (16) of the second verse paragraph is manifestly one of contrast, and yet both women embody a creative force. This force is vital for the creativity which the poet imagines for himself in the poem's final chant. This chant occupies a perpetual conditional tense as it reconstructs the events of the poem, seeing them as symbols for a shadowy, original act of creation, in which the poet "would build that dome in air, / That sunny dome! those caves of ice!" (46–7). Coleridge plays on the idea of "castles in the air," a familiar phrase for illusory dreams, in his imagining of that "dome in air," and yet this "dome in air" seems like a supreme possibility conjured up by the lyric's compacted romance. As in *The Rime of the Ancient Mariner*, the romancer takes center-stage at the poem's close, a figure who in this case induces through his state of rapt ecstasy a "holy dread" (52) in the onlooker. As in the *Rime*, the reality principle, which Harold Bloom, in his account of Freud and Romantic quest, sees as summoned into being for the founder of psychoanalysis by the longings of romance, is embodied in a listener, who marvels at the poet-figure, without plucking out the heart of his mystery.[7]

In a late letter written in 1825, Coleridge produces a virtual allegory of the war between enchantment and reality principle in his poetic romances. Describing his career in terms drawn from romance, he begins by saying that:

> In Youth and early Manhood the Mind and Nature are, as it were, two rival Artists, both potent Magicians, and engaged, like the King's Daughter and the rebel Genie in the Arabian Nights' Enternts. [Entertainments], in sharp conflict of Conjuration – each having for its object to turn the other into Canvas to paint on, Clay to mould, or Cabinet to contain.

Such a "conflict of Conjuration" runs through Coleridge's work, as he himself recognized. In a tour de force too long to be quoted here, he charts and enacts the movement from the mind's triumphs, resulting in "Christabels & Ancient Mariners set to music by Beethoven," to Nature's revenge. Nature, characterized in romance terms as "a wary wily long-breathed old Witch . . . is sure," Coleridge comments with sad wryness, "to get the better of Lady MIND in the long run" and "mocks the mind with its own metaphors" (534). The passage reads like a tragicomic meditation on the fate of Coleridge's own shaping spirit of imagination, never so vividly alive as when declaring its imminent demise. Here, metaphor allows the poet an escape route from depression, and reminds us that, in Coleridge's hands, romance serves as a vehicle for recording the mind's triumphs and tribulations, its involvement in "conflict of Conjuration" with all that opposes imaginative conquest.

At a subliminal level such a conflict is present in *Christabel*, a Coleridgean romance at home with the unhomely, driven to dwell among imaginings of trespass. If Coleridge never quite persuades the reader that *Kubla Khan* is a fragment, he manages in *Christabel* to compose a poem that dallies among complexities and shadows, refusing through its bewitching ambivalences to emerge into a state of moral daylight. The heroine's goodness and innocence may seem the stuff of romantic stereotype, but they are unable to hold at bay the serpentine corruptions brought into the poem by the powerfully presented Geraldine. Geraldine finds entrance into Christabel's home, sleeps with her in a scene that mingles sorcery and hints of lesbianism, and turns her father against her. And yet she, too, seems to struggle with a force beyond her control. Before she lies beside Christabel, the narrator comments:

> Ah! what a stricken look was hers!
> Deep from within she seems half-way
> To lift some weight with sick assay,
> And eyes the maid and seeks delay.
>
> (256–9)

The triplet rhyme sympathizes with the longing for "delay" from what appears here to be a task imposed on the "stricken" Geraldine. Good and evil swap places in a poem that is at its most uncanny in its narrator's attempts to affirm a straightforward trust in the scheme of things. So, at the close of the conclusion to Part 1, the narrator chooses to interpret Christabel's smiles and tears, and unquiet movement, not as the result of the disturbing influence of Geraldine, but of the heroine's knowledge "That saints will aid if men will call: / For the blue sky bends over all!" (330–1). There, the "For" of the last line is strikingly unearned and presupposes the very belief in all-guiding goodness which the poem subverts. The narrative structures of romance may traditionally be engaged in a "search," as Frye has it, "for some kind of imaginative golden age in time or space" (1957: 186), but Coleridgean romance aches with nostalgia for some state of Edenic harmony which the very presence of nostalgia reveals as ultimately lost. In the case of *Christabel* we have another example (along with *The Rime of the Ancient Mariner*) of a kind of nostalgia for the pieties associated with religious belief at its most unquestioning. This belief is figured throughout the poem as a medieval Catholicism, replete with invocations of saints, Mary, and guardian spirits, and it may be that Coleridge's imagination was more at ease imagining the frailty of religious spells in the face of evil when those spells were associated with a form of religion (Catholicism) which he did not profess.

As a narrative, *Christabel* is remarkable for its attention to atmosphere and mood, and reluctance to tell a straightforward tale. The attention to atmosphere and mood is at its most overt in the opening in which an air of foreboding and disquiet arises from the narrator's question-and-answer routine ("Is the night chilly and dark? / The night is chilly, but not dark," 14–15) and communicates itself to the subtly unsettled and unsettling meter of the poem. For examples of narrative reluctance, one might consider the two conclusions to the two parts, both of which meditate in more or less oblique ways on what has preceded them. So, in the second conclusion, the brusque behavior of Sir Leoline, who has been influenced by Geraldine's machinations, toward his much-loved daughter catalyzes reflection on the vagaries of paternal feeling; Coleridge depicts a father who delights in his child so much "that he at last / Must needs express his love's excess / With words of unmeant bitterness" (663–5). In this romance perversity becomes natural; the "unmeant" stands in for the heart's deepest feelings. The writing here spins itself out with unmoralistic effectiveness, seeming only mildly surprised by the impulse "To dally with wrong that does no harm" (669); in its capacity to induce a quiet horror at the unnaturalness of human nature, the passage illustrates in miniature the poem's subversive dealings with romance. The certainties of the genre are devastatingly mimicked and turned upside down, until it seems appropriate that the poem should fail to advance beyond sly, elusive surmises about the murky depths of the human psyche and the discontents of civilization.

Keats

Keats's imaginings center on the poetic vocation itself, and romance in his work serves to register the intoxication, and sometimes the sobering aftermath, induced by these imaginings. In the sonnet "When I have fears that I may cease to be," he associates death with an end of writing; no longer will he "trace" (7) the "shadows" (8) that he sees in the night sky "with the magic hand of chance" (8). That "magic hand of chance" rhymes serendipitously with the "Huge cloudy symbols of a high romance" (6) which it both perpetuates and is inspired by, and the phrasing brings out Keats' sense of romance as beckoning toward new thresholds, barely apprehended but valuable intimations. In another sonnet, "On sitting down to read *King Lear* once again," he invokes "golden-tongued romance" (1) as a seducing "syren" and "queen of far-away" (2), before banishing it in favor of tragedy, evoked in a grimacing line as "The bitter-sweet of this Shaksperean fruit" (8). Despite this assertion of a traditional generic hierarchy, Keats is able, in his use of romance, to bring his poetry into contact with tragic experience.

Endymion, which received the scorn of many of Keats' contemporaries, the polite indifference of later critics, and the author's self-criticism, comes into focus luminously when viewed through the lens of romance. Subtitled "A Poetic Romance," it uses its seemingly erratic plot-line – concerned with Endymion's love for the moon-goddess and eventual discovery of satisfied love when the heavenly Diana and the earthly Indian maid turn out to be one and the same at the close of Book 4 – to track Endymion's and Keats' adventures in consciousness. "The quest romance of *Endymion*," writes Stuart Curran, "figures forth the quest for poetic identity of its singer" (1986: 150). Indeed, Keats writes of the poem in terms which suggest its very composition and reception are forms of romance: the poem is

> a test, a trial of my Powers of Imagination and chiefly of my invention which is a rare thing indeed – by which I must make 4000 Lines of one bare circumstance and fill them with Poetry... Do not Lovers of Poetry like to have a little Region to wander in which they may pick and choose, and in which the images are so numerous that many are forgotten and found new in a second Reading...? (1995: 266)

This extract is often quoted, but the suggestions for readings it contains are rarely acted on; Keats' romance is, the letter hints, a teeming galaxy of "Poetry," a "Region to wander in," packed with inventive "images." It is scarcely fanciful to see the poem as an ocean whose every poetic wave is a romance in miniature, an adventure in enchantment and discovery. The poem's true meaning is best sought by attending to local details and felicities rather than to some supposed overarching allegory; it is the way such details and felicities ramify that creates the poem's larger meanings.

A few examples must suffice. The poem's opening radiates throughout the work, since the view that "A thing of beauty is a joy for ever" (Book 1, line 1) is both fought for in the wording of each line and contested by the fear that, in fact, the "loveliness" (Book 1, l. 2) of such things of beauty will "Pass into nothingness" (Book 1, l. 3). Epiphany and absence are the poles between which the couplets of this poem waver. The poet's task is greedily to absorb and make available to his readers the "glories infinite" (Book 1, l. 29) of imaginative experience, glories that may originate in the ordinary but are changed by Keats' verbal alchemy. "They alway must be with us, or we die" (Book 1, l. 33), he writes at the close of this opening, making clear what is at stake in this apparently almost extempore performance. Later in Book 1, when Endymion tells his sister Peona of his visionary encounters with a goddess-figure, he avoids the hackneyed through images that ally romance with credible sensuous experience, as when he says: "I felt upmounted in that region / Where falling stars dart their artillery forth, / And eagles struggle with the buffeting north / That balances the heavy meteor-stone' (Book 1, ll. 641–4). The pressure to imagine, shown in the assonantal patterning here ("*fa*l*ling*" and "*forth*" folding in a chiastic embrace round "*stars*," "*dart*," and "*ar*tillery"), is at work throughout the romance.

At the same time, romance in *Endymion* is alert to the dangers of enchantment. Keatsian ambivalence about "dream," both a gateway to vision and a possible form of delusion, is central to his individual reworking of romance, and it shows itself in *Endymion* when, near the close, the hero asserts: "I have clung / To nothing, lov'd a nothing, nothing seen / Or felt but a great dream!" (Book 4, ll. 636–8). On the face of it, the plot will prove this outburst to be mistaken; the "dream" he has loved has, indeed, been "great." But the repeated use of "nothing" speaks eloquently of the undertow of possible disenchantment that runs below the poem's surface. At this moment Endymion saves himself, one might argue, from the predicament of Shelley's Poet in *Alastor* (1816), a poem which seems to be a point of departure for *Endymion*. Shelley's Poet clings to the "nothing" of a visionary dream so tenaciously that it costs him his life. The mixed tonalities of *Alastor*, involving admiration for as well as criticism of the Poet's extremism, duplicate themselves throughout romances in the Romantic period. Keatsian and Shelleyan romance enters the mirage-world of narcissism in poetically expressive ways. When Endymion seeks to grasp his beloved in Book 4, his action gives rise to a scenario of vanishing and despair: "Despair! despair! / He saw her body fading gaunt and spare / In the cold moonshine. Straight he seiz'd her wrist; / It melted from his grasp: her hand he kiss'd, / And, horror! kiss'd his own – he was alone" (506–10). The beloved is no more than "cold moonshine," where the colloquial sense of "moonshine" ("foolish or visionary ideas," *OED*) peeps through as disconcertingly as the discovery that the kissed hand is the hero's own hand. In this context, the scene in Book 3, where Endymion helps Glaucus reawaken the spell-bound, sleeping lovers, assumes particular importance. In this episode Endymion lives for others and is saved from solipsism, just as the genre of romance (for Keats) must forsake the merely marvelous. And yet the lovers can only be saved when there is someone (Glaucus) who "*utterly / Scans all the depths of magic, and expounds / The meanings of all motions, shapes, and sounds*" (Book 3, ll. 696–8). The poem wishes to escape the mirror-world of self-concern that threatens romance, yet it privileges the ability to explore "*all forms and substances / Straight homeward to their symbol-essences*" (3, 699–700); abundance of "*meanings*" lures the imagination into construing a world of "*symbol-essences*" that contrives not to be insubstantial or shadowily Platonic. The budding poet values romance as a source of magical power and as a means of exploring the proper function of poetry.

In later work Keats uses the form of romance to take to new levels of expressiveness the tension between enchantment and disenchantment explored in *Endymion*. In "La Belle Dame Sans Merci" he weds the conventions of romance – love-blighted knight haunted by his encounter with "a faery's child" (14) – to obsessions which recur in his poetry, especially when he is writing about poetry. The poetry's use of the ballad form is spare and sophisticated. Keats avoids pastiche and confessional lyricism alike. Artfully suggesting the atmosphere of a medieval lay about the meeting of human and supernatural beings, he simultaneously detemporalizes his figures, so that they refuse simply to belong to an age that has passed. The poem's uncanniness derives, in part, from the way knight and lady belong in and out of time; we read a poem that has been thrown free from the poet's subjectivity and yet is profoundly concerned with subjectivity. The poem is strong on effect (palely loitering figure with anguish-moistened brow), but short on cause, creating intense pathos out of the gap. There is, we feel, a connection between what happened in the "elfin grot" (29) and the knight's nightmarish vision of enthralled, "death pale" (38) victims of "La belle dame sans merci," but we are hard pressed to say what the connection is. This lyric romance works its magic on us by obliging us to follow in the knight's footsteps. Powerful submerged concerns with sexuality and gender relations press themselves upon us without allowing us to condemn la belle dame as seductive sorceress or the knight-at-arms as guilty of male projection. The pendulum of control (if that is what it is) swings unexpectedly from the knight ("And there I shut her wild wild eyes / With kisses four," 31–2) to la belle dame ("And there she lulled me asleep," 33), but the absence of condemnation in the poem is striking; the knight's perceptions have an unanswerable as well as inexplicable authenticity, and his experience adds up to a destiny rather than an episodic diversion.

When he attempts to explain, the knight makes us aware of fumbling attempts to clarify what is evidently the source of continual bewilderment and residual enchantment. As the speakers glide into one another from stanza 3 to stanza 4, an effect created by absence of speech marks, it is clear that the knight's "I met a Lady in the Meads" (13) is at once an answer to the question "O what can ail thee . . . ?" (1) and a recognition that any answer must involve compulsive rehearsal of an incomprehensible experience.

Subsequent efforts by the knight to explain only promote further confusion. His assertion that "sure in language strange she said / I love thee true" (27–8) couples certainty with enigma. We wonder whether "sure" means "definitely" or "surely"; we wonder, too, whether the heart-piercing directness of "I love thee true" tells us more about the knight's need to hear than about the words spoken by the "faery's child." Her "language strange" depends for its comprehension on his wish-fulfilling translation. At the poem's close the knight's sophomoric "this" – "And this is why I sojourn here" (45) – bears witness to his inability to explain what has happened to him or why it has had such an impact on him. This is not to say that the poem uses romance to convey an impression of incomprehensibility for its own sake. It is, rather, that the knight has had an experience but missed its meaning, to adapt T. S. Eliot: or, more accurately, it is to suggest that missing the meaning may be a key to the significance of an experience of great intensity, one that cannot but link itself, through the emphasis on love, language, infatuation, and dream, with the romance between poet and muse.

The three narrative romances contained in Keats's 1820 volume – *Isabella*, *The Eve of St. Agnes*, and *Lamia* – sustain and amplify these explorations of imaginative experience. Keats grew to dislike the first two poems, describing *Isabella* as "smoke-able," that is, vulnerable to mockery, and displaying "too much inexperience of life, and simplicity of knowledge" (1995: 296), and doing his best to revise *The Eve of St. Agnes* in ways that subvert his immersion in the poem's romance. In fact, both poems balance delicately between surrender to and critique of the genre of romance. In doing so, they show that romance is able to be the medium for the imagination's self-apprehension. *Isabella* makes notable play of the fact that it is a retelling for the modern age of a past tale, a story from Boccaccio's *Decameron*; the telling of the tale oscillates between the straightforward and the self-conscious, never allowing the reader the luxury of a secure position. Keats might have said in his "Dear Reynolds, as last night in bed I lay" that he would "from detested moods in new romance / Take refuge" (111–12), but *Isabella* cannot wholly free itself from the "detested." Romance comes into contact with mercantilist capitalism in the form of Isabella's two brothers, who murder Lorenzo, their sister's lover, and with deranged obsession, when Isabella dotes on Lorenzo's severed head out of which her basil plant grows. The narrator's interventions focus self-consciously on his inability to retain the simplicity of telling to be found in the original tale. When Isabella discovers Lorenzo's corpse and digs it up, Keats intervenes, before she and her "aged nurse" (343) cut off the head, with the following stanza:

> Ah! wherefore all this wormy circumstance?
> > Why linger at the yawning tomb so long?
> O for the gentleness of old Romance,
> > The simple plaining of a minstrel's song!
> Fair reader, at the old tale take a glance,
> > For here, in truth, it doth not well belong
> To speak: – O turn thee to the very tale,
> And taste the music of that vision pale.

> (385–92)

The stanza establishes *Isabella* as second-order romance, remote from "the gentleness of old Romance." All Keats' synesthetic powers may be devoted to exhorting us to engage in appreciation of the original and "taste the music of that vision pale." And yet the reader both wishes to taste such music and is detained by Keats' own latter-day concern with "wormy circumstance," with the bereaved Isabella caught in all the unglamorous reality of obsessed grief as she digs up her lover's dead body, "nor stay'd her care, / But to throw back at times her veiling hair" (375–6). The poem's *ottava rima* does not have a Byronic knowingness (Byron will use the same form with effective wit in *Beppo* and *Don Juan*), but Keats exploits the possibilities it offers of prolonged attention and changes of direction.

The Eve of St. Agnes takes the concern shown by romance with antitheses and opposites to a compelling extreme. Cold is set against warmth; religion, old age, and death against youth and sexuality; the suspension of disbelief against the awareness of illusion; the deeply sensuous against the self-consciously fictive; the folkloric against the highly literary. Keats immerses himself in the legend of St. Agnes' Eve, which tells how a maiden retiring to bed without supper is rewarded with dreams of a future lover; at the same time he is self-aware about the attractions of make-believe, evoking "the argent revelry" (38) who attend the feast in the castle where Porphyro, Romeo-like, braves the hostility of ancient foes to win Madeline's love, and conceding that this group of revelers is "Numerous as shadows haunting fairily / The brain, new stuff'd, in youth, with triumphs gay / Of old romance" (39–41). Fleetingly but tellingly, the lines lay bare the imaginative process we witness in the poem, as the poet's "brain" freshly recreates "triumphs gay / Of old romance." Keats' capacity for feeling his way into his subject drives the poetry's "triumphs," whether its rhythm is limping in sympathy with the hare "trembling through the frozen grass" (3), or the poem's hero is pictured "Brushing the cobwebs with his lofty plume" (110), or its heroine is captured falling asleep in "her soft and chilly nest" (235). The result is a sumptuous and in-felt occupation of a world that is a heightened version of our own and a pure incarnation of the spirit of romance, where romance means surrender to the enchantment of the past.

Keats' past world, however, unmoors itself from history (it is impossible to date or place his castle, save in some vaguely medieval age), even as it comments with possible secular irony on the modes of religious belief current in the poet's contemporary culture. The poem has been read as exalting transcendental ecstasy (Earl Wasserman) and as exposing the voyeuristic designs of a near-rapist and the life-denying refusal of life of a hoodwinked dreamer (Jack Stillinger).[8] The fact that it can sustain both readings indicates Keats' ability to inhabit the very genre (romance) which he seems at times to subvert. The peculiarity and greatness of the poem derive from the presence in its diction of high intelligence as well as sensuous intensity. The sleeping Madeline, for example, is no heroine out of Henry James; we attribute to her no great complexity of moral or emotional consciousness. But as a figure who is at once "*Blissfully* haven'd both from joy and pain" (240) and "*Blinded* alike from sunshine and from rain" (242) (emphases added), she is the subject of juggling acts of judgment, envied and yet criticized for her retreat from the contraries of human experience. Again Porphyro, concealing himself in Madeline's bedroom, may seem less gallant hero than voyeur as he watches the heroine undress (stanza 26). Keats, however, refuses simply to hand him over to our tut-tutting disapproval, entering into Porphyro's feelings with an ungiving power. "Noiseless as fear in a wide wilderness" (250) in Madeline's bedroom, Porphyro manages not to recall Iachimo in *Cymbeline*; rather, the writing attributes to him something of the "slumberous tenderness" (247) that he listens to in the sleeping Madeline.

At the poem's climax, romance and the reality principle battle it out. Madeline, before making love with Porphyro, expresses her disappointment that he is not the man of her dreams. After the love-making, "the frost-wind blows / Like Love's alarum pattering the sharp sleet / Against the window-panes" (322–4), breaking in upon the spellbound world of romance. But during the love-making itself opposites converge and coalesce, especially in the wording of the unrevised and received reading where it is said of Porphyro that "Into her dream he melted, as the rose / Blendeth its odour with the violet, – / Solution sweet" (320–2). Here Keats finds a way of talking about sexual intercourse that is also a means of describing a marriage between "dream" and reality. The dreams of romance are actualized and made real by lover and poet. The balance here does not hold, and the poem's ending leaves the reader unsure whether the love depicted in the poem will last. Above all, it questions our own involvement in the romance. In the final stanza we leave the castle with the lovers, and then find that the lovers have left us, as the narrator whisks us away from a world in which we have been absorbed: "And they are gone: ay, ages long ago / These lovers fled away into the storm" (371–2). That "storm" might be "an elfin-storm from faery land, / Of haggard seeming, but a boon indeed" (342–3), as Porphyro professes, but it spells an end to Keats' imaginative inhabiting of "faery land" in the poem.

Indeed, *The Eve of St. Agnes* marks the high point of Keats' engagement with romance. In *Lamia*, the serpent-woman heroine embodies the ambivalences of romance with jaunty painfulness; she is a series of riddling oxymorons, a shape-changing illusion doomed to be unmasked by Apollonius, embodiment of reason at its most reductive. In this poem, Keats, schooled by Dryden, rehearses his tug toward and mistrust of romance with a kind of self-lacerating mockery. In some of the most impressive writing the reader witnesses an effect of destroyed illusions (the final section in which Lamia is literally seen through by Apollonius' gaze is a case in point). *The Fall of Hyperion* (1819), Keats' unfinished reworking of the first *Hyperion*, sees a renewed and severe reengagement with romance. Dream is castigated by the poet's muse, Moneta, incarnation (among many things) of the poet's superego and an eloquent, proleptic spokesperson for Freud's reality principle. At the same time, the poem is subtitled "A Dream." The warning against romance, the imagination, dream, and enchantment is delivered in a poem that is still in thrall formally and imaginatively to these things. Keats or his muse denigrates a poetry of mere "dream" and opposes "The poet and the dreamer" as "Diverse, sheer opposite, antipodes" (199, 200); yet he is nowhere more indebted to romance than in this late Dantean piece, in which the adventures of consciousness made possible by romance take on a tragically sobered coloring.

See also: chapter 3, THE POPULAR ENGLISH METRICAL ROMANCES; chapter 4, ARTHURIAN ROMANCE; chapter 16, ROMANCE AND THE ROMANTIC NOVEL; chapter 18, VICTORIAN ROMANCE: TENNYSON; chapter 19, VICTORIAN ROMANCE: MEDIEVALISM.

Notes

1. Preface to *Alastor*, in *Shelley's Poetry and Prose*, ed. Donald H. Reiman and Neil Fraistat (2002), p. 72. This edition is used for all quotations from Shelley's poetry.
2. *Biographia Literaria*, ch. 14, in *Samuel Taylor Coleridge*, Oxford Authors, ed. H. J. Jackson (1985), p. 314. Unless indicated otherwise, this edition is used for all quotations from Coleridge's writings.
3. "Ode to a Nightingale," l. 70; quoted from John Keats, *Selected Poems*, ed. Nicholas Roe (1995). This edition is used for all quotations from Keats' poetry.
4. Northrop Frye, *The Secular Scripture* (1976: 48). See the same work, p. 47, where Frye contrasts the "'and then' narrative" of romance with the "'hence' narrative" of realism.
5. Quoted from Wordsworth and Coleridge, *Lyrical Ballads*, ed. with intro. R. L. Brett and A. R. Jones (London: Methuen, 1969), p. 277.
6. The Preface to "Kubla Khan" is quoted from the Oxford Standard Authors edition, ed. E. H. Coleridge (1912), pp. 296, 295, since the Oxford Authors edition does not include a full text.

7. See Harold Bloom on Freud and "the reality principle" in Bloom's "The Internalization of Quest Romance" (1971: 23).
8. See Jack Stillinger, *"The Hoodwinking of Madeline" and Other Essays on Keats's Poems* (Urbana: University of Illinois Press, 1971), and Earl R. Wasserman, *The Finer Tone: Keats' Major Poems* (Baltimore, MD: Johns Hopkins University Press, 1953). For further discussion of Keatsian romance and its deconstructive ability to celebrate and criticize romance in the same breath, see Tilottama Rajan, *Dark Interpreter* (1980). See also Jacqueline M. Labbe, *The Romantic Paradox* (2000). Labbe reads Keats' romances as seeking to "challenge the viability of . . . masculinity" (2000: 86).

References and Further Reading

Texts

Byron, George Gordon, Lord (1986). *Byron*, ed. Jerome J. McGann. Oxford Authors. Oxford: Oxford University Press.

Coleridge, Samuel Taylor (1985). *Samuel Taylor Coleridge*, ed. H. J. Jackson. Oxford Authors. Oxford: Oxford University Press.

Hemans, Felicia (2002). *Selected Poems, Prose, and Letters*, ed. Gary Kelly. Peterborough, Ontario: Broadview.

Keats, John (1995). *Selected Poems*, ed. Nicholas Roe. London: Dent.

Scott, Sir Walter (1904). *Scott: Poetical Works*, ed. J. Logie Robertson. Oxford Standard Authors. London: Oxford University Press.

Shelley, Percy Bysshe (2002). *Shelley's Poetry and Prose*, ed. Donald H. Reiman and Neil Fraistat. 2nd edn. New York and London: Norton.

Wordsworth, William (1984). *William Wordsworth*, ed. Stephen Gill. Oxford Authors. Oxford: Oxford University Press.

Criticism

Auden, W. H. (1951). *The Enchafèd Flood; or, The Romantic Iconography of the Sea*. London: Faber and Faber.

Bloom, Harold (1971). "The Internalization of Quest Romance." In *The Ringers in the Tower: Studies in Romantic Tradition*. Chicago: University of Chicago Press.

Cox, Jeffrey N. (1998). *Poetry and Politics in the Cockney School: Keats, Shelley, Hunt and their Circle*. Cambridge: Cambridge University Press.

Curran, Stuart (1986). *Poetic Form and British Romanticism*. New York: Oxford University Press.

Duff, David (1994). *Romance and Revolution: Shelley and the Politics of a Genre*. Cambridge: Cambridge University Press.

Frye, Northrop (1957). *Anatomy of Criticism: Four Essays*. Princeton, NJ: Princeton University Press.

Frye, Northrop (1976). *The Secular Scripture: A Study of the Structure of Romance*. Cambridge, MA: Harvard University Press.

Kucich, Greg (1991). *Keats, Shelley, and Romantic Spenserianism*. University Park: Pennsylvania State University Press.

Labbe, Jacqueline M. (2000). *The Romantic Paradox: Love, Violence and the Uses of Romance, 1760–1830*. Basingstoke: Macmillan.

Lowes, John Livingston (1978). *The Road to Xanadu: A Study in the Ways of the Imagination*. London: Picador. [First published in 1927, revised in 1955.]

Newlyn, Lucy, ed. (2002). *The Cambridge Companion to Coleridge*. Cambridge: Cambridge University Press.

O'Neill, Michael (1997). *Romanticism and the Self-Conscious Poem*. Oxford: Oxford University Press.

Perry, Seamus (1999). *Coleridge and the Uses of Division*. Oxford: Oxford University Press.

Rajan, Tilottama (1980). *Dark Interpreter: The Discourse of Romanticism*. Ithaca, NY: Cornell University Press.

Wolfson, Susan J. (1986). *The Questioning Presence: Wordsworth, Keats, and the Interrogative Mode in Romantic Poetry*. Ithaca, NY: Cornell University Press.

Wolfson, Susan J., ed. (2001). *The Cambridge Companion to Keats*. Cambridge: Cambridge University Press.

18

Victorian Romance: Tennyson

Leonée Ormond

Alfred Tennyson might be surprised to find himself included in this volume. Arthur E. Baker's *Concordance* of Tennyson's work as poet and dramatist lists only three usages of "romance," two from poems and the third from a play (1914: 589, 1057). Two of these date from the final decade of Tennyson's life, and both reflect contemporary disquiet about popular fiction and its possible effects upon young female readers. For the older Tennyson, "romance" was what Gillian Beer has defined as "lightweight commercial fiction deliberately written to flatter day dreams" (1970: 1).

In "The Wreck," a poem published by Tennyson in 1885, a woman tells of her flight from her husband.[1] When her lover, Stephen, dies in a storm at sea, she blames herself for destroying him. Her elopement, she tells her mother, did not arise from "animal vileness":

> for all but a dwarf was he,
> And all but a hunchback too; and I looked at him, first, askance,
> With pity – not he the knight for an amorous girl's romance!
>
> (III, 125)

The woman's reference to a "knight" as the likely object of a girl's fanciful desire is an appropriate one for, by this date, Tennyson's own *Idylls of the King* had done much to popularize courtly romances of knights and ladies.

In his village tragedy, *The Promise of May*, first performed in 1882, Tennyson used the word with much the same meaning. The heroine, Dora, has failed to recognize that her fiancé is her dead sister's seducer. Sensing that they have very different attitudes to life, she ponders the wisdom of her choice, concluding her soliloquy with another question: "But may not a girl's love-dream have too much romance in it to be realised all at once?" (Act III; Tennyson 1953: 741).

Tennyson had referred to "romance" on one earlier occasion, in a sonnet of 1877 addressed to Victor Hugo. The poem expresses gratitude to Hugo for his kindness to Tennyson's son, Lionel, during a visit to Paris. In its first version, the opening read:[2]

> Victor in Poesy, Victor in Romance,
> Cloud-weaver of phantasmal hopes and fears.

(III, 24)

Reprinting the poem three years later, Tennyson altered "Poesy" to "Drama," a substantial change, but one which retains the reference to "Romance" as Hugo's defining characteristic. From private comments, it is clear that this was the aspect of Hugo's "unequal genius" which Tennyson most admired (H. Tennyson 1897: II, 422).

Another of Hugo's admirers, Robert Louis Stevenson, writes of the important part played by the French writer in the development of the nineteenth-century prose romance. For Stevenson romance was "the poetry of circumstance" (1887: 250), an appropriate genre both for accounts of adventure and for the highest flights of the imagination. Hugo himself had pondered the meaning and derivation of the word, concluding that his early poems showed the influence of medieval romances. The "Préface" to his *Odes et Ballades* of 1824 considers the relation of "romantic" literature to the romance: "D'où lui vient ce nom de *romantique*? Est-ce que vous lui avez découvert quelque rapport bien évident et bien intime avec la langue *romance* ou *romane*?" (Hugo 1884: 10–11).

Tennyson had read Hugo in his twenties, after the death of his close friend Arthur Hallam; Hugo's work is well represented in Tennyson's library at Lincoln. An avid reader of novels and journals, Tennyson would have understood the issues in the critical debate later in the century on the distinction between romance and realism as modes of fiction, a debate in which Stevenson was to prove such an important contributor. Few of Tennyson's own copies of novels seem to have survived, but he is known to have admired Ann Radcliffe's Gothic fictions, *The Mysteries of Udolpho* and *The Romance of the Forest*. Poems published in 1827, when he was 17, are annotated with quotations from these two novels and from another early favorite, Charlotte Smith's *The Old Manor House*, with its secret threatened world of love, its isolated heroine and rescuing hero. Another much read author was Walter Scott, and there is a large selection of Scott novels in Tennyson's library. The boy Tennyson wrote poems inspired by Scott, one based on *The Bride of Lammermoor*, an important influence on his later *Maud*, with its story of lovers from warring families. Later, Tennyson was to describe Scott as "the most chivalrous literary figure of this century" (H. Tennyson 1897: II, 372). He also admired Thomas Hardy's early novel, *A Pair of Blue Eyes* of 1873, included by Stevenson in his list of modern romances.

Tennyson was familiar with many earlier works which are described as romances today, although he might not have recognized them under that designation. Both as a boy and as a young man, he read stories of all kinds, whether in verse or prose, and his reactions to them often found an outlet in his poetry. Throughout his career, Tennyson was, for all his outstanding lyric gifts, very much a poet of narrative. There are recognizable story poems, including *The Princess*, "The Revenge," or *Enoch Arden*, but more meditative poems, like his masterpiece, *In Memoriam*, are often lit up by glimpses of familiar human stories, used as points of comparison with the poet's own emotion. This was an age of storytelling, not only in fiction but also in poetry, the fine arts, and music.

Tennyson's involvement with the romance narrative was life-long, beginning with fairy tales, and continuing through classical and eastern texts, medieval and Renaissance writing, to the age of the novel. A surprising proportion of Tennyson's early poems are personal reinterpretations of romances of different types. His own major contribution to the genre, however, came through his versions of chivalric romance, inspired by his reading of Arthurian legend. Tennyson wrote his first Arthurian poem around 1830, and his last in the 1880s. The tendency to return to well-worn subjects or modes is one of Tennyson's most notable characteristics, and he reinvented the romance in different ways throughout his life.

At the same time, Tennyson developed the practice of insetting some of his romance poems into prologues and epilogues, frame tales of nineteenth-century life. This habit seems to have sprung from a wish to incorporate more modern subject matter in his work, as though the sensitive poet believed that it was a part of his calling to tackle the pressing issues of his own age. An early example of this is "The Day Dream." In 1830, while still a student at Cambridge, Tennyson published a short piece, "The Sleeping Beauty," in *Poems, Chiefly Lyrical*. He gives a pictorial impression of the sleeping princess in Charles Perrault's story, embalming the girl at the heart of the legend as a static image, not as part of a narrative:

> She sleeps, nor dreams, but ever dwells
> A perfect form in perfect rest.
>
> (II, 52)

In the two years that followed, Tennyson completed a sequence of poems to surround his original evocation of the sleeping princess. The first describes the palace, sunk in sleep; birds, insects, plants, barons, butler, and king are all frozen into stillness, with only a hint in the final stanza of their eventual release from stasis:

> When will the hundred summers die,
> And thought and time be born again,
> And newer knowledge, drawing nigh,
> Bring truth that sways the soul of men?
> Here all things in their place remain,
> As all were ordered, ages since.
> Come, Care and Pleasure, Hope and Pain,
> And bring the fated fairy Prince.
>
> (II, 51)

Plate 3. "The Rose Bower," from the *Legend of Briar Rose* series, painted by Sir Edward Coley Burne-Jones, completed in 1890. (The Faringdon Collection Trust, Buscot Park, Oxfordshire.)

Edward Burne-Jones' *Briar Rose* series of pictures, painted in different versions from the 1860s to the 1890s, are the perfect counterpoint to this poem, again expressing an implied wish that "Care and Pleasure" will never return, so that the romance of the "Sleeping Beauty" can be left to its own perfection. Tennyson, unlike Burne-Jones, completed the poem with the arrival of the Prince, the waking of the Princess, and an onomatopoeic evocation of the disturbances of normal life:

> The parrot screamed, the peacock squalled,
> The maid and page renewed their strife,
> The palace banged, and buzzed and clackt,
> And all the long-pent stream of life
> Dashed downward in a cataract.

(II, 54)

The Prince and Princess depart, in a scene reminiscent of the end of Keats' *Eve of St. Agnes* (a favorite poem with Tennyson). Unlike Keats, who concludes his poem with storm and death, Tennyson leaves us free to imagine the best for the lovers' future, while the outcome remains open:

> And o'er the hills, and far away
> Beyond their utmost purple rim,
> Beyond the night, across the day,
> Through all the world she followed him.

(II, 56)

Tennyson employs many of the characteristics of the romance in his retelling of a familiar story. The setting is a palace, the lovers are prince and princess. Stained glass, clothes, jewelry, even the bedclothes, are fine and costly. The characters are not defined as personalities, but left to play their parts in a preordained story. However, hostile criticism of the 1830 volume convinced Tennyson that this was not enough. According to his friend, the poet Edward Fitzgerald, he added a prologue and epilogue after 1835, as he did with the "Morte D'Arthur," "to give a reason for telling an old-world tale" (H. Tennyson 1897: I, 194). Tennyson's Prologue, Moral, Envoi, and Epilogue do not, however, take him far away from the atmosphere of his original poem. The extended work is now entitled "The Day-Dream" and the poet addresses an aristocratic woman, Lady Flora, who, like the poet, has been asleep. After telling her of his own dream, he addresses his poem to her, mocking his own temerity and speculating on her reactions. As Christopher Ricks comments, each of the changes weakened the original impulse: "even the felicities of phrase now lack the tautness, the tension, which the isolated sleeping beauty created" (Ricks 1972: 135).

"The Sleeping Beauty" is only one instance of the effect on Tennyson's poetry of his early reading. When the available evidence is assembled, it is clear that he grew up reading "romance," and that he *would* probably have recognized his own place in a tradition defined by a modern, rather than a late nineteenth-century, meaning of the term. Such a concept of romance would have carried Tennyson back to the roots of his creativity, to his Lincolnshire childhood, to his days as an undergraduate at Cambridge, and to his friendship with Arthur Henry Hallam.

We know that, as a boy, Tennyson read *The Arabian Nights* in Galland's French translation. This compilation of stories from different Middle Eastern traditions is often accounted a treasury of romance. In "Recollections of the Arabian Nights," published in Tennyson's 1830 volume, he tries to evoke the excitement of an exotic Eastern locale without narrating the stories themselves. Tennyson was influenced by a number of the tales, but there are few precise narrative details, for all his repeated references to Haroun Alraschid. The figure in the boat carried down the Tigris is very much the poet, carried back into the world of romance literature:

> Thence through the garden I was drawn –
> A realm of pleasance, many a mound,
> And many a shadow-chequered lawn
> Full of the city's stilly sound.
>
> (I, 229)

The young Tennyson read poetry with his mother, and it may have been with her that he first encountered "The Sleeping Beauty" and the *Arabian Nights*. It was with his father, however, that he studied Homer.

George Tennyson was the father of a large family, and he taught them all (girls and boys) the classical languages. For scholars of romance, Homer's *Odyssey* is the "archetype, not only of Greek, but of all great romance" (McDermott 1989: 12). Alfred Tennyson drew upon the *Odyssey* for two of his finest early poems, "The Lotus Eaters" and "Ulysses." Both raise issues about whether the protagonists should move forward or "rust unburnished" ("Ulysses," I, 617), questions which were troubling Tennyson personally. As in all Tennyson's later developments of romance material, his *Odyssey* poems reconstruct Homer's narrative by exploring the psychology of the characters, and by relating this exploration to a detailed account of the natural world.

Homer's *Iliad* is not usually interpreted as a romance, but it could be argued that Tennyson extracted one of the "romance" elements from the narrative for his poem on "Oenone," the first love of Paris, abandoned for Helen. Tennyson's main source, however, was Ovid's *Heroides*. As in other instances, he was to return to the material. "The Death of Oenone" was published posthumously in 1892.

The *Heroides* was one of Geoffrey Chaucer's sources for his "Legend of Good Women," another favorite work of Tennyson's youth. Tennyson published his own "recollection" of Chaucer, "A Dream of Fair Women" of 1832. The poet imagines himself falling asleep over a volume of "The Legend" by "Dan Chaucer, the first warbler" (I, 481). Here, however, Tennyson did not foreground his own emotional reactions to the narrative but, taking Chaucer's dream structure, he wrote his own poem, introducing new female characters: Helen of Troy, Iphigenia, Jephtha's daughter, and Fair Rosamond. As Tennyson noted, one figure in his poem *had* appeared in

"A Dream of Fair Women": "From among these Cleopatra alone appears in my poem" (I, 480). He is careful to point out, however, that his major source for the Egyptian queen was Shakespeare, not Chaucer. Tennyson's account of Fair Rosamond, Rosamond Clifford, mistress of Henry II, places his poem within the romance tradition. Legend has it that Rosamond was murdered by the king's wife, Eleanor of Aquitaine, within the palace garden at Woodstock. Her fate clearly captured Tennyson's imagination, as Fair Rosamond reappeared in his play, *Becket*, rejected for the Lyceum by Henry Irving in the 1870s, and not performed in the poet's lifetime.

Literature was not the only route to romance for the Tennyson children. George Tennyson had collected a number of Old Master paintings, mainly good early copies of Italian and Dutch works. The poet's niece, Agnes Weld, spoke of one in particular, a version of a subject from the *Gerusalemme Liberata* of Torquato Tasso: "Both my uncles Alfred and Charles have often told me of the influence exerted upon their minds by the poetic dreams that were suggested to them by the beautiful picture of 'Armida and Rinaldo with the Decoying Nymph'" (Weld 1903: 12). The painting, which is unidentified, probably came into the possession of Tennyson's younger brother, Charles, inspiring him to write a sonnet recalling its early "influence" on him:

> Dear is that picture for my childhood's sake, –
> The man asleep, so near to love or harm;
> The winged boy, that stays Armida's arm,
> The siren-girl, all hushed lest he awake.
>
> (Tennyson Turner 1868: 18)

The picture evidently showed the Christian knight, Rinaldo, asleep, watched over by the witch Armida, who has vowed revenge upon him, but now falls in love with him.

George Tennyson's two copies of *Gerusalemme Liberata*, both in Italian, are now at Lincoln. One, published in Padua in 1726, was acquired by Tennyson after his father's death, and twice annotated with his own name. The first of these inscriptions is dated "Somersby 1835" and the second simply reads "Farringford," Tennyson's home from 1853. By that time, he was also the owner of a two-volume copy of the famous English translation of Tasso by Edward Fairfax, the gift of a Cambridge friend, Robert Tennant. A new translation, by Alexander Cunningham Robertson, was published in 1853, and this also entered Alfred Tennyson's collection.

Tennyson's interest in Tasso emerges in his long poem about a women's university, *The Princess* of 1847. Here the framing "Prologue" to the knightly jousts and battles tells of a group of nineteenth-century characters who entertain one another with a serial story in the manner of Chaucer's pilgrims or of Boccaccio's exiles from Florence. A broken statue is propped against the country-house wall at Vivian Place. Its subject is an ancestor, Sir Ralph, who fought with Richard I during the Crusades and was present at his victory over the Saracens at Ascalon. Walter Vivian tells the poet the story of Sir Ralph:

> "A good knight he! we keep a chronicle
> With all about him" – which he brought, and I
> Dived in a hoard of tales that dealt with knights,
> Half-legend, half-historic, counts and kings
> Who laid about them at their wills and died.
>
> (II, 189)

Among these earlier warriors was

>   a lady, one that armed
> Her own fair head, and sallying through the gate,
> Had beat her foes with slaughter from her walls.
>
> (II, 189)

The chronicle describes how this "miracle of noble womanhood" swept out "like a thunderbolt," "her arm lifted, eyes on fire" (II, 190). This tale of the warrior woman has an obvious relevance to Tennyson's story of a female university, with its analysis of woman's place in the world. At the same time, through its relation to Walter's narrative of the crusading Sir Ralph, it suggests an association with Tasso's epic account of the knightly battles for Jerusalem and of the warrior women who fought there. *Gerusalemme Liberata*, rather than Malory's *Morte Darthur*, may have been a source for the broadly sketched picture of a medieval political system in *The Princess*. Tasso's Clorinda, one of the leading warriors in the Saracen army, is killed by the man who loves her, the Christian knight, Tancred. Tasso's description of Clorinda riding out to battle suggests a closer parallel than even Spenser's Britomart with the warrior woman of Vivian Place:

>   against her foes on rode the Dame,
> And turn' their backs against the winde and raine,
> Upon the French with furious rage she came,
> And scorn'd those idle blowes they stroke in vain.
>
> (Tasso 1981: 270)

Tennant's gift of Tasso's poem seems to have been part of an exchange of books. A five-volume Latin edition of the *Decameron*, the mid-fourteenth-century sequence of stories by Giovanni Boccaccio, loosely connected through a frame tale of flight from plague-stricken Florence, is now in Tennyson's library. It was originally given to Tennant by Tennyson, and was presumably returned after Tennant's death in 1842. Tennyson's father owned an Italian edition, which would have been available to his son. It is likely that the poet was inspired to explore the text by his friendship with Arthur Hallam, a passionate Italophile, who is said to have introduced the younger Tennysons to Italian poetry. One of Alfred's therapeutic activities in the immediate aftermath of Hallam's death was to work hard on his Italian. Years later, he recalled how the Somersby maid washed away the Italian phrases which he had carefully written out on his fireplace.

Tennyson later told his son that he had begun a poem drawing upon Boccaccio's "The Lover's Tale" when he was 17, which would have been around 1827, the year in which he arrived at Cambridge. Elsewhere, he says, more convincingly perhaps, that he was 19, which would place the writing of the poem after his meeting with Arthur Hallam.

As with other romance authors whom he encountered in youth, Tennyson returned to Boccaccio much later in life, writing a play on another subject from the *Decameron*, *The Falcon*, when he was nearly 60. Many stories in the *Decameron* were renowned for their bawdiness. Tennyson was, however, attracted to two tales which belong to a more courtly romance tradition. They have in common the narrative of a young man who seeks the love of a woman, apparently in vain. In both cases she is married to another, although in the story from which *The Falcon* is taken, the husband is now dead. Both of the spurned lovers behave with exemplary generosity and nobility of spirit, demonstrating the highest ideals of romance.

In Boccaccio's fourth story for the tenth day, from which *The Lover's Tale* comes, Gentile loves another man's wife, Catalina. When she dies he goes to her tomb and, placing his hand upon her breast, realizes that she is still alive. He takes her home, where his mother revives and saves her. Having promised to preserve her honor, Gentile asks Catalina to allow him to return her to her husband in his own time. Shortly afterwards, she gives birth to a son. Gentile asks his friends to dinner, and sets them to decide whether a man who finds and revives a servant left for dead is entitled to keep the servant. When Catalina's husband declares that the servant must belong to the man who found and restored him, Gentile brings in his wife and child. Husband and wife are reunited, and Gentile remains a close friend of the family.

In "The Lover's Tale," Tennyson writes of a young man, Julian, who grows up and falls in love with a cousin Cadrilla, later renamed Camilla because Tennyson thought that Cadrilla sounded like "quadrille." The lengthy passage on their childhood, narrated by Julian, is entirely absent from the original Boccaccio text, and Tennyson thus moves the emphasis of the story away from a courtly love tale of passion for a married woman to an account of early love, set within a richly evoked landscape of hills and the sea. Camilla tells Julian that she loves another man, Lionel, a theme to which Tennyson was to return in his *Enoch Arden*. After Camilla's marriage, Julian despairs. Then he hears of her death, and makes his way secretly to the chapel where her body lies, in order to take farewell of her. As in Boccaccio, he finds that she is still alive, and, her husband being away, brings Camilla to his home where she bears her child. Tennyson had apparently written this part of the story when it was set up in print for publication with his 1832 volume of poems. Then, despite the appeals of Arthur Hallam and other friends, he withdrew it, feeling that it was too flawed to appear in its present form. Only in 1869 did he publish the final section, "The Golden Supper," and then only as a result of his outrage at the circulation of pirated copies of the 1832 version. "The Golden Supper" is narrated by another speaker, and it is he who describes Julian's return of the wife to the husband, and his departure from the area. In the original story, Gentile had remained close to the couple, but, perhaps responding to Victorian morality, Tennyson banishes his hero. The whole poem appeared in a revised form in 1879.

The older Tennyson was in the habit of reading aloud to his wife in the evenings and Boccaccio's name sometimes appears in her diary entries for the 1870s. Unfortunately, Emily Tennyson does not list the stories selected for reading, but those which inspired *The Lover's Tale* and *The Falcon* were perhaps among them. Tennyson's dramatic adaptation of Boccaccio's ninth story for the fifth day, *The Falcon*, was one of his most successful ventures in the theater. His full-length play, *Queen Mary*, had run for only 23 performances in 1879, but, by contrast, his two shorter plays, *The Falcon* and *The Cup*, were very well received in 1879 and 1881. For *The Falcon*, Tennyson retained the names of Boccaccio's characters. The impoverished but noble Federigo loves the widowed noblewoman, Giovanna. He has spent all his money on presents for her, but she will not accept his suit. Hunting with his falcon is now his only pleasure, and a source of food. Giovanna visits him to ask him to gratify her sick son's wish to see his falcon. Federigo, having nothing else to give her, has, however, killed the falcon in order that Giovanna can dine. Won over by his generosity, she accepts him.

Tennyson took the bare outline of Boccaccio's story, and then, as with *The Lover's Tale*, he gave the characters defined personalities, deepening the simple stereotypes of the romance tale. He introduces Federigo's female servant and his foster brother, Filippo. Both characters have a function as storytellers, and they also provide the dramatist with another means of underlining the nobility of Federigo's behavior. Concentrated within a single act, the drama of misunderstanding leads to a happy ending, as Giovanna decides to accept Federigo. Tennyson removes the dark note with which Boccaccio ends his story, the death of Giovanna's son and her inheritance of her husband's fortune. At the same time he reduces the importance of Giovanna's brothers, whose desire to keep her fortune in their own family is a feature of the original story. For Boccaccio's readers, such an ending would have represented an assurance that the couple could live in a style appropriate to their rank. In Tennyson's drama, however, there is a gentler ending, as Federigo promises Giovanna:

> We two together
> Will help to heal your son – your son and mine –
> We shall do it – we shall do it.
>
> (Tennyson 1953: 723)

If anything, *The Falcon* follows more closely in the traditions of romance than the original story by Boccaccio.

With William and Madge Kendal in the leading roles, the play ran for 67 performances at the St. James's Theatre. The sets, by the painter Marcus Stone, were much praised. Some idea of his designs for Giovanna's dark red costume, decorated with gold and green jewels, can be gained from Val Prinsep's painting of Madge Kendal in the title role at the Garrick Club, London.

We do not know what prompted Tennyson to return to Boccaccio's stories after a long interval of years. Malory, on the other hand, is known to have been a lifelong favorite. Tennyson's Arthurian poems were a product of the revival of interest in the *Morte D'Arthur* which emerged at the turn of the eighteenth and nineteenth centuries. The first significant figures in this revival were Walter Scott and Robert Southey, and Southey wrote an introduction to an authentic Caxton text which was published in 1817. Two cheap editions had, however, already appeared in the previous year. Tennyson owned the three-volume edition published by R. Wilks, and a single volume of the other 1816 edition, published by Walker and Edwards, a gift from Leigh Hunt, is in the library at Lincoln (see Simpson 1996: 97–9). Roger Simpson points out that Tennyson favored Malory over other Arthurian sources, setting a trend which influenced most treatments of the story during the second half of the nineteenth century (Simpson 1990: 225). Tennyson himself told Edward Fitzgerald:

> Of the Chivalry Romances ... I could not read "Palmerin of England" nor "Amadis", nor any other of those Romances through. The "Morte d'Arthur" is much the best: there are very fine things in it, but all strung together without Art. (H. Tennyson 1897: I, 194)

He did, however, use the story of Geraint from the second volume of Lady Charlotte Guest's translation of Welsh stories, which she entitled *The Mabinogion* and published in 1840.

Through his father, the young Tennyson had access to a number of scholarly works about the historical Arthur. In his biography of his father, Hallam Tennyson tells us that the poet had "[f]rom his earliest years ... written out in prose various histories of Arthur" (1897: II, 121). One of Tennyson's first adaptations of Arthurian material, printed by Hallam Tennyson, is a plan for a religious allegory (possibly inspired by the movement in favor of Catholic Emancipation) with Arthur as faith, Merlin as science, Mordred as scepticism, and two Guineveres as primitive Christianity and Roman Catholicism respectively. The opposing Guineveres may have been influenced by Spenser's treatment of Una (true religion) and Duessa (Falsehood or the Roman Catholic Church) in *The Faerie Queene*. Another, and very different, prose plan has King Arthur in Camelot, with his bards singing to him, while the hostile forces of Saxons draw closer. A third scheme was for a five-act masque in which the Lady of the Lake was to have played a major role.

Two fragments of a "Ballad of Sir Lancelot" are believed, like these Arthurian schemes, to date from the early 1830s. Arthurian subject matter was often used for burlesque purposes at this period, and Tennyson's friends are reported to have enjoyed the humor of his poem. Twenty years later, Tennyson told the Duke of Argyll that he had composed a poem on Lancelot's Quest for the Grail in his head, but had since forgotten it. The brief sections which survive are a few lines of a love-song from Lancelot and a description of Lancelot and Guinevere riding through the woodland in spring (to the dismay of Merlin and of Lancelot's son, Sir Galahad). At this early stage in his career, it would seem that Tennyson was experimenting with a range of different approaches to the Arthurian legend: chivalric and nationalistic, burlesque, romance, and religious.

"The Lady of Shalott," published in 1832, was both Tennyson's first published Arthurian poem and, at the same time, his first important romance poem. The poet had read of the Donna di Scalotta in an Italian novella, and told a friend that "the web, mirror, island, etc., were my own. Indeed, I doubt whether I should ever have put it in that shape if I had been then aware of the Maid of Astolat in *Mort Arthur*" (Rossetti 1903: 341). Roger Simpson has demonstrated that Tennyson was not the first poet to turn to this source, and that, in comparison with his contemporaries, he achieves his effect "through a reduction of an orthodox story line ... His deliberate suppression of narrative thread presents the action in a staccato series of tableaux" (1990: 198). This "tableau" effect is characteristic of Tennyson's treatments of Arthurian subjects from "The Lady of Shalott" to the *Idylls*. Here the Lady's tower (a familiar feature of romance narrative) is set in a pastoral landscape, and the "lighted palace" of Camelot is briefly evoked with a townscape of houses, towers, gardens, and wharfs. Nor are these tableaux purely pictorial: sounds, whether of the wind in the leaves, Lancelot's ringing armor and his song, the Lady's haunting death lament, or "royal cheer" (I, 395), are an essential part of the effect.

The elements of a romance are present here, the knight in armor, the lady in the tower. Both play their parts in the story, but, as in a romance, we have few details of their appearance and less knowledge of their personalities. The sight of Lancelot, which leads to the Lady's death, is a fleeting one. His armor is described in most detail, and we hear of his "broad clear brow" and his "coal-black curls" (I, 392). The Lady herself is pictured as no more than "a lovely face" and not until Lancelot sees her lying dead in her barge (I, 395).

The concept of the prohibition at the heart of the Lady's story is a common feature of romance, but Tennyson's "curse" is an indefinite and oblique one:

> She has heard a whisper say,
> A curse is on her if she stay
> To look down to Camelot.
> She knows not what the curse may be.
>
> (I, 390)

We have a story of love in "The Lady of Shalott," but without the usual "happy ending." Many explanations for the Lady's story have been put forward, all intended to fill the gaps in the narrative. One of the more convincing, because it relates to other early Tennyson poems, sees the "Lady of Shalott" as a questioning of the poet's vocation, whether to live in a tower or to descend into the world of everyday life.

Scenes of battle and single combat were an almost invariable element in chivalric romance. Tennyson, however, had little taste for describing such episodes at any stage in his career. In the dream that precedes "A Dream of Fair Women," the poet finds

Plate 4.   La Mort d'Arthur, painted by James Archer, 1860. (Manchester City Art Galleries.)

himself about to strike a blow, but the focus rapidly moves away, and the stroke is never made:

> And once my arm was lifted to hew down
> A cavalier from off his saddle-bow,
> That bore a lady from a leaguered town;
> And then, I know not how,
>
> All those sharp fancies, by down-lapsing thought
> Streamed onward, lost their edges, and did creep
> Rolled on each other, rounded, smoothed, and brought
> Into the gulfs of sleep.

(I, 483)

In Tennyson's early "Morte D'Arthur" poem, begun in 1833 and published in 1842, the account of the last great battle of Arthur and his knights is compressed into the ringing opening line: "So all day long the noise of battle rolled" (II, 5). When

Tennyson placed the poem within the setting of the final book of the *Idylls*, "The Passing of Arthur," he gave a fuller, if highly impressionistic, account of the "last weird battle in the west" (III, 549). The original poem opens with Arthur mortally wounded, and with his knights fallen around him. Only Sir Bedivere remains. The death of great men was a favorite subject with nineteenth-century writers and painters, and Tennyson's personal grief for Arthur Hallam went hand in hand with this to inspire one of his finest poems.

J. M. Gray has made a close comparison of the text with the relevant passages of Malory's eighth book, showing how the poet takes, not only the outline of events, but also some of the most telling physical details from *Morte D'Arthur* (Gray 1980: 10–12). The dying Arthur sends Bedivere to throw the sword Excalibur back into the lake where the Lady of the Lake once gave it to him. From Malory's brief reference to the jeweled sword and a ruined chapel Tennyson creates a night setting with characteristic effects of light and sound, deepened through onomatopoeia and alliteration:

> So saying, from the ruined shrine he stept
> And in the moon athwart the place of tombs,
> Where lay the mighty bones of ancient men,
> Old knights, and over them the sea-wind sang
> Shrill, chill, with flakes of foam. He, stepping down
> By zig-zag paths, and juts of pointed rock,
> Came on the shining levels of the lake.
>
> There drew he forth the brand Excalibur,
> And o'er him, drawing it, the winter moon,
> Brightening the skirts of a long cloud, ran forth
> And sparkled keen with frost against the hilt:
> For all the haft twinkled with diamond shafts,
> Myriads of topaz-lights, and jacinth-work
> Of subtlest jewellery.

(II, 7–8)

While the subject of Tennyson's "Morte D'Arthur" is not, strictly speaking, the stuff of romance, his debt to the form and his legacy to its future development is clear here. The symbolic object is of importance in the romance and here the sword stands for kingship, and for Arthur's renunciation of it after the fall of the Round Table. But what readers will remember from the passage is the haft shining in the moonlight and the contrast between the bleak scene and the brilliant weapon.

For publication in 1842, Tennyson set his poem into a frame tale (like that for the later *Princess* and for "The Sleeping Beauty"). "The Epic" is an account of a Christmas Eve party, where the guests discuss the relation between the modern world and that of the past. A poet, Everard Hall, reads the "Morte D'Arthur" poem aloud. He tells his audience that it is the only remaining part of his 12-book Arthurian epic, the rest having been burnt as deemed unsatisfactory.

> "Why take the style of those heroic times?
> For nature brings not back the Mastodon,
> Nor we those times; and why should any man
> Remodel models? these twelve books of mine
> Were faint Homeric echoes, nothing-worth,
> Mere chaff and draff, much better burnt."
>
> (II, 2–3)

"The Epic" light-heartedly dramatizes Tennyson's own doubts about creating a 12-book "epic." He wrote in 1858 that he would "be crazed to attempt such a thing in the heart of the 19th Century" (1981–90: II, 212). The less challenging title, *Idylls of the King,* was given to the sequence of poems about Arthur and his knights, the first of which was published in 1859 and the last in 1885. Tennyson did not write the books in chronological order, and when the sequence was eventually finished it was clear that the overall emphasis was on the later years of Arthur's reign and the gradual disintegration of the kingdom. Gillian Beer has written of the "increased role of women and the emphasis on sexual love" which "chiefly distinguish the Arthurian romance from earlier related Carolingian literature [epics or *chansons de geste*]" (1970: 25). Tennyson takes this process further in his *Idylls.* The four books published in 1859 all bore female names in their titles, "Vivien" (later "Merlin and Vivien"), "Elaine" (later "Lancelot and Elaine"), "Guinevere", and "Enid" (later divided into "The Marriage of Geraint" and "Geraint and Enid"). In each the emphasis falls upon "sexual love." Some of the later books continue this pattern, among them "Gareth and Lynette," published in 1872 and "Pelleas and Ettarre" of 1869. Other books, written later, are more concerned with the history of Arthur himself. "The Coming of Arthur" and "The Passing of Arthur," both of 1869, introduce and conclude the cycle. "The Last Tournament" and "Balin and Balan" both represent important elements in the overall theme of disintegration.

Of all the books, Tennyson himself found "The Holy Grail" the most disturbing. He told the Duke of Argyll, "I doubt whether such a subject could be handled in these days, without incurring a charge of irreverence" (1981–90: II, 244), but, once he began, it took him only ten days in 1868 to write it. Tennyson's reluctance can be related to the comparative absence of the supernatural from the *Idylls,* a departure from earlier romance versions of the story, including Malory's. He eventually solved a part of his problem with "The Holy Grail" by writing most of it as a dramatic monologue, told by Sir Percivale, and so shifting the burden of proof and belief away from the poet himself. Although Tennyson visited many of the places associated with the legends of Arthur, he was deliberately indefinite about locations in his poem and was not to be drawn into the arguments about the identity of the original Arthur, or about the religious significance of the Grail quest.

Malory's *Morte Darthur* has been described both as a romantic epic and as an Arthurian romance. It could be argued that Tennyson's version of the story, which draws upon a variety of sources, is closer to romance than that of Malory. Tennyson's avoidance of the description of violent action, for example, means that such passages as this have no place in the *Idylls*: "Anon sir Arthure ran to anothir and smote hym downe and thorow the body with a spere, that he felle to the erthe dede" (Malory 1967: I, 129).

The original Arthurian legends contain much which belongs to the romance tradition. Arthur's origins, for example, are mysterious. Is he the son of Uther Pendragon, and therefore the rightful heir by birth, or is he a supernatural figure? Tennyson includes both possibilities. In "The Coming of Arthur" Guinevere's father, Leodogran, King of Cameliard, needs to know that Arthur is of noble birth if he is to accede to his marriage proposal. He is given two answers to his question. Either Uther married King Gorlois' queen, immediately after killing her first husband in battle, and Arthur was conceived legitimately, or, as in Bedivere's version of the story, drawn from Merlin's master, Bleys, the child Arthur was washed onto the shore from a ninth wave. More than one of Tennyson's poems speak of human life as lying between two seas, so that the second possibility can be interpreted metaphorically. In Merlin's words: "From the great deep to the great deep he goes" (*CA*, 410; III, 278).

The Arthurian cycle is, of course, essentially aristocratic, dealing with the lives of kings, queens, great knights and ladies. Romance frequently stresses ritual and ceremony, appropriate to the ordered court at Camelot, with Arthur giving judgment on questions of law and order and of knighthood. Tennyson describes such scenes at court, with the king sitting in state on his throne. One of the most stately examples comes in "Lancelot and Elaine," as Sir Lavaine and Sir Lancelot arrive at the joust. The prize is a diamond, the last taken from a dead king's crown found by Arthur in the years before he became king. In this passage, Tennyson's description of Arthur's robes and of his throne reflect the aestheticism of the late 1850s and 1860s, probably showing the influence of his friendship with the painter George Frederic Watts and with the Holland House circle. Such rich accounts of the symbolic accoutrements of kingship are also entirely in keeping with the traditions of romance. Lavaine sees

> the clear-faced King, who sat
> Robed in red samite, easily to be known,
> Since to his crown the golden dragon clung,
> And down his robe the dragon writhed in gold,
> And from the carven-work behind him crept
> Two dragons gilded, sloping down to make
> Arms for his chair.
>
> (*LE*, 430–6; III, 434)

Tennyson has been criticized, in his own time and today, for overdoing the descriptions of dress in the *Idylls*, but they are entirely appropriate for romance. In "The Marriage of Geraint" and "Geraint and Enid," much is made of Enid's clothes. When, in her poverty, she first meets Geraint, she wears "faded silk" (*MG*, 762: III, 347). After Geraint has defeated her father's enemy, her mother takes out a fine dress "All branched and flowered with gold" (*MG*, 631; III, 343), stolen from them three years before. Geraint, however, demands that she wear the "faded silk." Guinevere has declared that she alone will dress his bride for her wedding and, keeping her promise, the Queen "clothed her for her bridals like the sun" (*MG*, 836; III, 349). In her married life at Camelot, Enid, to please her husband, wears "some fresh splendour" every day, sometimes arrayed by the Queen herself, "In crimsons and in purples and in gems" (*MG*, 14 and 10; III, 324). As so often in romance, the pattern is then repeated in "Geraint and Enid." Mistrusting his wife, Geraint demands once more that she put on her "worst and meanest dress" and ride away with him (*MG*, 130; III, 328). Obeying him, Enid chooses the "faded silk" in which she traveled to Camelot. Later in the story, when her husband has been wounded and seems likely to die, Earl Doorm, who has captured her, demands that she wear

> a splendid silk of foreign loom,
> Where like a shoaling sea the lovely blue
> Played into green, and thicker down the front
> With jewels than the sward with drops of dew,
> When all night long a cloud clings to the hill,
> And with the dawn ascending lets the day
> Strike where it clung: so thickly shone the gems.
>
> > (*GE*, 686–92; III, 368)

Enid, of course, refuses the dress and insists on remaining as she is. When her situation seems desperate, Geraint recovers, and strikes off Doorm's head. On their return to Camelot, the Queen once more clothes Enid in "apparel like the day" (*GE*, 947; III, 374). Here, Enid's clothes are indications of her state of mind and of her situation. The revolving changes reflect the whole passage of a narrative which ends with qualified happiness, since Geraint, now suspicious of Guinevere, cannot take the same pleasure in her choice of garments for his wife.

Among the books of the *Idylls of the King* some are nearer to the pattern of romance than others. The two "Geraint" stories provide one example and "Gareth and Lynette" another. The princely Gareth, at the request of his mother, disguises himself as a kitchen boy. Arthur, discovering that Gareth is his nephew, promises him that he shall undertake the next quest which comes to Camelot. He is held to his word when Lynette entreats that Sir Lancelot shall rescue her sister, Lyonors. Instead, she finds herself given a scullion as a champion. The form of the story is easily recognizable, and has its roots in folk tale. Gareth even compares himself to "Cinderella":

> and thou wilt find
> My fortunes all as fair as hers who lay
> Among the ashes and wedded the King's son.
>
> > (*GL*, 880–2; III, 308)

For "Gareth and Lynette" Tennyson drew upon Malory's "Tale of Sir Gareth" from the eighth book of the *Morte Darthur*, making a number of significant changes from the original story. Stepping out of the romance tradition, he added a wealth of natural description, typical of his own style as a poet. In one of the best of his Virgilian metaphors drawn from nature, Tennyson describes the time of day:

> Nigh upon that hour
> When the lone hern forgets his melancholy,
> Lets down his other leg, and stretching, dreams
> Of goodly supper in the distant pool.
>
> (*GL*, 1154–7; III, 317)

Stylistically, Tennyson gives his work an archaic effect by retaining some of Malory's distinctive usages. These include linking words like "so," "for," "and," and "but" at the beginnings of lines and sections, and certain prefixes like "mis" and "un." Gareth, for example, tells Lynette that he does not want her to "missay me and revile" and Merlin speaks "Unmockingly" to Gareth (*GL*, 923 and 288; III, 309 and 289; see also Gray 1980: 84–9; 77–8).

Another important change, characteristic of all Tennyson's adaptations of romance, is his deepening of the characters' psychology. One example comes in the first 430 lines of his poem when the poet describes Gareth's appeal to his mother, Queen Bellicent, that he should be allowed to follow his brothers, Gawaine and Mordred, to Camelot. By adding this opening section, Tennyson humanized the story into a family drama of mother and son. He told his wife, jokingly, that he would "describe a pattern youth" for their two young sons (E. Tennyson 1981: 297).

Tennyson's revised opening eliminates one element of suspense. Malory's narrative begins with Arthur in his Whitsuntide court, and with Sir Gawaine failing to recognize Gareth as his own brother. Malory's readers might have known the story already, or have taken the hint that Gareth (known as Beaumains) is not what he seems, but it is only considerably later in the story that, having defeated Sir Persant in battle, Malory's Gareth declares: "my name is Sir Gareth of Orkenay, and Kynge Lott was my fadir" (1967: I, 317). Tennyson reduces the number of Gareth's brothers from four in Malory to two, Gawaine and Mordred. In Malory's version, Mordred is Gareth's half-brother, Arthur's own son, incestuously fathered on his half-sister. Mordred's destruction of the Round Table becomes a fitting punishment for Arthur's sin in begetting him. In Tennyson's sequence of poems, Arthur is presented as the perfect king and an Arthur who committed incest would be an impossibility.

This opening of "Gareth and Lynette," which constitutes about a third of the whole, includes a lengthy description of the gate of Camelot:

> The dragon-boughts and elvish emblemings
> Began to move, seethe, twine and curl.
>
> (*GL*, 229–30; III, 288)

Gareth's quest is like a carefully constructed ritual. He has to defeat the unpleasant Sir Kay, rescue a man who has been attacked by "six tall men" (*GL*, 791; III, 305), and then fight a series of knights who stand between him and Lyonors' castle. In Malory there are eight, but Tennyson, again compressing the original, cuts them down to four. Three, representing the ages of man, guard the bends of the river, and, at the castle itself, stands the fourth and final Knight, Death.

This quest is punctuated by the gibes of Lynette, who constantly mocks her companion. Tennyson clarifies Malory's structure, showing how Lynette slowly begins to respect Gareth. When he defeats his opponents, and they beg for their lives, Gareth asks her to petition for them, and, when she does so, spares them and sends them to Arthur's court. This courtesy (which forces Lynette to acknowledge his existence) is not found in Malory, where Gareth usually kills his opponents. Lynette's teasing songs, reflecting each of Gareth's victories, become an indication of her changing emotions. The pattern is predictable, the outcome apparently certain, until, in his final lines, the poet pulls the carpet from under our feet, breaking the illusion, by declaring that there are variant versions of this story, Malory's and his own:

> And he that told the tale in older times
> Says that Sir Gareth wedded Lyonors,
> But he, that told it later, says Lynette.
>
> (*GL*, 1392-4; III, 323)

Not quite an open ending, perhaps, since we have to assume that Gareth weds Lynette, but still a conscious break with the expectations of the older romance. In Malory's version it is Lyonesse (Lyonors), whom Gareth marries, after a long passage where his love makes him ill with longing. Tennyson omitted the whole of this passage, too strong for a Victorian audience, and ends, crisply, with a marriage which rounds off his own narrative. Tennyson's development of Lynette's personality probably reflects his liking for contemporary fiction. Spirited heroines are certainly not unknown in the earlier romances, but Lynette's particular blend of pride and insouciance has a distinctly nineteenth-century quality. Instead of presenting the reader with two women, often sharply contrasted like Spenser's Una and Duessa, Tennyson creates one flawed but appealing young woman, who learns from experience and eventually metamorphoses into a Victorian heroine. This is a new-style romance, where the girl who rides alongside the hero becomes his bride, not the one who waits in the tower for the rescuing hero.

See also: chapter 3, The Popular English Metrical Romances; chapter 4, Arthurian Romance; chapter 6, Malory and the Early Prose Romances; chapter 12, "Gothic" Romance; chapter 13, Women's Gothic Romance; chapter 16, Romance and the Romantic Novel; chapter 17, Poetry of the Romantic Period; chapter 19, Victorian Romance: Medievalism; chapter 26, Twentieth-century Arthurian Romance.

Notes

1. All references to Tennyson's poetry are to *The Poems of Tennyson*, ed. Christopher Ricks, 3 vols. (1987). The volume number is given, followed by the page number. References to *The Idylls of the King* also include abbreviated titles and line numbers: *CA* is "The Coming of Arthur"; *GL* is "Gareth and Lynette"; *LE* is "Lancelot and Elaine"; *MG* is "The Marriage of Geraint."

2. I should like to acknowledge the help of Caroline Corbeau, who first drew my attention to this quotation.

References and Further Reading

Baker, Arthur E. (1967, reprint). *A Concordance to the Poetical and Dramatic Works of Alfred, Lord Tennyson*. London: Routledge and Kegan Paul.

Beer, Gillian (1970). *The Romance*. London: Methuen.

Campbell, Nancie, ed. (1971–3). *Tennyson in Lincoln: A Catalogue of the Collections in the Research Centre*. 2 vols. Lincoln: Tennyson Society.

Culler, A. Dwight (1977). *The Poetry of Tennyson*. New Haven: Yale University Press.

Frye, Northrop (1976). *The Secular Scripture*. Cambridge, MA, and London: Harvard University Press.

Gray, J. M. (1980). *Thro' the Vision of the Night: A Study of Source, Evolution and Structure in Tennyson's Idylls of the King*. Edinburgh: Edinburgh University Press.

Hugo, Victor (1884). *Odes et Ballades*. New edn. Paris: Hachette.

Malory, Thomas (1967). *The Works of Sir Thomas Malory*, ed. Eugène Vinaver. 3 vols. 2nd edn. Oxford: Clarendon Press.

McDermott, Hubert (1989). *Novel and Romance: The Odyssey to Tom Jones*. Basingstoke: Macmillan.

Ormond, Leonée (1993). *Alfred Tennyson: A Literary Life*. Basingstoke: Macmillan.

Paden, W. D. (1942). *Tennyson in Egypt: A Study of the Imagery in his Earlier Work*. Lawrence: University of Kansas Press.

Ricks, Christopher (1972). *Tennyson*. Rev edn. Basingstoke: Macmillan. [Revised version published in 1972.]

Rossetti, William Michael, ed. (1903). *Rossetti Papers*. London: Sands.

Simpson, Roger (1990). *Camelot Regained*. Cambridge: D. S. Brewer.

Simpson, Roger (1996). "Tennyson, Leigh Hunt and the Giant: A Speculative Note." In *Essays in Memory of Michael Parkinson and Janine Dakyns*, ed. Christopher Smith. Norwich Papers IV, 97–9.

Slater, Michael (2000). *Tennyson in the Theatre*. Tennyson Society Occasional Paper, no. 10. Lincoln.

Stevenson, Robert Louis (1887). "A Gossip on Romance." In *Memories and Portraits*. London: Chatto and Windus, pp. 247–74.

Tasso, Torquato (1981). *Godfrey of Bulloigne*, trans. Edward Fairfax, ed. K. M. Lea and T. M. Gang. Oxford: Oxford University Press.

Tennyson, Alfred (1953). *Poetical Works including the Plays*. Oxford: Oxford University Press.

Tennyson, Alfred (1981–90). *Letters of Alfred, Lord Tennyson*, ed. Cecil Y. Lang and Edgar F. Shannon, Jr. Oxford: Oxford University Press.

Tennyson, Alfred (1987). *The Poems of Tennyson*, ed. Christopher Ricks. 3 vols. London: Longman.

Tennyson, Emily (1981). *Lady Tennyson's Journal*, ed. James O. Hoge. Charlottesville: University Press of Virginia.

Tennyson, Hallam (1897). *Tennyson: A Memoir*. 2 vols. London: Macmillan.

Tennyson Turner, Charles (1868). *Small Tableaux*. London: Macmillan.

Tillotson, Kathleen (1965). "Tennyson's Serial Poem." In G. and K. Tillotson, *Mid-Victorian Studies*. London: Athlone Press, pp. 80–109.

Weld, Agnes (1903). *Glimpses of Tennyson*. London: Williams and Norgate.

Wright, Herbert G. (1957). *Boccaccio in England from Chaucer to Tennyson*. London: Athlone Press.

19

Victorian Romance: Medievalism

Richard Cronin

"By *romantic* poems," wrote Thomas Arnold in 1862, "we mean, poems in which heroic subjects are epically treated, after the manner of the old romances of chivalry" (1862: 285). Almost all the poets that we think of as Romantic wrote such poems – Coleridge's "Christabel," Wordsworth's *The White Doe of Rylstone*, Byron's *Childe Harold's Pilgrimage: A Romaunt*, Shelley's *Laon and Cythna* – Scott collected and edited old romances, and Southey translated them. But after 1862 the term Romantic changed its meaning. It came to refer to a literary movement that began in England on or before 1798, when *Lyrical Ballads* was published, and ended in 1824, when Byron died, or shortly afterwards, and it was not a movement that seemed to those who first defined it helpfully characterized by a taste for old romances. The romance was removed from Romanticism, and one of the effects was to obscure the links that connected the poets of the early nineteenth century with their successors – the Brownings, the Rossettis, Arnold, Morris, Swinburne, and Tennyson – all of whom wrote major poems in which "heroic subjects are epically treated, after the manner of the old romances of chivalry."

The Victorian interest in romance was strengthened by the philosophy of the Pre-Raphaelites. The Pre-Raphaelite Brotherhood was founded in 1848; its chief members were John Everett Millais, William Holman Hunt, and Dante Gabriel Rossetti, and its chief principle was an insistence on scrupulous realism, but in a study of Victorian romance it is the second incarnation of the Brotherhood that is the more important. This was formed in 1856, when the young Oxford students William Morris, Edward Burne-Jones, and Algernon Swinburne met D. G. Rossetti, and located in medieval art a healthful corrective to the ugliness, industrialization, and commercialism of the nineteenth century.

The two chief influences on Victorian romance were Scott and Keats, and it is best to start with them. Scott's narrative poems were written as a flamboyant assertion that it could not be said of Britain as his mentor, Edmund Burke, had said of France, that "the age of chivalry is gone." In the series of poems that began with *The Lay of the Last*

Minstrel (1804), the "thousand bright swords" that failed in Paris to protect Marie Antoinette from being manhandled by a brutal mob are drawn from their scabbards in a lively demonstration that Britain, unlike France, remained true to its past. In these poems Scott establishes himself, in the words of his son-in-law, J. G. Lockhart, as "the 'mighty minstrel' of the Anti-Gallican war" (Lockhart 1837: 2, 155). Poems written "after the manner of the old romances of chivalry" become vehicles through which Scott expresses the newly concentrated patriotism of a nation at war. In 1812, with the publication of *Childe Harold*, Byron usurped Scott's place as Britain's most popular poet by offering his own "very *unknightly*" Childe as a more authentic representative of the spirit of the nation:

> So much for chivalry. Burke need not have regretted that its days are over, though Marie Antoinette was quite as chaste as most of those in whose honours lances were shivered, and knights unhorsed. (Preface to Cantos I and II)

Scott and Byron agree that the present state of the nation is best mapped by tracing its links to the period in which the nation was born. They differ in the maps that they draw, and their difference was echoed throughout the century as "the old romances of chivalry" were appropriated by proponents of almost every shade of political and ethical opinion. But it was also in Scott's poems that the romance first registered the character that it was to retain throughout the century, as a poetic form at once epic and escapist, at once solemnly public and playfully irresponsible.

In the introductory epistles of *Marmion* Scott offers his poem to its readers as "an old romance," a tale sheltered from the urgencies of contemporary life. The epistles offer a definition of romance that associates it with the country rather than the city, with the childish rather than the adult, and with play rather than work. In the very first epistle Scott represents Nature as teaching him his unworthiness for the "high theme" that he had once aspired to:

> Meeter, she says, for me to stray
> And waste the solitary day,
> In plucking from yon fen the reed,
> And watch it floating down the Tweed.
>   (*Marmion*, Introduction to Canto First, 235–8)

But as soon as he has characterized the writing of romances as an aimless, pastoral activity, Scott is prompted to defend them:

> They gleam through Milton's heavenly theme:
> And Dryden in immortal strain
> Had raised the Table Round again,
> But that a ribald King and Court
> Bade him toil on to make them sport.
>   (*Marmion*, Introduction to Canto First, 275–9)

Spenser, Milton, and Dryden were, Scott claims, dedicated to the romance tradition, but they also constitute the great line of England's national poets. The argument has turned so completely that Dryden's distraction from romance can be described in exactly the same terms as Scott's devotion to it, as a retreat from serious labor to "sport." A similar ambivalence marks almost all Victorian invocations of the romance tradition, whether in poetry, pictures, architecture, or sculpture.

Keats' contribution is, on the face of it, more straightforward. He made romance pictorial, so that to read through *The Eve of St. Agnes*, the romance that most strongly influenced the Victorians, is at once to follow a story and to wander through a gallery of pictures. At the end of the poem the lovers make their escape from the castle, and as they do so they withdraw into a legendary past:

> And they are gone: ay, ages long ago
> These lovers fled away into a storm.
>
> (370–1)

In a sense, of course, they have always been remote, as removed from us as the figures in one of D. G. Rossetti's medieval watercolors, but not consistently so. Keats' poem is intensely visualized, but repeatedly the appeals to the eye are complicated by appeals to other senses, most powerfully the sense of touch, and whenever this happens the effect is to render the figure with an urgent physical immediacy. When Madeline undresses, "Of all its wreathed pearls her hair she frees," and her action lends her a distant charm, but immediately she "unclasps her warmed jewels one by one," and the verse thrills with the contact of hard stone on soft skin. The effect is to render Madeline momentarily with an intense bodily palpability. Alternately removed from us and brought close, she shimmers through the poem "like shot-silk" (Tennyson 1969: 1463). The phrase is Tennyson's, describing *Idylls of the King*, a poem which repeatedly rehearses the Keatsian effect.

It was Tennyson, as Leonée Ormond points out in this volume, who, more than anyone else, was responsible for the introduction of Arthurian romance to the nineteenth century. It seemed to many of his first readers a bizarre project. After all, in 1833, the very year in which Tennyson began to write "Morte d'Arthur," Coleridge had opined, "As to Arthur, you could not by any means make a poem national to Englishmen. What have *we* to do with him?" A number of Tennyson's reviewers agreed, including John Sterling, who commented, "The miraculous legend of 'Excalibur' does not come very near us, and as reproduced by any modern writer must be a mere ingenious exercise of fancy" (Jump 1967: 119). It was a comment wounding enough to prevent Tennyson for many years from pursuing his project to write an Arthurian epic in 12 books even though he had it "all in [his] mind," and "could have done it without any trouble." But Tennyson's enthusiasm for knights at arms, though a distinctive taste, was not an isolated one. Malory's *Le Morte Darthur*, on which his own poem was closely based, had not been in print since 1634 until a new edition appeared in 1816, followed a year later by another (edited by Southey), after which the book remained in print throughout the century. In 1819 Scott published *Ivanhoe*, five dramatized versions of which appeared on the London stage in the following year. In 1829 Kenelm Digby's *The Broad Stone of Honour*, in which he represented the chivalric code as providing the one true guide in all ethical and political matters, had reached the form in which it was eagerly assimilated by Benjamin Disraeli and the "Young England" party to which he attached himself. By 1835, when Tennyson's uncle changed his name to Charles Tennyson d'Eyncourt and began to refashion the family seat, Bayons Hall, into Bayons Manor, the fairy-tale castle derided by his nephew in *Maud*, the fashion for a medievalizing architecture was already well established, and in 1839 Lord Eglinton organized the first full-scale tournament to have been held in Britain for more than 200 years, only to find all his costly preparations nullified by a cloudburst. In the Arthurian poems that he published in 1842 Tennyson might reasonably have imagined that he was appealing not to a recent fashion but to one that had been firmly established for 25 years. But, as Tennyson was aware long before he read Sterling's review, it was a taste than ran counter to the much more widespread as well as more vociferous view that it was the duty of the poet to take his subject matter from his own age.

Arthurian poetry became the test case in this debate, the exemplary resource of poets unable to recognize the imaginative potential of the age in which they lived. As Elizabeth Barrett Browning put it:

> Nay, if there's room for poets in this world
> A little overgrown (I think there is),
> Their sole work is to represent the age,
> Their age, not Charlemagne's, – this live, throbbing age,
> That brawls, cheats, maddens, calculates, aspires,
> And spends more passion, more heroic heat,
> Betwixt the mirrors of its drawing-rooms,
> Than Roland with his knights at Roncesvalles.
> To flinch from modern varnish, coat or flounce,
> Cry out for togas and the picturesque,
> Is fatal, – foolish too. King Arthur's self
> Was commonplace to Lady Guenever;
> And Camelot to minstrels seemed as flat
> As Fleet Street to our poets.
>
> (*Aurora Leigh*, 5, 200–13)

Some demurred, most powerfully Matthew Arnold in the preface to his 1853 *Poems*, some, such as Ruskin, argued on both sides of the question, but very few poets, as opposed to reviewers, were single-minded on the matter. Barrett Browning herself, after all, wrote medievalist poems. Nevertheless, the debate serves to focus attention on the question of why so many nineteenth-century poets persisted, despite strongly voiced objections, in choosing subject matter pointedly remote from the age in which they lived. One answer is implicit in Tennyson's very first Arthurian exercise, "The Lady of Shalott."

The lady enclosed in her tower, exercising an art that is contingent on her refusal to gaze at life directly, has always, and perhaps inevitably, been understood as a type of the poet. "Tennyson, we cannot live in Art," Tennyson remembers R. C. Trench telling him (1969: 400). It is the thought, he notes, that prompted him to write "The Palace of Art," in which the Soul, like the Lady of Shalott, becomes "half sick of shadows." "The Lady of Shalott" adds only the wry postscript that, if we cannot live in Art, we cannot live without it either, for the Lady leaves her tower, and floats down the river to Camelot only to die. The poem was first drafted in October 1831, at the height of the debate preceding the passing of the Great Reform Bill. Tennyson turns away from the great national question to weave, from a few brief hints found in a fourteenth-century Italian novella, a poem the chief business of which seems to be to question its own propriety. By 1831, when he began to write the poem, it was hard for any poet to believe in the importance of his profession. By then Edward Moxon was the only London publisher prepared to accept volumes by living poets, and he insisted that the poet bear the full cost of publication (Erickson 1996). Poetry, unlike the novel, did not sell. Moxon was disappointed by the sale of the volume in which "The Lady of Shalott" first appeared. Tennyson's "poetry is 'popular at Cambridge,'" he told Browning, "and yet of 800 copies that were printed of his last, some 300 only have gone off" (Browning and Browning 1984: 3, 134). Two conclusions are suggested. First, medievalism is a mode favored by poets who recognize themselves as anachronisms, practitioners of an art that could neither claim influence over the day-to-day business of life nor earn them a living. The novelists, it must have seemed, had displaced the poets as effectively as the mechanical looms had displaced the handloom weavers whose craft the Lady of Shalott so decoratively parodies. Second, the concealed subject of medievalist poems is the gap that separates the world of the poem from the world in which the poem is written.

In "Morte d'Arthur," the fragmentary epic ends as Arthur's barge recedes from view, becoming

> one black dot against the verge of dawn,
> And on the mere the wailing died away.
>
> (271–2)

The lamentations of the three queens fade into silence, and, as they cease, so too does the voice of the poet who has summoned them into their brief life. The magical sword, the great battle, and Arthur himself are released back into the distant past, which reclaims them. The poem's audience, all except the parson who has been asleep, resume their everyday identity:

> Then Francis, muttering, like a man ill-used,
> "There now – that's nothing!" drew a little back,
> And drove his heel into the smouldered log,
> That sent a blast of sparkles up the flue.
>
> (284–7)

The young men go to bed, and dream, but the matter of the dream is not so much the poem as the long lapse of years that separates them from it. The narrator dreams of the barge returning, bringing Arthur back to nineteenth-century England dressed "like a modern gentleman."

The name for what is produced by writers and their sympathetic readers when confronted by a discrepancy between a fictional structure and the structures of meaning with which they are familiar, a discrepancy between sign and significance, is allegory. So, the admirer of Everard Hall's poem understands it as an allegory in which Hall delineates in the person of Arthur the characteristics of the ideal Victorian gentleman. In *The Return to Camelot*, Mark Girouard presents this as the central allegory underlying all Victorian medievalism. The rich young aristocrats who hired suits of armor from Samuel Pratt's showroom in Lower Grosvenor Street so that they might cut a proper figure at the Eglinton Tournament were dressing up as allegorical representations of themselves, as they were or as they aspired to be. This is the allegorical reading that Tennyson himself appealed to when he dedicated *Idylls of the King* to the memory of the Prince Albert, who was "scarce other than my own ideal knight," a tribute swiftly modified when Swinburne retitled the poem "Idylls of the Prince Consort" (Jump 1967: 339) to "scarce other than my king's ideal knight." But, as Girouard recognizes, the allegorical possibilities were various. They might, for example, be satirical rather than celebratory, as in Carlyle's *Past and Present*, Pugin's *Contrasts*, or Ruskin's *The Nature of Gothic*, in which the disparity between the medieval and the nineteenth century exposes the woeful inferiority of modern economic or political or aesthetic systems, or, as in Peacock's *Maid Marian* or Mark Twain's *A Connecticut Yankee at the Court of King Arthur*, the procedure might be reversed. So, the relationship between the medieval and the modern might be one of likeness or one of difference, and either might support any shade of political and ethical opinion, from the Romantic Toryism of Disraeli to the revolutionary socialism of William Morris. The only constant is the allegoric mode.

When Tennyson first began to meditate an Arthurian epic in 1833 he wrote a memorandum in which he tried to work out his allegory in some detail: "K. A. religious faith"; "Modred, the sceptical understanding"; Merlin, "Science"; "The Round Table: Liberal Institutions" (1969: 1461). The contemporary responses to the poem that Tennyson most approved, by J. T. Knowles and Henry Alford, understood it allegorically. For Knowles, for example, Arthur represents the "king within us," and the episodes of the poem "the perpetual warfare between the spirit and the flesh." As we read, "we see the body and its passions gain continually greater sway, till in the end the Spirit's earthly work is thwarted and defeated by the flesh. Its immortality alone remains to it, and, with this, a deathless hope" (Jump 1967: 313). More modern readings remain true to the allegoric method, their differences pro-pelled, one suspects, by a diminished interest in the twentieth century in battles between the spirit and the flesh, and a diminished faith in immortality. So, for John D. Rosenberg, in 1973, Tennyson's poem is inflected throughout by a sad pessimism, until it becomes "the subtlest analysis of the failure of ideality in our literature," a

"doom-laden prophecy of the fall of the West" (1973: 11, 1). Or, still more influen-
tially, in 1983 C. Y. Lang concluded, "The real subject of this great poem is the
British Empire." Arthur's business is to impose, through his Round Table, which
serves "as model for the mighty world," civilization on all the globe:

> And Arthur and his knighthood for a space
> Were all one will, and thro' that strength the King
> Drew in the petty princedoms under him,
> Fought, and in twelve great battles overcame
> The heathen hordes, and made a realm and reign'd.
>
> ("The Coming of Arthur," 514–18)

Arthur forging his kingdom of Britain figures in this reading the destiny of his nation
in the nineteenth century, which was to rule the world.

But Tennyson himself was as likely to resent as to invite allegorical reading – "I
hate to be tied down to say, '*This* means *that*'" (1969: 1463). Allegory justifies the
nineteenth-century poet who chooses to write "after the manner of the old romances of
chivalry," because allegory allows an event set in the past to have a meaning for the
present, but nineteenth-century poets remained distrustful of allegory, because it was
a mode that seemed to assume that facts might yield values, and that some stable
connection might be formed between the public world in which signs have their
being and the private world in which meanings are forged.

In the nineteenth century Arthurian poems are alternately merely decorative and
pregnant with deep meaning. Hence the oddity that the figures in the poems tend to
shimmer, alternately removed from us, as if they were pictures of pictures of people, and
rendered with an oddly palpable intimacy. So, when Elaine's brother sees for the first time
"the peopled gallery" erected to view a tournament, it "Lay like a rainbow fallen upon the
grass" ("Lancelot and Elaine," 429). The simile takes all those women in their bright
dresses and dissolves them into a play of colored light, as if in a confession that they were
never more than a figment of the imagination. Tennyson's intense focus on the sound of
his lines, what Whitman calls his "finest verbalism," works to the same effect: it invites us
to linger on the words too long to avoid an experience that Tennyson knew well:

> As when we dwell upon a word we know,
> Repeating, till the word we know so well
> Becomes a wonder, and we know not why.
>
> ("Lancelot and Elaine," 1020–2)

And yet there are quite different moments, as when a "churl" speaks "sputtering"
through newly broken teeth, which are "Yet strangers to the tongue" ("The Last
Tournament," 66). This is Tennyson in Keatsian mode, inviting the reader tentatively
to flick a tongue over unfamiliar roughnesses, but it also has a temporal dimension.
Tennyson is, after all, summoning an experience that became commonly available
only in the nineteenth century, only after a visit to the dentist. The poems occupy an

odd place, as the verbal equivalent of the medievalist paintings that wealthy collectors hung on the walls of their Victorian living rooms, pictures that delight by opening a window into a world so different from the world occupied by those who inhabit the room. But these are magic pictures, pictures that may at any moment become so vivid that the room's inhabitants are made to feel oddly unreal. It is a thought that seems to lie behind a strange and compelling passage in Matthew Arnold's Arthurian poem, *Tristram and Iseult*. In the bedchamber where Tristram lies dying, tended by his young wife, there is a tapestry showing a huntsman with his pack, but the huntsman is imagined gazing into the room with a "flurried air," as of a man who finds himself by some enchantment transported out of the forest which is his proper place into a room where he and his pack of dogs have no place:

> How comes it here, this chamber bright,
> Through whose mullioned windows clear
> The castle-court all wet with rain,
> The drawbridge and the moat appear,
> And then the beach, and, marked with spray,
> The sunken reefs, and far away
> The unquiet bright Atlantic plain?

(2, 168–74)

The huntsman depicted on the tapestry comes alive, and looks at the room in which he hangs as if it were itself a painting, a domestic scene of a room with a window opening onto a landscape that recedes into the far distance of the sea.

The key moments in *Idylls of the King* are those when "New things and old" seem "co-twisted, as if Time / Were nothing" ("Gareth and Lynette," 222–3). So, when Geraint enters the castle of Enid's father, he sees

> A shattered archway plumed with fern;
> And here had fallen a great part of a tower,
> Whole, like a crag that tumbles from the cliff,
> And like a crag was gay with wilding flowers.

("The Marriage of Geraint," 316–19)

The lines, Tennyson noted, "were made at Middleham Castle" (1969: 746), and the effect is to produce an odd anachronism, in which a past world and the ruined vestiges of it that have been preserved into the nineteenth century coincide. In "Morte d'Arthur" the narrator, trying to explain his admiration of the poem, suggests, "Perhaps some modern touches here and there / Redeemed it from the charge of nothingness," but in that poem and in the later *Idylls* the poetic effect is located not in the "modern touches," but in their juxtaposition with the long gone. Guinevere, lying guiltily awake "Beside the placid breathings of the King" ("Guinevere," 944), is at once a figure far removed in time and intimately contemporary – any Victorian wife living the nightmare of adultery. Geraint and Enid, in their estrangement, are like figures on a shield, and are also suffering the pain of isolation within an intimate relationship that is peculiar to bourgeois marriage:

> the two remain'd
> Apart by all the chamber's width, and mute
> As creatures voiceless thro' the fault of birth,
> Or two wild men supporters of a shield,
> Painted, who stare at open space, nor glance
> The one at other, parted by the shield.
>
> ("Geraint and Enid," 265–9)

Idylls of the King is Tennyson's most decorative and also his most novelistic poem. When, at the end of "Gareth and Lynette," he draws attention to his revision of Malory in having Gareth marry Lynette rather than her sister, he is attentive to the conventions of the novel. Lynette in her railing at Gareth, the "kitchen-knave" who "smellest all of kitchen-grease," is like Estella railing at Pip – "And what coarse hands he has! And what thick boots!" – until her behavior modulates to reveal a hidden affection, when she becomes more like Mary Garth, who speaks roughly to Fred Vincy because she loves him, but needs him to prove himself worthy of her love. Geraint falls in love with Enid, in medieval fashion, at first sight, but, when she serves him his food, and he is overcome by a desire to "stoop and kiss the tender little thumb / That crost the trencher as she laid it down" ("The Marriage of Geraint," 394–5), his fascination seems oddly Victorian, like Mr. Thornton unable to remove his eyes from Margaret Hale's bracelet as it repeatedly falls down over her wrist and is pushed up again (*North and South*, chapter X). Enid, who as a married woman becomes the victim of Geraint's groundless jealousy, is a medieval type, a version of patient Griselda, but what most struck Walter Bagehot in the poem was the "whole story of the dress" (Jump 1967: 227), the shabby dress that Geraint insists that his bride wear when he first takes her to the court of Camelot, and the dress that she chooses to put on once more when she becomes the object of his suspicions:

> But Enid ever kept the faded silk,
> Remembering how first he came on her,
> Drest in that dress, and how he loved her in it,
> And all her foolish fears about the dress,
> And all his journey toward her, as himself
> Had told her, and their coming to the court.
> And now this morning when he said to her,
> "Put on your worst and meanest dress," she found
> And took it, and arrayed herself therein.
>
> ("Geraint and Enid," 841–9)

As Leonée Ormond notes, all through the poem Enid's changes of dress function emblematically, as "indications of her state of mind," and yet at this moment the emblematics seem very Victorian. Enid is revealed as a contemporary of Dickens' Amy Dorrit who comes to the Marshalsea to nurse Arthur Clennam wearing the old dress in which he had first seen her:

> "I hoped you would like me better in this dress than any other. I have always kept it by me, to remind me: though I wanted no reminding." (*Little Dorrit*, chapter XLV)

Walter Bagehot notes in his review that nothing separates the medieval romance from the nineteenth century more dramatically than the relations between men and women. In Malory, for example, women may be represented as the exalted object of a reverential love, but rather more often they are simply trophies – if an errant knight is overthrown any woman accompanying him is likely to be appropriated by the victor as one of the spoils of battle. A poem such as William Morris' "The Haystack in the Floods" gains its grim power by introducing into the Victorian library a savage world in which Robert's mistress, Jehane, defends herself from being raped by the knight who has taken captive her lover by warning him that a woman can "strangle" or "bite through [the] throat" of a sleeping man, and is then forced to watch her assailant "bend / Back Robert's head" and cut his throat. Swinburne locates sadism in the women as well as the men of the old romances. In "The Tale of Balen," Balen, unwittingly engaged in the battle with his brother in which both will die, looks up and sees that the murderous conflict is being eagerly watched by "ladies blithe and fair," who have crowded the towers to view it. Malory's Arthur seems utterly unlike Tennyson's in chiefly regretting his wife's adultery because it lost him the fellowship of his knights. But such contrasts always admit alternative readings. One reader may focus on the difference between the present and the past, another may understand the past as unashamedly revealing a truth that moderns prefer to disguise. It is quite possible, after all, to read Tennyson's as a poem in which the crucial function of women is to secure the bonds of friendship between men on which civilization depends. Guinevere fulfills that role when she allows Lancelot to love her, and calamitously fails to do so when she allows him to have sex with her.

The women poets of the period seem especially interested in tracing their continuity with their medieval forebears. For example, in Barrett Browning's "Romance of the Swan's Nest," it is not clear whether "little Ellie," who dreams of being won by a knightly lover who proves his devotion by a succession of knightly exploits, is herself a girl of the Middle Ages, or, as her name suggests, a nineteenth-century child with a taste for old romances. The point is that it does not matter. She thinks to reward the knight by revealing to him her most treasured secret, a "swan's nest among the reeds," and, whether she is a child of the fourteenth or the nineteenth century, the poem tells the story of how a child's dream world may be shattered before ever she emerges from her girlhood. Ellie visit the swan's nest every day, until one day she finds that the "wild swan had deserted, / And a rat had gnawed the reeds!'" In "The Romaunt of the Page," the hastily married bride who accompanies her husband to the wars disguised as his page is clearly a figure from the past, but she finds that her husband holds to the conventional view that "womanhood is proved the best / By golden brooch and glossy vest / The mincing ladies wear." By donning masculine clothes and engaging in the masculine business of war she has forfeited any chance that he might return her love. The husband's views seem scarcely distinguishable from those of many of Barrett Browning's contemporaries. The comedy of Christina Rossetti's "The Prince's Progress" depends upon a similar effect. It traces the journey of a prince to the tower in which his lady lives immured, awaiting his coming. The prince sets off "in the joy of his strength," and had "journeyed at least a mile" before he sees a "wave-haired milkmaid, rosy and white" and "Grew athirst at the sight." He is "strong of limb if of purpose weak," but after dallying with the milkmaid until dawn he sets out again, only to find the waste land through which he travels a "Tedious land for a social prince." When the waste land is traversed and he finds himself in a green landscape once more, he "Loitered a while for a deep stream bath" and "Yawned for a fellow man." Finally arrived at his lady's palace, he finds himself oddly reluctant to enter. He wonders whether it might be too late for a visit, and whether the princess will be ready to "open the crimson core / Of her heart to him" in the manner that he would wish. While he lingers by the gate it opens, and a funeral cortège emerges. Tired of waiting for him, the princess has died.

The "modern touch" that makes Rossetti's poem medievalist rather than medieval is that she bestows upon her knight the refined indolence of a character like Dickens' Eugene Wrayburn. In this, she is wholly typical. Victorian poets very often impose on figures taken out of old romances a wholly modern burden of self-consciousness. When Tennyson's Merlin broods upon events to come he becomes quite different from Malory's character: it is not the future that is opened up so much as the deep recesses of his inner life:

> So dark a forethought rolled about his brain,
> As on a dull day in an Ocean cave
> The blind wave feeling round his long sea-hall
> In silence.
>
> ("Merlin and Vivien," 228–31)

That kind of deep interiority becomes a necessary condition of Arthurian characters when they are transported into the nineteenth century, and often enough it is an uncomfortable condition. When Tennyson's Arthur discovers his wife's adultery, he generously informs Guinevere, "Lo! I forgive thee, as Eternal God / Forgives," and the effect is to shine a cruel light not on Guinevere's wifely failings but on her husband's monstrous self-righteousness. Tennyson clearly imagines that he is bestowing on his King a divine capacity for forgiveness, but the reader who grants Arthur a modern self-consciousness is far more likely to be struck by Arthur's failure to match the ideal of gentlemanly conduct displayed by Dickens' Sir Leicester Dedlock when he makes a similar discovery, and by 1859 it was difficult not to grant a fictional character such a consciousness. One solution was to take that discrepancy between medieval romance and modern self-consciousness and make it the point of the poem.

Robert Browning's "Childe Roland to the Dark Tower Came" is only vestigially a romance: throughout, narrative is subordinated to landscape, the protagonist is deprived of all knightly appurtenances except for a once-mentioned spear, even the name by which he is conventionally known is given him only by inference from the poem's title, the line from *King Lear* which becomes the war-cry that ends the poem. It is a quest poem, but Browning's interest is focused not on the outcome of the quest, which remains untold, but on the consciousness of the questor. The poem begins, as it ends, *in medias res*. The knight meets a cripple, and responds to him with a spasm of disgust and hatred that reveals that the knight is himself the true cripple, deformed not in body but in mind. The rest of the poem serves simply to clarify the diagnosis, as the knight travels through a meager landscape that becomes the stuff of nightmare only because it is so fully saturated by the self-disgust that he projects upon it. A thinly sown meadow becomes for him the symptom of a horrifying disease: "As for the grass, it grew as scant as hair / In leprosy." All suffering prompts loathing rather than pity, as when he sees a "stiff, blind horse, his every bone a-stare":

> Seldom went such grotesqueness with such woe:
> I never saw a beast I hated so –
> He must be wicked to deserve such pain.
>
> (82–4)

The physical deformity of the horse is eclipsed by the truly grotesque moral deformity of an observer who can respond to suffering only by supposing that it is deserved. This is a speaker, one deduces, engaged in a quest the condition of which is that he remain free from worldly stain, with the inevitable consequence that his world is transformed into a site of infection. He is hopelessly and hideously neurotic, and yet he remains an everyman of the nineteenth century, a Christian soul, any Christian soul, committed to the pursuit of an ideal that his world cannot accommodate, which is why there is a true heroism, sad but more moving than the heroism that Tennyson's Arthur or any of his knights rise to, when in a lightning flash he sees "all the lost adventurers, [his] peers . . . ranged along the hill-sides," met to witness him repeat their failure:

> Dauntless the slug-horn to my lips I set
> And blew. *"Childe Roland to the Dark Tower came."*
>
> (203–4)

Browning embraced self-consciousness as the necessary condition of his modernity. But few of his contemporaries were so single-minded. For Arnold, for example, medieval subject matter appealed, one suspects, precisely because it offered the possibility that a modern poem might present something other than an "allegory of the state of one's own mind" (Arnold 1965: 598–9). In *Tristram and Iseult*, for example, the lovers converse in rhymed quatrains that seem expressly designed to present their love operatically rather than to follow the movement of their feeling, and in the narrative sections Arnold borrows from Coleridge's "Christabel" a meter that works to confine the poem within a world of romantic enchantment. But, even in this poem, self-consciousness intrudes, most markedly in the poem's third part. Iseult les Blanche Mains is living a life of exile in Cornwall, lonely despite the presence of her two children, keeping vigil, presumably, over the grave of her husband and his lover, the other Iseult. The narrative in this part of the poem expands into pentameter lines, and, as it does so, Iseult begins to suffer from a nineteenth-century, very Arnoldian world-weariness:

> No, 'tis the gradual furnace of the world,
> In whose hot air our spirits are uncurled
> Until they crumble, or else grow like steel –
> Which kills in us the bloom, the youth, the spring –
> Which leaves the fierce necessity to feel,
> But takes away the power –
>
> (3, 119–23)

Iseult, who is represented by Arnold as an angelically forgiving wife, frees herself from her spiritual torpor long enough to entertain her children with a story, and remarkably the story she tells is of Merlin and Vivien, and how Vivien so beguiled the sage that he divulged to her the spell with which she imprisoned him "till the judgment-day" in a little "daisied circle." It is impossible not to read the tale as a wife's bitter comment on her husband's fatal infatuation with the other Iseult. It is as if she has slipped her angelic mask and revealed herself as a woman in full agreement with the narrator that the romantically absolute love for which Tristram lived and died is only a "fool passion" that men are sadly prone to:

> Being in truth but a diseased unrest,
> And an unnatural overheat at best.
> How they are full of languor and distress
> Not having it; which when they do possess,
> They straightway are burnt up with fume and care,
> And spend their lives in posting here and there
> Where this plague drives them; and have little ease,
> Are furious with themselves, and hard to please.
>
> (3, 135–42)

In moments like this Arnold's Iseult gains an unexpected depth, by which I mean that the reader is induced to credit her with the interiority that in nineteenth-century writing becomes the mark of human depth. Other poets, notably William Morris and Swinburne, were more successful than Arnold in avoiding any such illusion.

They wished to do so, I suspect, for two reasons. First, to open up interior spaces is inevitably to separate the mind from the body, and hence it is a technique that lends itself too easily to the kind of representation of human experience that J. T. Knowles was happy to identify in *Idylls of the King*, which he saw as illustrating "the perpetual warfare between the spirit and the flesh." Neither Morris nor Swinburne was willing to accept that spirit and flesh ought to be at war with one another. Second, inner consciousness is, in the nineteenth century, scarcely distinguishable from conscience. Victorian novelists, George Eliot most emphatically, were ready enough to denounce the moral crudity of a fictional economy that offered worldly rewards for virtuous conduct, most often wealth and marital happiness. Such a system represented right conduct not as a moral imperative but simply as a good investment. To open up the inner space of a character's consciousness has the happy effect of removing any need to offer material punishment to the wicked and material rewards for the virtuous because the reader's demand for justice can be fully satisfied on a psychological level. Tennyson's Arthur does not threaten, like Malory's, to burn Guinevere at the stake, because Tennyson can represent Guinevere as undergoing a more exquisite torture within the fires of her own conscience. But Tennyson's Guinevere was first exposed to the Victorian public in 1859, a year after Morris had presented them with a queen who differs from Tennyson's in much more than the spelling of her name.

"The Defence of Guenevere" is remarkable in that Guenevere all but accepts the truth of the charge of adultery Gauwaine brings against her, and yet still insists that Gauwaine lies. The one proof she offers is that she does not, like Tennyson's Guinevere, feel guilty: "A great queen such as I / Having sinn'd this way, straight her conscience sears / And afterwards she liveth hatefully." But Guenevere lives in the warm glow of a self-adoration that she sees unwillingly reflected in the faces of all her male accusers. From the time that she first saw Lancelot, she explains,

> I grew
> Careless of most things, let the clock tick, tick,
> To my unhappy pulse, that beat right through
> My eager body.
>
> (74–7)

She experiences her marriage – "I was bought / By Arthur's great name and his little love" – as threatening that union of body and spirit in which she recognizes her life, as a subordination of the vital rhythm of her pulse to the mechanical ticking of a clock. Lancelot gives her back herself, and it is that self that she offers to her accusers. Her defense consists of a provocative, theatrical act of self-display: she speaks "With passionate twisting of her body there," but she speaks only as a way of commanding the gaze of her auditors. She acts out for them her own ravishing physicality:

> If I had
> Held out my long hand up against the blue,
> And, looking on the tenderly darken'd fingers,
> Thought that by rights one ought to see quite through,
> There, see you, where the soft still light yet lingers,
> Round by the edges.
>
> (120–5)

She offers that delicate collusion of light and flesh as a wholly sufficient rejoinder to all those who would represent the body as sinful, and virtue as the product of its conquest by the spirit. She holds her hand up to the sun as a more lively demonstration of a truth that she first offers in a parable. An angel asks a man to choose between two cloths, "one blue / Wavy and long, and one cut short and red / No man could tell the better of the two." After "a shivering half hour" the man chooses "heaven's colour, the blue," only to be told that he has chosen hell. It is Guenevere's confession of the fatal mistake of her choice of husband, a satire on those who dignify aesthetic preferences by representing them as moral choices, and a rich joke at the expense of all those who believe that arbitrary human conventions, such as the notion that blue rather than red is heaven's color, are in perfect accord with a divine order. In all its aspects it is a parable that Morris' friend, Swinburne, would have much enjoyed.

Swinburne's own Arthurian poems, *Tristram of Lyonesse* and *The Tale of Balen*, are his attempt to purge the romance tradition of Victorian accretions. Tennyson's Arthur assures Guinevere, "I was ever virgin save for thee" (554), though Tennyson's sources agree that Modred, with whom he is about to do battle, is Arthur's son by his half-sister, and Tennyson will not have it that Galahad is Lancelot's son by Elaine. Arnold is so anxious to deny that Tristram's marriage with the second Iseult is sexless that he gives her two children. In all such cases Swinburne is happy to revert to "the grand old compilation of Sir Thomas Malory" (340). Tennyson, he claims, has "deformed" materials that offered him in outline a story of Aeschylean tragic grandeur, all hinging on "the incestuous birth of Modred from the connexion of Arthur with his half-sister, unknowing and unknown," and the effect of his revisions is to reduce "Arthur to the level of a wittol, Guenevere to the level of a woman of intrigue, and Launcelot to the level of a 'co-respondent'" (Jump 1967: 318–19). *Tristram of Lyonesse* is an aggressive response to Tennyson's *Idylls*, but not an unprovoked one. In "The Last Tournament," first published in 1871, Dagonet, Arthur's fool, represents Tristram as, like Swinburne and D. G. Rossetti, a member of the fleshly school of poetry: "Spat – pish – ," he says of one of Tristram's songs "the cup was gold, the draught was mud" (298). Swinburne retorted by labeling "Merlin and Vivien" obscene, "An elaborate poem describing the erotic fluctuations and vacillations of a dotard under the moral and physical manipulation of a prostitute." Ten years later, in 1882, he issued a more measured response in his own version of the Tristram legend, in which Merlin is not the victim of a malicious plot, but rather is given by Nimue a "guerdon gentler far than all men's fate," enclosed in a place where he

> Takes his strange rest at heart of slumberland,
> More deep asleep in green Broceliande
> Than shipwrecked sleepers in the soft green sea
> Beneath the weight of wandering waves.
>
> (*Tristram of Lyonesse*, 2877–81)

Swinburne here, of course, is further from Malory than Tennyson was, but what he prizes in Malory is precisely his inconsistency, the manner in which he represents Nimue as either malign or benevolent, and a character such as Lancelot as at once an ideal knight and lover, and a false friend to his king.

Tennyson rewrites Malory to bring him into conformity with Victorian proprieties, hence his insistence on acquitting Arthur of the charge even of unwitting incest. But when Swinburne rewrites Malory, when he represents Merlin's imprisonment as Nimue's love gift to him, he is asserting his right to impose on Malory values the only authority of which rests on their authenticity, because for Swinburne the universe is indifferent, and human experience allows only the precarious dignity that is won when one asserts one's own wholly individual values in the face of a world that pays them no heed:

> How should the skies change and the stars, and time
> Break the large concord of the years that chime,
> Answering, as wave to wave beneath the moon
> That draws them shoreward, mar the whole tide's tune
> For the instant foam's sake on the turning wave –
> For man's sake that is grass upon a grave?
>
> (*Tristram of Lyonesse*, 1705–10)

The universe mocks any human demand that it embody human values, and the only dignity left us is to accept that and ourselves to mock the universe, as Tristram teaches Iseult in his songs:

> And each bright song upon his lips that came,
> Mocking the powers of change and death by name,
> Blasphemed their bitter godhead, and defied
> Time, though clothed round with ruins as kings with pride,
> To blot the glad life out of love: and she
> Drank lightly deep of his philosophy.
>
> (*Tristram of Lyonesse*, 1393–8)

She learns well enough to assert in her loneliness at Tintagel that the proof of her love for Tristram is that she would happily give up on his account her hope of Heaven. She entertains the notion that she might best display that love by agreeing to be separated from Tristram, him in Heaven, her in Hell, only to dismiss the notion as an absurdity. Her own marriage seems as unreal to her as her marriage to Linton seems to Emily Brontë's Catherine, and for the same reason:

> God, give him to me – God, God, give him back!
> For now how should we live in twain or die?
> I am he indeed, thou knowest, and he is I.
>
> (*Tristram of Lyonesse*, 2364–6)

Love, romantic love, is represented as the one absolute value to which human beings can lay claim, and as occluding all other human duties and obligations. The second Iseult, the woman inveigled by Tristram at the age of 16 into a sexless marriage, is understandably reluctant to recognize the virtue that Tristram displays in refusing to allow her children. She kills her husband with a lie, by telling him that the boat landing at the shore flies black sails rather than white, signifying that Iseult of Cornwall is not aboard. "I suppose you have taken the *sails* as the issue of your story," Arnold wrote to him; "a beautiful way of ending, which I should perhaps have used, had I known of it, but I did not." But it is hard to see how he could have done so without admitting the notion that romantic love might not be an "unnatural overheat," that it might rather embody a value in the face of which Iseult of Brittany's wholly understandable resentment is revealed as nothing more than shrewishness.

It is no coincidence that the romances to which Victorian poets were most powerfully drawn were romance stories that hinged on adultery, for, as Tony Tanner points out in his seminal study, *Adultery in the Novel*, adultery is the great theme of nineteenth-century fiction. Tennyson can offer the *Idylls* as at once a poem about marriage and a national epic because he is an adherent of the view that the marriage bond is both the type and the guarantee of the whole system of bonds through which civilized society is maintained. Guinevere sins with Lancelot, which "wrought confusion in the Table Round," with consequences as baleful as they are inevitable, culminating in "that last weird battle in the West," and a wave breaking across a field peopled only by the dead. Arnold, Morris, and Swinburne do not share Tennyson's interest in the national implications of the topic, but, like him, they are preoccupied by the notion of adultery, a love that demonstrates its intensity through, perhaps a love the intensity of which depends upon, its transgression of the most central of social taboos. Tanner's study is European in its range of reference: Rousseau, Goethe, and Flaubert provide him with his major examples (*Anna Karenina* is the most surprising omission), and necessarily so, because Tanner can recall only one Victorian novel, George Meredith's little-known *One of Our Conquerors*, that takes adultery as its theme. In British novels it is much more usually the case that "adultery is just, but sedulously, averted," as in *Wuthering Heights*, *Jane Eyre*, and *Daniel Deronda* (Tanner 1979: 12). The conclusion seems clear. Tanner is right to insist that adultery is a central theme of the Victorian novel, but it is a theme that Victorian novelists were inhibited from addressing directly. So were the poets, again with the single and startling exception of Meredith in his *Modern Love*, but it was a subject matter that became available to them if they agreed to write "after the manner of the old romances of chivalry."

Victorian medievalism is, no doubt, most often either decorative or complacent or illustrative; either offered as a delightful contrast to the mundane drabness of modern life, or as a means of ennobling a life, like Prince Albert's, given over to patient committee work, by locating within it knightly virtues, or as a means of recommending to one's contemporaries a superior social order by locating that order, whether it be conservative and hierarchical or proto-socialist, in some imagined medieval past. But, for the poets, medieval subject matter was at its most vital when "new things and

Plate 5.   "How They Met Themselves," watercolor by Dante Gabriel Rossetti, 1864. (Peter Nahum at
the Leicester Galleries, London.)

old" could be most tightly "co-twisted," and this was the possibility that they found in the adulterous romances of Lancelot and Guinevere, and of Tristram and Iseult, in which a subject matter of central modern significance, and a subject matter that the novelists found difficult or impossible to address directly, became available to them. These are the poems that realize a possibility that D. G. Rossetti seems to intimate in one of his watercolors, "How They Met Themselves." A young man and woman dressed in medieval clothes take a walk in the forest, and, in a shocking encounter that makes the woman swoon, meet a pair of young lovers and recognize that the young lovers are themselves.

See also: chapter 3, THE POPULAR ENGLISH METRICAL ROMANCES; chapter 4, ARTHUR-IAN ROMANCE; chapter 6, MALORY AND THE EARLY PROSE ROMANCES; chapter 16, ROMANCE AND THE ROMANTIC NOVEL; chapter 17, POETRY OF THE ROMANTIC PERIOD; chapter 18, VICTORIAN ROMANCE: TENNYSON; chapter 26, TWENTIETH-CENTURY AR-THURIAN ROMANCE.

References and Further Reading

Texts

Arnold, Matthew (1965). *The Poems of Matthew Arnold*, ed. Kenneth Allott. London: Longmans.

Browning, Elizabeth Barrett (1992). *Aurora Leigh*, ed. Margaret Reynolds. Athens: Ohio University Press.

Browning, Elizabeth Barrett (1996). *Selected Poems*, ed. Colin Graham. London: J. M. Dent.

Browning, Robert (1996). *The Poems*, ed. John Pettigrew, completed by Thomas J. Collins. 2 vols. Harmondsworth: Penguin.

Morris, William (1858). *The Defence of Guenevere and Other Poems*. London: Reeves and Turner.

Rossetti, Christina (1979–90). *The Complete Poems of Christine Rossetti*, ed. R. W. Crump. 3 vols. Baton Rouge: Louisiana State University Press.

Swinburne, A. C. (1925–7). *The Complete Works*, ed. Sir Edmund Gosse and T. J. Wise. 20 vols. London: Heinemann.

Tennyson, Alfred (1969). *The Poems of Tennyson*, ed. Christopher Ricks. London: Longman.

Criticism

Arnold, Thomas (1862). *Manual of English Literature, Historical and Critical, with an appendix of English metres*. London: Longman.

Browning, Robert, and Elizabeth Barrett (1984–). *The Brownings' Correspondence*, ed. Philip Kelley and Ronald Hudson. Winfield,

KN: Wedgestone Press; London: Athlone Press. [14 volumes published by 2004.]

Erickson, Lee (1996). *The Economy of Literary Form: English Literature and the Industrialization of Publishing, 1800–1850*. Baltimore, MD, and London: Johns Hopkins University Press.

Girouard, Mark (1981). *The Return to Camelot: Chivalry and the English Gentleman*. New Haven and London: Yale University Press.

Harrison, Antony H. (1988). *Swinburne's Medievalism: A Study in Victorian Love Poetry*. Baton Rouge and London: Louisiana State University Press.

Jump, John D., ed. (1967). *Tennyson: The Critical Heritage*. London: Routledge and Kegan Paul.

Lang, Cecil Y. (1983). *Tennyson's Arthurian Psycho-Drama*. Tennyson Research Centre. Lincoln: Tennyson Society.

Lockhart, J. G. (1837). *Memoirs of the Life of Sir Walter Scott*. Edinburgh: Robert Cadell; London: John Murray and Whitaker.

Rosenberg, John D. (1973). *The Fall of Camelot: A Study of Tennyson's* Idylls of the King. Cambridge, MA: Harvard University Press.

Tanner, Tony (1979). *Adultery in the Novel: Contract and Transgression*. Baltimore, MD: Johns Hopkins University Press.

Tennyson, Alfred (1969). *The Poems of Tennyson*, ed. Christopher Ricks. London: Longman.

20

Romance and Victorian Autobiography: Margaret Oliphant, Edmund Gosse, and John Ruskin's "needle to the north"

Francis O'Gorman

Victorian life writers felt the lure of the romance. They also felt its limits. Understood as a progress narrative, a history of attainment, the romance plot could easily be assimilated into a dominant discourse of early and mid-Victorian culture. The narratives of self-improvement and self-advancement, potent in their appeal and in their possibilities for ironization, have long been recognized as having helped define working-class identity in the mid-nineteenth century, giving new, culturally specific life to the narrative of attainment. Such trajectories lay beneath the influential exhortations of Samuel Smiles' *Self-Help, with Illustrations of Character and Conduct* (1859), and his later encouragements to manly fidelity in *Duty with Illustrations of Courage, Patience, & Endurance* (1880), both key documents in the middle of the period's construction of a nonprofessional male identity.[1] The history of progress, fashioned into a plot of quest and conquest over adversity, the arduous search for reward and fulfillment (often sexual) was a tempting paradigm for some fictional autobiographers from the middle classes in the early part of the Victorian period, who were often also interested in the vectors of class. Charlotte Brontë explored something of its potential in *Jane Eyre* (1847), fusing it with a version of the *bildungsroman*; Dickens tested its serviceability for a critique of modern classed identity and its intersection with the determining power of sexual desire in *Great Expectations* (1861–2).

Romance offered an enticing mythic structure to the fictional autobiographer: a narrative of accomplishment, a plot of progress, which could, as in *Great Expectations*, be tellingly ironized. But for the most interesting of the real autobiographies of the second half of the period, this dimension of the romance was important insofar as it was denied. Eloquent autobiographical statements from both men and women from the 1870s onward derived their energy partly from the refusal of the subject's life to submit readily to its terms. Such autobiographers, finding little to suit their purposes in plots of attainment, and certainly not in heroic achievement, did not sustain the romancer's preference for the otherworldly either. *Jane Eyre* gestured toward a mysterious world of miraculous communication across great distances, suggesting the force of human desire to transcend material impediments, and the Gothic dimension enabled further engagement with things beyond the earthly. But for those nonfictional autobiographers who discerned no meaningful connection between their own lives and the achievement conventions of romance, writing autobiography necessitated the contemplation of patterns of existence that were sharply different from the otherworldly. These texts meditated on the irruption of an unruly reality in the fabric of human lives, the place of the grubby facts of quotidian existence or the punctures made by disaster. William Hale White's *The Autobiography of Mark Rutherford, Dissenting Minister* (1881), Margaret Oliphant's *Autobiography* (1899),[2] and Oscar Wilde's *De Profundis* (1905) are examples. Oliphant's *Autobiography*, intended for her relatives, resisted linear narrative, comprising fragments of memorial text recording a life continually ruptured, like the linearity of her plot, by disabling calamity. Bereavement after bereavement was recounted in this private narrative, only recently made available in its original form, and Oliphant ended her manuscript with the somber statement: "And now here I am all alone. I cannot write any more" (Oliphant 1990: 154). Leaving the reader a glimpse of the solitary author's grief, this terminal point offered neither catharsis nor a clear sense of authorial achievement. The central figure wrote – or ceased writing – at her conclusion alone, deprived of the family matrix that was fundamental to her sense of identity and literary purpose. Each of her children and her husband were dead before her. The romance narrative's investment in accomplishment, and its preference for otherworldly conditions preserved apart from the ungainly, disruptive contingencies of reality, were far from Oliphant's mind.

The purposive narrative frame implied by the romance, with its satisfactions and conquests, is, in Oliphant's autobiography, a resonant absence. Gillian Beer has discussed the place of unsuccessful or incomplete reading, modifying the paradigm of reading provided by Harold Bloom's *The Anxiety of Influence: A Theory of Poetry* (1973), in the patterns of literary influence in *Arguing with the Past: Essays in Narrative from Woolf to Sidney* (1989: see especially 6–10). But a text's deliberate efforts at contesting a genre, the "unsuccessful" presence of unwanted generic limits in the new work, can also be a characteristic feature of the literary identity of a new text. John Ruskin's autobiography *Praeterita: Outlines of Scenes and Thoughts Perhaps Worthy of Memory in my Past Life* (1885–9), a text with a complex relation with Victorian autobiographical traditions in general, transacted with the romance plot with peculiar subtlety, and his self-writing gained part of its distinctive literary identity from its refusal of the logic of progress that may be thought part of the Victorian inheritance of the medieval romance (of which Ruskin was himself a ready, if not an expert, reader). Yet *Praeterita*'s dealings with romance went beyond this. Romance, variously and conflictingly understood, played a role in the text's articulation of major issues about veracity and imagination, truthfulness and memory, and the relationship between seeing and knowing. Indeed, romance was at the core of the book's polygonal intellectual debate, as well as pertinent for its provocative narrative organization. It provided Ruskin, who was in various ways rewriting his life against a reader's expectations, with an idea for reinforcing themes of what he called in *Modern Painters* I (1843), "the Beautiful and the True,"[3] of which he had made his life's work.

Praeterita suggested its involvement in a world of romance from its memorable opening pages. Ruskin's first statement in the autobiography – "I am, and my father was before me, a violent Tory of the old school; – Walter Scott's school, that is to say, and Homer's" (35, 13) – invoked Scott as a guiding influence in a way that *Praeterita* would later confirm, then problematize. Certainly, Scott enabled Ruskin at the beginning, in the serene manner that was as characteristic of the text as it was uncharacteristic of Ruskin's usual vivid multiplicity of modes as a writer, to locate his own politics in a heroic context and to imbricate his Toryism with a noble romance world, associated with his now long-dead father ("I do not mean this book to be in any avoidable way disagreeable or querulous," 35, 49; see also 35, 38). Toryism, he said economically, was "a most sincere love of kings, and dislike of everybody who attempted to disobey them" (35, 14). Provocatively phrasing his enduring conviction in the virtues of obedience, heroic leadership, and divinely appointed hierarchy, Ruskin reminded his readers that such kingship was no privilege but required a life of greater labor than other men. As he expressed it with regard to Scott, and speaking of a favorite Scott novel, "Redgauntlet speared more salmon than any of the Solway fisherman" (35, 14). In doing so Redgauntlet, the eponymous hero of Scott's 1824 novel, affirmed a fraction of his true heroism, and Scott revealed something of his admirable understanding of the duties and burdens of leadership. The specific issue of Scott's association with romance – and Scott's debt to medieval romance was, as Jerome Mitchell patiently detailed in 1987, considerable – became further thematized as *Praeterita* moved on. But at its beginning, Ruskin's use of the novelist to identify, with a muted voice that was not his most familiar, his political convictions with the heroic world of chivalrous labor, insisting that its values had a place in the politics of the present, invited the reader to see a correspondence between Ruskin's life story and romance that the autobiography would extend and complicate.

Like Oliphant's autobiography, *Praeterita* resisted the logic of the attainment narrative, though in its continued defiance it paradoxically reminded the reader of the formal patterns it was eschewing. Romance insinuated itself into the reader's mind through the text's refusal to be seduced by its reassuring teleology. This was partly to do with the distinctive structure of the volume. Ruskin's mode of self-revelation, as many critics have noted (for example, Helsinger 1979; Sawyer 1985), was one that continually curled back on itself. "Whether in the biography of a nation, or of a single person, it is alike impossible to trace it steadily through successive years" (35, 169), Ruskin remarked at the beginning of chapter 10, and he returned many times, commenting on those returns, to add further perspectives to what he had already said, as if textually acting out the impossibility of following the trail of a unitary, progressive narrative. He noted at the beginning of chapter 3 that he had misleadingly overemphasized the place of good books in his early account of his childhood (35, 51); he returned to hint at his entrancement with Venice (35, 295) long after he had tried to deny the significance of the city in his work (35, 156); he observed at the end of chapter 2 that "I shall have to return over the ground of these early years, to fill gaps, after getting on a little first" (35, 49–50), preparing the reader for the habit of revision that would distinguish the whole sweep of the book.

Returning, doubling back in a serpentine movement, complicated the chronological movement of *Praeterita*, leaving the reader with a sense of the potential incompletion of its statements, the continual ripeness of its analysis for reconsideration. Ruskin's multiple depictions of what might have appeared to be turning points in his life – points one might have expected, in a hurried reading, to be moments of consequential change – also worked alongside this "involute"[4] patterning to resist the logic of progress that could be associated with the romance Ruskin evoked at the beginning. Ruskin pointed to moments of significance in his life, but he did so with such frequency that they became in aggregate less significant. Henry Telford, his father's business partner, presented him, soon after its publication, with the illustrated copy of Samuel Rogers' *Italy* (1830), which included vignettes by the painter who would subsequently consume Ruskin's energy as a critic of art: J. M. W. Turner. Ruskin remarked that "This book was the first means I had of looking carefully at Turner's work: and I might, not without some appearance of reason, attribute to the gift the entire direction of my life's energies" (35, 29). But this apparent turning point – James Dearden (1970: 70–6) reminds us that it was probably not Ruskin's actual first sight of a Turner – was, for a start, only one of a plurality of moments of consequence. There were many others. They included his first sight of the Alps (35, 116); the opening of the door of the Scuola di San Rocco in Venice and his acquaintance with the art of Tintoretto (35, 371–2); his conversion to realism in art on the road to Norwood in 1842 (35, 311); and his second conversion to realism in Fontainebleau that same year (35, 314–15). Weighted with different loci of significance, Ruskin's text cumulatively implied the failure of conversion points or moments of apparent revelation to have purchase on his consciousness. What was rather affirmed was the consistency of the self beneath the surface events and its insulation from external occurrences of seeming consequence.

These moments were not equivalents of Pip's first meeting with Estella, or Jane Eyre's first encounter with the injured Rochester, or Edmund Gosse's first serious question as a child about the efficacy of prayer in *Father and Son* (1907) or his realization that Philip Gosse was not infallible. The self of *Praeterita* was not so constituted, and was not to be diverted by events. Ruskin was careful to warn his reader to avoid the trap of believing moments of first sight were points of individual transformation. It was only with some *"appearance* of reason" that the gift of Rogers' *Italy* seemed central to his passion for Turner. Beneath surface occasions of human contingency was an enduring identity, a self that was a fixed point that firmly impeded any notion of a progress narrative:

> It is the great error of thoughtless biographers to attribute to the accident which
> introduces some new phase of character, all the circumstances of character which gave
> the accident importance. The essential point to be noted, and accounted for, was that I
> could understand Turner's work, when I saw it; – not by what chance, or in what year, it
> was first seen. (35, 29)

Critics of Ruskin, especially from North America, have been disappointed by *Praeterita*'s avoidance of a plot of personal progress. Wanting, like Sandra Gilbert and Susan Gubar in their approach to *Jane Eyre*'s "pilgrimage" in *The Madwoman in the Attic* (1979: 347), to identify a kind of Whig history, they have found *Praeterita* psychologically frustrating. Elizabeth Helsinger remarked (1979: 87) that the "book seems deliberately to refuse the minimum we expect from autobiography: a retrospective account of the writer's life which discovers some order, consistency, and purpose in past actions, a progress towards the present self." Paul Sawyer was more dispirited. "As a record of development," he said, "*Praeterita* is . . . a defeated and in many ways a depressing book" (1985: 312). But these perspectives overlook the political and theological issues at stake in Ruskin's self-presentation as static. In lamenting, as Helsinger does, that there "is no growth, no progress, no change" (1979: 89), they do not take into account Ruskin's Carlylean ontology. Ruskinian selfhood was, as he understood it, determined *ab initio* and independent of fortunes and accidents. For it to be otherwise would have placed it in tension with his acceptance that each individual was divinely ascribed a place in the social body and endowed with the powers necessary to fulfill the responsibilities of that place, however humble, middling, or grand. Only obliquely suggested by *Praeterita*'s unshakeable faith in kings, Ruskin's principle of order, the "natural pre-eminence of one man over another" (16, 121), was built on acknowledgment of the fixed ranks and correspondent obligations of men and women, and the natural "inequality" that flowed from that. It was this that gave foundation to the political and economic critique of the 1860s and 1870s as much as, in a different way, it lay behind the self-construction of the autobiography. "That your neighbour," Ruskin said in *Unto this Last* (1860):

> should, or should not, remain content with *his* position, is not your business; but it is
> very much your quantity of pleasure that may be obtained by a consistent, well-
> administered competence, modest, confessed, and laborious. We need examples of
> people who, leaving Heaven to decide whether they are to rise in the world, decide
> for themselves that they will be happy in it, and have resolved to seek – not greater
> wealth, but simpler pleasure; not higher fortune, but deeper felicity; making the first of
> possessions, self-possession; and honouring themselves in the harmless pride and calm
> pursuits of peace. (17, 112, italics in original)

Praeterita inscribed a secure self because Ruskin understood his own consciousness and faculties in relation to an ordained hierarchy like the one that underpinned the class critique of *Unto this Last* and the social structure of the Guild of St. George, Ruskin's alternative agrarian community planned in the 1870s. Surveying the difference between himself in 1886 and his youth in 1837 in the "Roslyn Chapel" chapter of *Praeterita*, Ruskin's conclusion, couched with wit and bathos, was an effect of this same ontology. "I find myself," he wrote, "in nothing whatsoever *changed*. Some of me is dead, more of me stronger. I have learned a few things, forgotten many; in the total of me, I am but the same youth, disappointed and rheumatic" (35, 220, italics in original).

This paradigm of human identity, growing from Ruskin's acknowledgment of a divinely ordained order in human society, took the individual out of time, even if time moved around it to bring, as *Praeterita* frequently lamented, deprivation to buildings and landscapes (see, for example, 35, 259). Ruskin invited perception of his own unchanged self, not in relation to the temporal but the eternal, and in this he deepened the connections between *Praeterita*'s literary strategies and the medieval. For in constructing an identity that was to be conceived *sub specie æternitatis*, Ruskin forged a link between the representation of his selfhood and the medieval practice of figuring persons and objects regarded in the light of eternity, not in relation to a human-centered viewpoint that required the adoption of perspective, or in accordance with an aesthetic that privileged the relation of sublunary things to time. Associated with pre-Renaissance aesthetics and theology in this way, the changeless self of *Praeterita*, at the root of the autobiography's avoidance of a romance-like plot of attainment, was embedded in the Christianized aesthesis of the medieval in a way strikingly coherent with Ruskin's continual preference for the age of faith, as he saw it, over the arrogance and errors of the Renaissance.

Consistent with medieval aesthetics and with Ruskin's broader thinking at one level, this conception of self in *Praeterita* was not without paradox at another, for it was also to be associated with the medieval genre that was precisely the subject of its contestation. The romance plot may have been one of achievement, but it was not one of development in what the nineteenth century would come to understand as the domain of the psychological. Romance heroes did not undergo growth in any kind of pre-psychological inner life. Ruskin, preoccupied in later texts like *The Bible of Amiens* (1880–4) and *Valle Crucis* (published in 1894) with the integrity of historical figures from the Middle Ages, framed himself in his autobiography as akin to such resolutely consistent men who understood their own God-given powers and how to fulfill their determined responsibilities. By extension, he also associated himself with the heroes of literary romance from the Middle Ages, sharing with them their characteristic of possessing "not a developing personality but an *essence*," as Paul Sawyer rightly observed (1985: 312, italics in original). Ruskin, fashioning his own subjectivity in the autobiography in aesthetic and theological terms absorbed from the medieval, the period that, since *The Seven Lamps of Architecture* (1849), he had constructed as the locus of the spiritual, moral, and political ideal, complicated the relationship between the autobiography and the idea of romance with gestures that at once spurned and welcomed it.

The relation between romance and the postures of *Praeterita* was similarly double in the text's discussions of literary and painterly truthfulness. Romance was both *self-consciously* excluded and also, redefined, of the essence. It was not, taking the first side of this relationship, merely romance's association with the progress narrative, but its identification with the fantastical and otherworldly that mattered in the veiled negotiations of *Praeterita*. Romance, in this sense, played a role in the expression of one of the text's central themes, connected to the binary of life and death that figured in Ruskin's mature work and was a key feature of the rhetoric of his alternative political economy in *Unto this Last*. The insubstantial world of fanciful imagination was inseparable from Ruskin's understanding of romance as he presented it in chapter 8, conceived as part of the potentially treacherous corpus of the untrue. But if there was paradox in the relation of the Ruskinian self as it was constructed in *Praeterita* to the romance, then there was a further paradox in the relation between the author's dedication to faithful representation *contra* romance and his self-construction in romance terms. Loosely associating his own role with the heroic, dragon-slaying St. George in his political work in the 1870s, Ruskin offered himself silently in the autobiography as a quasi-romance figure engaged in a dauntless, resisted campaign for the veracious against the misleading. He appeared in the person of a romance hero struggling against the truthlessness of the romance.

The chapter "Vester, Camenae" was partially given to a discussion of the faithfulness of Byron's poetry. A serious reader of Byron from his youth, Ruskin insisted in *Praeterita* on the poet's representations of people and human emotions as real. There was, he said, an "unquestionable reality of person in his stories, as of principles in his thoughts" (35, 150). This truthfulness had taken hold of Ruskin from his childhood. Byron had made Venice, for instance, alive for him from the first, by bringing back to life – and Ruskin usually thought of Venice as distinctively dead – its past history, tragic or inglorious, bidding him "seek first in Venice – the ruined homes of Foscari and Falier" (35, 150). In the Queen of the Adriatic, the place that was to the young Ruskin the "Paradise of cities,"[5] Byron had made the stones echo with the sound of the living dead. The poet "told me of, and reanimated for me, the real people whose feet had worn the marble I trod on" (35, 151). Not even Shakespeare had done this, Ruskin realized, retrospectively considering what of use he had learned from his early reading. Shakespeare's perception of Venice had been merely "visionary" (35, 151), not in the sense that it was revelatory but in the sense that it was misleading. Such absence of verity was discerned in the writing of Scott, from whom Ruskin had emblematically "learned" his Toryism and who remained a source of instruction and delight throughout his life. Byron was distinguished by the "unquestionable reality of person in his stories" (35, 150), whereas neither Scott nor Samuel Rogers was capable of such fidelity to human fact:

> Romance, enough and to spare, I had learnt from Scott – but his Lady of the Lake was as openly fictitious as his White Maid of Avenel: while Rogers was a mere dilettante, who felt no difference between landing where Tell leaped ashore, or standing where "St. Preux has stood." (35, 150–1)

It is Ruskin's admiration for Scott that is usually remembered. But he was consistently impatient with the falsity of many of his representations of the human.

This association between romance, however enthusiastically read, and the unreliable in Scott's writing was a part of the literary debate in *Praeterita* about sincerity itself, and it meshed with the text's major engagement with questions of clear sight, truthful representation, and honesty in vision and principle. Certainly, *Praeterita* proclaimed its own commitment to autobiographical veracity as part of its more ample statement about the primacy of truth-telling. Ruskin reminded his readers of his fixed resolve to narrate his own life dependably as befitted the son "taught to speak truth"[6] by a devoted father. But such reminders could be fretted with concerns about the kind of knowledge that "truthful" writing imparted. The truthless world of Scott's romance, with its "openly fictitious" (35, 151) people, was in danger of contaminating the autobiographical writing that was dedicated to a Byronic depiction of a real self. "In my needful and fixed resolve," Ruskin said in volume II, "to set the facts down continuously, leaving the reader to his reflections on them, I am slipping a little too fast over the surfaces of things" (35, 279). The anxiety about the misleading nature of previous factual narratives, or apparently factual narratives, gave fresh momentum to Ruskin's habitual revisiting of previously narrated material to augment and modify it. Ruskin parried the misleading element of Scott's romances by endeavoring to find a mode of narrating the self that did not compromise its history by imposing either an artificial linearity or a false clarity.

Faithful in its efforts to depict autobiographical fact, *Praeterita* offered a man entranced by the real beyond the self, possessed of vision that did not belong to a faithless literary mode. Ruskin's "honest desire for truth" (35, 226) required the capacity to see the material universe without error, the faculty that Ruskin had celebrated in the great painters, especially Turner, to whose work he had dedicated the first half of his career. *Praeterita* was restating an aesthetic and moral commitment that, since *Modern Painters* (1843–60), was in nothing whatsoever *changed*. In the third volume, Ruskin had anticipated *Praeterita*'s suspicion of truthless romance, once again associated with Scott. Walter Scott's characters and domestic scenes were perfectly done, Ruskin said, "But his romance and antiquarianism, his knighthood and monkery, are all false, and he knows them to be false" (5, 337). The painter who saw without such impediment possessed a lucidity of vision that was potentially revelatory. Turner, Ruskin said in *Modern Painters* I, certainly did. At the level of empirical perception, he saw with clarity different from that of any previous artist. He

> is the only painter, so far as I know, who has ever drawn the sky... all previous artists having only represented it typically or partially, but he absolutely and universally. He is the only painter who has ever drawn a mountain, or a stone; ... the only painter who ever drew the stem of a tree... the only painter who has ever represented the surface of calm, or the force of agitated water; who has represented the effects of space on distant objects, or who has rendered the abstract beauty of natural colour. (3, 252)

Yet romance was never only falsity for Ruskin. Although romance was "sometimes taken as synonymous with falsehood" (12, 53), as he said in 1853, it was not to be associated with the feigned alone, and with the kind of vision Turner repudiated on his canvases. Material fact was neither the sum of Ruskin's "honest desire for truth," nor of what he regarded as rightful in art. If romance was to be dismissed by *Praeterita* in some senses, it was to be cherished in another. Indeed, romance, separated from the idea of falsity, was to be associated with the core of Ruskin's relationship with landscape in the autobiography, with its interweaving of memory and revelation. The material world properly perceived was one in which the imagination discerned the presence of spirit. Part of the wisdom one might learn from the shape of the earth and the truths of its landscapes lay in the discernment of the unseen. Ruskin's terrains, the topographies described in *Praeterita* – the titles of chapters hinted at the extent of its engagement with topography as most were the names of places[7] – and consistently in his writing beyond it, were intelligible in mythic terms. Romance, associated with the visionary, assumed that the spiritual was visible through the fabric of materiality; it involved wonder and was akin to myth. Both shared the territory of religion.

"Every soul of us has to do its fight with the Untoward," Ruskin said in the chapter on "Fontainebleau," "and for itself discover the Unseen" (35, 306). For him, the discovery of the Unseen was partly the comprehension of divine intention in mountain form. In *Praeterita*, Ruskin's response to the Alps was a matter of understanding the revelation of the hills as prepared by God for human witness. Ruskin perceived amid the eternal snows the divine will, the moral meaning of Alpine form, reading the relationship between nature and God's intention in the way he had most extensively explored – in ornithology, geology, and botany – in his science textbooks in the 1870s: *Love's Meinie* (1873–81), *Deucalion* (1875–83), and *Proserpina* (1875–86). "The first sight of the Alps," Ruskin said in *Praeterita*, characteristically returning to comment on an event he had narrated already earlier in the book (35, 116):

> had been to me as a direct revelation of the benevolent will in creation. Long since, in the volcanic powers of destruction, I had been taught by Homer, and further forced by my own reason, to see, if not the personality of an Evil Spirit, at all events the permitted symbol of evil, unredeemed; wholly distinct from the conditions of storm, or heat, or frost, on which the healthy courses of organic life depended. In the same literal way in which the snows and Alpine roses of Lauter-brunnen were visible Paradise, here, in the valley of ashes and throat of lava, were visible Hell. If thus in the natural, how else should it be in the spiritual world?

To read the Alpine contours in this almost Dante-esque frame was to understand the romance of the natural world – to adapt a phrase from Philip Gosse (1860) – in all its moral force.

The connection between a sense for romance, the robustness of individual moral judgment, and a particular quality of sight had been made earlier in Ruskin's writing in a way that would still resonate in *Praeterita*'s later definitions. In the *Lectures on Architecture and Painting*, delivered in Edinburgh in November 1853, Ruskin had told his fashionable audience that the "instinctive delight in, and admiration for, sublimity, beauty, and virtue," was "the truest part of your being" (12, 54). This capacity to take pleasure in morally worthy scenes or events was something to be encouraged against the dominant model of masculinity that required "practical men" to shut down all their capacity for "poetical enthusiasm" (12, 54). It comprised an alternative form of manly perception and consciousness, the allowance of that eight-eenth-century formulation of "poetical enthusiasm," and was associated in Ruskin's mind with an innate sense for romance. He told his listeners that so long as "the feelings of romance endure within us, they are unerring, – they are as true to what is right and lovely as the needle to the north; and all that you have to do is to add to the enthusiastic sentiment, the majestic judgment – to mingle prudence and foresight with imagination and admiration, and you have the perfect human soul" (12, 55).

Ruskin variously applauded the awareness of romance in visual perception as a moral faculty, whether as a sense of the "lovely and right" as he put it in 1853, or cognition of a mountain's revelation as he understood it in *Praeterita*. An understand-ing of romance as pertaining to that which was more than the material was also part of the dynamic of personal maturation in the celebrated autobiographical account by the literary critic and biographer, Edmund Gosse, of his childhood experience with the Plymouth Brethren. *Father and Son* (first published in 1907), is another instance of the way romance, reimagined, played in the patterns of signification in Victorian auto-biography. Ruskin's interest was in the romance of the world beyond the self; Gosse traced his development in terms of the imaginary of his inner life. He cherished an unseen world not visible in nature but released by literature, which was valuable because its relationship with the daily restraints that constituted his ordinary life was one of contrast. The first fictional work Gosse, as a child, was allowed to read – his allowance up to that point had been theological – was Michael Scott's "noisy amorous novel of adventure,"[8] *Tom Cringle's Log* (1833). Like a glass of brandy to a baby, the romance's effect was drastic intoxication. But it also offered a suggestion of more lasting promise. With its "long adventures, fighting and escapes," it discovered to "my inner mind a sort of glimmering hope . . . that I should escape at last from the narrowness of the life we led at home, from this bondage to the Law and the Prophets" (1986: 171). Romance hinted at the limits of the present, suggesting how its boundary could be breached in futurity. Imaginary writing of different kinds later disclosed to the young Gosse how those limits could be mentally transcended, revealing that a route out of the confines of the present lay in the mind. His first reading of Shakespeare, which his father quickly forbade, brought him to "the seventh heaven of delight" (177); Dickens' *Pickwick Papers* (1836–7) prompted such pleasures it inspired entranced repetition: "I must have expended months on the perusal of *Pickwick*, for I used to rush through a chapter, and then read it over again very slowly, word for word, and then shut my eyes to realize the figures and the action" (191–2).

The formation of an imaginative life, the nurturing of imagination in the interior spaces of the mind, enabled at first by a romance, allowed Gosse's withdrawal from the emotional and intellectual demands of life among the Brethren. It facilitated inde-pendence, beginning the transformation of life under the "Law and the Prophets" into one in which there was room for self-development. Gosse was finally, as he phrased it at the close of *Father and Son*, to take "a human being's privilege to fashion his inner life for himself" (251) and that inner psychology was partly brought to realization by his consciousness of the pleasures of the literary. But this was not only about *self-definition*. Announcing in the first sentence of his autobiography that his story was almost the record of a "struggle between . . . two epochs" (35), Gosse's account of the young child detaching himself via romance from the stern pre-Darwinian theology of his devout father invited the reader to understand the narrative as a history of a painful but necessary sea change, a transition that was not only personal but cultural. *Father and Son* constructed a view of historical periodization, suggesting that its protagonists were representative of a process of historical change in which radical difference was prioritized over continuity and any more complex relation of moment to moment. The fault-lines of past and present, the early Victorian and the late, and the Victorian and the modern, were, Gosse suggested, clearly legible in this narrative of a man born "to fly backward" and a child who could not help "being carried forward" (35). The individual development of the young Gosse was, the text encouraged its readers to see, partly a representation of the emergence of the historically new. The discovery of romance was, in this broader narrative, the moment of the modern. Peter Allen argued (1988: 501) that Gosse, in *Father and Son*, had found "a way of speaking indirectly through the restrictions of current literary codes [chiefly about class], and he was certainly not the last proponent of modernism to have done so." But Gosse's relationship with modernism was more than this. The paradigm of difference that *Father and Son* advanced for mapping the change from one "epoch" to another as a matter of marked differences would prove tempting for Bloomsbury and the modernists. Anxious to define their own newness, they would dramatically exploit a myth of the modern as a radical departure from the previous era to make a bold claim about their own difference from the Victorians, now being thoroughly reassessed.[9]

Gosse's realization through a romance of the presence of the imaginary in an existence otherwise deprived of it was freighted with a claim about the patterns of history as well as with the desire to preserve a "hard nut" (168) of individuality disguised from the external world.[10] Ruskin's sense of romance, the romance that was proper to morally acute vision, was also bound up with a historical argument, but one in which, unlike for *Father and Son*, the past was privileged over the new as the locus of value. Realizing romance in vision for Ruskin was inseparable from moral apprehension, but was also associated with the memorial. Especially in his later years, Ruskin affirmed the healthiness of the human imagination that found in nature not only divine truths but human histories. He suggested that regarding the land, or the built environment, was, for those of a healthy moral nature, inhabiting a community of justice and faith, to enter imaginatively into association with an ancestral heritage. W. S. W. Anson observed in his introduction to Wilhelm Wägner's *Epics and Romances of the Middle Ages* (first published in English in 1883) that the late nineteenth century was seeing a rise of interest in romance, a tendency "to enquire into these old tales, nay beliefs, of our common ancestry."[11] Ruskin valued a form of romance perception that involved the remembrance of ancestry that was itself a sign of belief, a testimony to a community's faith in greatness and historical continuum. To see properly was to recall the history of one's race – Ruskin was not narrowly nationalistic in confining his argument to England – as if it was written on the land. At the times of their greatest virtue, Ruskin said in his inaugural lecture as Slade Professor of Fine Art at Oxford in February 1870, all communities made such connections, understanding their land as commemorative. This, he declared, in the Sheldonian Theatre – which was, appropriately, rich with his own memories of 30 years before[12] – "is one of the loveliest things in human nature":

> In the children of noble races, trained by surrounding art, and at the same time in the practice of great deeds, there is an intense delight in the landscape of their country as *memorial*; a sense not taught to them, nor teachable to any others; but, in them, innate; and the seal and reward of persistence in great national life; – the obedience and the peace of ages having extended gradually the glory of the revered ancestors also to the ancestral land; until the Motherhood of the dust, the mystery of the Demeter from whose bosom we came, and to whose bosom we return, surrounds and inspires, everywhere, the local awe of field and fountain; the sacredness of landmark that none may remove, and of wave that none may pollute; while records of proud days, and of dear persons, make every rock monumental with ghostly inscription, and every path lovely with noble desolateness. (20, 36, italics in original)

Increasingly in Ruskin's later years, this form of memory was approved as a part of the romance of vision, a way of seeing by which the present was made stable through anchorage in the past.[13] Ruskin's memory of his own family ancestry in *Praeterita* was, however, he realized with distress, failing – he chastized himself for being guilty of "profanely" (35, 127) neglecting the traditions of his people. The resulting sense of dislocation from personal history, as I have discussed elsewhere (O'Gorman 2001b), was a distinctive and painful way in which the autobiography defined terms that would be exploited by the modernists with their concern with the deracinated consciousness, detached from place and history. Ruskin's self-construction in the 1880s helped generate an element of the cultural frame for modernism in the new century, and such correspondence was an example of one of the many crossovers between the historical periods of writing, the textual links between "epochs," which the inheritors of Edmund Gosse's historical paradigm of difference would endeavor to deny.

Praeterita both warded off and celebrated romance. Central features of Ruskin's thinking about self, art, and landscape were involved in the text's multiple transactions with it. While the notion of romance that Ruskin inherited came chiefly from Sir Walter Scott, it would be misleading to suggest that he, deeply committed to the medieval in various ways, and even shaping his own selfhood in *Praeterita* in terms of a medieval aesthetic, was without knowledge of actual medieval romance in the period that saw, according to David Matthews, the foundation of the modern idea of Middle English and the establishment of the canon of Middle English literature (see Matthews 1999; 2000: especially 8–12). Ruskin, an original subscriber to the Early English Text Society, listed Chaucer in *Modern Painters* III as one of the finest of poets of whom it was true that "the greatest fruits of their work are gathered out of their own age" (5, 127); he told his readers in letter 17 of *Time and Tide* (1867) that Chaucer gave direction in the contemporary question of the best forms of labor: he, like all poets of sense, agreed in his "scorn of mechanic life" (17, 402). In the 1870 inaugural lecture at Oxford, Ruskin further proposed Chaucer as the "most perfect type of a true English mind in its best possible temper" (20, 29). Chaucer's translation of the *Romance of the Rose* served other specific purposes. Silently invested with associations of Ruskin's love for Rose La Touche,[14] the work was, Ruskin believed, alluded to in the title of his book on English and Greek birds, *Love's Meinie*. Ruskin added at the beginning of the October 1873 installment of *Fors Clavigera* (1871–84), the series of open letters principally on politics, that Chaucer's translation offered the best descriptions of the two noble forms of human love from which the contemporary world could usefully learn – "that of husband and wife, representing generally the family affections, and that of mankind, to which, at need, the family affection must be sacrificed" (27, 626). The language of Chaucer's romance was evoked as serviceable for the politics of 1873 and as a contribution to a debate about the role of the "sentimental" (27, 627) in political judgment. But the commerce between *Praeterita* and ideas of romance was certainly more than this. Ruskin offered himself as a romance hero rejecting the falsity of romance; as a romance consciousness, a divinely given essence free from time, in an autobiography that avoided the romance plot of attainment. He wrote against the truthlessness of romance at the same time as he rejoiced in the moral faculty of romance vision that was unerring in its recognition of the spiritual, moral, and memorial dimensions of the environment God had given to human beings. Recognizing these plural facets of *Praeterita* is to observe how deeply a Victorian autobiography could go in its dealings with romance; it is also to discover a particularly sophisticated feature of Ruskin's many-sided textual settlement, so consequential for his work at large, with an idea of the medieval, here inherited through Scott, and absorbed into the patterns of his own distinctive mind.

See also: chapter 16, Romance and the Romantic Novel; chapter 18, Victorian Romance: Tennyson; chapter 19, Victorian Romance: Medievalism; chapter 21, Victorian Romance: Romance and Mystery; chapter 22, Nineteenth-century Adventure and Fantasy.

Notes

1. On the role of particular forms of narrative in classed identities in the period, see Regenia Gagnier, *Subjectivities: A History of Self-Representation in Britain, 1832–1920* (1991).
2. *The Autobiography and Letters of Mrs M. O. W. Oliphant Arranged and Edited by Mrs Harry*

Coghill was published in 1899. Elisabeth Jay assembled and edited the complete text, including passages omitted in the original in *The Autobiography of Margaret Oliphant: The Complete Text*, ed. Elisabeth Jay (1990).

3. *The Complete Works of John Ruskin* (Library Edition), ed. E. T. Cook and Alexander Wedderburn, 39 vols. (London: Allen, 1903–12), 3, 4. Subsequent references to this edition are in the main text.

4. I use the word in the sense discussed by Lindsay Smith in "The Foxglove and the Rose: Ruskin's Involute of Childhood," in Dinah Birch and Francis O'Gorman, eds., *Ruskin and Gender* (Basingstoke: Palgrave, 2002), pp. 57–8.

5. *The Diaries of John Ruskin*, ed. Joan Evans and J. H. Whitehouse, 3 vols. (Oxford: Clarendon Press, 1956–9), I, 183.

6. 17, lxxvii – a quotation from the inscription Ruskin wrote for his father's grave in Shirley churchyard, near Croydon.

7. A contemporary response to this feature of the autobiography is John Riddy's collection of photographs of many of the title places published as *Praeterita* (Oxford: Ruskin School of Drawing and Fine Art, 2000).

8. Edmund Gosse, *Father and Son: A Study of Two Temperaments* (1986), p. 171. All subsequent references are in the main text.

9. The question of Ruskin's relation with modernism is treated in Dinah Birch, "Ruskin's Multiple Writing: *Fors Clavigera*" (1999: 175–87); Francis O'Gorman, *Late Ruskin: New Contexts* (2001: 143–66); Francis O'Gorman, "Ruskin's Memorial Landscapes" (2001: 20–34); and *Ruskin and Modernism*, ed. Giovanni Cianci and Peter Nicholls (2001). An early important text on the relation of Victorian and modern poetry was Carol T. Christ, *Victorian and Modern Poetics* (1984).

10. There is a discussion of Gosse's strategies of disguise and necessary duplicity in Howard Helsinger, "Credence and Credibility: The Concern for Honesty in Victorian Autobiography," (1999: 56–61). See also Allen 1988.

11. W. S. W. Anson's "Introduction" to Dr. W. Wägner, *Epics and Romances of the Middle Ages*, adapted by M. W. Macdowell (London: Sonnenschein, 1884, first published 1883), p. 10.

12. On 12 June 1839 Ruskin read his Newdigate Prize-winning poem *Salsette and Elephanta* to the University in the Sheldonian Theatre. William Wordsworth received an honorary degree in the same ceremony. Ruskin comments on the experience in MS passages intended for *Praeterita*, reproduced in vol. 35, pp. 613, 614.

13. Stephanie Barczewski has usefully discussed the role of romance narratives themselves in the formation of English national identity in the last two decades of the nineteenth century in *Myth and National Identity in Nineteenth-Century Britain* (2000: 93–5).

14. Ruskin's relationship with Rose La Touche is best approached in *John Ruskin and Rose La Touche: Her Unpublished Diaries of 1861 and 1867*, ed. Van Akin Burd (Oxford: Clarendon Press, 1979), and Tim Hilton, *John Ruskin: The Later Years* (New Haven: Yale University Press, 2000).

References and Further Reading

Allen, Peter (1988). "Sir Edmund Gosse and his Modern Readers: The Continued Appeal of *Father and Son.*" *ELH* 55, 487–503.

Barczewski, Stephanie (2000). *Myth and National Identity in Nineteenth-Century Britain.* Oxford: Oxford University Press.

Beer, Gillian (1989). *Arguing with the Past: Essays in Narrative from Woolf to Sidney* London: Routledge.

Birch, Dinah (1999). "Ruskin's Multiple Writing: *Fors Clavigera.*" In Dinah Birch, ed., *Ruskin and the Dawn of the Modern.* Oxford: Oxford University Press, pp. 175–87.

Burd, Van Akin, ed. (1979). *John Ruskin and Rose La Touche: Her Unpublished Diaries of 1861 and 1867.* Oxford: Clarendon Press.

Christ, Carol T. (1984). *Victorian and Modern Poetics.* Chicago: University of Chicago Press.

Cianci, Giovanni, and Peter Nicholls, eds. (2001). *Ruskin and Modernism.* Basingstoke: Palgrave.

Dearden, James S. (1970). *Facets of Ruskin: Some Sesquicentennial Studies.* London: Skilton.

Gagnier, Regenia (1991). *Subjectivities: A History of Self-Representation in Britain, 1832–1920*. New York: Oxford University Press.

Gosse, Edmund (1986). *Father and Son: A Study of Two Temperaments*. Harmondsworth: Penguin. [First published in 1907.]

Gosse, Philip (1860). *The Romance of Natural History*. London: Nisbet.

Hilton, Tim (2000). *John Ruskin: The Later Years*. New Haven and London: Yale University Press.

Helsinger, Elizabeth (1979). "The Structure of Ruskin's *Praeterita*." In George P. Landow, ed., *Approaches to Victorian Autobiography*. Athens: Ohio University Press, pp. 87–108.

Helsinger, Howard (1999). "Credence and Credibility: The Concern for Honesty in Victorian Autobiography." In George P. Landow, ed., *Approaches to Victorian Autobiography* (Athens: Ohio University Press), pp. 39–63.

Matthews, David (1999). *The Making of Middle English, 1765–1910*. Minneapolis: University of Minnesota Press.

Matthews, David (2000). *The Invention of Middle English: An Anthology of Primary Sources*. University Park: Pennsylvania State University Press.

Mitchell, Jerome (1987). *Scott, Chaucer, and Medieval Romance: A Study in Sir Walter's Scott's Indebtedness to the Literature of the Middle Ages*. Lexington: University Press of Kentucky.

O'Gorman, Francis (2001). *Late Ruskin: New Contexts*. Aldershot and Burlington, VT: Ashgate.

O'Gorman, Francis (2001). "Ruskin's Memorial Landscapes." *Worldviews: Environment, Religion, Culture. Special Edition: Writing, Landscape, and Community* 5, 20–34.

Oliphant, Margaret (1990). *The Autobiography of Margaret Oliphant: The Complete Text*, ed. Elisabeth Jay. Oxford: Clarendon Press.

Ruskin, John (1903–12). *The Complete Works of John Ruskin*, ed. E. T. Cook and Alexander Wedderburn. Library Edition. 39 vols. London: Allen.

Ruskin, John (1956–9). *The Diaries of John Ruskin*, ed. Joan Evans and J. H. Whitehouse. 3 vols. Oxford: Clarendon Press.

Sawyer, Paul L. (1985). *Ruskin's Poetic Argument: The Design of the Major Works*. Ithaca, NY: Cornell University Press.

Smith, Lindsay (2002). "The Foxglove and the Rose: Ruskin's Involute of Childhood." In Dinah Birch and Francis O'Gorman, eds., *Ruskin and Gender*. Basingstoke: Palgrave, pp. 48–63.

Wägner, W[ilhelm] (1884). *Epics and Romances of the Middle Ages*. Adapted by M. W. Macdowell. London: Sonnenschein. [First published in 1883.]

21

Victorian Romance: Romance and Mystery

Andrew Sanders

In the preface Dickens added to the completed serialization of *Bleak House* in August 1853 the novelist insisted that he had "purposely dwelt on the romantic side of familiar things." The phrase seems to have puzzled, even dismayed, generations of subsequent readers of the novel. To Dickens' contemporaries the "familiar things" described in *Bleak House* were doubtless the death, the disease, and the dirt which were pervasive elements in the urban framework of the London which lies at the core of the novel. But what did Dickens mean by emphasizing the "romantic" side of the familiar? Was he perhaps claiming that he had written a love story, which, once it had been developed out of London's potential deathliness, might serve to show that positive human forces could counter negative ones? Or was he telling his readers that his "purpose" had been to construct a complexly plotted and distinctively modern narrative around the problems familiar enough in contemporary life? *Bleak House* does indeed have a love story, albeit a somewhat subdued one. It finally unites a good doctor, Alan Woodcourt, to that determined sweeper away of cobwebs, Esther Summerson, but the novel could scarcely be described as a love story *tout court*. What readers most remember about *Bleak House* is its double narrative and the sense in which the two narratives gradually coalesce having separately unraveled the complex strands of the plot. Those same readers might be more inclined to classify the novel as a mystery than as Esther's love story. It was certainly as a mystery that many of Dickens' contemporaries and immediate successors seem to have read it. When stage versions of *Bleak House* were produced in the nineteenth century they were variously retitled as *Lady Dedlock's Secret*, *The Dedlock Secret*, and *Chesney Wold*, thus largely excluding Esther's dominant part in the narrative. The silent film version of the novel, produced in 1920, dwells almost exclusively on Lady Dedlock's story with Esther appearing merely as a complicating factor in her mother's fraught love life.[1]

There had been an informed critical discussion about the distinction between a novel and a romance in the closing years of the eighteenth century and the first half of the nineteenth, though by the time of the publication of *Bleak House* the term "novel" seems to have been universally applied to works of fiction with contemporary settings and with pretensions to "realism" in their plots and settings. Ann Radcliffe had conspicuously chosen to describe both *The Mysteries of Udolpho* (1794) and *The Italian* (1797) as "Romances" and it was as "the Shakespeare of Romance Writers" that she was hailed by Nathan Drake in his *Literary Hours: or Sketches, Critical, Narrative and Poetical* of 1798. In seeking to explore and define the nature of terror in literature, Drake distinguishes between "objects of terror...which owe their origin to the agency of superhuman beings" and "that thrilling sensation of mingled astonishment, apprehension, and delight so irresistibly captivating to the generality of mankind" which is linked to a "sublime or pathetic sentiment" or to "the uncertain and suspended fate of an interesting personage." For Drake, Radcliffe had alleviated "the wild landscape of Salvator Rosa" with the "softer graces of Claude [Lorrain]." She had thus "softened down" scenes of terror with an "intermixture of beautiful description, or pathetic incident" so that "pleasurable emotion is ever the predominating result" (Drake 1798: 269–74).[2] A "Romance" was thus likely to be seen as containing elements of terror and of the sublime, whether in terms of its physical setting or in relation to the predicament of its characters. For the writer of romance, engaged in stimulating "pleasurable emotion" in his or her readers, "realism" was neither requisite nor necessarily desirable.

It is perhaps in the light of Radcliffe's determination to describe her fiction as "romances'" that we can grasp why it was that Thomas Holcroft should give his *Anna St. Ives* of 1794 the subtitle "a novel." The same description was added by Jane Austen to the title pages of her *Sense and Sensibility* (1811), *Pride and Prejudice* (1813), *Mansfield Park* (1814), and *Emma* (1816). Later in the nineteenth century this descriptive subtitle was also given to Harriet Martineau's *Deerbrook* in 1839, to Wilkie Collins' *The Woman in White* in 1860, and, perhaps most famously, to that "novel without a hero," Thackeray's *Vanity Fair* of 1847–8. Elsewhere in early and mid-Victorian fiction we commonly find authors employing either the vague description "a Tale" (as in Gaskell's *Mary Barton: A Tale of Manchester Life* of 1848 and Dickens' two historical novels, *Barnaby Rudge: A Tale of the Riots of 'Eighty* of 1841 and *A Tale of Two Cities* of 1859) or adopting Henry Fielding's term "history" (used by Dickens for the "Personal History" of David Copperfield in 1849–50 and by Thackeray for his *History of Pendennis* in 1848–50). Otherwise we have the much more specific attempts to convey an illusion of realism: "an Autobiography" (used by Charlotte Brontë for her *Jane Eyre* in 1847 and by Kingsley for his *Alton Locke* of 1850) or "Memoirs" (used by Thackeray for the new edition of *Barry Lyndon* in 1856 and for *The Newcomes* of 1853–5). Interestingly enough, the one writer who seems to have declined to eschew the term "romance" was William Harrison Ainsworth who so subtitled his *Rookwood* of 1836 and his *Jack Sheppard* of 1839 and went on to style his popular stories *The Tower of London* (1840), *Guy Fawkes* (1841), *Windsor Castle* (1843), and *St. James's or the Court of Queen Anne* (1844) as "Historical Romances." Ainsworth proved to be more ambiguous when it came to his once celebrated story, *The Lancashire Witches*, which was called "A Novel" on its first appearance in 1849 "for

Private Circulation," but which was resubtitled "A Romance of Pendle Forest" when it was issued for the general public later in the same year. He was, nevertheless, to continue to use the term "Historical Romance" to describe his less commercially successful stories of the 1860s (such as *The Constable of the Tower* of 1861 and *Cardinal Pole, or the Days of Philip and Mary* of 1863).[3]

Although William Spalding's *History of English Literature* of 1853 (written "For the use of Schools and of Private Students") draws little distinction between novels and romances,[4] when Margaret Oliphant published her astute *Literary History of England in the End of the Eighteenth Century and Beginning of the Nineteenth Century* (1882), she seems to have taken it for granted that readers would assume that the "romance" was largely an eighteenth-century form, which had been rendered redundant by the "novelists" of the early nineteenth century. In writing of the work of Maria Edgeworth, Jane Austen, and Susan Ferrier, Oliphant draws out a contrast with the work of Elizabeth Inchbald:

> It is curious to note the difference between their contemporary Mrs. Inchbald and these ladies of the new light. The *Strange Story* [*A Simple Story*], with its graceful talent and individuality, belongs to the eighteenth century altogether. It deals with no definable development of human nature, and it has no real study of life. It is a surprise to us to realise that *Pride and Prejudice* was actually written earlier than that curious romance, though it did not till some time after see the light. Mrs. Inchbald is of the past, her production is almost archaic; but Jane Austen belongs to humanity in all periods, and Miss Edgeworth is even more clearly natural and practical.[5]

"Romance" is therefore to be distinguished from a novel, a higher class of fiction that shows a "definable development of human nature," a "study of life," and a quality of representation that is "clearly natural and practical."

In March and April 1858 David Masson, who was Professor of English Literature at University College London, gave a series of lectures on "British Novelists and Their Styles" to the Philosophical Institution at Edinburgh. In the course of these lectures, which were published a year later, Masson confessed, somewhat reluctantly, that there was a real enough distinction between romances and novels. He went on to explain to his audience that these long-established terms could be usefully seen as older and newer types of fiction:

> I have not hitherto recognized this distinction, nor do I care to recognize it very distinctly, because, after all, it is one more of popular convenience than of invariable fitness. A Romance originally meant anything in prose or in verse written in any of the Romance languages; a Novel meant a new tale, a tale of fresh interest. It was convenient, however, seeing that the two words existed, to appropriate them to separate uses; and hence, now, when we speak of a Romance, we generally mean "a fictitious narrative, in prose or verse, the interest of which turns upon marvellous and uncommon incidents;" and, when we speak of a Novel, we generally mean "a fictitious narrative differing from the Romance, inasmuch as the incidents are accommodated to

the ordinary train of events, and the modern state of society." If we adopt this distinction, we make the prose Romance and the Novel the two highest varieties of prose fiction, and we allow in the prose Romance a greater ideality of incident than in the Novel. In other words, where we find a certain degree of ideality of incident, we call the work a Romance.[6]

This is a useful distinction and it is one that might perhaps explain why that admirer of Walter Scott, William Spalding, had been disinclined to distinguish between romance and novel, and also why that fanciful follower of Scott, Harrison Ainsworth, had so determinedly clung on to the idea of the "historical romance."

Towards the end of his lectures, having surveyed the history and development of the novel in Britain, Masson went on to "classify" what he saw as 13 categories of "recent" fiction. By "recent" he meant developments in fiction since the death of Sir Walter Scott, and he began (appropriately for his Edinburgh audience) with "The Novel of Scottish Life and Manners," most of which had been written under the direct influence of Scott. To this category he added the related varieties of Irish and English novels, including mention in the latter of what we might now call the English "provincial" novel (the Brontës, Gaskell, Kingsley). He then glanced at "The Fashionable Novel" (which we might call the "Silver Fork Novel"), the "Illustrious Criminal Novel" (now often typed as "Newgate" fiction), and the "Traveller's Novel," dividing that category into the two subspecies of "The Novel of American Manners and Society" (in which he included the work of Frances Trollope and Dickens' *Martin Chuzzlewit*) and "The Oriental Novel" (mentioning the now largely forgotten work of James Justinian Morier and James Baillie Fraser). There followed the "Military and the Naval Novel," the "Novel of the Supernatural Phantasy" (*Frankenstein*, Bulwer Lytton's *Zanoni*, and Dickens' "Christmas Books"), the "Art and Culture Novel" (supposedly inspired by Goethe's *Wilhelm Meister*, but of which Masson finds few significant home-grown examples), and finally the "Historical Novel." Modern critics and readers might not choose to recognize, let alone define, most of these categories when discussing Victorian fiction. What is interesting is that Masson describes all of his examples as "novels," even those such as *Frankenstein* that we might now see as a "romance" in the light of his own earlier definition of that term. To certain of these categories, and how they might relate to the continuing Victorian experiment with romance, we will return.

Before moving away from Masson's observations about the state of contemporary fiction, however, it is proper to pause over two further related aspects of his critical study. He notably draws a useful distinction between Dickens and Thackeray. Thackeray is described as "a novelist of what is called the Real school" while Dickens "is a novelist of the Ideal or Romantic school." This distinction is complemented by Masson's account of what he assumed was the "proper business of the novel" in the present day and how the form might develop in the second half of the nineteenth century. Put succinctly, this "proper business" was "the representation of social reality." At the time of his lectures, it should be remembered, Masson had as yet no knowledge of the work of George Eliot. Nevertheless, the last sentences of his published lectures seem to look forward to a newly flexible kind of social realism in the novel, one which might allow for a new kind of heroism which finds its proper ambience in a newly charged imaginative universe:

> I believe, however, that there may be vindicated for the literature of prose phantasy the liberty of an order of fiction different from the usual Novel of Social Reality, and approaching more to what has always been allowed in metrical poesy, and that, accordingly, those occasional prose fictions are to be welcomed which deal with characters of heroic imaginary mould, and which remove us from cities and the crowded haunts of men.[7]

This is manifestly not a prescription for George Eliot's future contribution to the nineteenth-century novel, let alone a prevision of Thomas Hardy's or Henry James's. Perhaps, after all, what Masson was aspiring to was a sense that the days of the romance were not numbered and, indeed, that its fullest realization might lie in the future.

In order to explore both the survival and the development of certain key aspects of "romance" in Victorian fiction it is useful to return to some of the categories that Masson delineated in 1859. According to his own definition, the interest of romance turns on "marvellous and uncommon incidents" and on an "ideality of incident" – when a writer might be said to have deviated from a narrative form centered narrowly on "the ordinary train of events and the modern state of society." It should therefore be possible to recognize a certain distinctiveness in those Victorian novels that broke away from a strict adherence to the norms of "realism." It is apposite therefore to look at selected examples of the kind of fiction that Masson categorizes under the headings of "the Historical Novel," "the Novel of Supernatural Phantasy," and somewhat less directly, "the Illustrious Criminal Novel" (which we might more usefully describe as "the mystery novel" or "the detective novel").

It was generally agreed in the nineteenth century that the historical novel had reached its apogee in the work of Sir Walter Scott, and his Victorian disciples, imitators, and admirers admitted that they were in awe of his achievement.[8] One practicing historical novelist, Edward Bulwer-Lytton, was prepared in his *Caxtoniana* of 1863 to proclaim that the creative artist in Scott outclassed the work of conventional historians because of his "impartiality," an impartiality derived from an incomparable "knowledge of the world":

> History, in its highest ideal, requires an immense knowledge of the world; it requires also something of the genius and heart of a poet, though it avoids poetical form – that is, the difference between an accurate chronicler and a great historian is to be found partly in knowledge, not only of dry facts, but of the motives and practical conduct of mankind, and partly in the seasonable eloquence, not of mere diction, but of thought and sentiment, which is never to be found in a man who has nothing in him of the poet's nature.

These are high ideals, and Bulwer goes on to distinguish between Scott and those admired historians, Hume and Macaulay:

> Scott, though a writer of romance, and having in his actual life political opinions quite as strong as those of Macaulay or Hume – yet, partly from a frank commune with the world in all its classes and divisions, partly from the compulsion of his art, which ordained him to seek what was grand or beautiful on either side of conflicting opinion, conveys infinitely fairer views of historical character than either of those illustrious writers of history. Scott, in a romance, could not have fallen into such Voltairean abasements of the grand principle of religious faith as those into which Hume descends when he treats of the great Puritans of the civil wars. Nor could Scott, in a romance, have so perverted the calm judicial functions of history as Lord Macaulay has done in that elaborated contrast between James II and William and Mary, which no pomp of diction can reconcile to the reader's sense of justice and truth.[9]

It is interesting that Bulwer has here chosen to use the word "romance" in order to suggest that Scott possessed an imaginative power akin to that of Shakespeare. The finest kind of historical fiction (or "romance") could therefore function in a narrative realm beyond the grasp of both the mere chronicler and the gifted, interpretative historian. In a sense, Bulwer is suggesting that the historical novelist does his or her job best when he or she understands the men and manners of the past in the same way that he or she understands the men and manners of the present. Rather than escaping into a charged and fantastic world, the novelist recreates the complex fabric of the past for readers by the refined force of his or her understanding of how character and environment interact in the present. It is the result of a symbiosis of imaginative freedom and disciplined psychological understanding. There was not much room there for the "ideality of incident" that David Masson saw as characterizing the romance.

Scott's influence on those Victorian novelists who wrote at least one historical novel (Bulwer himself, Dickens, Thackeray, Gaskell, Reade, Eliot, Hardy, Stevenson) was to prove profound. Rather than looking at a new generation of novelists who took their task and their art seriously (sometimes *too* seriously), it is worth considering the now somewhat neglected, but definitely *not* underrated, William Harrison Ainsworth (1805–82). As we have seen, Ainsworth was insistent that his works should properly be described as "historical *romances.*" *The Tower of London* of 1840 shows Ainsworth writing at his most vigorous. It might also be conceded, even by the most sanguine of modern critics, that the novel still has a degree of innovative daring about it, though its innovations were not to prove influential over another generation of writers. It was certainly a popular enough book in its time, passing through five editions between 1840 and 1845 and reaching a belated sixth edition in 1853. It was reissued in weekly penny numbers a year later and again in 1858–9 and had been translated into Dutch and Spanish in the 1840s and into French in 1858.[10] The novel originally had the advantage of being illustrated by a remarkable series of etchings and woodcuts by George Cruikshank (the most darkly memorable plate is perhaps the one that shows

Plate 6. "Mauger Sharpening his Axe," etching by George Cruikshank for William Harrison Ainsworth's *The Tower of London* (London: Richard Bentley, 1840). (Photograph © British Library.)

the executioner, Mauger, grimacing as he sharpens his axe). What rendered the
narrative of *The Tower of London* distinctive, however, was its combination of a
sensational plot, set in a particularly charged historical period, with a good deal of
topographical and architectural detail. It was a formula that Ainsworth would repeat
in *Windsor Castle* and *Old Saint Pauls*. In the preface he later added to *Rookwood*, his
story about the highwayman, Dick Turpin, the novelist had insisted that his chief
object in writing the story had been "to see how far the intrusion of a warmer and
more genial current into the veins of the old Romance would succeed in reviving her
fluttering and feeble pulses." Indeed, having named Horace Walpole, Ann Radcliffe,
Monk Lewis, and Maturin as his inspirations, Ainsworth went on to suggest through

an extended architectural metaphor that he might be the new artificer who was capable of restoring the old "fabric" of romance by clearing away the "rubbish which choked up its approach" and ensuring an "entire renovation and perfection."[11] *The Tower of London* seems to give substance to this architectural aspiration even more fully than *Rookwood*. Banished are the beetling Italian castles and the picturesque Salvator Rosa landscapes of Radcliffe, to be replaced by a singularly solid English building and a recognizable English ambience. Ainsworth sees the Tower as playing a vital role in the evolution of the myth of "Merry England," an England of roast beef and ale, of Bluff King Hal and Good Queen Bess. The great fortress was, moreover, a structure which was as familiar to Ainsworth's London contemporaries as it had been to their Tudor ancestors. As the novelist insisted to his readers, it was "the proudest monument of antiquity, considered with reference to its historical associations, which this country or any other possesses," and he was determined to weave a story around what he described as its triple historical functions as a palace, a prison, and a fortress.[12] This required rejecting Sir Walter Scott's example of a fictional intermixture of historical with invented characters, with the stress laid on the fortunes and the perceptions of the invented. Instead Ainsworth offered early Victorian readers an indiscriminate tangle of minor plots all of which took place in the Tower and most of which were variously spun around the story of the unfortunate Lady Jane Grey, her brief accession to the throne, her deposition, and her execution. It is not, however, in the retelling of the sad history of Lady Jane Grey that the "romance" of the story is primarily located, but in the love story of Cuthbert Cholmondeley and Angela, in the comic antics of the dwarf, Xit, and the giant yeomen warders (one of whom bears an uncanny resemblance to Henry VIII), and in the Gothic tergiversations of the jailors, Nightgall and Wolfytt, and the headsman, Mauger. *The Tower of London* never represents the kind of imaginative threat to the authority of a conventional chronicle to which Bulwer Lytton aspired. It attempts instead to explore a historical situation by reasserting a received and traditionally Protestant reading of events: Jane Grey is an innocent victim of the political maneuvers of others; Mary Tudor is an unlovable bigot, but she is an undoubted queen; her sister Elizabeth may be haughty, but even amid her misfortunes, she is learning to assume the role of Good Queen Bess. History moves inexorably forward toward a happier if less colorful future, with victims, villains, and victors alike pointing morals and adorning tales. But for Ainsworth the "history" is only one side of the "romance." With its creaking panels, its darkly mysterious vaults, its rattling chains, its jangling keys, its ghosts, and its grimacing villains, *The Tower of London* is often closer to a well-rehearsed and flamboyantly costumed pantomime than it is to a serious artistic challenge to Hume or Macaulay. Here at least "romance" may be said to have briefly triumphed to the detriment of "high" art.

   There is perhaps rather too much of what David Masson styled "supernatural phantasy" and too little of what he called "ideality of incident" in Ainsworth's historical fiction to render it a persuasive picture of the past for many modern readers. It is a different matter when it comes to the short, popular fiction that Masson recognized as properly falling within the category of "supernatural phantasy": Charles Dickens' "Christmas Books." These five tales, published between 1843 and 1848 were all designed for a specific seasonal market. The first and most successful of the tales, *A Christmas Carol, Being a Ghost Story of Christmas,* sold some 6,000 copies within days of its first appearance on December 19, 1843, and reached its seventh printing by the following May. The story was dramatized soon after its publication and there appear to have been at least eight further productions in the two succeeding months. Its steady popularity was also assured by the fact that its text formed the first of Dickens' own public readings on December 27 and 30, 1853 (each took three hours) and edited versions remained part of his repertoire throughout the rest of his reading career. The tale has retained its popularity and everyday familiarity into the twenty-first century. It also admirably demonstrates why David Masson was inclined to see Dickens as belonging to the "Ideal or Romantic school" of writers. Given its active afterlife and its many transmogrifications, many modern readers might find themselves disinclined to accept that *A Christmas Carol* truly is a key work of nineteenth-century fiction rather than some slim, shapely, fantastic alternative to the "loose baggy monster" of the realist Victorian novel. That may be due to the fact that we might more readily want to categorize the tale as a key Victorian *romance.*[13]

A Christmas Carol tells us a good deal about Charles Dickens' fictional preoccupations, and, despite its perennial hold on the imaginations of its readers, it also tells us a lot about the decade in which it was written. The 1840s have frequently been described as the "hungry forties." It was a period of industrial unrest and agricultural distress, one marked by the Irish famine, by strikes and lockouts, by the threat of Chartist-led insurrection, by the growth of urban squalor, and by the devastating spread of the diseases associated with the poverty of the slums: diarrhea, dysentery, phthisis, cholera, and typhus. It was by no means coincidental, therefore, that Dickens began work on his story shortly after a visit to Manchester in October 1843 and that his first public readings of the story should have taken place in Birmingham. The illustration of Scrooge confronted by the spectral children, "Ignorance" and "Want" shows the horrid encounter being enacted against a background of mills and smoking factory chimneys. Although ghost stories were regarded by Dickens' contemporaries as particularly suitable for the Christmas season, *A Christmas Carol* is rooted in contemporary problems and not in a desire to escape from reality. The story requires Scrooge to confront those problems, and, as far as he may, seek to remedy them. When the Ghost of Christmas Present shows Scrooge the "yellow, meagre, ragged, scowling, wolfish" children, Scrooge starts back "appalled" and asks the Spirit to whom they belong. "They are Man's," the Spirit replies:

> "This boy is Ignorance. This girl is Want. Beware them both, and all their degree, but most of all beware this boy, for on his brow I see that written which is Doom, unless the writing be erased. Deny it!" cried the Spirit, stretching out its hand towards the city. "Slander those who tell it ye! Admit it for your factious purposes, and make it worse. And bide the end." (Stave 3)

Dickens' tale uses fantasy, visions, and ghosts to point a modern moral and to remind his readers that the best hope for the proper reform of society lay in individual responsiveness. Scrooge's visions are not the result of a disturbance to his system due to "a slight disorder of the stomach." Rather, they appear to be vouchsafed by some benign supernatural force intent on reinforcing the true "spirit of Christmas." Scrooge's very human visitors in Stave One, the two portly gentlemen who come asking him for "liberality," describe Christmas as a season "when it is more than usually desirable that we should make some slight provision for the poor and destitute, who suffer greatly at the present time." If many Victorians would have agreed with David Masson that a novel, as differentiated from the romance, was primarily concerned with the "ordinary train of events and the modern state of society," Dickens was forcefully suggesting to readers of *A Christmas Carol* that modern society sometimes needed a representation of the extraordinary, or the "ideal," in order to address and then relieve its pressing problems. The real ghosts that haunted the 1840s were often all too substantial.

This leads us back to Dickens' claim in *Bleak House* to have dwelt on "the romantic side of familiar things." The "familiar things" with which the novel deals – death, disease, desuetude – were familiar indeed to those Victorians who chose to look into the lower depths of London or who fretted over the pervasive social and political anomalies of Britain as a whole. In many ways *Bleak House* was addressing what some unsympathetic readers considered to be over-familiar contemporary problems, and the central object of its criticism – the unreformed procedures of the Court of Chancery – had merely given Dickens, as one jaded contemporary commentator noted, "the opportunity of indulging in stale and commonplace satire upon the length and expense of Chancery proceedings."[14] In the case of the "pestiferous" and "obscene" urban graveyard in which Captain Hawdon is buried, Dickens was describing an unpleasant fictional phenomenon the reality of which had already been done away with, thanks to legislation in the 1830s and 1840s.[15] Moreover, despite the fact that its illustrations show characters dressed in the fashions of the 1850s, *Bleak House* is evidently set back some 20 years, with the effects of the Reform Bill either anticipated or imminently realizable and with the railway intruding itself into the English provinces. As Sir Leicester Dedlock's withdrawal from public life at the end of the novel indicates, he and his class have had their day and the world is opening up to the likes of Mr. Rouncewell, the northern "ironmaster." But this singularly unsentimental retrospect to the 1830s did not really give Dickens sufficient leeway to conceive *Bleak House* as a "historical romance." What the novelist may have meant by claiming that he had purposefully dwelt on the "romantic side of familiar things" was not that he was somehow "romancing" or "romanticizing" unpalatable elements in modern life, but that his complex *plot,* like that of *A Christmas Carol,* offered readers an imaginative way of resolving some of the social problems that the story had delineated. Dickens was, as Masson might have recognized, resorting to the "Ideal or Romantic" as a means of coming to terms in fiction with the "ordinary train of events" in "the modern state of society."

Bleak House is the first English novel to describe the work of a professional detective. Inspector Bucket, who is employed by Mr. Tulkinghorn to investigate Lady Dedlock's interest in the graveyard, and who later pursues that vagrant Lady on Sir Leicester's instructions, possesses the physical attributes of a good detective. He has an "attentive face," he is a "composed and quiet listener," he is methodical and he is painstaking. But Bucket is not the only detective in *Bleak House*, nor is he the prime reason why we might be tempted to see the novel as the first "detective story." This professional detective is complemented by a series of amateur investigators and snoopers (Tulkinghorn, Guppy, Krook, Smallweed) and the detective work around which the story is built contributes to the quest for self-knowledge undertaken from the beginning by Esther Summerson. Indeed, it is in the very idea of "quest" that we can attempt to recognize how the novel might properly be seen as akin to a modern "romance."

Bleak House was also to usher in a new fictional school. What David Masson had identified in 1858 as "the illustrious criminal novel" was later to be styled the "Sensation Novel." Dickens' association with this particular school of novel-writing was first formally identified by W. C. Philips in 1919 in his study *Dickens, Reade and Collins: Sensation Novelists*. Although later critics have been more disposed to look at the roles of dissident, and often criminally inclined, women in the so-called sensation novel, it is still valid to acknowledge that Dickens' work, from *Oliver Twist* onward, seems to have opened the door to the popular success of such novels of the 1860s as Collins' *The Woman in White* (1859–60) and *The Moonstone* (1868), Reade's *Hard Cash* (1863), and Mary Braddon's *Lady Audley's Secret* (1861–2). It is also by no means coincidental that these novels by Collins and Reade first appeared as serials in the pages of Dickens' own periodical, *All the Year Round*. So potent was the popular response to this new kind of criminal fiction that the Archbishop of York felt obliged to preach against it as "one of the abominations of the age."[16] The sensational thing about sensation fiction was that it appealed both to heightened emotion and to the intellect. It made new and, for some readers, excessive demands on its readers for it often required them to act as detectives themselves. Although Dickens is said to have found the startling appearance of Anne Catherick to Walter Hartright on the road from Hampstead to London in Wilkie Collins' *The Woman in White* one of the two most dramatic episodes in English literature, he was also inclined to feel that the "great pains" Collins had taken in constructing the complex plot of his novel were too emphatic.[17] He also complained, moreover, that his protégé was possessed of an unfortunate authorial disposition "to give an audience credit for nothing – which necessarily involves the forcing of points on their attention—which I have always observed them to resent when they find out – as they always will and do."[18] Collins was therefore guilty both of asking too much of his readers *and* of crediting them with too little speculative imagination.

Nevertheless, it was *The Woman in White* that Dickens selected to succeed the serialization of his own *A Tale of Two Cities* as the lead story in the pages of *All the Year Round*. Thus, in pride of place in the issue of November 26, 1859, the new story was introduced with the bold editorial assertion that "it is our hope and aim, while we work hard at every other department of our journal, to produce, in this one, some sustained works of imagination that may become part of English Literature." Dickens was astute enough to recognize that what Collins was offering to the reading public was precisely what that public had begun to crave: sensation. *The Woman in White* was to prove "the most popular novel of the century," according to the publisher George Smith (who signally failed to secure the opportunity of publishing it despite being told by a dinner companion that "everyone is raving about it . . . we talk 'Woman in White' from morning till night").[19] In the preface that Collins added to *The Woman in White* once the novel had completed its run, the novelist appealed to prospective reviewers not to "tell his story at second-hand," that is, to give away too much of his plot. He wanted new readers to discover the twists and concealments of that plot for themselves. The reviewer in *The Times* of October 30, 1860 (when the novel was already in its third edition) was insistent that it was, however, virtually impossible to give proper credit to Collins's achievement without revealing the plot:

> We are commanded to be silent lest we should let the cat out of the bag. The cat out of the bag! There are in this novel about a hundred cats contained in a hundred bags, all screaming and mewing to be let out. Every new chapter contains a new cat. When we come to the end of it out goes the animal, and there is a new bag put into our hands which it is the object of the subsequent chapter to open. We are very willing to stroke some of these numerous cats, but it is not possible to do it without letting them out.[20]

The *Times* reviewer has put his finger on precisely why the novel fascinated its original readers and why it continues to be a much admired model for writers of detective fiction. *The Woman in White* required a pleasurable delight in mystery and speculation, but it also offered gratification as the complex plot evolved itself and as the central mystery unwound after a succession of minor mysteries had been unraveled. Sensation fiction, like the long line of later detective/crime fiction that it engendered, tantalized as much as it satisfied. It exploited heightened emotion through a clever use of suspense, and, as much of Collins' best fiction does, it explored unusual states of mind, minds distorted by drugs, madness, revenge, and murderous desires. Above all, sensation novels returned fiction to the idea of the quest that figured so prominently in medieval romances. If the quest no longer had a spiritual end, the secular goals pursued by the writers of sensation fiction were to be achieved by a process of exploration, examination, and ultimately, resolution. This was a fiction that required steadfastness in its heroes and heroines in order that the disordering forces of sin might be defeated. Where crime had distorted the "ordinary train of events" the determined solver of crimes was endowed with a mission that restored the world to a kind of grace. It was perhaps uniquely through this kind of narrative that David Masson's ideal of "an order of fiction different from the usual Novel of Social Reality" was partly realized. If the sensation fiction of the 1860s contains relatively few "characters of heroic imaginary mould," it at least still succeeds in imaginatively removing readers from "familiar things," from the mundane and the commonplace, "from cities and the crowded haunts of men." This process of defamiliarization may indeed suggest that the romance had been transmogrified with a new questing energy in Victorian fiction.

See also: chapter 12, "GOTHIC" ROMANCE; chapter 13, WOMEN'S GOTHIC ROMANCE; chapter 16, ROMANCE AND THE ROMANTIC NOVEL; chapter 18, VICTORIAN ROMANCE: TENNYSON; chapter 19, VICTORIAN ROMANCE: MEDIEVALISM; chapter 20, ROMANCE AND VICTORIAN AUTOBIOGRAPHY; chapter 22, NINETEENTH-CENTURY ADVENTURE AND FANTASY.

Notes

1. For these versions of *Bleak House* see Philip K. Bolton, *Dickens Dramatized* (London: Mansell, 1987), pp. 349–67.

2. Nathan Drake, *Literary Hours*. 3 vols. 4th edn. (London, 1820), vol. 1, pp. 269–74. [First published in 1798.]

3. For these novels see S. M. Ellis, *William Harrison Ainsworth and his Friends*. 2 vols. (London: John Lane, 1911), vol. 2, pp. 356–83.

4. William Spalding, *The History of English Literature; with An Outline of the Origin and Growth of the English Language: Illustrated by Extracts* (Edinburgh, 1853). Spalding, who was Professor of Logic, Rhetoric and Metaphysics at the University of St. Andrews, is particularly impressed by Scott's fiction, but recognizes no distinction between "romance" and "novel" either in his work or in that of his successors; see pp. 363, 399.

5. Margaret Oliphant, *The Literary History of England* (1882), vol. 3, p. 205.

6. David Masson, *British Novelists and their Styles: Being a Critical Sketch of the History of British Prose Fiction* (1859), pp. 26–7.

7. Ibid., pp. 248, 308.

8. For a consideration of Scott and his heirs see Sanders 1978.

9. Edward Bulwer-Lytton, *Caxtoniana: A Series of Essays on Life, Literature and Manners*. 2 vols. (Edinburgh and London, 1863), vol. 2, pp. 301–2.

10. Ellis, *William Harrison Ainsworth and his Friends*, vol. 2, pp. 363–4.

11. W. H. Ainsworth, *Rookwood*. New edn. (1851), preface.

12. *The Tower of London: A Historical Romance* (1840), preface, p. iv.

13. For the afterlife of *A Christmas Carol* see Paul Davis 1990.

14. George Brimley in the *Spectator* (September 24, 1853). Reprinted in Philip Collins, ed., *Dickens: The Critical Heritage* (London: Routledge and Kegan Paul, 1971), pp. 283–4.

15. For this issue see A. W. C. Brice and K. J. Fielding, "*Bleak House* and the Graveyard," in Robert B. Partlow Jr., ed., *Dickens the Craftsman: Strategies of Presentation* (Carbondale: Southern Illinois University Press, 1970).

16. For the sensation novel see the useful entry in John Sutherland's *Longman Companion to Victorian Fiction* (1988), pp. 562–3.

17. See *The Recollections of Sir Henry Dickens K.C.* (London: Heinemann,1934), p. 54.

18. Letter of 7 January 1860. *The Letters of Charles Dickens*, ed. M. House, G. Storey, and K. Tillotson. 12 vols. (Oxford: Clarendon Press, 1965–2002), vol. 9, 1859–61, pp. 194–5.

19. Smith quoted by Kenneth Robinson in his *Wilkie Collins: A Biography* (London: Bodley Head, 1951), pp. 142–3.

20. Ibid., p. 148.

References and Further Reading

Ainsworth, William Harrison (1840). *The Tower of London: A Historical Romance*. London: Richard Bentley.

Braddon, Mary Elizabeth (1996). *Aurora Floyd*, ed. P. D. Edwards. World's Classics. Oxford: Oxford University Press. [First published in 1863.]

Braddon, Mary Elizabeth (1992). *Lady Audley's Secret*, ed. David Skilton. World's Classics. Oxford: Oxford University Press. [First published in 1861–2.]

Braddon, Mary Elizabeth (1999). *John Marchmont's Legacy*, ed. Toru Sasaki and Norman Page. World's Classics. Oxford: Oxford University Press. [First published in 1863.]

Brantlinger, Patrick (1982). "What is 'Sensational' about the Sensation Novel?" *Nineteenth Century Fiction* 37, 1–28.

Collins, William Wilkie (1975). *The Woman in White*, ed. Harvey Peter Sucksmith. London: Oxford University Press. [First published in 1860.]

Collins, William Wilkie (1982). *The Moonstone*, ed. Anthea Trodd. World's Classics. Oxford: Oxford University Press, 1982. [First published in 1868.]

Davis, Paul (1990). *The Lives and Times of Ebenezer Scrooge*. New Haven and London: Yale University Press.

Dickens, Charles (1994). *Bleak House*, ed. Andrew Sanders. Everyman Library. London: J. M. Dent; Vermont: Charles E. Tuttle, 1994. [First published in 1853.]

Dickens, Charles (2003). *A Christmas Carol and Other Christmas Writings*, ed. Michael Slater. Harmondsworth: Penguin.

Edwards, Philip D. (1971). *Some Mid-Victorian Thrillers: The Sensation Novel, its Friends and Foes*. St. Lucia: University of Queensland Press.

Hughes, Winifred (1980). *The Maniac in the Cellar: The Sensation Novel of the 1860s*. Princeton, NJ: Princeton University Press.

Masson, David (1859). *British Novelists and their Styles: Being a Critical Sketch of the History of British Prose Fiction*. Cambridge: Macmillan.

Oliphant, Margaret (1882). *The Literary History of England in the End of the Eighteenth Century and the Beginning of the Nineteenth Century*. 3 vols. London: Macmillan.

Sanders, Andrew (1978). *The Victorian Historical Novel 1840–1880*. London: Macmillan.

Sutherland, John (1988). *The Longman Companion to Victorian Fiction*. London: Longman.

22

Nineteenth-century Adventure and Fantasy: James Morier, George Meredith, Lewis Carroll, and Robert Louis Stevenson

Robert Fraser

I want us to consider some Victorian adventure romances, and before doing so it may be helpful to ponder awhile a distinction drawn by Northrop Frye 30 years ago between what he called "naive" and "sentimental" romance. Naive romance, Frye observed in his Charles Eliot Norton Lectures, was "the kind of story that is found in collections of folk tales" or *Märchen*, like Grimm's fairy tales. "Sentimental" romance by contrast consisted of "a more extended and literary development of the formulas of naive romance"; most of it in early and modern times had, Frye thought, "been in prose narrative" (1976: 3).

If this distinction possesses merit, it is of clear relevance to the mid to late nineteenth century. Readers, after all, had been made newly aware of "naive" romance in all its vigor and complexity. The tales collected in Germany by the brothers Jacob Ludwig Carl and Wilhelm Carl Grimm under the title *Kinder- und Hausmärchen*, for example, were in 1823 made available in English by George Cruikshank in his *German Popular Stories*. Perrault's French *contes de fées*, rendered into English by Robert Samber in 1729, were now inspiring a generation of folklorists, notably Robert Louis Stevenson's friend, the Scottish writer Andrew Lang. In 1840, moreover, Edward Lane issued his English "translations" of the Arabic cycle *Alif Laila wa Laila*. Though readers had long had access to the French redactions by Antoine Galland (1704–17), Englished by the Reverend Edward Forster in an edition with engravings by Robert Smirke in 1802, Lane's *Arabian Nights' Entertainments* or *A Thousand and One Nights* were stimulating a fresh appreciation of these exotic adventures. At about the same time the oriental vogue received added impetus through the translations of Henry Torrens and the orientalist William Hay Macnaghten (1838). Of course, a question lingered as to how close to the "naive" in Frye's sense these early versions were, how much they meddled with, sentimentalized and prettied up the originals, and how far they perpetrated the kind of orientalist gazing memorably described for a much later generation by Edward Said. Such questions were to prove all the more pertinent in the light of unexpurgated versions produced late in the century: in England by Sir Richard Burton (1885–8), and in France by J. C. Mardrus (1899).

The issue of authenticity, and its implications for our understanding of genre, seem especially relevant in the face of three salient facts. The first is the prominence ascribed by Frye among others to "mock" – or as he calls it "parody" – romance. The second is the emergence, during the eighteenth century, of the novel. The third is the appearance during the mid-nineteenth century of the alternative "realisms" associated in England with George Eliot and in France with Gustave Flaubert. It is widely recognized, for example, that the novel developed as a literary form when parodic procedures were applied to the subject matter of romance. Throughout the nineteenth century the two forms flourished side by side, and from 1880 onward they were deliberately portrayed as rivals. At much the same time, to save itself, romance turned parodic, developing its own habits of satire and self-reference. This was especially true at mid-century when the subject matter of romance sometimes ran remarkably close to that of the novel. Practitioners of both forms, after all, were interested in a similar social topics and institutions: nationality, the monarchy, Parliament, the class system, the Church, the law and marriage, and so forth. So as not to be absorbed by its feisty competitor, romance fashioned its own ways of dealing with these themes, ones in no danger of being swallowed up by the realist mode in which the novel had come to excel.

To cover all eventualities, we must embarrass this picture a little further. Parody romance, as Frye portrays it, has always tended toward self-conscious sophistication, the knowing smile. What then, one asks, of that procedure, dear to nineteenth-century writers, whereby "sentimental romance" attempts to look as "naive" as possible, relying on the reader's *nous* to detect its purported naivety as *faux*? This technique was frequently applied to both of the standard themes of the genre: love and travel. It is with travel adventure that I am principally concerned here. Applied to this subject, the procedure yields the following result. What look like literal journeys turn out, in the hands of certain romance writers, to be less physical expeditions than specialized acts of adventure across an internal or subjective – but always symbolic – space.

This was often the case no matter what the story's location, and even when its author's credentials as a traveler appeared unimpeachable. A precedent in these respects was set in the 1820s by the writer and diplomat, Sir James Justinian Morier. Born in Smyrna, Morier had served as secretary to two successive British ambassadors in Persia. After assisting Sir Hartford Jones to negotiate a treaty with the Shah, he settled in Tehran and published with the house of John Murray (well known for Murray's *Guides*) two volumes of his travels (1812 and 1818). Success, however, arrived with his third book in which he adopted the guise of Hajji Baba, successively beard-trimmer, doctor, executioner, and picaresque rogue. The jokes were many-sided. The name Hajji Baba alluded to one of the more familiar of Galland's tales, "Al Barba and the Forty Thieves," of doubtful Arabic authenticity though well known from pantomime. The protagonist of *The Adventures of Hajji Baba of Ispahan*, what is more, was a barber by occupation and in 1824, the date of publication of Morier's tale, the word could newly be applied to a rich fruit cake, a usage retained in the name of "rum baba" and giving rise to a mildly racist running joke. The Murray imprint lent the whole exercise a spurious solemnity, and in eighteenth-century fashion Morier had presented himself as mere editor and translator. Attentive readers, however, soon detected a strong resemblance between these fictitious travels and Morier's own as set out in two printed volumes. But Hajji himself was a rapscallion, a ruthless seducer and violator of the harem, and it was not long before the Persian minister in London had lodged an official protest with the Court of St. James. Four years later, Morier had his revenge. Again from Albemarle Street, he issued *The Adventures of Hajji Baba of Ispahan in England,* in which the protesting ambassador is converted into the impressionable Mirza Farouz and Baba into his scheming secretary (once more a surrogate for the author). They voyage to greet the Shah of England but, before they set out, the British Minister in Iran (a sly reworking of Hartford Jones) warns them against proffering their number one gift: a magnificent black man intended as Keeper of His Majesty's harem. As the Englishman carefully explains:

> "Our king has only one wife, and the whole of his government are guardians over her good conduct; they are his Mûrwaris."
> Upon this speech all the Persians laughed and cried out "La illahah illâllah! there is but one God!"
> "How," said the vizier, "only one wife? Then what is the use of his being king? What if he gets fed up with her? What then?" (Morier 1828: 29)

It was a question to which the private conduct of King George IV provided a ready answer.

When the delegation reaches England, they marvel at its sumptuous beds, its blatant democracy, its well-furnished inns, its codes of chivalry and, above all, its treatment of women. Despite – or perhaps because of – his years spent overseas, Morier comes across as John Bull's greatest fan. The result is a distanced vision of contemporary Britain, a nation viewed both as exotic and as almost comically advanced.

George Meredith and Counter-romance

Another writer theoretically and practically aware of the potential of such distancing techniques – particularly in the highlighting of sexual attitudes – was George Meredith. This is not surprising since, as Gillian Beer has pointed out, Meredith's literary career consisted of a progress – or perhaps a regress – from romance to realism, with many a glance backward. It was Meredith who in volume III of his triple-decker novel *Diana of the Crossways* (1885) was to spotlight an important difference between reality and the romance mode in depicting female characters. The context is a meditation by the infatuated young politician, Percy Dacier, on the book's resourceful and modern – its married but restless – heroine, Diana Merion. "She wouldn't be a bad heroine of Romance," Dacier remarks to himself at one point, "with little intuition of the popular taste." He provides an opportunity for the author to correct him, since:

> the right worshipful heroine of Romance was the front-face female picture he had won for his walls. Poor Diana was the flecked heroine of Reality: not always the same; not impeccable; not an ignorant-innocent, nor a guileless: good under good leading; devoted to the death in a grave crisis; often wrestling with her torrential nature nobly; and a growing soul; but not one whose purity was carved in marble for the assurance to an Englishman that his possession of the changeless thing defies time and his fellows; is the pillar of his home and universally enviable. Your fair one of Romance cannot suffer a mishap without a plotting villain, perchance many of them, to wreak the dread iniquity: she cannot move without him; she is the marble block, and if she is to have a feature, he is the sculptor; she depends on him for life, and her human history at least is married to him far more than to the rescuing lover. No wonder, then, that men should find her thrice cherishable featureless, or with the most moderate possible indication of a countenance. Thousands of the excellent simple creatures do; and every reader of her tale. On the contrary, the heroine of Reality is that woman whom you have met or heard of once in your course of years, and very probably despised for bearing in her composition the motive principle; at best, you say, a singular mixture of good and bad; anything but the feminine ideal of man. (Meredith 1885: III, 133–5)

This passage raises a number of questions concerning gender and genre. Romance, Meredith asserts, occurs when a narrator addresses himself or herself (himself if Meredith, herself if, say, the Scheherezade of the *Nights*) to male partialities and wants (a "romantic" adventure, for example, would be one that appeals to male fantasies). This is an incisive point, all the more so because it cuts across certain conceptions implicit, say, in the marketing of commercial twentieth-century "romance." The contention is best understood, however, in the frame of Meredith's larger argument. Characterization and narrative in romance, for Meredith, are products of superstition and awe. It is these very qualities, furthermore, that hold society – and women in particular – back. In Meredith, political and sexual power constitute twin forms of fantasy in which victor and victim are imaginatively caught up. The business of romance is to endorse this entrapment; the business of the novel to dispel it. Viewed from this controversial standpoint, romance is a retrograde and conservative form; the novel is a revolutionary one.

In turning aside the fond – the romantic – delusions of Sir Percy Dacier concerning his modern heroine, Meredith is thus committing himself to a polemic that one might well call *counter-romantic*. Indeed *counter-romance* (as opposed to, say, parody romance) is an apt description for much, if not all, of Meredith's fiction. His initiation in 1856 had been *The Shaving of Shagpat: An Arabian Entertainment*, whose very subtitle alludes to Lane's *Arabian Nights' Entertainments*. Its opening chapter, "The Thwackings" – with its joke genealogies, sonorous alliterations, and sustained parataxes – aims for a related atmosphere:

> It was ordained that Shibli Bagarag, nephew of the renowned Baba Mustapha, chief barber of the Court of Persia, should shave Shagpat, the son of Shimpoor, the son of Shoolpi, the son of Shullum; and they had been clothiers for generations, even to the time of Shagpat, illustrious.
> Now the story of Shibli Bagarag, and of the ball he followed, and of the subterranean kingdom he came to, and of the enchanted palace he entered, and of the sleeping king he shaved, and of the two princesses he released, and of the Afrite held in subjection by the arts of one and bottled by her, is it not known as 'twere written on the finger-nails of men and traced in their corner robes? As the poet says:
>
> > Ripe with oft telling and old is the tale,
> > But 'tis the sort that can never grow stale.
>
> Now, things were in that condition with Shibli Bagarag, that on a certain day he was hungry and abject, and the city of Shagpat the clothier was before him; so he made toward it, deliberating as to how he should procur a meal, for he had not a dirhem in his girdle, and the remembrances of great dishes and savoury ingredients were to him as the illusion of rivers sheening on the sands to travellers gasping with thirst. (Meredith 1856: 1)

This reads like parody romance of a very particular kind. To start off with, the pleasure that it affords depends on multiple acts of recognition. The pseudo-oriental prose style, for example, recalls less the work of Lane than Torrens' *The Book of the Thousand Nights and One Night*. Second, certain occupations stand out, and in doing so focus the attention. The oppressive Shagpat, for example, is depicted as a "clothier." To interpret this clue, it helps to have read Thomas Carlyle, whose *Sartor Resartus* (1833–4) had turned the semiology of vestments into a critique of contemporary Britain, and Charles Kingsley, who in *Alton Locke* (1850) had used the rag trade as a metonym for economic and social injustice. Later on we discover that Shibli Bagarag, the man who will liberate the city from Shagpat's power, is – like Morier's surrogate Englishman – a barber. He has vowed to cut a single hair on Shagpat's head – called the "identical" – by means of which this ruthless enchanter holds society in his thrall. Eventually, with the held of his fiancée Noorna bin Noorka, he succeeds. The hair of course represents superstition, awe, and false admiration. Uprooting these characteristics, and the mental attitudes on which they depend, Shibli liberates – perhaps modernizes – the city.

Thus construed, the setting of the book is less Persia than England. Its conclusion neatly runs, "So, ever fresh illusions will arise / And lord creation, until men are wise." It is no accident that Meredith nods toward that arch-critic of British society, Carlyle, since his purpose, beyond and through "entertainment," is satirical: partly of the *Arabian Nights* genre, but mostly of his own country with its subtle and arcane class distinctions, its barriers of caste and etiquette, its endearing but oppressive traditions. The means by which he achieves this objective is the extirpation of awe, that is, of fantasy and the romantic tendency. Already therefore, at the very beginning of his writing career, Meredith's mode is a precocious form of anti-romance.

The equation between form and meaning in Meredith's writing, and its counter-romantic tendency, grew subtler as he switched surface allegiance to the comedy of social manners. As Gillian Beer has also pointed out, there are several reversals in, say, *The Adventures of Harry Richmond* (1870) that depend on a recall of the romance mode, a style its author had officially abandoned. *Harry Richmond* is a picaresque tale whose episodic form recalls Smollett and very early Dickens; its theme once more is the emancipation of its characters from delusion, social fantasy, and obsequious forms of deference. The principal culprit this time is Harry's spendthrift and opportunistic father, obsessed with rank and royal connections. Much revered by his only son, Richmond senior tours Europe, determined to hitch Harry to a foreign aristocrat. Eventually he finds a likely candidate in the shape of Princess Ottilia, daughter of a German princeling. It is while the parent is pursuing a match of his own back in Bath, however, that the son gains an insight into his temperament and into the "ostentatious displays" that have landed him heavily in debt. Unsurprisingly, all his plans come to nothing. Harry weds the far more appropriate Janet Ilchester; the father dies, romantically, in a fire.

Again fantasy and romance are confounded in the interests of reality and potentially of a liberating politics. Romance endorses the values of the aristocrat and parvenu; the novel the aspirations of the decent middle class. Romance is implicitly portrayed as a Tory, a hierarchical form, the novel as Whig and radical. Romance is an inflationary genre – inflationary of hopes, expectations, of stocks and shares. In an age devoted to the railways and to fiction, it is boom and bust. The novel, meanwhile, steadies the nerves with the reasonable – George Eliot-like – prospects of incremental progress and reform.

It is a view Meredith was to elaborate to increasing effect. In his comic masterpiece of 1879, *The Egoist*, orientalist echoes cohere around a ceramic metonym: the willow-pattern plate (though, as the American scholar Robert D. Mayo long ago explained, neither the popular willow pattern, nor the situation it apparently depicts, are oriental, properly speaking). Willow-pattern dishes had been manufactured by the Coughley works in Shropshire since 1780 in vague imitation of Chinese porcelain. 1849 saw the appearance of the legend in the first volume of *The Family Friend*; two years before *Shagpat,* it reached the stage as an extravaganza entitled *The Mandarin's Daughter*, performed at the Strand Theatre in London in 1851. This told of a mandarin and widower with a riverside mansion and a beautiful daughter named Koong-see. He has promised her hand to a rich suitor called Tajin, but she prefers her father's secretary, a penniless scholar, to whom she pledges her heart beneath the weeping willow tree. The dreadful parent thereupon incarcerates her in the pavilion seen center right, but she and her lover escape across the bridge and by means of the boat. Eventually, in token of their mutual devotion, they are transformed into birds, seen hovering in the sky.

This *faux naïf* fable incorporates several of the traditional themes of romance literature: the angry parent, disapproved love, the escape, metamorphosis, and so on. In the design as employed in plates and dishes, these elements are made even more appealing by rendering them at a point of stasis. An impression of serenity and prettiness derives from a decorous balance of uprights and obliques, and a deep, almost indigo, blue. The escaping birds too seem emblematic of a perfect middle-class marriage. Via such endlessly reproduced images, Victorian couples were able to view themselves reflected on their place mats as free spirits and escapees.

In *The Egoist* Meredith takes this fake *chinoiserie* and turns it into a paradigm of deception and moral bombast. The "pattern" in this instance is both an ideal of social protocol and the name of the book's sonorously self-congratulatory hero, Sir Willoughby Patterne. Patterne plays the part of Tajin, his intended Clara Middleton is the girl, her father Professor Middleton the obsequious mandarin, the studious Vernon Whitford, with whom she eventually elopes, the lucky scribe. Willoughby gets his girl in the shape of Laetitia Dale, a bright woman under no illusions as to his worth. A pseudo-romantic plate design thus becomes a dance of liberation whereby false romance is confounded while a deeper, more satisfying pattern is confirmed. Escape, and settling down together, neatly coincide.

Lewis Carroll and the White Knight

A somewhat different case is provided by Lewis Carroll, alias the Reverend Charles Lutwidge Dodgson, Lecturer in Mathematics at Christ Church, Oxford, all the more so because his romances appeared in the form of stories for, and about, children. That Alice Liddell, daughter of the Dean of Christ Church, was the first audience of the Alice stories has never been doubted. But the published version of *Alice's Adventures in Wonderland* (1865) – its sequel *Through the Looking-glass* (1872) was, of course, never anything but a written tale – was partly intended for Dodgson himself and the British bourgeoisie beyond him. Through the Alice books they were given access to Dodgson's versatile, playful, and in every sense fantastic mind, productive both of forthright letters to the newspapers and of textbooks such as *Euclid and His Modern Rivals* (1879). It was a mind, moreover, deeply energized, both by topical and organizational questions and by the logical principles underlying them. Through it romance became an intellectual – even an academic – form equipped with carefully placed screens of distance and burlesque, and instinct with proto-vaudeville and theater.

Again, Carroll's purposes have a lot to do with recognition and non-recognition, and with temporary displacements betwixt familiar and unfamiliar. From its opening page *Alice's Adventures in Wonderland* insists on this transmutation with the appearance of a speaking rabbit, of whom we read:

There was nothing so *very* remarkable in that; nor did Alice think it so *very* much out of the way to hear the rabbit say to itself "Oh dear! Oh dear! I shall be too late" (when she thought it over afterwards, it occurred to her that she ought to have wondered at this, but at the time it all seemed quite natural). (Carroll [1865] 1965: 25–6)

The context, of course is Alice's drowsiness on a summer afternoon, but the effect is to question the distinction between the "remarkable" (the province of romance) and the "natural" (boast of the realist novel); even the distinction – with a careful substitution of upper for lower case – between animal and human, Rabbits and rabbits. That rabbits are popular – and named – as domestic pets, serves to make this existential crisis more acute.

It is the same with the rabbit-hole down which Alice pursues the unpunctual mammal. From its very opening this chamber is an ambiguous space, since to enter it she would already have to have changed size; the vertical shaft instantly transforms the hole from an animal-made burrow into that man-made passage, a well. As Frye points out, Alice's descent corresponds to a standard motif of romance literature; in Carroll's treatment this trope turns into a quasi-scientific expedition. Speculation as to the likely effects of uninterrupted downward momentum had been rife since Galileo Galilei's dialogue *Ai due massimi sistemi* (*Concerning the Two Great Systems*) (1630); the remoter implications reach out toward Newton, proleptically even as far as Einstein. *Wonderland* exploits a fact of life of which Dodgson the teacher was well aware: ultimate scientific and philosophical questions commonly coincide with questions children ask. One year after the publication of Jules Verne's adventure quest *Voyage au centre de la terre* (1864), this episode also encroaches on science fiction or, as it was more usually known at the time, scientific romance. That the fissure down which Alice tumbles is lined with domestic items like marmalade jars only accentuates the puzzle. The suppressed panic in the writing is both agoraphobic and claustrophobic, since the sanctum that Alice has violated is a space both domestic and exotic. As Frye observes, her fall is a classic descent, but it is also a voyage inward as much as downwards and outwards. In one sense, Alice falls home.

Similar crossings of code and mode attend the drink Alice downs, outlandish yet a blend of reassuring nursery flavors ("cherry tart, custard, pineapple, roast turkey, toffee and hot-buttered toast"), and the door through which she is lured. This threshold, and the test its penetration requires, are in line with romance of the medieval sort; they also anticipate treatments of this theme in later science fiction such as H. G. Wells' parable of loss and choice, "The Door in the Wall" (1906). Once through the divide, however, Alice enters a caricature of an English garden featuring a tea party, a caterpillar, and a Cheshire Cat. Her focus of surprise fastens on these subjects in turn while their commonplace qualities are transformed into oddity, their oddity into common sense. Her encounters with successive creatures large and small leave her nonplussed: less, I should say, by their strangeness than by their ability to intensify ordinary childish curiosity. A reiterated vein is a travesty of adult conversational platitudes. Listen to the Mad Hatter (in real life, it seems, a successful Oxford

milliner) and his companions, the March Hare and the dormouse, as they ponder the
conundrum "Why is a raven like a writing desk?":

> "Come, we shall have some fun now!" thought Alice. "I'm glad they've begun asking
> riddles – I believe I can guess that," she added aloud.
> "Do you mean that you think you can find out the answer to it?" said the March Hare.
> "Exactly so," said Alice.
> "Then you should say what you mean," the March Hare went on.
> "I do," Alice hastily replied, "at least I mean what I say – that's the same thing, you
> know."
> "Not the same thing a bit!" said the Hatter. "Why, you might as well say that 'I see
> what I eat' is the same thing as 'I eat what I see!'"
> "You might as well say," added the March Hare, "that 'I like what I get' is the same as
> 'I get what I like'!"
> "You might as well say" added the Dormouse, which seemed to be talking in its
> sleep, that 'I breathe when I sleep' is the same thing as 'I sleep when I breathe'!" (Carroll
> [1865] 1965: 95)

In this veritable Socratic trialogue it is hard to tell who is master and student, teacher
or taught. Alice begins with a statement that is solecistic according to rules set by her
companions' too literal understanding of word and thought. Their rejoinders seem
bizarre to her and to us, though we recognize in them the eccentric banality of so
much adult logic. It is Alice who is out of step. Nonsense and sense coincide yet,
thanks to the donnish author's fidgeting with semantics, it is far from being clear, at
any given moment, just which is which.

The Mock Turtle and the Gryphon confront the girl with just as hard an ordeal. It
begins in trite inquiry:

> "Why, what are *your* shoes done with?" said the Gryphon. "I mean, what makes them
> so shiny?"
> Alice looked down at them, and considered a little while before she gave her answer.
> "They're done with blacking, I believe."
> "Boots and shoes under the sea," the Gryphon went on in a deep voice "are done with
> whiting. Now you know."
> "And what are they made of?" Alice asked in a tone of great curiosity.
> "Soles and eels of course," the Gryphon replied, rather impatiently: "Any shrimp
> could have told you that." (Carroll [1865] 1965: 136–7)

The subject of this disquisition is the logic – or illogic – of verification. Alice believes
her footwear to have been treated with black boot polish, *believes* rather than *knows* this
because, of course, it is a housemaid who has cleaned the shoes. The Gryphon offers
the empirical information that piscine shoes are polished with whiting, trumping this
assertion with an illogical double pun and that habitual fallback of the platitudinous
absurd, an appeal to public opinion: "any shrimp could tell you that." Alice and the
Gryphon rely for support on respective hierarchies of land and sea; both sound

unconvincing. The Gryphon and the Mock Turtle have themselves been abstracted from a bourgeois or collegiate setting, since the Gryphon has stepped down from a coat of arms and the Mock Turtle out from a tureen (mock turtle soup was a creamy *compôte* of lamb). Their whimsicality reinforces the silliness of Alice's daily world, even as she attempts to bolster it with clichés of her own.

The surreal stupidity – as well as the basic unfairness – of much social routine is further suggested by the sequence of rituals of passage with which *Wonderland* closes: the card games (implicit throughout), croquet on the lawn, dances, initiations, and, of course, the preposterous trial. In their distancing of everyday procedures, these episodes anticipate *fin-de-siècle* anthropological quest romance such as Rider Haggard's. Alice's petulant reaction when she finally spills the pack of cards represents an affront to the conventional order even as it purports to restore everyday reality. The playing cards become scattered leaves. Wonderland fades into what the author's sentimental coda calls Alice's childlife, both snug and strange, *gemütlich* and *unheimlich*. Unfamiliarity, or perhaps defamiliarization, is all.

The prevalent logic of *Through the Looking Glass* is that of reversal, which it applies to a chessboard. The board is a working model of the social system – like those miniature steam engines of which the Victorians were so fond, chugging away in imitation of a full-blown machine. The whole conception involves a complicated series of jokes concerning scale. These jokes, however, work contrary to one another since, though a microcosm of British society, the board, with its vast, almost geographically extended squares, itself occupies too grand a grid for a game.

Gratifyingly for the imagination, this too perfect set of correspondences (which in this book lie inside one another rather than, as in *Alice's Adventures in Wonderland*, side by side) continually breaks down. The result, however, is less a series of explosions – despite the efforts of Tweedledum and Tweedledee – than of implosions. Creatures, characters, scenes and episodes proliferate into smallness. One effect is a number of abrupt discontinuities in the narrative. Approaching the Third Square, for instance, Alice finds herself looking across a limitless landscape recalling Victorian visions of East Africa. She might be Burton or Speke:

> Of course the first thing to do was to make a grand survey of the country she was going to travel through. "It's something very like learning geography," thought Alice, as she stood on tiptoe in hopes of being able to see a little further. "Principal rivers – there *are* none. Principal mountains – I'm on the only one, but I don't think it's got any name. Principal towns – why, what *are* those creatures, making honey down there? They can't be bees – nobody ever saw bees a mile off, you know" – and for some time she stood silent, watching one of them that was bustling about among the flowers, poking its proboscis into them, "just as if it was a regular bee," thought Alice. (Carroll [1872] 1965: 215)

Running downhill and leaping into the valley, she discovers that the creatures are elephants. No sooner has she made this observation, worthy of report to the Royal Geographical Society, than Carroll inserts a pattern of asterisks, and the scale shrinks to a railway compartment in a train crossing, not from Cairo to the Cape, but from Didcot apparently, and to Oxford. Alice finds this change cramping ("I was in a wood just now – and I wish that I could get back there"), all the more because the insects she meets in the carriage are so small and their jokes so paltry. Even the typeface in which the text is set dwindles to make the point. In much the same way, when Alice attempts to enter the fourth square, the wood is transformed into a shop in St. Aldate's. The epitome of this process is the red king's reverie. He is dreaming of Alice who in turn is dreaming of him and so forth, in a nightmare of Berkeleian infinite regress to which the narrative constantly alludes. Identities prove fugitive and names constantly dissolve. Alice even forgets her own, her panicky reaction to which is to insist once more on the class system with its, to her, self-evident habits of deference: "If she" – as Alice tartly informs the Gnat concerning the governess – "couldn't remember my name, then she'd call me 'Miss' as the servants do" (Carroll [1872] 1965: 224).

But this insistence on social gradation proves as frustrating as everything else. As the White Queen, a sorry and flustered matron suffering a bad hair day, stresses, responsibility is no fun; in certain respects it's preferable to be a pawn. "When I was your age . . . Sometimes I've believed as many as six impossible things before breakfast" (Carroll 1872: 251). But now she's a mere monarch: which, of course, in the inexorable logic of chess, Alice the neutral pawn is destined or doomed to become. Momentarily her fate overawes her: "'Only it's so *very* lonely here!' Alice said in a melancholy voice; and at the thought of her loneliness, two large tears came rolling down her cheeks" (Carroll [1872] 1965: 250).

It is at this juncture that most readers recognize the quest for what it is: a parable of growing up, or maybe *down* and *in*. In this parody of *hamartia* the oysters are eaten "every one," the Lion beats the Unicorn, Humpty Dumpty falls off his wall. Magic and unpredictability fly away, their sole repository being the White Knight, who naturally is Dodgson himself with his madcap inventions, his academic and political obsessions and parodies of Southey and Wordsworth, the intertextual qualities of which Alice cannot be expected to follow. She walks away, leaving him to his quibbles and his quills. She becomes a Queen, a common or garden grown-up, while the chess game collapses into mere fretwork, with Dodgson's solitary, pedantic countenance peering sadly through:

> Still she haunts me, phantomwise,
> Alice moving under skies
> Never seen by waking eyes.
>
> (Carroll [1872] 1965: 345)

As Morton Cohen's fine biography of Carroll confirms, a very ordinary, not to say snobbish, woman is what Alice Liddell indeed became. The intimation of such a possibility in the story violates one of the prime conditions of romancing, as we perceive the forlorn, matter of fact face of the author staring through the ruined contract of the tale. This sorry sight lends the whole exercise perspective, but in so doing welshes on one important element in the traditional romance, which – as Gillian Beer once forcefully pointed out – was an evenness, or two-dimensionality, of texture. If we are to understand the romance method aright, Beer declares in her sharp book on the subject (1970: 21),

> we have to abandon the critical metaphor of perspective (with its suggestion of far and near) or depth (with its suggestion that what is deepest is most significant). Instead we are confronted with a thronging, level world, held at a constant distance from us, colourful, full of detailed particularity, ramifying endlessly outwards.

Ramifying constantly inward, Lewis Carroll's *Through the Looking Glass* tends by contrast toward an alternative mode: an inverted, closet picaresque.

The Divided Self: Robert Louis Stevenson

The picaresque, with its eighteenth-century antecedents, was developed in the following decade by Robert Louis Stevenson, whose work illustrates the peripatetic and inward-looking facets of romance by splitting them into a series of self-reflexive dualities, frequently embodied within one person, or between friends or relations.

During his Edinburgh childhood Stevenson had familiarized himself with the romance mode through his use of toy theaters, and by poring over *The Arabian Nights* in the Reverend Edward Forster's illustrated translation from Galland. Appropriately, after a series of charming travelogues, it was with a modern extension to the *Arabian Nights* cycle that Stevenson set out on his long expedition into fiction. His *New Arabian Nights* of 1882 updates the form by substituting for the ubiquitous Haroun Al-Rashid of the original *Nights* a figure called Prince Florizel of Bohemia, who thwarts various international crime rings: a private Suicide Club, a cartel devoted to the theft of an Indian diamond. It is with the sequel *The Dynamiter*, however, that the revolutionary aspects of this exercise were most fully explored. The circumstances of this work's composition are instructive since Stevenson was confined to bed with sciatica while staying with his American wife Fanny in a villa near cholera-infested Toulon. Every day Fanny ventured forth from his sickroom to shop in the pestiferous streets of the old town. On her return, play-acting Scheherezade, she told him a story in which she transformed herself in turn into a polygamous Mormon wife in Utah, or a Cuban slave. By this means she related the story of an anarchist cell that plants bombs in London and Glasgow; in the Vailima edition of Stevenson's works *The Dynamiter* appears under his name, but the inventions were joint ones. They also confirmed a deep-seated habit whereby adventure romance became both a refuge from sickness and a metaphor for his – and his culture's – temperamental restlessness. Like the later *Island Night's Entertainments* (1893) they exhibit a fresh sensation that was to become more and more a feature of the romance genre as the century progressed: vicarious muscular zest.

Stevenson's mature romances (it was a term he self-consciously employed), are characterized by three tendencies: claustrophobia, division, and flight. The flight (or fugue, to entertain a not inappropriate musical analogy) is an attempt to escape the other two experiences: a baffled attempt, since Stevenson's male protagonists carry their moral and psychological cargo with them, just as surely as Stevenson, in his own successive journeys around the globe, carried his diseased, tubercular body. As Karl Miller has persuasively argued in his book *Doubles* (1987), these cargoes were invariably freighted with Stevenson's Scottishness and his inherited Christianity. Time and time again, Stevenson splits himself into two: one half remains true to the virtues of the domestic hearth while the other sets forth treacherously to explore the bounds of morality or convention, be it at sea, in rural Scotland, or through the murky wynds and byways of the city.

In *Treasure Island* (1883) this tendency is already present in the tense but affectionate relationship between the high-minded young protagonist Jim Hawkins and the veteran pirate Long John Silver. By placing an adolescent male at the optic center of the tale, Stevenson achieves an important perspective. Silver is an out-and-out rogue, of course: looking at him, Hawkins is introduced not simply to the average complexities of human beings, but to an ambiguity in evil closely entwined with the ardent uncertainties of his own nature. Good is not straightforward in this book; nor is bad simply bad, much though the teller of the tale tries to maintain the distinction. The island is a free zone in which the sailors explore such alliances, betrayals, and temporary collusions as mere pragmatism demands. Captain Flint's treasure is a pretext and, once acquired, it is frittered away. Surprisingly, this twist is the opposite of disappointing, since by then the tale has developed its own momentum of excitement. Indeed it might plausibly be claimed that excitement supplies not merely the mood of this book, but its theme.

The methods of *Treasure Island* are applied with more thoroughness in *Kidnapped* (1886), considered by Henry James the finest of all Stevenson's romances. This claim holds despite its being intended – like *Treasure Island* – as reading matter for boys, and its action straying no further than Caledonia. These very limitations intensify the dizzying effect of a book firmly located both in place – the Lowlands, Highlands, and Inner Hebrides – and in time – the high summer of 1752, seven years after the second Jacobite rising. Once again we have a young male narrator, though David Balfour, the disingenuous youth at the center of it all, is 18, on the edge both of manhood and the inheritance of his ancestral property. He is tricked into service aboard the brig *The Covenant* at the instigation of his corrupt Uncle Ebenezer, who wishes to cheat him out of the estate of Shaws. Bound for the Carolinas, the ship is wrecked off Mull, where David falls into the company of the diminutive though rugged Jacobite, Alan Breck Stewart, engaged in conveying money to conspirators in France. The climax is a recreation of the murder of Colin Campbell of Glenure, a "factor" for the Hanoverian government, a crime of which, as a result of coincidences of time and place, David and Alan are unfairly suspected. Much of *Kidnapped* – the title is politically fortuitous – is thus set in an occupied land, for the Highlands of the Hanoverian age are depicted as a society reeling under the iron fist of a foreign power. Breck epitomizes the puny yet doughty resistance of the place: its humor, its irascibility, its resourceful ruggedness, and plain speaking. From him David is estranged both by language – he has Latin but no Gaelic – and by political allegiance, yet the growing friendship between them is the emotional center of the tale. The story is devoted to their flight southward, its theme nothing less than the personality and identity of Scotland, a nation newly eclipsed, newly divided. The crux of this division is language. Much of the narrative is carried in Scots, David's native tongue, into which his Highland friends are uncomfortably obliged to drop for his benefit. Aware of his inadequacies in this brutal yet proud environment, David takes refuge both in coy Calvinist propriety – he will not, for example, play cards with his Highlander hosts – and a pathetically resounding contempt. The moment when, fatigued beyond endurance, he turns on Alan and his people is one of the funniest, most revealing, and genuinely moving in nineteenth-century Scottish literature:

> "O!" says I, "I ken ye bear a king's name. But you are to remember, since I have been in the Highlands, I have seen a good many of those that bear it; and the best that I can say of them is this, that they would be none the worse of washing." (Stevenson [1886] 1986: 163)

The quarrel is made up; David proceeds toward his inheritance, and in the sequel *Catriona* (1893) toward love. The wound in the national psyche is harder to heal – as much of Stevenson's work attests.

The most luridly notorious exploration of doubleness in Stevenson's writing – perhaps in all British fiction – is *The Strange Case of Dr. Jekyll and Mr. Hyde*. It is not difficult to discern the reasons for the enthusiasm with which this short work was treated on its publication in 1886 by Sidney Colvin, F. W. Myers, and others. The setting is urban and modern, in contrast to the romances already discussed; the thought is scientific or at least pseudo-scientific, and the structure akin to that of a detective story. The plot originated in a dream, but Stevenson tore his first version up because, Fanny told him, he had missed the opportunity to construct an "allegory." The term is telling since, beneath its contemporary accouterments, *Jekyll and Hyde* possesses a theology less Calvinist than medieval. "I chose the better part" writes the respectable Dr. Jekyll, confessing in a written submission to his friend, the lawyer Utterson, the crimes he has committed in the person of Hyde, "and was found wanting in the strength to keep it up," thus echoing St. Paul in Romans 8 (Stevenson [1886] 1987: 68). He also speaks of "my original evil," much like Augustine's "original sin." Critics have sometimes missed this point, interpreting the doctor's split condition as abnormal: early commentators connected it with the theory, fashionable at the time, of the "multiplex personality"; more recently, largely by selective quotation, Elaine Showalter has construed Hyde's illegal acts as those of homosexual indulgence. In fact his is an instance of average cruelty exacerbated by medical intervention; his civil war with himself, moreover, is presented as a form of social conflict in miniature. He suffers, he says, a "perennial war among my members": as for the human race, "I hazard the guess that man will be ultimately known for a mere polity of multifarious, incongruous and independent denizens." The achieved allegory then is partly an ancient fable of moral damnation, and partly a modern case of civil strife, of society – as in Meredith – seldom at ease with itself.

Stevenson's last book, *Weir of Hermiston* (1897), on which he was working in Samoa on the day he died, bears the subtitle "An Unfinished Romance." It is usually interpreted as his subtlest study in division within the family: this time – in a proto-Freudian fashion – between father and son. It is better viewed, I think, as a battle within one strife-torn temperament. Archie Weir is young, yet bears within him both the censorious reflexes of his father, an irascible judge with a "droll formidable face," and the fastidiousness of his deceased, pious mother. Before she dies, mother and son conduct a revealing discussion on the subject of judgment. Apropos of his father's reputation as a relentless hanger of recreants, Weir throws in her face a favorite text from Christ's Sermon on the Mount: "Judge not that ye be not judged":

> It was 1801, and Archie was seven, and beyond his years for curiosity and logic, when he brought the case up openly. If judging were sinful and forbidden, how came papa to be a judge? to have that sin for a trade? to bear the name of it for a distinction?
> "I can't see it," said the little Rabbi, and wagged his head.
> Mrs Weir abounded in commonplace replies.
> "No, I canna see it," reiterated Archie. "And I'll tell you what, mamma, I don't think you and me's justifeed in staying with him." (Stevenson [1896] 1987: 92)

Yet 20 years later, when his friend Frank Innes counsels him against courting Kirstie Rutherford, a comely neighbor at Hermiston, it is Archie who turns judgmental. In the last completed chapter he upbraids himself for levity and breaks the relationship off. According to the uncompleted scheme, Frank was then to seduce Kirstie, upon which Archie ups and murders him, appearing at his trial before his father. Construed in this way, the tale is a fantasia on the contradictions of indictment, and of the Scottish temperament itself. It achieves all that *Kidnapped* manages and more, all within the physical confines of Edinburgh and one rural district.

Stevenson found the romance a free field for debate and improvisation; he left it a recognizable and distinct mode of writing with its own range of spirited effects, its props, its desired and quickening mood. Naive romance fell astern as literary romance sharpened on the horizon. It is to the period immediately following Stevenson – the decade or more of the *fin de siècle* – that we trace the beginnings of market genres: detective, science fiction, "whodunit," and what have you. What was to emerge in the age of Haggard, Conan Doyle, and Wells was a predominantly male form – both in its characterization and its audience – with a strong story line, a gripping, page-turning quality, full of movement and diversity, at war with quietude. In the later twentieth century the classifications were to broaden out once more, not always to their betterment. And "romance" as a library and bookseller's category would come to mean something altogether different. However, that's another story.

See also: chapter 18, VICTORIAN ROMANCE: TENNYSON; chapter 19, VICTORIAN RO-MANCE: MEDIEVALISM; chapter 20, ROMANCE AND VICTORIAN AUTOBIOGRAPHY; chapter 21, VICTORIAN ROMANCE: ROMANCE AND MYSTERY; chapter 23, INTO THE TWENTIETH CENTURY; chapter 24, AMERICA AND ROMANCE; chapter 27, ROMANCE IN FANTASY; chapter 28, QUEST ROMANCE IN SCIENCE FICTION.

References and Further Reading

Ali, Muhsin Jassim (1981). *Scheherezade in England; A Study of Nineteenth-Century English Criticism of the Arabian Nights*. Washington, DC: Three Continents Press.

Beer, Gillian (1970). *The Romance*. London: Methuen.

Beer, Gillian (1970). *Meredith: A Change of Masks*. London: Athlone Press.

Caracciolo, Peter L., ed. (1989). *The Arabian Nights in English Literature: Studies in the Reception of* The Thousand and One Nights *into British Culture*. Basingstoke: Macmillan Press.

Carroll, Lewis (1965). *The Annotated Alice. Alice's Adventures in Wonderland and Through the Looking-Glass Illustrated by John Tenniel*, ed. Martin Gardner. London: Penguin. [First published in 1865 and 1872.]

Cohen, Morton (1996). *Lewis Carroll: A Biography*. London: Macmillan.

Forster, Edward (1802). *The Arabian Nights* (from the French version of Antoine Galland, with engravings and pictures by Robert Smirke). London: William Miller.

Fraser, Robert (1998). *Victorian Quest Romance: Stevenson, Haggard, Kipling and Conan Doyle*. Plymouth: Northcott House in Association with the British Council.

Frye, Northrop (1976). *The Secular Scripture. A Study of Structure in Romance*. Cambridge, MA: Harvard University Press.

Lane, Edward William (1839–41). *The Thousand and One Nights*. London: Charles Knight.

Meredith, George (1856). *The Shaving of Shagpat: An Arabic Entertainment*. London: Chapman and Hall.

Meredith, George (1871). *The Adventures of Harry Richmond*. London: Chapman and Hall.

Meredith, George (1979). *The Egoist*. Norton Critical Edition. New York and London: Norton. [First published in 1879.]

Meredith, George (1885). *Diana of the Crossways*. London: Chapman and Hall.

Miller, Karl (1985). *Doubles: Studies in Literary History*. Oxford and New York: Oxford University Press.

Morier, James (1824). *The Adventures of Ali Baba of Ispahan*. London: John Murray.

Morier, James (1828). *The Adventures of Hajji Baba of Ispahan in England*. London: John Murray.

Said, Edward W. (1978). *Orientalism*. New York: Pantheon.

Showalter, Elaine (1991). *Sexual Anarchy: Gender and Culture at the Fin de Siècle*. London: Bloomsbury.

Stevenson, Robert Louis (1882). *The New Arabian Nights*. London: Chatto and Windus.

Stevenson, Robert Louis (1986). *Kidnapped and Catriona*, ed. Emma Letley. World's Classics. Oxford: Oxford University Press, 1986. [First published in 1886 and 1893.]

Stevenson Robert Louis (1987). *The Strange Case of Dr Jekyll and Mr Hyde* and *The Weir of Hermiston*, ed. Emma Letley. World's Classics. Oxford: Oxford University Press, 1987. [First published in 1886 and 1896.]

Stevenson, Robert Louis (1995). *Treasure Island*, ed. Emma Letley. World's Classics. Oxford: Oxford University Press. [First published in 1883.]

Torrens, Henry (1838). *The Book of the Thousand Nights and One Night*. London: W. H. Allen.

Wells, H. G. (1906). "The Door in the Wall" in *Selected Short Stories*. London: Penguin, 1958.

Yeatzell, Ruth Bernard (2000). *Harems of the Mind: Passages of Western Art and Literature*. New Haven and London: Yale University Press.

23

Into the Twentieth Century: Imperial Romance from Haggard to Buchan

Susan Jones

The term "imperial romance" encapsulates a complex group of fictions appearing in Britain between the 1880s and the 1920s, which were devoted to narrating adventure in colonial settings. The phrase arises from the influence of postcolonial literary criticism, initiated by Edward Said in the 1970s, where literature emerges as an important textual source for understanding the construction of imperialist ideologies and the relationship of the "imperial subject" to the colonized "other" (see Said 1978; 1993). However, the two components of the phrase, "imperial" and "romance," need to be understood in their individual contexts. While the adjective "imperial" conveniently describes the generic mode of this kind of fiction, we need nevertheless to be alert to the historical complexities that lie behind the word itself, and the dangers of too readily schematizing such a varied and ambivalent range of texts. In a historical sense, the term "imperialism" is both fluid and problematic, as etymological shifts in the meanings and associations of the word occurred throughout the nineteenth century. In fact, the word "imperialism" began to be used by contemporaries to describe British overseas expansion only in the last decades of the century.[1] This usage coincided with specific shifts in economic, political, and philosophical thinking about empire in the late nineteenth century, when conflicting ideas about the future of British overseas development created the conditions for a range of literary responses to the historical moment. Britain's commercial lead began to disappear in the middle of the century, and contests over economic policy with regard to the empire arose from the need to consolidate resources in the face of Britain's decline as a world power. In fact, nostalgia for the "romantic quest" at the end of the century arose partly out of an anxiety about Britain's waning economic position.

In response to economic conditions at home, an energetic wave of overseas expansion occurred during this period, but Britain encountered fierce competition from other growing European powers for the conquest of hitherto unexplored territories.

Imperial romance thus developed within a complex political context, and, as we shall see, frequently offered an ambivalent reaction to expansionist policy. Writers like Robert Louis Stevenson, Henry Rider Haggard, Rudyard Kipling, and Joseph Conrad drew to varying degrees on the tradition of boys' own adventure established during the nineteenth century by G. A. Henty, Mayne Reid, Frederick Chamier, Frederick Marryat, and R. M. Ballantyne. Such novels had emphasized plot and action,[2] while frequently exploiting situations and landscapes of empire, and assuming the prominence of "England as a vanguard nation, leading the world to the future."[3] Yet a shift in presentation in the later writers' work often produced a less unified and far more equivocal understanding of imperial ideology than that of their predecessors.

Many texts of this period reflected their authors' first-hand experience of empire. Some, like Haggard or Kipling, wrote from a position of fundamental belief in its continuity, despite their complex attitudes to imperialism. Haggard had gone to work for the British colony of Natal in 1875; Kipling became a journalist in India in 1866. A later writer, John Buchan, was in charge of land settlement in South Africa in 1902, following the Boer War, and at the time of his death in 1940 he was Governor-General of Canada. He carried narrative traditions associated with Henty and Marryat well into the twentieth century, showing a nostalgia for waning imperialist values in the face of the First World War and beyond. Others, like Joseph Conrad, a Polish *émigré* whose parents had joined the resistance to Russian hegemony in Warsaw in the 1860s and had been exiled to northern Russia, offered a skeptical view of imperial ideology as it was understood during this period. E. M. Forster's *A Passage to India* (1924) was partly written out of the author's pre- and post-war experience of the country, but, in its reflection of turn of the century political and economic debates about the future of the colonies offers no comfortable closure. On the one hand, Forster's liberal background, and his often biting critique of the English ruling classes in *A Passage to India*, often sound curiously close to the ideal of mutual dependency envisaged by the late nineteenth-century "constructive imperialists."[4] Yet, despite his ideological proposition of potential harmony within the empire, Forster never really addresses the issue of Indian rights to self-determination, and the novel remains unresolved in its proclamation of " 'No, not yet' . . . 'No, not there' " (Forster [1924] 1989: 316).

As the genre developed into the twentieth century, imperial romance generated as many anxieties about imperialism as it encouraged readers to uphold its values. Conrad's, and to some extent Forster's, narrative strategies also suggest that the proto-modernist novel developed out of the adventure tradition as much as setting itself in opposition to the form. Henry James referred to the romance of adventure in his 1908 preface to *The Portrait of a Lady* (1881), when he situated the composition of this work relative to debates about realism and romance in the period. He had wished to make Isabel Archer's psychological adventure as "interesting" as "the surprise of a caravan or the identification of a pirate" (James [1908] 1981: 17). Gesturing to the successful genre of the adventure novel, James was intent on extending the parameters of the realist novel to express the interior "adventure" of its characters. Likewise, writers of adventure fiction may have written within the romance tradition, setting the story in Africa, India, or the Far East, but their methods cannot so readily be distinguished from the experimental aesthetics associated with the rise of the modernist novel.

The genre offered a versatile and malleable framework, accommodating many forms of "exploration" (encompassed by the sensation novel, the detective or spy story, science fiction, and the Gothic novel). The dominant theme of the romance quest of exotic and imaginative adventure intersected with a wide variety of contemporary issues, ranging from anthropology, physics, and evolutionary theory to feminist politics and vivisection. Thus Marie Corelli's *The Romance of Two Worlds* (1886), or H. G. Wells' *The Island of Dr Moreau* (1896), extend notions of colonization to comment on theological or scientific exploration in the period. John Buchan's *The Thirty-Nine Steps* (1915), fundamentally a spy story set in London and Scotland, shares certain features of the romance of adventure, while departing from the foreign settings of Haggard or Kipling. On the other hand, Conrad's *Nostromo* (1905) shares with Buchan's *The Courts of the Morning* (1929) an entirely fictional geographical space while commenting (albeit from quite different ideological positions) on actual imperialist practice regarding the United States' interventions in South America in the early twentieth century. Imperial romance provided a highly flexible locus of experimentation, distinguished by the fluidity of the form, its hybridity, and its radical as well as conservative tendencies.

Genre

Recurring generic features of imperial romance find their antecedents in older forms. Most of the novels under discussion illustrate the function of the journey as it appears in medieval romance quests. They also encompass the properties of the travel narrative, whose origins can be found in texts describing sixteenth- and seventeenth-century voyages of discovery. As in earlier paradigms, the identity of the protagonist is at stake, he undergoes a "test," a number of trials and temptations in the encounter with the "other" in exotic and hazardous locations, and ideally (but by no means exclusively) remains secure and attached to the mores of his society on the return. If Haggard generally upholds the principles of Victorian imperial ideology at the close of his novels, his protagonists are often more problematic than we might expect, exhibiting something of the restlessness and anxiety of a Gawain, whose return is unsettled and unresolved. As Alan Sandison argues throughout his study of the genre (1967), the imperial adventure story ostensibly confirms the superiority of the imperialist authority, but on close reading, many exhibit an anxiety about this reductive view. In fact, Conrad's novels often read like anti-romances. At the beginning of *An Outcast of the Islands* (1896), the male protagonist "stepped *off*" (my italics) the familiar path of his career as a colonial trader rather than embarking on a noble quest.[5] And Conrad's novels never offer the traditionally comic closure of the genre in the technical sense.

One of the most enduring features of the romance novel during this period is closely related to the nineteenth-century reconstruction of medievalism, encompassing Victorian responses to ideas about chivalry and the concept of honor. The heroes of Marryat and Henty unselfconsciously uphold ideals of male heroic behavior. But many of the romances of the later period express anxiety about the decline of heroic adventure, nostalgia for older forms of chivalric behavior rather than confidence in the imperialist quest. Writers become increasingly self-conscious about the form, especially with the rise of feminism and the suffragist movement. Ford Madox Ford relates the tale of *female* knights jousting in the lists to determine the conquest of a husband in his medieval time-travel fantasy, *Ladies Whose Bright Eyes* (1911; based loosely on Mark Twain's *A Connecticut Yankee at King Arthur's Court* [1889]). In *Chance* (1913), Conrad deliberately divides the novel into two parts entitled "Damsel" and "Knight," while undercutting the chivalrous gestures of its dramatized narrators, who attempt to impose on the story their ideal of romance. The "Knight" is a sea captain whose extremes of heroic behavior lead to the non-consummation of his marriage, while the female protagonist resists the role of damsel in distress. Both these texts ironize the romance form while peripherally alluding to imperial romance in their exploration of domestic rather than territorial conquests.

A crisis of subjectivity in the protagonist commonly coincides with traditions of romance. Disguise, cross-cultural dressing, and inter-racial relationships abound, but these novels nearly always suggest the issue of "going native," as in Buchan's *Greenmantle* (1916; the character of Sandy Arbuthnot was inspired partly by the author's acquaintance with T. E. Lawrence), or of miscegenation as in Conrad's *Outcast*. Closely connected to this issue is the question of gender, which is problematized by the romance of empire, paradoxically by the almost exclusive emphasis on the identity of a male protagonist. Several critics have suggested that the ideology behind the novel of adventure finds its origin in the social structures of the public school, an observation borne out by the novels of Haggard, Kipling, and Buchan in particular (see Sandison 1967; Green 1979; Bivona 1998; Fraser 1998). Women are either absent altogether or, as in Haggard's *She* (1887), represent a male Victorian anxiety about female power and sexuality that survives through to Buchan's *Greenmantle*, whose Teutonic *femme fatale* threatens to undermine the hero's loyalties to the British effort in the First World War. Wells' attitude to women is often sympathetic, but his emphasis on female identity appears more frequently in domestic romances, such as *Ann Veronica* (1909), than in science-fiction novels such as *The Time Machine* (1895), *The War of the Worlds* (1898), or *The Island of Doctor Moreau* (1896; the novel explores the implications of vivisection), works that respond, or relate more directly to the adventure tradition and imperialist romance by encompassing a critique of Victorian explorations in biology and physics. Conrad, who appears to follow the tradition of male exclusivity (foregrounding the subjectivity of Marlow, Kurtz, and Jim in *Heart of Darkness* [1902] and *Lord Jim* [1900]), often undermines traditional assumptions about women, his discussions of imperial adventure extending to an indictment of the way in which women have been excluded not only from the active life of adventure, but also from its critique. On the other hand, popular fiction also produced its female adventurers, proving the exception to the predominantly masculinist emphasis of adventure romance. However sentimental and conservative in tone, a highly successful writer like Marie Corelli gave the female protagonist the role of the quest in her extravagant travels into space in *The Romance of Two Worlds* (1886).

The content of the romance genre in the late nineteenth century also depended on a number of contemporary advances in evolutionary theory, theology, and anthropology. First, the publication of Charles Darwin's *Origin of Species* in 1859 initiated anxieties about human origin. Both Haggard and Kipling touched on the issue of origins, drawing on Darwinian ideas that destabilized Victorian confidence in theological certainties. Their narratives are imbued with references to Darwin's legacy of "the accidental variation from which the species developed" (in Sandison 1967: 26). Such thinking also leads to moral relativism in discussions of foreign customs and manners, a relativism that derives from a much longer philosophical tradition (such as John Locke's critique of innate ideas, or the philosophy of David Hume). In *She*, the narrator of the novel observes "how the customs of mankind . . . vary in different countries, making morality an affair of latitude, and what is right and proper in one place wrong and improper in another" ([1887] 1998: 82). At the same time, earlier racialist theories of history (such as Robert Knox's *The Races of Men* [1850]), used to bolster Britain's mid-century image of industrial and imperial prominence, were reinvigorated by Darwin's thesis of evolutionary competition. The social Darwinism of the late nineteenth century gave new energy to ideas of white racial superiority and spurred on the jingoistic patriotism accompanying aggressive late-century expansionism.[6] Whereas an early Victorian adventure writer such as Marryat in *Masterman Ready* (1841) took English superiority for granted, late nineteenth-century imperial romance frequently reflects a deep anxiety about the savagery of late imperial conquest, and about the proximity of "civilized" humanity to its primitive origins. In this respect Stevenson's *The Ebb Tide* (1894) and Conrad's *Heart of Darkness* (1902) assume a remarkably similar tone, where both texts deal with the moral precariousness associated with the white man's unconscious assumption of European racial superiority. They share an epistemological skepticism that places both writers in a transitional moment on the cusp of literary modernism.

The predominantly Gothic register of the late nineteenth-century period arises from a number of different textual influences. Responses to historiography and developments in anthropology intersect with romance traditions, so that Haggard's interest in Egyptology surfaces in his references to the origins of *She*, Kipling experiments with an imaginative version of social history in *Kim* (1901), and Buchan refers closely to aspects of First World War history in *Greenmantle* and *Mr. Standfast* (1919). The rise of occultism, spiritualism, and theosophy had a fundamental influence on late Victorian romance. Victorian religious doubt and conflict in attitudes to a new burst of expansionism accompanied the publication of such texts as Madame Blavatsky's *Isis Unveiled* (1877) and A. P. Sinnett's *The Occult World* (1881). Interest in alternative religions to Christianity followed the success of Edwin Arnold's *The Light of Asia* (1879), and Sinnett's *Esoteric Buddhism* (1883), reflected in the almost religious quality of Kipling's "faith" in empire in his poetry (as in "Recessional," 1897) and in his images of decline and reversal of civilized behavior in "Mark of the Beast" (1890), where an Englishman desecrates a Hindu temple and turns into a werewolf. Variations on the imperial Gothic theme appear in Bram Stoker's *Dracula* (1897), an exploration of human regression and vampiric conquest, and in Stevenson's *The Strange Case of Dr. Jekyll and Mr. Hyde* (1887), which Brantlinger reads as an urban version of "going native." Occultism produced both serious and skeptical responses. Conan Doyle and W. T. Stead expressed a sense of certainty in matters paranormal, while Sigmund Freud, in *The Future of an Illusion* (1927), presents occult phenomena as the unconscious workings of the mind. Andrew Lang, a close friend of Haggard, was interested both in anthropology and in psychic phenomena, and typifies the late Victorian conflict between empiricist beliefs and fascination with superstition and the spiritual. With the dawn of the twentieth century, a complex analogy can be made between occultism and imperialist ideology. Contact with the dead offers a new form of conquest, just as the notion of empire itself is in question, while communication without frontiers encapsulates the borderland position of the imperialist, who is both from the mother country and away from it (see Brantlinger 1988: 251–3).

Texts

The novels of Henry Rider Haggard (1856–1925) provide some of the most striking examples of mainstream adventure fiction of the late Victorian period, written predominantly against the late nineteenth-century background of the scramble for Africa.[7] Ostensibly delivering his fictions in a pro-imperialist voice, we learn from Haggard's biography that he himself had nevertheless endured a fate shaped by a repressive English ruling class that looked on the colonies to provide opportunities for the less successful products of a public-school education. The Carlylean ethos (expressed in his 1839 pamphlet, "Chartism") promoted overseas expansion with its potential for emigration. Carlyle saw the empire as an essential economic development to alleviate civic problems in Britain and to create openings for the "surplus" of the ruling class. As the son of an English country gentleman, Haggard had failed miserably at school and was sent by his father to South Africa in 1875 to work on the unpaid staff of Sir Henry Bulwer in the British colony of Natal. Later he used his experiences in Africa to generate successful yarns of boys' own adventure and imperial quests. His novel *King Solomon's Mines* (1885) offers a fictional parallel to the opening up of Africa and the epistemological challenges of the unknown, previously supplied by nonfiction texts such as Mungo Park's *Travels* (1798) and, by the nineteenth century, Henry Stanley's *How I Found Livingstone* (a bestseller by 1872).[8] Haggard's novels also intersect with developments in racialist and evolutionary doctrines in the field of natural history, as paradoxically, the "humanitarian" discourses of the "white man's burden" propagated the myth of the Dark Continent. An anthropological quest to understand human origins went hand in hand with the colonialist desire for expansion and prospecting for trade. As the narrator of *She* proclaims, Africa houses "the relics of long dead and forgotten civilizations,"[9] a phenomenon that Haggard explores again in novels such as *Cleopatra* (1889) and *Ayesha, the Return of She* (1905).

In political terms, Haggard's *She* offers an intriguing response to the contemporary African situation. The story is narrated by Ludwig Horace Holly, a Cambridge scholar who decides to accompany his friend Leo Vincey on a quest to follow the path of Leo's ancestors on an African adventure. Landing on the coast of Mozambique, they discover the Amahaggar tribe (roughly based on contemporary knowledge of the Lovedu people of southeast Asia), which is ruled by a woman, Ayesha, whose ancestry connects her to the founding of the Egyptians. Reversing the situation of the Lovedu, Haggard provides the Amahaggar with a social structure based on matrilinearity, and in Ayesha, "She-Who-Must-Be-Obeyed," an autocratic leader with the gift of immortality (see Chrisman 1990). Both Holly and Leo are seduced by Ayesha's beauty, yet resist her cruelty and terrorizing power (which includes a threat to conquer Britain and usurp Queen Victoria's power). After surviving many hair-raising adventures, the men finally persuade Ayesha to practice Christian compassion – at which point she loses her immortality and dies.

As a popular romance, *She* provides a fantasy of travel where upright young Englishmen take up the challenge of exploration to a largely unknown continent. But what the travelers find in darkest Africa is more unsettling than the usual tales of warring tribes – they discover an intransigent, immortal, white woman whose reign of terror over the local people hardly conforms to the ideal of the "white man's burden." From a Freudian perspective, the narrative displays all the classic symptoms of male anxiety about female power. Yet in a number of respects the text fails to conform precisely to the reading of "She" as an archetypal *femme fatale* provided by Gilbert and Gubar (1989). In fact Haggard makes this kind of analysis almost too easy by telling us how the adventurers had to penetrate cave-like structures whose shape "was meant to roughly symbolise or suggest the female form" ([1887] 1998: 261). Yet the tone in which Ayesha's story is conveyed is mixed – parodic, yet also empathetic, and on some occasions introducing an element of music-hall and bur-lesque. The complexities of representations of imperialism in which images and positions are written against one another preclude any straightforward reading of the tale. Haggard's narrator, for example, shows considerable empathy for the tortured meditations of Ayesha. And while Ayesha herself is ultimately destroyed before she can take over the British empire, we could argue that a radical subtext emerges, pointing to the story as an allegory or moral exemplum of British imperialism itself. Like Ayesha, Victoria was a white woman ruling over subject peoples, open to the dangers of "overreaching."

Of the contemporary evolutionary ideas impinging on Haggard's novel, the most striking intertextual resonances occur with Darwin's *Origin of Species* (1859), his *Descent of Man* (1872), and Thomas Huxley's *Man's Place in Nature* (1863). These resonances play an important role in shaping the generic register of the romance. It is true that Huxley refutes the idea of the African as "missing link" or evolutionary stage between the anthropoid ape and civilized white man. Nevertheless, Huxley suggests a proximity between African, chimpanzee, and gorilla. Haggard plays with and undermines some of the implications of Huxley's theories by alluding quite directly to the connection between the intellectual "superiority" of the white man and his "primitive" ancestry. In *She*, Holly initially describes himself as "short, thick-set and deep-chested almost to deformity, with long sinewy arms, heavy features, deep-set grey eyes" ([1887] 1998: 7–8). He is affectionately termed the "Baboon" by Billali and Ayesha. Paradoxically, he possesses extraordinary intellectual powers, and proves to be the only real match for Ayesha (in spite of her physical attraction to the Adonis-like, but rather dull, Leo). When Ayesha herself is consumed by the flames of the eternal Pillar of Fire, she is reduced to the physical dimensions and appearance of a monkey. Thus Haggard offers a tragic, even absurd subversion of the comic closure of romance. The "natural" pairing between the two beauties (Ayesha and Leo) is undesirable in terms of the moral framework of the novel, and the intellectual pairing (between Holly and Ayesha) realized physically only at the point of Ayesha's death. Contemporary anxieties about civilized man's proximity to his primitive origins emerge. And in spite of its ostensibly "happy ending" (with Ayesha dead, the British empire is left intact) the closure of *She* offers a far more uneasy treatment of imperialist and feminist politics than we might expect.[10]

Furthermore, we can see how Haggard provided the springboard for modernist experimentation with exotic romance. For example, Conrad offers a striking response to the genre in his early fiction. Haggard's male protagonists explore "the heart of the darkness" ([1887] 1998: 261) of Ayesha's Africa, remarking how "three modern Englishmen . . . seemed . . . out of tone with that measureless desolation" (70), and we hear echoes in Conrad as he repeats the sense of dislocation experienced by Marlow in *Heart of Darkness*, or by the white man on entering the lagoon in his early Malay story of that name, "The Lagoon," collected in *Tales of Unrest* (1898). With his first two novels – *Almayer's Folly* (1895) and *An Outcast of the Islands* (1896) – Conrad brings the influence of French realism (from his reading of Flaubert, Maupassant, and Pierre Loti) to imperial romance. Resisting the evocation of a fantasy of adventure, an "empire of the imagination" (*She* [1887] 1998: 175), he sets these tales in a bleak world of colonial opportunism. Nina Almayer's conflicted identity, split between the influences of a Europhile father and a native mother, disturbs the harmony of the romance closure, while her father Almayer's futile dreams suggest a highly skeptical perspective on imperialist attainment. But the shifting narratorial perspectives of *Outcast* show an even more direct response to Haggard's *She*, allowing the reader to question the function of the *femme fatale* of imperial romance. It seems to be no accident that Conrad's heroine is called Aïssa, although she is native Malay, not white like Haggard's heroine, and she possesses principally sexual, not political power. Nevertheless she increasingly disrupts political negotiations between white and native factions in the novel. Here Conrad comments on the way in which women are denied access to the action of the masculine world of romance, while the female presence in the novel represents both the white European male's desire for romantic oblivion and the threat of the "other" whom he wishes to overpower and colonize. We follow the adventures of Willems, the male European protagonist, whose experiences comply to some extent with the trope of male abandonment of identity to the enchanting but deadly threat of the *femme fatale*. But Aïssa's sense of Willems' alterity is presented with equal force, complicating the notion of a fixed imperial subject embodied in the European male, who in Haggard's novels returns to the mother country with a modicum of restlessness, but with a relatively unscathed sense of identity and of the righteousness of imperial practice.

Willems also learns little from his encounter with the "other," but rather than supplying the staple closure of harmony, Conrad shows how his hero's misunderstanding of the relationship leads only to tragedy. He fails to concede any autonomy to Aïssa. He takes exception to her cultural and religious customs as a Muslim, "tearing off her face-veil" and trampling on it "as though it had been a mortal enemy" ([1896] 1992: 39). He expects her to abandon her people and offers her neither Christian compassion nor honesty in return, failing to inform her that he already has a wife and child. Instead it is she who momentarily attains the kind of recognition usually accorded to the Conradian hero, realizing Willems' moral weakness and "the tremendous fact of our isolation" (250). Yet ultimately her tragedy, like Willems', emerges from a failure of vision. Betrayed by her lover, she shoots him in despair. Aïssa's crime of passion initiates a recurring theme in Conrad's fiction in which women play an important role in the critique of imperialism, one that helps to shift the focus of imperial romance toward an increasingly skeptical as well as modernist perspective. In both *Nostromo* and *Victory* (1915), novels that borrow from imperial romance their exotic settings, the female protagonists (Emilia Gould, Lena) act as the moral repositories of the novel, where materialist drives and imperial quests lead only to the moral isolation of the male subject.

Conrad continued his exploration of the imperial subject in *Lord Jim*. Published in 1900, this novel encapsulates more than any other Conradian narrative the author's rigorous interrogation of the ideals underpinning romance. Developing the ironic register of the early Malay novels, Conrad describes the disillusionment of the British sailor whose obsession with the heroic quest is acquired during his childhood reading of adventure tales (of the type written by Marryat or Henty) and ends in failure to live up to his self-imposed ideals. The narrative repeatedly focuses on the incident of Jim's jumping from a sinking ship transporting a party of Muslim pilgrims from Singapore to Jeddah – an act with which he cannot or will not come to terms. Conrad's complex narratorial strategies in presenting the moment of Jim's desertion as a dislocation of consciousness mark the novel as one of the most striking early instances of modernist writing in English. The narrative also extends Conrad's ongoing critique of imperialism, established in *Heart of Darkness* (of course, we have to remember that, with one eye on the marketplace, and with the debt Conrad felt to a "borrowed" homeland, he carefully orchestrated the settings of his fiction to suggest more explicit criticism of empires other than the British). But in this novel imperialism is a driving force that he associates more directly with the futility of romantic idealism (he will return to the theme again in *Victory*, where the male protagonist's father is a Nietzschean philosopher). In the last section of *Lord Jim*, the hero gets his final opportunity to absolve himself of guilt by taking on the role of protector of the island community of Patusan. The emphasis throughout the novel on Jim as a "white figure," with his Christ-like or angelic qualities, is suggestive, especially in this last section, of his role as the benevolent white colonialist of the Victorian imagination. The degree to which this image may be distinguished from the reality of actual imperialist practice is suggested here. Conrad complicates the reading experience by offering a number of narratorial perspectives on Jim's tale, including those of Marlow, who also appeared in *Heart of Darkness*, and a "privileged reader" (roughly corresponding to the typical reader of *Blackwood's Magazine*, a journal of conservative, sometimes jingoistic tones, in which *Lord Jim* initially appeared). With Marlow's recollection of the privileged reader's overtly racist claim that "giving your life up to them," referring to anyone who was not white, "was like selling your soul to a brute,"[11] Conrad finally places Jim's dilemma not only within the context of romanticism, but in the context of the Victorian imperialist's perspective on "the white man's burden." Recent studies have drawn on the arguments of postcolonial critics such as Said, Gayatri Spivak, and Homi Bhabha to show how we might also read *Lord Jim* from the perspective of late nineteenth-century European anxieties about the colonial encounter (see Parry 1983 and GoGwilt 1995). The text of *Lord Jim* occupies an equivocal position in turn-of-the-century discussions of imperialism. Its narrative complexity exposes and displaces "orientalist" discourses of empire, yet in other ways its representations preserve the seductive power of a romanticism which has often consolidated assumptions about imperialist hierarchies. Conrad may present a shift toward twentieth-century thinking about representations of race and nation, but *Lord Jim* offers no easy transformation of values, and often sustains a problematic continuity with, as well as a critique of, imaginative reconstructions of the imperial subject. Just as Conrad's proto-modernist engagement with issues of identity demands an equivocal response, his presentation of the colonial encounter, registering as it does the tone of both romantic and skeptic, ultimately leaves with the reader, in modernist fashion, the onus of interpretation.

Rudyard Kipling's *Kim* appeared one year later, in 1901. Like *Lord Jim*, this novel straddles the centuries in terms of its ambivalent generic status. It offers a paradigm of late nineteenth-century imperial adventure even as it anticipates (however obliquely) twentieth-century concerns about the complexities and problems of identity experienced by the imperial subject. However, in tone it sounds very different to the bleak skepticism of Conrad's narrative. In spite of the well-established commonplace that associates Kipling with a love of tradition and empire, the novel celebrates excess, subversion, diversity, its form anticipating a kind of playful postmodernism. It tells a rites of passage story – the tale of a young boy's maturation set against the exotic landscape and the social complexity of imperial India. Yet the experiences of the young Kimball O'Hara, the poor orphaned white son of an Irish soldier, brought up by his dead mother's mixed-race sister, hardly conform to a preference for the secure and unambiguous subjectivity of the white colonial hero. In its simplest form the story shows how Kim survives his upbringing in the native quarter of Lahore. He befriends an aged lama, the proverbial wise man, whom he joins in wandering through India, over the Grand Trunk Road, until he is adopted by the Irish regiment in which his father served and is given an English education. The book revels in the adventures of a young boy of mixed race, whose shifting identities perfectly qualify him for participation in the "Great Game" (a term Kipling uses ironically) of treachery, betrayal, and spying for the British. Kim's versatility, cunning, his performative nature, and survival skills provide a textual *jouissance* that carries the reader through a series of boyish escapades set against the complexity of Indian and imperialist British politics. The exoticism of the tale arises from the proliferation of Indian settings and landscapes. Its presentation of India's multicultural society draws the British reader's attention to the many grand narratives residing outside Christianity (one of which is represented by the lama's mystical quest to "attain freedom from the Wheel of Things").[12] The characterizations of Kim and his friends may not seem as psychologically searching as those of Conrad's novels, but nevertheless they undermine any secure assumptions about identity as we see Kim caught between cultures (Kim speaks in the vernacular, thinks in Hindi, and is proficient in communicating with English or Indian, Christian, Buddhist, or Muslim). Kipling offers sometimes strikingly critical insights into the structures and complexities of India under British imperial rule.

Kim demonstrates many of the traditional generic functions of romance – it is a quest narrative, outlining the conflicts of identity of the hero, the threat of disruption of social order, the differences between pagan and Christian social and moral structures. We are constantly made aware of complex moral codes impinging on Kim's life, as the lama's ethics frequently conflict with those required by the "Game" of espionage. At the same time, these elements represent the ways in which the romance form has been adapted during this period, absorbing features of the travel narrative and spy story to illustrate and comment on the specific conditions and problems associated with the experience of empire. It shows its contemporaneity in its interest in ethnography and the history of anthropology. Kim's British employer, Colonel Creighton, is working on "the Indian Survey" and has an ambition to write "F.R.S." after his name ([1901] 1983: 157). He had "bombarded" the Royal Society for years with "monographs on strange Asiatic cults and unknown customs" (157). At the same time, Kipling gestures back to earlier English forms of romance as we delight in Kim's disguises – he moves as easily around the bazaar in his various assumed personae as Moll Flanders went undetected around the streets of London.

Kipling may ultimately condone imperialist structures of control, but it could also be argued that his narrative strategies evince a more ambivalent perspective, not least in their open-endedness. Like Conrad in *Lord Jim*, Kipling frequently plays with the notion of "belonging" to a British imperial hegemony as he toys with the notion of Kim's becoming "one of us" (188). But Kim's empathy with the alternative ways of the lama are confirmed at the close of the novel, when he is ready to join the adult world just as the lama is ready to leave it. Kipling finally suggests Kim's refusal to capitulate entirely to the yoke of the British ruling class. In the last pages of the novel, following the lama's death, Kim contemplates dropping his secret service connections at the very moment he qualifies for full admission to "the club."

Another "hybrid" novel of the period, Conrad and Ford Madox Ford's collaboration, *The Inheritors*, appeared in 1901. This work, which is not well known, shows the way in which generic experimentation so often grew out of the structures of "imperial" romance. The most widely known collaboration of these writers, itself entitled *Romance* (1903), was a deliberate attempt to produce a Stevensonian bestseller. However, their first collaboration, *The Inheritors*, draws on a wider range of forms – it is a political satire commenting on the rise of a new breed of ruthless modern politicians who have exploited the influence of mass communications and speculative capitalism to overthrow a flawed administration, one that survived by sustaining dubious imperialist practices. Yet its mixed generic form also engages intriguingly with the burgeoning interest in late Victorian scientific romance – a genre that itself crosses uneasily the boundaries of highbrow and lowbrow fiction, and that commutes imperial romance's emphasis on conquest of new territories for a fear of conquest from lands beyond earth. In *The Inheritors*, Conrad and Ford allude to a plethora of late Victorian scientific romances and political novels – perhaps most obviously, to those of H. G. Wells, with references to Darwinist theory, the Nietzschean *Übermensch*, anxieties about degeneration and entropy, and recent developments in mathematics and physics. We rarely associate either Ford or Conrad with the genre of science fiction, but *The Inheritors* turned out to be a story full of *fin de siècle* anxiety about the future and references to the invasion of Earth by inhabitants of the future. Drawing on the ubiquitous presentation of the *femme fatale* of Haggard's *She* and others, Conrad and Ford invent a beautiful but deadly female from the Fourth Dimension who exploits a power vacuum in British politics by exposing the atrocities committed during the colonization of Greenland, a project that has been undertaken in the name of progress (as in *Heart of Darkness*, there is a clear critique of Boer War policies and King Leopold II's investment in the Belgian Congo). Although it was never a great public success, this novel appropriately exemplifies the intersection of several generic relations of imperial romance during this period.

Perhaps less obviously, but most strikingly, it offers a critique of Marie Corelli (the pseudonym of Mary or Minnie MacKay) – a prolific novelist who successfully tapped into late nineteenth-century popular taste. Her first publication, *A Romance of Two Worlds* (1886), was a fantasy novel, and in its own way offered an alternative to the boys' own adventure of imperial romance by presenting a female adventurer who explores the territories of the future. Like Wells, Corelli responded to developments in mathematics and the physical sciences such as electricity, photography, X-rays, and the new geometry. Yet, couched in a tone of sentimental, quasi-religious idealism, drawing on the discourses of *fin-de-siècle* spiritualism, her work converts the "science fiction" novel into a highly salable product that ultimately gratified the conservative tastes of a wide romance-reading public, and offers her readers a sentimental but unconvincing closure of romantic harmony. The tone of *The Inheritors* is in fact closer to that of earlier satires of contemporary evolutionary theory and politics. It responds to works like Max Nordau's novel *Degeneration* (1885), or Wells' undermining of evolution in *The Time Machine* (1895), or his use of the metaphors of invasion, conquest, and colonization in *The War of the Worlds* (1898). But in *The Inheritors*, where the hero is a writer forced to take hack work, and the female protagonist is a cold and ruthless woman who is determined to "inherit the earth," Conrad and Ford demonstrate the literary intellectual's anxiety, not just about the "new imperialism," but about the success of popular romance writers, especially a woman like Corelli, whose novels sold as well as those of Haggard and Henty. In the satire of Conrad and Ford we may hear a hint of how the romance form continued to engage writers in the twentieth century in the debate initiated by James and others over the future of the novel.

John Buchan, on the other hand, never seemed overly anxious about the status of romance, although his texts engage reflectively with the form itself. His novels are plot-driven and his style follows that of late nineteenth-century imperial romance. With the publication of *The Thirty-Nine Steps* (1915), Buchan produced a thoroughly "ripping yarn" in the spirit of the boys' own adventure tradition. However, in a very changed political climate, set against the background of the First World War, his novel appears to depart from the genre in its reversal of the location of imperial romance. Rather than beginning the story with the hero venturing out to the colonies, we first meet Richard Hannay on his *return* from service in the South African *veld*. In London, Hannay exhibits all the restlessness and sense of displacement experienced by Haggard's protagonists on their return to Britain at the end of *She*. His sense of disappointment and unease is not dissimilar to that of Marlow returning to the "sepulchral city" at the close of *Heart of Darkness*. Thus Buchan's tale takes off from the point at which the imperial romance closes. His hero starts off by threatening to go back to South Africa, a place where he felt his participation in a life of adventure had been guaranteed. But he soon becomes inveigled into a spy narrative of equally nail-biting dimensions (Buchan himself worked in intelligence and propaganda for the Foreign Office and War Office during the First World War). By transposing the structuring principles of anticipation and thrill of discovery familiar to readers of imperial romance onto domestic locations in London and Scotland, Buchan updates the adventure story to accommodate the modern context in which men like Buchan himself had returned from the colonies to participate in the European war. However, Buchan constantly signals his indebtedness to the context of imperial romance. His hero identifies himself as "A Colonial"[13] and alludes to the conflict between free trade and protectionism, even if it does appear as a dimly distant and little understood concept. One character presumes that the hero is "a Free Trader and can tell our people what a wash-out Protection is in the Colonies" ([1915] 1993: 41), but Hannay admits to himself that "I had very few notions about Free Trade one way or the other" (42). Hannay talks nostalgically of the "fragrant sunniness of the South African veld" (49) in relation to the Scottish landscape, and invokes the name of his former Boer scout, Peter Pienaar, as if it were a kind of mantra encapsulating the ideal of boys' own adventure. In *Greenmantle* (1916) the setting more closely resembles the exotic locations of imperial romance as Hannay, Pienaar, and Sandy Arbuthnot (loosely modeled on T. E. Lawrence) embark on a spying expedition for the British government that takes them eventually to Erzerum and the northeastern frontier of Turkey. The story is based on Germany's actual relationship with Turkey during the Great War and offers an interesting historical footnote to ongoing European relationships with the Middle East, given the heroes' attempts to thwart a German plot to exploit Islamic fundamentalism to facilitate their eastward drive. In both novels Buchan's male protagonists, like Haggard's or Henty's, survive their adventures intact, and while they take on a series of aliases and disguises that echo the performativity celebrated in Kipling's earlier spy story, *Kim*, they rarely become disaffiliated or "go native." In *Greenmantle*, Hannay's upright identity is compromised by his attraction to the scurrilous siren, Hilda von Einem, and by his fascination with Stumm's decadent lifestyle (both of which he claims to abhor but nevertheless describes in loving and sensuous detail). The homoerotic overtones of his relations with Peter and Sandy emerge in Buchan's curiously ambivalent handling of passages of considerable sensuality – reminiscent of late nineteenth-century romance's frequent association with *fin de siècle* decadence.

On the other hand, Buchan's first-person narrator in *The Thirty-Nine Steps* self-consciously plays with the kind of subjective modernist strategy employed by writers like Conrad and Ford, as Hannay muses to himself: "I seemed to be another person, standing aside and listening to my own voice, and judging carefully the reliability of the tale" (45). And when, in an extraordinary passage, given the political context, Hannay reveals an implicit empathy with Kaiser Wilhelm, Buchan attempts both to inform his readership and to "modernize" the romance, problematizing the notion of the "other" by suggesting a less schematic image of the enemy than that accorded to the popular presentation of the Kaiser as the personification of evil.

Buchan's novels show the way in which the imperial romance survived well into the twentieth century, proving it to be a hardy and enduring sub-genre. Many examples of the genre, popular in their day, have, however, failed to survive shifts in literary taste and canonization. The first half of the twentieth century was influenced by the hegemony of modernist literary aesthetics and the rise of the New Criticism in the 1940s and 1950s, which promoted pejorative views of romance as inferior literary material. Many romance and adventure novels produced between the 1880s and the 1920s were subsequently neglected. For example, the now infrequently read W. H. Hudson (*Green Mansions*, 1904) reached wide audiences among his contemporaries, whereas Joseph Conrad struggled to achieve popularity during much of his career, but has since been absorbed into the canon of the experimental or modernist novel. Henry Rider Haggard, extraordinarily successful during his lifetime, was neglected during the mid-twentieth century, but with the rise of feminist criticism and cultural studies has returned to prominence in recent years. A reverse critical trend occurred in the late twentieth century, initiated by the influence of cultural, postcolonial, and gender studies, and has led to a recovery of many formerly neglected texts. The versatility of the form is apparent, exposing the fact that despite debates about the novel that attempt to distinguish realism and romance, the two are often interdependent. We see how romance forms have been subjected to skeptical and modernist treatments, and how they often intersected with many of the debates that subsequently occupied the modernist writers. Thus the importance of the map as a signifier of potential (and imaginary) conquest in Stevenson's *Treasure Island* returns in Conrad's *Heart of Darkness* as a metaphor for white Europeans' arrogance and greed in their attempt to fill in the "blank spaces" of unconquered territory during the nineteenth-century scramble for Africa. Stevenson delights the reader with the innocent boyish hunt for treasure (although his presentation of colonialist practices sometimes implies darker impulses). Conrad emphasizes Marlow's disillusionment with the methods of the imperialist quest that sustain corrupt practices in the search for ivory in *Heart of Darkness*. The image of the "blank spaces" returns in Conan Doyle's *The Lost World* (1911) where the male protagonist, a young journalist, is told by his girlfriend that he must become a hero of adventure before she will marry him. His editor, however, sees how difficult a quest this would be, suggesting that the blank spaces in the map have now been filled and that the romance of adventure has lost its place in the contemporary context. With this remark, Doyle's character summarizes the position of the genre as it moved into the twentieth century. Its most conservative variations looked back to an ideal of heroism and conquest confirming secure identities under imperial British rule or celebrating the energy of late Victorian discovery and exploration. Elsewhere, transformations of the genre suggest a far more skeptical turn, as the romance finally foresees the end of empire and embraces the uncertainties of the future in the modern world.

See also: chapter 20, Romance and Victorian Autobiography; chapter 21, Victorian Romance: Romance and Mystery; chapter 22, Nineteenth-century Adventure and Fantasy; chapter 24, America and Romance.

Notes

1. In the early nineteenth century the word often had a pejorative connotation, and was not associated with problems of the British empire specifically. See Richard Koebner and Helmut Dan Schmidt, *Imperialism* (1964: 1). Koebner and Schmidt trace the introduction of the word "imperialism" into the English language as a gloss on the French Second Empire and the autocratic policy of Napoleon III, a political structure that maintained "its hold on the French during the period 1852–70." See also J. S. Richardson, "*Imperium Romanum*: The Language of Power" (1991: 1–9); Robert J. C. Young, *Postcolonialism* (2001),

chapter 3, "Imperialism," pp. 25–43. I am very grateful to Dr. Simon Potter, National University of Ireland, Galway, for helpful conversations about the historical context of the British empire in the late nineteenth century.

2. Robert Louis Stevenson followed their lead and defended the status of romance fiction against the moral seriousness of the realist novel, believing that the novel should distinguish itself "by its immeasurable distance from life." Quoted in Malcolm Bradbury, *The Modern British Novel* (1993: 44).

3. Patrick Brantlinger, *Rule of Darkness* (1988: 239). Ideas about colonial rule in the early nineteenth century remained traditionally conservative, underpinned by the notion of the British as a "governing race." Humanitarian movements, developing from the abolitionism of the 1830s (Emancipation Act of 1833), and frequently fueled by Christian evangelical movements whose rhetoric outlined "the white man's burden," offered alternative perspectives on the government of colonial dependencies, often embracing respect for indigenous traditions and visualizing eventual self-government. But the outcome of the Indian Mutiny in 1857 was effectively to squash arguments for the independence of the mainly nonwhite parts of the empire, and an "illusion of permanence" emerged in relation to the British occupation of India. See also Francis Hutchins 1967.

4. See Peter Cain, "The Economic Philosophy of Constructive Imperialism" (1996: 42–65). Cain uses the term "constructive imperialism" to describe the ideology giving rise to the form of protectionism that came into its own with the conservative Joseph Chamberlain's tariff reform campaign in 1903. Support for reform was partly aided by the resurgence in interest in the empire during the South African Wars, and partly occurred in spite of criticism leveled against the British handling of relations with the Boers. "Constructive imperialism," in one form or another, endured into the first half of the twentieth century, but ultimately failed because of the domestic sacrifice involved in offering the colonies favorable import arrangements. It also failed to accommodate many British interests that already accepted Britain as a post-industrial nation more closely linked to Europe than to the empire. Against this background, we can read much of E. M. Forster's early writing, and trace his enduring position in *A Passage to India*.

5. Joseph Conrad, *An Outcast of the Islands* ([1896] 1992), 4. Hereafter all references to this novel are from this edition and its page numbers quoted in the text.

6. Early twentieth-century socioeconomic theorists, like J. A. Hobson (who was influenced by John Ruskin and Richard Cobden) and Joseph Schumpeter, saw imperialism as a retrogressive stage of economic and political development. See Schumpeter, *Imperialism and Social Classes* ([1919] 1951), p. 84: "imperialism is ... atavistic in character." See also Brantlinger 1988: 227–53.

7. Among the explanations for the political context, Thomas Pakenham (*The Scramble for Africa*, 1992) observes that by the mid-1870s, much of Africa still represented an unexplored, mysterious, and unknown territory. Political historians have posed differing theories for the forces behind expansionism in Africa. Some (from John Hobson to Lenin) offer a Eurocentric explanation, suggesting that surplus capital in Europe held the key to expansionist policies. Eric Williams, in *Capitalism and Slavery* (1944), suggests that Britain could afford to abolish slavery once it had provided the surplus capital to support an industrial take-off. Others prefer an Afrocentric explanation, looking at sub-imperialisms within Africa itself, where sufficiently destabilized environments facilitated colonialist projects. Ronald Robinson and John Gallagher, in *Africa and the Victorians* (1961), prefer a combination of these two theories.

8. The literary antecedents for writing about Africa can be found in the work of the Romantics of the late eighteenth and early nineteenth centuries. These texts, however, constituted a strong political critique, associating Africa with the inhuman violence of the slave trade (Wordsworth's *Prelude*; Blake's "Little Black Boy"; Coleridge's "Greek Prize Ode on the Slave Trade"; and, anticipating an

aspect of Conrad's *Heart of Darkness*, Southey's "To Horror"). Influenced by Enlightenment beliefs (that all people should be treated equally under the law), Rousseau's philosophy of the noble savage, and anti-abolitionist propaganda, pre-Victorian writers envisioned Africans living freely and happily without interference. A shift in perspective occurred during the transition from the British campaign against the slave trade and the imperialist partitioning of Africa that dominated the last quarter of the century. During this period, the myth of the Dark Continent developed, fueling a market for romances of male adventure expressing the Victorian preoccupation with the quest to conquer unknown territory. See the *Pall Mall Gazette*, February 10, 1895, for example, which notes the extreme competitiveness arising between nations in their "scramble" for territory at the end of the century: "In times past . . . the whole of heathendom . . . was our inheritance . . . All that has changed . . . the world is filling up around us . . . and Europe throws off ever increasing swarms to settle in other continents."

9. Henry Rider Haggard, *She* ([1887] 1998), p. 62. Hereafter all references to this novel are taken from this edition and its page numbers quoted in the text.

10. See Andrea White, *Joseph Conrad and the Adventure Tradition* (1993: 99): "Haggard initiated a certain shift in the genre of adventure fiction that subverted some of its most traditional claims concerning the imperial subject."

11. Joseph Conrad, *Lord Jim* ([1900] 1983), p. 212. Hereafter all references to this novel are from this edition and its page numbers quoted in the text.

12. Rudyard Kipling, *Kim* ([1901] 1983), p. 9. Hereafter all references to this novel are from this edition and its page numbers quoted in the text.

13. John Buchan, *The Thirty-Nine Steps* ([1915] 1993), p. 41. Hereafter all references to this novel are taken from this edition and its page numbers quoted in the text. Buchan can also be identified as part of a specifically Scottish tradition whose antecedents were Scott and Stevenson.

References and Further Reading

Bivona, Daniel (1998). *British Imperial Literature 1870–1940: Writing and the Administration of Empire.* Cambridge: Cambridge University Press.

Bradbury, Malcolm (1993). *The Modern British Novel.* London: Secker and Warburg.

Brantlinger, Patrick (1988). *Rule of Darkness: British Literature and Imperialism, 1830–1914.* Ithaca, NY: Cornell University Press.

Buchan, John (1993). *The Thirty-Nine Steps.* Oxford: Oxford University Press. [First published in 1915.]

Cain, Peter (1996). "The Economic Philosophy of Constructive Imperialism." In *British Politics and the Spirit of the Age: Political Concepts in Action*, ed. C. Narvari. Keele: Keele University Press, pp. 42–65.

Chrisman, Laura (1990). "The Imperial Unconscious? Representations of Imperial Discourse." *Critical Quarterly* 32:3, 38–58.

Conrad, Joseph (1983). *Lord Jim.* Oxford: Oxford University Press, 1983. [First published in 1900.]

Conrad, Joseph (1992). *An Outcast of the Islands.* Oxford: Oxford University Press. [First published in 1896.]

Forster, E. M. (1989). *A Passage to India.* London; Penguin, 1989. [First published in 1924.]

Fraser, Robert (1998). *Victorian Quest Romance.* Plymouth: Northcote House.

Gilbert, S., and S. Gubar (1989). *No Man's Land: The Place of the Woman Writer in the Twentieth Century.* Vol. 2, *Sexchanges.* New Haven: Yale University Press.

GoGwilt, Christopher (1995). *The Invention of the West: Joseph Conrad and the Double Mapping of Europe and Empire.* Stanford, CA: Stanford University Press.

Green, Martin (1979). *Dreams of Adventure, Deeds of Empire.* New York: Basic Books.

Haggard, Henry Rider (1998). *She*. Oxford: Oxford University Press. [First published in 1887.]

Hutchins, Francis (1967). *The Illusion of Permanance: British Imperialism in India*. Princeton, NJ: Princeton University Press.

James, Henry (1981). *The Portrait of a Lady*. Oxford: Oxford University Press. [First published in 1881; preface added in 1908.]

Kipling, Rudyard (1983). *Kim*. New York: Bantam Books. [First published in 1901.]

Koebner, Richard, and Helmut Dan Schmidt (1964). *Imperialism: The Story and Significance of a Political Word, 1840–1960*. Cambridge: Cambridge University Press.

Parry, Benita (1983). *Conrad and Imperialism: Ideological Boundaries and Visionary Frontiers*. London: Macmillan.

Richardson, J. S. (1991). "*Imperium Romanum*: The Language of Power." *Journal of Roman Studies* 81, 1–9.

Said, Edward (1985). *Orientalism: Western Representation of the Orient*. Harmondsworth: Penguin. [First published in 1978.]

Said, Edward (1993). *Culture and Imperialism*. London: Chatto and Windus.

Sandison, Alan (1967). *The Wheel of Empire*. London: Macmillan.

Schumpeter, Joseph (1951). *Imperialism and Social Classes*. New York: Augustus M. Kelly. [First published in 1919.]

White, Andrea (1993). *Joseph Conrad and the Adventure Tradition*. Cambridge: Cambridge University Press.

Young, Robert J. C. (2001). *Postcolonialism: An Historical Introduction*. Oxford: Blackwell.

24

America and Romance

Ulrika Maude

Moonlight, in a familiar room, falling so white upon the carpet, and showing all its figures so distinctly, – making every object so minutely visible, yet so unlike a morning or noontide visibility, – is a medium the most suitable for a romance-writer to get acquainted with his illusive guests . . . A child's shoe; the doll, seated in her little wicker carriage; the hobby-horse; – whatever, in a word, has been used or played with, during the day, is now invested with a quality of strangeness and remoteness, though still almost as vividly present as by daylight. Thus, therefore, the floor of our familiar room has become a neutral territory, somewhere between the real world and fairy-land, where the Actual and the Imaginary may meet, and each imbue itself with the nature of the other. (Hawthorne [1850] 1986: 35)

Hawthorne's meditations could perhaps best be paraphrased by Elissa Greenwald's observation that "romance reveals the margin of reality which is transformed by consciousness. That consciousness is, of course, historically constructed and partly determined by ideology" (1989: 7). Although the propensity for romance in the American novel was singled out early by authors such as William Gilmore Simms, Nathaniel Hawthorne, Herman Melville, and Henry James, the actual romance theory of American fiction was elaborated in the mid-twentieth century by critics such as F. O. Mathiessen, Lionel Trilling, Charles Feidelson, and, most prominently, Richard Chase. The theory, in other words, is by no means new. Nor, as we shall see, is it universally accepted, as a result of what has variously been considered its nationalistic or gendered bias or, indeed, the problematic categorization of modern prose into the genres of realism and romance. Contentious as the theory may be, "'romance' is the word that Brown, Irving, Poe, Hawthorne and Melville used to describe what they at least thought they were doing" (Bell 1980: xii). This chapter will map some of the major definitions of American romance over the past 50 years, and trace the main outlines of the American romance debate.

In 1948, Lionel Trilling argued that while the English novel emphasized social texture and verisimilitude, the American prose romance did not place equal emphasis on the portrayal of society. Trilling wrote (1981: 200): "the novel in America diverges from its classic intention, which . . . is the investigation of the problem of reality beginning in the social field. The fact is that American writers of genius have not turned their minds to society. Poe and Melville were quite apart from it; the reality they sought was only tangential to society." The main emphasis in Trilling's study, however, was not on the merits of individual authors, but on the specifically national characteristics of the literature written on the new continent. Indeed, "[u]ntil a tradition of American literature developed its own inherent forms, the early critic looked for a standard of Americanness rather than a standard of excellence" (Baym 1981: 125–6). This bias is reflected in most of the major critical studies of the period, most prominently, perhaps, in Richard Chase's highly influential book, *The American Novel and Its Tradition*, published in 1957. In his study, Chase consolidated the more tentative ideas laid out by early critics. Where Trilling had written about the Americans' "resistance to looking closely at society" (1981: 201), Chase argued that "since the earliest days the American novel, in its most original and characteristic form, has worked out its destiny and defined itself by incorporating an element of romance" (1957: viii). For Chase, the American tradition differed from the European, and specifically the English one, in being "freer, more daring, more brilliant" (1957: viii) than the latter, which tended to conform more fastidiously to realist conventions.

While the American tradition of fiction sprang from England, Chase's argument ran, it parted company with that tradition by incorporating a far more noticeable degree of romance than the English novel. By romance in the specifically American context, Chase was referring to what he called:

> an assumed freedom from the ordinary novelistic requirements of verisimilitude, development, and continuity; a tendency towards melodrama and idyl; a more or less formal abstractness and, on the other hand, a tendency to plunge into the underside of consciousness; a willingness to abandon moral questions or to ignore the spectacle of man in society, or to consider these things only indirectly or abstractly. (Chase 1957: ix)[1]

While one could argue, as Nina Baym has done (1981: 132), that we may "look in vain for a way to tell a believable story that could free the protagonist from society or offer promise of such freedom, because nowhere on earth do individuals live apart from social groups," the "large tracts of wilderness" the pioneers originally encountered in America made the idea much less implausible. Hence, in Chase's formulation, the "essential quality of America" is found in the "unsettled wilderness," which offers the individual the opportunity to inscribe onto the landscape "his own destiny and his own nature," which in turn could develop more independently on the new continent than in the socially restrictive old world (Baym 1981: 132).

Chase argued (1957: 2) that it was the "profound poetry of disorder" that distinguished the American novel from the English one. While the American novel had obviously developed from its English counterpart, at least in its earlier stages, it was, unlike its English precursor, stirred "by the aesthetic possibilities of radical forms of alienation, contradiction, and disorder" (Chase 1957: 2).[2] The English novel was "a kind of imperial enterprise, an appropriation of reality with the high purpose of bringing order to disorder" (Chase 1957: 4). The American novel, in turn, had merely aimed to "discover a new place and a new state of mind. Explorers see more deeply, darkly, privately and disinterestedly than imperialists, who must perforce be circumspect and prudential," Chase wrote (1957: 5). Contrary to several previous critics' views, many of the best American novels, Chase proposed, achieved "their very being, their energy and their form, from the perception and acceptance not of unities but of radical disunities" (1957: 7).[3] Chase cites the example of James Fenimore Cooper, often considered the first successful American novelist, and more specifically his novel *The Prairie*, originally published in 1827, which according to Chase was

> not inspired by an impulse to resolve cultural contradictions half so much as by the sheer romantic exhilaration of escape from culture itself, into a world where nature is dire, terrible, and beautiful, where human virtues are personal, alien, and renunciatory, and where contradictions are to be resolved only by death. (Chase 1957: 7)

Chase's own inflated rhetoric reveals his identification with romance, which he felt to be the quintessentially national characteristic of American prose.

For Chase, the contradictions that American fiction seemed to accommodate could be accounted for by the solitary position of the individual in American society, itself in turn triggered by frontier conditions and the doctrines of Puritanism. New England Puritanism, Chase argued, rested on "grand metaphors of election and damnation," "the kingdom of light and the kingdom of darkness," and the "eternal and autonomous contraries of good and evil" (1957: 11). Furthermore, Chase felt, "the New England Puritan mind itself seems less interested in redemption than in the melodrama of the eternal struggle of good and evil, less interested in incarnation and reconciliation than in alienation and disorder" (1957: 11). The final and perhaps most obvious contradiction inherent in American culture could be found in the "dual allegiance of the American," perched as he or she was between "the Old World and the New" (1957: 11).

Romance, for Chase, was a genre that lent itself to a "radical skepticism about ultimate questions" (1957: x). Another way of putting it might be to say that American fiction parted company with the British empirical tradition, whose obvious fictional manifestation was realism. This subversion in American letters, however, came with a price, for despite its more relaxed accommodation of ambiguities, Chase argued, American fiction lacked the complexity of the English novelistic tradition. This very lack of complexity, according to Chase, was one of the defining features of the romance novel. In the English realist novel, Chase proposed, character, with all its contextual references, took precedence over action. In American romance, it was action that took center stage, while character became "abstract and ideal, so much so in some romances that it seems to be merely a function of the plot" (1957: 13).

Chase cites the examples of Hawthorne's *The Scarlet Letter* and Melville's *Moby Dick*, where "the characters and events have actually a kind of abstracted simplicity about them. In these books character may be deep but it is narrow and predictable. Events take place with a formalised clarity" (1957: 5). Henry James makes a similar point about *The Scarlet Letter* in his biography of Hawthorne: "The people strike me not as characters, but as representatives, very picturesquely arranged" (1879: 114).[4] Fantastic events, which have a "symbolic or ideological, rather than a realistic, plausibility" tend to occur in romance novels (Chase 1957: 13). While Chase cautions the reader against any excessively rigid definitions of the American prose romance, he does state that since romance as a genre is less committed to verisimilitude than the novel, it tends to veer more toward myth, allegory, and "symbolistic forms" (1957: 13).

Chase refers to the American romance as a literary hybrid: "unique only in [its] peculiar but widely differing amalgamation of novelistic and romance elements" (1957: 14). For the American romance, while stemming from the European novel tradition, evolved into a new genre under diverse cultural conditions and aesthetic aspirations. Chase quotes at length William Gilmore Simms' 1853 preface to *The Yemassee*, originally published in 1835, where Simms argues that American romance could be considered the modern-day equivalent of the epic, an amalgam of the novel and the poem. Like the epic, the romance

> invests individuals with an absorbing interest – it hurries them rapidly through crowding and exacting events, in a narrow space of time – it requires the same unities of plan, of purpose, and harmony of parts, and it seeks for its adventures among the wild and wonderful. It does not confine itself to what is known, or even what is probable. It grasps at the possible; and, placing a human agent in hitherto untried situations, it exercises its ingenuity in extracting him from them, while describing his feelings and his fortunes in his progress. (Simms [1853] 1962: 6)

Romance, in short, parts company with Aristotelian poetics which lead to a realist aesthetic, a point also taken up by Hawthorne in his famous 1851 preface to *The House of the Seven Gables*. While Aristotle urged that literature should portray not the possible but the probable, Hawthorne exempted the author of romance from this constraint, for the author of romance, Hawthorne wrote, "has fairly a right to present that truth under circumstances, to a great extent, of the writer's own choosing or creation" ([1851] 1998: 1).

Likening romance to the epic had appropriately nationalistic connotations for a nation in search of its own artistic voice. Chase mentions a number of other American novels that bring to mind epic literature, amongst them Cooper's *The Prairie*, Herman Melville's *Moby Dick*, and Mark Twain's *The Adventures of Huckleberry Finn*. The psychological possibilities of romance, however, are nowhere as fully realized, Chase argues, as in the work of Nathaniel Hawthorne, who consolidated and helped theorize the generic prevalence of romance in American letters.

Chase argued that in the prefaces to his longer prose works, Hawthorne formulated a theory that identified romance as a " 'border' fiction," whether between "civilization and the wilderness" or, as in Hawthorne's own work, one that found its locus in "the borderland of the human mind where the actual and the imaginary intermingle" (Chase 1957: 19). An example of this intermingling can be found in one of Hawthorne's most famous shorter fictions, "Young Goodman Brown," first published in 1835. In the short story, set in seventeenth-century Puritan America, Goodman Brown, the protagonist, leaves his house late one evening against his wife Faith's wishes. He heads toward the forest, where he encounters a man "in grave and decent attire," who carries a "staff, which bore the likeness of a great black snake, so curiously wrought, that it might almost be seen to twist and wriggle itself, like a living serpent" (Hawthorne 1974: 75–6). In a tone of ambiguity endemic to Hawthorne, the narrator nonetheless hastens to add that this "must have been an ocular deception, assisted by the uncertain light" (1974: 76). To Goodman Brown's surprise, the mysterious man not only greets him but appears to know him and, what is more, is familiar with the protagonist's (Puritan) family, including his grandfather, who had "lashed the Quaker woman so smartly through the streets of Salem" (1974: 77).[5] Goodman Brown also encounters a pious villager, Goody Cloyse, who had "taught him his catechism, in youth, and was still his moral and spiritual adviser" (1974: 78). To the protagonist's horror, Goody Cloyse addresses Goodman Brown's traveling companion as "your worship," and as the narrative unfolds, he discovers that the entire village are heading for an initiation ceremony in which "there is a nice young man to be taken into communion to-night" (1974: 79). The young man turns out to be Goodman Brown himself, who encounters his entire community, both the pious villagers as well as the criminal or morally dubious ones, at the ceremony. The protagonist, distressed to find even his own wife and father at the temple in the rocks, witnesses the Devil inaugurate the ceremony:

> "Lo! there ye stand, my children," said the figure, in a deep and solemn tone, almost sad, with its despairing awfulness, as if his once angelic nature could yet mourn for our miserable race. "Depending upon one another's hearts, ye had still hoped, that virtue were not all a dream. Now are ye undeceived! Evil is the nature of mankind. Evil must be your only happiness. Welcome, again, my children, to the communion of your race!" (1974: 87–8)

The pious Goodman Brown resists temptation and turns his back on the ceremony. When he wakes up the following morning, he sees the villagers in their usual tasks. What has changed are not his friends and companions but Goodman Brown himself. The protagonist, who turned his back on the Devil, appears himself to have become the true victim of the incident:

> A stern, a sad, a darkly meditative, a distrustful, if not a desperate man, did he become, from the night of that fearful dream. On the Sabbath-day, when the congregation were

singing a holy psalm, he could not listen, because an anthem of sin rushed loudly upon his ear, and drowned all the blessed strain. When the minister spoke from the pulpit, with power and fervid eloquence, and, with his hand on the open Bible, of the sacred truths of our religion, and of saint-like lives and triumphant deaths, and of future bliss or misery unutterable, then did Goodman Brown turn pale, dreading, lest the roof should thunder down upon the gray blasphemer and his hearers. Often, awakening suddenly at midnight, he shrank from the bosom of Faith, and at morning or eventide, when the family knelt down at prayer, he scowled, and muttered to himself, and gazed sternly at his wife, and turned away. And when he had lived long, and was borne to his grave, a hoary corpse, followed by Faith, an aged woman, and children and grandchildren, a goodly procession, besides neighbors, not a few, they carved no hopeful verse upon his tomb-stone; for his dying hour was gloom. (1974: 89–90)

As George Dekker has observed (1990: 133), the story, "although historically grounded in the doctrines, repressions, and anxieties of frontier New England, [does] not purport to determine or 'explain' the subsequent course of regional or national history." Rather, its concerns are private and belong to "studies of the psychology of guilt" (Dekker 1990: 134). Moral values are rendered ambiguous in the story, for the reader is left pondering whether the sin has its origin in the villagers or, indeed, in Goodman Brown's own mistrustful mind. The story, in other words, compels the reader to question whose moral integrity is finally at stake.

From a contemporary perspective, one could argue that by rendering moral values questionable, Hawthorne's story in fact foregrounds not only its own fictionality, but the ambiguous nature of any representation of experience. In contrast, the English realist novel, in keeping with the empirical tradition, purported to be an accurate portrayal of the world in which it was set. Perhaps for these very reasons Chase felt that Hawthorne's formulation of romance as a type of liminal fiction that did not "swerve aside from the truth of the human heart" offered the perfect definition of a quintessentially *national* mode of writing (Hawthorne [1851] 1998: 1; Chase 1957: 19). Hawthorne's own work exemplified his point perfectly, by staging the complexity of the moral and psychological dilemmas its characters faced. What Chase seemed to be suggesting, in other words, was that Hawthorne's style portrayed a psychological or moral *realism* missing from the English novelistic tradition, and perhaps for these reasons, Chase felt that Hawthorne's self-conscious and experimental writing announced the "definitive adaptation of romance to America" (Chase 1957: 19). Hawthorne, Chase argued, was the first writer to respond to the specificities of the American imagination, managing to mirror what he called the American mind. "[T]he word 'romance,'" Chase summed up, "begins to take on its inevitable meaning, for the historically minded American reader, in the writing of Hawthorne" (1957: 20).

Chase's eagerness to conclude that American romance was finally a form of realism, albeit one "'of the human heart'" (1957: 19), is revealing in itself, for nineteenth-century Puritan America experienced a deep sense of moral unease about fiction, and especially romance, which was seen as "pure and dangerous fantasy" (Bell 1980: 14).

The subversive, even radical, undertones of romance can best be explained by recalling Frye's theorizing of the genre as the epitomization of Utopian longings. Fredric Jameson's much later interpretation is similarly suggestive of the genre's radical potential, for Jameson argued that it offered the reader "the possibility of sensing other historical rhythms" that were free "from that reality principle to which a now oppressive realistic representation is the hostage" (1981: 104). Romance, Jameson added, offered the reader "demonic or Utopian transformations of a real now unshakably set in place" (1981: 104).[6]

Due in part to the unease experienced about the potentially subversive nature of the genre, nineteenth-century definitions of romance did not always observe the distinction between fiction and fact. This, Michael Bell argued, manifested itself in a tendency, witnessed in such writers as Poe, Irving, and Melville, "to find in 'real' objects, scenes, or actions qualities associated with literary romance, especially the air of imaginative susceptibility induced or recalled by romantic literature" (1980: 15). Bell went on to say:

> By attributing to reality itself the "romantic" or "poetic" qualities of subjective imagination, American writers, influenced by associationist aesthetics and by the example of Scott, attempted to bridge the chasm between fantasy and experience, fiction and fact. It is in this sense that we should understand the vogues of historical romance and romantic history. They offered an apparent mode of reconciliation; they provided a rationale for... the conservative theory of romance by viewing "romance" as a "historical" or "realistic" mode whose "reality" just happened, luckily, to be "poetic" or "romantic".

In order to keep the gulf between fact and fiction as masked as possible, in other words, authors tended to set their stories in the "'misty past'": "[t]he more recent past or the present, by their insistent 'reality,' reopened the chasm between fact and fancy, revealing once again the primary fictionality of romance" (Bell 1980: 15–16). This was why Hawthorne, who tended to set his stories in seventeenth-century America, felt the need to apologize for the contemporary setting of *The House of the Seven Gables* (Bell 1980: 16). In the preface to the work, Hawthorne referred to "Romance" as an "exceedingly dangerous species of criticism," for it brought "fancy-pictures almost into positive contact with the realities of the moment" ([1851] 1998: 3). Bell therefore argued that what he coined "the nineteenth-century conservative theory of romance," which grew out of associationist aesthetics and the nation's moral objection to fiction, was ultimately little more than "a theory of realism, of rational mimesis" (Bell 1980: 19). Bell's argument, in other words, questioned Chase's categorization of nineteenth-century fiction into novel and romance, and picked up on the inevitable slippage in all romance theories of American literature.

Bell's corrections to the romance theory of American literature have not been unique. By foregrounding the difference between the English and American traditions, Chase's ideas served to emphasize the insularity of national literatures and so to promote a specifically American mode of writing. As several critics have remarked, Chase's agenda was clearly an ideological one, and his book triggered an ongoing debate about the romance theory of American fiction, which has most prominently been contested by the so-called New Americanists' revisionist critique.[7] In 1984, Nina Baym, who had a few years earlier prominently contested the gendered bias of the American canon, published what has now become a classic dissenting essay, "Concepts of the Romance in Hawthorne's America."[8] Baym argued that the romance theory had not only been "the single most powerful theoretical concept in modern American literary history and criticism," but also that it had been "indispensable for constructing a canon of major works; membership in the romance category has been a significant criterion for inclusion or exclusion" (Baym 1984: 426). Baym added that the dichotomy of novel and romance was far less pronounced than critics such as Chase had suggested, and that the two terms were in fact used interchangeably in the nineteenth century: "the term romance was deployed in the main, indeed massively so, simply as a synonym for the term novel" (1984: 430).

Baym, furthermore, argued that Hawthorne's own works did not fall naturally within the category of romance. Before *The Scarlet Letter*, Hawthorne had written only shorter fictions, which did not pertain to the genre of romance, due to their "interiority, slow pacing, relative lack of action, and heavy proportion of meditative prose" (Baym 1984: 438). Again, one might mention "Young Goodman Brown," with its brooding moral commentary, as an example. Furthermore, "if *The House of the Seven Gables* [a longer prose work originally published in 1851] departed in significant ways from Hawthorne's earlier practice, surely it did so in the direction of a greater contemporary realism and attention to surface finish, attributes which would create works different from but no more romancelike (in his age's terms) than his earlier fiction" (Baym 1984: 438). Baym went on further to attack Chase for his claim that in the preface to *The Marble Faun*, a romance Hawthorne had written in Italy, the author described romance as "the predestined form of American narrative" (Chase 1957: 18). To prove the problematic nature of Chase's claim, Baym cited the following passage from the preface to *The Marble Faun*, in which Hawthorne (referring to himself and his experiences in Italy in the third person) discussed precisely the difficulty, if not impossibility, of writing romance in the American context:

> Italy, as the site of his Romance, was chiefly valuable to him as affording a sort of poetic or fairy precinct, where actualities would not be so terribly insisted upon, as they are, and must need be, in America. No author, without a trial, can conceive of the difficulty of writing a Romance about a country where there is no shadow, no antiquity, no mystery, no picturesque and gloomy wrong, nor anything but a common-place prosperity, in broad and simple daylight, as is happily the case with my dear native land. It will be very long, I trust, before romance-writers may find congenial and easily handled themes either in the annals of our stalwart Republic, or in any characteristic and probable events of our individual lives. Romance and poetry, like ivy, lichens, and wall-flowers, need Ruin to make them grow. ([1860] 1990: 3)

As Michael Bell has observed, Hawthorne is pointing out that "conservative romance – the sort of integrative, 'related' romance linked with Europe – will be impossible in

America. We don't yet have enough 'reality' that is already 'romantic'" (Bell 1980: 20). One could add, in support of Baym's argument, that subsequent critics such as Larry J. Reynolds, Jonathan Arac, and Sacvan Bercovitch have suggested that prose works such as *The Scarlet Letter*, which *are* set in the past, namely in seventeenth-century Boston, clearly react to such mid-nineteenth-century developments as the question of slavery, "the European revolutions of 1848," and the Women's Rights Movement (Reynolds 2001: 4), which would render Chase's claim of the lack of social commentary in American letters, and in particular in Hawthorne, problematic.

Baym's major point was that Chase's romance theory was a retrospectively constructed misrepresentation. In the context of postwar America, it conveniently catered to nationalistic and other ideological needs, rather than actually corresponding to the nineteenth-century literary climate, where the dominant genre was in fact the novel. As Thompson and Link aptly (albeit unsympathetically) put it (1999: 3):

> Chase is charged [in Baym's article] with wanting to write a book about a uniquely American tradition that would help to "reconstruct" an American cultural and nationalist solidarity after the internally rupturing experience of World War II. To that end [Chase] layered American cultural history with a nationalistic bias that finds its literary analogue in the romance tradition.

Several critics have suggested that during the nineteenth century, the distinction between romance and the novel was "far less important than the more general distinction between *all* fiction and what conventional thought took to be 'fact.'... The avowed 'romancer' admitted or proclaimed what the 'novelist' strove to conceal or deny: that his fiction was a figment of imagination" (Bell 1980: xii). Hence the "bloated imagination" Thomas Jefferson referred to in his 1818 letter to Nathaniel Burwell on "the inordinate passion prevalent for novels":

> When this poison infects the mind, it destroys its tone and revolts it against wholesome reading. Reason and fact, plain and unadorned, are rejected. Nothing can engage attention unless dressed in all the figments of fancy, and nothing so bedecked comes amiss. The result is a bloated imagination, sickly judgement, and disgust towards all the real business of life. (Jefferson quoted in Bell 1980: 6)

The distinction between romance and the novel has also been seen as one of subject matter or theme rather than form, mode, or style (Poirier 1966: 8–11). In much debate, the determining characteristics are indeed clearly emotional rather than literary (Bell 1980: 15).

Critics have also found other cause to contest the romance theory of American fiction. The Americanist, Elissa Greenwald, argues that marked genre boundaries between romance and realism can and ought to be questioned, and George Dekker (1990: 15–16) goes as far as to state that the dichotomy appears so over-simple "as a scheme for discriminating between the major kinds of modern prose fiction that its survival seems something of a scandal. Even if it has some validity in theory, those who employ the distinction often press it so hard as to be very misleading about actual practice." This seems especially pertinent, as we have seen, in relation to Chase's argument that the American novel is less suited to the study of social issues or historical reality than the English, realist one. Elissa Greenwald, in her study of realism and romance (1989: 1), reminds us of the problematic supposition that realist novels should be seen "primarily as transcriptions of a society around them." The assumption that one *can* identify a reality outside the realm of the text is a contentious one to begin with, as poststructuralist theorists and critics of the past decades have so persuasively argued. Poststructuralist theory has not only questioned received assumptions about the representational nature of literature, but it has also forced us to reevaluate the validity of dichotomies, such as the one currently at stake. Greenwald suggests instead, as many others have done before her (including, one might argue, Hawthorne himself), that realism has firm links with romance, and it would therefore be more accurate to discuss the "interpenetration of romance and realism" in American fiction (Greenwald 1989: 4). This is something that even Chase acknowledged in his inclusion both of what he called "the novel" (i.e. realism) and the romance in the tradition of American fiction (Greenwald 1989: 4), and even more explicitly, in his endorsement of romance as a form of realism "of the human heart" (Chase 1957: 19). Greenwald takes Chase's point a step further (1989: 4), arguing that "romance is not so much a repudiation of mimesis as a particular way of viewing reality," which again renders romance a peculiar subcategory of realist fiction.

American fictional prose, the received reading goes, follows a trajectory or genealogy from Hawthorne to James. James, in this view, is seen to take off from where Hawthorne leaves his novels, perfecting the art, "fleshing out [Hawthorne's] themes, characters, and plots," and in the process, creating the American realist novel (Greenwald 1989: 3). The point was first made by T. S. Eliot, and further elaborated by Marius Bewley and Robert E. Long, all three of whom argue that James transforms Hawthorne's romance into realism. Greenwald, however, argues that Hawthorne's romance has an air of interiority that could be characterized as a form of psychological realism. "Young Goodman Brown" could again be cited as a case in point, since the story questions the origin of the darker forces and impulses it stages, suggesting to the reader that Goodman Brown's attitudes toward his fellow villagers could as plausibly be triggered by his own mistrustful nature as by the actions of the villagers themselves. Furthermore, "symbolism may be a consequence of repression which suppresses any literal meaning that is threatening or forbidden" (Greenwald 1989: 4). The most obvious example of this kind of symbolism would be the scarlet letter in Hawthorne's most famous novel, which functions as a sign or Rorschach blot that stands for a variety of repressed cultural motifs. Hawthorne, Greenwald sums up (1989: 4), "dramatizes the essential subjectivity of romance by showing how its projections are frequently the products of neurosis or self-contained introspection on the part of the characters." Where Henry James, the psychological realist, most resembles Hawthorne is precisely in his emphasis on interiority. Greenwald writes (1989: 4):

> [I]f James's adaptation of Hawthorne's romance forwarded the aims of realism, it also
> subtly undermined them from within, for romance blurred the line between inner and
> outer worlds, leading to the modernist undermining of the belief in a stable realm
> outside the self or even a stable self.

Furthermore, an "illusion of verisimilitude" is preserved in romance, for even though
it is clearly a "fanciful" genre, it nonetheless presents to the reader a familiar world,
unlike, say, fantasy literature (Greenwald 1989: 5).

Gary Thompson and Eric Link open their book on the American romance controversy (1999: 4) by pointing out that for "many revisionists, the American romance
tradition has . . . become a corroborative side-issue to a much larger one: the reinterpretation of the political ideology of mid-twentieth-century American culture as a
whole." In what amounts to an attack on the New Americanists' critique, the authors
argue that questions of gender, race, and ethnicity have, in the last two decades, taken
precedence over questions of genre: the romance theory, they write, is seen "as a
manifestation of conservative consensus politics intent on maintaining some post-war
anti-Stalinist, indeed, anticommunist 'Americanness'" (Thompson and Link 1999: 6).
New Americanists, they add, are unhappy about the elevation of practitioners of "the
'escapist' genre of romance" to "cultural or artistic idols," and instead see themselves
as restoring the voices of different kinds of minorities (1999: 6).

The self-named New Traditionalists start their counterargument by pointing out
that the "novel/romance distinction" was not invented in 1950, nor indeed in 1850,
but was in use before 1690. In addition, a hybrid amalgamation, often referred to as
"*modern romance*" or "*new romance*," can be found "from at least the late eighteenth
century," which further complicates a debate that has been approached too schemat-
ically (Thompson and Link 1999: 8). Thompson and Link give evidence of the
manner in which the novel/romance distinction was consistently employed in a
number of American magazines, and they discuss at length the hybrid nature of
modern romance, whose prime representatives are Poe and Melville. The latter's work,
they argue, "resulted in perhaps the most complex and sophisticated theoretical
rendering of the actual and the imaginary in antebellum America" (Thompson and
Link 1999: 107). The "New Traditionalists" stress that

> the novel tends toward representation of the "actual" or everyday world. The romance
> tends toward representation of an "imaginary" world or *a combination of the two*. The
> latter was precisely Hawthorne's understanding when he wrote in the preface to *The
> Scarlet Letter* that the province of romance is a kind of "neutral territory" somewhere
> *between* the real world and an enchanted world. The key phrase bears repeating: the
> romance is a discursive space "where the Actual and the Imaginary may meet, and *each
> imbue itself with the nature of the other.*" (Thompson and Link 1999: 15)

The slippage between realism and romance is hence always already built into
Hawthorne's own formulations, which "directly reflect the dominant understanding
in mid-nineteenth-century America of the two main varieties of modern prose fiction"

(Thompson and Link 1999: 14–15). The reader is reminded of Chase's original formulation of romance as a literary hybrid, consisting both of "novelistic and romance elements" (1957: 14).

Thompson and Link further argue that New Americanists have overlooked crucial aspects of the work of critics such as Mathiessen, Trilling, and Chase. They point out that Mathiessen stressed "the *necessary* connection between aesthetic and political concerns," as indeed did Trilling. Not only did the latter maintain that "the aesthetic and the ideological were intimately connected," but also he subtitled his book "*Essays on Literature and Society*" (Thompson and Link 1999: 8). The New Americanists' revisionist rendering of the American romance tradition, the authors argue, has hence itself been a misconstruction. Persuasive as some of the arguments Thompson and Link present may be, speculations of "male dominance in nineteenth-century romance [being] an *accident* of American literary history" do seem to thwart and undermine their thesis and reveal the authors' own ideological bias (Thompson and Link 1999: 185). The New Traditionalists' approach could be seen as indicative of the trend in some recent criticism of distance from theoretical and political concerns.

As we have seen, the debate about America and romance has come full circle. It began in the mid-twentieth century as a means of singling out the predominant characteristics of the writing of canonized authors, and at the same time, and perhaps more importantly, as a way of consolidating a specifically national tradition in American letters. With the new theoretical and political awareness that gained ground in the academy in the 1980s, New Americanists such as Michael Bell, Nina Baym, and Elissa Greenwald either qualified or vigorously contested Chase's romance theory of American fiction. Finally, New Traditionalists, such as Thompson and Link, have returned to the origins of the debate. They have found the need, in turn, to qualify the New Americanists' revisionist ideas, while reverting back to original ideas about the American canon. The last word about America and romance is far from said; the debate continues.

In "The Custom House" preface to *The Scarlet Letter*, Hawthorne, as we have seen, referred to romance as a "neutral territory" ([1850] 1986: 35). One cannot, with hindsight, miss the irony of Hawthorne's comment, for in the latter half of the twentieth century, American romance became anything but a neutral ground: "Apparent dichotomies between realism and romanticism, between novel and romance have become a critical, theoretical, historical, and, above all, political battleground" (Thompson and Link 1999: 4). Whether scholars have contested the theory on the grounds of its exclusion of women, racial or ethnic minorities, cold war ideological conflicts, ambiguous genre boundaries, or more recent developments in literary theory, or whether, alternatively, they have felt the need to defend original ideas of canonicity, the question of America and romance has, for the past 50 years, been the site of heated, often cutting, controversy and debate.

See also: chapter 12, "Gothic" Romance; chapter 20, Romance and Victorian Autobiography; chapter 21, Victorian Romance: Romance and Mystery; chapter

22, Nineteenth-century Adventure and Fantasy; chapter 23, Into the Twentieth Century.

Notes

1. Critics have, of course, taken issue with Chase's narrow definition of romance, and it should be noted that Chase himself often appears to part company with it in his analysis proper.

2. Chase argues that until 1880 or 1890 the English novel functioned as the model for the American one. Thereafter, American novelists tended to turn more to French and Russian influences (Chase 1957: 3).

3. Chase is referring here to D. H. Lawrence's argument regarding a reconciliation in American letters of opposites such as Dionysian energy and genteel spirituality, or Van Wyck Brooks' theory of the manner in which American prose collapses the distinction between "highbrow" and "lowbrow" culture.

4. James, no doubt, was referring to a lack of psychological depth and development in Hawthorne's work which James himself is famous for having contributed to the American novel.

5. This is no doubt an autobiographical reference, for Hawthorne's own great-grandfather, John Hathorne, acted as a judge in the Salem witchcraft trials.

6. Jameson is, of course, referring here to the context of late capitalism, but given the new nation's recently won independence from Britain, and the political possibilities this

seemed to offer, his thoughts seem to apply to the nineteenth-century American context.

7. In a now famous article entitled "Whose is American Romance?" Frederick Crews (1988) gives the following definition of New Americanists: "New Americanists are broadly post-structuralist in sympathy; they refuse to draw categorical distinctions between literature and history, foreground and background, art and advocacy, and they distrust all 'foundational' claims, whether they be for fixed aesthetic quality, authorial autonomy, a specifically literary kind of discourse, or scholarly detachment...For a New Americanist, social struggle must always be kept in view, and any concepts obscuring it – concepts, for example, of the 'American Character,' of the representative masterpiece, of the impish freeplay of signifiers – are to be not just rejected but exposed as ideology."

8. Baym's article, "Melodramas of Beset Manhood: How Theories of American Fiction exclude Women Authors," argued that authors canonized by such critics as Trilling "turn out – and not by accident – to be white, middle-class, male, of Anglo-Saxon derivation or at least from an ancestry which had settled in this country before the big waves of immigration which began around the middle of the nineteenth century" (Baym 1981: 129).

References and Further Reading

Arac, Jonathan (1986). "The Politics of the Scarlet Letter." In Sacvan Bercovitch and Myra Jehlen, eds., *Ideology and Classic American Literature.* Cambridge, MA: Harvard University Press, pp. 247–66.

Baym, Nina (1981). "Melodramas of Beset Manhood: How Theories of American Fiction exclude Women Authors." *American Quarterly* 33, 123–39.

Baym, Nina (1984). "Concepts of Romance in Hawthorne's America." *Nineteenth-Century Fiction* 38, 426–43.

Bell, Michael Davitt (1980). *The Development of American Romance: The Sacrifice of Relation*. Chicago and London: University of Chicago Press.

Bercovitch, Sacvan (1988). "Hawthorne's A-morality of Compromise." *Representations* 24, 1–27.

Bewley, Marius (1952). *The Complex Fate: Hawthorne, Henry James, and Some Other American Writers*. London: Chatto and Windus.

Brooks, Peter (1995). *The Melodramatic Imagination: Balzac, Henry James, Melodrama, and the Mode of Excess*. New Haven: Yale University Press.

Chase, Richard (1957). *The American Novel and its Tradition*. Garden City, NY: Anchor-Doubleday.

Cooper, James Fenimore (1988). *The Prairie*. London: Penguin. [First published in 1827.]

Crews, Frederick C. (1988). "Whose American Romance?" *New York Review of Books Online* 35: 16.

Dekker, George (1990). *The American Historical Romance*. Cambridge and New York: Cambridge University Press.

Eliot, T. S. (1918). "The Hawthorne Aspect." *Little Review* 5, 47–53. [Reprinted in F. W. Dupee, ed., *The Question of Henry James*. London: Allen Wingate, 1947, pp. 123–33.]

Fiedelson, Charles, Jr. (1953). *Symbolism and American Literature*. Chicago: University of Chicago Press.

Frye, Northrop (1957). *Anatomy of Criticism*. Princeton, NJ: Princeton University Press.

Greenwald, Elissa (1989). *Realism and the Romance: Nathaniel Hawthorne, Henry James, and American Fiction*. Ann Arbor: UMI Research Press.

Hawthorne, Nathaniel (1974). *Mosses of an Old Manse*. The Centenary Edition of the Works of Nathaniel Hawthorne, vol. X. Ohio: Ohio State University Press. [First published in 1846.]

Hawthorne, Nathaniel (1986). *The Scarlet Letter*. New York: Penguin. [First published in 1850.]

Hawthorne, Nathaniel (1990). *The Marble Faun*. New York: Penguin. [First published in 1860.]

Hawthorne, Nathaniel (1998). *The House of the Seven Gables*, ed. Michael Davitt Bell. Oxford: Oxford University Press. [First published in 1851.]

James, Henry (1879). *Hawthorne*. English Men of Letters. London: Macmillan.

James, Henry (1999). *The American*. World's Classics. Oxford: Oxford University Press. [First published in 1877.]

Jameson, Frederic (1981). *The Political Unconscious: Narrative as a Socially Symbolic Act*. London: Methuen.

Long, Robert E. (1979). *The Great Succession: Henry James and the Legacy of Hawthorne*. Pittsburgh, PA: University of Pittsburgh Press.

Mathiessen, F. O. (1941). *American Renaissance: Art and Expression in the Age of Emerson and Whitman*. New York: Oxford University Press.

Poirier, Richard (1966). *A World Elsewhere: The Place of Style in American Literature*. New York: Oxford University Press.

Reynolds, Larry J. (1985). "*The Scarlet Letter* and Revolutions Abroad." *American Literature* 57, 44–67.

Reynolds, Larry J., ed. (2001). *A Historical Guide to Nathaniel Hawthorne*. New York: Oxford University Press.

Simms, William Gilmore (1962). *The Yemassee*, ed. Alexander Cowie. Hafner Library of Classics 26. New York: Hafner. [First published in 1835.]

Thompson, G. R., and Eric Carl Link (1999). *Neutral Ground: New Traditionalism and the American Romance Controversy*. Baton Rouge: Louisiana State University Press.

Trilling, Lionel (1981). *The Liberal Imagination: Essays on Literature and Society*. Oxford: Oxford University Press.

25

Myth, Legend, and Romance in Yeats, Pound, and Eliot

Edward Larrissy

The use of myth, legend, and romance in Yeats, Eliot, and Pound is intimately bound up with ideas of renewal. This renewal is simultaneously sexual and social; indeed, it connects the sexual and social. At the same time, the use of these resources, in a context where the authority of traditional beliefs is being eroded, occurs in such a way that it emphasizes the insecurity and alienation of a world deprived of agreed myths, and this fact in itself colors the ambition of social renewal. Myth and romance can be used to offer a wide-ranging interpretation including the hope of renewal, but also one which, being embodied in imagery rather than the drily discursive, offers a surrogate for the lost aura associated with the sacred, and thus enacts a vital aspect of that very renewal.[1]

The most striking contribution Yeats made to the reinterpretation of myth and romance was to give new and vital shape to the matter of Ireland. There was one general advantage in turning to Irish tradition, apart from the mere fact that it was Irish, and this was that it had not grown stale with over-use in the way that classical matter might be claimed to have done. Indeed, Yeats compared the use he was able to make of it with the arduous freedom of William Blake's personal mythology, which was rooted in his experience of the London streets around him. Blake could speak of how "I see in deadly fear in London: Los raging round his anvil / Of death" (*Jerusalem* 15: 21–2, Erdman edition). As Yeats says, "[Blake] was a symbolist who had to invent his symbols . . . Had he been . . . a scholar of our time [he would] have gone to Ireland and chosen for his symbols the sacred mountains, along whose sides the peasant still sees enchanted fires" (1961: 114). Yeats, in the first poem in *The Wind Among the Reeds* (1899), describes the host of the Sidhe (or fairies) "riding from Knocknarea," a hill visible from Sligo town: one of the sites of his youthful wanderings, and also one of the sacred mountains to which he refers.

This comparison may remind us of the personal associations Irish myth and legend acquired in Yeats' work, Maud Gonne, for instance, becoming like a fairy enchantress. The right relationship of man and woman, that venerable topic of romance, is a prime preoccupation of Yeats, and it is scarcely surprising that this should be expressed in a combination of personal and universalizing tendencies. This combination can be related to Yeats' early use of the word "mood" in referring to his use of symbolism: he sees the symbolism of poetry, and thus the figures of which he makes use, as evoking moods that are themselves the expression of eternal supernatural powers. This emphasis on "mood" can be related also to the contemporary aesthetic context. It is reminiscent of the symbolist ideal of finding a formula for the *état d'âme*. It is also congruent with a certain impressionism, fashionable in the 1890s, and evident in the poems of Yeats' friend Arthur Symons. Indeed, so un-Yeatsian an artist as Joseph Conrad in 1897, in the preface to *The Nigger of the Narcissus*, appeals to the idea of "mood." In these tendencies we can also find the basis for an instructive contrast with Blake, to supplement our earlier comparison: for while the nineties tended to misrepresent Blake as a purveyor of ineffable symbolism, it is clear that Blake himself attributed definite, if complex, meanings to his mythological creations.[2] As it happens, Yeats, who really knew his Blake, and was the co-editor of the first serious edition of his poetry (1893, with Edwin Ellis), is less of an offender than many others in the period. Nevertheless, it remains the case that Yeats in general gives relative priority to suggestion and musicality as compared with Blake. And here we have the measure of a difference between the modern and the Romantic employment of romance. In the modern period, romance becomes involved in the same tendencies that arise in relation to mythology or merely personal symbolism: the quest for immediacy of presentation balanced by indirectness about intellectual meaning.

The matter of Ireland is voluminous and various. It might be found in a number of different sources. One of the most important for Yeats is the Ulster cycle of sagas in Old Irish, which for the most part recite the heroic deeds of Cuchulain, champion warrior of a legendary Iron Age king of Ulster, Conchubar. Much, though not all, of this story is to be found in the *Táin Bó Cuailnge* ("The Cattle Raid of Cooley"). The events described in these sagas are generally supposed to have occurred sometime near the beginning of the Christian era, but the earliest of the surviving versions of the *Táin* is in language dated to the ninth century. In a number of important poems, and in a cycle of plays, Yeats interprets Cuchulain as a symbol of selfless, but ultimately tragic, heroism; he also fashions him into an image of the heroic spirit of Ireland. In "Cuchulain's Fight with the Sea," the hero unknowingly kills his own son in battle. King Conchubar, "the subtlest of all men," realizes that, when he has brooded for a while, Cuchulain will slay him and his whole court in mindless rage and grief.[3] He therefore persuades his Druids to "Chaunt in his ear delusions magical" so that when he awakes he will fight with the sea, and indeed, Cuchulain proceeds to fight "the invulnerable tide" (36). This poem introduces the idea, expounded in the plays, that Cuchulain represents an honest, deeply felt, and selfless commitment to the heroic ethos, but one in which lack of self-regard may sometimes verge on the heedless and foolhardy. Conchubar, by contrast, is always seen as "subtle" and sometimes as cunningly self-serving. One of the plays, *On Baile's Strand* (1904), gives a fuller version of the story of Cuchulain's fight with the sea. By the addition of two low and venal characters, the Fool and the Blind Man, Yeats is able to develop the theme of Cuchulain's nobility: while he fights the waves, they occupy themselves in stealing from the ovens. (This is the incident to which Yeats refers years later in "The Circus Animals' Desertion.") Since Cuchulain is also a symbol of Ireland's heroism, it is reasonable to see some connection between the ideas in this play and the castigation of modern Irish materialism in *Responsibilities* (1914), where, in "September 1913," Yeats' refrain announces bitterly that "Romantic Ireland's dead and gone, / It's with O'Leary in the grave" (108–9). For Modern Ireland is inclined only to "fumble in a greasy till / And add the halfpence to the pence." The contrast between this spirit and that of true nobility is suggested in other poems from this volume, for instance, in "Beggar to Beggar cried," where the only ambitions are for comfort and ease: "And though I'd marry with a comely lass / She need not be too comely" (114–15). The heroism of the Easter Rising of 1916 surprised Yeats and won his slightly qualified admiration; and thinking, years later, in "The Statues," about one of its leaders, Patrick Pearse, he remembered him in the final hours of resistance "summon[ing] Cuchulain to his side" (337).

The great tragic story of Deirdre comes from the same body of material as the tales of Cuchulain, and refers to the same location and personages as those to be found in the *Táin*. In Yeats' play (1907), which bears her name, she becomes a female counterpart to Cuchulain. Yeats also takes the opportunity to develop the idea of Conchubar's ruthless cunning, since he desires Deirdre, who herself loves the handsome young warrior, Naoise. When the young lovers flee to Scotland, Conchubar tricks them into returning and has Naoise killed. Deirdre commits suicide. In fact, Deirdre is a female counterpart of Cuchulain both in point of heroism and as a symbol of Ireland. There was already a long tradition of symbolizing Ireland as a woman: Yeats' own Cathleen ni Houlihan is another example.

The Ulster cycle consists of heroic sagas. But an equally important source is of a somewhat different character. For Yeats also draws heavily upon the medieval Fenian cycle of romances, centering on the figure of Finn mac Cumhaill (Finn McCool) and his warrior band. The earliest matter in this tradition is to be found in manuscripts composed in Middle Irish, and dating from around the year 1200. To this body of material belong the legends of Oisin, or Ossian, the poet son of Finn, who was the basis for the figure of Ossian in the eighteenth-century pastiches of James Macpherson, and the subject of Yeats' first ambitious long poem, *The Wanderings of Oisin* (1889), which is also, as it happens, his first major foray into the matter of Ireland. Stories of Finn and Oisin remained part of the stock in trade of traditional Gaelic-speaking storytellers, both in Ireland and Scotland, into the early years of the twentieth century.

This should serve to remind us that oral tradition is another important source for Yeats: a source of folklore, especially about the fairies. He himself would seek this knowledge directly from the lips of the common people, although he might supplement what he discovered in this way by studying the researches of learned antiquarians. In fact, Yeats himself may be seen as an amateur folklore researcher. His *Fairy and Folktales of the Irish Peasantry* (1888), for instance, draws upon stories and legends recounted to him by people he met in the Sligo region.

Before considering the substance of *The Wanderings of Oisin*, one needs to note the significance of writing about this figure in the contemporary Irish context. Since the Scottish Ossian was based on Oisin, most of whose original adventures took place in Ireland, the Irish had long nursed a certain patriotic pique on the score of Macpherson's encouragement of "Scotland's pretensions to Ossian," as James Hardiman put it in the preface to his *Irish Minstrelsy* (1831). One of the Irish sources upon which Yeats could draw was the Dublin-based *Transactions of the Ossianic Society*, the title of which is intended to imply the true location of Ossian.

The Ossianic connection sheds an interesting light on the way in which Yeats hoped to assist Irish cultural renewal, for the figure of Ossian was still a romantic one in the late nineteenth century. It seems that many Irish writers, including Yeats, thought that Ireland should enjoy its proper prestige as the true source of a legend that had exerted an influence over the writers of Europe and North America for over a century: Goethe, Chateaubriand, and Whitman had been admirers. In at least one place, Yeats implies that the Celticism he espouses is influenced by Macpherson, for the original title of the poem now known as "The Rose of Battle" is a slight misquotation of a phrase from one of Macpherson's "Ossian" poems: "They went forth to the Battle but they always fell" (37). The poem depends upon a romantic cliché about the noble defeat of the Celt in the modern world. Yet the context of this poem, amid Yeats' own reworkings of the Fenian material, makes it clear that Ireland is the true source of the Celtic spirit.

Despite its late nineteenth-century subjectivist aspect, to which we have already referred, Yeats' "Celtic Twilight" (his phrase) can be appreciated for his achievement in transmitting to a wider readership the disturbing uncanniness of Irish romance. This quality offered Yeats, as an Anglo-Irish Protestant who lived in London for much of his youth, a way of conveying both his distance from, and his intimacy with, Ireland. Many knowledgeable commentators have derided Yeats' efforts as a falsification of the directness and simplicity of the best medieval Irish poetry. But the picture changes if one examines the Fenian romance material, and not just the kind of selection of early medieval verse which ends up in modern anthologies. It is from romance that Yeats takes his interest in Faery, and when this is understood, he seems to be an authentic mediator.

Typical of this uncanny quality is the lyric poem, "Song of the Wandering Aengus" from *The Wind Among the Reeds*. This has undoubted connections with Irish mythology and romance. As Yeats says in his notes to this volume, Aengus is "The god of youth, beauty and poetry. He reigned in Tir-nan-Oge, the country of the young."[4] Aengus goes out in the twilight of dawn into the hazel wood, because "a fire" is in his head. He cuts and peels "a hazel wand" and hooks a berry to a thread and fishes with the rod thus fashioned. There are undoubtedly magical overtones to the use of the word "wand," since Yeats also informs us that "The hazel tree was the Irish tree of Life or Knowledge, and in Ireland it was doubtless, as elsewhere, the tree of the heavens."

The language of the poem is compellingly evocative, in line with Yeats' interest in conveying "mood." For instance, the uncertain light of twilight is cunningly evoked: the words "flickering," "glimmering," and "brightening" chime together suggestively, and Yeats offers a vivid, impressionistic image of the flickering of the moths and that of the stars echoing and intensifying each other. Aengus catches a fish, which immediately turns into a woman whose magical potency is revealed when she calls him by his name and he has to follow her for the rest of his life. Yeats' note confirms that she is of the fairy kind, for "the Tribes of the Goddess Danu [the *sidhe* or fairies] can take all shapes, and those that are in the water take often the shape of fish." Of course, this is an allegory of falling in love, as well as of the connection between love and the poet's song. But it is also an accurate reflection of the way in which the Fenian romances show that the strangeness of the other world is never more than a breath away. A cogent way of supporting this assertion is to look at the use of Irish legend and myth by a quite un-Yeatsian contemporary Irish poet, Seamus Heaney. A poem that draws on a fantastic Irish legend is "Lightenings: viii," from *Seeing Things* (1991). This recounts how "The annals say" that when the monks of Clonmacnoise were at their prayers, a ship appeared above them, the anchor dragging along beneath, so that it caught itself in the altar-rails. A crewman came down a rope and struggled to release it, but the abbot pointed out that he could not bear their life beneath the boat and would "drown." So the monks assist him, and the man climbs back, "Out of the marvellous as he had known it." This quality of using romance to underline the strangeness of the ordinary is something that Heaney shares with Yeats: Heaney's version of the medieval romance of Sweeney (*Sweeney Astray*) provides a more impeccable example, generically speaking.

One can see a comparable quality in Yeats' *The Wanderings of Oisin*. As in the extensive tradition upon which it draws, this poem recounts how a woman of Faery, Niamh, rides across to Ireland from her home in Tír na nÓg ("The Land of the Young," i.e. of the immortal *sidhe* or fairies) because even in that other world she has heard of the fame of Oisin's prowess both as poet and warrior, and she wants him for her lover. Oisin cannot resist her unearthly beauty, and he rides off with her to the other world, where he will himself be immune from ageing as long as he remains there. In a passage near the end of the first part, already in the other world, Oisin discovers a broken lance-haft from his own mortal world lying in the foam on the seashore.

> When one day by the tide I stood,
> I found in that forgetfulness
> Of dreamy foam a staff of wood
> From some dead warrior's broken lance:
> I turned it in my hands; the stains
> Of war were on it, and I wept,
> Remembering how the Fenians stept
> Along the blood-bedabbled plains,
> Equal to good or grievous chance.

(365)

Of course, this passage emphasizes the mortality which is essential to the world he has left, and insinuates the point that humanity may love the beautiful but bitter mortal world they inhabit more intensely than some immutable ideal, which by its very nature may be alien to them. But equally noteworthy is the fact that the spear is broken: what he holds in his hand is, in fact, the broken haft. This fragment of his past has the effect of making the world he is in seem stranger, while at the same time its own appearance, part of an object once familiar to the warrior Oisin, also makes the world he has left seem strange. It operates like a quotation taken out of context. The effect is indubitably uncanny, in a way that may be illuminated by reference to Freud's discussion of E. T. A. Hoffmann's *The Sandman,* with its strange doublings and its beloved who turns out to be a mechanical doll (1919). For Freud, the ambivalence of what is *unheimlich* (literally, "un-homelike") lies in its paradoxical closeness to what is *heimlich* ("known" or "home-like," but also "secret" in a sinister way). The repetition of the familiar may be consoling, in that it buttresses the ego and its construction of the world. But it may also be unsettling when it installs something familiar precisely in the place where one should not expect it. This quality of the strangeness of the familiar is a characteristically modernist one, and may be contrasted with the postmodernist use of romance to be found in Paul Muldoon's "Yarrow," from *The Annals of Chile* (1994). Here we encounter not only Deirdre and Cuchulain, but also the Knights of the Round Table, though it is clear that personages from Muldoon's own youth are in some sense adopting these roles. In a characteristically self-conscious postmodernist way, the point is about the inseparability of identity from already existent signs and narratives.

As it happens, there must be a case for seeing Yeats' brilliant reworking of the Oisin story as reflecting his own Anglo-Irish identity. The son of a middle-class Protestant family, he spent much of his childhood in London, going for long summer holidays in the profoundly different world of Sligo, with its striking, legend-filled landscape and its storytelling peasantry. His *Autobiographies* recount how he felt at home in neither world, a condition which bears comparison with Oisin's. An important part of the Oisin tradition, reflected in Yeats' version, is the contrast between modern and ancient Ireland, and this is relevant to the comparison of nineteenth-century Ireland and England. Like a number of its precursors, Yeats' *Oisin* includes a colloquy between Oisin and St. Patrick which happens after Oisin has returned from the other world and grown old. In the intervening years, Ireland has been converted to Christianity, and Oisin ruefully and proudly recalls the heroic spirit of pagan Ireland. Arguably, newly Christianized Ireland can stand for England and modernity; and pagan, Fenian Ireland for the Celtic spirit which is still alive in the Sligo countryside. Yeats shared with other Celticists the hope that this spirit would be renewed and would triumph, in a new age, over the rationalism and materialism which had come to dominate Western society, not least the British empire. This means that Celticism is not only relevant to Celts, and it shows how Yeats' Celticism is paralleled by the later ideas about renewal to be found in modernism. The hope specifically for the renewal of Ireland's Celtic spirit becomes apparent in some of the Fenian poems of *The Wind Among the Reeds*.

The influence of the Fenian cycle on this volume is more substantial than it now appears, for the titles of a number of poems in the first edition, and in several subsequent editions, made references, which Yeats subsequently erased, to characters in Irish tradition, including Fenian ones. Thus, the original title of "He Thinks of his Past Greatness when a Part of the Constellations of Heaven" was "Mongan Thinks of his Past Greatness." Yeats' original note, when the poem was first published in *The Dome* (October 1898), explains that Mongan was "a famous wizard and king who remembers his past lives." But Mongan's best-known past life was as Finn mac Cumhaill, as Yeats could have discovered from a couple of sources; one of these, Kuno Meyer and Alfred Nutt's translation of *The Voyage of Bran* (1895), contains the information that "Mongán, however, was Find [Finn], though he would not allow it to be told."[5] Yeats, in a spirit of hermetic symbolism, keeps Mongan's secret and makes it part of the larger and only half-secret message of the first edition of *The Wind Among the Reeds*: namely, that the spirit of Finn is still alive, regrets the loss of its past glory, and, as we learn from other poems such as "The Valley of the Black Pig," may well be able to bring about an apocalyptic renewal of Ireland's destiny.

As we have seen, the symbolist lyrics of *The Wind Among the Reeds* contain much Fenian material. This volume was supplied with lengthy notes, taking up some third of its extent, and explaining the Irish material by reference to James Frazer's *Golden Bough*. While this fact is little known to contemporary readers, who are used to the various collected editions, which banish the notes to the back, it was for many years a given of knowledge about Yeats. This must have been true for Eliot, whose footnotes to *The Waste Land* (complete with reference to Frazer) are in part a comment on Yeats' use of myth and legend: a comment emphasizing the relative universality and centrality of Eliot's concerns, among which the Celtic plays its part, but in the more "European" form of the Arthurian legend. (Another way of looking at the footnotes is in a Scriblerian light, as both a satire on Yeats' romanticism, and a self-conscious parade of dry scholarship which is intended to be seen in relation to the poems' themes of sterility and the broken word.)

Of Eliot's works, *The Waste Land* is obviously the poem to which the topics of romance and myth are most relevant. Nevertheless, one has to confront the question of how centrally important they are to it. Notoriously, the notes were added only in order to fill the number of pages so that the printer could make a viable volume. Contemplating the anxiety they occasioned, Eliot remarked that he was sorry he had sent readers on "a wild goose chase after Tarot packs and the Holy Grail" (1957: 110). Yet in the notes there is a prioritization of some sources over others. Jessie L. Weston's *From Ritual to Romance* (1920) is given pride of place in the opening remarks; and Tiresias is said to be the chief personage, uniting all the rest. These references, and others, can undoubtedly be linked to themes within the poem. We need to realize that Eliot's remarks about the "wild goose chase" are intended to remind the reader of the proper function of poetry and the correct way of understanding its relationship to tradition. In the second section of "Tradition and the Individual Talent," Eliot asserts that "The effect of a work of art upon the person who enjoys it is an experience of a different kind from any experience not of art." The emphasis on the experience of art relegates to a secondary level those references which the poet may make to other works: "[The work] may be formed out of one emotion, or may be a combination of several; and various feelings, inhering for the writer in particular words or phrases or images, may be added to compose the final result." Above all, Eliot is telling us, the work of art brings about an aesthetic effect. If it provides us with information, this may be of interest or use to us, but it has nothing to do with what should be the poet's primary intention. The poem may also refer to other works; but to be successful, it needs to make these participate in "compos[ing] the final result" – which is an aesthetic effect. Whether or not we accept Eliot's modernist aesthetic, his admission that art does indeed take feelings, phrases, and images as its material means that he cannot exclude referentiality, and we are entitled to ask such questions as, "What are these 'feelings' about?"

The prominence Eliot gives to Jessie L. Weston bears directly on the title and the central subjects of the poem. Not only does she employ the term "Waste Land" (two words) but in the fertility myths she examines, a recurring figure is the Fisher King, impotent and reigning over a land which has become waste because it reflects his condition. He and the land can be saved by the arrival of a stranger who will put or answer certain ritual questions. Weston notes that the Grail legend, with its pure knight who performs the same role as the stranger, has strong similarities with the myths of the Fisher King. It is obvious that both sets of legends belong to the sort of mythological materials examined by Frazer. Of course, Frazer's positivism in relation to the genesis of the myths of dying gods is not shared by either Yeats or Eliot. Frazer sees such myths as representing primitive ritual practices whereby the king's sexual potency symbolizes and guarantees fertility. He has to be ritually sacrificed in order to be replaced by a new young king and thus maintain the cycle of fertility. For Yeats, in contrast, as for Blake and Shelley, vegetative myths represent a universal structure of spiritual death and resurrection, of which the poet should be the prophet. In Yeats' case one might almost say that priest, or at least magus, was a better word. Eliot takes a different but parallel course. The objective implication of *The Waste Land*, even though its composition predates his conversion, is that the Christian narrative is the most significant example of the myth of the dying god because it embodies the idea of spiritual renewal linked to the objectivity of ethical truth, and transcending the subjective vision of the poet.

The specifically sexual elements in the Fisher King story are also of undoubted importance. For Eliot, as for Yeats, the relationship of man and woman is a central preoccupation. Whether it be Tiresias, or Oedipus, or Hamlet, or the Fisher King impotently presiding over a wasteland, Eliot's preferred myths, legends, and romances are centrally concerned with sexual anxiety and disturbance. Eliot uses this material to represent the mutual alienation of the sexes, and to suggest that this is a concomitant of loss of faith, which assists in the destruction of the creative word. The last pages of *The Waste Land* make a link between the failure to communicate in sexual love and the waiting – possibly hopeless – for a new spiritual dispensation. Indeed, failure specifically of communication between the sexes is a frequent theme, from *Prufrock* via "Portrait of a Lady" to *The Waste Land* itself. Central to this failure is the failure of the speaker, his inarticulacy: "It is impossible to say just what I mean." At the same time, the image of women is often very negative, though in their case the malady seems to take a different form. This may be unsettling but empty articulacy: the women who "come and go / Talking of Michelangelo," or who fix the speaker with a verbal pin in *Prufrock*. Or it may be some indefinable quality that goes beyond words but is still threatening – something of which her scent may be an acceptable symbol, as with the perfume which "confused ... the sense" in *The Waste Land*. Or it may be a sense of threat so powerful that it has to be conveyed in terms of a figurative castration, as with the image of John the Baptist's head in *Prufrock*. The connection of sexual and spiritual malaise encouraged by Weston facilitates Eliot's own links between his array of troubled themes, and hints at a religious solution which might offer a unifying redemption, and a renewed grounding, of the self.

There had already been hints in Eliot's earlier work, unsupported by romance and myth in a strict sense, but alluding to Dante, that modernity as such could be conceived as a kind of Hell, and the poem as a kind of *Inferno*. Already in *The Love Song of J. Alfred Prufrock* the city is the locus of industrial pollutants which fill the air with "yellow fog," a fog with disturbingly soporific connotations: it seems somehow to muffle consciousness in its impenetrability, and appropriately enough it "curls once about the house / And falls asleep." Thematically parallel with this image is that of the evening sky as "a patient etherised upon a table." As with the yellow fog, this presents an extinction of consciousness in which an artificial chemical element plays its part. Such extinction figures Prufrock's infirmity of will and his entrapment within his own subjectivity to a pathological degree, unable to bring consciousness into a right relationship with action: unable to muster the decisiveness to speak the necessary word – a proposal, a declaration of love – to the difficult woman who is the object of his "love song." He bears a passing resemblance to the figure in the epigraph from Dante's *Inferno* XXVII, which directly precedes the opening of the poem. Guido da Montefeltro is to be found in the Circle of the Deceivers, for which reason the tip of his tongue trembles symbolically. The concern of one of the damned that his reputation should not suffer is comical in the original text, and along with his location in Hell, it raises a question about the difference between the appearance and the reality of the speaker. Prufrock, however, is not so much a deceiver because he intends to be one, but because of what he does not know about himself. In the essay "Hamlet and his Problems," Eliot speaks of the failure of Shakespeare's play as being caused by the incoherence of the presentation of the character of the prince. It fails to offer an "objective correlative" for the emotions expressed by Hamlet, that is to say, a formula for these emotions made up of "actions, events and objects," which we can decode, or which allows us to apprehend them. Specifically, "Hamlet the man is full of some stuff which he could not drag into the light and contemplate." This stuff is to do with his desire for and fear of the mother; in other words, there is an unconscious and unexamined Oedipal problem in Hamlet's character. Prufrock expressly disclaims a comparison of himself with Hamlet: "No! I am not Prince Hamlet, nor was meant to be." Yet there is one comical similarity to Hamlet in Prufrock's strongly emphasized indecision. The other similarity is in the "stuff" which he, like Hamlet, cannot contemplate.

It is inappropriate to psychoanalyze Eliot, however. This is not so much because he knows what he is doing (though he does) as because Prufrock's lack of self-knowledge is part of the very meaning of the poem, so that to treat the poem as a kind of unconscious dream-text is to misunderstand it, and to lay oneself open to misapprehension of its strategies. Eliot is attempting to provide an objective correlative for Prufrock's emotions, and in the process he must reveal his lack of self-knowledge. A good test case for asking whether or not Eliot is, in general, master of these materials is provided by the prose-poem "Hysteria" from the same volume: "I was drawn in by short gasps, inhaled at each momentary recovery, lost finally in the dark caverns of her throat, bruised by the ripple of unseen muscles." It is not credible that Eliot should be unconscious of the sexual connotations of these words.

It is important, however, to answer the question of why this kind of sexual disturbance should be an essential characteristic of Eliot's Hell of Modernity; why, that is, the fear of woman should have this role alongside the infernal sordidness of the modern city and the sense of disconnectedness and alienation which is inseparable from it. And the answer appears to lie in the nature of modern woman. At the same time, it is important to grasp that sexual disturbance appears to be the prime, founding disturbance. The myth of Tiresias, which Eliot's notes claim is so important to an understanding of *The Waste Land*, ends with Juno blinding him and Jupiter giving him the gift of prophecy and long life in return. Eliot is telling us that the poetic voice of the poem is enabled by a figurative castration. It is a broken voice, however; "uniting all the rest," it cannot conceal the patent fragmentation and multivocality of a poem of which the working title had been "He do the police in different voices." This fact might serve to remind us of a striking ambiguity in Eliot's technique: is the poem "a heap of stony rubbish" and a pile of "fragments," or is it an innovative poem whose fragmentariness is a daring employment of the modernist collage principle? It is both, of course; we do not have to choose. We can, indeed, attempt to bring the two perspectives together in one view; and Eliot has offered hints enough to enable us to do so: *The Waste Land* is comparable to the *Inferno* in attempting to be a poem about Hell which offers us an objective correlative. To put it more crudely, a good poem about Hell must be hellish in its manner. This realization should help to remind us that the negative associations of inarticulacy in the speaker, and of something indefinable and irrational in woman, may, ironically, be related to the radical formal qualities of the poetry. In any case, Tiresias is an appropriate uniting principle precisely because he cannot unite the words of the poem. He is there to embody the sterility, emptiness, failure of communication, and sexual failure which are its subject; as it says, "I can connect nothing with nothing." It is Jessie L. Weston and the Grail legend that suggest the possibility of another way of speaking. The myths themselves contain the clue: the Fisher King or the Grail

Knight has to "put or answer certain ritual questions"; that is, they have to find words which will effect a connection with the truth – in the case of the Grail Knight, with transcendent truth.

Despite the Hell of Modernity, however, myth and romance in Eliot are not used in a one-sided, mock-heroic manner to show up the paltriness of the modern world. Admittedly, there is that element in the way they are used: one might add the filthiness of the river sweating oil and tar, or the supposedly mindless simplicity of the ragtime music in *The Waste Land*, which are contrasted with the beauty and seriousness of the art and society of the past. Yet the past is also full of corruption and spiritual emptiness, as the stories to which we have referred make clear. An unfriendly view would be that Eliot seeks to have it both ways, so to speak: to condemn modernity, while also bewailing fallen human nature. A more measured view would be that he sees human nature as irredeemably fallen throughout history, but appraises the modern world as an exceptionally troubled and endangered era.

On this showing, Eliot was ready enough for a return to the faith. After the absolute inanition of meaning in *The Hollow Men*, the rediscovery of the framework of sacred truth provided by Christianity permits a new and positive image of woman influenced by the figures of the Blessed Virgin Mary and Beatrice, at the same time that the recognition of the Word permits a renewed sense of the possibilities to be found in poetic words in *Ash Wednesday*. At least in the thinking that lies behind this poem, it could be claimed that Eliot, in contrast to the direction suggested by Jessie L. Weston's book, has traveled from romance to ritual.

The ambition of universality, found in Eliot's attempt to represent a moment of Western culture, should lead into a consideration of the extent to which myth, for modern poets such as Pound and Eliot, offers a way of achieving a profound understanding of experience in a world characterized by alienation, absence of agreed narratives, and the overturning of the sacred. In this light, it is interesting to remember the way in which the body of myth and legend in Pound subsists alongside the emphasis on clarity and accuracy of perception to be found not only in his imagist phase but throughout his work: such an emphasis, however, tends to reinforce the sense of the observer's isolation (e.g. "In a Station of the Metro") and the difficulty of achieving coherence, and this can obviously be illustrated from *The Cantos*.

Yet again, as in Yeats and Eliot, one finds that myth and romance in Pound are deployed to suggest the possibility of the rediscovery of a right relation between man and woman, as in the tales of troubadours or some of the stories from Ovid upon which he draws. Again, as in Yeats and Eliot, sexual renewal is impossible to separate from social renewal: when it is said, at the beginning of Canto LXXXI, that "Zeus lies in Ceres' bosom," this is a reminder of the Emperor's relationship to the sky-god and the earth (which he can save from being a wasteland). At the same time, the particular stress on Ovid's *Metamorphoses* is a reminder of the way in which for Pound, and for his friend H.D., as for Yeats and to some extent Heaney, the recreation of myth, legend, and romance can be a way of representing the irruption of the strange and marvelous into creation.

The nature of Pound's engagement with romance can in large part be deduced from his *The Spirit of Romance* (first published in 1910). What Pound means by this spirit may well have something to do with "strangeness," for he quotes Pater on the addition of "strangeness" to "beauty" in romantic art, and there is no disapproval implied.[6] Indeed, as Peter Makin points out (1985: 8), the book is "thoroughly imbued with Paterism, in its language (key words are 'fine,' 'subtle'), its choice of materials (small, private, craftsman-like objects, such as Arnaut Daniel's lyrics and the church of San Zeno), and its hidden assumptions," which are that the objects of criticism possess particular "virtues" or "qualities." "Strangeness" is admitted: Pound refuses to get involved in the debate of classic against romantic, which might have led to a supposedly classical rejection of this quality. Nevertheless, the chief impetus behind the book lies elsewhere, in defining that characteristic "virtue" which belongs to romance: this is the "spirit" to which the title refers. A central point for this definition is raised in relation to Dante, a figure of surpassing importance for Pound, not least in the *Cantos*. Pound remarks that Dante is the culmination of the Middle Ages rather than the beginning of the Renaissance, and we are entitled to infer at the very least that this indicates a preference for those medieval works which can be seen as conveying the spirit of romance (166). He goes on to suggest the aesthetic difference involved: "In architecture, mediaeval work means line: Renaissance work means mass" (166). And although he concedes that "the analogy in literature is . . . inexact," he notes, as if there is a connection with the idea of "line," that Dante "sought to hang his song from the absolute, the center and source of light" (166). The "virtue" of romance consists in a kind of keen purity, which ultimately becomes one with Pound's later, bracing critical dicta, not least those relating to Imagism, with their horror of superfluous words. Since this is the case, it is scarcely surprising that Pound thinks of this quality as one that is "modern," citing the example of Villon (167).

This raises the question of how far the aesthetic values that Pound prizes are seen by him as trans-historical. The question has particular relevance, since it bears on the "modern" relationship to romance. In the preface ("Praefatio ad Lectorem Electum"), Pound offers an insight into his sense of how one artistic period can be like another:

> It is dawn at Jerusalem, while midnight hovers above the Pillars of Hercules. All ages are contemporaneous. It is B.C., let us say, in Morocco. The Middle Ages are in Russia. The future stirs already in the minds of the few. This is especially true of literature, where the real time is independent of the apparent, and where many dead men are our grandchildren's contemporaries, while many of our contemporaries have been already gathered into Abraham's bosom, or some more fitting receptacle. (1952: 8)

An inadvertent reading might fasten on the statement that all ages are "contemporaneous" and assume that it implied some kind of universal homogeneity. Yet the passage is clear that different cultures are usually at different stages: when it is dawn at Jerusalem, it is still midnight at the Pillars of Hercules. The point is rather that, despite these differentials, the virtue of good art cannot be tied to one period. On

Pound's reading, the spirit of romance goes back at least as far as the late classical period, and reawakens at various points, including the modern age.

Accordingly, Pound uses a long time-span from which to demonstrate the qualities of romance. Of central importance is the relationship of literary language to the language of the people. Taking his cue from Apuleius, author of *The Golden Ass*, Pound attempts to trace a tradition of Latinity, going back to the late Roman empire, which is substantially founded in a conscious use of the vernacular:

> Apuleius writes in a style not unlike Rabelais, a style that would, they tell us, have offended Tacitus and disgusted Cicero and Quintilian. Like Dante and Villon, he uses the tongue of the people, i.e. an incult Latin. The language of the Roman court was then Greek. The Troubadours, Dante and Apuleius, all attempt to refine or to ornament common speech. (12–13)

This is another characteristic that we may relate to what Pound calls "modern." A related point is that, while not necessarily making a fetish of it, Pound nevertheless values highly a certain quality of rough-hewn outspokenness. Villon receives high praise, and he is introduced by means of a contrast with some of the "fine gentlemen" of the romance tradition; his "unvarnished, intimate speech" is noted; but this attribute is firmly tied to certain elements in Provençal poetry (167). Pound's emphasis here can be related to his prizing of the martial qualities of the verse of the troubadour Bertrans de Born: it is not for "his love songs that he is most remembered, but for the goad of his tongue, and for his scorn of sloth, peace, cowardice, and the barons of Provence" (45).

These qualities are understood by Pound as essentially masculine. It is for this reason that they are intimately related to the softer aspects of romance and courtly love. "Psychology and Troubadours," written in 1916 and not to be found in the first edition of *The Spirit of Romance*, relates the troubadour phenomenon to fertility myths and what may be learnt from them: immortal truths about the psychology of sex, with sexual division constituted as a dynamic polarity. Pound remarks that he believes in "a sort of permanent basis in humanity, that is to say, I believe that Greek myth arose when someone having passed through delightful psychic experience tried to communicate it to others" (92). Sex is at the heart of this experience; and the polarities may be "positive and negative," "North and South," "sun and moon'" (93). In the "chivalric" mode, these poles produce a "charged surface" between "the predominant natural poles of two human mechanisms" (94). These beliefs were to remain at the heart of Pound's work, early and late.

The presentation of a virile persona, and notions of the feminine that complement it, are constants in the poetry and associated criticism, and their original basis is in Pound's reading of romance. The link can be made by looking at an early example, "Sestina: Altaforte," which was originally read aloud in a suitably assertive manner to a group of poets, and to the admiring Henri Gaudier-Brzeska, in the Eiffel Tower restaurant in Soho. The persona is that of Bertrans de Born:

The man who fears war and squats opposing
My word for stour, hath no blood of crimson
But is fit only to rot in womanish peace
Far from where worth's won and the swords clash.
For the death of such sluts I go rejoicing.

(Pound 1968: 29)

When we have moved on to the more modernist phase of vorticism, the vortex is said to impregnate the "passive vulva" of London (Pound 1960: 204). The energy of troubadour art derives from the masculine or positive pole, so we should not be surprised to find that, in a letter to John Quinn, Pound describes the energy of another vorticist, Wyndham Lewis, as "jism bursting as white as ivory... Spermatozoon, enough to repopulate the island with active and vigorous animals."[7]

It is not only the best art that is masculine. The ruler should also be, as Pound described Mussolini, "a male of the species." In *Hugh Selwyn Mauberley* the turpitude of the modern age consists in choosing "a knave or an eunuch / To rule over us." In this connection, it should be noted that in Canto LIV the right order of things under the Fourth Dynasty (Tsin) is threatened by eunuchs, who become powers behind the throne, singing "emptiness is the beginning of all things." The link between the eternal truth about sexuality and what Pound sees as political sanity is succinctly made at the beginning of Canto LXXXI: "Zeus lies in Ceres' bosom / Taishan is attended of loves." The sky-god fertilizes the goddess of the crops: each part of the order of nature reflects the eternal polarity, and this is the only basis of fruitfulness in the cosmos. Taishan is the sacred mountain of China where the Great Emperor of the Eastern Peak lived. The Emperor is a living expression of the sky-god, enjoying "the mandate of heaven."

The line about Zeus derives from Pound's inventory of fertility myths. The reason why Ovid's *Metamorphoses* is so important a presence in the *Cantos* is partly to do with its status as a repository of such myths. However, there is another point to bear in mind, a related one about the power of sexual passion to induce ecstasy or frenzy: a power for transformation, and a dangerous one. Canto IV, for instance, brings together the story of Philomela (lines16–20) with that of the troubadour Cabestan (Guillen da Cabestan, lines 21–31), who fell in love with the lady Soremonda. Her jealous husband killed him and served up his heart cooked. Soremonda vowed never to eat again and threw herself out of a window. Then we have the story of Actaeon (ll. 32, 57–64), who, having been turned into a stag by Diana because he had seen her bathing, ended up being torn to pieces by hunting dogs. This is followed by a reference to the story of Piere Vidal, another troubadour, who fell in love with the Lady Loba ("she-wolf") and went mad. He dressed in wolfskins and ran wild in the woods, where he was hunted by dogs. Apart from the emphasis on metamorphosis, it is clear from these juxtapositions that Pound is intent on asserting the equivalence of the spirit of romance with that of the Greek myths. In this respect he is at one with Yeats and Eliot. The reason for this tendency within modernism has much to do with the point at which we started: modernism is not much concerned with distinctions between myth and romance – or, if you like, between texts and traditions that recount myths on the one hand, and the body of texts that can be called "romances" on the other. It is more concerned to draw myth and romance into the activity of providing a surrogate for the fading aura of the sacred. In the process, it eschews pedantry about the sources and employment of its imagery in favor of a reworking in the light of the poet's vision.

See also: chapter 3, THE POPULAR ENGLISH METRICAL ROMANCES; chapter 17, POETRY OF THE ROMANTIC PERIOD; chapter 18, VICTORIAN ROMANCE: TENNYSON; chapter 19, VICTORIAN ROMANCE: MEDIEVALISM; chapter 23, INTO THE TWENTIETH CENTURY; chapter 24, AMERICA AND ROMANCE; chapter 29, BETWEEN WORLDS.

Notes

1. An account which owes something to Fredric Jameson in his "Romance and Reification: Plot Construction and Ideological Closure in Joseph Conrad," in *The Political Unconscious: Narrative as a Socially Symbolic Act* (London: Methuen, 1981), pp. 206–80.

2. For a comparison and contrast of the ways in which Blake and Yeats represent aspects of the mind, see Edward Larrissy, "Zoas and Moods: Myth and Aspects of the Mind in Blake and Yeats," in *Myth and the Making of Modernity*, ed. Bell and Poellner (1998: 25–34).

3. W. B. Yeats, *The Poems: A New Edition*, ed. Richard J. Finneran, 2nd edn. (London and Basingstoke: Macmillan, 1989), p. 35. All subsequent references to Yeats' poetry will be from this edition and cited by page number.

4. Some of Yeats' notes may be found near the end of collected editions of his poems, but the easiest way for contemporary readers to find the full original version is to consult the variorum edition of the poems.

5. Kuno Meyer and Alfred Nutt, *The Voyage of Bran Son of Febal to the Land of the Living* (1895–77), I, p. 52. The meaning of the Mongan connection is discussed by Edward Larrissy, *Yeats the Poet* (1994: 73).

6. Ezra Pound, *The Spirit of Romance* (1952: 14). All subsequent references to this work will be from this edition and cited by page number.

7. Quoted in Richard Humphreys, "Demon Pantechnicon Driver: Pound in the London Vortex, 1908–1920," in *Pound's Artists* (1985: 58).

References and Further Reading

Bell, Michael, and Peter Poellner, eds. (1998). *Myth and the Making of Modernity: The Problem of Grounding in Early Twentieth-Century Literature*. Amsterdam and Atlanta, GA: Rodopi.

Eliot, T. S. (1957). *On Poetry and Poets*. London: Faber.

Eliot, T. S. (1920). *The Sacred Wood*. London: Methuen, pp. 42–53. ["Tradition and the Individual Talent" first published in 1919.]

Freud, Sigmund (1919). "The Uncanny." Translated in *The Standard Edition of the Works of Sigmund Freud*, ed. James Strachey, vol. 17. London: Hogarth Press, 1953, pp. 217–56.

Humphreys, Richard (1985). *Pound's Artists: Ezra Pound and the Visual Arts in London, Paris and Italy*. London: Tate Gallery.

Larrissy, Edward (1990). *Reading Twentieth Century Poetry: The Language of Gender and Objects.* Oxford: Blackwell.

Larrissy, Edward (1994). *Yeats the Poet: The Measures of Difference.* Hemel Hempstead: Harvester Wheatsheaf; New York: Prentice Hall, 1995.

Makin, Peter (1985). *Pound's Cantos.* London: George Allen and Unwin.

Meyer, Kuno, and Alfred Nutt (1895–7). *The Voyage of Bran Son of Febal to the Land of the Living.* 2 vols. London: David Nutt.

Pound, Ezra (1952). *The Spirit of Romance.* 2nd, rev. edn. London: Peter Owen.

Pound, Ezra (1960). *Pavannes and Divagations.* London: Peter Owen.

Pound, Ezra (1968). *Collected Shorter Poems.* 2nd edn. London: Faber.

Smith, Stan (1994). *The Origins of Modernism: Eliot, Pound, Yeats and the Rhetorics of Renewal.* Hemel Hempstead: Harvester Wheatsheaf.

Surette, Leon (1993). *The Birth of Modernism: Ezra Pound, T. S. Eliot, W. B. Yeats, and the Occult.* Montreal and Kingston: McGill-Queen's University Press.

Weston, Jessie L. (1920). *From Ritual to Romance.* Cambridge: Cambridge University Press.

Yeats, W. B. (1961). *Essays and Introductions.* London: Macmillan.

26

Twentieth-century Arthurian Romance

Raymond H. Thompson

Through the centuries since its inception in the Dark Ages, Arthurian legend has endured in a variety of forms. Each has left its mark, but none more than the chivalric romance of the Middle Ages, for it is in this form that the legend has exercised its greatest influence upon later writers. In the pages of Sir Thomas Malory's *Morte Darthur* and the many retellings based upon it, new generations have discovered the magical world of King Arthur and his Knights of the Round Table. Thus captivated, they have ventured yet further afield, encountering Malory's antecedents: Welsh heroic tales and poems, Latin chronicles and saints' legends, verse and prose romances in French and almost every other language of Europe. Acquaintance with the literature has led in turn to curiosity and speculation about its historical basis. Yet despite this range of material, it is the romance form of Arthurian legend that continues to wield the most powerful influence, not only through Malory's fifteenth-century compilation, but increasingly through such diverse romances as Chrétien de Troyes' *Lancelot* and Béroul's *Tristan* (French, twelfth century), Wolfram von Eschenbach's *Parzival* and Gottfried von Strassburg's *Tristan* (German, thirteenth century), *Sir Gawain and the Green Knight* and *The Wedding of Sir Gawain and Dame Ragnell* (English, fourteenth to fifteenth century). These and others have provided, not only a fruitful source of material to reshape and imitate, but also models of how to treat that material. As a result the romance has permeated other literary forms whenever they deal with Arthurian legend.

Even when the authors react against their romance models, moreover, deliberately choosing gritty realism and an anti-romantic mood, they find it almost impossible to escape its influence entirely. The characters that they create have, after all, been shaped by romance. To change them too radically would sever their links with Arthurian legend. Tristan may be a vicious thug or a sensitive poet, but he may not escape his fatal attraction for Isolde; Merlin may be a scheming politician or a divinely inspired seer, but he may not abandon his responsibility to help Arthur win the throne; for his part, Arthur may be a brutal tyrant or a compassionate ruler, but, however reluctant or belated he may be in novels like Tim Powers' *Drawing of the Dark* (1979), where he is reincarnated in a later age, he may not refuse his destiny to lead the heroic struggle against the dark tide that must eventually overwhelm whatever he holds dear. When a reborn Arthur does, in fact, reject his destiny in Mercedes Lackey's "Once and Future" (1995), the result, unsurprisingly, is a rather short story.[1]

The dilemma is articulated by Rosemary Sutcliff, one of the finest historical novelists of the twentieth century. Sutcliff is noted for the authenticity of her creations of the past, and when she wrote about Arthur in *Sword at Sunset* (1963), she sought beneath the "mediaeval splendours" for "a Romano-British war-leader" in "an attempt to recreate . . . the kind of man this war-leader may have been, and the story of his long struggle" (vii), as she explains in her "Author's Note." She continues,

> Certain features I have retained from the traditional Arthurian fabric, because they have the atmosphere of truth. I have kept the original framework, or rather two interwrought frameworks: the Sin which carries with it its own retribution; the Brotherhood broken by the love between the leader's woman and his closest friend. These have the inevitability and pitiless purity of outline that one finds in classical tragedy, and that belongs to the ancient and innermost places of man. I have kept the theme, which seems to me to be implicit in the story, of the Sacred King, the Leader whose divine right, ultimately, is to die for the life of the people.

Sutcliff's instincts are, as usual, sound. It is Arthur's destiny to lead, and die for, the people, and that is one important reason why his story continues to fascinate down through the ages. But by retaining these traditional features, she introduces not only the world of tragedy, but also that of romance.

The romance form evolved in many different directions in the twentieth century, including most strikingly Gothic and historical romance, mystery and romantic fiction, science fiction and fantasy.[2] The last has been particularly welcoming to Arthurian legend, since it so readily accommodates the element of the marvelous (see Hume 1984: 152–9). Although not essential to romance, this does account for some of the favorite motifs in the legend, such as the Sword in the Stone, the Sword from the Lake, Tristan and Isolde's love potion, and the voyage of the mortally wounded Arthur to Avalon, to say nothing of the Holy Grail. The growth of fantasy has also led to the proliferation of magic-workers and a variety of supernatural creatures. In the medieval romance, enchanters were relatively marginal figures, sources of advice and creators of challenges for the hero to overcome and thus prove his worth; and though they occasionally play an important role, as does Merlin in Tennyson's *Idylls of the King* (1857–86) and Edwin Arlington Robinson's *Merlin* (1917), so they largely remained until the rise in the popularity of fantasy in the second half of the twentieth century. Merlin was the first to attain real prominence, serving as Arthur's tutor in T. H. White's *Sword in the Stone* (1938), but he has since been joined by the Lady of the Lake, Morgan le Fay, and her sister Morgause. Indeed Merlin and Morgan have both been protagonists of series as well as individual novels.

The qualities that identify the romance are, like all literary definitions, more elusive than at first might appear to be the case. In *Anatomy of Criticism* (1957), Northrop Frye, the most influential among the theoreticians who have examined the form, categorizes it, not as a genre, but as a mode. "Fictions," Frye maintains, "may be classified . . . by the hero's power of action" (33). He continues,

> If superior in *degree* to other men and to his environment, the hero is the typical hero of *romance*, whose actions are marvellous but who is himself identified as a human being. The hero of romance moves in a world in which the ordinary laws of nature are slightly suspended: prodigies of courage and endurance, unnatural to us, are natural to him, and enchanted weapons, talking animals, terrifying ogres and witches, and talismans of miraculous power violate no rule of probability once the postulates of romance have been established.

Romance dominated literature during the Middle Ages, but it has given way to other modes since. "During the last hundred years," Frye observes, "most serious fiction has tended increasingly to be ironic in mode" (1957: 34–5).

This seems clear enough, though it unfortunately implies that post-medieval romance is not serious fiction, an attitude that has pervaded the study of the novel since at least F. R. Leavis' *The Great Tradition* (1948). According to Frye (1957: 304):

> The essential difference between novel and romance lies in the conception of character-ization. The romancer does not attempt to create "real people" so much as stylized figures which expand into psychological archetypes . . . a suggestion of allegory is constantly creeping in around its fringes.

What gives us pause, however, is Frye's later acknowledgment (1957: 305):

> "Pure" examples of either form are never found; there is hardly any modern romance that could not be made out to be a novel, and vice versa. The forms of prose fiction are mixed . . . In fact the popular demand in fiction is always for a mixed form, a romantic novel just romantic enough for the reader to project his libido on the hero and his anima on the heroine, and just novel enough to keep these projections in a familiar world.

To complicate matters still further, Gillian Beer argues not only that "unstable blending of the actual and the symbolic is typical of the romance method" (1970: 20), but also that some novels move from romance to realism as the hero matures (71–2); for her part, Diane Elam pronounces that "each text must redefine what it means by 'romance'" so that "we are never quite sure what romance may mean" (1992: 7).

In practice as opposed to theory, therefore, it will not be easy to decide the extent to which a given novel is a romance. Yet this decision is important, for as Frye points out (1957: 305): "a great romancer should be examined in terms of the conventions he chose . . . If Scott has any claims to be a romancer, it is not good criticism to deal only with his defects as a novelist."

This concern is doubly important in twentieth-century Arthurian fiction, moreover, because it is the legend itself that is often the main source of romance elements. If it is to avoid condemnation by comparison with more realistic novels, its virtues as romance must be established. Otherwise, the Arthurian legend per se will be deemed to be a contamination, responsible for the "defects" in any novel where it appears.

The most recognizable of the features that identify romance is the treatment of character. As Frye and others have observed, the hero is superior in degree to other men, the characters stylized: idealizations beneath apparent realism. When Arthurian figures are first encountered in a work of fiction, they may seem as individualized as the characters found in the pages of other novels, even those that have won praise for their realism. In *The Mists of Avalon* (1982) by Marion Zimmer Bradley, the various female narrators reveal their frustrations and anxieties as they struggle to cope with domestic problems: controlling parents and headstrong children, complicated love affairs and unhappy marriages, the unfortunate and sometimes disastrous consequences of all too human errors in judgment, however well meant or reluctantly undertaken. The list could be drawn just as easily from any Jane Austen novel. As Parke Godwin's *Firelord* (1980) opens, Arthur promises, "I want to write of us the way we were before some pedant petrifies us in an epic and substitutes his current ideal for ours. As for poets and bards, let one of *them* redecorate your life and you'll never be able to find any of it again" (2). Similar promises to reveal stark reality rather than reinforce the public's romantic perception might have been offered by Marlow in Joseph Conrad's *Heart of Darkness* (1899), based as it is so closely on the author's own harrowing experience in the Congo. While it might be argued that the fiction of both Austen and Conrad fits the pattern of romance more closely than most scholars have recognized, both authors are, nevertheless, ranked by Leavis among the four novelists in a great tradition noted for its realistic, rather than romantic, view of life.

The Arthurian characters, however, soon stand out as far from ordinary. In Bradley's novel, Morgaine is chosen to play the part of the Mother Goddess in the Great Marriage, and as she lies in the darkness awaiting the Horned One, "the Goddess surged inside her, body and soul . . . dazed, terrified, exalted, only half conscious, she felt the life force take them both" (178–9). Years later, in Arthur's hall, "She felt the rushing downward of power, felt herself standing taller, taller, as the power flooded through her body and soul . . . filling her like the chalice with the sacred wine of the holy presence" (770): thus transformed, she bears the Grail about the hall, seen by some as "a maiden clothed in shimmering white" (770). In Godwin's novel, Arthur too experiences visions, but it his deeds that mark him out: the valor of his assault, with Bedivere and Geraint, upon Saxon raiders, "three against eighty" (25); the compassion that he feels for the people, for whom he learns "To love, to care, to be small as well as great, gentle as well as strong. . . . To be a king, to wear a crown, is to know how apart and lonely we are and still exist and *dare* to love in the face of that void" (90–1).

Such figures loom larger than life, stirring the heart and firing the imagination with the glimpse of something nobler. As he lies for the last time in Morgaine's arms, the dying Arthur in Bradley's novel murmurs, *"I will always see the Goddess with your face"* (868); in Godwin's novel, Merlin tells the king, with cheerful understatement, "You didn't do badly at all, Arthur. If I hadn't been at this for ages, I might even boast a bit" (391). These heroes are indeed superior in degree to other men (and women).

Both of these novels, however, are fantasies, one of the modern genres of romance in which we might expect to encounter such figures. It might, therefore, be more appropriate to consider the extent to which the heroes are "one of us," characters typical of what Frye calls "the *low mimetic* mode . . . of realistic fiction" (1957: 34). To a large extent, this is how they function when they deal with the day-to-day problems of ordinary life. Medieval romance grandly ignores such petty demands, dealing instead, in Henry James's oft-quoted words, with "experience disengaged, disembroiled, disencumbered, exempt from the condition that we normally know to attach to it and . . . drag upon it."[3] The discomforts of pregnancy, the pain of childbirth, the ailments of children, all trouble Morgaine and the other mothers in *The Mists of Avalon*, much as they do mothers today, but medieval romance passes over such matters other than, for example, to mention (briefly) a mother's death so that Tristan's name and problematic relationship with his stepmother can be explained. In the romances, the knights' vigor remains undiminished except for (brief) interludes while combat wounds heal; in *Firelord*, however, Arthur and his companions suffer from cold and fatigue as they patrol beyond the Roman Wall, and they feel the effects of advancing age, as Arthur ruefully acknowledges: "my sword belt let out a reluctant notch or two. I tended to weary earlier in the evening after a hard day" (246). Nor do their ladies fare better: "Guenevere rejoiced that age didn't thicken her own delicate frame, but even as she chortled over Yseult's corpulence, the lines deepened and the flesh wrinkled about her own mouth" (246).

The heroes of twentieth-century Arthurian fantasy, thus, may sometimes prove superior in degree both to other men and women and to their environment, but most of the time they are as human as are we. They rise above us when touched by their destiny: Bradley's Morgaine when infused by the power of the Goddess; Godwin's Arthur when inspired by his Merlin-haunted visions of a more glorious world. For as W. R. J. Barron declares, "Romances represent life as it is and as it might be, imperfect reality and imagined ideal in one" (1987: 6).

This mixture of modes is no more than we would expect after the warnings of Frye and others. Indeed one can discern not only Frye's low mimetic mode, in which the hero is "superior neither to other men nor to his environment," but also his high mimetic mode, in which the hero is "superior in degree to other men but not to his natural environment" (1957: 33–4). This is the hero of most tragedy and epic, and both Bradley's Morgaine and Godwin's Arthur do rise to these heights at times. Morgaine's struggle to preserve the worship of the Goddess in the face of an intolerant and repressive Christian faith leads to the death of many for whom she cares deeply: Accolon, Kevin, Nimue, Mordred, and others, as well as Arthur. Yet she courageously accepts responsibility for her actions: *"I had loosed this monster upon the world . . . and all I had sought was in ruin"* (865, 867). She even recognizes her own fault: *"It was not she {the Goddess} but I in my pride who thought I should have done more"* (876). Where Bradley's Morgaine sometimes sounds the tragic notes, Godwin's Arthur sounds the epic, for he proves, time after time, to be an inspiring leader, outmaneuvering foes and rivals with unexpected actions like his heroic race from Scotland to save Eburacum (York), snatching victory against high odds in battle after battle, from Neth Dun More to Badon.

Sometimes, however, the notes in *Firelord* are ironic, for Arthur has a mischievous sense of humor, and since he finds particular glee in deflating the pretensions of others, he frequently targets conduct found in romance. In medieval romance, Galahad, the destined winner of the Holy Grail, is notable for his effortless virtue; of the infant son of Lancelot and the self-righteous Eleyne of Astolat (in *Firelord* a fusion with the figure of Elaine of Corbenek), Arthur irreverently observes, "Galahalt's wide, complacent stare looked from birth on a fixed cosmos where God sat ringed about with the house of Astolat, the archangels somewhere below the salt" (238). Extraordinary signs mark the birth of heroes in romance, but when Arthur hears the Saxon story that Cerdic was born with a sword in his hand, he quips, "Symbolic, of course, but awkward for his mother. God help a king without a sense of humor. He may stand close to his legend, but he should never lean on it" (111).

The irony is even more pervasive in fantasies like Naomi Mitchison's *To the Chapel Perilous* ([1955] 1999) and Thomas Berger's *Arthur Rex* (1978). Like Donald Barthelme's *The King* (1990), the former meets Elam's definition of a postmodern romance: "Flagrant anachronisms appear as the common effect of the disruption of historical boundaries by postmodern romance . . . these anachronisms challenge conventional modernist understandings of history" (12–13). Mitchison not only provides keen insight, but also achieves comic effect by introducing the press into Arthur's court, then sending reporters with modern professional standards to find the truth behind some of the stories that comprise the often contradictory body of Arthurian legend. The targets of Mitchison's humor include both the modern press and the conventions of medieval romance: the traditional damsel and her accompanying dwarf are employed as the reporter and photographer for the *Camelot Chronicle* newspaper, and comedy results when the two worlds collide. The newspaper is published by none other than Merlin, for do not newspapers, mergers, and the like, he recognizes, come "from a fantastic world" (196)?

Berger has an even sharper eye for the ridiculousness inherent in so many romance conventions, observing that churls "died from the plague and other maladies of the common folk (whereas knights did perish only in battles and ladies from love)" (168). The proof of this observation is Elaine of Astolat, who rejects Gawaine and pines away from unrequited love for Launcelot, much to the latter's perplexity:

> "But now, what are we to do with poor Elaine, if I can not love her, and she can not love thee, and thou canst love no other?" He frowned in compassion and said, "I do not speak in intentional absurdity."

"Yet, of course 'tis absurd," said Gawaine sorrowfully, "the which is proved merely by hearing it said. And thou and I have better things to do, no doubt . . . " (184)

This situation recalls another of Frye's modes (1957: 34): "If inferior in power or intelligence to ourselves, so that we have the sense of looking down on a scene of bondage, frustration, or absurdity, the hero belongs to the *ironic* mode."

The blending of irony and romance dates from the very origins of chivalric romance in the Middle Ages, and it occurs in some of the greatest works of medieval literature, like the *Lancelot* of Chrétien de Troyes and *Sir Gawain and the Green Knight*. That it has continued to flourish in the twentieth century, particularly in the form of Ironic Fantasy (see Hume 1984: 154–6; Thompson 1985: 139–62) confirms Frye's opinion that pure examples of the romance and novel are never found. Nor is it always easy to discern which is the dominant mode in an individual work of fiction, nor even when a mode changes. Is Godwin's Arthur the hero of romance or epic during his desperate races across the country, or his surprising victories against overwhelming odds? Is his devoted companion Bedwyr a low mimetic or ironic figure when he responds with outrage to his daughter's suitor's concern for his "advanced years" (248)?

But what of historical novels as opposed to fantasies? Some, like Chester Keith's *Queen's Knight* (1920) and Lord Ernest Hamilton's *Launcelot* (1926), follow their medieval romance sources in characterization as well as plot, but others, like Edward Frankland's *Bear of Britain* (1944), Bernard Cornwell's Warlord Chronicles (1995–7), and Sutcliff's *Sword at Sunset* strive to create credible Dark Age people. In the process, they discard many of the traditional figures from Arthurian romance. Frankland preserves the anti-romantic perception, derived from Gildas' sixth-century diatribe *De Excidio Britanniae* (*On the Ruins of Britain*), of a brutal world of pillage, rape, and murder. But if the setting seems far removed from the world of romance, the characters are another matter. Arthur's doomed struggle to save Britain marks him as an epic hero in Frye's high mimetic mode, while the very excesses of his foes, who give free rein to cruelty and lust, treachery and ambition, make them larger than life. Men like Cerdic, Medraut, and the British princes who squander Arthur's hard-won victories are as monstrous as any ogre, as archetypal as any villain in romance.

Cornwell also creates a world which has largely shed its Roman heritage, but here again the characters keep bursting out of their low mimetic guise. Not only do the ambition, hatred, and cruelty of Arthur's enemies go far beyond the bounds of reason, rejoicing in acts of torture and the slaughter of innocents, but the response of Arthur and his followers can be just as extreme. Unlike their enemies, they wish "to treat folk well, to give them peace and offer them justice" (*Excalibur* [1997]: 314), but once aroused they wage war "with a savage joy in defeating the enemy" (192). Thus the narrator records,

> It is the beguiling glory of war, the sheer exhilaration of breaking a shield wall and slaking a sword on a hated enemy. I watched Arthur, a man as kind as any I have known, and saw nothing but joy in his eyes. Galahad, who prayed each day that he could obey Christ's commandment to love all men, was now killing them with a terrible efficiency. Culwch was roaring insults ... while Taliesin was singing as he killed the enemy wounded left behind by our advancing shield wall. You do not win the fight of the

shield wall by being sensible and moderate, but by a Godlike rush of howling madness. (423)

Sutcliff, by contrast, depicts a post-Roman world that is fighting to preserve what remains of the order and civilization of a bygone age, as the titles of her two Arthurian novels proclaim: *The Lantern Bearers* (1959) and *Sword at Sunset* (1963). Her characters are less extreme than those of Frankland and Cornwell, but they too stand out from the ordinary throng. In *Sword at Sunset*, the half-sister who seduces Artos reminds him of a witch or a fairy from the Otherworld, like Keats' "La Belle Dame Sans Merci": "Are you afraid to wake in the morning on the bare mountain side, and find three lifetimes gone by? . . . Are you afraid to hear the singing of Rhiannon's Birds that makes men forget?" (37). The hate that she learned from her mother, and that she in turn teaches their son, Medraut, who will eventually destroy all that Artos has fought to preserve, is the stuff of darkest nightmare, and indeed Artos comments grimly to the friends he meets after this encounter, "I have dreamed evil dreams in the night" (43).

By contrast, the companions who follow Artos display devotion and self-sacrifice: "'They will not grow old,' I said. 'The flame is too bright.' And I knew the grief that I suppose all commanders know from time to time, when they look about them at the men who answer to their trumpets; grief for the young men who will never grow old" (86). It would be an injustice to Sutcliff's craft to reduce her characters to a simplified division between good and evil. Nevertheless, the romance roots of her material have left their mark, reinforced as they are by the contrasting light and dark imagery. As Frye observes (1957: 195): "The characterization of romance follows its general dialectic structure . . . Characters tend to be either for or against the quest. If they assist it they are idealized as simply gallant or pure; if they obstruct it they are caricatured as simply villainous or cowardly." Such figures tend to become archetypes, like those analyzed by C. G. Jung. Among them Frye lists "the witch . . . appropriately called by Jung the 'terrible mother,' and he associates her with the fear of incest . . . . The faithful companion . . . has his opposite in the traitor" (1957: 196). By preserving the traditional pattern of Arthur's sin and its retribution, Sutcliff unavoidably preserves something of its romance origins.

The theme of the "Leader whose divine right, ultimately, is to die for the life of the people" is another mark of romance, as well as the high mimetic mode, for it creates a hero who is very far from ordinary, however he is depicted. The devotion that Artos inspires in his followers is not just a tribute to his success in battle, though it is important to a warrior that his leader be lucky; nor to his personal charisma, a quality more noticeable in *The Lantern Bearers*, since it is told from a different point of view; nor to his willingness to lead by example: "I must not bide long . . . taking for myself the freedom for my own pleasure that I had denied to . . . the rest. I think that few of them would have grudged it to me if I had, but it was not in the bargain" (66). Like Bedwyr these young men abandon other plans, like Gwalchmai they leave behind a secure environment, all to follow the dream that Artos offers, to build a Britain strong and united by the bonds of love and sacrifice.

For as I have argued in *The Return from Avalon* (1985: 47–8), Artos stands out as a hero who genuinely cares for others, protecting younger followers as much as possible, feeling deeply the death of his beloved hounds, of his brave warriors, and of close friends like Aquila, Gwalchmai, and Ambrosius. The role of Sacred King is one that he willingly embraces, and before the last battle he reflects, "could only hope that my death might serve also as a ransom for the people" (464). In the battle itself, he sacrifices his own life to buy time for reinforcements to win through, and when he finds a "good place for a last stand," he tells the handful of companions with him, "My most dear, we have fought many fights together, and this is the last of them and it must be the best. If it is given to men to remember in the life we go to, remember that I loved you, and do not forget that you loved me" (474). To which the youngest replies, "We have good memories, Artos the Bear" (474). At such times, Artos stands out as more than an ordinary man. He represents a nobler way of life, a vision from "the romance mode which could inspire hope and raise aspiration, moderated but undaunted by the likelihood of failure . . . of life both as it is and as it might be" (Barron 1987: 6, 25).

As in fantasy, it can be difficult to decide whether the characters of historical novels belong to epic or romance when they rise out of the low mimetic mode. Indeed, it might be argued that their excesses are no more than another attempt at realism, merely a mirror of life itself. Is the savage cruelty of Arthur's enemies in the novels of Frankland and Cornwell but the conduct typical of a barbaric age, like that of the Nazis rather than the monsters of romance? Is the "savage joy" and "Godlike rush of howling madness" in Cornwell's novel the berserker rage of Dark Age warriors or the supernatural possession of romance? Is the self-sacrifice of Sutcliff's Artos the heroism of which many are capable or the idealism of romance? In one sense, it does not matter, for down through the ages the polarities and idealism of romance have both reflected and shaped the reactions of men and women. The distinction between epic and romance is more problematic, but the sharp division between the dream-inspired heroes and their helpers on the one hand, and their hate-filled adversaries on the other, is a clear mark of characterization in romance: "The enemy may be an ordinary human being, but the nearer the romance is to myth, the more the attributes of divinity will cling to the hero and the more the enemy will take on demonic mythical qualities" (Frye 1957: 187). Moreover, as Frye points out, "while one mode constitutes the underlying tonality of a work of fiction, any or all of the other four may be simultaneously present" (1957: 50).

The setting in which these characters move satisfies another criterion of romance, for it is certainly remote in time (see Beer 1970: 12; Wilson 1976: 57), whether placed in the historical Dark Ages or the High Middle Ages pictured in chivalric romance. Even when events unfold in a later or contemporary setting, the past is invoked by the Arthurian figures, whether reincarnated, like Arthur in Tim Powers' *The Drawing of the Dark* (1979), or immortal like Merlin in Susan Cooper's series *The Dark Is Rising* (1965–77). Sometimes Arthur may return from Avalon, as he does in Pamela F. Service's *Winter of Magic's Return* (1985); and Merlin may be released from an imprisoning oak tree, as he is in Simon Hawke's *Wizard of Camelot* (1993), or revived from a long sleep, as he is in C. S. Lewis' *That Hideous Strength* (1945).[4] Even when events are placed in a future era, as envisaged in C. J. Cherryh's science-fiction novel *Port Eternity* (1982), the Arthurian past retains a powerful presence.

In Cherryh's novel, the recreation of an Arthurian microcosm in a marooned spaceship is integral to the exploration of the complex relationship between illusion and reality. How closely the plot matches that of conventional romance is revealed by Frye in *The Secular Scripture*: "In science fiction the characters may be earthlings, the setting the intergalactic spaces, and what gets wrecked in hostile territory a spaceship, but the tactics of the storyteller generally conform to much the same outlines" (1976: 5). Influenced by Tennyson's *Idylls of the King*, Dela, the wealthy owner of the luxury space craft which she names "Maid of Astolat," not only has the interior decorated to look like a medieval hall, but also has it staffed by "made people" modeled on Arthurian characters. "Made people" are cloned from special genetic combinations, then conditioned with "deepteach" tapes to create a special "psych-set." Since "the greatest joy" in Dela's life "was to pretend" (11), for the benefit of their owner they "play out the old game" (12), allowing her to escape from the pressures of business and politics into the "idyllic" world of romance (see Frye 1957: 43). But though it starts out as an illusion, a game, an escapist fantasy, the Arthurian pattern gradually enmeshes all the characters, "made" and "born people" alike, leaving them stranded at the end, outside of normal time and space, in an ironic recreation of Avalon: "Whether we dream, still falling forever, or whether the dream has shaped itself about us, we love . . . at least we dream we do" (191).

This dream world, moreover, is invested with nostalgia, another trait of romance according to Frye: "The perennially childlike quality of romance is marked by its extraordinarily persistent nostalgia, its search for some kind of imaginative golden age in time or space" (186). This nostalgic note is sounded, not only in novels that play with illusion and reality as does *Port Eternity*, but also, most hauntingly, in those that are narrated in the first person, at moments when the narrator realizes just how precious was the world that has been lost. Thus in *Firelord*, Arthur remembers "Gwen and I walking by the river, watching twilight turn the water to purple and ink against the wheat-colored far bank" (207). In Gillian Bradshaw's *In Winter's Shadow* (1982), Gwynhwyfar recollects:

> the memory of Camlann [Camelot] in the morning, the sun shining from the snow on the roof of the feast hall, the smoke of the morning fires, the feasts in the great dim building, the glitter of much gold, the strains of the harp. Whatever the bitterness that mingles with the memories, what we had in Camlann was the dream that the hearts of all men have ever longed for . . . Of course the loss of that is bitter, more bitter than the loss of all the world. But I cannot wish to forget that it was there for a few years. No, I wish to forget none of it: Arthur's smile and clear eyes, Bedwyr's warm gaze, the friendships and loves and the astounding beauty of the world we were making anew. (376–7)

Such recollections are typical of Frye's fifth phase of romance, in which "the mood is a contemplative withdrawal from or sequel to action ... it presents experience as comprehended" (1957: 202).

To North American readers, the Arthurian setting is also remote in place, but even British readers no longer feel as close as they once did to a social organization along tribal or feudal lines, or to a rural landscape dominated by villages and walled towns, villas and farms, forts and castles. The difference is most noticeable in novels involving time travel. In *The Third Magic* (1988) by Welwyn Wilton Katz, *The Minstrel Boy* (1997) by Sharon Stewart, and the many stories loosely derived from *A Connecticut Yankee in King Arthur's Court* (1889) by Mark Twain, such as *A Kid in King Arthur's Court* (1995), a novel by Anne Mazer based on the screenplay of the Disney film, modern teenagers awaken in an Arthurian world in which they must struggle to survive.

Arthurian fiction in the twentieth century provides much more detail about the setting than does medieval romance, which is usually vague on geography and highly selective in its choice of details (Auerbach 1946: 115–21). This may be explained not only by the conventions of the novel genre, but also by the need to describe a world that is unfamiliar to the reader, whether set in the remote past, the distant future, or the realm of fantasy. The Arthurian story in chivalric romance, by contrast, is placed in a contemporary setting, the world of the High Middle Ages. Clothing and armor, feasts and pastimes, castles and chapels, all mirror the latest fashions, and their description served to impress the audience with the splendor of the romance world. There was no need to offer detail about ordinary objects and people.

The chivalric romance reveals hardly anything about the living conditions of the lower classes (Auerbach 1946: 121). These were largely ignored, apart from shadowy servants who carry food and wine to the table, and uncouth herdsmen who give directions to questing knights. Indeed dogs, horses, and even falcons usually play a larger role in events (as Frye drily remarks, these creatures are "incurable romantics" [1957: 36]). Modern readers, however, not only have more democratic leanings (A. and B. Lupack 1999: 326), but also find the details of an ancient way of life interesting, perhaps even exotic in an era that enjoys historical recreation.

As a result, a fuller picture of the past is drawn in Arthurian fiction, embracing different classes and eras. Events are narrated, not only by the high-born, but also servants and slaves. Indeed, in some novels the protagonists change status, closely observing the new surroundings that they, like the reader, view with unfamiliar and curious eyes. In Sutcliff's *The Lantern Bearers*, Aquila, a Roman officer and son of a landowner, is captured by Jutes and toils among them as a slave for nearly two years; in Bradshaw's *Kingdom of Summer* (1981), the narrator, Rhys ap Sion, leaves the family farm to become Gwalchmai's servant on quests and embassies throughout the realm; in Monica Furlong's *Juniper* (1990), the daughter of King Mark of Cornwall becomes apprentice to a wise woman living in a humble cottage; and Gareth, like his namesake in Malory's *Morte Darthur*, journeys from the court of Orkney to serve in the kitchens of Camelot for a year in several novels that include his adventures, such as *Gareth of*

Orkney (1956) by E. M. R. Ditmas and (very humorously) Thomas Berger's *Arthur Rex*. Other novels follow the lives of their heroes as they learn the duties of page and squire, often in new surroundings, as is the case in *Arthur: The Seeing Stone* (2000) and *Arthur: At the Crossing-Places* (2001) by Kevin Crossley-Holland.

While historical romances from the earlier part of the century, like Clemence Housman's *Sir Aglovale de Galis* (1905) and John Erskine's *Galahad* (1926), and even some fantasies like Berger's *Arthur Rex*, follow their chivalric romance models in paying slight attention to the setting, the trend in Arthurian fiction throughout the twentieth century has been toward a much fuller picture. Often the challenges posed by a new environment are crucial to the learning process that the characters undergo: like Aquila in Sutcliff's *The Lantern Bearers* and Guenevere in Godwin's *Beloved Exile* (1984), they may be made callous by suffering as slaves, then redeemed by love; conversely, they may learn compassion for the less fortunate after exposure to the hardships of life either among the lower classes, as does Arthur in Crossley-Holland's series, or among the outcasts of society, as he does in Godwin's *Firelord*. This concern to provide a wider range of realistic detail in the setting reveals how the novel genre and low mimetic mode have modified the influence of chivalric romance in Arthurian fiction of the twentieth century, balancing such elements as the remote setting in time and place and the nostalgia for a lost golden age.

Plots too may seem more realistic, dealing as they do with political struggles among the powerful, hunger and hardship among the poor. Yet here too romance motifs lurk close to the surface. This is unavoidable whenever traditional stories are used as source material, no matter how loosely. They remain highly visible even in transpositions of Arthurian legend to a modern setting, in novels like *The Natural* (1952) by Bernard Malamud and *Castle Dor* (1961) by Arthur Quiller-Couch and Daphne du Maurier.

The first of the "six isolatable phases . . . in a romantic hero's life," discerned by Frye (1957: 198), is the account of his birth, and the more closely an author follows this pattern, the deeper he or she moves into the romance mode. Features such as conception outside wedlock by royal parents, rearing by people of humbler status than his own, threats upon his life by powerful authority figures, and eventual acceptance and acknowledgment of his rights recur in novels about Arthur (Mary Stewart's *The Hollow Hills*, 1973, and Jack Whyte's series *A Dream of Eagles*, 1992–); Merlin (Stewart's *The Crystal Cave*, 1970, and Jane Yolen's *Young Merlin* trilogy, 1996–7); Mordred (Stewart's *The Wicked Day*, 1984); Gwalchmai (Bradshaw's *Hawk of May*, 1980); Perceval (Dorothy James Roberts' *Kinsmen of the Grail*, 1963); Tristan (Hannah Closs's *Tristan*, 1940).

Frye's second phase, "the innocent youth of the hero" (1957: 199), is most poignantly portrayed in White's *Sword in the Stone*, with its idyllic description of Arthur's childhood: haymaking in "real July weather, such as they only had in old England" ([1938] 1963: 10); celebrating Christmas at the Castle Sauvage with "the old English wolves wandering about slavering in an appropriate manner, or sometimes peeping in at the keyholes with their blood-red eyes" (192); transformed by

Merlyn's magic into various creatures to learn about them; and roaming throughout the castle:

> The place was, of course, a complete paradise for a boy to be in . . . He knew everything, everywhere, all the special smells, good climbs, soft lairs, secret hiding-places, jumps, slides, nooks, larders and blisses. For every season he had the best place, like a cat, and he yelled and ran and fought and upset people and snoozed and daydreamed and pretended he was a Knight, without ever stopping. (48)

Frye's other phases also appear: the fourth, "maintaining the integrity of the innocent world against the assault of experience" (1957: 201), is seen in attempts to conceal the adultery of Lancelot and Guenevere from public view in novels like White's *The Once and Future King* (1958); the "idyllic view" (202) of the fifth pervades the nostalgic recollections of Camelot noted above; the "movement from active to contemplative adventure" (202) in the sixth marks Merlin's disengagement from the world in novels like Stewart's *The Last Enchantment* (1979). Most widespread in modern Arthurian fiction, as in medieval romance, however, is the third phase. This is the quest theme in which the hero must slay the dragon, rescue the princess, or win some other talisman of power, then return to rule over the kingdom that he has saved (Frye 1957: 189). Anne Wilson, in *Traditional Romance and Tale*, discerns that these stories were "disguises" behind which lurked "subject-matter which was apparently violent and frightening, and that hate, incest, patricide and other such concerns, appeared to be present" (1976: ix). This cycle of events, which she calls a "move" (a term borrowed from Vladimir Propp's *Morphology of the Folktale*), may be repeated with variations (59). In *Symbolic Stories*, Derek Brewer outlines the basic "family drama" behind the quest: at its core lie three characters, the protagonist, the father, and the mother. Most other characters are " 'repeats' or 'splits' of the main three . . . what the male protagonist has to do is kill his father, dodge his mother, and win his girl" (1980: 9).

Obviously, any narrative can be reduced to a quintessential core, but this particular one lies disturbingly close to the surface in Arthurian legend. As Brewer points out, "failure to grow up, that is failure to escape from the parents, is usually the basis of tragedy" (1980: 11); moreover, the "dangers of dominating mother-love" (12) are much greater than the hostile father figure. Thus while Arthur defeats such displaced father figures as Loth of Orkney (his half-sister's husband) and Ryons, the king/ogre who collects the beards of subject kings (thereby keeping them symbolically in a state of perpetual childhood), he is trapped in an incestuous relationship with his half-sister Morgause (or sometimes Morgan le Fay). This act sows the seed for the tragic fall of Arthur's kingdom in the majority of novels that deal with this final phase of the legend (see Frye 1957: 36–7). Furthermore, Morgause proves to be a devouring mother figure for her own sons in *The Once and Future King* by White and elsewhere, notably the novels of Stewart and Bradshaw. In Bradley's *The Mists of Avalon*, Morgaine is more caring, but the endearments with which she comforts the dying Arthur, *"my brother, my baby, my love"* (868), reveal the maternal aspect of her role.[5] In

Reading the Romance, Radway acknowledges the "blissful symbiotic union between mother and child that is the goal of all romances despite their apparent preoccupation with heterosexual love and marriage" (1984: 156).

Other quests, fortunately, prove more successful. After escaping from controlling mothers and slaying or propitiating various hostile father figures, Gareth rescues and marries the Lady of Lyonnesse in Ditmas' *Gareth of Orkney*, Gwalchmai wins the acceptance of Arthur and his court in Bradshaw's *Hawk of May*, and Perceval finds the Holy Grail in Roberts' *Kinsmen of the Grail*.

Anne Wilson remarks that "nearly all the romances are 'hero' stories, not 'heroine' ones" (1976: ix). Twentieth-century Arthurian fiction, however, has introduced the heroine, or female hero,[6] in increasing numbers. Her quest, according to Brewer, is "to dodge her father, and if not kill at any rate pretty severely neutralise her mother, and make it possible for her man to get her" (1980: 9): in other words, the Cinderella story. This is the typical formula of romantic fiction (see Radway 1984: 212), and the last decade of the twentieth century has witnessed a veritable explosion of such novels with Arthurian links, often thinly disguised as fantasies by their use of the supernatural: they may be set in Arthur's day, like *Enchantress* (1996) by Barbara Benedict; or encompass later ages as well, like *Merlin's Legacy*, a series (1996–9) by Quinn Taylor Evans; or even take place in the contemporary world, like *The Enchanter* (1990) by Christina Hamlett, which involves time travel and a reincarnation of Merlin.

The Cinderella pattern is also attached to Arthur's queen. In Nancy McKenzie's *The Child Queen* (1994), she must survive the machinations of her aunt and jealous cousin (Elaine), who try to prevent, then break up, her marriage to Arthur; in Godwin's *Firelord*, she defies the authority of her father to help Arthur win the throne and her hand in marriage; in Helen Hollick's *The Kingmaking* (1994), she takes violent action against the enemies who stand between her and Arthur. Not only does she escape unaided after Melwas' abduction, knocking him out and killing the guard, but she then leads Arthur's men to rescue their lord from prison and there slays Melwas herself.

Such modifications of the Cinderella pattern to allow the female hero more initiative became increasingly popular as the century drew to a close,[7] culminating in the formidable female warriors who are the protagonists of *Dawnflight* (1999) by Kim Headlee and *The King's Peace* (2000) by Jo Walton. Yet this development was anticipated as early as 1930 in W. Barnard Faraday's *Pendragon*. The Princess Gwendaello (Guenevere) leads her warriors, first against the Irish invaders, then in a desperate race to save Artorius at Badon. There she sweeps onto the field of battle like a wild war goddess, scattering the Saxons before her: "in front of all the others was a chariot driving with wild horses, with manes and tails blowing about, and in it a figure with red hair streaming in the wind, holding a spear and shrieking aloud in fury" (281). When Artorius tells her she has saved Britain, she replies, "'And also something that I value even more. For I have come, and mine with me, forty miles this day that I may keep it.' Then with a fine cloth she wiped the blood from my face and softly kissed me" (281). These Cinderella figures may look harmless and vulnerable, but those who threaten their relationship with their chosen mates learn to their cost just how misleading that impression can be.

These heroine tales produce female heroes no longer content with the passive role allotted high-born ladies in chivalric romance: they choose instead to wield political power both indirectly and directly, rather than merely entertain Arthur's guests at banquets; they free themselves, rather than await rescue by another. The tales produce a different kind of male hero as well. Traditional virtues like courage and loyalty, which mark the knights of chivalric romance, are augmented by increased sensitivity and intelligence. In novels like *The Dragon and the Unicorn* (1996) by A. A. Attanasio, Ygrane turns from the brutal, patriarchal Gorlois to the sensitive, considerate Theo (who takes the name of Uther when he succeeds to the throne).

The Savage Damsel and the Dwarf (2000), an ironic fantasy by Gerald Morris, humorously exposes the limitations of the more conventional hero and heroine: though handsome and valiant, Gareth is rather stupid; though beautiful, Lyonesse is self-centered and manipulative. By contrast, Gaheris, though a poor fighter, displays a keen wit and willingness to sacrifice himself for others; and Lynet, though less beautiful than her sister, displays not only more initiative, but also more intelligence and consideration for others. These, increasingly, are the qualities that distinguish the hero and heroine of modern Arthurian romance. Fortunately, Gareth and Lynet are intelligent enough to recognize that each other's merits are worth more than the physical beauty of their siblings (trying to envision married life with Gaheris, Lynet wonders, "What would they talk about?" [153]). At the end of the story they set off together to manage his family's lands: Gaheris to "see to the crops, take care of my tenants, put the estates back in good repair" (195), Lynet to heal the sick with her newly discovered magical powers.

In hero, as opposed to heroine, stories, modern Arthurian romance also yields new qualities in the hero and heroine. Arthur is readier to sacrifice himself for the people than to pursue honor and glory; and rather than exterminate pagans and drive out invaders as in medieval literature, he is much readier to tolerate religious and ethnic differences.[8] Thus he pursues a policy of peaceful coexistence in novels like Cornwell's *Enemy of God* (1996) and Diana L. Paxson's *The Hallowed Isle: Book Two: The Book of the Spear* (1999), even at the cost of alienating his more fanatical followers. He is, moreover, more likely to seek a soul-mate who will share the burden of rule, as in Godwin's *Firelord*, than a dynastic match with a peerless beauty. When he does marry merely for the sake of a political alliance, as in Sutcliff's *Sword at Sunset*, it ultimately proves disastrous.

Arthurian romance has flourished throughout the twentieth century, spreading into new genres with astonishing vigor. The romance mode not only dominates genres like fantasy, but even penetrates more mimetic genres like the historical novel. While the extent to which romance elements are present varies from text to text, the power of association created by Arthurian legend ensures that they remain inescapable in even the most anti-romantic novels. Indeed, in their efforts to reveal the brutal reality behind the romantic image, these may create characters as exaggerated as any encountered in romance. Moreover, as another century begins, Arthurian romance shows every sign of adapting itself to the aspirations of a new generation. Just as the chivalric romances of the Middle Ages produced different heroic ideals – warrior knights like Kay, knights errant like Gawain, courtly knights like Lancelot, Grail knights like Galahad – so the romances of later centuries have in their turn created heroes who reflect changing social values. In the twentieth century and beyond, as in earlier centuries, Arthurian romance thereby reveals it is "always concerned with the fulfilment of desires" (Beer 1970: 12).

There does, however, appear to be some divergence from such fulfillment. Hero stories present tolerant heroes who strive to reconcile conflicting demands as reasonably as possible, and to accomplish this task they want heroines who will provide them with support, both practical and emotional. Heroine stories present independent-minded female heroes, striving to take control over their own lives, and they are looking for considerate heroes who will respect their aspirations. The potential for a fruitful partnership exists, but whether it can be established amid the pressures that life exerts remains to be seen. The betrayal of Artos by Ygerna and Guenhumara in Sutcliff's *Sword at Sunset* reveals the dangers of neglecting to care enough for the feelings of women, but betrayal of the hero brings not happiness but suffering, to them as well as others. Godwin's *Firelord* shows what a good working partnership between Arthur and Guenevere can achieve, though it is Morgan who fulfills his deepest emotional needs, Lancelot hers. When the pressures are too great, even our best efforts do not suffice, it would seem.

Yet Arthurian romance offers the hope of a better world, even if only for a while, and that is better than a bleak existence. "Do not weep my friend," the dying Arthur tells Sir Bedivere in Berger's *Arthur Rex*. "Rather thank God in joy that for a little while we were able to make an interregnum in the human cycle of barbarism and decadence" (495). Sometimes, too, like Lynet and Gaheris in Morris' *The Savage Damsel and the Dwarf*, like Lienors and Dalyn in Mitchison's *To the Chapel Perilous*, we can find happiness if we turn away from fashionable values to follow a path that is truer to our selves. We may even be fortunate enough to find a soul mate with whom to travel on that journey. And that is the eternal promise of romance.

See also: chapter 3, THE POPULAR ENGLISH METRICAL ROMANCES; chapter 4, ARTHURIAN ROMANCE; chapter 6, MALORY AND THE EARLY PROSE ROMANCES; chapter 17, POETRY OF THE ROMANTIC PERIOD; chapter 18, VICTORIAN ROMANCE: TENNYSON; chapter 19, VICTORIAN ROMANCE: MEDIEVALISM; chapter 24, AMERICA AND ROMANCE; chapter 27, ROMANCE IN FANTASY; chapter 28, QUEST ROMANCE IN SCIENCE FICTION; chapter 30, POPULAR ROMANCE AND ITS READERS.

Notes

1. For the varied treatments of these and other Arthurian figures in modern literature, see character entries in *The New Arthurian Encyclopedia*, ed. Lacy et al. (1996); also Raymond H. Thompson, "Conceptions of King Arthur in the Twentieth Century," in Edward Donald Kennedy, ed., *King Arthur: A Casebook* (New York and London: Garland, 1996), pp. 299–311.

2. For a discussion of the Arthurian legend in these and other genres, see _The New Arthurian Encyclopedia_ and Thompson 1985.

3. Henry James, _The American_, 2 vols. (1883); the quotation is from the preface, first published in the New York edition (1907–17), vol. 2.

4. For the motif of Merlin's revival see Thompson, "The Enchanter Awakes: Merlin in Modern Fantasy," in _Death and the Serpent: Immortality in Science Fiction and Fantasy_, ed. Carl B. Yoke and Donald Hassler (Westport, CT: Greenwood, 1985), pp. 49–56; substantially revised and expanded as "The Enchanter Awakes: Merlin in Modern Fiction," in _Merlin: A Casebook_, ed. Peter Goodrich and Raymond H. Thompson (New York and London: Routledge, 2003), pp. 250–62.

5. See Thompson, "The First and Last Love," in _The Arthurian Revival: Essays on Form, Tradition and Transformation_, ed. Debra Mancoff (New York: Garland, 1992), pp. 230–47; reprinted in Fenster 1996: 331–44.

6. See Maureen Fries, "Female Heroes, Heroines and Counter-heroes," in _Popular Arthurian Tradition_, ed. Sally K. Slocum (Bowling Green, OH: Bowling Green State University, Popular Press, 1992), pp. 5–17; reprinted in Fenster 1996: 59–73.

7. See Barbara Ann Gordon-Wise, _The Reclamation of a Queen: Guinevere in Modern Fantasy_ (Westport, CT: Greenwood, 1991), pp. 119–39; Elisabeth Brewer, "The Figure of Guenevere in Modern Drama and Fiction," in _Arturus Rex: Acta Conventus Lovaniensis_, ed. Willy Van Hoecke, Gilbert Tournoy, Werner Verbeke (Leuven: University Press, 1991), vol. 2, pp. 479–90; reprinted in Fenster 1996: 307–18.

8. See Thompson, "Darkness over Camelot: Enemies of the Arthurian Dream," in _New Directions in Arthurian Studies_, ed. Alan Lupack (Cambridge: Brewer, 2002), pp. 97–104.

References and Further Reading

Auerbach, Erich (1957). _Mimesis: The Representation of Reality in Western Literature_, trans. Willard R. Trask. Garden City, NY: Doubleday. [First published in German in 1946, translated 1953.]

Barron, W. R. J. (1987). _English Medieval Romance_. London: Longman.

Beer, Gillian (1970). _The Romance_. London: Methuen.

Berger, Thomas (1978). _Arthur Rex_. New York: Delacorte Press/Seymour Lawrence.

Bradley, Marion Zimmer (1982). _The Mists of Avalon_. New York: Knopf.

Bradshaw, Gillian (1982). _In Winter's Shadow_. New York: Simon and Schuster.

Brewer, Derek (1980). _Symbolic Stories: Traditional Narratives of the Family Drama in English Literature_. London: Brewer; Totowa, NJ: Rowman & Littlefield.

Cherryh, C. J. (1985). _Port Eternity_. New York: DAW.

Cornwell, Bernard (1997). _Excalibur: A Novel of Arthur_. London: Joseph.

Elam, Diane (1992). _Romancing the Postmodern_. London and New York: Routledge.

Faraday, W. Barnard (2002). _Pendragon_. Oakland, CA: Green Knight. [First published in 1930.]

Fenster, Thelma S., ed. (1996). _Arthurian Women: A Casebook_. New York and London: Garland.

Frye, Northrop (1957). _Anatomy of Criticism: Four Essays_. Princeton, NJ: Princeton University Press.

Frye, Northrop (1976). _The Secular Scripture: A Study of the Structure of Romance_. Cambridge, MA: Harvard University Press.

Godwin, Parke (1980). _Firelord_. Garden City, NY: Doubleday.

Hume, Kathryn (1984). _Fantasy and Mimesis: Responses to Reality in Western Literature_. New York and London: Methuen.

Lacy, Norris J., et al., eds. (1996). _The New Arthurian Encyclopedia_. New York and London: Garland. [First published in 1991.]

Lupack, Alan, and Barbara Tepa Lupack (1999). _King Arthur in America_. Cambridge: Brewer.

Mitchison, Naomi (1999). _To the Chapel Perilous_. Oakland, CA: Green Knight. [First published in 1955.]

Morris, Gerald (2000). _The Savage Damsel and the Dwarf_. Boston: Houghton Mifflin.

Radway, Janice A. (1984). *Reading the Romance: Women, Patriarchy, and Popular Literature.* Chapel Hill and London: University of North Carolina Press.

Sutcliff, Rosemary (1963). *Sword at Sunset.* London: Hodder and Stoughton.

Thompson, Raymond H. (1985). *The Return from Avalon: A Study of the Arthurian Legend in Modern Fiction.* Westport, CT: Greenwood.

White, T. H. (1963). *The Sword in the Stone.* New York: Dell. [First published in 1938.]

Wilson, Anne (1976). *Traditional Romance and Tale: How Stories Mean.* Ipswich: Brewer; Totowa, NJ: Rowman & Littlefield.

27

Romance in Fantasy through the Twentieth Century

Richard Mathews

Twentieth-century fantasy writing preserves many of the appealing surfaces and philosophical depths of the romance tradition while creating new structural and thematic dimensions of its own. The modern fantasy novel originated in the work of William Morris and George MacDonald in the second half of the nineteenth century. It evolved rapidly through a variety of popular literary forms during the next hundred years, reaching a high point with the publication of J. R. R. Tolkien's *The Lord of the Rings* in the mid-twentieth century. After Tolkien's epic fantasy unmistakably established a peak in the new terrain, fiction writers in the latter half of the century explored and plotted uncharted ranges as the seismic aftershocks of fantasy unsettled and reshaped contemporary fiction from avant-garde to mainstream and rocked popular literary culture through such modes as horror in the works of Stephen King, scientific romance in book and screen versions of Michael Crichton's *Jurassic Park*, and a slew of groundbreaking fantasy films including *Peter Pan*, *Raiders of the Lost Ark*, *The Princess Bride*, *Harry Potter*, and the stunning Peter Jackson cycle adapted from *The Lord of the Rings*.

Romance is at the core of these and other works of twentieth-century fantasy. The prominent literary critic Northrop Frye has even suggested that "romance is the structural core of all fiction" (1976: 15), but the term "romance" would not readily come to mind today for most fans of the fantasy genre. In common usage "romance" may conjure love, mystery, and idealism, but in the latter decades of the twentieth century, the general public understood "romance" fiction as meaning something else entirely. What most readily would come to mind were bookstore shelves and airport news-stands brimming with paperback "romance novels," their covers aglow with poster boys such as Fabio, replete with Lancelot haircut but appealing to sensibilities more attuned to soap opera than to complex literary traditions.

Nonetheless, literary romance survived the century surprisingly well – especially when one considers that for most US baby-boom generation readers – even those of us earning doctoral degrees in English literature – romance as a special genre had disappeared from the academic curriculum as well as from popular culture. It simply was not taught in the classrooms of high schools and universities. And, ironically, given its historically firm roots as a genuinely popular as opposed to an academic mode, the very lack of validation in the halls of academe may have helped to keep romance's true identity alive in popular culture.

After World War II the serious contemporary novel became a hot literary property in bookstores, bestseller lists, and university classrooms. During this period there was an interesting and healthy movement to open university curriculums to reform. By the 1960s most colleges and universities included postwar novels and current fiction as well as classics and milestone period pieces. Within this atmosphere graduate students learned to trace the rise of the novel from the epistolary works of Richardson through Fielding and Sterne in the eighteenth century, followed, in the United Kingdom, by Jane Austen, the Brontës, and Charles Dickens, and in the United States by Washington Irving, Nathaniel Hawthorne, Mark Twain, and Henry James ... and leaping forward to John Steinbeck and Ernest Hemingway, Graham Greene and Iris Murdoch, John Updike and Saul Bellow, Flannery O'Connor and Eudora Welty. American academia embraced a host of recent fiction by applying analytical New Critical methods that worked magic with works of realism, social realism, and even surrealism. But no one spoke of romance, though the French and German languages preserve its importance for modern fiction in their word for "novel" – *roman* – a term for narratives written in the vernacular or popular "romance" languages.

While reviewing lists of literary terms for my doctoral examinations, I suddenly realized that I had never been taught the meaning of "romance" as a literary form. When I asked what I ought to know about it, one of my favorite professors patiently explained that the prose romance had been a more or less dead-end, allegorical mode of writing, a kind of fiction writing that never amounted to much. He suggested I read Sir Philip Sidney's *Arcadia* if I wanted to find a representative example. It was thought to be allegorical, bucolic, artificial. It was a type of writing that might once have been of interest to court dandies and landed gentry more attracted to pretense and affectation than to realism, but it had nothing to say to a modern reader. I dutifully read Sidney's charming narrative, mastered the necessary definitions, and gave "romance" relatively little further thought at that time.

Yet far from the academic spotlight, with little fanfare, romance was regrouping and gathering crowds of devoted readers. There was a flowering of fantasy and science fiction that by the mid-twentieth century began to attract the notice of publishers and readers, if not traditional professors of English literature.[1] Popular audiences seemed determined to enjoy variations of romance in a variety of guises – from books written for children but clearly meant for adults to appreciate, to works of horror and the supernatural in a lineage descending from the Gothic novel, to works that tamed fantasy with the rules of science and emerged qualified by a veneer of realism as "science fiction" (separately discussed by Katherine Hume), and including works that challenged the borders of the real – by consorting with superhuman "savages" such as Tarzan or Conan; by exploring alternative realms within and without from faerie to

Middle Earth to Earthsea; by traversing the space–time continuum in alternative realities that embraced *The Once and Future King* and fostered our ability to see infinity in a grain of sand with William Blake or "Galaxies Like Grains of Sands" with the multi-talented, multi-modal contemporary British author Brian Aldiss.

It seems surprising in retrospect that the very fans and readers creating and increasing a popular market for supernatural stories, science fiction, and fantasy would not have conceived these works as "romance." H. G. Wells had called his books "scientific romances" and the two British writers most responsible for shaping modern fantasy also used the term "romance." George MacDonald subtitled his innovative grown-up fairy tale *Phantastes*, "A Faerie Romance for Men and Women," and William Morris spent the final years of his life writing and publishing prose romances.[2]

Romance, then, flourished in the twentieth century through two of its most vibrant and creative stepchildren: science fiction and fantasy. Both of them arose in the mid-nineteenth century, and they were to some extent mutually supportive. Some authors, including writers as diverse as H. G. Wells, Jules Verne, Ray Bradbury, Ursula Le Guin, and Piers Anthony have comfortably written in both genres, but this essay will focus primarily on the survival of romance in fantasy.

Fantasy today represents a triumph of romance in spirit, myth, and marketplace. With the Harry Potter films and book revenues setting records for a market that includes virtually all ages, and Peter Jackson's epic cinematic rendering of J. R. R. Tolkien's *The Lord of the Rings* bringing new generations of twenty-first-century readers to appreciate the work of the most scholarly of the great twentieth-century fantasy writers, it looks as if romance will turn out to be one of the dominant modes in twentieth-century literary history.

The Origins of Modern Fantasy

Converging factors offered fertile grounds for fantasy. The nineteenth century witnessed the rapid growth of printed media and literacy, thanks in part to the influence of guilds and unions and the spread of working-men's colleges. A rising middle class had wealth and an interest in reading works both old and new. And as the industrial revolution swept through all aspects of society, it increased our abilities to look both backward and forward in time. For one thing, the pace of change itself had accelerated to the point where it could not be ignored.[3] Families in earlier generations had accustomed themselves to gradual social, political, and personal change. Most parents took it on faith that there would be slow but steady *progress*, but they could rest easy with the assurance that – barring the drastic intervention of good fortune or disaster – their children's lives would be on the whole quite similar to their own.

By the middle of the nineteenth century, they could no longer enjoy that comfort. Landscapes and urban environments were transformed before their eyes. Inventions and conceptions not only multiplied, but *awareness* of the changes became pervasive.

And simultaneously, along with revolutionary changes toward the future, there were major breakthroughs in awareness of the past. Translations of ancient texts proliferated; hieroglyphics were deciphered, opening new doors to ancient Egypt; archaeology uncovered layers of ancient history; and folklorists collected tales and legends that memory and oral traditions had preserved for centuries. Science fiction was part of the literary impulse to cope with all these changes and discoveries through the projection of potential scenarios to emulate or to avoid; fantasy was a similar kind of literary coping mechanism, offering escape from change by creating the opportunity to enter a completely different reality for a while.[4]

Another way of understanding the impulse toward fantasy is that it helped set rapid historical change in perspective by presenting entirely different scales of existence and possibilities for transformation. Whether fantasy depicted diminutive worlds of fairies, small animals, and little people, or vast terrains, great armies, and larger than life heroes, changes in the actual world became relatively inconsequential when compared to complete bodily metamorphoses, the rise and fall of empires, the cosmic clash of good and evil, or the conquest of all time and space through magic or rebirth or resurrection. These matters were on planes beyond mundane existence, and they called for a reassessment of temporal and material alterations. Traditional religious institutions that might otherwise have fulfilled this function seemed overwhelmed, but as Harold Bloom observes, "Theology, whether orthodox or heretical, finds its last literary refuge in classic and modern fantasy" (1994: xii). Amid a great age of scientific and technological discovery accompanied by the rediscovery of ancient cultures through archaeology, exploration, and the translation of texts, literary artists and a wide audience of popular readers felt the need to set forth and explore unknown worlds – precisely as the known world was more completely encompassed and explained. There was a thirst for the unexplainable and unpredictable, an omnivorous desire to cope with and enjoy the unfathomable.

The contours of modern fantasy arising from works by Morris and MacDonald in the mid-nineteenth century formed a clearly shaped genre by the early decades of the twentieth century. As various authors suggest in this volume of essays, the truth of the matter is that this popular new fiction signaled the rebirth of one of the oldest modes of imaginative writing. Romance was reincarnated and revitalized in brilliant works of modern fantasy. The landmark nineteenth-century works of prose romance include Lewis Carroll's *Alice's Adventures in Wonderland* (1865) and its sequel *Through the Looking Glass and What Alice Found There* (1872), which Bloom describes as "the still unmatched masterpiece of prose fantasy in English" (1994: xi). Other milestone nineteenth-century works include Mary Shelley's *Frankenstein* (1818); Washington Irving's *The Sketch-Book of Geoffrey Crayon* (1819–20) (especially "Rip Van Winkle" and "The Legend of Sleepy Hollow"); Nathaniel Hawthorne's *Twice-Told Tales* (1837); Charles Dickens' *A Christmas Carol* (1843); William Morris' "The Hollow Land" (1856) and other stories; George Meredith's *The Shaving of Shagpat: An Arabian Entertainment* (1856); George MacDonald's *Phantastes* (1858); George Eliot's "The Lifted Veil" (1859); Carlo Collodi's *Pinocchio* (1882); H. Rider Haggard's *King*

Solomon's Mines (1885) and *She* (1886); Mark Twain's *A Connecticut Yankee in King Arthur's Court* (1889); and Bram Stoker's *Dracula* (1897).[5]

Themes and techniques abound, but Morris and MacDonald established a cluster of defining characteristics: a break with conventional reality; a clear struggle of good against evil; a hero called to high purpose; episodic plot structures in which apparently unrelated events coalesce into clusters of significance; and a revolutionary fluidity of form, time, causality, language, and reality. MacDonald can be said to have fathered the "faerie romance" and fantasies grounded in religious vision. Morris provided the pattern of heroic, politically radical, secular, and epic fantasy. MacDonald's influence is clearly seen in the writing of David Lindsay, C. S. Lewis, Owen Barfield, and Charles Williams, and it reaches a twentieth-century climax of sorts in John Crowley's *Little, Big* (1981) and in his related *Aegypt* series.[6] Morris' influence is found in the works of Lord Dunsany, Henry Newbolt, Fritz Leiber, E. R. Eddison, Robert E. Howard, J. R. R. Tolkien, Stephen Donaldson, and other epic fantasy writers who chose a scale far larger than Faerie, which found a natural culmination in Robert Holdstock's *Mythago Wood* (1984) and his *Mythago Cycle*.[7] Of course, neither genetic strand is pure; C. S. Lewis, J. R. R. Tolkien, and others directly acknowledge the influence of *both* of these founding fathers of fantasy, but their differing techniques and assumptions also suggest divergent paths.

Approaches to Modern Fantasy

Of the innumerable schema offering means to organize the unfolding of romance in twentieth-century fantasy, the micro and macro perspectives that can be extrapolated from the techniques of MacDonald and Morris respectively seem especially fertile. The turn toward applied science in the Victorian age opened special avenues for the romantic sensibility. Whether one navigates the streets with a magnifying glass or field-glasses, one gains new knowledge – and the differences revealed by the lenses may reflect differing philosophies and sensibilities.

In fact, one way of conceiving the two strands of modern fantasy is through the contrast of little and big, a technique exploited by Jonathan Swift in the two contrasting books of *Gulliver's Travels*. The MacDonald lineage yields a type of fantasy on the scale of Lilliput that seems to move inward. In fantasy of this type one often enters an unknown world through a diminutive or interior location – the back of a cupboard or wardrobe, a door in a garden wall, or some other small and domestic space. The Morris model by contrast often extends on an epic scale – at once ancient and infinite. Such Brobdingnagian realms tend to call for heroes with larger than life strengths and virtues. Often the story depicts a monumental struggle that sprawls across vast landscapes and seems to touch primordial sources. In truth, both modes resonate with elements that are primordial or archetypal, and it is telling that in the last quarter of the twentieth century Northrop Frye dedicated his Charles Eliot Norton lectures at Harvard University to "a study of the structure of romance," published as *The Secular Scripture* (1976). The construction of romance was a building of meaning relevant to an increasingly secular society in much the way scriptures or sacred texts served older generations. Here were fables and parables removed from daily life in which one could discover truth.

The Quest for Belief in Romance

The religious impulse specifically – and systematic philosophy generally – found itself under attack by the rational and applied successes of science as the industrial revolution gathered steam. In the mid-nineteenth century, the minister and editor George MacDonald found ways to approach intuitive truths through imagined realms where his religious principles could capture the imagination. The result was a startling first novel: *Phantastes: A Faerie Romance for Men and Women* (1858). In this book MacDonald successfully transplanted the fairy tale to the grown-up world with fluid, free-associative themes and plot elements. While the context remains commonplace and modest in scale, the issues and implications expand outward; *Phantastes*, like subsequent works in its tradition, embodies the paradox that what seems at first small may in fact be large. Yet despite the unexpected forests and dimensions that open within MacDonald's fantasy, it remains a world of restriction and constraint, although it was written at about the same time that Morris composed epic fantasy set in elemental landscapes.

Fantasy introduces several radical ideas drawn from the romance tradition. First, it makes countercultural assertions about the nature of progress. Morris looked back to an idealized Middle Ages, a time when superstition and religion commanded stronger allegiances than science and logic. While not entirely rejecting the idea of progress (Morris and others imagined the enactment of utopian ideas in the future as well as the past),[8] the writing nonetheless does not presuppose that "new" is "better." It seeks preservation or "restoration" of the fragile elements of a golden time. Often there is a hint of Plato in the orientation of fantasy – a suggestion that the truest learning is remembering – which would imply an education more tied to the past than to the present and future.

Fantasy writers are likely to presuppose a fall from perfection as part of history, with the present day viewed as not necessarily an improvement from an earlier condition. Often there is reference to a golden age or a prelapsarian time before the fall. Fantasy challenges our impulse to consider the present as "the best of times." Morris borrowed many of his utopian ideas from the lost values he saw in a more hopeful past, and he devoted much of his life to a reaffirmation and reinterpretation of the Gothic; Tolkien's *oeuvre* makes the point repeatedly that though lost light will never be fully recovered, each teller of tales can record and repeat its story and thereby retain or reclaim a part of its radiance.

In the emerging fantasy tradition the loss of great light does not necessarily mean the present must be overwhelmed by darkness. The genre of Gothic romance traditionally dated from Horace Walpole's *The Castle of Otranto* (1765) had suggested the potential for powerful evil presences, partly sustained through atmosphere and mood, supernatural elements, and the presence of ghosts linked to a tradition of such stories, but in the end most fiction flowing directly in that lineage led to weird tales, Gothic novels, or horror fiction. There are trace elements of idealism in their convoluted visions, but they evolve in a tradition driven by response to fear and outside the main legacy of romance and fantasy.

One supernatural predecessor more akin to fantasy was Charles Dickens' immensely popular seasonal tale, *A Christmas Carol* (1843), in which the ghost story combined with allegory to turn toward a vision of hope and renewal. This fiction moved toward fantasy, and it was a movement toward the rejection of materialism and cynicism, toward affirmation of renewal and belief.

Darker supernatural elements formed a core in the fiction of Edgar Allan Poe, and he began reshaping the short-story form to include more overwhelming supernatural elements, leaning toward dangerous, powerful, uncontrollable, and ominous aspects, which would eventually be expressed in dark romance fantasies. Poe pioneered techniques and themes of supernatural fantasy in stories such as "The Manuscript Found in a Bottle" (1833), "The Fall of the House of Usher" (1839), and "The Masque of the Red Death" (1842). This strand was taken up in the late Victorian period by Bram Stoker and others, carried into the pulp era in fiction by such writers as H. P. Lovecraft and Clark Ashton Smith, and survives today in the novels and stories of Anne Rice and Stephen King. But this movement toward the dark side was not the mainstream strength of the romance tradition, nor has it been at its heart.

While technology was rapidly obliterating the constraints of space and time by creating fast and ubiquitous modes of transportation, fantasy writers proved they could similarly break transport barriers with even greater dramatic success. In the United States in 1900, L. Frank Baum introduced modern mythic figures that were peculiarly American – the Scarecrow, the Tin Woodman, the Cowardly Lion, and the rest of the cast. He moved his characters through space in both plausible and implausible ways (a tornado or a long walk to Oz; a magical flight by mythical creatures or magical transport home). J. M. Barrie introduced Peter Pan in 1902 in *The Little White Bird*, later elaborating the invention in theatrical productions beginning in 1904, which were developed in *Peter Pan in Kensington Garden* (1906), and finally shaped into a fully fledged children's book in *Peter and Wendy* (1911). The story of the boy who could fly was not only a reminder of the fairy-tale tradition, but also gave each individual the power of flight. Furthermore, Barrie implicitly addressed issues of ageing and mortality through the idea of choosing whether or not to enter a land of eternal youth – and through his unspoken recognition that children's stories broke barriers of age and mortality every day. Both these authors clearly understood that their stories reached adults as well as the children the adults reared and read to – that they spoke not only to "children of all ages," but that they spoke directly to all ages.

Another living influence touching on the ageless appeal these writers sought has roots in the increased awareness of folklore and oral traditions previously mentioned.

Jakob and Wilhelm Grimm had published their influential collection of *Kinder- und Hausmärchen* (popularly translated as *Fairy Tales*) in 1812–13; mythic tales from the north were collected in Finland by Elias Lonnrott and published as *Kalevala* in 1835; Welsh tales from *The Mabinogion* were translated and published in English between 1838 and 1849. By the start of the twentieth century, the devoted work of scholars and translators had not only succeeded in preserving these and other fascinating tales and legends, but had also shown that these stories had compelling attractions of a timeless quality. And they appealed to audiences of virtually all ages. Including parables and cautionary tales, tragic and comic visions, and characters who ranged in age from infants to ancients, in kind from animals to magicians, in wisdom from the fool to the wise, and in social station from beggar to king, they became perfect complements to the industrial revolution. They were fruits of scholarship that offered ways of preserving alternative modes of knowledge from the past and important transitional support for societies immersed in science and realism. Rooted in the work of the past was the persistent and disturbing message that the reality that is most real cannot be seen; the truths most true cannot be proven. Many writers of fantasy built on the examples of old tales with their different systems of knowledge, faith, and belief. These qualities, though difficult to articulate clearly, form a characteristic expression of romance in fantasy moving forward through a skeptical age. They are exemplified most obviously in such works as G. K. Chesterton's *The Man Who Was Thursday* (1908); Charles Williams' *The Place of the Lion* (1931); C. S. Lewis' *The Lion, the Witch, and the Wardrobe* (1950); Gene Wolfe's *The Book of the New Sun* (1980–3), a hybrid science-fiction fantasy; and Orson Scott Card's *Seventh Son* (1987) and Alvin Maker tales.

These matters of faith and belief also haunt the edges and complicate the depths of other twentieth-century books in less explicit ways. *The Cream of the Jest* (1917), *Jurgen* (1919), *Figures of Earth* (1921), and the other interlocking works that comprise the 18-volume masterpiece of James Branch Cabell, known collectively as *The Biography of Manuel*, employ folk motifs and brilliant wit to turn intellect upon itself; Mervyn Peake's *Titus Groan* (1946), *Gormenghast* (1950), and *Titus Alone* (1959), sometimes referred to as the *Gormenghast Trilogy*, combine Gothic settings and surreal vision with humor and intelligence to create a masterpiece that seems simultaneously to inhabit both real and fantastical realities. *The Last Unicorn* (1968), by Peter Beagle, also combines intellectual self-consciousness and humor with romantic simplicity to fold fantasy back upon its own traditions in a story that is paradoxically beautiful, funny, and sad.

A Century of Fantasy and New Technologies

Just as changes in technology shaped the development of fantasy in the nineteenth century, new technologies shaped its evolution in the twentieth. Improved techniques of mass production and the development of new, cheaper, and faster printing and

binding processes affected everything from the composition of type and the manufac-
ture of paper to the systems of marketing and distribution of the finished printed
works. In addition, the rapidly developing mass media of film, radio, and television
fostered new techniques of writing while enhancing a writer's ability to reach huge
numbers of people quickly. Romance as a true child of popular culture thus acquired
new characteristics and dimensions.

American publisher Frank A. Munsey led a manufacturing change to cheaper
printing papers made from wood pulp with his magazine *The Argosy* in the 1880s.
By the turn of the century, this trend resulted in a proliferation of popular magazines
selling for very low cover prices and catering to special interests.[9] Munsey helped to
usher in a period of "pulp fiction" that lasted through the turn of the century and into
the 1950s. Thanks to the audiences created by the pulps, important new markets for
fantasy writers emerged. One of the best known of these magazines, *All-Story*, had
originally been edited for children (as *Argosy* had been), but it began publishing
fantastic stories for adults in 1905. In the days before scientific market research, good
editors found ways of combining the adventures and fancies appealing in childhood
with works that also engaged older readers. By 1920 Munsey had merged *All-Story*
with *Argosy* to become *Argosy All-Story Weekly*. Edgar Rice Burroughs launched his
career in the pages of *All-Story*, where *Tarzan of the Apes* made its debut in 1912. It was
also where Burroughs published his immensely popular Barsoom series, beginning
with *A Princess of Mars*, also in 1912, and the Pellucidar series, starting with *At the
Earth's Core* in 1914. While some critics classify Burroughs' stories as science fiction,
since most events in his tales are explained without magic, his work made the
essential pattern of romance immensely popular and accessible. Whether set on
Mars, or in the jungles of Africa, or at the Earth's very core, a Burroughs story
presented imaginative situations and ideas that were virtually if not actually impossible. Tarzan, in particular, is an immensely influential fantasy invention, a figure
possessing the larger than life elements necessary to qualify as fantasy hero. He
prefigured Conan the Barbarian, another of the great superhuman characters in fantasy
to have emerged from the pulps. And his appeal to youngsters as well as older readers
endures not only in continuing paperback sales, but also through comic books,
cartoons, films, and other media.

Another contributor to *All-Story* who rivaled Burroughs for popularity was A.
Merritt, whose work appeared there regularly from 1917 through to the 1930s.
Merritt, a journalist and editor of Hearst's *American Weekly* newspaper supplement,
was perhaps the most popular fantasy novelist of his day. He wrote in a lush, poetic,
and artificial style, contributing to the tradition of a special language for fantasy
worlds. His books, including *The Moon Pool* (1919), *The Ship of Ishtar* (1926), and
Dwellers in the Mirage (1932), have sold millions of copies.

The first magazine devoted specifically to fantasy and horror was *Weird Tales*
(1925–54). Especially during the long tenure of its most influential editor, Farns-
worth Wright, it published a varied and significant body of fantasy writing, including the Conan stories of Robert E. Howard. Other important authors whose work was

published in *Weird Tales* were H. P. Lovecraft, Ray Bradbury, and Robert Bloch. The success of a healthy number of pulp magazines nourished a talented group of writers who understood their readers' appetite for entertainment, escape, and expansion. Together these creative and commercial forces went a long way toward ensuring that the development of fantasy depended more on popular or mass appeal than it did on intellectual or highbrow approval.

It also demonstrates another interesting way in which changes in technology have continued to shape and influence fantasy. Throughout the twentieth century, however primitive a fantasy hero such as Tarzan or Conan might appear, it was generally cutting-edge technology that served to deliver new romance permutations to mass audiences. At the same time, the very structure, content, and style of romance were changed by the media. The language of the writing was tailored to speed, and the writing style became less important than the creations and events unfolding. Newspaper comics and comic books began both to support and exercise influence on fantasy as graphic artists told enormously complicated stories in pictures, and legions of new superheroes emerged. Tarzan appeared in a comic strip drawn by Harold Foster in 1929. "The Phantom," by Lee Falk and Ray Moore, began in 1936. "Superman," the creation of writer Jerome Siegel and artist Joe Schuster, appeared in *Action Comics #1* in 1938. *Marvel Comics #1* appeared in 1939. Thereafter, visual conceptions of scene and action in fantasy coexisted with comic-book "frames," and the nonverbal abilities of comic-book artists exerted new influences on writers of fantasy.

Alternative Languages for Alternative Worlds

One thematic strand in the evolution of fantasy had always been its usually unstated but implicit attempt to transcend words. Sometimes this took the form of artificial language, as in the writings of Morris, Cabell, or Merritt, but there were other methods ranging from minimalism to free association, from the spare chapters of Italo Calvino in *Cosmicomics* (1963; translated 1968) to the sprawling prose visions of Gene Wolfe in *Nightside the Long Sun* (1993) and *The Book of the Long Sun* series. Moreover, the technologies and collaborative sensibilities that gave rise to comic books nurtured and advanced this impulse. Even more important, however, the collaborative potential of the fantastic and visual imagination was released and explored in the new mass medium of film. Important early milestones include *The Avenging Conscience* (1914), a film version of Poe's "The Tell-tale Heart"; *Tarzan of the Apes* (1918), which brought Edgar Rice Burroughs to the screen; and F. W. Murnau's *Nosferatu* (1922), which began a series of haunting vampire movies, with a bumper crop of Dracula films to follow. In 1931 a Mark Twain fantasy made it to the screen with *A Connecticut Yankee*, and that same year marked the first release of *Frankenstein* and *Dracula*. Lewis Carroll's *Alice in Wonderland* appeared on screens in 1933, as well as *The Invisible Man* and *King Kong*, and toward the end of the 1930s two immensely important films were released: the first full-length animated feature film by Walt

Disney, *Snow White and the Seven Dwarfs* (1937), a breakthrough achievement opening up new possibilities for fantasy on the screen, and *The Wizard of Oz* (1939), in which directors Victor Fleming and King Vidor combined color and sepia camera work, appealing special effects, and a superb musical score and cast, to give a whole new meaning to fantasy with enduring appeal for "children of all ages."[10] From these early popular successes, writers, directors, producers, and actors learned through new technologies the same powerful message that fantasy conveys through one of the oldest of human technologies, our written language: that it is characteristic of high art for a medium to transcend itself. And just as fantasy writers had always sought effects in writing that occurred beyond the limits of language, artists using photography – a medium made to capture and reproduce what was *really* there – discovered that some of their greatest achievements lay in conveying the fantastic and unreal through this medium.

There is no space here to discuss the fascinating evolution of fantasy through film, but the popularity of Hollywood fantasy, the astounding growth of special effects, and the cross-fertilization of television and film will be at least somewhat familiar to most readers. New technologies continue to unfold new realms for fantasy, as computers have led to fluid new interactive forms of digital language. The infant industry of video games has opened virtual spaces for interactive fiction and role-playing that join writers, visual artists, programmers, and audiences in participatory acts of mutually constructed fantasy. The technologies metamorphose as quickly as shape-shifters have in fantasy from Ovid's *Metamorphoses* right through to Piers Anthony's heroine in *A Spell for Chameleon* (1977) or the genie in Walt Disney's *Aladdin*. As if to illustrate this point, the film fantasies referred to at the start of this essay – Peter Jackson's *Lord of the Rings* and Chris Columbus' *Harry Potter* – have been released on digital video disks with additional scenes and interactive features. Marketed separately are "game" versions of both feature films.

Many of the seminal works in twentieth-century literary fantasy are also about the limits of language. Morris surmounted the constraints of Victorian English by turning to the simple words and rough cadences of its Anglo-Saxon roots. H. G. Wells took note of this achievement in his review of *The Well at the World's End* in the *Saturday Review*: "To those who write its pages will be a purification, it is full of clean strong sentences and sweet old words. 'Quean' and 'carle,' 'eme,' 'good sooth,' yeasay' and 'naysay' . . . 'fain' and 'lief' and 'loth' and 'sunder,' and the like good honest words will come all the readier after this reading" (Wells 1896: 413). Other writers, including Tolkien, invent entire language systems and syntax or selected sets of new vocabulary. Implied by these inventions is the underlying sense that the most essential elements we grapple with are things for which we have no words – or for which our ordinary words are inadequate or obfuscating. There is no rule about how the limits of language should be attacked or overcome. Some of the complex multiple systems, such as one finds in Tolkien's work, may suggest that we are capable of imagining whole language universes we have never seen before. Other writers who employ apparently similar but imprecise clusters of invented words, such as Lewis or

Le Guin, may indicate that the addition of mere fragments of new language can transform our perceptions of reality.

Lewis, like MacDonald and much of the fantasy tradition in antiquity and the Middle Ages, created a fusion of fantasy and the religious vision. In fact, the Oxford Inklings (including Lewis, Williams, and Tolkien) collectively shared and developed a complex and multilayered body of fantasy rooted in Christian belief. Lewis' intuition of joy, beauty, justice, and infinite perfection led to his profound Christianity; Morris' and Moorcock's dissatisfaction with society, politics, and stereotypes led to counter-cultural and revolutionary secular idealism – utopian in Morris and anti-heroic in Moorcock. Fantasy opens possibilities of transformation even in the hands of the iconoclastic Moorcock, whose heroes such as Elric, Hawkmoon, and others in the *Eternal Champion* novels mock and satirize Conan and other prior superheroic characters, using irony that ultimately turns upon itself to advocate ideals while eroding brute strength and certitude.

In a century driven by rationality tempered by irony or satire, fantasy offered a way out – a glimpse of some perfection beyond the surfaces of reality. The position is beautifully captured in the central metaphor of an H. G. Wells story, which also becomes the title of a touchstone book: "The Door in the Wall" (1906, 1911). This title – and this book itself as an artifact – encapsulate the essence of modern fantasy. The American publisher Mitchell Kennerley achieved a publishing breakthrough embracing cutting-edge print technology and fantasy fiction. In what must surely have been in part homage to Morris, whose fantasy novels were handset in types of his own design and illustrated with prints and decorations harking back to Johann Gutenberg, Kennerley commissioned his own type design from Frederic Goudy and created a book of fantasy that would use the most realistic artistic medium – photography – to enhance a work of modern romance. The photographs of Alvin Langdon Coburn were printed to extraordinary effect to illustrate the pure fantasy of H. G. Wells. And the combination rings true to the airy idealism of Wells' prose:

> There was something in the very air of it that exhilarated, that gave one a sense of lightness and good happening and well being; there was something in the sight of it that made all its colour clean and perfect and subtly luminous. In the instant of coming into it one was exquisitely glad – as only in rare moments and when one is young and joyful one can be glad in this world. And everything was beautiful there. (9)

This heightened perception of pure joy prefigures C. S. Lewis' later articulations in his Christian apologetics and his fiction of how transient intuitions can lead one to romantic visions. The narrator in Wells' story is transformed in a moment of profound perception:

> In the very moment the door swung to behind me, I forgot the road with its fallen chestnut leaves, its cabs and tradesmen's carts, I forgot the sort of gravitational pull back to the discipline and obedience of home, I forgot all hesitations and fear ... . I became in a moment a very glad and wonder-happy little boy – in another world. It was a world

Plate 7 The Door in the Wall, title-page spread for H. G. Wells' book (1906), illustrated with photographs by Alvin Langdon Coburn (New York: Mitchell Kennerley, 1911). The title is taken from Wells' 1906 short story that begins the collection. (George Eastman House.)

> with a different quality, a warmer, more penetrating and mellower light, with a faint clear gladness in its air, and wisps of sun-touched cloud in the blueness of its sky. And before me ran this long wide path, invitingly, with weedless beds on either side, rich with untended flowers, and these two great panthers. (9)

Wells presents this in terms that might describe epiphany in fantasy fiction more generally:

> an abnormal gift ... that in the guise of wall and door offered him an outlet, a secret and peculiar passage of escape into another and altogether more beautiful world ... By our daylight standard he walked out of security into darkness, danger and death. But did he see like that? (24)

The structure can be epic or fragmentary: Tolkien's *The Lord of the Rings* or his *Unfinished Tales*; Cabell's *Biography of Manuel* or Calvino's *Cosmicomics*; Burroughs' *Pellucidar* and *Tarzan* or Borges' *Ficciones* and *Dreamtigers*. Fantasy has proven its imaginative and literary effectiveness at virtually every generic length. It reminds us that our tendency to interpret change through time as "improvement" or "progress" must be questioned, for the oldest stories have such power still that they call each new generation not only to read them but to retell them – as Morris retold classical epics, Old French romances, Welsh tales, and Norse legends; as T. H. White and others have retold Arthurian legends (see the chapter on Arthurian romance); as Evangeline Walton and Lloyd Alexander have retold the *Mabinogion*; as John Barth or Salman Rushdie adapt and renew the *Arabian Nights*... the list could go on and on.

And especially in the last decades of the twentieth century, romance found ways to incorporate reflexive self-consciousness, irony, experimentation, and gamesmanship. It evolved a variety of alternatives to rational and linear realistic fiction, dissociating its stories from necessary correspondence to reality. One finds examples in works by Barth and Rushdie as well as those of innovators such as Brian Aldiss, William Burroughs, Angela Carter, Harlan Ellison, Thomas Pynchon, John Updike, and many others. Their alternative approaches to fiction eschewed correlation with literal or scientific truth while avoiding the neat symbolic correlations of allegory. A variety of resulting styles and forms offered authors the virtually unlimited freedom to cross the borders of conventional fiction and romance in order to explore philosophical, political, and social alternatives.

William Gibson's *Neuromancer* (1984), discussed by Katherine Hume, crosses boundaries of another order as it blazes a fusion of scientific and fantastical elements in ways that brilliantly exemplify the "new romancer": the hero who shares many of the pure strains of the traditional romance hero described by Ray Thompson, but combines these in surroundings that conspire (ultimately unsuccessfully) toward the ironic mode. Here is the traditional journey of romance undertaken at both the macrocosmic, global level and the microcosmic internal neurons of inner space. And here in the fusion of inner and outer body – the neurons of the individual at play in a limitless global or ultimately cosmic network of the wired information matrix – the new romancer finds not hard science but ghosts and magic within the machine as voodoo entities and mythic archetypes surface and mystify, haunt and disappear elusively beyond the hero's grasp or understanding.

Like H. G. Wells – one of the fathers of science fiction who also nurtured romance in an outpouring of fantasy stories at the start of the twentieth century – Gibson and other trans-genre authors reminded us at the century's end that no genre – and no hero – faces the twenty-first century alone, unmixed, and pure. Yet the inexhaustible wellsprings of romance continue to provide us with sources for purifying transformation in modes of fantasy that remain fluid, inspiring, metamorphic, and that always tantalizingly lead us further into the unknown.

Notes

1. Most notable and influential among the publisher responses in the US was the Ballantine Adult Fantasy Series. Riding on the coat-tails of the popularity of Tolkien's novels in paperback, the Ballantines tested a few fantasy reprints starting in 1966. Betty Ballantine and Lin Carter then officially initiated the Ballantine Adult Fantasy Series that eventually included some 60 volumes, published between May 1969 and April 1974.

2. Morris published these first pure romances with Reeves and Turner: *A Tale of the House of the Wolfings, and All the Kindreds of the Mark Written in Prose and in Verse* (London: Reeves and Turner, 1889) and *Roots of the Mountains, Wherein Is Told Somewhat of the Lives of the Men of Burgdale Their Friends Their Neighbours Their Foemen and Their Fellows in Arms* (London: Reeves and Turner, 1890). His other prose romances were published in brilliant, hand-printed, hand-bound editions at his own Kelmscott Press: *The Story of the Glittering Plain, Which Has Been Also Called the Land of Living Men or the Acre of the Undying* (Hammersmith: Kelmscott Press, 1891 – the first book printed at the Kelmscott Press); *News from Nowhere: or, An Epoch of Rest, Being Some Chapters from a Utopian Romance* (Boston: Roberts Brothers, 1890 – the actual unauthorized first edition; London: Reeves and Turner, 1891; Hammersmith: Kelmscott Press [sold by Reeves & Turner], 1893); *The Wood Beyond the World* (Hammersmith: Kelmscott Press, 1894); *Child Christopher and Goldilind the Fair* (Hammersmith: Kelmscott Press, 1895); *The Well at the World's End* (Hammersmith: Kelmscott Press, 1896); *The Water of the Wondrous Isles* (Hammersmith: Kelmscott Press, 1897); and *The Sundering Flood* (Hammersmith: Kelmscott Press, 1898).

3. This point was suggested to me in a conversation with book historian and antiquarian bookseller Sean Donnelly, Tampa, Florida, April 17, 2003.

4. Ibid.

5. The indispensable source for tracing the evolution of the genre in America is Brian Attebery's *The Fantasy Tradition in American Literature: From Irving to Le Guin* (Bloomington: Indiana University Press, 1980).

6. The series currently includes *Aegypt* (1987), *Love & Sleep* (1994), and *Daemonomania* (2000).

7. Also known as the Ryhope Wood series, the Mythago series currently includes *Lavondyss: Journey to an Unknown Region* (1988), *The Hollowing* (1993), a collection of related short stories in *Merlin's Wood* (1994), the title story in *The Bone Forest* (1991), and *Gate of Ivory, Gate of Horn* (1997).

8. Morris composed two major utopian novels, both set in England: *A Dream of John Ball*, set in the Middle Ages, and *News from Nowhere*, set in the twenty-first century.

9. Frank Andrew Munsey (1854–1925) was a self-made millionaire who built a newspaper and magazine empire, including *The Argosy*, *The All-Story*, *The Cavalier*, *Munsey's Magazine*, and others. In addition to shaping the pulp paper and size format (about 7 by 10 inches), Munsey also led the way in converting publications to an all-fiction content, eliminating the mixture of articles, poems, and curiosities found in the traditional magazine.

10. John Grant notes in *The Encyclopedia of Fantasy* that this was not the first time Baum's land of Oz had been filmed. The silent film versions he mentions are *Dorothy and the Scarecrow of Oz* (1910), *The Land of Oz* (1910), *The Patchwork Girl of Oz* (1914), *His Majesty, The Scarecrow of Oz* (1914), the only version produced by Baum himself, *The Magic Cloak of Oz* (1914), and *The Ragged Girl of Oz* (1919).

References and Further Reading

Attebery, Brian (1992). *Strategies of Fantasy.* Bloomington: Indiana University Press.

Barron, Neil (1990). *Fantasy Literature: A Reader's Guide.* New York: Garland.

Bloom, Harold, ed. (1994). *Classic Fantasy Writers.* New York: Chelsea House.

Bloom, Harold (1995). *Modern Fantasy Writers.* New York: Chelsea House.

Clute, John, and John Grant (1997). *The Encyclopedia of Fantasy.* New York: St. Martin's.

Frye, Northrop (1967). *Anatomy of Criticism: Four Essays.* New York: Atheneum. [First published in 1957.]

Frye, Northrop (1976). *The Secular Scripture: A Study of the Structure of Romance.* Cambridge, MA: Harvard University Press.

Le Guin, Ursula K. (1979). *The Language of the Night: Essays on Fantasy and Science Fiction,* ed. Susan Wood. New York: Putnam.

Magill, Frank N. (1983). *Survey of Modern Fantasy Literature.* Englewood Cliffs, NJ: Salem Press.

Manlove, C. N. (1975). *Modern Fantasy: Five Studies.* Cambridge: Cambridge University Press.

Mathews, Richard (1997). *Fantasy: The Liberation of Imagination.* New York: Twayne; London: Prentice-Hall.

Pringle, David, ed. (1995). *The St. James Guide to Fantasy.* New York and London: St. James Press.

Rabkin, Eric S. (1976). *The Fantastic in Literature.* Princeton, NJ: Princeton University Press.

Wells, H. G. (1896). Review of *The Well at the World's End. Saturday Review* (London), 17 October 1896. [Reprinted in *William Morris: The Critical Heritage,* ed. Peter Faulkner. London: Routledge and Kegan Paul, 1973, pp. 413–15.]

Wells, H. G. ([1911] 1980). *The Door in the Wall and Other Stories.* With Photographs by Alvin Langdon Coburn. Boston: David R. Godine. [Reproduction of the edition first published in 1911 by Mitchell Kennerley; story first published in 1906.]

28

Quest Romance in Science Fiction

Kathryn Hume

Science fiction has produced its epics, its utopian and dystopian satires, and the occasional comic or tragic plot, but most readers associate the form with the quest romance. Early in the history of the genre such romances were mainly adventure stories, but now they tend to explore either technological or scientific problems, or they investigate social patterns (human or alien). In any event, they adhere to the hero monomyth pattern. Initial equilibrium is shattered by the call to adventure; the hero crosses the threshold into a special world; he or she struggles with various adversaries and problems, and returns to the normal world, more mature and more firmly integrated into his or her society, usually as some kind of leader.

For a varied sample of texts that follow the pattern, consider Isaac Asimov's *Fantastic Voyage*, Gregory Benford's *Timescape*, John Brunner's *Shockwave Rider*, Arthur C. Clarke's *Fountains of Paradise*, Philip K. Dick's *Ubik*, Joe Haldeman's *Forever War*, Ursula Le Guin's *The Dispossessed*, Alexei Panshin's *Rite of Passage*, Bruce Sterling's *Islands in the Net*, John Wyndham's *Day of the Triffids*, and Roger Zelazny's "The Doors of His Face, the Lamps of His Mouth." The science-fiction form of the pattern tends to assume a focal hero, a futuristic setting, and an emphasis on technology that would logically preclude highly skilled hand-to-hand fighting, though one finds routine violations of those and other commonalities: a group protagonist in Clarke's *Rendezvous with Rama*; significant hand-to-hand combat combined with space travel and elaborate ecochemistry in Herbert's *Dune* series; something akin to the Dark Ages in Hoban's *Riddley Walker*, although the protagonist interacts with the technological researchers of his day; refusal to return to normal existence in McIntyre's *Superluminal*. These variants, however, also exist in earlier romance and folktale, where we have triadic heroes (or leader and 12 companions), and the poor third son of a peasant who wins a princess and understandably stays in her realm rather than returning to his father's hovel.

Science-fiction plots thus have clear structural affinities with earlier romances. Furthermore, one can argue that many scientific inventions function within the plot exactly as various magic gimmicks do in romances and fantasies. N-space drive is operationally equivalent to stepping through a mirror or to wandering a year and a day and finding your destination at that symbolic moment. They move the protagonist by unusual and maybe uncanny means to a special world, where adventures can happen that would not take place back in the normal world.[1]

My question grows out of this uneasy equivalence of science and magic. If at least some science exists to fulfill quest romance plot functions, is science fiction just updated medieval romance, or does its eponymous claim to science justify itself by opening up the form to something new? If it does manage to add something new to this very widespread popular tradition, what might the novelties be? I shall argue that the human body and what animates that body – basics in any culture's imaginary – change fairly radically between the earlier quest romance and science fiction.

Bodies and Souls

Much of the Western tradition's quest romance was established by medieval romances, and the culture they reflected was Catholic. Hence, they assume that a human consists of a soul and a body. Most Middle English romances show the protagonist fighting various opponents or, on occasion, making moral and psychological choices. By defeating the opposition and making the right decisions, he or she ends up well established in this world and well prepared for the next. Without being particularly pious, the English strain of romance usually maintains an orientation toward the good health of the soul. *Sir Amadace* and *Amis and Amiloun* illustrate the popular pattern, *Sir Gawain and the Green Knight* its more sophisticated form.

The medieval hero's body conforms to the accepted limitations of everyday existence. It may be stronger and less easily destroyed than an ordinary person's, but it remains realistic in its limitations.[2] All of the bodily transformations I can think of are undergone by secondary characters.[3] They may be powerful secondary characters like the Loathly Hag of the *Wife of Bath's Tale* or the Green Knight himself, but many figures that alter physically – such as the shapeless lump of meat that becomes a child in *The King of Tars* – are undistinguished parts of the background tapestry against which medieval English protagonists work out their destiny.[4] In Old Norse *fornaldarsögur*, the occasional irascible and avaricious warrior is transformed into a mound-dwelling *dráugr* upon death so that he may guard his treasure, and Bothvar Bjarki can shapeshift into bear form – but that ability to transform oneself comes from the pre-Christian world, and it remains as a cherished bit of folklore rather than as an option available to the Christian hero of later tradition, at least in England. The romance's focal figure is not able to transform his body – hence the occasional need for disguise and subterfuge, as in *Amis and Amiloun* and *The Erl of Toulous*. Nor can he alter what animates him; he can only try to prepare it for salvation.[5]

When we look at the quest romances that emerge in the world defined by science, we find basic shifts. Humans are no longer bodies with souls attached (or souls with bodies attached, as C. S. Lewis and various Catholic writers insist).[6] They combine body and mind, with mind consisting above all of intelligence. Intelligence plays a role completely absent in the Middle Ages; a science-fiction protagonist is unlikely to boast with the Carpenter in the *Miller's Tale*, "Ye, blessed be alwey a lewed man / That noght but oonly his bileve kan!" (ll. 3455–6). While intelligence that trips itself up can be sneered at in any era, Hendy Nicholas in the same tale would have felt at home with engineering pranksters at MIT.[7]

Furthermore, in the modern quests, both body and mind have become malleable, transformable, and even transcendable. Margaret Wertheim treats this as neurotic escapism in *The Pearly Gates of Cyberspace* (1999: 253–82), although she seems to consider the same longings within a religious framework not to be neurotic, or at any rate less escapist because linked to moral obligations. If one does not believe in a soul, heaven, and hell, however, one may consider such cravings to reflect the intersection of scientific experience, a different emphasis on what matters about humans, and a pliable literary form. Religions offer answers to those willing to accept their premises, but we may prefer different starting points. What would we change about ourselves as biological beings if we had the scientific power to do so? And if we kick those ideas about, might something – someday – come of them, and would that be a good idea or not?

Changing the Body

Bodily transformations take many forms. Invisible changes to internal reproductive apparatus would make an all-female world possible – a result that no longer seems exotic in the wake of the sheep Dolly. Various forms of immachination occur, by which human body or brain is combined with a machine; we already experience temporary immachination when deep-sea diving or orbiting earth, and any attempt to cross space would make that the rule of life, but mechanism and flesh can also combine intimately, indivisible except by surgery, as in a cyborg.[8] We also find the sentient machine, whether still human-shaped or a computer; when its mind can pass the Turing test, we tend to see it as "human," and this gives us a departure from the current limitations of our bodies. Finally, some authors hybridize humans with aliens. Although a number of these fantasies offer breakaway possibilities in the war between the sexes, others seek the ideal political ruler or explore the politics of miscegenation.

A variety of animals can be induced to produce all-female offspring without any male contribution. The implications of such a biological fact provide the basis for all-female clone lines in "Houston, Houston, Do You Read?" (1976) by James Tiptree (pseudonym for Alice B. Sheldon) and in Suzy McKee Charnas' *Motherlines* (1978), in which a bit of chemistry and congress with stallions are able to trigger that all-female reproduction in women. The women in both these worlds live without men, and both worlds treat that as a desirable state of affairs, the extant men being shown to have the worst male traits from various feminist perspectives.[9] The same desirability of an all-female society is upheld in Joanna Russ's "When It Changed" (1972), but there the women merge ova in the lab and continue to create genetic diversity, a higher-tech solution, and one with biological advantages, although the clone-lines in the other stories explore the implications of knowing or having access to the records of hundreds of women with your own body and that part of your mind that is inherited. While one-gender communities were commoner in the Middle Ages than now, and monks in particular congratulated themselves on not having to deal with the evils of women, such living arrangements did not truly posit the possibility of continuing humanity by new means. Within medieval romances, all-female communities were likely to be prisoners, as in, for instance, Chrétien de Troyes' *Yvain*, all too eager to be rescued by a man. No romancer I know of wondered whether an all-female community would produce a kinder, gentler world (Tiptree), or whether the all-female world might be far from utopian, yet cherished because it offered freedom to be what you could make of yourself without regard to male patterns (Charnas, Russ) – a state of affairs not seen as desirable in the medieval context.[10]

Immachination, the spectrum stretching from machine with artificial intelligence to slightly cyborged human, opens up the possibilities of a body enhanced by or replaced by mechanical and electronic parts. Anne McCaffrey explores brainships – spaceships governed by human brains that have been born into bodies so defective they could not live in the regular world. They face genuinely new problems when, for instance, someone feeds a computer virus to the shipboard computer (*PartnerShip*). The creation of androids so humanoid that they can become sexual partners of humans can serve the purpose of showing us notions current in different eras of the ideal woman ("Helen O'Loy" by Lester Del Rey) and ideal man (*He, She, and It* by Marge Piercy). More important, however, they raise philosophical issues. If an android has become so good a male human as to fall in love, has his creator the right to send him to death for the good of the community, even if he was originally created to defend that community? Should the android be paid for his services? In the Jewish community of *He, She and It*, the question of whether the android could make up a minyan (a prayer group that requires 10 Jewish males over 13 years of age) sent the rabbis off, ferociously cheerful at the chance to argue such a fine question. Because mind does not define the human in the Middle Ages, any creature not born of woman could not gain baptism, have a soul, or ever deserve human rights, such as those were. For recent writers, mind rather than soul defines humanity, so the future might yield such human equivalents, even if artificial intelligence has not developed nearly as quickly as was first hoped.

Robert A. Heinlein pushes the human-machine hybrid into the realm of politics in *The Moon is a Harsh Mistress* (1966). At one level, his protagonist is a workable combination of human and machine, with his enhanced and adaptable prosthetic arm. As *Homo faber*, he represents one ideal. When Heinlein looks for the perfect ruler, he explores combining human with machine and comes up with a sentient computer, Mike, friend to Manny of the arm, but this thought experiment turns into a trap. This electronic ruler counts the votes to come out as he deems best, and can manipulate any computerized record or process (control oxygen, light, and pressure in this Lunar corridor culture). Everything the computer does seems approved by the author, but Heinlein felt compelled to kill off the computer's sentience, leaving just electronic functionality. Humanity had been rendered superfluous, infantilized by this superior being. Manny's quest has all the usual hero monomyth trappings, including descent into a special world (Earth) and love interest, but in his attempt to help bring about a revolution, he comes up against human inferiority to the logic possible for a computer. If only the machine could keep humanity from its more stupid impulses and handle some of the boring mechanics of rule yet still give humans freedom! However, Heinlein could see no long-term way of combining the human and machine-like logic at the political level. Our stupidity seems weightier than our intelligence overall, so his Lunar society cannot be saved from red tape, coercion, police, and other incursions into personal freedom. Within the medieval world, human stupidity operating in the world (as opposed to sinning – a kind of stupidity – and its effect on the individual) is not such a daunting problem, politically speaking.

Changes in the body that truly alter the form yet remain entirely biological are the subject of Octavia Butler's *Xenogenesis* trilogy. A space-faring species that mixes and alters genes as easily as we digest a meal saves that fragment of humanity not killed off by atomic catastrophe and proceeds to mingle genes with the remaining humans. Butler's Oankali bear about the same technological superiority to humans that white Europeans and Americans bore to Africans during slave-trading days. The Oankali ensure chemically and genetically that never again can a child be born that is purely human, without an admixture of the "master's" blood.

What Butler's change to our biological form permits is a totally different mode of interacting with the universe around us, and she may thus explore the possibility of a family unit that involves two races – human and Oankali – and three genders – male, female, and ooloi. That one should wish to understand the universe by direct access to molecular information would, of course, not have been thinkable in earlier literature. Nor would a medieval writer have felt that gathering such information was both a pleasure and a good in its own right; that curiosity and desire derive from our scientific world. Curiosity, after all, was a sin in the Middle Ages, a subspecies of Pride. Indeed, Butler's third sex, the ooloi, embody a kind of scientific specialist and doctor combined, in that they not only understand molecularly and lust to learn more, but also can alter such molecules at will. They mix and mingle human male and female genetic material with Oankali male and female material to produce the hybrid offspring of five parents, and they perform chemical manipulations to heal any malfunctioning parts of the body.

The protagonists of each novel follow quest romance patterns, but these patterns aid their coming to terms with sexual behaviors and biological cravings that readers have never experienced. Indeed, Butler attributes the human trajectory toward mass destruction to an internal contradiction between our high intelligence and our strong hierarchical drive. With intelligence not a prime medieval desideratum and medieval technology not up to mass destruction, the human hierarchical drive functioned largely unchallenged by intelligence in that era. Butler's values thus differ from any values possible for early European romancers, and while the growing-up pattern in her novels still involves a sense of achievement and stability upon reaching maturity, she offers us an original and intriguing notion of what maturity might mean were we to change physically.

Transcending the Body

The body irritates our intelligence with its limitations. The clumsy physical entity cannot do all we want. It grows ill and old, and will die. Its orgasms are inadequate, and its capacity for ecstasy is not easily enough invoked. Our intelligence can imagine and desire that these not be so, hence the drive to transcend this body.

One of the simplest forms of this improved body comes in Kate Wilhelm's *Welcome, Chaos*. When inoculated with a serum, half of the world's population dies, but those who survive find themselves immortal, all the damage to their tissues repaired, their health perfect. Wilhelm does not explore the long-term effects of such a change, but focuses on the acute tensions involving the transition.

Another quick way to transcend the body is for the mental faculties to survive the death of the body. In Arthur C. Clarke's *2010: Odyssey Two* (1982), Dave Bowman becomes a disembodied spirit, able to exist as pure energy. This ability is evidently given to him by the higher powers that established the black monolith, the focus for *2001: A Space Odyssey*. According to Clarke, those original explorers of Earth

> had long since come to the limits of flesh and blood; as soon as their machines were better than their bodies, it was time to move. First their brains, and then their thoughts alone, they transferred into shining new homes of metal and plastic ...
>
> But the age of the Machine-entities swiftly passed. In their ceaseless experimenting, they had learned to store knowledge in the structure of space itself, and to preserve their thoughts for eternity in frozen lattices of light. They could become creatures of radiation, free at last from the tyranny of matter. (274)

Clarke has long been interested in doing away with bodies, and in this novel, that becomes possible for humans. In his transcended form, Dave Bowman is able to enter computers and read their contents, make an image of himself appear and talk on a television screen, telekinetically explode an orbiting nuclear device, and telekinetically comb his dying mother's hair. With a bit of help from the master beings, he also saves the essence of the computer HAL from destruction, and the artificial intelligence responsible for all the trouble in the previous book thus becomes his disembodied companion. Mind in a computer is held to be equivalent to a human mind, and both, with the right help, can escape any physical embodiment.

Particularly famous for its portrayal of body transcendence is William Gibson's *Neuromancer* (1984). A good many of the characters in this book are trying to avoid death in one fashion or another. Julie Deane has his DNA "reset" each year, and preserves an active life at 135 with hormones and serums. The Tessier-Ashpool family use clones of themselves and periodically disappear into cryogenic storage so as to extend the period of their existence. A famous hacker, the Dixie Flatline, is preserved as a downloaded entity, and can be brought back to electronic life to run a hacker-raid on the Tessier-Ashpool computers. The protagonist, Case, transcends his body in two fashions. One is temporary, but it constitutes the experience he lives for. While "the meat" remains sitting at a keyboard, his mind enters the matrix, something like today's Internet, and can "read" electronic signals. Data banks are geometric shapes of various colors, and one navigates visible pathways. While the body is still connected to that mind (and its fingers continue to use the keyboard), Case's mind essentially leaves his body. When his mind's own neurological network is deliberately damaged by an enemy to make jacking into the matrix impossible for him, he feels this to be a "fall" into the meat. He follows a self-destructive pattern of behavior, life not being worth living to him without the rush and challenge of hacking. Drugs (which he indulges in frequently) and sex are both poor substitutes for jacking into the special world of the matrix and traveling its strange pathways.

When he deals with one of the massive artificial intelligences that governs half the matrix, Neuromancer, he is offered the chance of continuing to live, but only in a portion of this "consensual hallucination" that is the matrix. During a few seconds when he is flatlined (brain-dead), he spends days on a "terminal beach" with a former girlfriend, also dead. He is assured that he could stay in this electronic world if he gave up his work for the other artificial intelligence, Wintermute, but he refuses in order to pursue his quest. However, when the quest is done and the two AIs have been merged, he jacks in, and among the colorful geometric shapes, "he saw three figures, tiny, impossible, who stood at the very edge of one of the vast steps of data. Small as they were, he could make out ... [a human form used by Neuromancer]. Linda still wore his jacket; she waved, as he passed. But the third figure, close behind her, arm across her shoulders, was himself" (270–1). Also, although the tape of the Dixie Flatline was erased at his own request, Case hears Dixie's laugh as he sees those three figures. Thus at the end Case exists in at least two independent forms; one is electronic and its doings are no longer known to the mind/body of that name who plies his trade as a hacker. Linda and Dixie are both dead yet appear alive in the matrix.

At the end of Clarke's *2061: Odyssey Three*, Heywood Floyd finds that Dave Bowman has taken Floyd's consciousness and disembodied it, yet has left the body and consciousness alive for what life remains to the old man. In both *2061* and *Neuromancer*, we thus find the mind being "copied" and set free of the body, leaving the body and the original mind intact. In neither instance is the freed mind augmented or made more intelligent, though Dave Bowman's example suggests that Floyd will be acquiring a phenomenal mass of new knowledge. Basically, though, in these novels the body is the limit that the authors wish to escape. The mind will succeed if only it can be freed from the meat, from age and death.

Retaining the Body but Transcending the Mind

Some authors seem less bothered by age and death than by other limitations, and those they propose solving through various forms of extra-sensory perception and action, including in the more extreme forms, telekinesis and teleportation. These in some sense extend the body's powers, yet they are interpreted as mental. Telekinesis lets you move some object across the room or across the city – but this and other effects are achieved by mind. They extend the mind's range in that the mind may be able to see or hear what is going on somewhere apart from the person with such mental powers. Few of these authors have tried imagining true changes in the mind in terms of consciousness or thinking capability, in part because increased intelligence or truly different consciousness are both difficult to make literarily real. These minds are still ordinary as far as thoughts and concerns; they have, though, extended their powers. Many authors have focused on the problems that would arise if the untalented majority of people had to compete with the psi-talented minority and the all too likely witch-hunts that might result from such an evolutionary differentiation in the human species.

When the Rhine Institute appeared to validate a certain telepathic and clairvoyant possibility in humans, and as this was reinforced by rumors of the Russian army (and later, the American army) using psychics to find such items as downed planes, telepathic abilities edged into the realm of science and could be explored as potentially scientific. Since then, a few of the later experiments have been exploded as fraudulent and no talents have emerged at the readily usable, close to infallible level seen in fiction (at least as far as is known to the public): telepathy and related abilities tend now to be the purview of fantasy.

McCaffrey's Federated Telepath and Teleport agency in her *Gwyn-Raven-Lyon* series serves not only the solar system but Deneb and Iota Aurigae and planets around other G-type stars in our galaxy. People and cargo can be transported instantaneously through the mental efforts of the Talented, who augment their power by means of ordinary electrical generators. Mercedes Lackey's Valdemar heralds all have minor mental talents, and a few have such "mental magic" to a much more powerful degree – telekinesis for small objects, far-seeing, far-sensing, some foresight, fire-starting, and the like. Unlike McCaffrey's Talented, the heralds live in a pre-industrial world, and represent pure fantasy, with no science-fiction admixture. In the goody-goody worlds these two authors imagine, such mental powers are strenuously controlled by highly moral administrations, the few rogue users getting their minds reamed and talents removed. The untalented may occasionally grumble, but they stand to gain in safety, security, or money, so learn to put up with the disparity in abilities. In the works of both authors, at least some new talent springs from untalented parents, so ordinary people can hope their descendents will not be cut off from this evolutionary breakthrough, if that is what it is. These people may instead be just a talented tenth, individuals born with a characteristic like left-handedness, in which case the authors put them to the service of their civilized worlds and do not make the disparity of power into a political issue.

Back in a more scientific world, the skepticism about moral use of the talents shows itself. Wilson Tucker's *Man from Tomorrow* shows an evolutionary breakthrough when at least two families produce multi-talented offspring, the equivalent to the Cro-Magnons who will eventually supplant the Neanderthals. The man foolish enough to let his talents become obvious while he is in the army is forced into government service – well paid, but totally involuntary. He is used as the communications center for a spy network because he can follow the spies in his mind, learn what they learn, all without any conventional communication. He learns from his earlier mistake and keeps to himself his development of telekinesis, which allows him to escape with his life from the double-agent spymaster. Paul heads off to an obscure Caribbean island with his similarly talented partner (who has kept hers secret), and they will presumably beget the next generation of talent on this island paradise. Unlike such talents in fantasy writing, these emerge in a political context and are used in a dog eat dog world. Parallel to this new power is the development of atomic bombs; Paul is first being recognized for what he is while Hiroshima is being vaporized, and he must disentangle himself from the spy network about the time that Russia is discovered to have bombs; this is also the time that he discovers the talented woman – proliferation! Wilson Tucker treats such talent as power, and recognizes its political import; the fantasists mentioned prefer keeping it apolitical or put it to the service of an implausibly moral government.

Transcending the mind is tempting as a daydream, but may not prove so wonderful in practice. In "It's a *good* life," a story that has no romance happy ending, we see what happens when an infant is born with full telekinetic abilities. He kills anyone who angers him. No one can teach the boy any sort of restraint or humanity, and no one can approach the child to kill him because the murderer's thoughts are perceived. The little town in which this child was born finds itself yanked into some frame of existence that cuts it off from the rest of the world. People keep getting killed while the rest must try to think good thoughts because the child responds viciously to anger or negative thoughts. Jerome Bixby beautifully combines the unreasoning and unsocialized impulses of a small child with total power; the result is a horrible monster.

Similarly, in "Flowers for Algernon," Daniel Keyes depicts a mind that transcends itself when a retarded man undergoes an operation that triples his IQ, taking it into the genius range; regrettably for him, the effects of the operation are not permanent, and his journal throughout this experiment documents his rise, first into literacy, then into abstract mathematical and philosophical work, and then his agonizing devolution back into mental retardation. This attempt to show a mind going beyond the norm is quite unusual. Charlie's experience does follow a quest-romance pattern, gruesomely so, in that his final equilibrium shows him almost happy again, no longer aware of all that he has lost.

Transcending both Body and Mind

The problem of showing the mind transcended – at least in terms of intelligence – has proved very difficult. The solution most often tried is that of joining one mind to a mass mind, a shared consciousness. This may occur without the mind permanently leaving the body, as it does for a secondary character in Russell Hoban's *Riddley Walker*, and it is achieved in the course of abandoning the body in Arthur C. Clarke's *Childhood's End*, though that experience is denied to the hero, so we are given no sense of what it might feel like.

We find an attempt to create that experience for body and mind, however, in Spider and Jeanne Robinson's *Stardance*, *Starseed*, and *Starmind*. The amount of science in these books is minimal, aside from the many observations of what weightless life would be like. The framework, however, is space stations and life in space, not the religious rapture described by Pat Robertson in his evangelical apocalypse, *The End of the Age* (1995), in which his good Christians rise to heaven in bodily form. The Robinsons' characters eventually rise from Earth without any machine helping them, but to join a group of humans who have already made the transitions into bodies that can live floating in space, fueled by solar energy, their body chemistry enabled by a symbiote. The transition made by the first half-dozen is relatively easy because they have all been good friends and lovers, so when their minds also become one mind, the joining has just extended the closeness that they have already experienced as a temporary telepathic phenomenon. As the rest of humanity starts to make the transition, the effect puts vastly more strain on the mind because the mass mind is so much greater. Way-stations with meditational techniques and space-walk training are encouraged to help prepare ordinary egos for psychological impact and spatial vertigo.

Stardance, the most successful of the three volumes, follows quest romance patterns, the hero being a modern dancer deprived of his profession by a smashed hip that healed badly. He not only becomes a dancer again in the special world of zero gravity, but also mends his shattered life and joins with the other dancers into the first stage of the starmind, the first humans to make the evolutionary transition. What that transition does physically is to free him from earth and all bodily limits – though death by violence is still possible – and expand his mind, making it happy, moral, compassionate, loving, and infinitely efficient. The improved morality for those who make the transition would obviously be approved in a medieval romance, but the other gains, especially with regard to efficiency and knowledge, would not have seemed so important in the earlier period. Much is made in the state of weightlessness of the lack of hierarchy, so maybe this is a way of escaping one of the forces creating the human dilemma in Octavia Butler's analysis, a dominant force in the medieval period. The Robinsons might put it that the transcended humans finally learn how to live intelligently rather than hierarchically, not prey to the irrational forces that so greatly influence humanity in its current form. As several people – Albert Einstein and Harlan Ellison among them – are credited with saying, "The two commonest substances in the universe are hydrogen and human stupidity." Stupidity, not sin. Stupidity becomes such an issue only when humans are primarily defined as mind rather than body or soul.

So what do contemporary writers of romance do that truly goes beyond the realm of medieval romance? One can write off space travel as just another form of special travel, and monsters change form without necessarily changing function. Some pseudo-scientific trappings seem operationally indistinguishable from magic. In "On Science Fiction," C. S. Lewis lambasts space opera if all it can achieve is love story or crime story in disguise (1966: 61), and he prides himself on exploring truly different landscapes in his planetary trilogy. However, as anyone knows who has taught *Out of the Silent Planet* (1938) back to back with Spenser's *Faerie Queene* Book I, he has not truly touched on differences proffered by science. His shared religion keeps him from getting beyond the medieval and Renaissance quest romance, although he generates some lusciously strange landscapes.

Defining humanity in terms of intelligence rather than soul does produce some new stories. Intelligence not born of man and woman but compatible with humans is limited only by the human authors' imaginations. In her bispecies hybrids, Octavia Butler definitely pushes toward new sensations, sexualities, cultures, and new modes of knowing the material universe. Putting off death or avoiding it altogether also constitutes new situations. While immortality seems implausible (unless minds prove downloadable), putting death off for decades might one day be achieved, and will presumably owe everything to intelligence if it happens. Heinlein goes into multi-century long lives in *Time Enough for Love* (1973), and the possibility also faces the characters in *Welcome, Chaos*; *2010*; *Starmind*; and *Childhood's End*. One might eventually get tired enough of life to choose to die – but that would be a major breakthrough for humanity and a radical change in the nature of human life. If sufficiently stimulating new forms of knowledge come into being, and one finds new worlds to conquer (literally or figuratively), ennui might be held at bay for an indefinite time. Whatever the ultimate result, death is being reconfigured in these romances, and the promise is not of heaven, but of a life as long as one wishes – of necessity, a life with no severe financial problems.

The contemporary romances are also changing the nature and centrality of love. Not only is it sometimes not heterosexual, but the emphasis on mind has meant that hormonal obsessions have not always been upheld as the true center of life nor even its most obvious goal. The growth of more flexible sexual mores in the 1960s has led to the depiction of more temporary sexual alliances, and reduced the burning import once attached to finding a spouse. Projects relating to learning, understanding, and achieving tend to rank much higher in science-fiction quests. While many medieval romances similarly treat love as a generic given rather than a major passion, many are cast in terms of boy wins girl, and that pattern is surprisingly peripheral to these contemporary romances. The science-fiction quest is a quest pursued by the intelligence, and that conception of mind affects the generic sense of what matters most in life. In the world of mental activity, romance is secondary.

See also: chapter 3, The Popular English Metrical Romances; chapter 4, Arthurian Romance; chapter 12, "Gothic" Romance; chapter 13, Women's Gothic Romance; chapter 22, Nineteenth-century Adventure and Fantasy; chapter 26, Twentieth-century Arthurian Romance; chapter 27, Romance in Fantasy; chapter 30, Popular Romance and its Readers.

Notes

1. Even when n-space drive or diving down wormholes is treated as a viable means of transport, such means cannot help but seem a bit uncanny for readers, who have reason to doubt that these methods will ever be feasible. For other discussions of the relationship between SF and romance, the hero monomyth, and Northrop Frye's mythoi, see Delany, Hume (1974, 1982), Kagle, Lomax, Parrinder, and Stevenson.

2. As Raymond H. Thompson points out, medieval heroes "rarely possess supernatural powers, and when they do it is usually a minor feature that survives from sources in legend, like the strength of Gawain," which in some tales fluctuates with time of day (1982:220). Superior and supernatural powers are commonplace in modern fantasy, and appear at times in scientific guise in science fiction.

3. Melusine, the serpent/woman in the *Romauns of Partenay*, might be a partial exception, since Melusine is the central figure in one portion of that long tale; she is, though, female and, in many versions of the story, a fairy and therefore not Christian.

4. The roles of the secondary characters in that tapestry were analyzed psychologically by Derek Brewer in *Symbolic Stories* as parental forces and splits of the hero. Applications of this escape from mimetic assumptions are made in the essays in *Studies in Medieval English Romances: Some New Approaches*.

5. Velma Bourgeois Richmond (1975: 58–85) discusses an arguable exception to this rule: characters who struggle to make their fiendish souls redeemable. These include Sir Gowther and Robert the Devil.

6. See for instance, C. S. Lewis in "The Weight of Glory": "There are no *ordinary* people. You have never talked to a mere mortal. Nations, cultures, arts, civilization – these are mortal, and their life is to ours as the life of a gnat" (1949: 15); see also Walter M. Miller, Jr., in *Canticle for Leibowitz*, "You don't *have* a soul, Doctor. You *are* a soul. You *have* a body, temporarily" (1959: 272).

7. Gary K. Wolfe's definition of science fiction – the transformation of chaos into cosmos by applying the scientific method (1979: 4) – and Darko Suvin's emphasis on the necessity of a cognitive novum (1979: 4) both point to the germinal role of intelligence as central to the form.

8. Despina Kakoudaki (2000) charts the combinations of human and artificial.

9. They do not take into account the long-term drawbacks of cloning, although these are treated in *Where Late the Sweet Birds Sang* by Kate Wilhelm (1976).

10. Christine de Pisan, writing in the fifteenth century, was one of the few medieval writers who did consider a community in terms of female virtues, though she focused on denying negative stereotypes more than on creating an alternative society.

References and Further Reading

Asimov, Isaac (1969). *Fantastic Voyage.* New York: Bantam. [First published in 1966.]

Benford, Gregory C. (1981). *Timescape.* New York: Pocket Books. [First published in 1980.]

Bixby, Jerome (1971). "It's a *good* life." In Robert Silverberg, ed., *Science Fiction Hall of Fame.* New York: Avon, pp. 523–42. [Story first published in 1953.]

Brewer, Derek (1980). *Symbolic Stories: Traditional Narratives of the Family Drama in English Literature.* Totowa, NJ: Rowman and Littlefield.

Brewer, Derek, ed. (1988). *Studies in Medieval English Romances: Some New Approaches.* Woodbridge, Suffolk: Boydell and Brewer.

Brunner, John (1976). *Shockwave Rider.* New York: Ballantine. [First published in 1975.]

Butler, Octavia (1989). *Xenogenesis* Trilogy. New York: Popular Library. [*Dawn* first published in 1987; *Adulthood Rites* first published in 1988; *Imago* first published in 1989.]

Charnas, Suzy McKee (1978). *Motherlines.* New York: Berkley.

Clarke, Arthur C. (1953). *Childhood's End.* New York: Ballantine.

Clarke, Arthur C. (1968). *2001: A Space Odyssey.* New York: Signet.

Clarke, Arthur C. (1973). *Rendezvous with Rama.* New York: Harcourt Brace Jovanovich.

Clarke, Arthur C. (1978). *Fountains of Paradise.* New York: Harcourt Brace Jovanovich.

Clarke, Arthur C. (1982). *2010: Odyssey Two.* New York: Ballantine.

Clarke, Arthur C. (1989). *2060: Odyssey Three.* New York: Ballantine. [First published in 1987.]

Del Rey, Lester (1971). "Helen O'Loy." In Robert Silverberg, ed., *Science Fiction Hall of Fame.* New York: Avon, pp. 62–73. [Story first published in 1938.]

Delany, Samuel R. (1987). "The Gestation of Genres: Literature, Fiction, Romance, Science Fiction, Fantasy...." In George E. Slusser and Eric S. Rabkin, eds., *Intersections: Fantasy and Science Fiction.* Carbondale: Southern Illinois University Press, pp. 63–73.

Dick, Philip K. (1991). *Ubik.* New York: Vintage. [First published in 1969.]

Gibson, William (1984). *Neuromancer.* New York: Ace.

Haldeman, Joe (1976). *The Forever War.* New York: Ballantine. [First published in 1974.]

Heinlein, Robert A. (1968). *The Moon is a Harsh Mistress.* New York: Berkley. [First published in 1966.]

Heinlein, Robert A. (1974). *Time Enough for Love.* New York: Berkley. [First published in 1973.]

Herbert, Frank (1982). *Dune.* New York: Berkley. [First published in 1965.]

Hoban, Russell (1982). *Riddley Walker.* New York: Washington Square Press. [First published in 1980.]

Hume, Kathryn (1974). "Romance: A Perdurable Pattern." *College English* 36, 129–46.

Hume, Kathryn (1982). "Medieval Romance and Science Fiction: The Anatomy of a Resemblance." *Journal of Popular Culture* 16, 15–26.

Kagle, Stephen Earl (1971). "The Societal Quest." *Extrapolation* 12, 79–85.

Kakoudaki, Despina (2000). "Pinup and Cyborg: Exaggerated Gender and Artificial Intelligence." In Marleen S. Barr, ed., *Future Females, The Next Generation: New Voices and Velocities in Feminist Science Fiction Criticism.* Lanham, MD: Rowman and Littlefield, pp. 165–95.

Keyes, Daniel (1971). "Flowers for Algernon." In Robert Silverberg, ed., *Science Fiction Hall of Fame.* New York: Avon, pp. 603–35. [Story first published in 1959.]

Le Guin, Ursula K. (1975). *The Dispossessed.* New York: Avon. [First published in 1974.]

Lewis, C. S. (1965). *Out of the Silent Planet.* New York: Macmillan. [First published in 1938.]

Lewis, C. S. (1965). *The Weight of Glory and Other Addresses.* Grand Rapids, MI: William B. Eerdmans. [First published in 1949.]

Lewis, C. S. (1966). "On Science Fiction." In *In Other Worlds: Essays and Stories.* New York: Harcourt Brace Jovanovich, pp. 59–73.

Lomax, William (1989). "Landscape and the Romantic Dilemma: Myth and Metaphor in Science-Fiction Narrative." In George E. Slusser and Eric S. Rabkin, eds., *Mindscapes: The Geographies of Imagined Worlds.* Carbondale: Southern Illinois University Press, pp. 242–56.

McCaffrey, Anne, and Margaret Ball (1992). *PartnerShip*. Riverdale, NY: Baen Books.

McCaffrey, Anne, and Mercedes Lackey (1992). *The Ship who Searched*. Riverdale, NY: Baen Books.

McIntyre, Vonda N. (1984). *Superluminal*. New York: Pocket Books. [First published in 1983.]

Miller, Walter M., Jr. (1976). *A Canticle for Leibowitz*. New York: Bantam. [First published in 1959.]

Panshin, Alexei (1968). *Rite of Passage*. New York: Ace.

Parrinder, Patrick (1980). *Science Fiction: Its Criticism and Teaching*. London: Methuen.

Piercy, Marge (1993). *He, She and It*. New York: Ballantine. [First published in 1991.]

Richmond, Velma Bourgeois (1975). *The Popularity of Middle English Romance*. Bowling Green, OH: Bowling Green University Popular Press.

Robertson, Pat (1995). *The End of the Age*. Dallas, TX: Word Publishing.

Robinson, Spider, and Jeanne Robinson (1991). *Stardance*. New York: Baen Books.

Robinson, Spider, and Jeanne Robinson (1991). *Starseed*. New York: Ace.

Robinson, Spider, and Jeanne Robinson (1995). *Starmind*. New York: Ace.

Russ, Joanna (1989). " When It Changed." In Ben Bova, ed., *The Best of the Nebulas*. New York: Tor, pp. 204–10. [Story first published in 1972.]

Sterling, Bruce (1989). *Islands in the Net*. New York: Ace. [First published in 1988.]

Stevenson, Lionel (1971). "The Artistic Problem: Science Fiction as Romance." In Thomas D. Clareson, ed., *SF: The Other Side of Realism: Essays on Modern Fantasy and Science Fiction*. Bowling Green, OH: Bowling Green University Popular Press, pp. 96–104.

Suvin, Darko (1979). *Metamorphoses of Science Fiction: On the Poetics and History of a Literary Genre*. New Haven: Yale University Press.

Thompson, Raymond H. (1982). "Modern Fantasy and Medieval Romance: A Comparative Study." In Roger C. Schlobin, ed., *The Aesthetics of Fantasy Literature and Art*. Notre Dame, IN: University of Notre Dame Press, pp. 211–25.

Tiptree, James [alias Alice Sheldon] (1989). "Houston, Houston, Do You Read?" In Ben Bova, ed., *The Best of the Nebulas*. New York: Tor, pp. 420–60. [Story first published in 1976.]

Tucker, Wilson (1955). *Man from Tomorrow* [original title, *Wild Talent*]. New York: Bantam. [First published in 1954.]

Wertheim, Margaret (1999). *The Pearly Gates of Cyberspace: A History of Space from Dante to the Internet*. New York: W. W. Norton.

Wilhelm, Kate (1985). *Welcome, Chaos*. New York: Berkley. [First published in 1983.]

Wilhelm, Kate (1977). *Where Late the Sweet Birds Sang*. New York: Pocket Books. [First published in 1976.]

Wolfe, Gary K. (1979). *The Known and the Unknown: The Iconography of Science Fiction*. Kent, OH: Kent State University Press.

Wyndham, John (1951). *The Day of the Triffids*. New York: Fawcett Crest.

Zelazny, Roger (1989). "The Doors of His Face, the Lamps of His Mouth." In Ben Bova, ed., *The Best of the Nebulas*. New York: Tor, pp. 36–61. [Story first published in 1965.]

29

Between Worlds: Iris Murdoch, A. S. Byatt, and Romance

Clare Morgan

Visions, you know, have always been my pasture; and so far from growing old enough to quarrel with their emptiness I almost think there is no wisdom comparable to exchanging what is called the realities of life for dreams. (Hugh Walpole)[1]

Intuition and the Need for Completeness

Cassandra, the bluestocking sister of successful novelist Julia in A. S. Byatt's *The Game* (1967),[2] muses on the nature of her relation with romance. She had come as a student to Oxford, "having read indiscriminately in Walter Scott, Tennyson, Morris and Malory, looking for a life as brightly coloured as books" (18). Her interest was not at that stage "in the conventions of the courtly love of the *Roman de la Rose*" (18). Her preoccupation was with "the feelings of Launcelot and Guinevere" (18). But something has happened, those feelings are no longer the central focus of her attention. In the intervening 20 years (she is now a don at an Oxford women's college) she has become "dry and informative" (109), "enveloped in the folds of a black gown . . . like a bundle of old stuff" (107). The shift of her interest from feelings to conventions comes not, she believes "from Ritual to Romance, but in the other direction, from romance to ritual."[3] The exchange is not a positive one, as the change from upper to lower case indicates: "Her feeling for completeness had betrayed her to a way of life she had not quite chosen . . . She had cultivated her walled-garden skills at the expense of any other she might have had" (18).

Iris Murdoch is similarly concerned with the perniciousness of the human need for "completeness" as it issues in the "facile merging tendencies of the obsessive ego"[4] which manufactures false causalities to account for the events of life. *The Flight from the Enchanter* (1956)[5] is largely taken up with these tendencies and this ego, epitomized in the historian Peter Saward's quest (akin to Casaubon's for the key to all mythologies in George Eliot's *Middlemarch* [1876]) to decipher the key to an ancient Babylonian language. His "obsession" with the deciphering of the Kastanic script has led him to a life of minute ritual, "divid[ing] his working day into four sections" (22), carefully organized and rigidly adhered to, culminating in the return of "the night again, which would be preceded by a period of contemplation, during which, in a kind of prayer, the problems were summoned up which were to be committed to the care of the darkness and put to the question during the hours of sleep" (22). This ritual of daily living, "varied only by occasional evening visits from friends" (22), is, like Cassandra's, not conducive to a full or fruitful existence. Saward's room, so dark as to be "cavern"-like, encompasses "vitality" (21) only in the form of "an anonymous-looking green plant" which produces "a luxuriance of green leaves but no flowers" (21). In the end, Saward's quest, like his plant, is shown to be fruitless. A "bilingual" tablet is discovered which preempts his endeavors and "tells every-thing" (*FE*, 286).

Both Murdoch and Byatt are raising important questions about the nature of knowledge, in particular how rational and intuitive knowledge should be differen-tially valued. The blow of chance delivered by the tablet's discovery not only means that all Saward's work has been, in Rosa's words, "for nothing" (286); it also shows that he was "off the track anyway" (286). Those "intuitions" at the heart of "imagin-ation and conjecture" that he paradoxically fostered by night and criticized so rigorously by day (*FE*, 24) have been proved worthless. Worse still, the tablet reveals that his Kastanic script contains nothing of significance, giving only "accounts of battles – quite interesting" (*FE*, 286). As Saward puts it, "One reads the signs as best one can . . . it's never certain that the evidence will turn up that makes everything plain" (*FE*, 287).

Both writers could be seen, perhaps, as merely extending the long-standing debate which found voice in such texts as Virginia Woolf's *To the Lighthouse* (1927) where, in her examination of the Ramsay family, Woolf favorably contrasts Mrs. Ramsay's "intuitive" approach to life with Mr. Ramsay's (masculine) desire to follow the path of rationality in his dictionary-writing and "reach R."[6] But whereas Woolf's balancing of reason against feeling issues in the final artistic vision of Lily Briscoe's completed painting, for Byatt and Murdoch resolution, even a resolution couched as ambigu-ously as Lily's closing exclamation, "I have had my vision!" (*TL*, 306), is impossible. Cassandra's hold on reality becomes loosened into a kind of madness which overcomes her when she finds herself existing within the latest novel her sister has written. Saward reverts to recounting, as though it were a fairy tale, the geography of Mischa's displaced upbringing (*FE*, 287).

Competing Systems of Knowledge

What both novelists present to their readers is an epistemological hall of mirrors, where not only are the relative values of rational and intuitive knowledge almost impossible to distinguish, but also the power of competing systems of knowledge, and their relevance to human existence, are disputed. In *Flight from the Enchanter*,

Mischa Fox is an up and coming media baron; John Rainboro is a product of the value and power systems of the old school tie elite; Saward stands for an academic intellectual elitism. In *The Game*, media power is compared to that of academe and religious belief. In *Possession*, academic knowledge (in all its factionalism) is pitted against itself, and against the opposed knowledge system of contemporary commerce, which Roland's girlfriend Val enters through economic necessity, but under the influence of which she blossoms from drab frustration to a position of sexual and social fulfillment.

This evident preoccupation with knowledge and power encourages discussion of both novelists in terms of what Jean-François Lyotard famously refers to as "the postmodern condition" (1984). Peter Saward's phrase about reading the signs tangentially anticipates Jacques Derrida's concern with signs and signifiers, with what came to be seen as a false "logocentric" confidence in language as the mirror of nature, founded in the illusion that the meaning of a word has its origin in the structure of reality itself.[7] On its more obvious level, in Saward's expectation of coherent linkages, the utterance indicates a belief in rational patterning, those fixed and logical connections which emanate from that "'Cartesian' clarity of exposition which [postmodernists] said arose from a suspect reliance on 'bourgeois' certainties concerning the world order" (Butler 2002: 8). The novels' attention to competing systems of knowledge (epitomized by the Oxford dinner party in *The Game*) can be related to Foucault's pronouncements on the relation between discourse, power, and the state of society.[8] We can see perhaps in Cassandra's ultimate disintegration, as in Murdoch's "schematic" characters (Sage 1992: 76), shades of Seyla Banhabib's assertion that, under postmodernism, "You and I are the mere 'sites' of such conflicting languages of power" (1992: 23). As Byatt puts it, "[postmodern] writers are attracted by the idea that perhaps we have no such thing as an organic, discoverable, single Self" (2000: 31). This problematized view of the self Byatt refers to as the "post-romantic, post-realist idea of the human individual." For both novelists the possibility of any stable knowledge is investigated, not only in terms of an incremental relativism of the self or subject, and the relation of that relativism to the systems of knowledge and power which appertain in society, but also in terms of the essentially contingent nature of the reality on which human beings attempt (more or less vainly) to impose some kind of coherence.

"Realism" and the Condition of England

The extent to which Murdoch and Byatt are "post-realist" is the subject of continuing discussion. Lorna Sage (1992: 72) sees Murdoch as "inhabit[ing] . . . the realist territory of nineteenth-century novelist tradition – more authoritatively than any of her contemporaries." Peter Conradi, however, in his biography has denied Murdoch's explicitly stated debt to George Eliot (2001: 596). And while Byatt is more immediately categorizable as "post-realist" in, for example, *Possession*'s self-reflexive discussion of the possibilities of the novel form,[9] she can also be seen as inhabiting a tendency in which "the postwar novel in Britain is characterized by a conscious recoil from the stylistic and formal artifice of modernist fiction, and by a return to the demands and responsibilities of realism" (Connor 1996: 45). These demands and responsibilities consist in a resurgence of "the nineteenth-century aspiration to diagnose and display in fiction the 'condition of England' through focusing on a closely particularized community as representing the whole of society" (Connor 1996: 45). Both Murdoch and Byatt do focus on "the condition of England." Through her microcosm of London society in the aftermath of the Second World War, Murdoch contrives to create the sense of a fractured society of displaced persons fatally distanced from the powers that control them. Closer social ties are also in the process of disruption: Annette, attempting a *Bildungsroman* progression from girlhood to womanhood, discovers that estrangement from familial connections casts her dangerously adrift, to the extent that in the absence of any effective role model she ultimately (if somewhat comically) attempts suicide. Mid-twentieth-century feminist concerns permeate the narrative in the comparison of the thrall of Rosa, Nina, Annette to Mischa Fox, with the rise in power (inexplicable and inimical to Rainboro, from his "old school tie" perspective) through the SELIB office of his personal assistant, Miss Casement (*FE*, 86). Byatt similarly addresses feminist issues, specifically in terms of women's education and sexuality, her two intellectual women, Cassandra in *The Game* and Maud in *Possession*, both eschewing enactment of their sexuality in the light of unsatisfactory love affairs. Changing class patterns are reflected in Rosa's working in a factory because she "wants to be in touch with the People" (*FE*, 15) while the homeless of London are brought, in *The Game*, directly and disastrously into Julia's middle-class domesticity. Unstable notions of the importance of Englishness find voice in Annette's rejection of her Kensington "finishing school," viewed by her diplomat father as an establishment which would produce in his "cosmopolitan ragamuffin . . . sufficient of the surface of a young English lady" (*FE*, 8) for her to find a suitable husband "in one, or at the most two, seasons" (*FE*, 7). If the residual hegemony of the British empire seems to apply in her father's feeling that "it was essential" that her education should "reach its climax in no other place than London" (*FE*, 8), the new world order is reflected in his apprehension that he "thoroughly disliked the place, which he found . . . both tedious and oppressive" (*FE*, 8). Indeed, the seat of power in the novel is found not in any English institution, but in the stateless, placeless figure of Mischa Fox: "No one knows where he came from . . . Where was he born? What blood is in his veins? No one knows" (*FE*, 35). In *Possession*, the internationalism of the academic community gives Byatt ample scope for a humorous discussion of a different kind of imperialism in the rivalry for possession of the Ash/LaMotte papers between an impoverished English academe and an American academe funded by global capitalism.

The condition of England and a degree of associated "realism" are significant attributes of both Byatt's and Murdoch's fictions, but are far from adequate in capturing their flavor or complexity. This is partially because realism itself has been increasingly identified as "internally fissured, frequently conscious of its own contradictions and constantly mutating into new forms."[10] This view of realism's multiple character has been counterpointed in critical discourse by a sense of the fluctuating forms and attributes of that modernism in opposition to which it has so often been situated (see, for example, Nicholls 1995). The postmodern temper's abhorrence of distinct boundaries and static divisions is reflected in the increasing acknowledgment of the provisional nature of such categorization, and inevitably presents challenges in delineating relations between different literary moments and tendencies. Perhaps, in Byatt's words, the need is "to keep thinking of new – even deliberately provisional – ways to read and compare what we have read" (2000: 3).

The inadequacy of "realism" (or of modernism or postmodernism) as terms in which to approach the complexities of Murdoch's and Byatt's work has already been more or less overtly or covertly acknowledged. As Richard Todd puts it, Murdoch, "who has rightly been called a 'fabulator' by Robert Scholes, is not creating an innocent realism" (1984:14). We can read her novels, he believes, "less as examples of traditional realism than as manifestations of curiosity about the elements and assumptions which made the novel a serious form of art." Lorna Sage qualifies her view of Murdoch as realist, in her admission that she has found herself exploring "a fascinating latter-day defence of what I think of as 'matriarchal realism'" (1992: x), a statement she later elucidates by her assertion that Murdoch "presents the paradox of the realist under siege" (1992: 75). Byatt similarly acknowledges that she was in the 1950s attempting to find her way through and around a "realism" which she no longer believed adequate to the novelist's purpose. She is, as she puts it, "trying to find a way between the 'sensibility' of Woolf, Lehmann, Bowen, and the 'jokey social comedy' of Kingsley Amis and John Wain" (1964: xi).

What siege is Murdoch as realist under? What ways around realism does Byatt negotiate? Walpole's extolling of the virtues of "vision" indicates a fruitful approach in attempting to answer these questions, which are of fundamental importance not only to the role of romance in the work of both writers, but also to a fuller apprehension of the nature of the novel in Britain after the Second World War.

The Influence of Neo-Romanticism

Byatt, seven years younger than Murdoch, shares with her an immersion in the mid-twentieth-century resurgence of romanticism that came to be known as the Neo-Romantic movement, which extended from around 1928[11] to the mid-1950s. Both writers place in their list of significant influences the figure of Samuel Palmer. Palmer's 1830 *Cornfield by Moonlight with the Evening Star* which appears on the cover of the 1991 Vintage edition of Byatt's first novel *The Shadow of the Sun* (1964)[12] is, she makes explicit in her preface, the "visual image that always went with the idea" of this first novel. Walpole's "vision" is inextricable from Byatt's vision of Palmer: a central character of the novel, Henry Severell, is, she admits: "partly simply my secret self...Someone who saw everything too bright, too fierce, too much, like Samuel Palmer's overloaded magic apples, or the Coleridge of the flashing eyes and floating hair, or the Blake who saw infinity in a grain of sand" (*SS*, x).

Palmer's significance for Murdoch is made clear in her eulogy for her close friend, the painter and engraver Reynolds Stone (July 1979), whose work she compares to Palmer's, which she characterizes as "precise, visionary, spiritual" and praises for "proceeding unselfconsciously from an intensely personal privacy," to give that "shock of beauty which shows how close, how in a sense ordinary, are the marvels of the world" (Conradi 2001: 510).

Samuel Palmer is one of the central influences on Neo-Romanticism. Geoffrey Grigson's seminal article "Samuel Palmer at Shoreham,"[13] which appeared in *Signature* in 1937, forms in its insistence on a pastoral infused by the Gothic and by witchcraft, part of a group of writings which have come to be seen as the "manifesto" of the Neo-Romantic movement. The Neo-Romantic movement has generally been regarded as short-lived, contained, and minimal in its influence: in short, a kind of mid-century aberration. Critics call upon David Jones and the early Dylan Thomas as witness to its Celtic excesses (and indeed to its parochialism); on John Minton to demonstrate its solipsistic and escapist tendencies; and, perhaps, on Mervyn Peake's *Gormenghast* (1950), or J. R. R. Tolkien's *Hobbit* (1937) or *The Lord of the Rings* (1954–5), to exemplify the fantastical aspects of a movement which is usually seen as being "over" by the mid-1950s.

The influence of Neo-Romanticism is, however, considerably more profound and far-reaching than its critics have so far acknowledged. Neo-Romanticism in certain of its aspects creates for Byatt and Murdoch a world between what can be broadly termed the modern and the postmodern sensibilities. In particular, it creates a ground where both writers can negotiate some of the questions of character, narrative form, audience, which came to be central preoccupations of postwar novelists (see, for example, Connor 1996: 12). But the figure of Samuel Palmer alone would hardly make a convincing enough connection for the importance of the movement in Murdoch's and Byatt's work to be accepted.

There is other circumstantial evidence linking the two writers to the Neo-Romantic movement. Murdoch had read, as early as 1943, the "New Apocalyptic" poets (Conradi 2001: 154). Raymond Mortimer, that early identifier of "the romantic revival," was soon to pick out the "surreal and dreamlike elements" in her work, which have "a dreamlike conviction" (Conradi 2001: 416). She sent (and had rejected) Queneau's *Pierrot Mon Ami* in translation to John Lehmann, publisher of *Penguin New Writing* in the 1940s and a leading figure in the Neo-Romantic movement (Conradi 2002: 232). Byatt's links are evident in her belief that J. R. R. Tolkien is still ruling the landscape of the imagination in the 1960s.[14] She acknowledges him as a significant influence on *Babel Tower* (1997) in that "The Tower in *Babbletower*, the book-within-a-book that is tried in *Babel Tower* derives...from Tolkien – the Company retreating from danger across a rocky landscape to a safe place."[15] It is, however, in the theoretical rather than the circumstantial, in the terms of the movement rather than its manifestations, that the significance of the connection between Byatt, Murdoch, and Neo-Romanticism can be found.

Most important among these terms, for the purposes of this discussion, are those that deal with time, space, and imagination. In 1937, John Piper sets out the Neo-Romantic conception of spatiality in the following way: aerial photography, he believes, has changed our "consciousness of spaces and vistas":

> From the air, hills flatten out ... the sea has become something new to the senses; it is like nothing we have ever known ... or any writing or painting about waves or cliffs or ships that was ever thought of. The significant thing being that our *horizons vanish*.[16]

Time, Space, and Meaning

Vanishing horizons presuppose vanishing boundaries. Delineation between near and far is called into question, and along with this questioning doubt must be cast on any traditional apprehension of the relations between things. Allied to this destabilization is what Paul Nash, in his exposition of the surreal elements of Neo-Romantic art in 1937, identifies as "a combination of irrational circumstances giving a sense of nightmare or hallucination."[17] The link between space and imagination implicit in Nash's definition is made explicit in John Piper's grounding of the apocalyptic elements of the movement in the notion of "nightmare"; nightmare is transmuted into a "Gothic revival" fueled by such artists as Graham Sutherland in his attention to elemental forms, via on the one hand a "vastness of ... mass" and on the other an "intense and prophetic vision" such as that he applauds in the late Turner.[18] Geoffrey Grigson sees art as resisting the exigencies of time and existing in a kind of eternal present. The Neo-Romantic is an art, he believes, in which "we are placing ourselves somewhere behind the contradictions of matter and mind, where an identity ... may more primitively exist."[19] If modernism had already appropriated the primitive, Neo-Romanticism sought to utilize it in the construction of a world that questioned its own boundaries. Herbert Read in his *Philosophy of Modern Art* (1952), in which he sets out some of the main strands of Neo-Romantic thought, makes explicit the links between Neo-Romanticism, "folk" culture, and the Jungian "collective memory." For Jung, transcending time is essential to the construction of meaning. Jung asks himself the question "from what source do we derive meaning?" and answers:

> The forms we use for assigning meaning are historical categories that reach back into the mists of time – a fact we do not take sufficiently into account. Interpretations make use of certain linguistic matrices that are themselves derived from primordial images. From whatever side we approach this question, everywhere we find ourselves confronted with the history of language, with images and motifs that lead straight back into the primitive wonder-world. (Hauke 1999: 4)

Just as Read theorizes Neo-Romanticism in terms of the universal symbols accessible to the collective human unconscious, so Lévi-Strauss updates Jung in the service of the postmodern sensibility:

> We might say, therefore, that the preconscious is the individual lexicon where each of us accumulates the vocabulary of his personal history, but that this vocabulary becomes significant, for us and for others, only to the extent that the unconscious structures it according to its laws and this transforms it into language . . . The vocabulary matters less than the structure. (Hauke 1999: 196)

Jung's "primitive wonderworld" and Lévi-Strauss's "preconscious" are realms where the rational structures of language intersect with the instinctual patterning mode of time accumulated. Each can be seen as a permeable membrane through the fabric of which the collective past and the individual present are forever passing and repassing in the process of deforming and reforming themselves and one another. Peter Saward's to and fro movement between the "light" of his rationally structured daily research rituals to the "dark" of the night-time (unconscious) where he hopes, paradoxically, for an illumination which escapes him (*FE*, 22), can be seen as a metaphor for this process. Cassandra's ultimately life-denying immersion in ritual at the expense of romance gestures toward the dangers of ignoring the potentialities of this cross-over world.

The importance of the place this world occupies in Byatt's thinking becomes apparent in her assertion that the Palmer images "of harvest are also an intricate art of my *private-universal* imagery" (*SS*, xvi, my emphasis). This importance can also be seen in her analysis of the Romantic movement, *Unruly Times: Wordsworth and Coleridge in their Time* (1997). Coleridge's concentration on the concrete and particular, Byatt believes, was balanced by "a mode of connecting himself to the deepest roots and underlying patterns of behaviour, language and expression" (1997: 280). The Romantic sensibility needed a "mode of vision which would combine the particular life of individual vision with the sense of underlying form and unity that could be abstracted." Coleridge looks toward this in his letter to "an unknown correspondent" after Wordsworth had criticized his *Hymn Before Sunrise in the Vale of Chamouny* as a specimen of the mock sublime:

> From my very childhood I have been accustomed to *abstract* and as it were unrealize whatever of more than common interest my eyes dwelt on; and then by a sort of transfusion and transmission of my consciousness to identify myself with the Object. (Byatt 1997: 280)

This transfusion of consciousness to identify with the object is closely akin to the structuring of Jung's "collective unconscious," and, via Read's appropriation of it for mid-twentieth-century art, to the Neo-Romantic movement itself.

Art and Magic

Murdoch's attachment to a similar between-world is made explicit in *The Fire and the Sun* in a set of paradoxical arguments about the nature and value of art. On the one hand "aesthetic form has essential elements of trickery and magic"; on the other, "magic in its unregenerate form ... is the bane of art" (*FS*, 78–9). Countering "the high temperature fusing power" of the Romantic imagination is the idea that "dream is the enemy of art and its false image" (*FS*, 79). The dream and the magic which Murdoch abhors are products of the "facile merging tendencies of the obsessive ego" (*FS*, 79) mentioned above. Murdoch is at one, in the realm of "false causality," with Jean-Paul Sartre, whose reliance on the notion of "contingency" is closely akin to Murdoch's belief that what the artist needs to be aware of are the "wandering causes" and the "mystery of the random" (*FS*, 80). But, for Murdoch, insurmountable difficulties of abstraction face such writers as Sartre. Murdoch is circumspect about "what level of generality" the artist is to operate on. "Great discoveries are made at great levels of generality" but, at the same time, "the lack of detail" can leave the reader unconvinced that he is really seeing "human life" and not the "ghostly ballet of bloodless categories" (*FS*, 81). The existential novel exemplifies, for Murdoch, such "ghostly ballet." Her preoccupations are similar to those Byatt points out in relation to Coleridge. How to combine the particular and the general? How to avoid abstraction and at the same time to contain any tendency to unleash the obsessive ego in an unwelcome solipsism that would fail, perhaps, to tell any general truth?

For Murdoch a partial answer lies in her own responses to the questions she raises about characterization in "Against Dryness" (1961). Between what she sees as "crystalline" and "journalistic" modes of writing (broadly speaking, symbolic and realist) a way forward that at once embraces and eschews both needs to be found. The nature of that way forward is set out in *The Fire and the Sun*, through the exposition of an aesthetic form which includes "ambiguity and playfulness" (*FS*, 85), akin to the "creative reveries of the Demiurge where truth and play mysteriously, inextricably mingle" (83), an arena in which "we see in a dream that art is properly concerned with the synthetic *a priori*, the borderland of *dianoia* and *noesis*, the highest mental state described in the *Republic*" (*FS*, 80).

Dianoia and *noesis*, "knowledge by experience" and "intuitive knowledge": this borderland where rational meets intuitive is remarkably akin to the realm in which the "transfusion and transmission" of Coleridge's consciousness in the cause of identifying himself with the "Object" takes place. As Byatt also points out (*UT*, 280):

> This kind of abstraction *deeper* than the recognition of the concrete idiosyncrasy of objects is also recognizable in Wordsworth's description of the "abyss of idealism" he experienced in childhood which is recalled in the glorious light images of the *Immortality Ode*: "I communed with all that I saw as something not apart from, but inherent in, my own material nature."

Byatt characterizes this "tension between the identity of subject and object," between the "blank misgivings of a creature moving about in worlds not realized" and the concrete realization of individual aspects of the world, as the material out of which Wordsworth and Coleridge created their greatest poetry. It is also, arguably, the material out of which Byatt and Murdoch create fictional worlds which surpass the realms available to the concrete apprehension of the realist eye.[20] In its mediation between rational and intuitive, particular and general, object and subject, it can be plausibly described as a liminal land where collective unconscious meets the contingent realm of everyday experience and event.

Authority and Freedom

"Wandering causes" and the "mystery of the random" (*FS*, 80), a mixture of generality and detail interposed with "ambiguity and playfulness" (*FS*, 85) – these are some of the characteristics of the fictional world Murdoch perceives as suitable for negotiating the rational and the intuitive. Byatt turns to the fairy story, as "related to dreams, which are maybe most people's first experience of unreal narrative, and to myths." This she opposes to "Realism [which] is related to explanations and orderings." Byatt believes the novel should encompass both modes, because "Great novels, I believe, always draw on both ways of telling, both ways of seeing."[21] Byatt's objection to "ordering" being of itself a sufficient means for fiction is illuminated in her views on Coleridge. Romanticism's interest in medieval life is more than mere nostalgia. The desire for the relative rigidity of old ways (Cassandra's walled garden comes to mind) is counterpointed by "the corollary of unleashed human energy" (*UT*, 131) of the feudal system. Hazlitt observed of Scott's historical novels that:

> As we read, we throw aside the the trammels of civilization, the flimsy veil of humanity...The wild beast resumes its sway within us. We feel like hunting animals...the heart rouses itself in its native lair, and utters a wild cry of joy, at being restored once more to freedom and lawless, unrestrained impulses...here are no...impassable Parallellograms, no long calculations of self-interest – the will takes its instant way to its object. (*UT*, 133)

The postwar novel had to take into account comparable oppositions between authority and freedom, between the "trammels of civilization" and the "wild beast" within us. The holocaust and the atomic age had cast fresh doubt on the grand narratives of science and humanism; an increasingly secular society questioned the foundational efficacy of religion as a healing force. And, fueled by existentialist claims for the possibilities of freedom and self-determination, patterns of social division were loosening, and the rights and duties of authority structures based in a paternalist apprehension of human relations were being undercut. A gradual commercialization of the culture industry meant that "increasingly, novels looked for *rapprochement* with the forms, languages and modes of address of mass culture, as well as ways of distinguishing themselves from it" (Connor 1996: 13).

Murdoch's desire to avoid "bloodless categories" and Byatt's belief in the need for the novel to encompass both real and unreal are both, perhaps, manifestations of a wish for such a *rapprochement*. It is a wish that issues, in their work, in an emphasis on archetypes, the patterning not of cause and effect, but of mythic or symbolic transcendence. In Byatt, this patterning is founded in Celtic and Norse myth, the "world of Loki the Deceiver, Fenris the Wolf, the Wild Hunt and the wanderings of Odin,"[22] and forms the basis of her statement that her writing centers on "the old, the new and the metaphor" (Wallhead 1999: 34). Murdoch creates, as Conradi says of *The Unicorn*:

> a fantastical, fairytale, Gothic world, with a Platonic topography, a bog that floods at seven-year intervals, an ocean that kills, a megalith "seemingly pointless yet dreadfully significant" and an imprisoned heroine out of a fairy tale. (Conradi 2001: 448).

It is a world of distance and displacement which mediates between the narrative commonality of folktale and the radical critique of the human condition encountered in the theater of the absurd.[23]

Narratives of Enchantment

High modernism's reliance on myth to accommodate artistic expression of what T. S. Eliot called "the futility and anarchy which is contemporary history"[24] would seem to suggest myth as inimical to the kind of mediations the postwar novel was faced with.[25] Northrop Frye in his discussion of archetypal criticism (1957: 133–40) compares realism, "an art of implicit simile," with myth, "an art of implicit metaphorical identity." Myth isolates the structural principles of literature; realism fits these same structural principles "into a context of plausibility." A bringing together of the two – mythical structure in realist fiction – creates problems which are solved by what he calls "displacement." This area of displacement, lying between myth at one end of the continuum and naturalism (extreme realism) at the other, is "the whole area of romance." Romance, in these terms, "is the tendency . . . to displace myth in a human direction and yet, in contrast to 'realism' to conventionalize content in an idealized direction." Romance fiction is characterized by "analogy, significant association, incidental accompanying imagery, and the like." This fiction is, Frye believes, "realistic enough to be plausible in its incidents yet romantic enough to be 'a good story'." In this he seems to be identifying precisely the tendency of postwar fiction to mediate between high and low art that Murdoch and Byatt exemplify.

Byatt sees *Flight from the Enchanter* as "a fantasy-myth" which "is moving towards a fictional representation of the reality of the contingent, the accidental" (1994: 38–9). The novel's mythic aspect lies in its playing off of *dianoia* and *noesis*, knowledge by experience and intuitive knowledge. The social realist novel of experience encapsulated in Annette's erratic trajectory from girlhood to womanhood is inscribed on a horizonless realm of conflicting intuitions where boundaries lose meaning. Habitual notions of spatiality are undercut in Mischa's house, which faces in all directions simultaneously. Divisions between human characters, and between the human and the archetypal, have no meaning. Calvin Blick's career of blackmail and pornography is carried on in Mischa's basement. Blick is the last line one has to cross before reaching Mischa; he fulfills a role somewhere between minder and alter ego. But Mischa himself inhabits the text as a fluid presence, the Minotaur at the heart of the labyrinth, the spider Hunter envisions in (quasi)delirium (all the characters are in one way or another bound up in his web), yet at the same time Mischa as human is portrayed sometimes as gentle and life-saving, sometimes as the ultimate destructive force in his magnetism and in his demands.

Murdoch's dissolution of boundaries allows her to construct a narrative of enchantment on two interconnected levels. The fluidity of character identity within and between realms (real and unreal) facilitates her portrayal of Mischa as shape-shifter, weaving a magical pattern between past and present, actual and imagined, concrete and fantastic. All worlds meet in Mischa, he is the hub of such diverse existences as Nina's (precarious refugee), Annette's (spoiled debutante), Rainboro's (government official). His eyes (one brown, one blue) see into an impossible diversity of worlds, those who inhabit the worlds fearing always that he can magically divine their intentions and acts. He has the compelling power of a wizard, like Merlin, turning up at unexpected times and places, and with an inscrutability that defies any attempt at prediction of intent.

False Causalities

There is a sense in which his all-seeingness reflects the postwar political climate of totalitarian opposition, of espionage and surveillance. Yet Murdoch employs it also to mount a critique of epic proportions on "the facile merging tendencies of the obsessive ego" (*FS*, 79) discussed above. The compelling aspect of Mischa's ubiquity is constructed by those around him in terms of a stultifying matrix of cause and effect which can be read on one level as exemplifying that "personal fantasy and egoistic anxiety" which is no more than "the fantastic doctoring of the real for consumption by the private ego" (*FS*, 79). This Murdoch abhors and holds in opposition to a desirable "education in moral discernment" (*FS*, 83). *The Flight from the Enchanter* deals with a world where people construct and live by images of false causality. The novel shows the disaster of this, in that a world thus constructed is destructive and pernicious: the "good" (as far as we know) character, Nina, destroys herself because Rosa is too enmeshed in her own false causalities (her obsession with Mischa, her subjugation to the Lusiewicz brothers' supposed power) to let her know that her fear of new rules about the status of aliens causing her deportation is groundless. True, Rosa is at her sick brother Hunter's bedside, so we might think she has his good at heart; but she soon abandons him to pursue Mischa, an act of apparent selfishness that she later justifies through the fact that she "knew" her brother would soon recover. Hunter becomes "a sick man" (*FE*, 259) through his belief that a kind of spell has been cast on him. Rainboro constructs false causes in the form of conspiracy theories, casting his women colleagues as demons and furies, within these constructions finding himself acting without knowing why or how. Murdoch extends her critique of false causalities in an examination of the pernicious aspects of romantic love. The compelling quality of Mischa's ubiquity is constructed by those around him in terms of an all-encompassing sexual and emotional attraction. Rosa and Annette in particular fall under his spell, both attachments shown ultimately as having a delusory, and highly destructive, content. Beyond the realist streets of well-heeled Kensington lie equally the fear and poverty and displacement of refugee existence, and the contingent realm of desire, with its interconnected self-delusions inextricable from the false logic of "obsession [which] shrinks reality to a single pattern" (*FS*, 79).

In place of any single pattern (akin perhaps to the "single reality" of J. P. Stern's realism) Murdoch formulates her warning against enchantment through the very means of enchantment itself. Her boundary-less world of permeable realms is constructed around interlinking themes of personal, social, moral, and political displacement. But at the same time, displacement in terms of Frye's definition of romance (myth in a human direction, content in an idealized direction) is self-evidently taking place. Murdoch's novel seems to fit well with Frye's further apprehension of the nature of what he calls "ironic literature" as a subdivision of romance. "Ironic literature," he believes, "begins with realism and tends towards myth, its mythical patterns being as a rule...suggestive of the demonic" (1957: 133–40). There is irony in Murdoch's presentation of the need to flee the enchanter (from Mischa, from "love," from self-love/ego) taking the form of romance, itself a deliberate version of a kind of enchantment. There is further irony in this form containing within it a critique of its own means: the difficulties of attempting to undertake what Murdoch calls a "discerning exercise of intelligence in relation to the real" (*FS*, 78) are made strikingly evident through the challenges confronting the reader in deciphering truth from falsehood in this romance text.

The Flight from the Enchanter as a Postmodern Text

Frye's work may be seen as a precursor of the French deconstructionist criticism which underpins postmodernist theoretical stances.[26] His delineation of the role of romance as mediator between mythic and realist, between high and low art, enables a view of *The Flight from the Enchanter* as an early postmodernist text, certainly in Patricia Waugh's terms of early postmodernism, as a "description of a range of aesthetic practices involving playful irony, parody, parataxis, self-consciousness, fragmentation" (1992: 41). There is another significant way in which the novel can be read as an early postmodernist text. Murdoch cites Plato (*The Republic* 395) as saying "that no one can write both comedy and tragedy" (*FS,* 81). She believes "There is a 'sublime absurd', comic or tragic, which depends on this insight into where the 'faults' of our partially failed, of our 'terrible and absurd' world come" (*FS,* 80). Lyotard, in his essay "What Is Postmodernism?",[27] sees both modern and postmodern "as operating under the sign of the sublime, in that the sublime is what attempts to represent the unrepresentable" (Larrissy 1999: 7). Murdoch's "sublime absurd" (what Byatt refers to as "a bitterly amusing social myth" [*DF,* 217]), neatly sums up what she is attempting to do in *Flight from the Enchanter.* Her construction of the text in the terms of romance enables her to develop a narrative which eschews both modernism and realism, to address, like Beckett, the "terrible and absurd" psychic state of the postwar age. One of the aspects of romance is that it is (as Beer says [1979: 53]) "anti 'duty'": "coincidence and magic create a kind of pagan freedom far removed from the world" where duty holds sway. Indeed, romance has been seen as on the side of individual free will in the opposition between "free will and determinism." But it is not this simple for Iris Murdoch. Murdoch's use of the enchanter motif allows her, like Conrad, to "invoke the supernatural and allegorical without ever relinquishing natural causes"; hence, like him, she "transforms romance into morality." She is using romance, in other words, to negotiate the difficult path between 1950s anti-authoritarianism and her own ethical system, in particular her belief that the "great artist, while showing us what is not saved, implicitly shows us what salvation means."[28]

The Politics of Narrative

A. S. Byatt's *Possession* is not only subtitled "a romance" but includes, by her own admission, "the medieval verse Romance, the modern romantic novel, and Hawthorne's fantastical historical romance in between" (2000: 48). The use of fairy story witnesses her desire to "play quite consciously with a postmodern creation and recreation of old forms." Byatt believes: "My fairy stories are postmodern, in that they reflect on the nature of narrative, and of their own narrative in particular. Narration is seen as the goal as well as the medium."

Part of Byatt's agenda is, then, the politics of narrative. In Patricia Waugh's terms (1984: 3), Byatt is a "metafictional" novelist in that she employs structural undermining of convention, using previous texts and systems on which to construct her tale. Several of the strands Waugh identifies as useful for exploring readers' expectations of the novel form are utilized in *Possession,* in particular the detective story, the romance, the comic, and the family saga. Byatt's postmodernism has been traced to European influences (Wallhead 1999: 34) and she acknowledges Umberto Eco, among others, as important in her development of *Possession*:

> I had already had the idea that *Possession* should be a kind of detective story, with the scholars as the detectives, when I read *The Name of the Rose* which combines mediaeval

theology, Church history, gleefully bloodthirsty horrors, reflections on the form of the novel, with a hero who is an avatar or precursor of Sherlock Holmes.[29]

Byatt's obvious use of romance motifs in her novel is acknowledged in its subtitle and evidenced in the quest theme, focused on romantic love and the acquisition of (factual) knowledge, with Maud as Lady, Roland as Knight (Byron's "Childe Roland" ironically shadows Byatt's often less than effectual "new man"), and the Baileys' ancestral home in Norfolk fulfilling the function of castle or tower, in which reside manifestations of the Grail, both in terms of the knowledge encompassed in Christabel's letters and the dawning attachment between Maud and Roland.

Uncritical conflation of the subtitle with the use of such motifs can lead, however, to an oversimplification of Byatt's ends and aims. Wallhead (1999: 100), for example, asserts that *Possession* has "no narrative intervention since it is a romance, like a fairy tale, told or repeated by yet another anonymous story-teller," whereas Byatt identifies three interventions by an omniscient narrator, which "tell what might be thought of as the most important, beautiful and terrible moments in the lives of the Victorian characters."[30] Byatt's use *of* romance tends in different directions from the ways in which the novel works *as* romance. The novel as romance is closely related to Frye's definition of a mediating form, particularly in his encapsulation of a "metaphorical organization" which he further identifies as "demonic" in his definition of mythical literature. Byatt acknowledges the importance to her conception of *Possession*, along with the sexual, of "both the daemonic and the economic." She describes how her "imagination is inexorably metaphoric."[31] This metaphoric quality is evident in her formulation of character. Maud's extreme fairness renders her humanity curiously ambivalent, and this ambivalence transfers across time (Christabel is equally fair) and across texts (the "heroine" of *Morpho Eugenia* is constructed as a similar archetype). Material surroundings are imbued with the excessive quality of the fairy tale: Maud's bathroom is described as "a chill, green, glassy place, glittering . . . shimmering . . . watery' (*P*, 56). Names take on metaphorical resonance: Maud for mad; Bailey for fortification; Ash for the ashes of death but also gesturing toward the rejuvenating role of the ash tree in Celtic mythology. Boundaries between past and present, real and unreal, are dismantled through a negation of the idea of horizon. In Piper's terms, we are presented simultaneously with a view from the air and a view from the earth, in the inscription on a potentially realist plot (a search for rational, academic evidence) of a radically shape-shifting, metaphorical world.

Imaginative Assent

It is this inscription, perhaps, that leads Steven Connor to feel *Possession* is "suspended somewhere between the conditions of . . . the historical novel and the historicized novel" (1996: 149). The historical novel's tendency toward realism is implicitly contrasted with the more radical potential of the novel that uses history to some other end. This contrast is reflected in Byatt's distaste for texts that require "historical belief" rather than "imaginative assent."[32] The imaginative assent Byatt refers to is related to her appreciation of Bruno Bettelheim's *Uses of Enchantment*, which suggests:

> The fairy-tale gives form and coherence to formless fears, dreads and desires. Recognising a fairy tale motif, or an ancient myth, Cinderella or Oedipus, in the mess of a life lived or observed gives both pleasure and security and the sense – or illusion – of wisdom.[33]

This comforting sense of a pattern understood refers not to the rational patterning of cause and effect (Cassandra's "ritual") but to those "primitive apprehensions and narrative motifs"[34] directly akin to the contents of Jung's collective unconscious; their value for Byatt lies in their causing us to "think consciously about human beings and the world."[35] Despite the caveat that we must recognize life as "a muddle, a conflict," the coherence of the fairy tale is necessary not only because such tales "delight," but because "they join us to each other."[36] The nature of this joining is elucidated in *Portraits in Fiction*, where Byatt discusses Roland's take on Randolph Ash, as represented in the three visual versions available to him:

> He remembered talking to Maud about modern theories of the incoherent self which was made up of conflicting systems of beliefs, desires, languages and molecules. All and none of these were Ash and yet he knew, if he did not encompass, Ash.[37]

The nature of "knowing" here belongs to Cassandra's realm of feeling, rather than the rational proclivities of her walled-garden self. Just before this passage, Byatt describes how Roland "thinks about how the images we see, the painters who made them, are part also of those who see and read. My imaginary Manet, my imaginary Watts, my imaginary poets, are part of Roland, and they are all of course part of me" (*PF*, 93).

The imagination (in Murdoch's terms, "the hot, fusing power of the romantic imagination") is what allows knowledge, of other human beings and (through the collective unconscious) of a common history and culture.

If *Possession's* use *of* romance tends toward the critical destabilization of the postmodern temper, *Possession as* romance transcends its own postmodern aspect. For the text revisits precisely those questions of connection addressed by both modernist experimentation and Neo-Romanticism's reconciliation of individual and collective, subject and object. Byatt has said, "I like change, not revolution. I like subtle distinctions within a continuing language, not doctrinaire violations."[38] The grounding of *Possession's* romance aspect within the "continuing language" of the Neo-Romantic movement casts light on the nature of that "narrative discovery" on which she believes "the pleasure of fiction is based."

See also: chapter 3, The Popular English Metrical Romances; chapter 16, Romance and the Romantic Novel; chapter 17, Poetry of the Romantic Period;

chapter 24, America and Romance; chapter 25, Myth, Legend, and Romance in Yeats, Pound, and Eliot; chapter 26, Twentieth-century Arthurian Romance; chapter 27, Romance in Fantasy; chapter 28, Quest Romance in Science Fiction; chapter 30, Popular Romance and its Readers.

Notes

1. Cited in Gillian Beer, *The Romance*. Critical Idiom series (London: Methuen, 1970), pp. 56–7.

2. A. S. Byatt, *The Game* (London: Chatto and Windus 1967; Vintage, 1992). Further references in the text are to *TG*.

3. Byatt is referring to Jessie Weston's *From Ritual to Romance* (Cambridge: Cambridge University Press, 1920). This text was a particular influence on T. S. Eliot.

4. Iris Murdoch, *The Fire and the Sun* (London: Chatto and Windus, 1977), p. 79. Further references in the text are to *FS*.

5. Iris Murdoch, *The Flight from the Enchanter* (London: Chatto and Windus, 1956; Penguin, 1977). All further references in the text are to *FE*.

6. Virginia Woolf, *To the Lighthouse* (1927; Harmondsworth: Penguin, 1996), p. 55. Further references in the text are to *TL*.

7. Murdoch's interest in the language theories of Ludwig Wittgenstein predispose her to problematize language in these terms. See Christopher Butler, *Postmodernism: A Very Short Introduction* (Oxford: Oxford University Press, 2002), p. 16.

8. See, for example, Michel Foucault, *Power/Knowledge: Selected Interviews and Other Writings, 1972–1977*, ed. Colin Gordon (Brighton: Harvester, 1980).

9. See, for example, Celia Wallhead, *The Old, the New and the Metaphor: A Critical Study of the Novels of A. S. Byatt* (London: Minerva, 1999). According to Christopher Butler, "The postmodern novel is characterized by a 'willingness to display to the reader its own formal workings'" (2002: 73).

10. Andrzej Gasiorek, *Postwar British Fiction* (London: Arnold, 1995), p. 12.

11. *The Dial* (February 28, 1928), 240. In his "London Letter" Raymond Mortimer states the case for there being: "Already the signs of a romantic revival ... everywhere perceptible," a revival which was "likely to react vigorously against the intellectualism of Bloomsbury."

12. *The Shadow of the Sun* was written in Cambridge between 1954 and 1957. References in the text are to *SS*.

13. "Samuel Palmer at Shoreham," *Signature* 7 (November 1937), 1.

14. See Byatt Writings from www.asbyatt.com: "Introduction to Babel Tower."

15. Ibid.

16. John Piper, "Prehistory from the Air," *Axis* 8 (Winter 1937), 5.

17. Paul Nash, "Surrealism and the Illustrated Book," *Signature* 5 (March 1937), 1.

18. John Piper, *British Romantic Artists* (London: William Collins, 1942), pp. 14, 28, 17. Piper quotes W. H. Pyne (1824) on Girtin.

19. Geoffrey Grigson, "Comment on England," *Axis* 1 (January 1935), 8.

20. Realism here is used in the terms suggested by J. P. Stern when he writes: "what [realism] implicitly denies is that in this world there is more than one reality." J. P. Stern, *On Realism* (London: Routledge & Kegan Paul, 1973), p. 54.

21. www.asbyatt.com: "Fairy Stories: The Djinn in the Nightingale's Eye."

22. Ibid.

23. Murdoch recounts Plato's comment in *The Republic* 395 that "no one can write both comedy and tragedy" (*FS*, 81). She is, however, strongly influenced by Samuel Beckett's existentialist tragicomedies, which demonstrate the inherited power of the theater of the absurd.

24. T. S. Eliot, "Ulysses, Order and Myth," *The Dial* LXXV (5 November 1923), 483.

25. Connor suggests the postwar novel is undergoing "conscious recoil from the stylistic and formal artifice of modernist fiction" (1996: 45).

26. See for instance K. M. Mewton, *Twentieth Century Literary Theory* (Basingstoke: Macmillan, 1998), pp. 100–1.

27. Appended by translators to *The Postmodern Condition: A Report on Knowledge* (Manchester: Manchester University Press, 1984).

28. Here she is endorsing Tolstoy's belief in "the universal" being "the proper province of the artist," *FS*, 80.

29. A. S. Byatt, www.asbyatt.com, "Choices: On the Writing of *Possession*."

30. Ibid.

31. www.asbyatt.com: "Introduction to Babel Tower." George Lakoff has postulated the metaphoric function as one which militates against the construction of boundaries and promotes expansive, fluid, and shifting notions of meaning: see George Lakoff and Mark Johnson, *Metaphors We Live By* (Chicago: University of Chicago Press, 1980).

32. www.asbyatt.com: "Fairy Stories: The Djinn in the Nightingale's Eye."

33. Ibid.

34. Ibid.

35. Ibid.

36. Ibid.

37. A. S. Byatt, *Portraits in Fiction* (London: Vintage 2002), p. 94. Further references in the text are to *PF.*

38. A. S. Byatt, "Give Me the Moonlight, Give Me the Girl," *The New Review II* (1975), 67.

References and Further Reading

Antonaccio, Maria (2000). *Picturing the Human: The Moral Thought of Iris Murdoch.* Oxford: Oxford University Press.

Banhabib, Seyla (1992). *Situating the Self: Gender, Community and Postmodernism in Contemporary Ethics.* Cambridge: Polity.

Beer, Gillian (1979). *The Romance.* Critical Idiom series. London: Methuen.

Butler, Christopher (2002). *Postmodernism: A Very Short Introduction.* Oxford: Oxford University Press.

Byatt, A. S. (1991). *The Shadow of the Sun.* London: Vintage. [First published in 1964.]

Byatt, A. S. (1991). *Possession: A Romance.* London: Vintage. [First published in 1990.]

Byatt, A. S. (1992). *The Game.* London: Vintage. [First published in 1967.]

Byatt, A. S. (1993). *Passions of the Mind: Selected Writings.* London: Vintage.

Byatt, A. S. (1994). *Degrees of Freedom: The Early Novels of Iris Murdoch.* London: Vintage.

Byatt, A. S. (1997). *Unruly Times: Wordsworth and Coleridge in their Time.* London: Vintage.

Byatt, A. S. (2000). *On Histories and Stories.* London: Chatto and Windus.

Byatt, A. S. (2002). *Portraits in Fiction.* London: Vintage.

Connor, Steven (1996). *The English Novel in History.* London: Routledge.

Conradi, Peter (2001). *Iris Murdoch: A Life.* London: HarperCollins.

Frye, Northrop (1957). *Anatomy of Criticism: Four Essays.* Princeton, NJ: Princeton University Press.

Foucault, Michel (1980). *Power/Knowledge: Selected Interviews and Other Writings, 1972–1977*, ed. Colin Gordon. Brighton: Harvester.

Gasiorek, Andrzej (1995). *Postwar British Fiction.* London: Arnold.

Hauke, Christopher (1999). *Jung and the Postmodern.* London: Routledge.

Larrissy, Edward (1999). *Romanticism and Postmodernism.* Cambridge: Cambridge University Press.

Lyotard, Jean-François (1984). *The Postmodern Condition: A Report on Knowledge.* Manchester: Manchester University Press.

Mellor, David (1987). *A Paradise Lost: The Neo-Romantic Imagination in Britain 1935–55.* London: Barbican Art Gallery.

Murdoch, Iris (1977). *The Flight from the Enchanter.* Harmondsworth: Penguin. [First published in 1956.]

Murdoch, Iris (1977). *The Fire and the Sun*. London: Chatto and Windus.

Nicholls, Peter (1995). *Modernisms*. Berkeley: University of California Press.

Piper, John (1942). *British Romantic Artists*. London: William Collins.

Sage, Lorna (1992). *Women in the House of Fiction*. London: Macmillan.

Sillars, Stuart (1991). *British Romantic Art and the Second World War*. London: Macmillan.

Todd, Richard (1984). *Iris Murdoch*. London: Methuen.

Wallhead, Celia M. (1999). *The Old, the New and the Metaphor: A Critical Study of the Novels of A. S. Byatt*. London: Minerva.

Waugh, Patricia (1984). *Metafiction: The Theory and Practice of Self-Conscious Fiction*. London: Routledge.

Waugh, Pat (1992). *Practising Postmodernism/ Reading Modernism*. London: Arnold.

Woolf, Virginia (1996). *To the Lighthouse*. Harmondsworth: Penguin. [First published in 1927.]

Yorke, Malcolm (1988). *The Spirit of Place: Nine Neo-Romantic Artists and their Times*. London: Constable.

30

Popular Romance and its Readers

Lynne Pearce

In her original proposal for this *Companion*, Corinne Saunders observed that: "Romance exists in *degenerate* form in works of the Mills and Boon type" (my italics). As the author given the responsibility for dealing with this end of the romance spectrum, some manner of defense was clearly called for, and my initial response – "yes, but what is most degenerate is also most *defining*" – has stood up well to the way this chapter has developed. Like it or not, it is the template originating in these mass-produced romances that has become the twenty-first-century's base-line definition of romance; and largely, I would contend, because they are where the "deep structures" (see Propp 1968), conventions, and clichés are laid most bare and become most repeatable. Impossible as it might be to define in terms of a more complex literary history, in this – its most popular and, indeed, most "degenerate" form – romance is a "story" that everyone knows.

The fact, moreover, that this most popular version of romance now exists in contemporary Western culture at the level of *discourse* also helps to explain why, in literary terms, its story is no longer confined to "Mills and Boon." Indeed, in preparing my material for the *Companion*, I quickly realized that it would be not only limiting, but anachronistic, to interpret my "popular" brief too narrowly: romance of the "degenerate" kind is now a staple point of reference for any amount of postmodern "literary" fiction and film, and its "ironic but not" treatment in such texts is, I feel, a measure of the extent to which contemporary culture is as obsessed with this particular "Ur"-narrative as ever: the story of how two lovers meet, become estranged, and are then reunited under the aegis of an "unconquerable love" has lost none of its appeal. At the time of writing, one film text to have proven massively successful in its recuperation of "degenerate romance" is Baz Luhrmann's *Moulin Rouge* (2001).[1] This is a movie in which the wildly extravagant parody of every romantic cliché in the book – a good deal of it centered on popular music of the 1970s and 1980s – works to validate, rather than to undermine, its central humanist message, which is: "To love and to be loved is the greatest thing of all." Bestselling author

Jeanette Winterson, likewise, has made a highly successful career out of unashamedly recycling a similar message, with her latest novel – *Powerbook* (2000) – walking the same tightrope between the clichés and the "holiness of the heart's affections" as her previous titles:

> I didn't answer. I had heard these arguments before. I had used them myself. They tell some truth, but not all the truth, and the truth they deny is a truth about the heart. The body can endure compromise and the heart can be seduced by it. Only the heart protests.
> The heart. Carbon-based primitive in a silicon world. (Winterson 2000: 40)

The basis of Winterson's credo is, of course, that somewhere, for all of us, love exists "in the original" and is "written in tablets of stone" (Winterson 1985: 170). In other words, the fact that love stories reproduce themselves endlessly is evidence not of postmodern "hyper-reality" but of the enduring power of that originary source ("We go back and back to the same scenes, the same words, trying to scrape out their meaning" [Winterson 2000: 78]).

While presumably differing in the degree of "essence" we afford this "Ur-story," there are surely few of us working in the field of popular romance who would not agree that it is a phenomenon the enduring "success" of which can ultimately only be understood in terms of the "deep structures" that enable its endless reproduction. Whether we then consider those structures an ideology or "false consciousness" that exists to be knocked down, or a psychic foundation with roots simply too deep to shake, matters less than this shared starting point. Certainly the most compelling writers on romantic love that I have encountered – such as Roland Barthes in *A Lover's Discourse* (1978) – give themselves up completely to the notion that here is a story and/or a set of conventions and clichés that none of us can escape, no matter how well we interrogate the manner of our entrapment. As for Winterson, the ultimate magic/ agony of romantic love for Barthes is the realization that that which appears most commonplace, most "accidental," is experienced by the desiring subject as that which is most fateful, most *un*repeatable, and most unique: "I encounter millions of bodies in my life; of these millions, I may desire some hundreds; but of these hundreds, I love only one" (Barthes 1978: 20).

In this chapter, then, I shall be focusing my attention largely on the "deep structures" that help to elucidate, if still not fully to explain, the "great enigma" of romantic love in its more popular literary and cultural manifestations. The first subsection thus offers a broad overview of the work of Tania Modleski (1982) and Janice Radway (1984) who, in the 1980s, were instrumental in making feminist and other scholars revise their opinion of popular romance in its more "degenerate" forms: first, by showing *why* the deep structures of such fiction have proven so compelling for women readers; and, second, by arguing that those readers must be considered *active*, rather than passive, consumers of the genre. This overview is followed by another on deep structure in which I suggest some new ways in which the compulsive reading/

viewing of romance texts can be explained by drawing, first, on the insights derived from recent "Trauma Theory" and, second, on Ernst Bloch's (1986) work on "day-dreams" and "anticipatory consciousness." As will be seen, these two models could hardly be more opposite in the ways in which they account for the workings of the human psyche, but both, I feel, help us to understand the narrativity of romantic love a bit more clearly (that is, *why* love exists "as a story").

Ernst Bloch's work on "anticipatory consciousness" (1986) also links with his interest in "beautiful foreign places," in the human subject's ability to create a "better world" for him- or herself, and I take this proposition as my lead for the final subsection of the chapter, which is about "Romantic Locations" and the role of space/place in popular romance texts. After exploring the implications of Bloch's utopianism with regard to the prevalence of exotic locations within the genre, however, I move into a discussion of how such an emphasis on space, place, and historical moment may also be read – quite oppositely – as a sign of their *cultural or historical specificity*. This final section of the chapter therefore acknowledges some of the main ways in which the popular romance genre has been transformed over the past 40 or 50 years, and raises the crucial question of to what extent romantic love can be liberated from the institutions and orthodoxies (in particular, heterosexual marriage and courtship) with which it is traditionally associated. While, for early feminist critics like Germaine Greer (1971) and Shulamith Firestone (1970), such a disassoci-ation of structure and ideology would be inconceivable (for them, romance was an "effect" of patriarchy, pure and simple), the insights of Queer theory (in particular) have shown us how cultural orthodoxies – like heterosexual romantic love – are both continually under threat *and* liable to reappropriation.[2]

This characterization of contemporary romance as fundamentally "unstable" also prompts me to end this introduction with a few words more on the problem of defining popular romance in generic terms; why, in particular, it would now seem wrong to focus simply on the "Mills and Boon" phenomenon. As I noted earlier, Jeanette Winterson's highly popular novels may easily be thought of under the heading of "popular romance" notwithstanding the fact that they are also classified as "literary," "postmodern," and – rather more controversially – "gay" or "queer." What distinguishes them, and similar titles, from the "Mills and Boon" class is that small, but crucial, twist of "knowingness" with which the romantic/sexual adventures are described and analyzed. What is striking about a text like *Powerbook*, however, is that – in terms of its key "ingredients," and the way in which they have been marketed – this product is *not* very far removed from romance in its more "degener-ate" form.

Putting to one side, then, the postmodern knowingness and irony in which Winterson's text is enfolded, a quick survey of what this text has in common with a classic Mills and Boon novel reveals why the depth of the structures/conventions linking them can also be used to explain the erosion of their generic boundaries, especially in terms of their readership. Apart from the fact that the core narrative tells the familiar story of a chance/fateful meeting between two lovers, a series of obstacles (husband/geographical separation), and reunion, what links this text with the common pleasures of popular romance are: its exotic locations (sixteenth-century Holland, Paris, Naples, London); its focus on the physical appearance of the heroine (in particular her "simple" but "expensive" clothing, 2000: 34); its sensual depiction of gourmet food (for example, artichokes, 49; rocket salad, 100; salsa di pomodori, 182–3). The "exotic location" element I shall return to in my later section on this theme, but I think it is worth registering the extent to which Winterson – like a good many other contemporary authors – seems to have realized (or perhaps it's her publishers who have realized) the appeal of glamorous "lifestyle" detail in their texts. The mingling of sexual fantasy with food fantasy, for example, has recently emerged as a new genre in its own right: what John Walsh in a cover story for the *Independent Review* identifies as "snack lit," i.e. "Sensuous fiction involving food, mysticism and lots of sex."[3] While Walsh undoubtedly had titles like Joanne Harris' *Chocolat* scathingly in mind when writing his pastiche, a random dip into any Mills and Boon novel (or, perhaps, in particular, one of the older, "classic" titles) reveals a similar exploitation of this order of fantasy. Take, for example, this (typical) extract from Violet Winspear's (1966: 26) *The Viking Stranger*:

> The crab-in-the-back was delectable, followed by chicken and salad with a guava sauce. They rounded off their meal with a mixture of island fruits served in hollowed pineapple shells and a coconut ice-cream. It rather surprised Jill that her host should have a sweet tooth, and she thought of something she had once read in a book, that there was a boy hiding inside most men. Be that as it may, it was obvious that the man facing her was enjoying every mouthful of his pineapple, papaya, mango and cream. As was she! It was exotic, tangy, mingling with the atmosphere of the restaurant and the champagne glow in her veins.

So, just a short step here, I would suggest, to Winterson's passion for artichokes ("The artichoke arrived and I began to peel it away, fold by fold, layer by layer, dipping it. There is no secret about eating artichoke, or what the act resembles. Nothing else gives itself up so satisfyingly towards the centre" [49]), though – in both instances – I would argue against reading these elaborate descriptions of food and dining as *merely* metaphors for the sexual act: equally important is the role they play in marking the cultural "commodity" appeal of the text. As I argue below vis-à-vis "romantic locations" the significance/pleasure associated with such *details* in the romance text is in excess of its relation to the love plot. Thus, while in other regards Winterson's text very clearly identifies itself as literary rather than popular (its lesbian/queer sexual politics; its philosophizing; its multiple story-lines; its typically postmodern "double" ending), in *marketing* terms it is effectively a "cross-over" title, designed to appeal to *Marie Claire* readers as well as university students.[4]

This mention of the British women's magazine *Marie Claire* may also be taken as the cue for further reflection on the "hybridization" of popular romance in the past ten years or so. As any visit to one of our high-street booksellers will reveal, popular romance of the Mills and Boon variety is now in serious – and possibly dwindling – competition with the category known as "contemporary women's literature," where sex and comedy would seem to have displaced "romance" per se, or – rather – to have assimilated both its conventions and its pleasures. The titles to be found in this category range from the "sex-romp classics" of Jilly Cooper and Judith Krantz through to the more thoroughly ironized *Bridget Jones's Diary* (Fielding 1997).[5] Indeed, it is clear that beneath this new umbrella heading any number of new subgenres are already lurking, though potential readers are clearly united in being (a) comparatively young and (b) hetero/sexually 'aware' (or desirous of becoming so). For John Walsh (see note 3), most of these titles could probably be included under the heading of "chick lit," but with respect to "the history of romance" it is clearly important to distinguish between the degrees of cynicism and irony with which that "love" is treated, and, most important, to what extent a discourse of eroticism may be seen to have displaced and/or transformed the discourse of romance. This last point clearly also has an important bearing upon the evolution/mutation of "Mills and Boon" titles in recent times (see below), yet what is most striking from the publishers' or readers' point of view is that what I perceive to be a particularly important distinction is barely registered. While, to my mind, romantic *love* is distinguished from erotic pleasure through traditional connotations of uniqueness, exclusivity, authenticity, permanence, unrepeatability, transcendence, in which sex itself plays a "sealing" rather than an instrumental role, today's texts/markets are happy to conflate these values with purely erotic ones. In the *Independent*'s list of "the 50 best romantic reads of all time," published on Valentine's Day 2002, for example, "classic romances" were listed alongside "period romances," "romantic comedies," "erotic romances," and "tear-jerkers." Thus, while on the one hand the *Independent* panel clearly registered a significant difference between these texts, it was nevertheless happy to yoke them under the umbrella of "romance." I turn now to a review of those structural elements that continue to make such groupings possible.

Rereading Popular Romance

Back in the 1980s, the work undertaken by Radway, Modleski, and other media/ cultural theorists on why women readers/viewers were such avid consumers of popular romance made what was, I feel, an incontrovertible case for the structural appeal of the "classic" narrative plot.[6] Drawing on Vladimir Propp's early twentieth-century structuralist study, *Morphology of the Folktale* (1968), Radway explains the appeal of these contemporary "fairy-stories" in terms of the way in which they convert initial loss and emptiness (the heroine is orphaned or abandoned; her prospective lover is sent away or estranged) into union and "completion" through the resolution of a problem/challenge (Radway 1984: 135), and then engages feminist insights into gender relations and the workings of patriarchy to explain what this "means" in terms of sexual politics. By returning to these deep narrative and psychic structures and investigating what they meant for actual readers (her ethnographic work for *Reading the Romance* centered on a group of readers from the small mid-west town of Smithton in the USA), Radway was instrumental in rescuing romance (and its readers) from the slur of escapism and "false consciousness." The sense of transformation/completion achieved by the heroines of such texts cannot fail to be compelling and/or compulsive to readers "ever hopeful" (see the discussion of Bloch below) of the same "adult autonomy, [a] secure social position, and the completion produced by maternal nurturance" (1984: 14). Influenced by the work of the feminist psychoanalytic theorist, Nancy Chodorow, Radway's initial hypothesis was, indeed, that what these readers found most compelling about their "ideal" popular romance was the emphasis on *nurturance*: that is, both the opportunity for nurturance afforded to the heroine and the nurturance bestowed upon her by a hero who was (ultimately) tender and attentive (1984: 13–14).

For Radway, this hypothesis was very much supported by the fact that her group of readers were very particular in what they wanted from their romances; indeed, the group had formed itself around bookseller Dorothy Evans' ability to identify and preselect the "best" titles (1984: 46–7). From an analysis of this vast pool of literature, Radway was eventually able to put together a template of what might be considered the "ideal" romance, which included: a "resolute focus on a single, developing relationship between heroine and hero" (1984: 122) (that is, with minimum attention paid to "interim" sexual partners or "rivals"); a heroine who distinguishes herself from other heroines through "unusual intelligence" or "an extraordinarily fiery disposition" (123) (and often to the extent that this undermines a more typical femininity); a heroine who is sexually inexperienced but develops a "natural" nurturing ability (127); a hero who is initially "hard, angular and dark" (128) but whose lust and aggression are transformed into love and tenderness by the heroine; a hero who is manifestly successful in public life (130). What would seem to typify Radway's ideal romance, then – in terms of both the "deep structure" of the plot (see her reworking of Propp's "functions," 134) and the characterization of hero and heroine – is a striking simplicity, and *singularity*, of purpose. The most intense pleasure, for these readers, would seem to lie in the growth and development of the heroine, the growing *intimacy* between the hero and heroine (in which sexual intimacy is only one factor), and finally, the transformation of the hero by the heroine through her love and nurturance.

As already mentioned, Radway initially turned to the theories of Nancy Chodorow to explain these preferences, concluding that "what the heroine successfully establishes at the end of the ideal narrative is the now familiar female self, the self-in-relation" (1984: 139). Like Tania Modleski, she also sees the heroine's ability to "tame" the hero as endemic to the success of the story at a more social or institutional level: "Because she manages this relation with a man who is not only masculine but redundantly so, the romance also manages to consider the possibilities of and difficulties of establishing a connection with a man who is initially incapable of satisfying a woman" (139). With more explicit reference to the cruelty or violence with which many popular romance heroes initially treat the heroines, Modleski added a further twist to this aspect of "reader-pleasure" by recognizing in it a spirit of *revenge*: "A great deal of our satisfaction in reading these novels comes, I am convinced, from the elements of a revenge fantasy, from our conviction that the woman is to bring the man to his knees and that all the while he is being so hateful, he is internally grovelling, grovelling, grovelling" (Modleski 1982: 45).

Rather less triumphantly, Modleski also sees the emphasis on masculine indifference, cruelty, and violence in popular romance fiction as a covert expression of pervasive *fear* and *trauma* – that "the desire to be taken by force (manifest content) conceals anxiety about rape and longings for power and revenge (latent content)" (48). Thus although, like Radway, Modleski sees the reading of romance fiction as an active and critical process on the part of the readers concerned, she is less sanguine about exactly what is being achieved or renegotiated in terms of individual empowerment and (hetero)sexual relations. Focusing primarily on romance reading as an "event" which enabled women to "indulge" themselves both materially (time off from the family) and psychically (through texts which performed fantasies of intimacy, nurturance, and self-actualization), Radway sees women's compulsive return to such texts as ultimately benign. Modleski, by contrast, sets us thinking about what the deep structures of story and psychology might mean when we start to read them "against the grain," and in particular, what they might mean in the patriarchal/misogynist cultures in which they are regularly performed.

Going Deeper: From "Trauma" to "Daydreams"

Modleski's concern, then, with the dark side of popular romance discovers in its "deep structures" the reiteration of events that – notwithstanding their subsequent resolution – are in themselves deeply traumatic. More recent feminist research into trauma and its "treatment" may thus be usefully employed to understand the nature of that trauma better, and the connection became explicit for me when – reading for another project – I was struck by the similarities in the way in which trauma victims and romantic lovers have been described and analyzed. In recent years, moreover, there has been an explosion of fiction in which the traumas of war or holocaust are interwoven with love stories which make those similarities explicit. Two especially affecting examples are Andrew Greig's *That Summer* (2000) and Ian McEwan's *Atonement* (2001), in which the "condition" of being in love is compared with the trauma of combat and bombardment both directly and indirectly. Take this example from Greig (2000: 147):

Two more sets of explosions, the rattle of machine-gun fire from above, a scream somewhere suddenly cut off. Then the sound levels dropped and the engines began to fade. I lay face down in the earth, almost comfortable, still trying to understand what had just happened to me. Something big had, for sure. I could feel the difference somewhere in under my ribs. It was almost like falling in love, as subtle, as undeniable, as irreversible.

This "life-stopping" event, in which the text's heroine narrowly escapes death during an aerial bombardment, mirrors similar descriptions of the hero, a fighter-pilot, in the midst of one of his raids. Both subjects register extreme temporal-spatial dislocation, and both are unable to order their experiences into anything resembling a story ("two minutes of blurred intensity, incoherent as a waking dream," 72). The implication, meanwhile, that "being in love" replicates these tendencies is most evident in the frequent descriptions of Len and Stella occupying a world which is a "time out of time"; a space/place of transcendent bliss that is nevertheless girded by imminent separation and/or death:

> It was a time out of the world, time we should have been asleep in bed, time rescued. Looking back, it was so strange and unconnected to anything else, I sometimes wonder if it happened at all or if it was a curious, overheated dream, a spurious imagining of another world, a world to come or that might have been, where we were lovers and the world was innocent. (Greig 2000: 104)

Here, then, we see the ironic parallels between dislocated "moments in time" that are, at once, so opposite and yet so similar, and which make an explicit link between the traumatic moment and our *inability* to render it into a meaningful and lasting "story."

This focus on the narrativization – or not – of the traumatic moment has, of course, become central to most accounts of what constitutes trauma and how it might be treated. It also moves us toward a further understanding of why romance fiction should be so invested in rendering all that is most "unspeakable" about the condition of "being in love" into a *story*. Dori Laub's description (below) of the limbo associated with the traumatic state certainly has a striking resonance with the passage from Greig's work quoted above, as well as with Barthes's celebrated account (1978: 188–94) of *ravissement* as a "hypnotic episode":

> While the trauma uncannily returns in actual life, its reality continues to elude the subject who lives in its grip and unwittingly undergoes its ceaseless repetitions and re-enactments. The traumatic event, although real, took place outside the parameters of "normal reality," such as causality, sequence, place, and time. The trauma is thus an event that has no beginning, no ending, no before, no after. This absence of categories that define it lends a quality of "otherness," a salience, a timelessness, and a ubiquity that put it outside the range of comprehension, or recounting, and of mastery. Trauma survivors live not with memories of the past, but with an event that could not, and did not, proceed through to its completion, has no ending, achieved no closure, and therefore, as far as the survivors are concerned, continues into the present and is current in every respect. (Felman and Laub 1992: 68–9)

In the same way, then, that – for trauma survivors – the means out of this impasse is to begin to narrativize the event through the facilitating presence of an auditor, or "witness," so the romantic reader/lover is compelled to return to situations ("real" or textual), in which the "timeless present" is kept painfully alive but would paradoxically seem to offer reassurance.

This last point raises further questions about the exact nature of romantic trauma given, especially, that it is retrospectively experienced by the desiring subject as the most intense *pleasure*. Reviewing the popular romance genre (and, indeed, many of its contemporary variants and mutations), it is clear that romantic love is preeminently a discourse defined by "misunderstanding" and "failed communication": romantic love, as it were, is *always* achieved in the face of obstacles that made it, at first, appear "impossible." In both classic romance (think of Brontë's *Jane Eyre*) and Mills and Boon novels, the worst trauma suffered by the heroines is usually associated with a cruel, cutting, or disparaging remark from the hero which can be experienced only as "rejection." Take, for example, this moment of heightened tension between the hero and heroine of *The Viking Stranger*:

> "You've not run up against any snags – or snares?" he drawled.
> Her head went back at that one and she met the full impact of his sardonic grey eyes. "What are you implying, Mr Norlund?" The words were out before she could stop them.
> "Am I implying something?" He peaked a flaxen eyebrow. "Surely that would mean I was taking more than a general interest in a member of my staff – do you consider that's what I'm doing?"
> She flushed at the bite to his words and shook her head. (Winspear 1966: 120)

Although, by the end of the story, Norlund's new tenderness toward Jill works to make us forgive and forget both this and his sexual aggressiveness, it would be fair to say that the palpable dislike and contempt that surfaces at such moments is never fully explained. In other words, although the narrative of such texts does a good job resolving practical obstacles and "impossibilities," the way in which these are also used to account for the psychosexual sparring that takes place between the hero and heroine is always rather less convincing.

What Lacanian (and other) psychoanalytic theory would advise us in this regard is, of course, that these "impossibilities" *persist* within relationships despite our attempts to create stories that will contain and "explain" them. We might therefore argue that it is the often cruel "illogic" of romantic sexual encounters that fuels our compulsion to return to those moments of confusion and "misunderstanding" with such obsession: the fact that s/he leaves me despite the fact s/he loves me; the fact s/he's cruel to me despite the fact s/he loves me; the fact s/he desires me *and* someone else. Although the classic/popular romance text might superficially reassure us with a narrative explanation for this ambiguous and irrational behavior, it could also be argued that it is – paradoxically – the (re)enactment of the traumatic "impossibilities" themselves that the subject/reader will continue to crave to the extent that this makes us feel less "alone" with our own miscreant experience.

Yet the appeal of the romance text in dealing with the perversity of our affections is also explained very persuasively – and rather more optimistically – by Ernst Bloch's work on daydreams and "anticipatory consciousness." In his utopian vision of human consciousness, culture, and society entitled *The Principle of Hope* (1986 [1959]), Bloch makes a powerful move against the "repressive burden" associated with Freud's "unconscious" (Bloch 1986: dust jacket) by arguing for the concomitant presence of a "not yet conscious" in every human subject. Rather than seeing all consciousness and unconsciousness as the product of what has gone before, Bloch identified a counter-tendency to think or dream that which has not yet happened, thereby eschewing the notion that our desires – sexual or otherwise – are always necessarily bound up in the past.

Such a proposition may be seen to impact upon our understanding of the deep structures of romance in a number of ways. Going back to the quasi-Lacanian explanation for the pleasure of such texts I offered above, for example, we might argue that rather than merely confirming the messy contradictoriness of our desires, the enduring success of romantic discourse is that it does, indeed, replace repressed, "past" emotions with new, anticipatory ones. Indeed, Bloch assists us in this regard by himself separating emotions into two distinct categories, "filled" and "expectant" (1986: 74):

> Filled emotions (like envy, greed, admiration) are those whose drive-intention is short-term, whose drive object lies ready, if not in respective individual attainability, then in the already available world. Expectant emotions (like anxiety, fear, hope, belief), on the other hand are those whose drive-intention is long-term, whose drive-object does not yet lie ready.

Positing romantic love as a mixture of "expectant" as well as "filled" emotions, we can, perhaps, begin to appreciate the struggle between retrogressive and repressive, and anticipatory and "not yet conscious" forces in romance texts in a newly utopian way. For the authors and readers of such stories, drives and emotions associated with the past are, ultimately, far less interesting than those associated with an unknown future. In other words, most romance texts deal in stories in which the "not yet conscious" ultimately triumphs over the conscious. And this, it could be argued, is *why* we return to them: not simply (as inferred from the trauma theorists cited above) in order to lay the ghosts of the past by making a story out of the "unspeakable," but – more positively – to displace that story (said or unsaid) by another which is a willful act of the imagination and exists *only* in the future. The central thesis of Bloch's book, indeed, is that the expectant, "unfilled" emotions will always necessarily triumph over the "filled" ones, and that the world of the "unconscious" is thus ever in competition with the "anticipatory consciousness."

The full measure of the difference between Freud's "unconscious" and Bloch's "anticipatory consciousness" is illustrated most concretely in the latter's chapter on the distinction between night-dreams and daydreams. This is also the section of the book that has most resonance for romance theory, since there is much in his characterization of the "daydreamer" that is also typical of the lover and, in particular, the lover's capacity for *seduction*:

> But clearly, people do not dream only at night, not at all. The day too has twilight edges, where wishes are also gratified. In contrast to the nocturnal dream, that of the daydream sketches freely chosen and repeatable images in the air, it can rant and rave, but also brood and plan . . . The daydream can furnish inspirations which do not require interpreting, but working out, it builds castles in the air as blueprints too, and not always as just fictitious ones. (Bloch 1986: 86)

For Bloch, then, the human subject's ability to make dreaming into an act/art of partly conscious "will" has profound implications – and for society as well as the individual. To survive and prosper, both individuals and societies need to be able to dream "that which does not yet exist," and our ability to do so is, indeed, "the principle of hope."

Romantic Locations

Another section of Bloch's book of particular interest for romance theory is that entitled "Beautiful Foreign Lands" (1986: 370–4) in which he links the subject's desire for travel "into the unknown" (real or imaginary) to his/her anticipatory consciousness. One of the features uniting popular romantic fiction – and here I include the postmodern, "literary" varieties alongside "Mills and Boon" – is its unerring recourse to exotic/strange/"other" locations: a tendency which, as I have noted elsewhere, is often the *only* significant variable in the texts concerned (see Pearce and Wisker 1998: 98–111) While there are clearly a good many ways of theorizing this investment in exotic locations in romance – including ones which look back to medieval romance – Bloch's theory returns us to deep structure by suggesting that these "foreign lands" are one of the strategic means by which the subject thinks or wills herself into an alternative future. A quick checklist of anyone's romance reading should support this speculation: how many romances *do not*, for example, involve some element of relocation before the subject/s can either "fall in love" or realize their love? In terms of the texts being used to illustrate this chapter, *A Viking Stranger* sees the orphan heroine, Jill, transported to sunny and glamorous California ("They landed in sunshine, to an un-English smell in the air, to a balmy warmth, and to voices that drawled . . . Jill saw that now she was on Californian soil. She breathed in the atmosphere and felt its vibrations" [Winspear 1966: 59]) while Winterson, with the self-conscious artistry of the postmodern author, has her central protagonist reflect upon the importance of romantic location thus (2000: 36):

> She said, "What about you? What brings you to Paris?"
> "A story I'm writing."

> "Is it about Paris?"
> "No, but Paris is in it."
> "What is it about?"
> "Boundaries. Desire."
> "What are your other books about?"
> "Boundaries. Desire."
> "Can't you write about something else?"
> "No."
> "So why come to Paris?"
> "Another city. Another disguise."

Implicit in this ironic exchange is, of course, the admission that romantic stories cannot do without their romantic locations. The protagonist here speaks of this need as a need for "disguise," with connotations of love as a "performance" that depends upon a changing backdrop to keep it fresh and new. Such "emotional tourism" could be read cynically (especially given the highly itinerant nature of Winterson's *oeuvre* as a whole), but the author herself – like Bloch – clearly takes the association between the "expectant emotion" that is love and "foreign lands" in good faith:

> If love is itself a journey, into entirely new life, then the value of foreign lands, experienced together, is doubled by it . . . Our own surprises are combined with those of the unknown land, of the foreign-beautiful city; then light falls in even the dullest minds, and the lively ones become full of figure. (Bloch 1996: 371)

> We went up to a little wooden bridge and lounged against the metal rail. The broad view of the river was a cine film of the weekend, with its amateur, hand-held feel of lovers and dogs and electric light and the spontaneous, unsteady movement of people passing this way and that . . . Frame by frame, that Friday night was shot and exposed and thrown away, carried by the river, by time, canned up only in memory, but in itself, scene by scene, perfect. (Winterson 2000: 36)

What is especially interesting – and typical – about this last Winterson extract is the way in which, once again, she combines a postmodern consciousness of time and place as simulacra with an undiminished "belief" in its beauty and necessity. The fact, in other words, that such "romantic locations" are experienced by us in mediated, hyper-real, and hyperbolic form does nothing to undermine their significance. In "memory," indeed, the clichéd "perfection" of Paris becomes the very "real" locus of the protagonist's loss:

> I thought of us, that afternoon in Paris, after we had escaped the rain. The sun came out and the pavements shone. It was as though the streets had been silvered into a mirror . . . Drops of rain fell from the hem of our coats and from the falling weight of your hair. (Winterson 2002: 230)

Romantic love, as Barthes observes (1978: 87), cannot exist without its "scene," and the anticipatory consciousness which defines romantic and sexual desire ensures that it will always exist in the lover's imagination as somewhere extraordinary and unique despite the fact it is also (necessarily) "typical."

This last point makes an important bridge between the utopian "romantic locations" I have been describing here and the traumatic spaces/places I described in the previous section. In one respect, indeed, we can see them as two sides of the same coin: the "time out of time" and "placeless place" that is typical both of the joy and the special quality of love *and* its violence and trauma. Rather than settling for this apparent paradox, however, I would propose that what is happening in most works of romantic fiction is an attempt to wrestle traumatic space *into* "ideal" space. The fact that there is such a fine line between the two in the experience of the lovers themselves is mirrored in the fact that a good many "romantic locations," as we have seen, are archetypal and/or "dream-like" rather than concretely observed. Winspear's California is a land of sun, and orange groves, and "golden" bridges; Winterson's Paris is a city of bridges, cafés, and glistening pavements. Yet, for all their "*sur-reality*," these places *are* named, recognizable locations that may be stitched into something resembling "history" and "story." Indeed, the real challenge for the romantic novelist, it seems, is to create a sense of place that is *both* "nowhere" and "somewhere"; a place which is both generic and specific; a place which is, therefore, both "uncanny" and safe. As the narrator of Greig's novel observes vis-à-vis Stella's photograph of Len taken during the summer of their romance: "With such details it could be anywhere in southern England. There's no one alive now who can say" (Greig 2000: 258).

And yet that is not at all the whole story. As I observed in the introduction to this chapter, popular romantic fiction is best understood as a genre in which deep structures and archetypes exist alongside the specificities of cultural and historical context. While I take the latter to include things like the institution of marriage and changing attitudes to homosexuality, it is best first observed with respect to the representation of space and place with which I have just been dealing.

Notwithstanding all that I have just written about the interest romantic fiction may be seen to have in creating rather "loosely observed" locations (spaces and places that are recognizable and yet *not*), it is clear that *popular* romance also has an interest in making its "scene-setting" more precise: an interest that might, indeed, be seen to distinguish the "popular" from the "classic" and "middle-brow" and which is probably best understood as the genre's more explicit commodification of romantic love. In other words, while the more classic romance may be seen to use its "romantic locations" to prompt or fulfill the desires and "expectant emotions" of the lovers, popular romance tends to make them into a "lifestyle statement" which is (in part) the undisguised *object* of the romance. We have already seen examples of this in the earlier quotations from *The Viking Stranger* in which Eric Norlund's personal charms are headily combined with expensive restaurants and minutely described gourmet food. Winterson too plies a similar trade in *Powerbook* where, in the later pages, the more generically romantic spaces of Paris and Capri give way to the "Costa Coffee Place" on Paddington Station (2000: 201). While this last detail could simply be taken as the novel's attempt to re/ground itself in contemporary realism, as lifestyle "branding" it will undoubtedly interpellate a large group of readers very effectively. In both these texts, it seems, the romance that is pursued is part and parcel of the lifestyle that supports it: "structure" and "surface" come together in what, for many readers, will be a compelling whole.

Conclusion

Yet, whatever its intentions, the political salvation of romance fiction is that it rarely manages to *sustain* this illusion of continuity between "structure" and "surface." From the works of Jane Austen, through Mills and Boon to certain postmodern titles, all those authors who have elected to set their romances within a recognizable social or historical space or place (that is, rather than keeping within the mythic/fantastical space of the fairy story) have had also to acknowledge the economic, social, and cultural materiality through which that romance is mediated or indeed produced. Moreover, while a good deal of popular romance may be seen to conspire with the capitalist and hetero-patriarchal institutions that have been heavily invested in these "transactions" of courtship and marriage for centuries, there are few texts which do not also hint, at least implicitly, at the corruption and inadequacy of these super-structures. Even those as apparently un-self-reflexive as Winspear's *Viking Stranger* covertly suggest that whatever Jill stands to gain through her marriage to Norlund (the romantic/glamorous lifestyle whose details the text has vaunted so tirelessly) she will "pay for" in terms of a 1960s marriage-contract which will limit her personal and social fulfillment to that of wife and, above all, mother (of numerous male children):

> Eric smoothed her hair with a large hand and she went even closer to him in growing confidence. "If you throw your kite over the moon and marry me, my love," he said, a wicked lilt in his voice, "you'll probably have the type of rogues who will pull girlish plaits right and left – have you thought of that?" (Winspear 1966: 189)

My point here, then, is that even in the most conventional and uncritical popular romantic fiction there is no attempt to disguise the fact that the resolution of the story in terms of its deep structures is also part of a socio-economic contract with quite other fulfillments – and demands. The exceptions to this are, of course, those romances that end in death, and – bearing in mind what I have just argued – it is not hard to see the appeal of this alternative formula for generations of writers not willing to "compromise" the integrity of their stories at a deeper level (see Pearce and Stacey 1995: 17). But death is not the favored resolution of the Mills and Boon or, indeed, the more contemporary "chick lit" romance variants, and readers are left to steer their own way through "endings" which combine deep, structural satisfactions with more debatable social ones.

Yet it would be misleading to suggest, as we enter the twenty-first century, that the writers of romance have not sought to respond to, or interrogate, the ideological superstructures in which the action of their stories takes place on a more conscious level. Even within the Mills and Boon genre, significant revisions have occurred, most especially with regard to the sexual desires and practices of the heroine. From the 1980s onward, Mills and Boon/Harlequin undertook a mass "liberalization" of their guidelines in this respect, spawning a host of new imprints like "Temptations," "Silhouette," and "Desire" which – as their titles suggest – move the erotic to the fore. As Janice Radway has observed in the revised 1991 introduction to *Reading the Romance*, however, it is highly significant that: (a) Mills and Boon/Harlequin have nevertheless felt the market need to retain what she describes as the more traditional "sweet" romances (16–17); and (b) that "in every case" the new-generation romances "refuse finally to unravel the connection between female sexual desire and monogamous heterosexuality" (16). In other words, the new titles are unable to (or, rather, are not "permitted" to) promote active female sexuality without the prospect of marriage and motherhood still beckoning in the future: "The stories therefore close off the vista they open up by virtue of their greater willingness to foreground the sexual fantasy at the heart of the genre" (16).

While the continuance of a deeply conservative ideology focusing on "the family" and "domestic fulfillment" is one way of reading the tensions and contradictions at the heart of these new imprints, however, it could also be argued that it is the incompatibility of erotic and romantic discourse per se that is the problem. As I intimated in the introduction to this chapter, erotica and romance constitute very different literary traditions and circulate in the world, even today, as very different stories and discourses. As we have already established, one of the key features of romantic love (and that which would seem to give its readers most pleasure) is the understanding that it is unique, exclusive, and non-transferable. For this reason, "contemporary" titles that seek the excitement of sexual adventure (usually involving several partners) *and* the fulfillment of a more traditional romantic love are almost certainly bound to fall between two stools. Even in terms of structure and plot they are unlikely to succeed, since the "hermeneutic" pleasure of the text (where obstacles, confusions, and misunderstandings are eventually resolved in a grand climax) are sacrificed for short-lived thrills and spills along the way. Reminding ourselves of these "readerly" consequences of deviating from the "Ur" morphology of the romance, it is no surprise that the more traditional imprints prosper alongside the new.

Apart from the market demand for more sexually active heroines, Mills and Boon/Harlequin have also made changes to the socio-economic profile of their heroines. From the 1980s onwards, especially, "career women" of different kinds have displaced "orphaned" teenagers (like Jill in *A Viking Stranger*) who work in menial jobs. For many of these new heroines, moreover, their work is extremely fulfilling, if not "all consuming" and, as Nikkianne Moody has observed, is frequently represented as "compensation," or a safe alternative, to an earlier, failed love affair (1998: 141–56). Indeed, the heroine's career now becomes the major test of commitment at the end of the story since, in most cases, she is faced to make a choice (or agree to a compromise) between her work and her "man" (1998: 146). Not surprisingly, Moody sees this persistent emphasis on marriage – notwithstanding the gestures toward the heroine's former socio-economic independence – as a "limit-point" of liberation as far as Mills and Boon popular romance is concerned. The heroines might have been granted more autonomy, relations between the sexes might have been modestly improved, but the ruling institution of hetero-patriarchy remains unchallenged.

As I said before, it is possible to read these latest mutations of the Mills and Boon genre more positively if we recognize the extent to which they rattle the orthodoxies of marriage and heterosexuality rather than consolidate them. In other words, these are texts that very conspicuously invite "reading against the grain" because of their profound structural/ideological internal contradictions. And while we cannot expect all readers of popular romance to engage in such openly political activity, the research of Radway and others was early proof that we should never underestimate the active and/or critical engagement of most of them. Indeed, what more recent Queer theory has taught us in this regard is that even as the "repetition" of key cultural orthodoxies works to uphold their status on the one hand, so does it expose their fragility: for gender and sexual norms to *remain* norms they need to be "performed" continually (see Pearce and Wisker 1998: 15–16). With this perspective in mind, it is not difficult to see contemporary romance – both as an eclectic whole and vis-à-vis its individual sub/ genres – as a category severely under stress. The discontinuities between romantic and erotic discourse on the one hand, and between "deep structures" and changing social/ cultural practices are ever present, even in the more superficially conservative texts. In addition, there is an ever growing list of titles – within that wider, eclectic, mutating pool of contemporary romance that I identified at the start of the chapter – that is actively seeking the discontinuities: texts whose lovers violate the norms of gender or sexuality or racial homogeneity, and which eschew coupledom, marriage, and children as the defining end point of their romance. As I have noted elsewhere, the most seriously radical of today's feminist and/or gay and lesbian romances are those that not only tell the stories of those positioned outside the ruling institutions, but also, simultaneously, *make visible* the means by which those institutions (re)produce them-selves (Pearce and Wisker 1998: 14).

Yet none of this detracts from this chapter's starting point, either: that the deep structures and "Ur" stories of romantic love remain as apparently unshakeable as ever. Indeed, reminding ourselves of the profoundly transformative, utopian potential of romantic love as a form of "anticipatory consciousness," we would surely not wish otherwise. Providing we can ensure – or, at least, strive toward – a situation in which *romantic desire* (as re/produced at the level of deep structure) can be disassociated from the *institutions of romance*, then we should remain free to play with this "most popular of *all* stories" to our hearts' content. Or should we? Contemporary postmodern authors like Jeanette Winterson clearly believe so, but maybe it is just *too hopeful* to believe that we may truly rewrite a love story without, at least, the ghosts of father, husband, and priest somewhere looking on.

See also: chapter 3, THE POPULAR ENGLISH METRICAL ROMANCES; chapter 7, GENDER-
ING PROSE ROMANCE IN RENAISSANCE ENGLAND; chapter 8, SIDNEY AND SPENSER;
chapter 12, "GOTHIC" ROMANCE; chapter 13, WOMEN'S GOTHIC ROMANCE; chapter
15, "INCONSISTENT RHAPSODIES"; chapter 24, AMERICA AND ROMANCE; chapter 25,
MYTH, LEGEND, AND ROMANCE IN YEATS, POUND, AND ELIOT; chapter 26, TWENTIETH-
CENTURY ARTHURIAN ROMANCE; chapter 27, ROMANCE IN FANTASY; chapter 28, QUEST
ROMANCE IN SCIENCE FICTION.

Notes

1. *Moulin Rouge*, directed by Baz Luhrmann, Twentieth Century Fox, 2001.
2. "Queer theory": I am referring in particular to the work of Judith Butler (1990, 1993) and Eve Kosofsky Sedgwick (1994), which has significantly advanced our understanding of how "normative" gender and sexuality are produced and sustained through the *repetition* of certain semiotic codes and behaviors, themselves dependent upon a visible distinction from the "deviant other" (see the introduction to Pearce and Wisker 1998).
3. John Walsh, "The Would-be Bestseller's Guide to Literary Stardom," *Independent Review* (2 July 2002), 4–6.
4. Winterson's *The Powerbook* is endorsed by the British women's magazine *Marie Claire*, which describes it as "beguiling, heart-rending."
5. An indication of the broad range of texts now marketed *alongside* "romance" is usefully illustrated by the *Independent's* "Fifty Best Romantic Reads": "The Information," *Independent* (9 February 2002), 4–11.
6. Readers unfamiliar with the "stages" of the classic romance plot are advised to check out Janice Radway's diagram, "The narrative logic of the Romance" (1991: 150).

References and Further Reading

Austen, Jane (1996). *Persuasion*. Harmondsworth: Penguin. [First published in 1818.]

Barthes, Roland (1979). *A Lover's Discourse: Fragments*, trans. R. Howard. Harmondsworth: Penguin. [Original work published in 1977.]

Belsey, Catherine (1994). *Desire: Love Stories in Western Culture*. Oxford: Blackwell.

Bloch, Ernst (1986). *The Principle of Hope*, trans. N. Plaice, S. Plaice, and P. Knight. Oxford: Blackwell. [First published in 1959.]

Carter, Angela (1977). *The Passion of New Eve*. London: Virago.

Carter, Angela (2003). *Nights at the Circus*. London: Vintage. [First published in 1991.]

Felman, Shoshana, and Dori Laub, eds. (1992). *Testimony: Crises of Witnessing in Literature, Psychoanalysis and History*. London and New York: Routledge.

Fielding, Helen (1997). *Bridget Jones's Diary*. London: Picador.

Firestone, Shulamith (1979). *The Dialectic of Sex: The Case for Feminist Revolution*. London: Women's Press. [First published in 1970.]

Greer, Germaine (1993). *The Female Eunuch*. London: Flamingo. [First published in 1971.]

Greig, Andrew (2000). *That Summer*. London: Faber and Faber.

Kureishi, Hanif (1990). *The Buddha of Suburbia*. London: Faber and Faber.

McEwan, Ian (2002). *Atonement*. London: Viking.

Modleski, T. (1985). *Loving with a Vengeance: Mass-produced Fantasies for Women*. New York and London: Routledge.

Moody, Nickianne (1998). "Mills and Boon's Temptations: Sex and the Single Couple in the 1990s." In *Fatal Attractions*, ed. Lynne Pearce and Gina Wisker. London: Pluto, pp. 141–56.

Pearce, Lynne, and Jackie Stacey, eds. (1995). *Romance Revisited*. London: Lawrence and Wishart.

Pearce, Lynne, and Gina Wisker, eds. (1998). *Fatal Attractions: Rescripting Romance in Contemporary Literature and Film*. London: Pluto.

Propp, Vladimir (1968). *Morphology of the Folktale*, trans. L. Scott. Austin: University of Texas Press. [First published in 1928.]

Radway, Janice (1991). *Reading the Romance: Women, Patriarchy, and Popular Literature*. Chapel Hill and London: The University of North Carolina Press.

Winspear, V. (1966). *The Viking Stranger*. London: Mills and Boon.

Winterson, Jeanette (1985). *Oranges Are Not The Only Fruit*. London: Women's Press. [First published in 1984.]

Winterson, Jeanette (2000). *The Powerbook*. London: Vintage.

Epilogue: Into the Twenty-first Century

Corinne Saunders

The essays in this volume have charted the various transformations of romance, from its inception in late classical narrative, to its diverse manifestations in the twentieth century. They demonstrate with clarity the power of romance as a mode: its origins seem in a sense natural, preceding the term itself. Medieval romance may be seen as formative in that it establishes both the great matters of romance, especially that of Arthur, and its great motifs – quest, adventure, otherworld journey, love. Thence each age adds to and rewrites romance, making the genre its own and yet retaining those crucial structures. In the writing of Sidney and Spenser, epic romance finds its flowering; in Shakespeare's last plays, romance attains a dramatic height never again reached; in the eighteenth century, romance gains a parodic force and at the same time enters the genre of the novel, most notably as the Gothic; in the Romantic period, it is rewritten once again, shaping and shaped by an intellectual and artistic movement of peculiar force; in the fiction and poetry of the Victorian period, the images and structures of romance are refracted through a distinctive moral lens; and in the twentieth century, romance inspires a series of sub-genres – imperial romance, contemporary fantasy, science fiction, popular romance, as well as influencing and shaping modern and postmodern poetry and fiction. It is easy to find constants in the recurrent motifs, most of all perhaps the power of the marvelous, which underpins the genres of fantasy and science fiction, but it is also imperative to recognize that romance finds its individual power through engagement with precise historical moments. This duality of historicity and timelessness seems to fuel romance, making it an enduring mode of infinite potential that can both reach beyond the everyday and remain firmly rooted in it.

Underlying the development of romance is this crucial issue of its relation to realism, and perhaps most of all romances of different periods are linked by their inclusion of nonrealist elements, often combined with a detailed mimetic quality. Thus the otherworlds of romance tend to be presented in carefully mimetic terms – political, social, and moral – and set against societies on the one hand distant, on the other rooted in the customs and behaviors of their audiences. Romance thus fulfills the function of escape literature, yet also allows for pertinent social comment – often through the contrast of ideal and real. The idealized world and its negatives are formed of conventional stereotypes, patterns, and motifs, but also particularized through original use of realistic detail. While the fantastic and exotic are crucial for their own sake, the function of romance goes beyond simple amusement. Its effect may be to create a social or moral awareness, sometimes of an acutely politicized kind, while at the same time the world of archetypes allows for exploration of the human psyche and engagement with the universals of human experience – kinship, love, loss, death. Romance addresses the human impulse away from realism, the desire to look into the depths of the psyche – yet this can only be effective when it is in some way rooted in the material, in the detailed mesh of the romance landscape, where realism intersects with familiar, stylized conventions. Such a mode can become hollow, offering escapist platitudes to its readers, and in these cases the universal emotions explored tend to be limited to formulaic expressions of romantic love. Yet in its more sophisticated versions, romance is highly energized, stimulating, and probing.

A random perusal of the shelves of a high-street bookshop could not demonstrate more clearly that romance is thriving as we enter the twenty-first century. This is in some ways startling in a highly secular age dominated by scientific explanation and discovery, in which genes and machines achieve more and more, and less and less is left to the imagination. Yet there is no doubt that the literary fever sweeping the Western world recently has been one of romance: *The Lord of the Rings* and *Harry Potter*. Both were initially aimed at children – yet both delight, it seems, at least as many adults. Tolkien's works, written over half a century ago, have gone in and out of fashion, but they have undergone another transformation in their rewriting for the medium of film, with its use of technological marvels, a new emphasis on love and the feminine, and the lessening of the didactic: the most powerful strands of the tale, however – the battle of good against evil, home and country against the invader, beauty against the monstrous, youth against age and death – remain more vivid than ever. J. K. Rowling uses many of the same ingredients in her presentation of Harry Potter, who as the ill-treated orphan with magical powers fulfills in his way the archetypal role of the exile, the "fair unknown" with unusual promise; Rowling also updates the boys' own adventure story in her depiction of "Hogwarts School of Witchcraft and Wizardry." These authors are not alone in their popularity. Philip Pullman's widely read *His Dark Materials* trilogy (1995–2000) offers another version of the battle of dark against light, the child of destiny against the powers of witchcraft. A recent bestselling novel by G. P. Taylor, *Shadowmancer* (2003), expresses in its title an engagement with romance archetypes: it too tells the tale of the ancient forces of evil, embodied in a sorcerer who attempts to control the universe. And Bernard Cornwell's popular historical novels, especially those treating the legend of Arthur, revisit the traditional matters of romance in contemporary terms.

Contemporary romance is by no means limited to fantasy. It is present in the light works of Jilly Cooper, such as *Pandora* (2002), which overtly plays with legend and is advertised as evoking "an alternative universe where love, sex and laughter rule," and in the novels of Joanne Harris, *Chocolat* (1999) and *Five Quarters of the Orange* (2001), which follow the kind of pattern discussed by Lynne Pearce, where erotic romance is combined with detailed evocations of other sensual pleasures, especially food and drink. But it is also present in more serious, self-consciously literary ways in a very diverse range of other works, spanning a variety of cultures: Paulo Coelho's *Alchemist* (1993), for instance, tells of an Andalusian shepherd boy's quest for treasure and his encounter with a mystical guide; Isabel Allende's *City of the Beasts* (2002) revives the structures of imperial romance in its narrative of a journey up a dangerous river; Vikram Seth's *A Suitable Boy* (1993) is also a quest romance, though of a very different kind. The archetypes of love and tragedy are rewritten in Gabriel Garcia Marquez's *Love in the Time of Cholera* (1991), with its quality of magic realism, and in Milan Kundera's *The Unbearable Lightness of Being* (1984). It is telling that the work which won the Booker Prize in 2002 was Ben Okri's novel *In Arcadia*. There is no doubt that many other writers pursue the contrasting mode of realism, sometimes to an uncomfortable extreme, yet romance seems to have had a powerful resurgence, so much so that recent popular film has returned to the romance matter of the earlier twentieth century, rediscovering, for example, Dodie Smith's *I Capture the Castle* (1949). There is no simple explanation, but perhaps a direct correlation may be found between the ebbing of romance away from everyday life and its surge into the imaginative life of the twenty-first century.

Romance, after all, speaks of imaginative possibility – the possibility of building castles in the air. Its tapestries of light and shadow address the ideal, not just to present an escape, but also to inspire belief in the potential, in the achievement of desire, in the embodiment of ideals, in the reconfiguration of the familiar – though not necessarily in a brave new world, for romance is often looking nostalgically to the retrieval of past glories. Romance allows us, at least while we turn its pages, to regain the promise and allure of "this rough magic," to achieve the vision of "The cloud-capped towers, the gorgeous palaces, / The solemn temples, the great globe itself," and to embroider the fabric of "this insubstantial pageant" with the many glowing colors of our dreams.

Index